STRESSFUL LIFE EVENTS

International Universities Press
Stress and Health Series

Edited by
Leo Goldberger, Ph.D.

Monograph 4

Stressful Life Events

edited by

Thomas W. Miller, Ph.D.

International Universities Press, Inc.
Madison   Connecticut

Library of Congress Cataloging-in-Publication Data

Stressful life events / [edited by] Thomas W. Miller.
     p. cm.—(Stress and health series ; monograph 4)
   Includes bibliographies and index.
   ISBN 0-8236-6165-2 :
   1. Life change events—Psychological aspects. 2. Stress
(Psychology) 3. Medicine and psychology. I. Miller, Thomas W.,
1943- . II. Series.
   [DNLM: 1. Behavioral Medicine. 2. Family. 3. Life Change
Events. 4. Mental Disorders—etiology. 5. Stress, Psychological. W1
ST799K monograph 4 / WM 172 S9159]
   RC455.4.L53S77 1989
   616.89'071—dc19
   DNLM/DLC   88-12907
   for Library of Congress   CIP

Manufactured in the United States of America

This book is dedicated to all of humankind who have experienced the trauma of stressful life events and who have come to know, understand, and adapt to the normative and catastrophic transitions that we encounter in our lives. And it is to my wife, my children, and my family that I dedicate this compendium of clinical research on stressful life events.

Contents

Contributors   xiii
Preface   xxi

PART I: THEORETICAL CONSIDERATIONS IN
         STRESSFUL LIFE EVENTS

  1. Recent Life Change Stress and Psychological
     Depression   5
     Richard H. Rahe, M.D.
  2. Life Events and Interdependent Lives: Implications
     for Research and Intervention   13
     R. A. Pruchno, Ph.D., F. C. Blow, Ph.D., and M. A.
     Smyer, Ph.D.
  3. Conceptual and Theoretical Problems in the
     Measurement of Life Stress   31
     Thomas W. Miller, Ph.D., A.B.P.P.
  4. Life Events and Schizophrenia: The "Triggering"
     Hypothesis   51
     R. Day, Ph.D.
  5. Why Do Unpredictable Events Lead to Reports of
     Physical Symptoms?   91
     Karen A. Matthews, Ph.D., Michael F. Scheier,
     Ph.D., Bradford I. Brunson, Ph.D., and Bernardo
     Carducci, Ph.D.

PART II: ASSESSMENT AND METHODOLOGICAL
          ISSUES IN STRESSFUL LIFE EVENTS

  6. Life-Event Scaling: Clinical Methodological Issues   105
     Thomas W. Miller, Ph.D., A.B.P.P.
  7. Reliability of Life-Event Ratings: An Independent
     Replication   123
     Glenys Parry, M.R.C., S.S.R.C., David A. Shapiro,
     M.R.C., S.S.R.C., and Lisa Davies, M.R.C., S.S.R.C.

 8. Reliability of Life-Event Interviews with Outpatient
    Schizophrenics   127
    Richard Neugebauer, Ph.D., M.P.H.
 9. Is There a Short-Cut? An Investigation into the
    Life-Event Interview   149
    P. McC. Miller, B.Sc., Ph.D., and D. P. Salter, M.D.
10. Personal Assessments of Life-Event Stress and the
    Near Future Onset of Psychological Symptoms   165
    D. G. Byrne, Ph.D.
11. The Stability of the State-Trait Anxiety Inventory
    Trait Anxiety Scale   181
    Melissa A. Elkind, M.S., and Anthony J. DeVito,
    Ph.D.
12. Stress as a Potential Barrier to the Search for Health   197
    R. Barker Bausell, Ph.D., and S. Petchel Damrosch,
    Ph.D.

PART III: LIFE STRESS AND BEHAVIORAL
           MEDICINE

13. Life Events and Myocardial Infarction   215
    G. Magni, M.D., A. Corfini, M.D., F. Berto, M.D.,
    R. Rizzardo, M.D., S. Bombardelli, M.D., and
    G. Miraglia, M.D.
14. Personal Determinants of Life-Event Stress and
    Myocardial Infarction   223
    D. G. Byrne, Ph.D.
15. Stressful Life Events Associated with Bulimia in
    Anorexia Nervosa: Empirical Findings and
    Theoretical Speculations   237
    Michael Strober, Ph.D.
16. Life Stress Measures and Reported Frequency of
    Sleep Disorders   257
    Zack Zdenek Cernovsky, Ph.D.
17. Dysfunctional Uterine Bleeding and Prior Life
    Stress   271
    Fred Tudiver, M.D., C.C.F.P.

18. End-Stage Renal Disease as a Stressful Life Event   281
    Edward Stodola, Ph.D., and Thomas W. Miller,
    Ph.D., A.B.P.P.
19. Life Events and Psychological Distress in
    Dermatologic Disorders: Psoriasis, Chronic
    Urticaria, and Fungal Infections   307
    Giovanni A. Fava, M.D., Giulia I. Perini, M.D.,
    Paolo Santonastaso, M.D., and Cleto Veller Fornasa,
    M.D.
20. Stress and Coping of Wives Following Their
    Husbands' Strokes   317
    Dennis Van Uitert, Ph.D., Raina Eberly, Ph.D., and
    Brian Engdahl, Ph.D.

PART IV: LIFE EVENTS AND MENTAL ILLNESS

21. Stress and Schizophrenia: Some Definitional Issues   329
    Bonnie Spring, Ph.D.
22. Recent Stressful Life Events and Episodes of
    Schizophrenia   351
    Bruce P. Dohrenwend, M.D., and Gladys Egri, M.D.
23. The Interaction of Life Events and Relatives'
    Expressed Emotion in Schizophrenia and Depressive
    Neurosis   377
    Julian Leff, M.D., and Christine Vaughn, Ph.D.
24. Life Events, Familial Stress, and Coping in the
    Developmental Course of Schizophrenia   393
    David Lukoff, Ph.D., Karen Snyder, M.A., Joseph
    Ventura, M.A., and Keith H. Neuchterlein, Ph.D.
25. Life Events and Personality Traits in Obsessive-
    Compulsive Neurosis   473
    Joseph McKeon, M.B., M.R.C.P.I., M.R.C.Psych.,
    Bridget Roa, B.Sc., and Anthony Mann, M.B.,
    M.R.C.P., M.R.C.Psych.
26. Life Events and Personality Characteristics in
    Depression   485
    H. Perris, M.D.

27. Life Events and Early and Late Onset of Bipolar
Disorder   499
Barry Glassner, Ph.D., and C. V. Haldipur, M.D.
28. Life Events Occurring Before and After Onset of
Depression in a Kenyan Setting—Any Significance?   507
D. M. Ndetei, M.D., and A. Vadher, M.D.

PART V: POSTTRAUMATIC STRESS: THE
VIETNAM EXPERIENCE

29. The Etiologies of Vietnam Posttraumatic Stress
Syndrome   519
Harry D. Silsby, M.C., and Franklin D. Jones, M.C.
30. Posttraumatic Stress Disorder: Psychometric
Assessment and Race   525
Walter Penk, Ph.D., Ralph Robinowitz, Ph.D.,
Dovalee Dorsett, Ph.D., William Bell, M.S., and John
Black, Ph.D.
31. Traumatic Stress Disorder: Diagnostic and Clinical
Issues in Psychiatry   553
Thomas W. Miller, Ph.D., A.B.P.P., and N. Donald
Feibelman, M.D.
32. Factitious Posttraumatic Stress Disorder: The
Veteran Who Never Got to Vietnam   573
Edward J. Lynn, M.D., and Mark Belza, M.D.
33. Chemotherapy of Traumatic War Stress   587
J. Ingram Walker, M.D.

PART VI: FAMILY AND LIFE SPAN
DEVELOPMENT: ISSUES IN STRESSFUL
LIFE EVENTS

34. Relationship of Family Life Events, Maternal
Depression, and Child-Rearing Problems   609
D. M. Fergusson, B.A. Hons., L. J. Horwood, B.A.,
B.Sc., and F. T. Shannon, F.R.C.P., F.R.A.C.P.
35. Family Life Events, Maternal Depression, and

Maternal and Teacher Descriptions of Child
Behavior   619
D. M. Fergusson, B.A. Hons., L. J. Horwood, B.A.,
B.Sc., M. E. Gretton, B.Sc., and F. T. Shannon,
F.R.C.P., F.R.A.C.P.
36. Stressful Life Events and Somatic Complaints in
Adolescents   633
John W. Greene, M.D., Lynn S. Walker, Ph.D.,
Gerald Hickson, M.D., and Juliette Thompson,
F.N.C.
37. Parenting Children in a Stressful Medical Situation   643
Joseph P. Bush, Ph.D., Barbara G. Melamed, Ph.D.,
and Carolyn S. Cockrell, Ph.D.
38. Contested Child Custody as a Stressful Life Event   659
Lane Veltkamp, M.S.W., and Thomas W. Miller,
Ph.D., A.B.P.P.
39. Factors Contributing to Teacher Stress   677
Robert G. Harrington, Ph.D., Judith A. Burry,
Ph.D., and Dennis Pelsma, M.S.
40. Coping with Stress: Differences Among Working
Families   697
Elaine A. Anderson, Ph.D., and Leigh A. Leslie,
Ph.D.
41. The 50-Year-Old Woman and Midlife Stress   711
Shirley Campbell, M.S.S.W.
42. Multifactoral Stressors in Life Change Events for the
Elderly Patient   729
Thomas W. Miller, Ph.D., A.B.P.P., and Louis L.
Jay, R.Ph.
43. Future Concerns and Recent Life Events of Elderly
Community Residents   749
Shayna Stein, Ph.D., Margaret W. Linn, Ph.D., Elisa
Slater, B.S., and Elliot M. Stein, M.D.

Concluding Thoughts on Stressful Life Events   759

Name Index   769
Subject Index   787

Contributors

Elaine A. Anderson, Ph.D., Assistant Professor, Department of Family and Community Development, University of Maryland, College Park, Maryland.

R. Barker Bausell, Ph.D., Professor, School of Nursing, University of Maryland and Prevention Research Center, Baltimore, Maryland.

William Bell, M.S., Psychology Service, VA Medical Center, Dallas, Texas.

Mark Belza, M.D., Research Psychiatrist, Stanford University Medical Center, Stanford University, Stanford, California.

F. Berto, M.D., Consultant Psychologist, Department of Cardiology, University of Padua School of Medicine, Padua, Italy.

John L. Black, Ph.D., Department of Psychology, VA Medical Center, Dallas, Texas.

F. C. Blow, Ph.D., Pennsylvania State University, College Park, Pennsylvania.

S. Bombardelli, M.D., Research Fellow, Department of Cardiology, University of Padua School of Medicine, Padua, Italy.

Bradford I. Brunson, Ph.D., Assistant Professor, Department of Psychology, Kansas State University, Manhattan, Kansas.

Judith A. Burry, Ph.D., Associate Professor, Department of Educational Psychology and Research, University of Kansas, Lawrence, Kansas.

Joseph P. Bush, Ph.D., Assistant Professor, Department of Psychology, Virginia Commonwealth University, Richmond, Virginia.

D. G. Byrne, Ph.D., Professor, Department of Psychology, The Australian National University, Camberra, Australia.

Shirley Campbell, M.S.S.W., Private Practice, St. Paul, Minnesota.

Bernardo Carducci, Ph.D., Associate Professor, Department of Psychology, Kansas State University, Manhattan, Kansas.

Zack Zdenek Cernovsky, Ph.D., Clinical Psychologist, St. Thomas Psychiatric Hospital, St. Thomas, Ontario, Canada.

Carolyn S. Cockrell, Ph.D., Department of Psychology, University of Florida, Gainsville, Florida.

A. Corfini, M.D., Research Fellow, Department of Cardiology, University of Padua School of Medicine, Padua, Italy.

S. Petchel Damrosch, Ph.D., Associate Professor, School of Nursing, University of Maryland, Baltimore, Maryland.

Lisa Davies, M.R.C., S.S.R.C., Research Psychologist, Social and Applied Psychology Unit, The University of Sheffield, England.

R. Day, Ph.D., Professor, Division of Mental Health, World Health Organization, New York, New York.

Anthony J. DeVito, Ph.D., Associate Director, University Counseling Center, Fordham University, New York, New York.

Bruce P. Dohrenwend, M.D., Professor of Psychiatry, Department of Psychiatry, Columbia University, New York, New York.

Dovalee Dorsett, Ph.D., Psychology Service, VA Medical Center, Dallas, Texas.

Raina Eberly, Ph.D., Counseling Psychologist, Psychology Service, VA Medical Center, Minneapolis, Minnesota.

Gladys Egri, M.D., Associate Clinical Professor, Department of Psychiatry, Columbia University, New York, New York.

Melissa A. Elkind, M.S., Graduate Assistant, University Counseling Center, Fordham University, New York, New York.

Brian Engdahl, Ph.D., Counseling Psychologist, Psychology Service, VA Medical Center, Minneapolis, Minnesota.

Giovanni A. Fava, M.D., Professor, Institute of Psychology, University of Bologna, Bologna, Italy.

N. Donald Feibelman, M.D., Chief Resident in Psychiatry, Department of Psychiatry, University of Kentucky, Lexington, Kentucky.

D. M. Fergusson, B.A. Hons., Director, Christchurch Child Development Study, Christchurch Hospital, Christchurch, New Zealand.

Cleto Veller Fornasa, M.D., Associate Professor, Department of Dermatology, University of Padova, Padova, Italy.

Barry Glassner, Ph.D., Professor, Department of Psychology, Syracuse University, Syracuse, New York.

John W. Greene, M.D., Professor, Department of Medicine, Division of Adolescent Medicine, Vanderbilt University, Nashville, Tennessee.

M. E. Gretton, B.Sc., Clinical Researcher, Child Development Study, Christchurch Clinical School of Medicine, Christchurch Hospital, Christchurch, New Zealand.

C. V. Haldipur, M.D., Clinical Psychiatrist, Hutchings Psychiatric Center, Syracuse, New York.

Robert G. Harrington, Ph.D., Professor, Department of Educational Psychology and Research, University of Kansas, Lawrence, Kansas.

Gerald Hickson, M.D., Professor, Department of Medicine, Division of Adolescent Medicine, Vanderbilt University, Nashville, Tennessee.

L. J. Horwood, B.A., B.Sc., Research Fellow, Child Development Study, Christchurch Clinical School of Medicine, Christchurch Hospital, Christchurch, New Zealand.

Louis L. Jay, R.Ph., Consulting Pharmacist and Graduate, University of Buffalo, Buffalo, New York.

Franklin D. Jones, M.C., Chief, Combat Stress Work Group, Neuropsychiatry, Walter Reed Army Institute of Research, Washington, D.C.

Julian Leff, M.D., Assistant Director and Professor, MRC Social Psychiatry Unit, Institute of Psychiatry, DeCrespigny Park, London, England.

Leigh A. Leslie, Ph.D., Department of Family and Community Development, University of Maryland, College Park, Maryland.

Margaret W. Linn, Ph.D., Director, Social Science Research, VA Medical Center and Department of Psychiatry, University of Miami School of Medicine, Miami, Florida.

David Lukoff, Ph.D., Director, Clinical Research Center for the Study of Schizophrenia/Rehabilitation Research and Training Center, Brentwood VA Medical Center, Los Angeles, California.

Edward J. Lynn, M.D., Chief, Psychiatry Service, VA Medical Center, University of Nevada School of Medicine, Reno, Nevada.

G. Magni, M.D., Clinical Assistant Professor, Department of Psychiatry, University of Padua School of Medicine, Padua, Italy.

Anthony Mann, M.B., M.R.C.P., M.R.C.Psych., Senior Lecturer, Institute of Psychiatry, Denmark Hill, London, England.

Karen A. Matthews, Ph.D., Associate Professor, Department of Psychiatry, University of Pittsburgh, Pittsburgh, Pennsylvania.

Joseph McKeon, M.B., M.R.C.P.I., M.R.C.Psych., Research Fellow, Institute of Psychiatry, DeCrespigny Park, Denmark Hill, London, England.

P. McC. Miller, B.Sc., Ph.D., Research Clinician, MRC Unit of Epidemiological Studies in Psychiatry, Royal Edinburgh Hospital, Scotland.

Barbara G. Melamed, Ph.D., Professor, Department of Psychology, Clinical Psychology Division, University of Florida, Gainsville, Florida.

Thomas W. Miller, Ph.D., A.B.P.P., Chief, Psychology Service, and Professor, Department of Psychiatry, College of Medicine, VA and University of Kentucky, Lexington, Kentucky.

G. Miraglia, M.D., Research Assistant Professor, Department of Cardiology, University of Padua School of Medicine, Padua, Italy.

D. M. Ndetei, M.D., Professor, Department of Psychiatry, Kenyatta National Hospital, Nairobi, Kenya.

Keith H. Neuchterlein, Ph.D., Research Clinician, Clinical Research Center for the Study of Schizophrenia/Rehabilitation Research and Training Center, Brentwood VA Medical Center, Los Angeles, California.

Richard Neugebauer, Ph.D., M.P.H., Professor, Gertrude H. Sergievsky Center, Columbia University Faculty of Medicine, New York.

Glenys Parry, M.R.C., S.S.R.C., Research Psychologist, Social and Applied Psychology Unit, The University of Sheffield, England.

Dennis Pelsma, M.S., Research Associate, Department of Educational Psychology and Research, University of Kansas, Lawrence, Kansas.

Walter Penk, Ph.D., Research Psychologist and Associate Professor, Department of Psychiatry, Tufts University School of Medicine and VA Medical Center, Boston, Massachusetts.

Giulia I. Perini, M.D., Professor, Institute of Psychology, University of Padua, Padua, Italy.

H. Perris, M.D., Professor and Clinical Director, Department of Psychiatry, Umea University, Sweden.

R. A. Pruchno, Ph.D., Miami Jewish Home and Hospital for the Aged, Miami, Florida.

Richard H. Rahe, M.D., Captain, Medical Corps, United States Navy, Washington, D.C.

R. Rizzardo, M.D., Research Assistant Professor, Department of Psychiatry, University of Padua School of Medicine, Padua, Italy.

Bridget Roa, B.Sc., Research Psychologist, St. George's Hospital, London, England.

Ralph Robinowitz, Ph.D., Clinical Psychologist, VA Medical Center, Dallas, Texas.

D. P. Salter, M.D., Research Clinician, MRC Unit for Epidemiological Studies in Psychiatry, Royal Edinburgh Hospital, Scotland.

Paolo Santonastaso, M.D., Professor, Institute of Psychology, University of Padua, Padua, Italy.

Michael F. Scheier, Ph.D., Assistant Professor, Department of Psychology, Carnegie-Mellon University, Pittsburgh, Pennsylvania.

F. T. Shannon, F.R.C.P., F.R.A.C.P., Clinical Researcher, Child Development Study, Christchurch Clinical School of Medicine, Christchurch Hospital, Christchurch, New Zealand.

David A. Shapiro, M.R.C., S.S.R.C., Research Psychologist, Social and Applied Psychology Unit, The University of Sheffield, England.

Harry D. Silsby, M.C., Deputy Commander, Chief of Professional Services, William Beaumont Army Center, El Paso, Texas.

Elisa Slater, B.S., Social Sciences Research, VA and University of Miami Medical Centers, Miami, Florida.

M. A. Smyer, Ph.D., Associate Professor, Pennsylvania State University, College Park, Pennsylvania.

Karen Snyder, M.A., Research Associate, Clinical Research Center for the Study of Schizophrenia/Rehabilitation Research and Training Center, Brentwood VA Medical Center, Los Angeles, California.

Bonnie Spring, Ph.D., Assistant Professor of Psychology, Department of Psychiatry, Harvard University, Cambridge, Massachusetts.

Elliot M. Stein, M.D., Director, Psychiatric Services, Douglas Gardens Community Mental Health Center, Miami Beach, and University of Miami School of Medicine, Miami, Florida.

Shayna Stein, Ph.D., Social Science Researcher, VA Medical Center and Department of Psychiatry, University of Miami School of Medicine, Miami, Florida.

Edward Stodola, Ph.D., Counseling Psychologist, Department of Counseling Psychology, University of Kentucky, Lexington, Kentucky.

Michael Strober, Ph.D., Professor, UCLA Neuropsychiatric Institute, School of Medicine, University of California at Los Angeles, Los Angeles, California.

Juliette Thompson, F.N.C., Clinical Nurse Specialist, Division of Adolescent Medicine, Vanderbilt University, Nashville, Tennessee.

Fred Tudiver, M.D., C.C.F.P., Professor of Family Medicine, Department of Medicine, Memorial VA of Newfoundland, St. Johns, Newfoundland.

A. Vadher, M.D., Professor, Department of Psychiatry, Institute of Medicine, Oxford University, England.

Dennis Van Uitert, Ph.D., Staff Psychologist, Center for Counseling, McKay-Dee Hospital Center, Ogden, Utah.

Christine Vaughn, Ph.D., Director, Family Factors Project Mental Health Clinical Research Center for the Study of Schizophrenia, Camarillo, California.

Lane Veltkamp, M.S.W., Professor and Director, Family Mediation Clinic, Department of Psychiatry, University of Kentucky, Lexington, Kentucky.

Joseph Ventura, M.A., Research Associate, Clinical Research Center for the Study of Schizophrenia/Rehabilitation Research and Training Center, Brentwood VA Medical Center, Los Angeles, California.

J. Ingram Walker, M.D., Staff Psychiatrist, VA Medical Center, Durham, North Carolina.

Lynn S. Walker, Ph.D., Clinical Psychologist, Division of Adolescent Medicine, Vanderbilt University, Nashville, Tennessee.

Preface

This book is designed to incorporate into this four-volume series on stress the latest information related to understanding stressful life events and their impact on our lives. Theoretical formulations and hypotheses, issues, and implications related to the validity and reliability of life stress measurement and its applications to both medical and mental health related concerns are addressed here. In addition, special attention is given to the individual and how that individual functions within the family in terms of stress and coping. This book views the person as both a producer of stress and a reactor to stress and attempts to identify a variety of sources of stress both from within and beyond the individual's life space.

This text is directed toward the myriad of health care deliverers and gathers together representative authorities in each of the areas presented. Many of these individuals have pioneered extremely fruitful research, and their understanding of certain pathogenic mainstream concepts that are useful in defining, analyzing, and treating stress-related disorders is broad based. There are several rich perspectives that effectively integrate the variety of generalizations about functional and dysfunctional aspects of stress.

Life-event research has become a focus of our understanding of the relationship between psychological stress and physical illness. Our purpose is to examine and summarize clinical and research evidence addressing the assessment of stressful life events, prominent scales for the measurement of stressful life events, and various issues and implications for both clinical and research application. A perspective on critical directions which might yet emerge in this most significant arena of study is offered in this text.

Traumatic experiences can create anxiety, stress, and tension sufficient to impact severely on one's psychological well-being. Identification and measurement of such stressful life events has gained considerable clinical and research interest. The medical and health-related professions have over the past decade begun to scrutinize the role and function of stressful life events as a correlate of illness. Examined herein are prominent measures of life events and the issues and implications which emerge when employing life events scaling in the process of researching psychological well-being.

The health profession has endeavored to address the importance of stress in life events through the inclusion of evidence as to the occurrence and severity of recent stressful events (Axis IV) in *The Diagnostic and Statistical Manual of Mental Disorders* (DSM-III). This is an important development by the health related professions to address the assessment of life stress as a precipitator or contributor to the onset of illness. Basic to an understanding of the effects of psychological or social data in precipitating illness is the distinction between necessary and sufficient cause. Some factor, which can be labeled the "necessary cause," must be present for disease or illness to occur, but its presence alone is not sufficient to produce disease. Other factors, one or more, must coincide with the necessary cause and provide the sufficient conditions for the disease state.

THE CONCEPTUAL MODELS OF STRESSFUL LIFE EVENTS

The experience of life events arises from an interaction between the individual and the situation—an asynchrony between change within the individual and change within the environment (Thomae, 1979; Chiriboga, 1982). In a real sense, an event is a special or significant occurrence. But what is a "significant," "stressful," or "critical" life event? Some investigators have restricted their definition of life events to "personal catastrophes" such as life-threatening illnesses (Hudgens, 1974), while others include a wide array of events "whose advent is either indicative of, or requires a significant change in, the ongoing life pattern of the individual" (Holmes and Masuda, 1974, p. 36). Such events may occur in school, work, love and marriage, children, residence, finances, social activities, and health. Some of these events are "negative" in a sense they are typically socially undesired, while others of them are socially desired and therefore "positive." In either case, they required adaptation and change on the part of the individual experiencing them.

There are several social psychological models of life stress processes that have been offered of late (Dohrenwend and Shrout, 1985). Such models reflect not only various types of psychopathology but also have application to health changes to be correlated with stressful life experiences. Dohrenwend and Martin (1979) suggest a model which argues that stressful life events cause psychopathology. This is based on empirical studies of extreme situations which often are life threatening, and it is referred to as the victimization model. A second model argues a predisposition approach wherein social conditions mediate the causal relation between stressful life events and resulting psychopathology; such a model argues that one has a vulnerability to stressful life experiences.

The additive burden model (Dohrenwend and Shrout, 1985) contrasts in ways with the vulnerability model in that it argues that personal dispositions and social conditions are portrayed as making independent causal contributions to the occurrence of psychopathology rather than mediating a stressful life experience.

The chronic burden model forgoes the issue of any recent life events but argues in favor of stable personal dispositions and social conditions which alone can cause the adverse changes in psychological and physical condition.

The proneness model suggests the presence of disorder leads to stressful life events which in turn exacerbate the disorder. This adds a new dimension to the directionality of the causal relationships between stressful life events and psycho-pathology. Each of these models provides a framework from which the more carefully assessed crucial issues in understanding the conceptualization of stressful life events. Of considerable concern to the clinical research area is the interaction between personal predisposition and social circumstances which is an estimate of the way in which any person adjusts to a stressful life experience.

Life events and how they are experienced vary from person to person and culture to culture. One major experimental approach to this problem has been to measure the amount of stress or behavioral change associated with different events (Dohrenwend, Krasnoff, Askenasy, and Dohrenwend, 1978). Researchers have done this by asking people to rate lists of life events. The widely used Social Readjustment Rating Scale (SRRS) developed by Holmes and Rahe (1967) to measure the stress of life events is illustrative of this approach. Holmes and Rahe provided the major impetus toward the systematic scaling of life events through quantifying the correlates between major life events and both physical and psychiatric disorders. More recently several research teams have contributed to what is now a significant element in the study of triggering factors which may result in major physical and psychiatric illnesses. Antonovsky and Katz (1967), Brown and Birley (1968), Paykel, Prusoff, and Uhlenhuth (1971), Myers, Lindenthal, and Pepper (1975), Dohrenwend and Martin (1979), have all generated life events scales and subsequent research to assess the validity and reliability of life events as a significant factor in precipitating change in the life functioning of human beings. There remains considerable variability among these researchers as to which life events weigh more significantly in assessing their impact on human behavior.

Brown and Birley (1968) formulated an inventory of life change events derived from interviews with individuals developing acute episodes of schizophrenia. Paykel et al. (1971) extended Holmes and Rahe's lists to 60 life change events while Myers et al. (1975) formulated a list of 62 events, based on items from the work of Holmes and Rahe (1967) and Antonovsky and Katz (1967). Rahe subsequently expanded his original list to 54 events, some of which had two to four options, making the actual number 76 events. Dohrenwend and Dohrenwend (1974) composed a life change list of 102 items. While the Dohrenwends rethought issues of sampling, completeness, and wording of life events, their list proved to be very similar to previous inventories.

Holmes and Rahe (1967) employed the Stevens (1974) technique of magnitude estimation in attempting to determine gradients of social and life change or readjustment. The technique focuses on the realization that specific events may cause change in the average person regardless of the desirability of the event. Examples of this include such life events as extremely pleasant life changes (such as marriage, inheriting a large sum of money, etc.) and were found to require nearly equal amounts of life adjustment as unpleasant events. It was because of this factor that life change events were originally scaled in terms of the amount of change they produced on a person's adaptability to stress producing events. The focus of current measurement research at the Life Change and Illness Research Project at the VA and UCLA is on examining universal and group specific elements of stressful life events. Group specific populations are being studied and the environmental differences and interaction effects which result from cultural variations are being explored.

It is hoped that this volume will contribute significantly to our understanding of life stress events and provide a conceptual clarity and scholarly direction in bringing together an international and multidisciplinary understanding of this concept.

REFERENCES

Antonovsky, A., & Katz, R. (1967), The life crisis history as a tool in epidemiological research. *J. Health & Soc. Behav.*, 8:15–21.

Brown, G. W., & Birley, J. L. (1968), Crisis and life changes and the onset of schizophrenia. *J. Health & Soc. Behav.*, 9:203–214.

Chiriboga, D. A. (1982), An examination of life events as possible antecedents to change. *J. Gerontol.*, 37/5:595–601.

Dohrenwend, B. P., & Shrout, P. E. (1985), "Hassles" in the conceptualization and measurement of life stress variables. *Amer. Psychol.*, 40/7:780–785.

Dohrenwend, B. S., Krasnoff, L., Askenasy, A. R., & Dohrenwend, B. P. (1978), Exemplification of a method for scaling life events: The PERI life events scale. *J. Health & Soc. Behav.*, 19:205–229.

——— Martin, J. L. (1979), Personal versus situational determination of anticipation and control of the occurrence of stressful life events. *Amer. J. Commun. Psychol.*, 7, 453–468.

Holmes, T. H., & Masuda, M. (1974), Life change and illness susceptibility. In: *Stressful Life Events: Their Nature and Effects*, ed. B. S. Dohrenwend & B. P. Dohrenwend. New York: John Wiley, pp. 45–72.

——— Rahe, R. H. (1967), The Social Readjustment Rating Scale. *J. Psychosom. Res.*, 11:213–218.

Hudgens, R. W. (1974), Personal catastrophe and depression: A consideration of the subject with respect to a medically ill adolescent, and a requiem for retrospective life-event studies. In: *Stressful Life Events: Their Nature and Effects*, ed. B. S. Dohrenwend & B. P. Dohrenwend. New York: John Wiley, pp. 119–134.

Myers, J. K., Lindenthal, J. J., & Pepper, M. D. (1975), Life events and psychiatric impairment. *J. Nerv. & Ment. Dis.*, 152:149–157.

Paykel, E. S., Prusoff, B. A., & Uhlenhuth, E. H. (1971), Scaling of life events. *Arch. Gen. Psychiat.*, 25:340–347.

Stevens, S. S. (1974), *Psychophysics: Introduction to Its Perceptual, Neutral and Social Prospects*. New York: John Wiley.

Thomae, H. (1979), The concept of development and life-span developmental psychology. In: *Life-Span Development and Behavior*, Vol. 2, ed. P. B. Baltes & O. G. Brim, Jr. New York: Academic Press.

Part I
Theoretical Considerations
in Stressful Life Events

At the forefront of today's understanding of events and their impact on the human organism are a variety of theories which argue either that stress lies within the environmental input, that it is couched in the cognitive appraisal, or that stress lies toward environmental input or that it is a multivariant, multiprocess system that views no single variable or process as the etiology, psychopathology in the organism. It is seen rather as a complex system of variables that address the environment, the personality of the individual organism and the impact of the stressful life event on both. Dr. Richard Rahe has distinguished himself and his work done in conjunction with Holmes and others for their thorough study of developmental input into the concept of life stress events. The initial contribution to this compendium is authored by Dr. Richard Rahe and looks at the historical roots of stress and how they reside within the realm of philosophy as well as medicine. Tracing as he did on the works of Descartes, counterbalancing Descartes' view with that of Spinoza, the noted religious philosopher, he guides the reader through the nineteenth century early psychophysiological efforts at understanding conceptualizing stress to the twentieth century experiments explaining a close integration of mind and body, of *psyche* and *some,* as critically important issues in our search for understanding of the importance and significance of how stress influences adaptational outcomes, social functioning, and a sense of well-being in the organism.

Drs. Pruchno, Blow, and Smyer of the Pennsylvania State

University address in chapter 2 a single life event and how this event has the capacity to effect and change not one but several lives. The central thesis of this chapter is that a single life event has the capacity to affect and change not one but several lives. This thesis is related to theory on attachment, roles, and convoys. The concept of life-event webs is introduced to capture the complex relations among individuals within networks such as families. Research challenges presented by the life-event web perspective include defining networks, assessing the impact of events on each member, and treating the web, not the individual, as the unit of analysis. The web perspective implies that intervention programs should be focused not on the individual but on the web.

Miller addresses conceptual and theoretical issues in stressful life events. Examined are research evidence addressing the assessment of life events, prominent skills for the measurement of stressful life events, and various issues and implications for both clinical and research application. Methodological questions and alternatives together with prospectives on critical directions necessary for the accurate measurement of stressful life events are discussed.

Dr. Day's presentation which addresses the "triggering" hypothesis looks at life events and their impact on psychopathology. It reviews the life event research specific to schizophrenia with the goal of assessing the extent to which recent empirical studies have implicated life stress variables as precipitants of acute episodes of this disorder. Different methodological strategies used in life event research are reviewed along with the substantive findings from quasi-experimental and controlled studies of schizophrenic patients. It is concluded that stressful life events have been found to be part of the pool of factors associated with the onset of acute schizophrenic episodes, but evidence is still lacking to indicate that this association is a necessary or direct one. Recommendations are made regarding the types of future studies required to fill the gaps in the existing literature.

The final article in this first section is authored by Drs.

Matthews, Scheier, Brunson, and Carducci and asks the question "Why do unpredictable events lead to reports of physical symptoms?" In Experiment 1, subjects performed a reaction time task while they listened to loud bursts of either predictable or unpredictable noise. As expected, reaction times were slower when the noise was unpredictable than when it was not. This finding suggests that more attention had been directed to the unpredictable than the predictable noise. In Experiments 2 and 3, subjects were exposed to either predictable or unpredictable noise and were either instructed to attend to the noise or given no special instructions. In both cases, subjects not instructed to attend to the noise reported more severe symptoms when the noise was unpredictable than when it was not, thus replicating the previous finding. Of greater interest, however, was the fact that equating the amount of attention directed to the unpredictable and predictable noise (by asking subjects to attend to the noise) eliminated the apparent benefits of predictability. Discussion of the findings centers on their theoretical and practical significance to stressful life events.

Chapter 1
Recent Life Change Stress and Psychological Depression

RICHARD H. RAHE, M.D.

The historical roots of stress concepts reside in the realm of philosophy as well as in medicine. For example, Descartes can be credited with the articulation of a dissociation between mind and body which still hampers modern day conceptualizations of stress and its effects. In the pursuit of his "philosophical reductionism" Descartes argued for the basic independence of the mind, especially in terms of thoughts and emotion, from the functions of the body. Counterbalancing Descartes' view was that of Spinoza, who emphasized the desirability of harmonious integration of a person's thoughts and emotions with his bodily functions and health. Spinoza, a noted religious philosopher, was influenced in his formulations by the religions of China and Japan.

In the nineteenth century, the Russian physiologist Ivan Pavlov repeatedly stated that the functions of the brain could be investigated in the same physiological manner as those employed in investigations of bodily functions. The French phys-

Acknowledgment. This chapter was first published in the *Rhode Island Medical Journal* (1980), 63/2:98–101, and it is reprinted by permission.

iologist Claude Bernard was impressed by the balance of physiological systems. His observations on the consistency of the "internal milieu" led him to conceptualize key elements pertaining to the body's maintenance of vital functions despite various environmental influences tending to alter these functions.

In the twentieth century, experiments which displayed the close integration of mind and body were conducted by physicians such as Walter B. Cannon and Hans Selye. By the mid-twentieth century, Harold G. Wolff's laboratory at Cornell University profoundly affected our thinking regarding measurement of life stress. Wolff, in turn, had been strongly influenced by the Swiss-American psychiatrist Adolf Meyer. During Meyer's tenure as Head of Psychiatry at the Johns Hopkins Medical School, he taught the use of his life chart in collating patients' biographical and biological health data. One of Dr. Wolff's colleagues, Thomas H. Holmes, extended work on the life chart approach, and in collaboration with sociologist David Hawkins devised the first recent life changes questionnaire. As a medical student the author worked with Dr. Holmes in revising Hawkins's questionnaire to specify more clearly the life change events being measured in order to achieve a sampling of events from five major aspects of life adjustment: health, work, family, personal, social, and financial. The author also initiated studies designed to determine estimations of magnitude for the various life change events on the questionnaire (Rahe, Meyer, and Smith, 1964).

RECENT LIFE CHANGES MEASUREMENT

Although it should be mentioned that there is no unanimity of opinion among researchers today as to a definitive list of recent life changes events, one of the first lists published was the one by Holmes and Rahe (1967). The original list contained 43 life change events. The revised list, which the author has used over the past two decades, contains 71 events. It was always the intent to sample events from key aspects of life adjustment, rather than to cover all possibilities.

The concept of change was used to quantify life events because of pioneering work by physiologists such as Bernard and Cannon. Assuming that a person's psychosocial adjustment is also maintained in some sort of balance, as in physiological homeostatic systems, psychosocial demands should cause temporary shifts in this balance with a return to a normal state after a period of time. Thus, the amount of change from previous psychosocial balance produced by recent life change events was used to determine our units of stress.

The results of our studies indicated that groups of individuals showed remarkable agreement as to average degrees of life change and readjustment engendered by each of the events on the list. Later cross-cultural studies confirmed these earlier findings (Rahe, 1969; Rahe, Lundberg, and Bennett, 1971).

RECENT LIFE CHANGE EVENTS AND DEPRESSION

We will now attempt to put in perspective the ways in which an individual's recent life change events may be related to the onset of psychological depression; examples derived from the science of epidemiology will be used. Life change events can be considered in many respects as an environmental "risk factor" for the development of depressive illness.

Most people are aware of how one's level of serum cholesterol is considered an environmental risk factor for development of coronary heart disease (CHD). When serum cholesterol data are viewed from an epidemiological point of view, it will be found that, although it's true that people who develop CHD generally have significantly higher serum cholesterol levels than people who remain free of this disease, the majority of persons with high serum cholesterol never develop CHD. This is a seeming paradox, until you realize that the universe of persons with elevated serum cholesterol levels is very large and the percentage of that universe who go on to develop CHD is quite small. Accordingly, there are far more false positives than true positives for this risk factor.

The same observations hold true for recent life change events and psychological depression. Depressed patients presenting at an outpatient clinic tend to report more recent life change events than do health controls (Paykel, Myers, and Dienelt, 1969). Inpatients with depressive disorders report even higher levels of recent life change. Suicidal patients report highest levels, a fourfold increase over control values (Paykel et al., 1969). Once again, the universe of persons with elevated recent life changes is very large. The majority of the persons in this universe remain in good spirits, and only a small proportion go on to develop depression. As with serum cholesterol and coronary heart disease, there are far more false positives than true positives with this risk factor.

RECENT LIFE CHANGE AND AN ILLNESS ONSET MODEL

Perhaps the best way to present the influence of recent life change events upon the onset of psychological depression is by the use of an optical model (Rahe and Arthur, 1978). If one conceptualizes subjects' recent life change events as a series of light rays passing through a number of lenses and filters, the distortion produced upon these light rays by the various lenses and filters represents the modifications by subjects' personal characteristics of the impact of these events. The first filter through which recent life change events pass is a polarizing filter. This polarizing filter symbolizes subjects' perceptions.

That is to say, some individuals perceive recent life change events as more, or less, difficult to adapt to than does the average individual. Thus, an individual may have a very different subjective interpretation of a recent life change event than does the average person, due to his own perceptive biases. Next in this model is a negative lens. This negative lens symbolizes psychological defenses. It has been demonstrated that some psychological defense mechanisms, such as repression and denial, essentially divert the normally arousing effects of significant recent life change events (Wolff, Friedman, and Hofer, 1964). However, most recent life change events of significant magnitude are both perceived by the individual and not totally defended against, causing some degree of physiological arousal.

The "energy" emanating from physiological arousal in the model then passes through a color filter. This color filter represents a person's coping capabilities. Coping capabilities may selectively "absorb" physiological arousal (symptoms) secondary to recent life change experience. The last lens in the model is a positive lens which represents illness behavior. A number of people perceive their recent life change events as significant, do not entirely defend against them, have some secondary physiological arousal, and fail completely to cope with resultant symptoms of a medical nature. Thus, these symptomatic persons never receive a diagnosis or medical treatment. It is only when individuals' illnesses are diagnosed and recorded that studies of recent life change events and illness cases can be carried out.

Once again utilizing the epidemiologic model, recent life change events in the lives of persons developing psychological depression (entered on medical records) represent only a small proportion of the universe of persons exposed to recent life change stress. Most persons so exposed either do not perceive these life changes as threatening, or successfully defend against them, or cope extremely well with resultant symptoms, or go on to become symptomatic, or any combination of these, but never report their symptoms to medical personnel.

SUMMARY

In this brief discussion some of the historical roots of stress concepts have been presented as well as information regarding the derivation of a questionnaire which measures recent life change experience as one aspect of recent life stress. Not only can recent life events be inventoried, but some estimation of the magnitudes of these events can be ascertained. Several studies have indicated that recent life change events occur more frequently in the lives of those subjects who report psychological depression than in normal controls. Although recent life change can serve as an environmental risk factor to identify those at elevated risk of developing psychological depression, far more false positives than true positives will be classified. Therefore, to evaluate persons' recent life stress for its possible influence leading to psychological depression, it is more helpful to trace the effects of recent life changes through the patient's perception, his psychological defenses, his coping skills, and his illness behaviors. Only after this has been done can the clinician obtain a clear understanding of an individual's recent life change stress and his illness susceptibility.

REFERENCES

Holmes, T. H., & Rahe, R. H. (1967), The Social Readjustment Rating Scale. *J. Psychosom. Res.*, 11:213–218.

Paykel, E. S., Myers, J. K., & Dienelt, M. N. (1969), Life events and depression. *Arch. Gen. Psychiat.*, 21:753–760.

Rahe, R. H. (1969), Multicultural correlations of life changes scaling. America, Japan, Denmark, and Sweden. *J. Psychosom. Res.*, 13:191–195.

——— Arthur, R. J. (1978), Life change and illness studies: Past history and future directions. *Hum. Stress*, 4:3–15.

——— Lundberg, U., & Bennett, L. (1971), The Social Readjustment Rating Scale: A comparative study of Swedes and Americans. *Psychosom. Res.*, 15:241–249.

——— Meyer, M., & Smith, M. (1964), Social stress and illness onset. *J. Psychosom. Res.*, 8:35–44.

Wolff, C. T., Friedman, S. B., & Hofer, M. A. (1964), Relationship between psychological defenses and mean urinary 17-hydroxycorticosteroid excretion rates: I. A predictive study of parents of fatally ill children. *Psychosom. Med.*, 26:576–591.

Chapter 2
Life Events and Interdependent Lives: Implications for Research and Intervention

R. A. PRUCHNO, PH.D., F. C. BLOW, PH.D., AND
M. A. SMYER, PH.D.

One woman gives birth to a child, another becomes a widow; one man suffers a serious heart attack, still another retires. Each incident has been the subject of intensive study (Rossi, 1968; Atchley, 1971; Lopata, 1973; Theorell, 1974). Such research is grounded primarily in two distinct world views: the mechanistic and the organismic. What these perspectives have in common is that a life event involves change in an individual's usual activities. Each fails, however, to consider the effect of an event beyond a single individual life, thereby neglecting the fact that the lives of people are intricately linked. The central thesis of this chapter is that a life event has the capacity to affect and change several lives. This proposition is grounded in the framework of the contextual or dialectical metamodel (Riegel, 1976). From this perspective, human development involves the coa-

Acknowledgment. This chapter was first published in *Human Development* (1984), 27:31–41, and it is reprinted by permission.

lescing of several dynamically interactive change processes (Riegel, 1975; Meacham, 1976).

The proposition that events have the capacity to affect several lives can be related to two long-established bodies of theory: (1) theories of attachment and interdependence which identify the "glue" which serves to unite people, and (2) theories of roles and convoys which define the ways in which relationships between people are operationalized. Previous life event research which has considered the role of people other than the target person has been limited to considering them as a mediating factor, capable of providing social support. Lowenthal and Haven (1968), for example, indicate that an intimate relationship with a confidant serves as a buffer against events such as retirement and widowhood. Similar findings are reported by Nuckolls, Cassell, and Kaplan (1972) with regard to the influence of the social network on pregnant women.

Individuals are linked together in complex ways, and therefore events have the capacity to affect networks or people. Positing multiple effects of life events will lead not only to a more thorough understanding of events themselves, but will ultimately help to explain developmental differences both between individuals as well as within a given individual. Such a proposition has important implications for the method of study, unit of analysis, and statistical analyses as well as for appropriate targets of intervention.

ATTACHMENT, INTERDEPENDENCE, AND ROLE PARTNERS

Although the concept of attachment occupies a central place in the literature on early childhood (Bowlby, 1969), its importance in the world of adulthood has only recently been addressed (Kahn and Antonucci, 1980). Originally construed as seeking proximity to the primary caretaker, especially in times of stress, attachment has come to be regarded more broadly.

Lerner and Ryff (1978), for example, apply the concept to the interpersonal relationships across the life span, while Kahn and Antonucci (1980) view attachment relationships as both a prototype of and precursor to supportive interactions in adulthood.

From a different though related perspective, Durkheim (1947) contended that happiness depends on the individual finding a sense of meaning outside himself. This can occur only in the context of group involvement. Similarly, Clark (1969) argued that social beings are interdependent organisms whose functional capacities, if not their very survival, depend on what they derive from others. The concept of interdependence among people provided the basis for the work of exchange theorists such as Homans (1980) and Kelley and Thibault (1954). Such theory assumes that exchange patterns are interactions between persons who psychologically exchange rewards and costs. As such, interdependence is viewed as vital to maintaining one's life. If interdependence among lives is assumed, it follows that a change in one life must have implications for others with whom one is connected.

The concept of roles is central to this assumption of interdependence. Roles define a set of activities expected of a person by virtue of a specific position in society. Thus roles serve to organize interactions among people (Merton, 1957). By definition, roles require role partners and may be used to describe the interconnectedness of individuals. Within this framework, people have partners who both influence and are influenced by one another. Thus, a man cannot be a husband if he does not have a wife, nor can he be a parent if he has no child.

LIFE-EVENT WEBS

Danish, Smyer, and Nowak (1980) argue for studying life events in a total life context. They contend that events per se do not cause change. Rather, a variety of event factors such as timing, sequencing, and duration must be considered. A salient aspect of the life context is the social world, especially that occupied by an individual's role partners. The term *life-event webs* captures the essence of an intricate linking of individual lives. Because entangled lives are sensitive to one another, they must bend and adapt to multiple events and changes. People are viewed as partners whose lives are so intricately interwoven that a life event has the potential to change not one but many lives. The extent of the effect which an event has depends on many considerations, including characteristics of the individuals involved, characteristics of the events, and the interaction between the two.

The study of life-event webs is concerned with change. Rather than focusing on one life, as has been traditionally the case, the concern becomes that of understanding the effect of a given event on multiple lives. The life-span orientation, reviewed by Baltes, Reese, and Lipsit (1980), is a useful perspective within which to develop these ideas. This perspective suggests that behavior change processes that fall under the rubric of development are viewed as a lifelong process. From this perspective, life events have both proximal and distal effects. The former produce their effects directly while the latter produce their effects through mediating variables.

These effects may be interpreted in two ways, both of which provide explanations for the vehicles of change. First, we may consider as proximal those effects experienced by the target individual, the focal concern of traditional life event research; and as distal, the effects on the rest of the family members. One aspect of the distal effects has been addressed by sociologists (Merton and Rossi, 1968) as anticipatory socialization. Defined as the patterned, but often unplanned, learning of a role in advance of assuming it, anticipatory socialization has been cited as a way of easing role transitions (Riley and Waring, 1976). Thus, a 50-year-old man may begin to understand the adaptations he will have to make upon retirement by observing an older business associate adjust to a new way of life.

Similarly, experiencing events through the eyes of others may serve as negative examples of anticipatory socialization.

Children may, for example, learn that they have little control over their environment as a result of living with parents who are relatively powerless and experience the loss of a job. Much of the literature on learned helplessness suggests such experiences as a preface to ineffectual modes of coping in the world (Schulz, 1979).

Hagestad (1981), referring to the anticipatory socialization function of families as role partners, contends that the family offers a unique "life-span reflector," one where members observe others in life phases, and anticipate the joys and sorrows of phases yet to come. One of the reasons it is often so painful for a middle-aged child to cope with a parent's failing health may be that the event sparks feelings of anticipation and dread regarding the middle-aged child's own future. Thus, using the distal-proximal distinction of Baltes et al. (1980), it is possible to understand how events which are distal in time may be considered antecedents to present developmental phenomena, as well as how events which are proximal may be dealt with as a function of how they were witnessed in the past.

A second interpretation of the proximal and distal effects focuses on the principle which Lerner, Skinner, and Sorrell (1980) term *evolving reciprocity*. This refers to the fact that changes in the given target level affect changes in all other levels, and in turn this influence provides feedback to the target level. Interactions are constant throughout time, thus return to the initial point is impossible.

Empirical evidence of this is reported by Sameroff (1975), who found that the quality and quantity of exchange relationships between mothers and their infants are important to understanding individual change in both. This finding is in direct opposition to traditional thought on the direction of socialization. The term *socialization* refers to the process by which an individual learns the rights and obligations associated with a new role (Riley and Waring, 1976), and has been viewed as a one-way process, with one individual being socialized and the other doing the socializing. For example, mothers were perceived as the agents of socialization, while the child's behavior was seen as the target of socialization.

Bengtson and Black (1973) and Bengtson and Treas (1980) discuss this principle in relationship to transmission between generations. They use the term *bilateral negotiation* to refer to the concept that socialization is not a unidirectional process, but rather each individual approaches the relationship as an agent of his or her own developmental interests, and each partner influences and is influenced by the socialization process and its outcomes. This suggests that socialization is a lifelong process (Brim and Wheeler, 1966), one that involves new learning in adulthood as well as in childhood.

If the principles of evolving reciprocity are considered over time, they suggest that when one person undergoes change, his or her role partners will also be affected by the change. Focusing on the family, a group whose lives are highly interconnected, it appears that "voluntary" transitions by one family member may create "involuntary" changes for another (Riley and Waring, 1976). Riley and Waring (1976) speak of this as "counter-transitions" and cite, as an example, the transition to motherhood. Motherhood is accompanied by the infant's entry into the role of child, by the husband's transition to fatherhood, and by the transformation of the couple's parents into grandparents. Similarly, the retirement of a business executive may change the lives of former office mates as well as the life of his or her spouse.

Hagestad (1981) speaks of these as "ripple effects." For example, "Marriage in one generation creates in-laws in another. Parenthood creates grandparenthood. Voluntary childlessness may create involuntary grandchildlessness" (p.12). Similarly, an involuntary transition by one family member may spark the opportunity for voluntary transition by another. For example, widowhood may provide a woman with the opportunity to resume a career or remarry. Elder's (1974) study of growing up during the Great Depression provides an example or how economic failure on the father's part led to the mother's search for employment, and shifted responsibilities in the children. It also served to increase the prominence of mothers in family affairs.

Komarovsky's (1940) study of the consequences of unemployment for the family and Hill's (1949) study of the effects of wartime separation also illustrate the phenomenon of evolving reciprocity within the family. In their study of how farm families cope with heart disease, Bubkoz and Eichhorn (1977) describe such far-reaching family changes as a redivision of labor and alterations in relationships between spouses as well as between parents and their children. Empirical research by Kerckhoff (1964) and Lipman (1961) revealed that wives' lives were greatly affected by their husband's retirement.

Evidence of a reciprocal change process which was not successfully negotiated is discussed by Bart (1968). She found a high incidence of depression among "empty nest" females hospitalized for the first time for mental illness. Linking these problems to the physical and emotional leave-taking of their children, Bart found that what these women had in common was that their lives had once been filled by the traditional role of mother and housewife. Once their children left home, their self-concepts were so threatened by loss of the maternal role that they needed outside help to adapt.

LIFE-EVENT WEBS: A DEVELOPMENTAL PERSPECTIVE

The developmental flavor of life-event webs is closely tied to developmental perspectives of attachment and roles. Individuals enter and leave numerous roles during their life courses, roles which provide the foundation for relationships with other people. Similarly, attachments to other people both endure and change over time (Lerner and Ryff, 1978). These concepts suggest that over the life course some members in a given network will change, while other members will remain stable. However, despite the stability of a given person in a network, the rest of the structure and the functioning of that network is subject to change over time. In addition, it must be remembered that at any given point in time, an individual may be involved in several networks. Over the life course, membership in these networks may change or remain stable.

The possibility of both stability and change in network membership has several results. Events which occur to a target person over time also have the potential to affect various significant others. Following changes in attachment and roles, some of these significant others will change over time, while others will remain the same. However, the structure of the total web of people affected as well as the way in which the web functions will likely change over time. For example, in the case of a five-year old child who starts school, other people affected by the event may include parents and siblings but also the lives of the spouse, the spouse's family, and their close friends.

If, on the other hand, we consider the involvement of a particular person in the life events which occur to other people, quite a different picture emerges. For example, an adolescent may be part of a web which experiences the death of a member. This death may change both the structure and functioning of the remaining network members. This same person years later may be involved in the web of an older associate facing retirement, and because of this involvement, have his or her own life changed.

A developmental perspective on life event webs would be incomplete without postulating cohort or historical effects. The social networks in which people are engaged are further embedded in the larger historical and cultural context. It can be predicted that cohorts will differ in the degree to which they are affected by events occurring within their webs. Swidler (1980), for example, has argued that cohorts of the 1940s and 1950s are less embedded in life-event webs than earlier cohorts, or at least are more willing to sacrifice the web for the sake of "personal growth."

RESEARCH IMPLICATIONS OF A WEB
PERSPECTIVE

The challenge of developing appropriate methods for the study of webs is a formidable one. Indeed, recent work in the areas of intergenerational relations (Hill, Foote, Aldous, Carlson, and MacDonald, 1970) and midlife divorce (Hagestad, Smyer, and Stierman, 1983) has illuminated some of the difficulties of studying systems of interacting lives. These studies have shown that major obstacles must be overcome before meaningful research on life-event webs can be undertaken. As is true for research in general, the problems and issues for methods of study must be guided by the questions to which answers are sought.

The search for an understanding of the multiple effects of life events on role partners presents a new set of research questions which previous paradigms have not considered. In this sense, we face a watershed, for the life-event web perspective focuses on substantively different questions and takes the development of the field in a new, different direction. Similar circumstances faced the field of psychotherapy when the concern switched from the individual to the family as the context for understanding developmental problems.

One set of research issues suggested by a life-event web perspective revolves around defining networks of people around which a web is spun. Researchers concerned with network analyses have struggled with a similar problem for decades. Wellman (1979), for example, found that only 36 percent of the surveyed intimates in a study reciprocally named the orginal target person as their own intimate. One successful approach to getting these data is to have the target person identified initially. Another approach might be to define webs, a priori, as comprised of family members. This facilitates member identification, yet excludes friends and neighbors who may be important, vital web members. It may also artificially include people in the web who are not involved in the target person's life. Perhaps the most parsimonious approach, especially if the issue is defining how life-event webs are spun, combines elements of both perspectives.

Once the web members are identified, the second challenge is that of assessing the impact of a specific life event on each member. This requires obtaining adequate subject participation. While researchers often have difficulty convincing individuals to participate in their studies, these problems would be compounded if the goal becomes collecting data from several members of a web.

The challenges of defining how life-event webs are formed as well as how events affect multiple lives are grounded in traditional research paradigms in which the unit of analysis is the individual. Here, data reduction and statistical techniques are available which permit analyses of individual data. When the issue shifts to how a given life event changes the structure and functioning of an existing network, the issues become more complicated. This orientation, which concerns the multiple effects of life events on networks of individuals, challenges the traditional unit of analysis of life-event research, namely, the individual. The unit of concern is no longer the individual, but rather the network members ensconced in the web.

A similar shift in the unit of analysis has been suggested by researchers concerned with intergenerational relations. Consideration of that literature reveals the array of problems associated with this new unit of analysis. Until recently intergenerational studies focused on the individual as the unit of analysis. Realizing that the goal of that research was not being met, and the questions were not being adequately addressed, some researchers such as Hill et al. (1970) and Bengtson (1975) sought to change the unit of analysis to the family.

Hagestad (1981), however, points out that while family researchers have devoted considerable time and effort to collecting family data (data from multiple members of the same family), the data are then analyzed in an aggregate group fashion which treats family members as unrelated groups of individuals. These aggregates of individuals are then stacked on top of one another to construct three-generational constellations. The problem with this approach is that all unique family variance is lost. Also, information about generational exchange, family interactions, and family support systems vanishes. Conclusions are made about the interconnections of generations within families even though family constellations have been destroyed in the process. Thus, despite theoretical concern with family process, the unit of analysis has remained the individual, and conclusions made from these data do not capture what is actually happening within the family.

In contrast to this perspective, an orientation which is concerned with the multiple effects of life events on networks of individuals calls for a change from the traditional unit of analysis that will account for the interweaving of lives. Hagestad and Dixon (1980) make the argument that in order to better understand individual careers and life events, it is crucial to study family constellations or "family clusters" of life stresses and supports. By studying the interconnections of family members and maintaining the integrity of the family constellation, a clearer picture of families may be obtained. As such, it is important not only to collect data on the webs of individuals in a social network, but also to maintain the integrity of the web in each step of the data analysis.

Traditional statistical analysis techniques are not appropriate for life-event web data. Since aggregating data only brings us back to the individual as the unit of analysis, additive linear approaches are not appropriate to compile and reduce data obtained on constellations of multiple lives. Hagestad and Dixon (1980) make the argument that in order to better understand individual careers and life events, it is crucial to study family constellations or "family clusters" of life stresses and supports. By studying the interconnections of family members and maintaining the integrity of the family constellation, a clearer picture of families may be obtained. As such, it is important not only to collect data on the webs of individuals in a social network, but also to maintain the integrity of the web in each step of the data analysis.

Traditional statistical analysis techniques are not appropriate to compile and reduce data obtained on constellations of multiple lives. This problem, along with the fact that computer data-analysis packages have not been developed which adequately handle such data, makes the study of multiple lives difficult. Tasks such as data coding, which are typically easy, soon become unmanageable when dealing with the many relationships among individuals in a life-event web.

The initial steps that must be taken in a new area of study revolve around the need for methods of data reduction which allow for description, methods whose aims are exploratory rather than confirmatory. There is generally a lack of life event web baseline information about the defining characteristics of the interconnections of lives. Such parameters include size, stability, homogeneity, symmetry, and connectedness of the existing networks (Kahn and Antonucci, 1980). In addition, properties of dyadic links within networks such as interaction frequency, type of interaction, and number of life domains included in the interactions may provide further insight into the workings of the network. Only after critical network parameters are identified may the impact which a given life event has on network members and their interrelationships be understood.

A more complicated question which further addresses the intricate linking of lives is the impact of a cluster of life events affecting members of a network at a common point in time. For example, within a network one member may directly experience losing a job, another member having a baby, and still a third leaving home. If the lives of these people are linked together, it is not unrealistic to expect that each member will be affected by all these events, and furthermore that the nature of their interrelationships will be altered by their previous experiences. The research problem becomes not one of identifying comparable clusters of events between groups of interlinked people, but rather one of understanding the unique characteristics and changes which occur within the network as a result of the events which its members experience. As such, the research issues may be seen as an expansion of the single-subject design or the factor-analytic P-technique.

Perhaps the greatest challenge to research oriented toward webs is identifying strategies for data reduction. The integrity of the network is central and must not be compromised. Cluster techniques or typologies which define networks and which are capable of showing change provide a starting point for making sense of some very rich data.

IMPLICATIONS FOR INTERVENTION

A web's approach to understanding the effects of life events calls not only for a reassessment of the way data are described and phenomena are explained, but also for a review of the tactics and goals of intervention. Because the target of change is the web, not the individual, traditional modes of intervention may no longer be appropriate.

Danish et al. (1980) have suggested that human development interventions can be arrayed along two dimensions: timing of intervention and level of intervention. It is the level of intervention for which this discussion is most central. While traditionally psychological and social interventions have focused on the individual level, during the past 20 years a growing number of theoreticians and practitioners have contended that our interventions should be targeted at other levels, including family, neighborhood, community, and social policy (Albee, 1959; Bryant, 1978; Goodstein and Sandler, 1978). A good example of this position is the work of Berger and Neuhaus (1977). They suggest that the focus of public policy and public intervention should be "mediating structures." They define these as "those institutions standing between the individual in his private life and the large institutions of public life" (p. 2). In their work, Berger and Neuhaus focus on four mediating structures which are particularly relevant for public policy: neighborhoods, families, churches, and voluntary associations. They suggest that the individual is "a migrant" between and among structures of varying complexity. In order to be most effective, therefore, public policy (and, by extension, interventions) must focus on the way-stations of the migrant, which are referred to as mediating structures.

A life-event web perspective for intervention suggests that intervention programs may be most helpful when focused on the web of individuals affected by a particular life stress. For example, in the case of kin-keeping of impaired elderly, it may be most useful to focus educational and therapeutic efforts not solely on the identified caretaker but on her or his spouse and children as well. One could envision developing educational programs which would help families anticipate the changing emotional and economic resources which will be available to each member as the older generation changes its needs for and demands on the support system.

Another example emerges from recent work on divorce in middle age (Hagestad et al., 1983). Hagestad et al. began by exploring the effects of divorce on adjustment among a group of middle-aged individuals. Their initial inquiries revealed, however, that the stress of midlife divorce had ripple effects on both the older and younger generation. For example, many of the middle-aged women turned to their children for economic and emotional assistance following a divorce in midlife. Others turned to their parents. For both the older and younger generations, these demands for support may have come at just the time in their lives when they were looking forward to support from the middle generation. In other words, the entire family may have been unprepared for the demands placed upon it. One of the lessons for intervenors which emerges from this work is that the entire family system—from the younger generation (children of midlife divorce) through the older generation (parents of midlife divorce)—should be the target of intervention. One could envision, for example, educational programs and preventive materials developed to alert the family system of the potentially important role families may play aiding adjustment to midlife divorce. In addition, materials which focus on some of the potential problems and difficulties which may face the family of midlife divorce, such as economic shortages and time conflicts, may ease the family transition as members face the process of midlife divorce together.

Not only do interventions targeted at the web level require innovative strategies, they are also subject to some of the same issues which plague research at this level. For example, it requires enlisting cooperation and active participation from multiple network members. This challenge may be formidable given that people identified by the target person may not consider themselves to be affected by a given life event. One possible solution to this problem is to let the target person, those the target identifies as involved in exchanges characterized by affect, affirmation, or aid, as well as family members who identify themselves as involved, participate in various intervention programs.

REFERENCES

Albee, G. W. (1959), *Mental Health Manpower Needs*. New York: Basic Books.
Atchley, R. C. (1971), Retirement and work orientation. *Gerontologist*, 11:29–32.
Baltes, P. B., Reese, H. W., & Lipsit, L. P. (1980), Life-span developmental psychology. *Amer. Rev. Psychol.*, 31:65–110.
Bart, P. (1968), Social structure and vocabularies of discomfort: What happened to female hysteria? *J. Health & Soc. Behav.*, 9:188–193.
Bengtson, V. L. (1975), Generation and family effects in value socialization. *Amer. Sociol. Rev.*, 40:358–371.
—————— Black, O. (1973), Intergenerational relations: Continuation in socialization. In: *Life-Span Developmental Psychology: Personality and Socialization*, ed. F. Baltes & W. Schaie. New York: Academic Press, pp. 59–66.
—————— Treas, L. L. (1980), The changing family context of mental health and aging. In: *Handbook of Mental Health and Aging*, ed. G. Birren & T. Sloane. Englewood Cliffs, NJ: Prentice-Hall.
Berger, P. L., & Neuhaus, R. J. (1977), *To Empower People*. Washington, DC: American Enterprise Institute for Public Policy Research.
Bowlby, J. (1969), *Attachment and Loss*, Vol. 1. New York: Basic Books.
Brim, O. G., & Wheeler, S. (1966), *Socialization After Childhood: Two Essays*. New York: John Wiley.
Bryant, T. E. (1978), Report to the President from the President's Commission on Mental Health. Washington, DC: Government Printing Office.

Bubkoz, M. M. J., & Eichhorn, R. L. (1977), How farm families cope with heart disease. In: *People as Partners*, 2nd ed., ed. L. Wiseman. San Francisco: Canfield Press.

Clark, M. (1969), Cultural values and dependency in later life. In: *The Dependencies of Old People*, ed. J. R. Kalish. Ann Arbor, MI: Institute of Gerontology Press.

Danish, S. J., Smyer, M. A., & Nowak, C. (1980), Life-span development and life skills. In: *Life-Span Development and Behavior*, Vol. 3, ed. M. Baltes & C. R. Brim. New York: Academic Press, pp. 312–317.

Durkheim, E. (1947), *The Division of Labor in Society*. New York: Free Press.

Elder, G. H., Jr. (1974), *Children of the Great Depression*. Chicago: University of Chicago Press.

Goodstein, L. D., & Sandler, I. (1978), Using psychology to promote human welfare; a conceptual analysis of the role of community psychology. *Amer. Psychol.*, 33:882–892.

Hagestad, G. O. (1981), Problems and promises in the social psychology of intergenerational relations. In: *Stability and Change in the Family*, ed. J. Fogel, W. Hatfield, V. Kiesler, & R. M. March. New York: Academic Press, pp. 211–218.

—— Dixon, R. A. (1980), Lineages as units of analysis: New avenues for the study of individual and family careers. Paper presented at the National Council on Family Relations, Portland, OR.

—— Smyer, M. A., & Stierman, K. L. (1983), Parent-child relations in adulthood: The impact of divorce in middle age. In: *Parenthood: Psychodynamic Perspectives*, ed. R. Cohen, D. Weissman, & B. Cohler. New York: Guilford Press, pp. 137–146.

Hill, R. (1949), *Familes Under Stress*. New York: Harper.

—— Foote, N., Aldous, J., Carlson, R., & MacDonald, R. (1970), *Family Development in Three Generations*. Cambridge, MA: Schenkman Books.

Homans, G. C. (1980), *The Human Group*. New York: Harcourt, Brace & World.

Kahn, R. L., & Antonucci, T. C. (1980), Convoys over the life course: Attachment, roles, and social support. In: *Life-Span Development and Behavior*, Vol. 3, ed. M. Baltes & C. R. Brim. New York: Academic Press.

Kelley, H. H., & Thibault, J. W. (1954), Experimental studies of group problem solving and process. In: *Handbook of Social Psychology*, Vol. 2, ed. M. A. Lindzey. Cambridge, MA: Addison-Wesley, pp. 97–108.

Kerckhoff, A. C. (1964), Husband-wife expectations and reactions to retirement. *J. Geront.*, 19:510–516.

Komarovsky, M. (1940), *The Unemployed Man and His Family*. New York: Dryden Press.

Lerner, R. M., & Ryff, C. D. (1978), Implementation of the life-span view of human development: The sample case of attachment. In: *Life-Span De-*

velopment and Behavior, Vol. 1, ed. P. B. Baltes. New York: Academic Press, pp. 230–246.

—— Skinner, E. A., & Sorrell, G. T. (1980), Methodological implications of contextual dialectic theories of development. *Hum. Dev.*, 23:225–235.

Lipman, A. (1961), Role conceptions and morale of couples in retirement. *J. Geront.*, 16:267–271.

Lopata, H. T. (1973), *Widowhood in an American City*. Cambridge, MA: Schenkman.

Lowenthal, M. R., & Haven, C. (1968), Interaction and adaptation: Intimacy as a critical variable. In: *Middle Age and Aging*, ed. F. Neugarten. Chicago: University of Chicago Press, pp. 78–84.

Meacham, J. A. (1976), Continuing the dialogue: Dialectics and remembering. *Hum. Dev.*, 19:304–309.

Merton, R. K. (1957), *Social Theory and Social Structure*. New York: Free Press.

—— Rossi, A. S. (1968), Contributions to the theory of reference group behavior. In: *Social Theory and Social Structure*, ed. R. K. Merton. New York: Free Press, pp. 321–333.

Nuckolls, K. B., Cassell, J., & Kaplan, B. (1972), Psychosocial assets, life crises, and the prognosis of pregnancy. *Amer. J. Epidem.*, 95:431–442.

Riegel, K. F. (1976), The dialectics of human development. *Amer. Psychol.*, 31:689–700.

Riley, M. W., & Waring, J. (1976), Age and aging. In: *Contemporary Social Problems*, 4th ed., ed. R. K. Merton & W. Nisbet. New York: Harcourt, Brace, Jovanovich, pp. 237–245.

Rossi, A. (1968), Transition to parenthood. *J. Marr. & Fam.*, 30:26–39.

Sameroff, A. J. (1975), Transactional models in early social relations. *Hum. Dev.*, 18:65–79.

Schulz, R. (1979), Learned helplessness and aging. Unpublished paper.

Swidler, A. (1980), Love and adulthood in American culture. In: *Themes of Work and Love in Adulthood*, ed. N. J. Smelser & E. H. Erikson. Cambridge, MA: Harvard University Press, pp. 74–83.

Theorell, T. (1974), Life events before and after the onset of a premature myocardial infarction. In: *Stressful Life Events*, ed. B. S. Dohrenwend & B. P. Dohrenwend. New York: John Wiley, pp. 324–336.

Wellman, B. (1979), The community question; the intimate networks of East Yorkers. *Amer. J. Sociol.*, 84:1201–1225.

Chapter 3
Conceptual and Theoretical Problems in the Measurement of Life Stress

THOMAS W. MILLER, PH.D., A.B.P.P

Tennant (1983) has addressed the issue of life-event stress in the onset of psychiatric disorder as being somewhat controversial, primarily because of methodological problems of retrospective studies. In essence, Tennant has suggested that problems of inaccurately dating events and illness to insure the events were antecedent has been prominent. Furthermore, the bias of "effort after meaning" tends to occur in which subjects search their past experience for some explanation for their distress. Tennant has encouraged prospective studies in which life event experience is assessed prior to the onset of illness and, therefore, can eliminate some of these problems.

Traumatic experiences can create anxiety, stress, and tension sufficient to impact severely on one's psychological well-being. Identification and measurement of such stressful life events has gained considerable clinical and research interest. Over the past decade the medical and health-related professions

Acknowledgment. This chapter was first presented to the Kentucky Psychological Association, Annual Conference, 1985, and it is reprinted by permission.

have begun to scrutinize the role and function of stressful life events as a correlate of illness; for example, through the inclusion of evidence as to the occurrence and severity of recent stressful events (Axis IV) in its *Diagnostic and Statistical Manual of Mental Disorders* (DSM-III).

Basic to an understanding of the effects of psychological or social data in precipitating illness is the distinction between necessary and sufficient cause. Some factor, which can be labeled the "necessary cause," must be present for disease or illness to occur, but its presence alone is not sufficient to produce disease. Other factors, one or more, must coincide with the necessary cause and provide the sufficient conditions for the disease state.

THE CONCEPTUAL MODEL OF STRESSFUL LIFE EVENTS

The experience of life events arises from an interaction between the individual and the situation—an asynchrony between change within the individual and change within the environment (Thomae, 1979; Chiriboga, 1982). In a real sense, an event is a special or significant occurrence. But what is a "significant," "stressful," or "critical" life event? Some investigators have restricted their definition of life events to "personal catastrophes" such as life-threatening illnesses (Hudgens, 1974), while others include a wide array of events "whose advent is either indicative of, or requires a significant change in, the ongoing life pattern of the individual" (Holmes and Masuda, 1974). Such events may occur in school, work, love and marriage, children, residence, finances, social activities, and health. Some of these events are "negative" in the sense they are typically socially undesired, while others of them are socially desired and therefore "positive." In either case, they require adaptation and change on the part of the individual experiencing them.

The type of life events and how they are experienced varies

from person to person and culture to culture. One major experimental approach to this problem has been to measure the amount of stress of behavioral change associated with different events (Dohrenwend, Krasnoff, Askenasy, and Dohrenwend, 1978). Researchers have done this by asking people to rate lists of life events. The widely used Social Readjustment Rating Scale (SRRS) developed by Holmes and Rahe (1967) to measure the stress of life events is illustrative of this approach. Holmes and Rahe provided the major impetus toward the systematic scaling of life events through quantifying the correlates between major life events and both physical and psychiatric disorders. More recently several research teams have contributed to what is now a significant element in the study of triggering factors which may result in major physical and psychiatric illnesses. Brown and Birley (1968), Antonovsky and Katz (1967), Paykel, Prusoff, and Uhlenhuth (1971), Myers, Lindenthal, and Pepper (1975), and Hough (1980) have all generated life-event scales and subsequent research to assess the validity and reliability of life events as a significant factor in precipitating change in the life functioning of human beings. There remains considerable variability among these researchers as to which life events weigh more significantly in assessing impact on human behavior.

Brown and Birley (1968) formulated an inventory of life change events derived from interviews with individuals developing acute episodes of schizophrenia. Paykel et al. (1971) extended Holmes and Rahe's list of 62 events, based on items from the work of Holmes and Rahe, and Antonovsky and Katz. Rahe subsequently expanded his original list to 54 events, some of which had two to four options, making the actual number 76 events. Dohrenwend and Dohrenwend composed a life change list of 102 items. While the Dohrenwends rethought issues of sampling, completeness, and wording of life events, their list proved to be very similar to previous inventories.

Holmes and Rahe (1967) employed the Stevens (1974) technique of magnitude estimation in attempting to determine gradients of social and life change or readjustment. The technique focuses on the realization that specific events may cause change in the average person regardless of the desirability of the event. Examples of this include extremely pleasant life changes (e.g., marriage, inheriting a large sum of money) and were found to require nearly equal amounts of life adjustment as unpleasant events. It was because of this factor that life change events were originally scaled in terms of the amount of change they produced on a person's adaptability to stress producing events.

The focus of current measurement research at the Life Change and Illness Research Project at the Veterans Administration and the University of California, Los Angeles (UCLA), is on examining universal and group specific elements of stressful life events. Group specific populations are being studied and the environmental differences and interaction effects which result from cultural variations are being explored.

SIGNIFICANT CONTRIBUTIONS TO LIFE-EVENT MEASUREMENT

Numerous measures have emerged which address the assessment of stressful life events. Consideration is given here to those that bear most directly on the clinical research appropriate to mental health and behavioral sciences.

Rahe and Holmes (1975) have processed their life-event scale through three major revisions. The Social Readjustment Rating Scale (SRRS) was devised in order to obtain numerical estimates of the average degree of life change and readjustment subjects assign to their recent life change events. These life changes involve modifications of an individual's sleeping, eating, social, recreational, personal, and interpersonal habits/events which require or are indicative of varying amounts of adjustment. The SRRS assigns magnitudes to each of 42 life change items, according to the amount, severity, and duration of adjustment each is perceived to require. The scaling instrument was found to be concordant among various segments of the American population and between Americans and other culturally significant populations where stress may vary due to life styles and eating habits.

Phase II realized the development of the Schedule of Recent Experience (SRE), a self-administered paper and pencil survey which lists life change events by year of occurrence. This measure is currently referred to as the Recent Life Changes Questionnaire (RLCQ). It includes 42 of the original life change questions of the SRE. Wording of questions was altered to provide greater clarity and allow for specific options of response. Test-retest reliability studies were instrumental in realizing these improvements in structure.

The use of instructions at the end of the questionnaire allowed subjects to self-scale their own subjective life change scores for each life change they had recently experienced. Patients completing the RLCQ then obtained at least three different life change scores for analyses with various illness criteria. First, subjects obtained a six-month life change unit (LCU) score for the SRE items. The second score obtained for subjects with respect to recent life changes was a sum of all recent life changes indicated in a six-month time period. This was called the "unit scaling method" and has proven to be as useful as the LCU method for samples of young subjects who, in fact, experience very few high LCU life changes. When dealing with samples of older subjects who may have had experienced life changes such as marriage, birth of a child, divorce, business readjustment, illnesses of family members, death in the family, and so on, it was recommended that the investigator use the LCU scoring system.

Phase III involved the use of a Subjective Life Change Unit (SLCU) score. This score yields a six-month SLCU total for the original SRE items, and for the entire list of 55 life change events. Using the SLCU methodology for the SRE life change questions permitted one to subtract SLCU scores from the standard LCU scores for the 42 questions. By doing so, the authors hypothesize, one could obtain a rough estimate of the subject's "defenses and coping" for these changes.

Coddington (1972) developed a modification of the SRRS

to assess stressful life events related to childhood. Different life experiences were constructed for the preschool age group, elementary school age group, junior high school age group, and senior high school age group. The method for producing each age group scale was that used in generating the Social Readjustment Rating Scale. The people who did the rating included teachers, pediatricians, and mental health workers. Interrater agreement was high with rank order correlations of $r = 90$. Using the new scale to quantify recent childhood experiences in 3,500 children, Coddington constructed an age-related curve of average social readjustment scores. Rubin, Gunderson, and Arthur (1971) employed the SRE to assess its predictive validity. A stepwise multiple regression analysis was employed with favorable results in predicting the onset of illness of Naval personnel. The scores derived from this statistical procedure yielded regression weights which resulted in improved predictability of future illness when compared with prior weights derived from an earlier civilian sample. Rahe, Mahan, and Arthur (1970) demonstrated a linear relationship between the mean illness rate of shipboard personnel and the magnitude of life change events.

Skinner and Lei (1980) conducted a factor analytic study using an interactive principal factor model with least squares estimate. The results suggest that relatively homogeneous subsets of life events can be identified among the 43 SRE items. The six factors are based on the occurrence of life-events during a 12-month period. Significant correlation coefficients ($p < .05$) are reported for the SRE total score as well as for the six factor scales suggesting that the internal consistency of the instrument is an acceptable measure of its reliability. Coefficient alpha measures the stability of responses to all life events in the scale, and it provides a lower bound estimate of the population reliability. The reliability of the SRE was $r = .80$, whereas the values for the six factor scales ranged from $r = .76$ to $r = .40$. Since the reliability of a scale is contingent on the number of items, all estimates for the factor scales were adjusted to a scale length of 43 items for comparison with the SRE. What this seems to suggest is that by increasing the number of events sampled under each factor, statistically significant reliability for the scales may be obtained.

Skinner and Lei (1980) found an internal consistency reliability estimate of .80 for the SRE in this clinical population. Often the 43 life events are scaled by social readjustment weights (SRRS) to yield a weighted total score in life change units (LCU). However, Lei and Skinner found virtual overlap between the SRE and LCU scores which had a highly significant correlation ($r = .97$). Also, the reliability estimate ($r = .72$) for the LCU scores was somewhat lower than the SRE. It should be noted that reliability and validity studies with the SRE have shown variable results. Three reliability estimates of the SRE which utilized college subjects and allowed only a week or so between test and retest all had high correlations—between $r = .87$ and $r = .90$. Hawkins, Davis, and Holmes (1957), and Rahe (1974a, c) reported that when the interval between test and retest was extended to six to nine months, resident physicians obtained correlations around $r = .70$, while U.S. Navy enlisted men obtained a correlation of $r = .55$.

Rahe (1974b) found that spouses separately agreed with their partner's scoring of recent life changes with correlations ranging between $r = .50$ to $r = .75$ over one to two years prior to testing. The SRE has been found to be concordant among various segments of the American population and between United States citizens and people of other cultures. Although it was essentially simplistic in its design, the life events approach has had its share of conceptual and methodological criticisms. The life span researcher is particularly concerned about the rather restricted range of events included in most events inventories as well as the frequent practice of combining both favorable and unfavorable events in a single global change score. Furthermore, the use of standard weights instead of those based on the individual's perception of the event have also been the object of criticism by Hultsch and Plemons (1979) and Chiriboga and Cutler (1980).

THE NEW HAVEN MEASURE

Paykel (1974) employed a checklist format of 60 items to ascertain events occurring within six months prior to the onset of the illness. Events were assessed by activity area (e.g., work, family, change in health) as well as by whether these life-event changes represented entrances or exits to a person's social field. A third rating was established to determine whether these events were of a socially desirable or undesirable nature. Weights were adjusted to accommodate degrees of desirability to the "average person" for comparability purposes. The weighted scores for events were summed to give an estimate of the life event stress experienced by the subject. Brown's research group (Brown and Birley, 1968) explored criteria for which life events should be regarded as most and least stressful. Identified criteria included (1) events; (2) changes in life circumstance; (3) role; (4) subject experiences; (5) health changes; and (6) a key ingredient—the personality and influence of relatives and members of his immediate living environment. Circumstances and critical life events were documented with date, context, and verification by significant others in the subject's environment. The second stage involved the research team rating the severity of the life events experienced by the subject and comparing it with the perceived threat this event might be to the average person. The subject's own reaction to the life event was not weighted in the rating. Brown and Birley were attempting in this maneuver to reduce or eliminate the bias confounding retrospective studies. Should the identification and scaling of such events be accomplished with satisfactory reliability, then these researchers have eliminated one of the key biases and strengthened the process of life events scaling which must accommodate the variability of circumstance and events which comprise our daily life experiences.

PERI LIFE EVENTS SCALE

The Psychiatric Epidemiological Research Interview—Life Events Scale (PERI-LES) was developed by Dohrenwend et al. (1978)

to measure life events, such as divorce, loss of job, or other more minor events. A number of life events have been shown to correlate with onset of medical and psychiatric illness. The PERI-LES was constructed as part of a study in New York City designed to develop methods for psychiatric epidemiological research in community populations.

A sample of life events that might be particularly characteristic of New York City was drawn from the experience of the local population. The list of 102 events was constructed by drawing on previous lists, on the researcher's own experiences, and on the events reported in the two Washington Heights studies. Excluded from the list were events that are subjective rather than objective in the sense that they are both theoretically and practically difficult or impossible to verify independently of subject's reports of their occurrence. Because earlier research suggested the importance of the desirability of events in predicting illness outcomes, attention was given by the authors to specifying this characteristic in the descriptions of events that were included.

Research has suggested that ratings obtained on the PERI-LES yield significant group differences, with more of these differences due to ethnic background than due to social class or sex variation. The PERI-LES has technical weaknesses which include reliability and generalizability. There is no reliability data on the frequency of occurrence of individual life events. The judges employed in assessing the rating of events were too few in number to assure that group differences were reliable. The strength of this scale is in its potential methodological rigor. Their expertise and the sophistication of this group of life-event researchers should yield improved revisions of their scale which will serve to provide clinical researchers with more valid and reliable methods for assessing stressful life events. It would appear that multiple measures incorporating lists of stressful life events, such as the Dohrenwend group has generated, must be assessed from a multivariate perspective with estimates of locus on control, state-trait anxiety, and perceived self-concept.

UNIVERSAL AND GROUP SPECIFIC
LIFE-EVENT SCALES

The VA/UCLA Life Change and Illness Research Project (Hough, 1980) has developed Universal and Group Specific Life Change Scales which include weights for their five scales. They include standardized weights derived from latent trait analysis of the qualities of scale items. The scales developed were from a survey of random sampling of adults between 21 and 60 years of age in El Paso, Texas, and a multistage cluster sample of similar adults from Ciudad Juarez, Mexico. Respondents were asked to rate the seriousness of 95 stressful life events. The 95 were chosen after a thorough review of the events used in previous life-event scales. Assessment criteria included interviewer reports on the respondent's ability to do the task, completeness of the responses, the rating of undesirable versus desirable events, the correlation of the individual's scores with his or her group's average, and case specific criteria. Scales for each ethnic group are included. These scales contain the Universal Scale items and items which were scaled for each ethnic group. Items kept in the scales met two criteria: small mean square error and agreement among groups on the change value due an item. The 51 items in the Universal Scale are therefore the ones whose response patterns fit the latent trait model and over which there was little disagreement among the ethnic groups sampled. The same criteria were applied with each of the ethnic groups to obtain the group specific change factors.

ISSUES AND IMPLICATIONS

Several issues emerge from the current state of life-event scaling. With respect to the specificity of the measures and scales which have emerged, much work needs to be done to improve the sophistication of the measures. Few have applied the rigors of sound validity and reliability studies. Numerous measures which are published but have not been included in this article report only face validity and simplistic estimates of test-retest reliability. Efforts to apply more soundly developed statistical procedures including multivariate analysis or variance to parcel out significant differences especially with respect to mediating variables must be considered by future investigators. Multiple regression analysis to assess the predictive quality of the measures to be tested must be encouraged. Measures of the internal consistency of the instrument should be completed and reported along with factor analytic studies.

Neugarten (1979) has hypothesized underlying dimensions of life events and empirically investigated through factor analytic studies the structure of life events and empirically investigated through factor analytic studies the structure of life-event scales. He has requested subjects to respond as to whether given events had happened to them within a certain time period. Studies employing such inventories, however, because covariance issues may well be unrelated to perceived stressfulness which is postulated as a crucial factor in disease onset and progression. One should not be discouraged, however, because multidimensional scaling techniques may well yield new and more empirically based multidimensional life stress event scales which could serve as a basis for hypothesizing specific events with specific outcomes.

There is a growing body of literature which assesses a relationship between major life events and psychological stress. Hyman and Woog (1982) have addressed carefully the assumption that stress, the organism's physiological and psychological response to life events, alters the organism's vulnerability and susceptibility and that this concept is a measurable dimension.

Rabkin and Streuning (1976) have pointed to the fact that several of the life stress scales have emphasized events more often related to life happenings for people in young adulthood. This may well reflect the considerable level of life stress in early adulthood; however, the rationale from the existing studies is unclear. Issues such as this argue for the idiographic development of life events unique to different age range groups within the study population and that life-event scales be designed to address the entire life span development.

With respect to scaling, several questions must be answered, including what life events are identifiable and rateable and whether or not there are mediating variables that have not been considered. All of this points to the necessity that life-event researchers first identify the onset of illness, the process of relapse, and map the pattern of disease. With this information, life events will assume significantly more impact when they are related to the point in the course of illness at which the events occur. The data must then be adjusted to an understanding of the psychological makeup and personality of the specific individual experiencing the illness and confronting the stressful life event.

There is a further consideration which deals with the definition of the universe to be scaled. Careful consideration must be given to the events listed in the life-event inventories, for these must be events for which individuals in the study population would be at risk in the time span over which they are required to report (Hurst, 1979). It is extremely difficult to conceptualize the universe of life events from a generalized perspective; furthermore, the inclusion of both desirable and undesirable events in the same measure has created some serious methodological concerns for researchers because undesirability rather than change factor appears to be more often associated with the gradients of change in health status (Mueller, Edwards, and Yarvis, 1977).

There are other issues which address life events and their impact on measurement. Cultural bias occurs in the perception and response to life stress situations. Paykel (1974) compared ratings by American and English samples on a 21-point scale. They obtained significantly higher ratings from the English sample on 19 out of 61 events and a statistically significant overall mean difference between the two samples of judges.

Several variables function as mediators for life events, including biological, psychological, social, and physical characteristics of the individual and the environment. There are large within and between person differences with respect to these variables. Palmore and Erdman (1979) found that adults adapted well to the occurrence of a single life event, as retirement, widowhood, departure of the last child from home, and illness but demonstrated poorer adaptation when any two events were clustered. Several investigators have hypothesized that the individual's social support system may help moderate or buffer the effects of life events upon his or her psychological state (Liem and Liem, 1978; Antonovsky and Katz, 1967; Thoits, 1982). While the emergence of a buffering hypothesis suggests that individuals with a strong social support system should better cope with major life stresses. Those with little or no social support may be more vulnerable to life changes, particularly undesirable ones, and no efforts in the scaling process have begun to accommodate this particular issue. Clearly, the hypotheses concern an interaction effect; that is, the occurrence of events in the presence of a social support system which should produce less stress than should the occurrence of events in the absence of social support systems. It becomes imperative that life-event scaling involve an interactive measurement dimension if the life scaling process is to be understood and accurately researched.

Numerous methodological questions which have come to the forefront of life-event research, the more notable of which includes the appropriate identification of events, the degree of distress experienced, and the measurement of responses of others to the impact of stressful life events on a subject population. Furthermore, the response to stressful life events must be examined from both a physiological perspective and from a social and cultural perspective. Dohrenwend and Dohrenwend (1974) have contended that life stress analysis is supported more by faith than by specific evidence. The Dohrenwends are correct. The state of the science of life events remains in its infancy. The several efforts to identify and analyze a significant aspect of our growing understanding of the impact of life events on psychological and physical adjustment must be viewed as initial steps in our comprehension of this study of life events.

Another issue addresses the question of how and why well-adjusted people deal with stressful life events and remain well adjusted in the process. Holmes and Rahe (1967) would argue that from their research efforts, the greater the life change, the more serious the likelihood of the occurrence of illness. They further suggest that the studies completed contribute to the etiology and the onset of illness. Systematic empirical study is necessary to assess idiographic components of the full range of psychologically adjusted persons as well as the multivariate treatment of stressful life events on each person in the range of stressful life events. A biosocial approach to understanding stress, life events, and individual differences among human beings is clearly warranted from the research and several studies which have emerged over the past two decades dealing with the life-event scaling process.

It is realized that variables which may affect life events include socioeconomic status, income, and interpersonal support systems including family and friends. Supportive interpersonal relationships may serve as resources for the individual to the degree to which they provide physical, psychological, or financial support (Adams and Lindemann, 1974). The availability of these resources is likely to vary over the life span.

For Levinson (1978), examination of events such as marriage, divorce, birth of a child, and retirement can only yield diverse biographies: (1) the person's sociocultural world, including social structures (family, social class, occupation, and political affiliation), and historic events such as war and the economy; (2) the person's participation in this world, including both specific roles, such as husband, friend, worker, and parent, and the life events related to those roles, such as marriage, birth of a child, promotion, and retirement; (3) aspects of the self including fantasies, moral values, talents and skills.

Life events must also be explored within the framework of interpersonal relations. Brown and Birley (1968), Vaughn and

Leff (1976), and more recently Kreisman (1979) and Herz and Syzamanski (1981) have focused on the development of measures to assess various aspects of family or significant others interaction or a precipitator of relapse with this patient population. Events and modes of expressed emotionality and response style must be viewed as stressful life events and explored in future research for their impact on a person in gaining a better understanding of their impact on triggering relapse in schizophrenia. Tennant (1985) and Andrews, Tennant, Hewson, and Vaillant (1978) have pointed to the large-scale prospective studies which do not substantially support a significant correlation between life events, stress, and illness. If this be the case, the significant relationships reported in retrospective studies could be attributable to the accuracy of patient reporting or the sensitivity of the instruments used in collecting and classifying the data.

Several of the life-event inventories have empirically relevant problems dealing specifically with the ambiguity, timing, and controllability of life events. Many of these inventories have been unidimensional (Paykel et al., 1971; Holmes and Masuda, 1974; Hurst, 1979). The unidimensional inventories generally have subjects rate events on a continuum defined a priori by the researcher and have come under criticism because the universe of life events is considerably more complex than a unidimensional total score might indicate. Dohrenwend and Dohrenwend (1974) have addressed the problem of complexity and have designed an a priori class of events and clusters relating to economic factors, separation, and/or death, interpersonal relations, and threat to life. This is seen as a positive first step in considering the multiplicity and complexity of life stress events as precipitators of disease entities and is valued as an improvement in the design of methodology of such inventories.

As Tennant (1983) suggests, the thrust of life stress research must continue with emphasis on prospective studies, using more sensitive measures of stress with appropriate short follow-up periods, and finally should include some assessment of both premorbid and present personality. There is cause to be optimistic in understanding the role and function of life events in interpreting psychological adjustments; yet those of us who continue to explore this area must be open to the possibility that stressful life events may be but extraneous variables. If we continue to focus only on generating lists of life events and apply them to various samples, we will have failed to recognize the important interchange which requires multivariate analysis of life events with locus of control, perceived self-esteem, state-trait anxiety, and numerous genetic, metabolic, and biochemical measures. These adjacent areas are in the larger scope of successfully assessing stressful life events.

REFERENCES

Adams, J. E., & Lindemann, E. (1974), Coping with long-term disability. In: *Coping and Adaptation*, ed. G. B. Coelho. New York: Basic Books, pp. 127–138.

American Psychiatric Association, Committee on Nomenclature and Statistics (1980), *The Diagnostic and Statistical Manual of Mental Disorders*, 3rd ed. Washington, DC: American Psychiatric Association.

Andrews, G., Tennant, C., Hewson, D. M., and Vaillant, G. E. (1978), Life event stress—Social support, coping style, and risk of psychological impairment. *J. Nerv. & Ment. Dis.*, 166/5:307–316.

Antonovsky, A., & Katz, R. (1967), The life crisis history as a tool in epidemiological research. *J. Health & Soc. Behav.*, 8:15–21.

Brown, G. W., & Birley. J. L. (1968), Crisis and life changes and the onset of schizophrenia. *J. Health & Soc. Behav.*, 9:203–214.

Chiriboga, D.A. (1982), An examination of life events as possible antecedents to change. *J. Gerontol.*, 37/5:595–601.

———— Cutler, L. (1980), Stress and adaptation: Life span perspectives. In: *Aging in the 1980s: Psychology Issues*, ed. L. Poon. Washington, DC: American Psychological Association.

Coddington, R. D. (1972), The significance of life events as etiologic factors in the diseases of children. Part 1. A survey of professional workers. *J. Psychosom. Res.*, 16:7–18.

Costa, P. T., Jr., & McCrae, R. R. (1980), Still stable after all these years: Personality as a key to some issues in aging. In: *Life-Span Development and Behavior*, Vol. 3, ed. P. B. Baltes & O. G. Brim, Jr. New York: Academic Press.

Dohrenwend, B. S., & Dohrenwend, B. P. (1974), *Stressful Life Events: Their Nature and Effects*. New York: John Wiley.
———— Krasnoff, L., Askenasy, A. R., & Dohrenwend B. P. (1978), Exemplification of a method for scaling life events: The PERI life events scale. *J. Health & Soc. Behav.*, 19:205–229.

Hawkins, N. G., Davis, W. G., & Holmes, T. H. (1957). Evidence of psychosocial factors in the development of pulmonary tuberculosis. *Amer. Rev. Tuber. & Pulmon. Dis.*, 75:768–780.

Herz, M. I., & Syzamanski, H. (1981), Assessment of life events in studying relapse in schizophrenia. Unpublished paper.

Holmes, T. H., & Masuda, M. (1974), Life change and illness susceptibility. In: *Stressful Life Events: Their Nature and Effects*, ed. B. S. Dohrenwend & B. P. Dohrenwend. New York: John Wiley, pp. 45–72.
———— Rahe, R. H. (1967), The Social Readjustment Rating Scale. *J. Psychosom. Res.*, 11:213–218.

Hough, R. L. (1980), Universal and group specific life change scales. Los Angeles: Life Change and Illness Research Project, University of California. Unpublished manuscript.

Hudgens, R. W. (1974), Personal catastrophe and depression. A consideration of the subject with respect to medically ill adolescent, and a requiem for retrospective life-event studies. In: *Stressful Life Events: Their Nature and Effects*, ed. B. S. Dohrenwend & B. P. Dohrenwend. New York: John Wiley, pp. 119–134.

Hultsch, D. R., & Plemons, J. K. (1979), Life events and life-span development. In: *Life-Span Development and Behavior*, Vol. 2, ed. P. B. Baltes & O. G. Brim, Jr. New York: Academic Press.

Hurst, M. W. (1979), Life changes and psychiatric symptom development: Issues of content, scoring and clustering. In: *Stress and Mental Disorders*, ed. J. E. Barrett. New York: Raven Press.

Hyman, R. B., & Woog, P. (1982), Stressful life events and illness onset. *Res. Nurs. & Health*, 5:155–163.

Jenkins, C. D., Hurst, M. W., & Rose, R. M. (1979), Life changes: Do people really remember? *Arch. Gen. Psychiat.*, 36:379–384.

Kreisman, D. E. (1979), Rejecting the patient: Preliminary validation of a self-report scale. *Schiz. Bull.*, 5/2:220–222.

Levinson, D. J. (1978), *The Seasons of a Man's Life*. New York: Alfred A. Knopf.

Lieberman, M. A. (1975), Adaptive processes in late life. In: *Life-Span Developmental Psychology: Normative Life Crisis*, ed. N. Datan & L. Ginsberg. New York: Academic Press.

Liem, R., & Liem, J. (1978), Social class and mental illness reconsidered: The role of economic stress and social support. *J. Health & Soc. Behav.*, 19:139–156.

Meyers, J. K., Lindenthal, J. J., & Pepper, M. D. (1971), Life events and psychiatric impairment. *J. Nerv. & Ment. Dis.*, 152:149–157.

Miller, T. W. (1981), Training schizophrenics and their families to communicate: A cognitive behavioral model. *Hosp. & Commun. Psychiat.*, 32/12:870–871.

——— Wilson, G., Dunas, M., & Miller, J. (1979), Development and evaluation of social skills training for schizophrenic patients in remission. *J. Psychiat. Nurs.*, 17:42–46.

Mueller, D. P., Edwards, D. W., & Yarvis, R. M. (1977), Stressful life events and psychiatric symptomatology. *J. Health & Soc. Behav.*, 18:307–317.

Myers, J., Lindenthal, J. J., & Pepper, M. (1975), Life events, social integration and psychiatric symptomatology. *J. Health & Soc. Behav.*, 16:421–427.

Neugarten, B. L. (1979), Time and the life cycle. *Amer. J. Psychiat.*, 136:887–893.

Palmore, E., & Erdman, R. (1979), Stress and adaptation in late life. *J. Gerontol.*, 34:841–851.

Paykel, E. S. (1974), Life stress and psychiatric disorders: Applications of the clinical approach. In: *Stressful Life Events: Their Nature and Effects*, ed. B. S. Dohrenwend & B. P. Dohrenwend. New York: John Wiley, pp. 135–149.

——— Prusoff, B. A., & Uhlenhuth, E. H. (1971), Scaling of life events. *Arch. Gen. Psychiat.*, 25:340–347.

Rabkin, J. G., & Streuning, E. L. (1976), Life events, stress, and illness. *Science*, 194:1013–1020.

Rahe, R. H. (1974a), The pathway between subjects' recent life changes and their near-future illness reports: Representative results and methodological issues. In: *Stressful Life Events: Their Nature and Effects*, ed. B. S. Dohrenwend & B. P. Dohrenwend. New York: John Wiley, pp. 73–86.

——— (1974b), A model for life changes and illness research. Cross-cultural data from the Norwegian Navy. *Arch. Gen. Psychiat.*, 31:172–177.

——— (1974c), Recent life changes, myocardial infarction, and abrupt coronary death. Studies in Helsinki. *Arch. Intern. Med.*, 133:221–228.

——— (1980), Recent life change stress and psychological depression. *R.I. Med. J.*, 63/4:98–100

——— Holmes, T. H. (1975), Social Readjustment Rating Scale revision. Unpublished paper.

——— Mahan, W. J., & Arthur, R. J. (1970), Prediction of near-future health change from subjects' preceding life changes. *J. Psychosom. Res.*, 13:401–405.

Rubin, R. T., Gunderson, E. K. E., & Arthur, R. J. (1971), Life stress and illness patterns in the U.S. Navy—IV. Environmental and demographic variables in relation to illness onset in a battleship's crew. *J. Psychosom. Res.*, 15:221–227.

Skinner, H. A., & Lei, H. (1980), The multidimensional assessment of stressful life events. *J. Nerv. & Ment. Dis.*, 168:535–541.

Stevens, S. S. (1974), *Psychophysics: Introduction to Its Perceptual Neutral and Social Prospects.* New York: John Wiley.

Tennant, C. (1983), Life events and psychological morbidity. *Psycholog. Med.,* 13:483–486.

——— (1985), Life events and schizophrenic episodes. *Austral. & N.Z. J. Psychiat.,* 19/4:327–329.

Thoits, P. A. (1982), Conceptual, methodological, and theoretical problems in studying social support as a buffer against life stress. *J. Health & Soc. Behav.,* 23/2:145–159.

Thomae, H. (1979), The concept of development and life-span developmental psychology. In: *Life-Span Development and Behavior,* Vol. 2, ed. P. B. Baltes & O. G. Brim, Jr. New York: Academic Press.

Vaughn, C. E., & Leff, J. F. (1976), The influence of family and social factors on the course of psychiatric illness. A comparison of schizophrenic and depressed neurotic patients. *Brit. J. Psychiat.,* 129:125–137.

Chapter 4
Life Events and Schizophrenia: The "Triggering" Hypothesis

R. DAY, PH.D.

Over the past 15 years, the relationship of stressful life events to the etiology, onset, course, and outcome of various psychiatric conditions (e.g., schizophrenia, depression, the neuroses, states of demoralization, etc.) has become the subject of intensive empirical research (Holmes and Masuda, 1974; Brown, 1974; Cleary, 1974; Murthy, 1975; Ratskin and Struening, 1976; Schless and Mendels, 1977; Paykel, 1978; Andrews and Tennant, 1978; Dohrenwend and Dohrenwend, 1978, 1980). The accumulated literature in this field indicates that the degree of causal significance and the character of the role to be accorded to life stress will vary in the case of different disorders. At the same time, a number of studies (Brown, Harris, and Peto, 1973a; Jacobs and Myers, 1976; Brown and Harris, 1978; Paykel, 1978; Leff and Vaughn, 1980) suggest that it may be possible to establish a certain syndromatic consistency in the associations to be found between life stress and specific features (e.g., onset, symptom severity, overall impairment, etc.) of var-

Acknowledgment. This chapter was first published in *Acta Psychiatria Scandinavia* (1981), 64:97–122, and it is reprinted by permission.

51

ious disorders. This chapter will review the life-event research
specific to schizophrenia with the goal of assessing the extent
to which recent empirical studies have implicated life stress
variables in the onset of acute episodes of this disorder. (The
controversial matter of diagnosis will not be discussed in the
body of the chapter, except to take note of the criteria used by
different authors.)

CONCEPTUAL AND METHODOLOGICAL ISSUES

Brown and Harris (1978) describe two fundamental positions
that may be taken with regard to the causal role of life events
in psychiatric illness.

One emphasizes the importance of predispositional factors and plays
down the influence of events. At most, events are seen as triggering
something that would have occurred before long for other reasons.
In terms of our discussion, an event merely aggravates a strong pre-
existing tendency. We refer to this as the *triggering effect*. An event
for the most part simply brings onset forward by a short period and
perhaps makes it more abrupt. The opposing position is that the onset
is either substantially advanced in time by the event or brought about
by it altogether. We refer to this as a *formative effect*. Of course, triggering and formative effects are the opposite ends of a continuum
rather than entirely different processes [p. 46].

In contrast to a number of other psychiatric conditions (e.g.,
depression, see Brown et al., 1973a; Brown, 1974; Brown and
Harris, 1978; Lloyd, 1980) in which life stress has been implicated as a predisposing (i.e., vulnerability) or formative factor,
the data on schizophrenia suggests that the primary role of life
events may be to "trigger" acute episodes of the disorder. The
idea of a "triggering effect" serves to emphasize the role of life
events as environmentally mediated precipitants acting on a
specific predisposition to the illness (Wing and Brown, 1970;
Wing, 1978) and stands in contrast to theoretical formulations

(Dohrenwend, 1975; Kohn, 1973) which indicate that life stress may provoke schizophrenic disorders in nonspecifically vulnerable or otherwise normal individuals. On a practice level the research in this area may lead to a better comprehension of the factors associated with the onset of acute schizophrenic episodes and have significant implications for the clinical management of these patients in the community (Beck and Worthen, 1972).

Previous studies have utilized two identifiable strategies for investigating the association between life stress and the appearance of psychiatric disorders. One strategy takes advantage of "natural" or "quasi-experimental" situations (Dohrenwend, 1975) presented by the environment. This strategy traces the effects of a single kind of obviously stress-provoking event, and most studies draw upon a population of subjects unselected for pathology. The second strategy emphasizes controlled studies of selected patient populations and focuses on the variety of potentially stressful events found in the routine course of everyday life. Studies of the second type were made possible by the development of instruments (e.g., questionnaires, event inventories, and interview techniques) that permit a retrospective evaluation of the life events occurring prior to the onset of the patient's illness.

One frequently cited source of quasi-experimental evidence for an association between life stress and mental disorder is the literature on "extreme situations"; for example, wartime combat situations, natural disasters, concentration camp environments, and the like (Hocking, 1965; Kinston and Rosser, 1974; Dohrenwend, 1975). For the most part, these studies deal with a sample of subjects drawn from the total population experiencing the event (i.e., the survivors) and describe transient, self-limiting sorts of conditions, the acute symptoms of which rapidly disappear once the individual has been removed from the stress-provoking situation. Conditions of this kind are perhaps best subsumed under Schneider's (1959) category of "psychic reactions." The evidence from this research for the proposition that "extreme situations" can provoke serious and long-standing types of clinical symptoms and disabilities in otherwise normal individuals is best described as inconclusive and contradictory.

Data from a quasi-experimental situation of a more relevant kind can be found in the epidemiological studies carried out by Steinberg and Durell (1968). In order to find out whether the necessity of adapting a stress-provoking life situation can precipitate schizophrenic symptoms, these authors compared the hospitalization rates for schizophrenia during the early months of military service with the rates found in subsequent periods over the first two years of active duty. The subjects for this study included draftees and voluntary enlistments, but they were restricted to individuals having less than two years' service prior to their hospitalization for schizophrenia. Men obligated for less than two years were excluded from the study cohort. These procedures were designed to ensure that the population at risk in the early months was comparable to the population at risk during subsequent periods.

The results from this study show a dramatic excess of cases in the first month and throughout the first year of military service when compared to the rates for the second year. Hospitalization rates were six times those of the second year during the first month of service and declined regularly thereafter. Patterns of rate change were similar among both categories of enlistments (i.e., draftees and volunteers), although the effects of the first month of service were more marked for the draftees.

In the analysis of the data, the authors were able to eliminate certain hypotheses that could be put forward to explain the high rates of hospitalization in the early months of military service. Excluded, for example, were hypotheses that the initial rates were a consequence of individuals who had joined the army as an early symptom of schizophrenia or the rapid identification of chronic cases. It was also determined that the observed temporal decline in attack rates after the first month of service could not be explained by the depletion at a constant rate of the pool of susceptible individuals, nor result from peculiarities in diagnostic and labeling practices. On the basis of these findings, Steinberg and Durell (1968) conclude that: "the hypothesis that seems most attractive . . . and with which the data are consistent is that the emotional stress associated with the necessity of making a social adaptation was effective in inducing schizophrenic symptoms" (p. 1099). By way of expanding upon this statement, the authors go on to add the following qualification:

[W]e cannot conclude that military service caused psychotic behavior to appear in men who otherwise would not have succumbed. Indeed, there is a suggestion that many of these men showed a predisposition to schizophrenia and might have broken down in civilian life, although we hold it unlikely that they would have become psychotic during the months in question in the same numbers [p. 1103].

Even though a quasi-experimental strategy of the kind used by Steinberg and Durell may produce convincing evidence for the existence of a relationship between life stress and the onset of schizophrenic disorders *under certain specific conditions*, it does not permit the investigators to readily address a number of critical secondary issues; for example, the magnitude of the association between life stress and illness onset, the range and character of life events that may precipitate an episode, intervening variables that buffer or aggravate the effects of events, and so on. Questions of the latter sort can be handled in a more precise manner through the second type of strategy outlined above.

Once the decision has been made to undertake controlled research with everyday life events, the investigator is forced to deal with a number of deceptively complex methodological issues. In contrast to quasi-experimental designs, the nature of the stress-provoking events to be studied, as well as their obvious meaning for the subjects, are no longer defined by the situation itself (e.g., imprisonment, disaster, combat, army induction, etc.). The investigator must now attempt to trace the effects of "unextraordinary events"; that is to say, events which are commonplace to the population under study (e.g., births, deaths, marriages, family disputes, economic and health changes, etc.) and events which may have an ambiguous meaning for the individuals to whom they occur. Reliable methods must be developed for defining, locating, recording, and assessing the pattern and meaning of these commonplace events as they occur in the everyday life of the investigator's subjects. Given the implications of these issues for the results of controlled studies, it is necessary to review some methodological properties of recent life-event instruments before moving on to a discussion of the empirical research on schizophrenic patients.

For the most part, prior research has been based on a commonsense definition of life events. It is clear, for example, that most investigators conceptualize life events as some kind of *stressful change* occurring in the previous pattern of the subject's life world. "Life events usually entail change and this they do to lives built around routine. . . . The significance of life events must be sought, we believe, in the interplay of the exceptional with the unusual" (Brown and Harris, 1978, p. 108). Handling each component of this definition in its widest sense, it may be observed that the idea of "stressfulness" implies the evocation of an unspecified, yet identifiable state of arousal on the part of the subject, while the concept of "change" assumes that the individual is required to make some kind of adaptive response to a new or unexpected interpersonal, physiological, or environmental situation. Beyond this emphasis on stressful change, there is an impulse to insist that the types of changes properly termed *life events* must be *datable* (in terms of impact or first awareness) and relatively nonrepetitive (as opposed to chronic) in nature. By way of summarizing these commonsense criteria for the definition of life events, it is valuable to quote from a paper by Dohrenwend, Krasnoff, Askenasy, and Dohrenwend (1978):

Investigators who have offered definitions of life events have either explicitly or implicitly been guided by . . . what they considered could reasonably be meant by stressful life events. For Holmes & Rahe (1967), stressful life events are those "whose advent is either indicative of or required a significant change in the ongoing life pattern of the individual." For Myers et al. (1972), "crises" or "events" are defined as experiences involving role transformations, changes in status or environment, or impositions of pain." Brown & Birley (1968) focus on "events which on commonsense grounds are likely to produce emotional disturbances in many people [and usually involve] either danger, significant changes in health, status, or way of life, promise of them or important fulfillments or disappointments." And Antonovsky & Kats (1967) refer to "life crises" consisting of "objective situations which, on the face of it, would seem to be universally stressful" and involving "an experience which either imposed pain or necessitated transformation." The common denominator of these definitions is objective occurrences of sufficient magnitude to bring about change in the usual activities of most individuals who experience them. This common denominator is about as close as we can come to a workable definition of what is to be sampled . . . in the context of studies of life stress [p. 209].

One of the earliest and, perhaps, the most influential of the current life-event instruments was developed by Holmes and Rahe (1967). The Social Readjustment Rating Scale (SRRS) originally contained 43 commonplace events, along with assigned weights; that is, life change units (LCU) indicating the relative degree of readjustment (defined as the amount and duration of change in the subject's accustomed pattern of life) associated with each event. Events included in the SRRS were extracted from the life charts of medical patients, while LCU ratings were obtained by averaging the relative scores for each event provided by a representative sample of individuals from the general population. Paykel and Uhlenhuth (1972) have observed that the rationale behind scaling "stressfulness" in terms of life change units is based on the proposition that:

[E]ven though events are multiplex in their detailed circumstances, and individuals may experience the implications of identical events in different ways, there is a common core to the way in which most people in any society experience an event, and this common core can be used to roughly quantify stress, independent of a specific subject's experience of it [p. 110].

Since its publication in 1967, the SRRS has generated an extensive body of research, as well as a number of similar instruments (e.g., Antonovsky and Kats, 1967; Dohrenwend and Dohrenwend, 1970; Myers, Lindenthal, Pepper, and Ostrander, 1972a; Paykel, Prusoff, and Uhlenhuth, 1971; Dohrenwend et al., 1978) based on the same rationale. Although influential as a model instrument, the validity of the SRRS has been questioned by Mechanic (1968, 1974), Brown (1974), Hinkel (1974), and Hudgens (1974). Among the most telling of the criticisms is Hudgens's (1974) observation that 29 out of the 43 events on the Holmes and Rahe (1967) list "are often the symptoms or consequence of illness." Expanding on this point, Brown and Harris (1978) have remarked that any claim regarding the causal effect of life events on psychiatric disorders cannot be finally accepted until a method has been found to ensure that the events in question were not brought about through the insidious development of the illness.

A second important criticism concerns the Holmes and Rahe technique of using cumulative LCU scores as an overall measure of stress. In brief, this procedure not only requires that we accept a number of rather tenuous assumptions about the simple additive properties of stress, but threatens to obscure the commonsense distinction between the stress resulting from a single event of major proportions (e.g., death of a child or spouse) and the cumulative effects of several more benign occurrences extending over a longer period of time.

A third criticism of the SRRS concerns the vague manner in which the event to be rated was specified for the judges in the calibration study.

The description used to rate degrees of readjustment (i.e. LCU scores) was exceedingly brief. A person simply "begins or stops work"; we do not know whether the change is voluntary, whether due to the birth of a baby, a husband's antagonism, or winning a lottery. Does it mean losing important ties or making new ones? Is the change the first or has it occurred many times before? [Brown and Harris, 1978, p. 166].

The uninformative quality of most of these descriptions required that each of the judges fill in the background situation which is necessary to meaningfully rate an event. This type of procedure can be assumed to produce multiple understandings of the same event, a pattern of variation that is further obscured by the decision to utilize the mean scores assigned by the judges. Moreover, it should be kept in mind that the LCU ratings derived from the judges may implicitly assume the existence of situational factors that cannot be directly compared to the circumstances characterizing a respondent's report. Once these multiple sources for error have been taken into account, it is very difficult to know how to interpret simple associations between illness reports and cumulative LCU scores.

Potential sources of error like the ones outlined above led Brown and his colleagues to develop improved procedures capable of avoiding the sorts of criticism leveled at the Holmes and Rahe instrument. Besides relying on an intensive personal interview, significant innovations introduced by Brown's group included contextual measures of stress and the concept of "independent" life events.

The use of a semistructured interview schedule permits the collection of detailed information, including data on the contextual factors determining the meaning and the impact of events. After carefully eliminating comments bearing on the respondent's personal reactions to the event, this material is given to independent raters for a commonsense assessment of impact (Brown, Sklair, Harris, and Birley, 1973b). It should be noted that this procedure, although more detailed than that of Holmes and Rahe, ultimately depends on the same rationale. The Holmes and Rahe judges were asked to make commonsense assessments of the stressfulness of events without knowledge of *either* the contextual situation *or* the respondent's personal reaction. Brown's raters are called upon to make equivalent sorts of commonsense judgments; their decisions, however, are facilitated by knowledge of the situational factors, while remaining likewise independent of any information about the respondent's personal reaction. Regardless of the extent to which contextual factors play a role in the rater's judgments, both procedures finally depend upon what Paykel and Uhlenhuth (1972) termed the *common core* to the way in which the people in any society experience an event.

Given the existence of this commonsense core for judging the impact or stressfulness of life events, the introduction of contextual factors simply permits a more precise and flexible application of the same culturally organized criteria that underlie the standard LCU ratings in the SRRS. For this reason, the procedure introduced by Brown et al. should be viewed as a substantial *improvement on* rather than an alternative to the original Holmes and Rahe methodology. At this point, it is important to comment on the reasoning which requires that the rater ignore the subject's personal reaction to an event. A number of studies (e.g., Scott, 1958; Garfinkel, 1968) have shown that the meaning of an event, when retrospectively assessed by the subject, is affected by the respondent's current situation and future expectations. In other words, any method of assessment that relies upon the respondent's subjective impressions about the impact or meaning of an event ultimately leaves the data vulnerable to the respondent's personal "search after meaning" (Brown, 1974). The simplest solution to this dilemma is the use of culturally organized, commonsense judgments of impact and stressfulness as provided by independent raters.

The final feature of the Brown et al. (1973b) procedure that requires comment is the concept of "independent" events. During their early research, Brown and Birley struck upon the idea of separately classifying all the events "which were apparently imposed on the subject and which for all practical purposes were outside his or her control: for example, learning about a father's serious illness, or discovering a burglary" (1968, p. 211). This subcategory of "independent" events represents a partial solution to the dilemma stated by Hudgens (1974). Since these events, by definition, are beyond the respondent's personal control, it is unlikely that they could have been brought about by the insidious development of the disease condition. Hence, the category of "independent" events provide the kind of data required to support causal hypotheses concerning the effects of life stress on psychiatric disorders.

Some of the technical innovations developed by Brown and his colleagues have been amalgamated into previously existing instruments. Most investigators, for example, now attempt to estimate the number and frequency of independent events experienced by their subjects. At the same time, serious problems will exist in areas like the scaling of impact or stress. Suffice it to say that several overlapping measures (e.g., readjustment, contextual threat, upset, undesirability, etc.) are in use today, and it is not at all clear to what extent they may be directly compared when assessing the results from different studies. In this connection, one recent investigator (Shrout, 1980; Lei and Skinner, 1980) observed that:

[T]here has not been conclusive proof that weighted life event indices are superior to unweighted counts . . . in predicting health status. Given this . . . and the related problem that weighted and unweighted indices are highly correlated, it might be tempting to dispense with the task of scaling life events and rely on unweighted . . . indices [p. 114].

By way of summarizing the above remarks, it may be suggested that the most significant contribution of the past 10 years of research has been the development of a coherent methodology for studying life events. Stated briefly, this methodology insists that life events must be defined and assessed with regard to a culturally patterned consensus about the kinds of occurrences that constitute stress-provoking changes, rather than in terms of an individual's subjective attitudes or idiosyncratic responses to the behavioral environment. It is this culturally organized consensus, together with the contextual factors determining the commonsense meaning of an event, that provide the necessary background required to decide upon whether or not any particular respondent has actually experienced an event and the degree of impact or stress that is normally associated with such an occurrence.

FINDINGS OF CONTROLLED STUDIES ON SCHIZOPHRENIA

Certain studies using mixed psychiatric samples, including schizophrenic patients, have been excluded from consideration in this review (Adamson and Schmale, 1965; Morrison, Hudgens, and Barehha, 1971; Hudgens, Robbins, and Delong, 1970; Eisler and Polak, 1973). This decision was based on the small size of the clinical sample of these studies or the difficulty involved in determining what portion of the data were collected from schizophrenic patients. Once these studies have been eliminated, it becomes evident that most of the available research on life events and schizophrenia has been done by two groups of investigators, one located in London, and the other in New Haven, Connecticut. These studies, when combined with a small body of additional research, more or less exhaust the relevant literature. The contributions from these sources are summarized in Table 4.1, which also serves as a guide to the articles mentioned in this review.

Perhaps the most influential body of research on the association between life events and the onset of schizophrenia has been done by Brown and his London-based colleagues. Refer-

Table 4.1
The Life-Event Literature on Schizophrenia

Camberwell Group	New Haven Group	Other Studies
Brown & Birley (1968)	Myers et al. (1972a, b)[a]	Beck & Worthen (1972)
Birley & Brown (1970)	Jacobs et al. (1976)	Harder et al. (1980)
Brown et al. (1973a,b)	Jacobs & Myers (1974)	
Leff et al. (1973)	Schwartz & Myers (1977)	
Brown (1974)	Paykel (1978)	
Leff & Vaughn (1980)		
Vaughn & Leff (1976a,b)[a]		
Leff & Wing (1971)[a]		
Hirsch et al. (1973)[a]		

[a]Indicates background studies

ring to the fundamental hypothesis motivating this work, Brown (Brown and Harris, 1978) has recalled that "we started with a somewhat vague belief that marked emotion of any kind—joy and excitement as well as distress and fear—could be enough to precipitate florid [schizophrenic] symptoms" (p. 184). The formal test of this belief (Birley and Brown, 1970; Brown and Birley, 1968) involved a sample of 50 schizophrenic patients and 325 community subjects. Patient selection for this study was handled in the following manner: "The first 50 patients whose onset had occurred within three months of admission and could be dated within a week were chosen from a total of 123 consecutive admissions diagnosed as suffering from schizophrenia" (Brown and Birley, 1968, p. 212). Of the 73 patients excluded from the clinical sample, 53 were rejected on grounds that they showed no change or only gradual deterioration during the three months before admission. Another 16 patients were eliminated because the changes occurring in the three months prior to admission could not be dated within a week, and four patients were dropped due to inadequate information (Birley and Brown, 1970).

All of the patients considered for this study were diagnosed on the basis of a standardized and comprehensive psychiatric interview (Wing, Birley, Cooper, Graham, and Isaacs, 1967; Wing, Cooper, and Sartorius, 1974). The clinical characteristics of the patients selected for the research are summarized in Table 4.2.

The clinical controls for this study consisted of 325 subjects drawn from six local firms in London's Camberwell district. They included clerical workers and building laborers as well as skilled, semiskilled, and unskilled factory workers. Brown and Birley (1968) note that two groups of subjects were roughly comparable in age, sex, nationality, and education, while demonstrating significant differences in marital status, family composition, and contacts with close relatives living outside the household.

The data-gathering phase of the research included separate interviews with each patient and a key relative concerning

Table 4.2
Clinical Characteristics of the Brown and Birley Sample[a]

Characteristics	No. of patients
1. Diagnosis	
a. Definite Schizophrenia	26
b. Probable Schizophrenia	24
2. Type of Onset	
a. Normal to Schizophrenic Symptons	29
b. Nonschizophrenic to Schizophrenic Symptons	8
c. Mild to Severe Schizophrenic Symptons	13
3. Prior Episodes	
a. First Episode	23
b. Relapse Episode	27
4. Prior Hospitalizations	
a. First Admission	24
b. Prior Admission	26

[a]Data derived from Birley and Brown (1970)

events occurring in the 3-month period prior to the onset of florid symptomatology. Subjects from the community sample were questioned in a similar manner about the three months leading up to the date of the interview.

Every reported event was subsequently classified as falling into one of four 3-week periods composing the temporal focus of the interview and categorized in terms of the extent to which it had either been imposed on the subject (i.e., independent events) or may have been brought about by the respondent's own behavior. The results from this analysis of the clinical and community control data are presented in Table 4.3.

From Table 4.3, it is clear that 46 percent of the patients in the study had at least one independent life event during the final 3-week period preceding the onset of the disorder. This figure compares with an average of 12 percent of the clinical sample experiencing similar events in any one of the earlier 3-week periods. In other words, the data indicate that members of the patient sample suffered a significant rise in the frequency of life events over the 3 weeks immediately before the onset of florid symptomatology.

Table 4.3
Percentage of Persons With at Least One Event in the Four
Three-Week Periods Before Onset (Patients, $N = 50$) and
Interview (General Population, $N = 325$)

	3-week Periods Before Onset/Interview			
	(furthest) 4th[b]	3rd[b]	2nd[b]	(nearest) 1st[a]
	Independent Events			
1. Patients	14	8	14	46
General Population	15	15	15	14
	Possibly Independent Events			
2. Patients	16	10	6	22
General Population	6	5	5	5
3. Patients	30	18	20	60
General Population	21	20	18	19

Derived from Brown & Birley (1968)
[a] For the first three-week period $p < 0.001$ ($1 df$) in all three groups (two-tailed 2 test)
[b] All nine comparisons not significant ($p < 0.05$)

The findings from the clinical subjects are substantially reinforced by the data from the community controls. Over the first 9 weeks covered by the interview, the average proportion of community subjects reporting events (14.7 percent) was roughly equivalent to the patient mean (12 percent) during the same period of time. Moreover, the community rate remains stable in the final 3 weeks of the study, whereas the patient sample demonstrates a significant rise in the proportion of patients experiencing independent life events. These data not only indicate that the temporal elevation of the patient's life-event rate cannot be attributed to lapses of memory, but would seem to suggest the operation of environmentally mediated causal factors during the 3 weeks prior to onset.

Equally significant results may be obtained by utilizing the data for life events that could not be rated as clearly independent of the subject's own behavior (i.e., possibly independent events). By demonstrating similar patterns of occurrence in both the clinical and community samples, these data further substantiate the conclusions based on the frequency of independent events.

With regard to the patient's clinical characteristics, Birley and Brown (1970) determined that differences in the type of onset, variations in symptomatology and diagnosis, as well as previous episodes and prior hospital admissions were unrelated to the occurrence of events in the 3 weeks before the acute onset of the disorder. The only variable that appeared to be related to the effects of life events was maintenance chemotherapy. Of the 13 patients reporting a reduction and/or cessation of medications in the 11 months prior to onset, only four were discovered to have had at least one life event during the final 3-week period of the study. In contrast, 23 of the 32 patients who had not taken any neuroleptics during the 12 months preceding acute onset reported at least one life event in the final 3-week period. The difference between these two groups is marginally significant ($p < 0.05$).

By way of summarizing their major findings in this study, Birley and Brown (1970) conclude that "life events and reducing or stopping phenothiazines contribute as precipitants of acute schizophrenia . . ." (p. 326).

In a subsequent paper, Brown et al. (1973a) (cf. Paykel, 1978) suggest a method for quantifying some of the above conclusions. Specifically, they put forward statistical measures designed to estimate both the proportion of patients in which life events appear to have a causal effect and the amount of time that the events can be assumed to advance the onset of the disorder. On the basis of the data collected by Brown and Birley (1968), it was estimated that life events had a causal effect in approximately 50 percent of the schizophrenic patients under study (calculations include independent and possibly independent events) and, in these cases, onset was "brought forward" on an average of 10 weeks. On commonsense grounds, it is argued that these calculations indicate an environmental-mediated "triggering effect" occurring in a substantial proportion of the Brown and Birley (1968) clinical sample.

Before leaving this study, it is worthwhile to review some of the subsidiary findings that emerged from the data. Brown and Birley (1968) point out, for example, that 70 percent of the patients experiencing an event during the final 3-week period before onset also reported at least one event in the other 9 weeks covered by the study. In contrast, only 35 percent of the patients who remained event-free during the final 3 weeks prior to onset reported more than a single event in the preceding 9 weeks of the study. Even though these figures may appear to suggest that life events have an additive effect, the authors observe that this may be a spurious correlation resulting from linked multiple events (e.g., quitting school in order to start a job). Once these linked events have been eliminated from the analysis, previous differences between the two groups of patients tend to disappear.

Brown and Birley (1968) also point out that patients reporting life events in the three weeks prior to the acute onset of the disorder are more likely ($p < 0.001$) to come from households with higher levels of chronic tension. With regard to these findings, the authors observe that "there remains the possibility that tension in the home can somehow bring about more independent events. . . ."

Before drawing conclusions from this study, it should be noted that Birley and Brown (1970) carefully restrict their findings to the subgroup of all "schizophrenic" patients that show a relatively abrupt onset of florid symptoms (Wing and Brown, 1970). Although the significance of this distinction is not completely clear, the authors appear to believe that the "acute" subgroup does not differ in any fundamental sense from other "schizophrenic" patients.

We believe . . . that several possible factors may have to combine to produce a "schizophrenic state"—for instance, some biological change in the brain, an acquired style of coping behaviour, and some difficulty or change in the environment. . . . At the onset of the illness the contribution of any particular factor may vary considerably. At times "inherent" factors, at others "exogenous" ones will be overriding [p. 325].

It is difficult as well to assess the significance of the authors' remarks concerning the possible effects of chronic household tension without the data from additional studies. We will return to these findings after discussing the extent to which the major conclusions of this study have been replicated in the work of independent investigators.

Birley and Brown's (1970) original findings concerning the relationship between life events, neuroleptic medications, and acute relapse episodes of schizophrenia were tested in a subsequent study by Leff, Hirsch, Gaind, Rhode, and Stevens (1973). This research was based upon a sample of 116 schizophrenic patients drawn from two placebo-controlled clinical trials. One of these trials (Leff and Wing, 1971) was predominantly concerned with acute patients (39 subjects), while the other (Hirsch, Gaind, Rhode, Stevens, and Wing, 1973) dealt solely with chronic patients (77 subjects).

Although the patients for this replication study were selected from the same kind of working class population (i.e., Camberwell and Southwark, London) used in the Brown and Birley research, it is difficult to accurately compare thier sociodemographic characteristics due to the paucity of information presented by Leff et al. (1973). Sociodemographic data is available for the chronic sample (Hirsch et al., 1973) and naturally appears skewed in the direction of older subjects with low levels of social adjustment, few friends, and little in the way of social activities. It may be assumed that the more extreme features of the chronic sample would be partially offset by the comparatively younger age and better level of social functioning to be expected among the acute patients.

During the course of the clinical traits, each one of the study subjects was interviewed with the Brown and Birley life-event schedule at the time of relapse, or at the end of the trial period if the patient remained well. On analysis, it was found that:

[I]n the three weeks before relapse or completion of the trial, 44% of the patients who relapsed while on active drug experienced an event, while the comparable rates for the other . . . groups varied between 7 and 25%. These differences did not reach significance [Leff et al., 1973, p. 660].

Further inspection of the data indicated that differences between the groups were increased by extending the period before relapse or completion of the trial from 3 to 5 weeks. The critical data for this 5-week period is displayed in Table 4.4.

Table 4.4 indicates that a somewhat smaller proportion of the Leff et al. sample experienced life events during the 5 weeks preceding onset than was reported in the Brown and Birley study. These differences, however, are not statistically significant and perhaps could have been predicted from the higher mean age and smaller household size found among the chronic patients (Brown and Birley, 1968).

With regard to the hypothesis under study, Table 4.4 suggests that, among patients maintained on placebo, there is no association between the timing of relapse episodes and the occurrence of life events in the 5-week period preceding onset. In contrast, a significantly greater proportion of the patients who relapsed while receiving an active drug had experienced a life event when compared to the subjects remaining well on

Table 4.4
The Occurrence of Events in the Five Weeks Before Interview

	Patients with an Independent Event	Patients with an Independent or Possibly Independent Event	Total Number of Patients
Relapsed:			
on placebo	8 (21%)	12 (31%)***	39
on drug	4 (44%)*	8 (89%)***	9
Well:			
on placebo	5 (31%)	6 (36%)**	16
on drug	7 (13%)*	24 (27%)***	52

$*p = 0.04$
**Derived from Leff et al. (1973)
$***p < 0.01$
    Significance determined by Fisher's Exact Test

active medications ($p < 0.001$). Leff et al. (1973) interpreted these findings in the following manner:

Schizophrenic patients living in the community and not taking drugs seem to relapse as a result of the disturbing effects of everyday social interactions. Out-patients on maintenance therapy are protected against the stress implicit in uneventful social intercourse, and are unlikely to relapse unless exposed to some additional stress in the form of one or another life event . . . [p. 659].

The data from this study provide substantial support for the Birley and Brown (1970) conclusion that stopping phenothiazines may contribute to relapse episodes among previously treated schizophrenic patients. Through a conservative application of the quantitative methods developed by Brown and his colleagues (Brown et al., 1973a), it is possible to estimate that there was a causal involvement of life events in the relapse of no more than 15 percent of the Leff et al. patients maintained on placebo; and among these patients, the onset of the disorder was probably "brought forward" by less than 11 to 12 days. [Calculations of "brought forward time" for the Leff et al. (1973) data were done by the authors of this paper on the basis of the formula in the Appendix to Brown et al. (1973a). The community controls used in these calculations were the Camberwell respondents from Brown and Birley (1968).]

At the same time, it should be noted that the author's remarks about the vulnerability of nonmedicated patients to the vicissitudes of uneventful everyday social interaction is an interpretive hypothesis that goes well beyond the data presented in the article. A similar point can be made with regard to the conclusions about the pathogenic effect of life events among patients receiving active medications. Given the small number of patients who relapsed while taking neuroleptics (nine patients), not to mention the paucity of data presented on the nature, frequency, and background of the reported events, it may be concluded that Leff et al. (1973) have shown an association between life events and relapse among medicated patients without, however, proving that the one phenomenon has *necessary and direct* causal implications for the other.

The material presented so far provides the necessary background for a more detailed discussion of the "triggering" hypothesis. In order to obtain additional comparative data on the association between life events and the onset of acute psychotic episodes, the following section draws heavily upon a series of independent studies with subjects from the area surrounding New Haven, Connecticut.

The study done by Jacobs and Myers (1976) is the closest in the current literature to a replication of Brown and Birley's (1968, 1970) research.[1]

Jacobs and Myers' study was undertaken with a series of 62 consecutive first admission schizophrenic patients drawn from three facilities (i.e., a state hospital, a community mental health center, and a general hospital ward) over a 6-month period. Screening criteria for diagnosis of schizophrenia were derived from Parkes' (1963) eight groups of positive symptoms, with the presence of two or more clusters being sufficient for inclusion in this study (Jacobs, Prusoff, and Paykel, 1974). According to the authors (Jacobs and Myers, 1976), these guidelines were productive of a group of patients that could be defined as schizophrenic by "broad standards."

Given the use of a consecutive admission strategy, it might be expected that this cohort of patients would be less representative of the acute subgroup of schizophrenics than the one

[1]An article by Harder, Strauss, Kokes, Ritzler, and Gift (1980) is relevant to the problems discussed here. Although these authors report on the life events among a sample of 35 diagnosed schizophrenic patients, they fail to control for the *date of onset of the illness* and instead utilize date of hospitalization for measuring the effects of life events. This procedure introduces a number of methodological problems having to do with the question of causality and makes it very difficult to draw valid conclusions from the data. The authors themselves point out that even though their data seem to confirm the work of Brown and Birley (1968, 1970), "it is possible that the increase in events shortly before hospitalization reflects a reverse causal effect, that is, the . . . psychotic experience produces more life events (Harder et al., 1980).

collected by Brown and Birley (1968). Yet, Jacobs and Myers (1976) report that:

[W]ith few exceptions, the interviewer psychiatrist was satisfied that he could date the acute illness onset to within a period of several days on the basis of the occurrence or exacerbation of symptoms and marked changes in social functioning [p.448].

With regard to sociodemographic factors, the Jacobs and Myers sample was relatively younger (mean age: 28 years) than the patients studied by Brown and Birley (mean age: 34 years), but both groups of clinical subjects were roughly comparable in terms of sex, marital status, and economic standing.

The control group for this research was drawn from the subjects in a random sample of 938 households originally chosen for a systematic population study of the New Haven mental health catchment area (Myers et al., 1972a,b). From this larger sample, it was possible to recruit 62 community subjects that could be matched with the schizophrenic patients on age, sex, socioeconomic standing, and ethnic background.

The list of events in this study was a modified and expanded version of instruments developed by previous investigators (Holmes and Rahe, 1967; Antonovsky and Kats, 1967; Paykel et al., 1971). During the data collection phase of the research, patients were interviewed concerning the 1-year period before the onset of their disorder, while the community controls were questioned about the 12 months preceding the date of the interview. Given the fact that the mean duration of illness among the patients was approximately 3 months, the period subject to recall during the interview averaged about 15 months. Since it was felt that most of the patients in the study "provided an accurate recollection of events," the investigators did not utilize Brown and Birley's method of interviewing a key relative in order to estimate the reliability of the information received from the clinical subjects.

Over the 12-month period covered by the interview, it was found that the schizophrenic patients reported an average of 3.2 events per person, as compared to an average of 2.1 events per person in the community controls. Although this difference in the average per person rates of life events appears highly significant ($p = 0.009$), it does not hold up when the same kind of analysis is done for independent events. Here the author notes that "a special classification of events designated to eliminate experiences that are conceivably the effects of illness failed to support the overall finding of a relationship between events and the onset of acute (schizophrenic) psychoses" (p. 446). In other words, the relative excess of events reported by the schizophrenic patients in Jacobs and Myers' study was primarily a product of the kinds of occurrences that may have been brought about through the insidious development of the patient's disorder.

Despite these apparently negative findings, the authors go on to point out that the patient group reported a significantly greater number ($p = 0.001$) of undesirable life events than their community sample. This data leads Jacobs and Myers to speculate about the relationship between life events and the network of social support available to the patients.

One wonders if the occurrence of undesirable life experiences in a setting where customary social supports are strained or unavailable . . . is the potent combination of factors that determines the consequences of experiences for schizophrenia prone individuals . . . [p.448].

These remarks suggest that life events alone are not sufficient to "trigger" the onset of a florid psychotic episode. According to Jacobs and Myers' line of argument, the critical factor creating a pathogenic situation is not the life event itself (whether independent, possibly independent, or probably illness-related), but the unavailability of customary social supports.

With regard to the factors which may account for the differences between their findings and the results from the Brown and Birley (1968) study, Jacobs and Myers observe that:

[T]ime analyses of the patient group alone document more events in the six months immediately before illness onset by comparison with the previous six months. It is possible, therefore, that the annual period used as the basis for comparison with normals diluted a real, greater difference [p. 453].

In two subsequent papers (Jacobs et al., 1974; Paykel, 1978) the authors calculated an average 6 months per person event rate of 2.5 for a subsample of 50 of the schizophrenic patients utilized in the present study.

It is also possible that the extended period of recall required in Jacobs and Myers' (1976) study left the results vulnerable to lapses of memory on the part of their subjects. In a study of event recall, Uhlenhuth, Balter, and Lipman (1977) found an average decrease in the number of reported events over an 18-month period of about 5 percent per month. Based on a test-retest design using the SRRS, Jenkins, Hurst, and Rose (1979) concluded that their findings "raise serious doubts about the validity of retrospective studies . . . when the period being reported is more than six months in the past" (p. 384).

An extrapolation of the expected 12-month rates from the data available in Brown and Birley's (1968) article provides further evidence for this hypothesis. Among the Camberwell patients, we could predict an average yearly rate of about 5.1 events (this includes independent and possibly independent events) per subject, while the general population sample may be expected to show a mean rate approaching 3.8 events per person. In other words, the Brown and Birley (1968) data would lead us to predict 60–80 percent higher per person rates on a yearly basis than is recorded in the Jacobs and Myers study. These remarks are underscored by the findings from an Anglo-American comparison of life events (Paykel, McGuiness, and Gomez, 1976). Paykel and his colleagues found that British patients and their relatives, when compared to a matched American sample, "tended to scale events more highly . . . but had experienced fewer events in the last year" (p. 243).

Similar evidence can be gathered from a subsequent study by Schwartz and Myers (1977). This research was based on a parallel sample of New Haven subjects and used a 6-month period of recall. Here the extrapolated data indicate an expected 12-month mean rate (includes all events) for the patients and the community controls that is somewhere between 50–100 percent higher than the figures in the Jacobs and Myers (1976) study. A summary of these extrapolated mean per person rates from the various available sources is presented in Table 4.5.

Besides the problem of recall, differences in the frequency of life events between the Brown and Birley (1968) and the Jacobs and Myers (1976) studies may in part be explained by the decision of the former investigators not to interview key relatives about the patients' experiences. Schless and Mendels (1978) found that interviewing significant others about patients' experiences could be expected to add approximately 29 percent more events to the number reported by the clinical subjects.

As part of their study, Jacobs and Myers (1976) also rated the events reported by their clinical and community subjects for social desirability, degree of upset, and required readjustment. The results from these impact measures suggested that even though a significant proportion of the schizophrenic patients (82 percent) reported at least one undesirable event, the majority of these events caused minor to moderate upset and required little or no readjustment on the part of the subjects.

Similar findings have appeared in a number of other studies. Beck and Worthen (1972), for example, asked a sample of 100

Table 4.5
Extrapolated Mean per Subject Life-Event Rates

Source	13 Weeks	26 Weeks	52 Weeks
Brown & Birley (1968)			
a. patients	1.74	2.86[a]	5.09[a]
b. controls	0.96	1.92[a]	3.84[a]
Jacobs & Myers (1974)			
a. patients	—	—	3.2
b. controls	—	—	2.1
Schwartz & Myers (1977)			
a. patients	—	3.25	6.5[a]
b. controls	—	1.51	3.02[a]

[a]Indicates extrapolated rates

community informants to give commonsense ratings for the
"degree of hazardousness" involved in the precipitating situations reported by 15 schizophrenic patients. Each rater was
supplied with a list of the events collected from the clinical
subjects and asked to score them in the following manner: "rate
1 if it would not be upsetting at all, 2 for slightly upsetting, 3
for pretty upsetting, 4 for very upsetting, and 5 for most upsetting thing that could happen" (p. 124). The resulting "hazardousness" scores ranged from just below slightly upsetting to
just above pretty upsetting, with an overall mean score of 2.70
for the patients in which a clear precipitating event could be
identified. After examining these data, the authors conclude
that: "as a group, schizophrenic patients are seen to decom-
pensate in the context of life situations which are independently
judged as not particularly hazardous" (p. 128). After some
years, Brown et al. (1973b) scored the data on their schizophrenic patients with a measure of impact. The measure utilized
was "contextual threat," a concept that relies upon commonsense judgments about the severity of an event's threatening
implications.

The consequences of many events are fairly completely resolved
within a week. . . . Others have more long-term implications for the
future. . . . The interviewer is required to make commonsense judge-
ments concerning how unpleasant or threatening the event would be
for most people one week after its occurrence. The rating takes into
account the circumstances surrounding the event . . . [p.174].

By applying this measure of impact to the schizophrenic data,
it was calculated that an average of 70 percent of all the clinical
subjects reporting an event during one of the 4 3-week periods
of the original study (Brown and Birley, 1968) had experienced
situations with "little or no threat." The lowest proportion was
found in the final 3-week period before onset where 53 percent
of the clinical subjects reporting events were rated as having
experienced situations of "little or no threat."

Even though the preceding measures of impact (undesirability, upset, hazardousness, readjustment, and contextual

threat) intersect and overlap in ways that are difficult to define, the cumulative findings indicate that at least half of the acute schizophrenic patients reporting life events prior to the onset of a disorder will report undesirable occurrences of a sort that provoke small to moderate upset and require little or no long-term readjustment.

In spite of the methodological problems discussed above, Jacobs and Myers' (1976) study suggests an important conclusion: the hypothesized association between life events and the onset of schizophrenic episodes is neither so robust nor so clear as might have been previously expected. The latter evidence, for example, concerning the large proportion of reported events having relatively low levels of impact tends to reduce the commonsense plausibility of a direct or necessary causal link. These data recall the earlier remarks of Brown and Harris (1978) and suggest that in a substantial proportion of cases life events simply play the role of a "final straw"; that is, they make onset more abrupt and/or accelerate the appearance of a condition that was bound to come about sooner or later for other reasons.

When we turn to the problem of quantifying the association between stressful life events and the onset of acute schizophrenic disorders, the estimates of "brought forward time" presented by Brown et al. (1973a) are probably the most informative in the literature. Paykel (1978) has reviewed the concept of "brought forward time" and noted some of its disadvantages.

It does not relate easily to the existing work on causative effects, or to epidemiological studies where incidence can be calculated. . . . It lacks any intuitive base. It is not immediately apparent what constitutes a high or low brought forward time [p. 116].

In this connection, Paykel (1978) suggests that a measure of "relative risk" (McMahon and Pugh, 1970) would solve many of the ambiguities inherent to "brought forward time." "Relative risk is the ratio of the rate of the disease . . . among those exposed to the rate among those not exposed" (p. 86). Paykel (1978) goes on to present a series of estimates of "relative risk" that compare the frequency of stressful life events among acute schizophrenic patients and members of the general community on the basis of published and unpublished data. Given the definition of "relative risk," however, it is possible to ask whether Paykel's procedure produces a meaningful estimate of what it is designed to measure. If it is assumed that schizophrenic patients are specifically predisposed or vulnerable to the illness, the "at risk" factor for onset resulting from life events cannot be usefully derived through a comparison of affected individuals with a sample of the general population. In this sense, Paykel's calculations seem to indicate that acute schizophrenia patients are 3–4.5 times more likely than members of the general population *to report a life event* over a specified period of time, but these figures tell us little about the relationship of life events to the onset of the disorder. A more adequate estimate of relative risk would seem to require two matched samples of schizophrenic patients, one that relapsed with florid symptoms and one that has remained in remission for a specified period of time. Since both samples may be assumed to be at the same risk for illness, a comparison of the frequency of life events across the two groups would produce a more meaningful measure of the relative involvement of life stress in the onset of the disorder. The data required for such a comparison are not presently available in the published literature.

By way of expanding upon these remarks, it is useful to examine one further piece of research by the New Haven group. Schwartz and Myers (1977) compared the life-event data from a sample of 132 posthospitalized schizophrenia patients with a matched group of 132 community controls. The clinical subjects in this study were interviewed while living in the community, 2 to 3 years after being discharged from one of six local inpatient units. Diagnostic validity was established by rating the New Haven Schizophrenia Index (Astrachan, Harrow, and Adler, 1972) from the data in the hospital records. Community control subjects were selected from the same epidemiological sample of 938 New Haven households described for Jacobs and Myers' (1976) research (Myers et al., 1972a,b). Both samples were matched for age, race, sex, and socioeconomic status.

Each one of the clinical and community subjects in this study was given a semistructured interview covering life events occurring in the previous 6-month period. Both samples were also given the Gurin Mental Status Index (Gurin, Veroff, and Field, 1960), while the patients alone were examined with the New Haven Schizophrenia Index and the Psychiatric Evaluation Form (Spitzer and Endicott, 1971).

When the two groups were compared with regard to the data from the life-event schedule, it was found that the patients reported a significantly higher ($p < 0.001$) mean per person rate of events than the community control subjects. Further analysis demonstrated that this overall difference held up for *both* "uncontrolled" (i.e., independent) and "controlled" (i.e., conceivably illness related) events. The schizophrenic subjects were also more likely ($p = 0.001$) to have experienced an "undesirable" event than the community controls.

In a subsequent part of this study, factor analysis was carried out on the items in the three clinical instruments (i.e., GMSI, NHSI, and PEF). This analysis yielded five distinct dimensions of symptoms: a neurotic factor, a schizophrenic factor, a motor retardation factor, a hallucinatory-delusional factor, and a turbulence factor. Next, a series of linear multiple regression analyses were undertaken to determine the differential impact of life events, treatment, natural history, and sociodemographic variables on the specific symptom dimensions isolated with the factor analysis. Based on the results of this work, Schwartz and Myers (1977) conclude that:

[I]n terms of total variance explained, life events do not appear to be as important in determining mental status factor scores as other predictive variables. However, it is clear that life events exert their greatest influence on symptom items that make up the neurotic factor (i.e., anxiety, depression, somatic concerns, etc.) [p. 264].

The data reported in this article raise two intriguing questions. Why are these posthospitalized community patients experiencing elevated rates of "uncontrolled" (i.e., independent) life events relative to the subjects from the general population? And to what extent do these findings raise doubts about the adequacy of the research design used in previous controlled studies; that is, studies which drew conclusions about the significance of life stress for the onset of schizophrenic episodes by comparing the frequency of events in a group of *hospitalized patients* with that found in a matched sample of community controls? In this connection, Schwartz and Myers make the following observation:

Our findings suggest that uncontrolled life stress does not necessarily lead to relapse and should be carefully examined in relation to other factors . . . in understanding the conditions of relapse as well as adjustment of schizophrenia [p. 269].

Unfortunately, the data as reported in this chapter cannot be reorganized in terms of the categories and criteria used by other investigators. It is impossible to tell, for example, the proportion of Schwartz and Myers' sample that would be considered actively psychotic by the standards found in other studies. Beyond noting that their community-based patients appear "to possess some measure of resilience in coping with the impact of life events" and suggesting that "the greater anxiety, depression and somatic symptoms" resulting from life stress "may increase vulnerability to the more severe symptoms characteristic of schizophrenia," the authors make few additional remarks about the implications of these findings.

Assuming the validity of Schwartz and Myers' data, the above findings provide strong evidence that certain intervening variables act to determine the final pathogenic quality of stressful life events. Hence it is worthwhile to recall that a number of the studies under review (Brown and Birley, 1968; Jacobs and Myers, 1976; Paykel, 1978; Dohrenwend and Dohrenwend, 1980) have suggested that the effects of life events on schizophrenic disorders are probably mediated by important features of the patient's social milieu. Brown and Birley (1968), for example, observed that patients reporting a life event in the 3-

week period prior to onset were more likely to come from households characterized by elevated levels of chronic tension. In a subsequent article, Leff and Vaughn (1980) come to the following conclusions:

We should systematically examine the hypothesis that for schizophrenic patients most life events serve to trigger the florid onset of symptoms in those who are predisposed and are experiencing tense and difficult situations either at home or at work or in some key relationship [p. 148].

A similar hypothesis was put forward by Jacobs and Myers (1976) when they suggested that schizophrenic individuals may be particularly vulnerable to undesirable life experiences occurring in "settings where customary social supports are strained or unavailable . . ." (p. 448).

Drawing on these accumulated observations, it seems reasonable to hypothesize that the schizophrenic individual's social network, and especially the intrafamilial milieu, is likely to be a critical locus for the intervening variables that help to explain the resilience in coping with life events shown by Schwartz and Myers' (1977) community-based patients.

There is but a single study in the literature that directly addresses this hypothesis. Leff and Vaughn (1980) assessed the interaction between life events and the emotional atmosphere found in the homes of 37 schizophrenic patients prior to the onset of the disorder. Life events were detected with the Brown and Birley (1968) schedule.

The emotional atmosphere [in the home] was assessed . . . from individual interviews with the relative or relatives within a week or so of the patient's admission to the hospital. . . . The crucial measures are of critical comments and emotional over-involvement, which are used to construct an index of Expressed Emotion (EE). About half of the patients returning to High EE relatives will suffer a relapse of schizophrenia within nine months, whereas no more than 15% of those returning to low EE relatives will do so [Leff and Vaughn, 1980, p. 152].

It was found that in the 3-week period preceding the onset of the disorder 56.3 percent (9 of 16) of the patients living in low EE households experienced at least one independent life event, while only 4.8 percent (1 of 21) from high EE households reported a similar event occurring in the same period. On the basis of these findings, Leff and Vaughn (1980) come to the following conclusions:

Episodes of schizophrenia in patients living with high EE relatives are not preceded by an excess of life events, whereas those in patients from low EE families are. Thus the onset or relapse of schizophrenia is associated *either* with high EE *or* with an independent life event [p. 153].

The results from this study fail to confirm previous hypotheses about the interaction between stressful life events and family milieu in the onset of acute schizophrenic disorders. An explanation for these divergent findings will have to await the completion of further research.

CONCLUSIONS

A close examination of the current literature suggests that stressful life events are part of the "pool of causal factors" (Bebbington, 1980) which have been found to be associated with the onset of acute schizophrenic episodes. Yet, there is little evidence to indicate that this association is a necessary or a direct one.

Three points are critical for this conclusion. First, the positive temporal correlations suggesting the hypothesized "triggering effect" (i.e., independent life events prior to onset) have been demonstrated to occur in only a relative minority of the patients studied by any investigator. Further commonsense doubt may be cast on the causal significance of these correlations by the large number of comparatively trivial events that find their way into current calculations.

Second, the data indicating that nonrelapse patients living

in the community may be characterized by elevated normative rates for life events have important implications. If these findings are substantially correct, it means that differences in life-event rates found between hospitalized patients and general population controls cannot be assumed to have a direct causal significance for the onset of acute schizophrenic disorders. Life events, for example, may be a nonspecific factor related to overall negative outcome and the variance found in relapse episodes may be explained by additional moderating or confounding factors (Bebbington, 1980; Susser, 1973) that have just begun to be studied (e.g., family atmosphere, social supports, etc.).

Third, the positive temporal correlations that do exist in the literature are based exclusively on retrospective sorts of studies, none of which has been fully or properly replicated. A situation of this kind creates numerous opportunities for subtle varieties of contamination and incidental forms of spurious findings; and even though no insuperable difficulties stand in the way of designing a prospective study, not one investigator has attempted to predict relapse on the basis of a prior life-event interview.

An additional matter to be considered is the problem of diagnosis. It has been suggested that the broadly defined clinical samples utilized in previous studies may include more than a single disorder. Jacobs and Myers (1976), for example, draw upon the concept of "schizophreniform or reactive psychoses" (Langfeldt, 1939; Faergeman, 1946, 1963; Stromgren, 1965; McCabe, 1975; Pandurangi and Kapur, 1980) in order to suggest that a specific subgroup of patients normally included under the rubric of schizophrenia may be distinguished by a tendency to report a higher frequency of events prior to onset of the disorder. Although certain investigators (e.g., Birley and Brown, 1970) have argued against this hypothesis, none of the current studies have attempted to apply carefully defined diagnostic criteria for "reactive purposes" of the sort provided by McCabe (1975).

Similar problems arise in connection with recent operationalized diagnostic approaches (Feighner, Robbins, and Guze, 1972; Spitzer, Endicott, and Robbins, 1975; American Psychiatric Association, 1980) that include symptom duration as an essential criterion for schizophrenia. A substantial number of the patients involved in previous studies would probably have been diagnosed as other than schizophrenic (e.g., schizophreniform, brief reactive, or atypical psychoses) using the stricter criteria contained in these schemata. At the present time, it is not at all clear whether these criteria may serve to distinguish relevant diagnostic subgroups that differ with regard to the frequency of reported life events (Tsuang, Dempsey, and Rauscher, 1976).

Until further studies have been carried out using available kinds of alternative diagnostic criteria, it is impossible to reject hypotheses which suggest that previous broader concepts of schizophrenia may contain identifiable subgroups of patients having a particular vulnerability to the effects of stressful life events.

Past work on life events and psychiatric disorders have produced an established methodology, increasingly reliable research procedures, and a variety of instruments that permit the continued accumulation of comparable data. At the same time, the current weaknesses and ambiguities in the literature on life events and schizophrenia suggest that relationships among the factors affecting the acute onset of this disorder are much more complicated than had been originally expected. Given the present state of the evidence, further progress in this area seems to require an emphasis on prospective sorts of research designs that (1) follow up and periodically reexamine cohorts of patients in the community; (2) control for additional variables (e.g., maintenance neuroleptics, social supports, etc.) implicated in the relationship between stressful life events and the onset of acute schizophrenic disorder; and (3) test alternative diagnostic criteria as a means of identifying subgroups of patients with a differential sensitivity to life stress. Even though time-consuming and difficult to carry out, studies of this form seem necessary to adequately address a number of the complex issues that have been raised in the course of prior research.

References

Adamson, J. D., & Schmale, A. (1965), Object loss, giving up, and the onset of psychiatric disease. *Psychosom. Med.*, 27:557–577.

American Psychiatric Association (1980), *The Diagnostic and Statistical Manual of Mental Disorders*, 3rd ed. Washington, DC: American Psychiatric Association.

Andrews, J. G., & Tennant, C. (1978), Life event stress and psychiatric illness. *Psychol. Med.*, 8:545–549.

Antonovsky, A., & Kats, R. (1967), The life crisis history as a tool in epidemiological research. *J. Health & Soc. Behav.*, 8:15–20.

Astrachan, B. M., Harrow, M., & Adler, D. (1972), Checklist for the diagnosis of schizophrenia. *Brit. J. Psychiat.*, 121:529–539.

Bebbington, P. (1980), Causal models and logical inference in epidemiology and psychiatry. *Brit. J. Psychiat.*, 136:317–325.

Beck, J. C., & Worthen, K. (1972), Precipitating stress, crisis theory, and hospitalization in schizophrenia and depression. *Arch. Gen. Psychiat.*, 27:123–129.

Birley, J. L. T., & Brown, G. (1970), Crises and life changes preceding the onset or relapse of acute schizophrenia: Clinical aspects. *Brit. J. Psychiat.*, 116:327–333.

——— Birley, J. (1968), Crises and life changes and the onset of schizophrenia. *J. Health & Soc. Behav.*, 9:203–214.

Brown, G. W. (1974), *Meaning, Measurement, and Stress of Life Events: Their Nature and Effects*. New York: John Wiley, pp. 217–244.

——— Harris, T. (1978), The social origins of depression. London: Tavistock.

——— ——— Peto, J. (1973a), Life events and psychiatric disorders. II: The nature of the causal link. *Psychol. Med.*, 3:159–176.

——— Sklair, F., Harris, T., & Birley, J. (1973b), Life events and psychiatric disorders. I: Some methodological issues. *Psychol. Med.*, 3:74–87.

Cleary, P. J. (1974), Life Events and Disease: A Review of Methodology and Findings. Report No. 37, Laboratory of Clinical Stress Research, Stockholm.

Dohrenwend, B. P. (1975), Sociocultural and sociopsychological factors in the genesis of mental disorders. *J. Health & Soc. Behav.*, 16:365–392.

Dohrenwend, B. S., & Dohrenwend, B. P. (1978), Some issues in research on stressful life events. *J. Nerv. & Ment. Dis.* 153:207–234.

————— ————— (1980), Life stress and illness: Formulation of the issues. Unpublished manuscript.

————— Krasnoff, L., Askenasy, A., & Dohrenwend, B. P. (1978), Exemplification of a method for scoring life events: The PERI life event scale. *J. Health & Soc. Behav.*, 19:207–234.

Eisler, R. M., & Polak, P. (1973), Soical stress and psychiatric disorder. *J. Nerv. & Ment. Dis.*, 154:88–104.

Faergeman, P. M. (1946), Early differential diagnosis between psychogenic psychoses and schizophrenia. *Acta Psychiat. Scand.*, 21:275–279.

————— (1963), *Psychogenic Psychoses*. London: Butterworths.

Feighner, J., Robbins, E., & Guze, S. (1972), Diagnostic criteria for psychiatric research. *Arch. Gen. Psychiat.*, 36:57–63.

Garfinkel, H. (1968), *Studies in Ethnomethodology*. Englewood Cliffs, NJ.: Prentice-Hall.

Gurin, G., Veroff, J., & Field, S. (1960), *Americans View Their Mental Health: A Nationwide Survey*. New York: Basic Books.

Harder, D., Strauss, J., Kokes, R., Ritzler, B., & Gift, T. (1980), Life events and psychopathology severity among first psychiatric admissions. *J. Abnorm. Psychol.*, 89:165–180.

Hinkel, L. E. (1974), The effect of exposure to culture change, social change, and the effects of interpersonal relationships on health. In: *Stressful Life Events: Their Nature and Effects*, ed. B. P. Dohrenwend & B. S. Dohrenwend. New York: John Wiley, pp. 9–44.

Hirsch, S. R., Gaind, R., Rhode, P., Stevens, B., & Wing, J. (1973), Outpatient maintenance of chronic schizophrenic patients with long-acting fluphenazine. *Brit. Med. J.*, 5854:633–637.

Hocking, F. (1965), Human reactions to extreme environmental stress. *Med. J. Aust.* 18/2:477–483.

Holmes, T. H., & Masuda, M. (1974). Life change and illness susceptibility. In: *Stressful Life Events: Their Nature and Effects*, ed. B. S. Dohrenwend & B. P. Dohrenwend. New York: John Wiley, pp. 45–73.

————— Rahe, R. (1967), The Social Readjustment Rating Scale. *J. Psychosom. Med.*, 11:213–218.

Hudgens, R. W. (1974), Personal catastrophe and depression. In: *Stressful Life Events: Their Nature and Effects*, ed. B. P. Dohrenwend & B. S. Dohrenwend. New York: John Wiley, pp. 119–134.

————— Robbins, E., & Delong, W. (1970), Reporting of recent stress in the lives of psychiatric patients. *Brit. J. Psychiat.*, 117:635–643.

Jacobs, S. C., & Myers, J. (1976), Recent life events and acute schizophrenic psychoses: A controlled study. *J. Nerv. & Ment. Dis.* 162:75–87.

—————Prusof, B., & Paykel, E. S. (1974), Recent life events in schizophrenia and depression. *Psychol. Med.*, 4:444–453.

Jenkins, C. D., Hurst, M., & Rose, R. (1979), Life changes: Do people really remember? *Arch. Gen. Psychiat.*, 36:379–384.

Kinston, W., & Rosser, R. (1974), Disaster: Effects on mental and physical state. *J. Psychosom. Res.*, 18:437–456.

Kohn, M. (1973), Social class and schizophrenia: A critical review and reformulation. *Schiz. Bull.*, 7:60–79.

Langfeldt, G. (1939), *The Schizophreniform States*. Copenhagen, Denmark: Munksgaard.

Leff, J. P., Hirsch, S., Gaind, R., Rhode, P., & Stevens, B. (1973), Life events and maintenance therapy in schizophrenic relapse. *Brit. J. Psychiat.*, 123:659–660.

——— Vaughn, C. (1980), The interaction of life events and relatives' expressed emotion in schizophrenia and depressive neurosis. *Brit. J. Psychiat.*, 136:146–153.

——— Wing, J. (1971), Trial maintenance therapy in schizophrenia. *Brit. Med. J.*, 5775:599–604.

Lei, H., & Skinner, H. (1980), A psychometric study of life events and social readjustment. *J. Psychosom. Res.*, 24:57–66.

Lloyd, C. (1980), Life events and depressive disorder reviewed. *Arch. Gen. Psychiat.*, 37:520–548.

McCabe, M. (1975), Reactive psychoses. *Acta Psychiat. Scand.*, Suppl. 259. Copenhagen, Denmark: Munksgaard.

McMahon, B., & Pugh, T. (1970), *Epidemiology: Principles and Methods*. Boston: Little, Brown.

Mechanic, D. (1968), *Medical Sociology*. New York: Basic Books.

——— (1974), Discussion of research programs on relations between stressful life events and episodes of physical illness. In: *Stressful Life Events: Their Nature and Effects*, ed. B. P. Dohrenwend & B. S. Dohrenwend. New York: John Wiley, pp. 87–97.

Morrison, J. R., Hudgens, R., & Barehha, R. (1971), Life events and psychiatric impairment. *J. Nerv. & Ment. Dis.*, 152:149–157.

Murthy, R. S. (1975), Methodological problems in the study of life stress and psychiatric illness. *Indian J. Psychol.*, 50:1–10.

Myers, J. K., Lindenthal, J., Pepper, M., & Ostrander, D. (1972a), Life events and mental status: A longitudinal study. *J. Health & Soc. Behav.*, 15:149–157.

——— ——— ——— (1972b), Life events and mental status: A longitudinal study. *J. Health & Soc. Behav.*, 13:398–406.

Pandurangi, A., & Kapur, R. (1980), Reactive psychoses: A prospective study. *Acta Psychiat. Scand.*, 61:89–95.

Parkes, C. M. (1963), Interhospital and intrahospital variations in the diagnosis and severity of schizophrenia. *Brit. J. Soc. Prevent. Med.*, 17:85–89.

Paykel, E. S. (1978), Contribution of life events to the causation of psychiatric illness. *Psychol. Med.*, 8:245–253.

────── McGuiness, B., & Gomez, J. (1976), An Anglo-American comparison of the scaling of life events. *Brit. J. Med. Psychol.*, 49:237–247.

────── Prusoff, A., & Uhlenhuth, E. (1971), Scaling life events. *Arch. Gen. Psychiat.*, 25:340–347.

────── Uhlenhuth, E. (1972), Rating the magnitude of life stress. *Canad. Psychiat. Assn. J.*, 17:93–110.

Ratskin, J., & Struening, E. (1976), Life events, stress and illness. *Science*, 194:1013–1020.

Schless, A. P., & Mendels, J. (1977), Life stress and psychopathology. *Psychiat. Dig.*, 38:25–35.

────── ────── (1978), The value of interviewing family and friends in assessing life stressors. *Arch. Gen. Psychiat.*, 35:565–567.

Schneider, K. (1959), *Clinical Psychopathology*. New York: Grune & Stratton.

Schwartz, C., & Myers, J. (1977), Life events and schizophrenia: Parts I and II. *Arch. Gen. Psychiat.*, 34:1238–1248.

Scott, D. H. (1958), Some psychosomatic aspects of causality in reproduction. *J. Psychosom. Res.*, 3:42–55.

Shrout, P. (1980), Scaling stressful life events. Unpublished manuscript.

Spitzer, R. L., & Endicott, J. (1977), Schedule for Affective Disorders and Schizophrenia (SADS), 3rd ed. New York: New York State Psychiatric Institute, Biometrics Research.

────── ────── Robbins, E. (1975), Research diagnostic criteria (RDC). *Psychopharm. Bull.*, 11:22–24.

Steinberg, H. R., & Durell, J. (1968), A stressful social situation as a precipitant of schizophrenic symptoms: An epidemiological study. *Brit. J. Psychiat.*, 114:1097–1105.

Stromgren, E. (1965), Schizophreniform psychoses. *Acta Psychiat. Scand.*, 42:483–488.

Susser, M. (1973), *Causal Thinking in the Health Sciences*. New York: Oxford University Press.

Tsuang, M. T., Dempsey, G., & Rauscher, F. (1976), A study of atypical schizophrenia. *Arch. Gen. Psychiat.*, 33:1157–1160.

Uhlenhuth, E. H., Balter, M., & Lipman, R. (1977), Remembering life events. In: *The Origins and Course of Psychopathology*, ed. J. Strauss, H. Babigian, & M. Roff. New York: Plenum Press, pp. 117–132.

Vaughn, C., & Leff, J. (1976a), The influence of family and social factors on the course of psychiatric illness. *Brit. J. Psychiat.*, 129:125–137.

────── ────── (1976b), The measurement of expressed emotion in the families of psychiatric patients. *Brit. J. Soc. Clin. Psychol.*, 15:157–165.

Wing, J. K. (1978), The social context of schizophrenia. *Amer. J. Psychiat.*, 135:1333–1339.

—— Birley, J., Cooper, J., Graham, P., & Isaacs, A. (1967), Reliability of procedure for measuring and classifying present psychiatric state. *Brit. J. Psychiat.*, 113:499–515.

—— Brown G. (1970), *Schizophrenia and Institutionalism.* London: Oxford University Press.

—— Cooper, J., & Sartorius, N. (1974), *Present State Examination.* London: Oxford University Press.

Chapter 5
Why Do Unpredictable Events Lead to Reports of Physical Symptoms?

KAREN A. MATTHEWS, PH.D., MICHAEL F. SCHEIER, PH.D.,
BRADFORD I. BRUNSON, PH.D., AND BERNARDO CARDUCCI, PH.D.

Unsurprisingly, perhaps, there is widespread support for increasing the predictability of aversive events in an essentially unpredictable world. Research has revealed that individuals generally prefer signaled stressors to unsignaled ones (Lanzetta and Driscoll, 1966; Perkins, Seyman, Levis, and Spence, 1966) and punishers delivered immediately rather than after some, usually variable, delay (Maltzman and Wolff, 1970). Consequently, it is not surprising that in other studies, regular stressors are rated as less aversive than irregular ones (D'Amato and Gumenik, 1960; Loviband, 1968). Predictability also appears to ameliorate the negative impact of aversive events on physical states. For example, relative to unpredictable noise bursts, people report less severe physical symptoms during predictable bursts (Weidner and Matthews, 1978). They also exhibit less

---

Acknowledgment. This chapter was previously presented at a symposium, "Cognitive Processes in the Reporting of Physical Symptoms," K. Matthews, Chair, during a meeting of the American Psychological Association, New York City, 1979.

actual symptomatology indicative of arousal than those experiencing unpredictable events (Loviband, 1968).

Unfortunately the benefits of predictability are not uniform. Indeed, for almost every study that reports a positive effect for predictability, there exists another study that suggests that predictability does not reduce the aversive consequences of the stressor. For example, several studies show that predictable stressors are not more preferable (Furedy and Chan, 1971; Furedy and Doob, 1972) or rated as less aversive (Furedy and Doob, 1972) than unpredictable stressors. What is more, even in the studies that confirmed the desirability of predictability, there is a substantial proportion of subjects who prefer unpredictable events (Lanzetta and Driscoll, 1966; Hare, 1966). Nor are the effects uniform with respect to physical states. At times, signals warning of an impending stressor actually increase its impact relative to no warning signals (Liddell, 1950; Brady, Thorton, and Fisher, 1962; Friedman and Ader, 1965; Averill and Rosenn, 1972). In sum, about the only thing that can be said with certainty about the effects of predictability is that they are unpredictable. Sometimes predictability is beneficial, sometimes it has no effect.

Clearly, these contradictory findings need to be reconciled. Although it is possible that they are due to chance, it is more likely that subtle but systematic differences exist in the execution of the various experiments and in the prevalence of relevant dispositional factors in them. Stated another way, the relevant factors that produce the differences between the effects of unpredictable and predictable aversive events may be absent in those studies in which the benefits of predictability are not apparent.

In this regard, we suggest that a critical factor in accounting for the differential effects of predictability is the individual's focus of attention. When persons are initially confronted by a stressor, they direct their attention toward it. Moreover, the amount of attention directed toward the stressor should be the same whether the stressor is predictable or not. However, as the stressor is repeatedly presented, attention is withdrawn more quickly from stressors that occur at regular intervals than those that occur at irregular intervals (Epstein, 1973; Epstein, Rosenthal, and Szpiler, 1978) because regularly occurring events are easier to process and to encode (Finkelman and Glass, 1970; Cohen, 1978). In other words, individuals experiencing predictable stress habituate or adapt more quickly than those experiencing unpredictable stress because they are attending to the aversive stimulus less. Consequently, they experience and report less negative consequences of the stimulus. According to our formulation, it is precisely this difference in the amount of attention allocated to predictable and unpredictable events that accounts for the differences between them in physical arousal, perceived unpleasantness, preferences, and reported symptoms.

In the case of studies showing no differences, we suspect that other factors within the situation or within persons may have caused an equal amount of attention to be allocated to both predictable and unpredictable stressors, thereby attenuating the benefits of predictability. An individual's focus of attention during an aversive event is affected not only by its predictability, but by a variety of other parameters as well. For example, the intensity of the stimulus should be relevant. The greater the intensity of a stimulus, the more attention it should command, other things being equal. When a stimulus reaches a high enough level of intensity, it may be impossible to withdraw attention from it, even a regularly occurring one (Graham and Clifton, 1966). Another parameter is the time course. Eventually an individual may withdraw his attention from even unpredictable events after frequent exposure to the particular event. Consequently, differences between regularly and irregularly occurring stimuli should disappear.

The analysis of previous research has thus far been completely post hoc. We will present a series of studies designed to obtain more systematic evidence concerning the role of attentional factors in response to unpredictability. As a first step, we chose to examine the ability of an attentional approach to account for a previously established finding in the unpredictability literature; that is, the finding that unpredictable events elicit reports of more severe physical symptoms of illness than predictable ones do (Weidner and Matthews, 1978). Our research strategy was twofold: we wished to demonstrate (1) that more attention was commanded by unpredictable than predictable events; and (2) that no differences in symptom reporting would occur between unpredictable and predictable events, provided that the amount of attention directed toward these events was roughly equal. To test the first part of the explanation, we examined how much attention 42 undergraduate subjects directed to a series of either unpredictable or predictable noise bursts while performing a subsidiary task for eight minutes. The subsidiary task required subjects to depress a response key upon the onset of several auditory signals superimposed on the audiotapes of noise bursts. We assumed that performance on the subsidiary task was a measure of attention to this task and that the amount of attention directed to the noise bursts was inversely related to the amount of attention available for extraneous events, in this case, for the subsidiary task. In other words, performance on the reaction time task should provide an indirect measure of the amount of attention directed to the noise bursts. We expected that because subjects were not forewarned of the predictability of the noise bursts, subjects listening to predictable noise would not initially know of its regularity. Consequently, performance on the subsidiary task should be equal for subjects experiencing predictable and unpredictable noise at the beginning of the noise series. As time progressed, however, we expected that performance on the subsidiary task would improve for subjects listening to predictable noise, because they should begin to habituate to the bursts and should have learned of the regular silent intervals during which time anticipation of noise onset was unnecessary. In contrast, we expected that subjects listening to unpredictable noises would not improve in their subsidiary task performance.

The relevant data are presented in Figure 5.1. As we can see, subjects experiencing predictable noise bursts improved in their subsidiary task performance from the first half to the

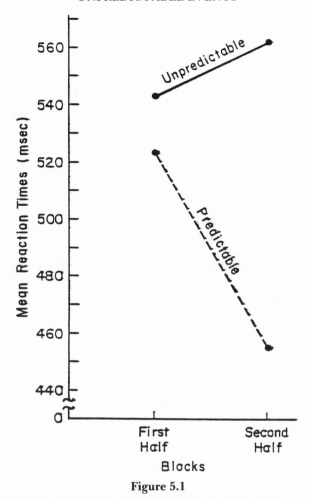

Figure 5.1

second half, whereas subjects experiencing unpredictable noise bursts did not, $F(1,40) = 13.38$, $p < .0008$, Predictability × Trial Blocks interaction. Assuming that subsidiary task performance is an indirect measure of attention to the noise bursts, the data strongly support that subjects withdrew their attention from predictable noise bursts over time. In contrast, subjects did not withdraw their attention from unpredictable noise bursts. Thus, the first part of our explanation was confirmed.

Our next step was to demonstrate that when an equivalent amount of attention is directed toward unpredictable and predictable noise bursts, there is no difference in symptom reporting between the two groups. But, when individuals are free to withdraw their attention from predictable bursts over time, they report less extreme symptoms than those experiencing unpredictable bursts. Thus, we expected that the benefits of predictability would be apparent only when individuals were not forced to attend to the event.

Experiment 2 tested this notion. Forty-seven subjects were asked to compute simple arithmetic problems while listening to unpredictable or predictable noise bursts for eight minutes. Half of each group were instructed to attend closely to the noise; the other half were given no instructions (control). At the end of the noise period, subjects completed a 14-item symptom checklist. If attention mediates the unpredictability-symptom reporting relationship, then subjects in the predictable-control group should report fewer symptoms than subjects in the remaining three groups.

The data presented in Table 5.1, Row 1, reveals that reported symptoms conformed fairly closely to the predicted pattern. Subjects in the predictable-control group did report less symptoms than the remaining subjects, $p < .001$. Also as anticipated, the two unpredictability conditions did not differ from each other; nor did the predictable attention group differ from the unpredictable control group, both ps $> .40$. Not anticipated,

Table 5.1
Total Reported Symptoms

| | Instructions to Attend to Noise | | | |
| | No (Control) | | Yes | |
Noise Bursts	Predictable	Unpredictable	Predictable	Unpredictable
Experiment 2	21.6	27.3	25.2	30.2
Experiment 3	26.7	33.0	35.5	31.6

however, was the slight, but nonsignificant ($p = .16$) tendency of subjects in the attention condition to report more intense symptoms when the noise was unpredictable than when it was predictable. Consequently, in order to examine both the reliability of symptom reporting in the unpredictable-attention to noise group and the general pattern of findings, we decided to repeat the second experiment.

Table 5.1, Row 2, reports the results of this experiment. As it reveals, the reported symptoms again conformed fairly closely to the predicted pattern. Subjects in the predictable control group did report less symptoms than the remaining subjects, $p < .02$. As before, the latter three conditions did not differ from one another, all $ps > .40$. But, in this experiment, there was no tendency for the attention-to-noise unpredictable group to report more symptoms. To determine whether unpredictable noise elicited more symptom reporting than predictable noise (as had previously been demonstrated [Weidner and Matthews, 1978] and existed in Experiment 2, $p < .05$), a final contrast testing the difference between the two control groups was computed and was also significant, $p < .05$.

Taken together, the findings of Experiments 2 and 3 replicate previous findings that unpredictable noise elicits greater symptom reporting than predictable noise. More importantly, they demonstrate that subjects who were prevented from withdrawing their attention from the predictable noise reported experiencing symptoms just as intensely as subjects for whom the noise bursts were unpredictable.

In sum, the results of the three experiments reported here offer strong support for the viability of an attentional explanation of the unpredictability-symptom reporting relationship. Experiment 1 suggested that subjects exposed to predictable noise were able to withdraw their attention from the stressor, whereas subjects exposed to unpredictable noise did not.

Experiment 2 and 3 subjects not instructed to attend to the noise reported more severe symptoms when the noise was unpredictable than when it was not, thus replicating the previous finding. As predicted, however, equating the amount of attention directed to the unpredictable and predictable noise (by asking subjects to attend to the noise) eliminated the apparent benefits of predictabilty. By extrapolation then, the present research also raises the possibility that attentional factors are not only important in our understanding of the effects of unpredictability on symptom reporting but also on ratings of aversity, preferences, and physiological arousal. Future research is planned to test this possibility.

The attentional explanation suggests under which circumstances increasing or decreasing attention to a negative event should have a positive, negative, or no effect on reports of physical well-being. Increasing attention to an *unpredictable* event is unlikely to enhance symptom reporting because individuals should already be attending to it at a near maximal level. In contrast, diverting attention is likely to decrease symptom reporting when the stressor is unpredictable. On the other hand, diverting attention from a *predictable* event is unlikely to reduce symptom reporting because individuals should be attending to it at a near minimal level, particularly after a substantial period of time has passed. In contrast, increasing attention to a predictable event should enhance symptom reporting.

Finally, we have discussed elsewhere the potential positive effects on physical well-being of increasing predictability for those at risk for disease, those diagnosed with an illness and undergoing treatment, or those experiencing major life changes such as is common for the elderly (Weidner and Matthews, 1978). The present data suggest that these positive effects may be realized only in certain types of situations. If the techniques for increasing predictability do not simultaneously require that the participants continue to attend to the aversive event, then such procedures should be beneficial. However, if the techniques do require or encourage such continual monitoring, then increasing predictability should be of no benefit to the well-being of the participants. Thus, it behooves us to pay careful attention to the specific parameters of the intervention programs designed to increase predictability of an aversive event.

Otherwise we may inadvertently eliminate the benefits of predictability.

REFERENCES

Averill, J. R., & Rosenn, M. (1972), Vigilant and nonvigilant coping strategies and psychophysiological stress reactions during the anticipation of electric shock. *J. Pers. & Soc. Psychol.*, 23:128–141.

Brady, J. V., Thornton, D. R., & Fisher, D. (1962), Deleterious effects of anxiety elicited by conditioned pre-aversive stimuli in the rat. *Psychosom. Med.*, 24:590–595.

Cohen, S. (1978), Environmental load and the allocation of attention. In: *Advances in Environmental Research,* ed. A. Baum, J. E. Singer, & S. Valins. Norwood, NJ: Lawrence Erlbaum.

D'Amato, M. E., & Gumenik, W. E. (1960), Some effects of immediate versus randomly delayed shock on an instrumental response and cognitive processes. *J. Abnorm. & Soc. Psychol.*, 60:64–67.

Epstein, S. (1973), Expectancy and magnitude of reaction to a noxious UCS. *Psychophysiol.*, 10:100–107.

———— Rosenthal, S., & Szpiler, J. (1978), The influence of attention upon anticipatory arousal, habituation, and reactivity to a noxious stimulus. *J. Res. Pers.*, 12:30–40.

Finkelman, J. M., & Glass, D. C. (1970), Reappraisal of the relationship between noise and human performance by means of a subsidiary task measure. *J. Appl. Psychol.*, 54:211–213.

Friedman, S. B., & Ader, R. (1965), Parameters relevant to the experimental production of "stress" in the mouse. *Psychosom. Med.*, 27:27–30.

Furedy, J. J., & Chan, R. (1971), Failures of information to reduce rated aversiveness of unmodifiable shock. *Austral. J. Psychol.*, 23:85–94.

———— Doob, A. N. (1972), Signalling unmodifiable shocks: Limits on human informational cognitive control. *J. Pers. & Soc. Psychol.*, 23:111–115.

Graham, F. K., & Clifton, R. K. (1966), Heart-rate change as a component of the orienting response. *Psychol. Bull.*, 65:305–320.

Hare, R. D. (1966), Psychopathy and choice of immediate versus delayed punishment. *J. Abnorm. Psychol.*, 71:25–29.

Lanzetta, J. T., & Driscoll, J. M. (1966), Preference for information about an uncertain but unavoidable outcome. *J. Pers. & Soc. Psychol.*, 3:96–102.

Liddell, H. (1950), The role of vigilance in the development of animal neurons. In: *Anxiety,* ed. H. Hoch & J. Zubin. New York: Grune & Stratton.

Loviband, S. H. (1968), The aversiveness of uncertainty: An analysis in terms of activation and information theory. *Austral. J. Psychol.*, 20:85–91.

Maltzman, I., & Wolff, C. (1970), Preference for immediate versus delayed noxious stimulation and the concomitant GSR. *J. Experiment. Psychol.*, 83:76–79.

Perkins, C. C., Jr., Seyman, R. G., Levis, D. J., & Spence, H., Jr. (1966), Factors affecting preference for signal-shock over shock-signal. *J. Experiment. Psychol.*, 72:190–196.

Weidner, G., & Matthews, K. A. (1978), Reported physical symptoms elicited by unpredictable events and the type A coronary-prone behavior pattern. *J. Pers. & Soc. Psychol.*, 36:1213–1220.

Part II
Assessment and Methodological Issues in Stressful Life Events

In theoretical terms, stress requires a precise definition, and the appropriate methodology must be attracted to systematically understand and define stress, its ideology, and its treatment. Research as an enterprise is a systematic development of empirically based theories. A theory is only as useful as its capability and methodology allows it to be understood within a particular framework. As an increasing number of researchers and health care professionals address the area of human stress, it is critically important that theory development be an essential component of any programmatic clinical research effort. As the scientific community embarks upon the assessment of stress, it must recognize that it is dealing with an abstract conceptualization, a construct if you will, which transcends symptomatology and identifying qualities common to stressful life experiences. It demands a greater understanding of human perception, of behavior, of biochemistry, and physiology. It requires a precise operationalization in order to effectively bridge the multiplicity of applications. It requires a multivariant paradigm which can be associated with stress factors and account for specific stress related responses.

Efforts toward the measurement of stress must deal with the issues of validity, reliability, and internal consistency. Research in this regard has a strong potential for yielding enormously useful information that can have a direct impact on the prevention or effective management of stress related disorders. In order to best understand these issues, a multidisciplinary approach to the assessment of stress and life events is imperative. A variety of issues relative to measuring life stress events within various diagnostic categories are explored in this section.

In chapter 6, Dr. Miller addresses clinical and methodological issues in the measurements of stressful life events. Examined and summarized are (1) research evidence addressing the assessment of life events; (2) prominent scales for the measurement of stress in life events; and (3) various issues and implications for both clinical and research application. Directions that may emerge in this significant area of clinical research are explored. In chapter 7, Drs. Parry, Shapiro, and Davies discuss reliability of life-event ratings. They note that there are two main methods of assessment: The first uses a standard checklist of events assigned a priori weightings derived from a rating sample and the semistructured interview which elicits information concerning life events and circumstances. Trained interviewers serving as raters, assess on Likert type scales the degree of "threat" associated with each event. With knowledge of subjects' social context, but ignorant of their psychiatric or emotional reactions, each rater makes three judgments: the event's short-term threat, its long-term threat (at the end of a week), and its focus (for example, "subject" or "other"). Raters then meet to pool judgments, and a consensus is reached.

In chapter 8, Dr. Richard Neugebauer addresses the reliability issues of life-event interviews and examines outpatient schizophrenics, using a 102-item structured checklist. Patients and one close relative were interviewed regarding events during the 12 preceding months. Interviewers were randomly assigned to patients, pair members were seen by different individuals. Mean intrapair agreement for all events combined was .22. Objective items exhibited greater reliability than subjective ones, but item ambiguity, event recentness, and stressfulness did not appear to influence agreement. Pairs evidenced low concordance on event dates. A greater number of events were recalled for the most recent six months than for the earlier period, and a pronounced interview effect on the number of reported events emerged. These findings, together with those from other reliability investigations, cast doubt on the validity of some retrospective studies of the relationship of life events to illness onset.

Drs. P. McC. Miller and D. P. Salter of the MRC Unit of Epidemiological Studies, Royal Edinburgh Hospital, Department of Psychiatry, Scotland, also discuss the life-event interview. They studied 42 men and 53 women patients at the Edinburgh Regional Poisoning Treatment Center. The interview covered life events and difficulties from six months before admission. For 43 patients it was in three stages: (1) a list of life events and difficulties to be checked off; (2) standard probing questions about each situation checked; (3) free flowing unstructured interviewing eliciting fuller contextual data about the stressful life situations. For individual patients more than 80 percent of the life situation information found after the final free flow stage had been obtained by the end of the probe stage. Furthermore, the final stage took something between a third and a half the interview time. On the other hand, it was clear that it would be unreasonable to end the interview after either the first free flow or the last stages, and the gain in information from probe to final stage was highly significant and potentially important. For individual life situations 75 percent underwent no further change in rating after the probe stage.

In chapter 10, Dr. Byrne reports data from two prospective studies of life-event measures with the focus being on psychological symptoms. This report presents data on prospective associations of life-event measures with psychological symptoms. Two issues in particular are addressed, the one relating to the causal influence of life events on symptom onset, and the other to the role of personal interpretations of life-event impact on this association. The latter issue derives from a consideration of the cognitive view of stress. Prospective associations did, indeed, emerge and were strongest where the individual was permitted to personally assess the impact of encountered life events. Temporal patterns of association varied with the kinds of symptoms (anxiety or depression) used as the dependent variable.

In chapter 11, Drs. Elkind and DeVito address the stability of trait anxiety under normal and examination-stress conditions using the State-Trait Anxiety Inventory. Correlation coefficients for those subjects receiving the STAI Trait Anxiety scale under normal and examination-stress conditions were highly significant and lend support to the State-Trait theory of anxiety which claims that trait anxiety is a relatively stable personality characteristic.

In chapter 12, Drs. Bausell and Damrosch study health seeking, affective, and demographic correlates of stress. Interviews obtained from a random sample ($N = 1,254$) of the American public indicated that the frequency with which severe stress was experienced was related both to compliance with recommended health seeking behavior (including not smoking, getting sufficient sleep, and several automotive safety practices) as well as demographic and affective (perceived importance of health behavior and perceived control over future health) variables. Although causality is difficult to determine, the combined effects of stress and noncompliance with recommended health practices may increase susceptibility to injury and disease.

Chapter 6
Life-Event Scaling: Clinical Methodological Issues

Thomas W. Miller, Ph.D., A.B.P.P.

Over the past decade, the medical, nursing, and health-related professions have begun to scrutinize the role and function of stressful life events as they relate to illness. This chapter examines the measurement of life events and the issues and implications for clinical and research applications.

In *The Diagnostic and Statistical Manual of Mental Disorders* (American Psychiatric Association, 1980), the psychiatric profession addresses the importance of stress in life events through evidence of the occurrence and severity of recent stressful events. This appears to be the first effort of the health professions to address life stress as a precipitator or contributor to illness even though, in 1975, Lehman considered the assessment of life stress information essential in the diagnosis and prognosis of illness.

However, the distinction between necessary and sufficient cause is basic to understanding the effects of psychological or social data in precipitating illness. A "necessary cause" must be present for disease or illness to occur, although its presence by itself is not sufficient to produce disease. Other factors must coincide with the necessary cause to provide sufficient conditions for the disease.

LIFE EVENTS: WHAT ARE WE
MEASURING?

Stress does not appear to reside within the particular life events or within the individual. Crisis arises from interaction between the individual and the situation; a simultaneous change takes place within the individual and within the environment (Elder, 1974; Riegel, 1976). The question is, what is a "significant," "stressful" or "critical" life event? Some investigators define life events as personal catastrophes such as life-threatening illnesses (Hudgens, 1974). However, a more common approach includes a wide array of events "whose advent is either indicative of or requires a significant change in, the ongoing life pattern of the individual" (Holmes and Masuda, 1974, p. 46). Some of these events are "negative" in the sense they are typically socially undesired, while others are socially desired and "positive." In all cases the events require adaptation and change on the part of the individual experiencing them.

Each person's life is characterized by various life events that are different in many ways. A major experimental approach has been to measure the amount of stress or behavioral change associated with events (Dohrenwend, Krasnoff, Askenasy, and Dohrenwend, 1978). To do this, researchers have asked people to rate lists of life events; the Social Readjustment Rating Scale (SRRS) developed by Holmes and Rahe (1967) is widely used to measure stress and is an example of this approach. Because of selection and sampling issues and the checklist approach to measurement, most studies of life events are prospective rather than retrospective in design.

THE MAJOR CONTRIBUTORS TO LIFE-
EVENT SCALING

Holmes and Rahe (1967) provided the major impetus toward the systematic scaling of life events by measuring the correlation of major life events and physical psychiatric disorders. Following Holmes and Rahe's initial efforts, several research teams contributed to the study of factors that may trigger major physical and psychiatric illnesses. Antonovsky and Kats (1967); Brown and Birley (1968); Paykel, Prusoff, and Uhlenhuth (1971); Dohrenwend and Dohrenwend (1978); and Hough (1980) also have generated life-event scales and subsequent research to assess the validity and reliability of life events as a significant factor in precipitation change in the life-functioning of human beings. These researchers vary as to what life events weigh more heavily than others in influencing life change.

Brown and Birley formulated an inventory of life change events from interviews with individuals who experienced acute episodes of schizophrenia. Paykel added to Holmes and Rahe's list, extending the count to 60 life change events, while Myers, Lindenthal, Pepper, and Ostrander (1972) gathered a list of 62 events based on items from the work of Holmes and Rahe and Antonovsky and Kats. Eventually, Rahe expanded his original list of 54 events, some of them having two to four options, making the actual number of events 76. Dohrenwend and Dohrenwend composed a life change list of 102 items, rethinking issues of sampling, completeness, and wording of life events; however, their list proved similar to previous lists.

Investigators Holmes and Rahe employed the Stevens (1974) technique of magnitude-estimation in an attempt to determine gradients of social and life change or readjustment. The Stevens technique focuses on specific events that may cause change in the average person, regardless of the desirability of the event. Pleasant life changes—for example, marriage, inheriting a large sum of money, and such—require nearly as much life adjustment as unpleasant events. Therefore, Holmes and Rahe scaled life change events in terms of the amount of change they produced in a person's state of life adjustment.

As life-event scaling matured, research at centers such as the Life Change and Illness Research Project at the Veterans Administration and University of California at Los Angeles (VA/UCLA) focused upon universal and group specific elements of stressful life events. Currently, populations are studied with environmental differences and interaction effects as the focus of measurement efforts. This chapter considers instruments that bear most directly on clinical-research application in nursing.

PROMINENT SCALES IN LIFE-EVENT MEASUREMENTS

THE SOCIAL READJUSTMENT RATING SCALE

In 1964 Holmes and Rahe devised the Social Readjustment Rating Questionnaire (SRRQ) to obtain numerical estimates of the average degree of life change and readjustment that subjects assign to life change events. Life changes studied involved those modifications of sleeping, eating, social, recreational, personal and interpersonal habits that required or indicated varying degrees of adjustment. The result of Holmes and Rahe's revision was the Social Readjustment Rating Scale (SRRS), which assigned magnitudes to each of 42 life change items, according to the amount, severity, and duration of adjustment each requires. The scaling instrument was found to be concordant among various segments of the American population and between U.S. citizens and people of other cultures.

Following this, Holmes and Rahe devised the Schedule of Recent Experience (SRE), a self-administered paper and pencil survey that listed life changes by year of occurrence. Now referred to as the Recent Life Changes Questionnaire (RLCQ), this updated version of the SRE retains the essence of the 42 original life change questions of the SRE, but the wording of questions has been altered for clarity and to allow for specific options of response. Test-retest reliability studies suggested these changes.

Instructions were placed at the end of the RLCQ so the subject could self-scale his own subjective life change scores for each life change he recently experienced. Patients obtained at least three different life change scores for analyses with various illness criteria. First, subjects obtained a six-month life change unit (LCU) score for the 42 SRE items. Second, they scored a sum of all recent life changes indicated in a six-month period. This was called the unit scaling method and proved to be particularly useful with subjects between 18 and 25 years of age, a group that usually experiences few high LCU life changes. (It is recommended the investigator use the LCU scoring system when dealing with samples of older subjects who may have experienced more life changes, such as marriage, birth of a child, divorce, business readjustment, illnesses of family members, death in the family, and so on.)

Finally a subjective life change unit (SLCU) score was obtained. This yielded a six-month SLCU total for the original 42 SRE life change questions permitted SLCU scores to be subtracted from the standard LCU scores for those 42 questions.

Coddington (1972) modified the Social Readjustment Rating Questionnaire to assess stressful life events related to childhood. Using the method in the Social Readjustment Rating Scale, he constructed a different list of experiences for each of the following groups: preschool age, elementary school age, junior high school age, and senior high school age. The 250 people who did the rating included teachers, pediatricians, and mental health workers. Interrater agreement was high, with rank order correlations or $r = .90$ or better.

Rubin, Gunderson, and Arthur (1971) assessed the predictive validity of the SRE. A stepwise multiple regression analysis was used with favorable results to predict the onset of emotional disturbance for Navy personnel. In another study, Rahe, Mahan, and Arthur (1970) demonstrated a linear relationship between the mean illness rate of shipboard personnel and the magnitude of life change.

Skinner and Lei (1980) conducted a factor analysis using an interactive principal factor model with least squares estimate. The results suggest that a relatively homogeneous subset of life events can be identified among the SRE items. The six factors isolated by Skinner and Lei are: (1) personal and social activities, (2) work changes, (3) marital problems, (4) residence changes, (5) family issues, and (6) school changes. The clinical population used by Skinner and Lei was 353 individuals who voluntarily sought help for alcohol and/or substance abuse.

Lei and Skinner found an internal consistency reliability estimate of $r = .80$ for the SRE with this clinical population. Often the 43 life events are scaled by social readjustment weights (the SRRS) to yield a weighted total score in life change units (LCU). However, Lei and Skinner found overlap between the SRE and LCU scores, a correlation of $r = .97$. Also, the reliability estimate $r = .72$ for the LCU scores was lower than the SRE. Reliability and validity studies with the SRE show variable results. Three reliability estimates of the SRE that used college subjects and allowed only a week between test and retest had high correlations between $r = .87$ and $r = .90$ (Hawkins, Davis, and Holmes, 1957; Rahe, 1974a). Rahe (1974b) and Rahe, Floistad, and Bergan (1974) reported that when the interval between test and retest was extended to six to nine months, resident physicians obtained correlations around $r = .70$ and the U.S. Navy enlisted men obtained a correlation of $r = .55$. Rahe, Romo, Bennett, and Siltanen (1974) conducted a study with spouses, who separately agreed with their partners' scoring of recent life changes over one to two years prior to testing; correlations ranged between $r = .50$ and $r = .75$.

The potential user of the most recent version of the SRE can consider a number of issues before applying the instrument to clinical and/or research use. The SRE instructions are limited and nonspecific, and not having carefully worked out pretested instructions is a concern when working with people who are experiencing stressful life events. Furthermore, the issue of social desirability and response sets must be assessed, since this issue is not addressed satisfactorily. The SRE could also be enhanced if it employed a Likert-type scale for items. The degree of severity must be assessed for individual items before valid comparability purposes, validity and reliability data might better be presented in tables rather than in the text of the articles. Disappointingly little information is available on the application of the SRE to both clinical and normal samples. Until more information is available, the SRE has limited application in clinical settings. While the SRE has done much to identify the importance of assessing stressful life events, it has not kept pace with the most recent measures available to be considered. The SRE requires more sophisticated measurement technology; however, it stands as an interesting and promising clinical and research tool.

HOSPITAL STRESS RATING SCALE

Based on the research efforts of Holmes and Rahe (1967), Volicer (1973) and Volicer and Bohannon (1975) developed a method of quantifying stress: a 49-item Hospital Stress Rating Scale (HSRS), for use with medical, surgical, and psychiatric patients. Volicer and Bohannon demonstrated that patients are capable and willing to order stressful life events and the rank ordering of events provides the mechanism by which the psychosoical stress experienced by hospitalized patients can be measured.

The HSRS satisfactorily estimates (1) content validity based on the assessment and appropriateness of items as rated by professionals familiar with stressful life events of hospitalized patients and (2) concurrent validity, obtained in correlation studies with an earlier version of the Hospital Stress Scale. Reliability of rank scores for various subgroups have ranged from $r = .90$ to $r = .96$ for all items on the scale. Test-retest reliability was reported at $r = .90$ for a sample of 50 medical and surgical patients interviewed two days apart; there was no tendency for scores to increase or decrease. The applicability to clinical research and generalizability of the HSRS require further systematic investigation.

THE PSYCHIATRIC EPIDEMIOLOGICAL RESEARCH INTERVIEW–LIFE EVENTS SCALE

The Psychiatric Epidemiological Research Interview–Life Events Scale (PERI-LES) was developed by Dohrenwend et al. in 1978 to measure such life events as divorce, loss of job, and other more minor events. A number of these life events have been shown to correlate with the onset of medical and psychiatric illness. PERI-LES was constructed as part of a New York City study designed to develop methods for psychiatric epidemiological research in community populations during which a sample of life events, characteristic of New York City, was drawn from the experience of the local population. The list of 102 events was constructed from previous lists, the researcher's own experiences, and the events reported in two Washington Heights studies. Excluded from the list were subjective events not easily identified or rated.

The Dohrenwend group accorded much research effort to the assessment of the applicability of their scale, and that research suggested that ratings obtained on the PERI-LES yield significant group differences. More of those differences were due to ethnic background than to social class or sex variation. However, the PERI-LES has technical weaknesses: (1) there is no reliability data on the frequency of occurrence of individual life events, (2) the samples that judges used in assessing the ratings of life events was too small to assure that group differences were reliable. The strength of this scale is its potential methodological rigor. Researchers should yield improved revisions of their scale, which will serve to provide clinical researchers more valid and reliable estimates of assessing stressful life events. Multiple measures incorporating lists of stressful life events, such as the Dohrenwend group generated, must be assessed from a number of perspectives. Estimates of psychological constructs can aid in understanding the interplay of multiple factors involved as the individual perceives and reponds to stressful life events.

UNIVERSAL AND GROUP SPECIFIC LIFE-EVENT SCALES

The VA/UCLA Life Change and Illness Research Project has developed Universal and Group Specific Life Change Scales, which include weights for their five scales. They include standardized weights derived from latent trait analysis of the qualities of scale items.

Hough (1980) and his colleagues developed the scales of life change events that can be applied to culturally heterogenous populations. The scales were compiled from a random sampling of adults, ages 21 to 60, from El Paso, Texas, and a multilevel clustered sampling of similar adults from Ciudad Juarez, Mexico. Respondents were asked to rate the seriousness of 95 stressful life events. The specific 95 were chosen after a review of events used in previous life-event scales. Assessment criteria included interviewer reports on the respondent's ability to do the task, completeness of the responses, the rating of undesirable versus desirable events, the correlation of the individual's scores with his or her group's average, and case specific criteria. Several scales were constructed on the basis of latent trait analysis. Scale I, the Universal Scale, contains 51 events seen as essentially alike by the ethnic groups studied.

There is a scale of life events for each ethnic group as well. These scales contain the Universal Scale items and items scaled for each ethnic group. Items in the scales met two criteria: small mean square error and agreement among groups on the change value due an item. The 51 items in the Universal Scale are those whose response patterns fit the latent trait model and over which there was little disagreement among the ethnic groups sampled. The same criteria were applied within each of the ethnic groups to obtain the group specific scale items. Statistical analyses suggest that the scales have a ratio quality. Hough and colleagues found ethnic differences similar to the Dohrenwend group. The use of the Hough scales have added a dimension to this early phase of assessing stressful life events and confirmed the importance of distinguishing between universal and group specific change variables.

SCHEDULE OF NURSE RESPONSE TO PATIENT DISTRESS

Graffam (1970) developed a research instrument specifically for use in studying nursing personnel response to patient's complaints of distress. The Graffam Schedule of Nurse Response to Patients' Complaints of Distress has been tested for validity, reliability, comprehensiveness, and applied appropriateness.

The Graffam Schedule is a checklist of items designed to elicit data on nine variables: type of distress, initiation of complaint, persons involved in communication, evaluation of complaint, referral for definitive action, implementation of physical measure of relief, use of psychological measures or approaches, evaluation of relief measure, and response timing.

Graffam (1969) reports that validity for this instrument was established for item content and occurred in the course of its development. Interrater reliability estimates are reported through two sets of information. First, two nurse educators jointly observed three events. For two of these events, there was .87 agreement on the 60 categories checked. For the third event, there was 100 percent agreement. Second, two other nurse educators jointly observed 15 events. In 10 of the events, there was 100 percent agreement; for the remaining five events, the percent of agreement ranged from .92 to .98 correlations. The significance of this instrucment is its development and recognition of significant others in effecting response to life change events.

OTHER LIFE-EVENT MEASURE

Paykel (1974) has employed a checklist format of 60 items to ascertain events occurring within the six months prior to the onset of illness. Events were assessed by activity area—including work, family, change in health—and whether these life-event changes represented entrances or exits to a person's social field. A third rating determined whether these events were socially desirable or undesirable. Weights accommodated degrees of desirability to the average person for comparability purposes. The weighted scores were summed to estimate the life-event stress experienced by the subject. Brown's research group (Brown and Birley, 1968) explored criteria for which life events should be regarded as most and least stressful. Identified criteria included events, changes in life circumstances, role, subject experiences, health changes, and the personality and influence of relatives and members of the immediate living environment—a key ingredient. Circumstances and critical life events were documented, with date, context, and verification by significant others in the subject's environment. In the second stage the research team rated the severity of life events experienced by the subject and compared it with the perceived threat this event might have to the average person. The subject's own reaction to the life event was not weighted in the rating. Brown and colleagues were attempting to reduce or eliminate the bias that confused previous studies. Should the identification and scaling of events be accomplished with satisfactory reliability, then researchers have succeeded in eliminating a key bias and have strengthened the process of life-event scaling by accommodating the variability of circumstance and events that comprises our daily life experiences.

Several issues and implications emerge from the current state of life-event scaling. Much work needs to be done to improve the sophistication of the measures and scales that have emerged. The rigors of sound validity and reliability studies have been applied to few. Several published measures that have not been included in this article report only face validity and simplistic estimates of test-retest reliabillity. Future investigators must apply soundly developed statistical procedures, including multivariate analysis of variance to parcel out significant differences, especially with respect to mediating variables. Multiple regression analysis to assess the predictive quality of the measures to be tested must be encouraged. Measures of internal consistency of the instrument need to be completed and reported along with factor analytic studies. We must know what is being measured and what the measures can offer from a research and a clinical perspective.

The contents of the life-event scales may merely represent a plateau in a process at a point when the individual gives up, having lost control, and is unable to maintain an internal locus of control, or the person may be experiencing system failure in coping with stressful life events. Clinicians and researchers alike must address this issue and the measures they use must be designed to assess and differentiate this critical variable.

From a scaling perspective, several questions need to be answered including: What life events are identifiable and rateable? Is the list complete? During what time frame have the life events provided intense stress? Are there mediating variables that have not been considered? If these are to be related to the onset of disease, life-event researchers must also identify the onset of illness, the process of relapse, and the pattern of disease. Life events may then assume significantly more impact. Data must be adjusted to the psychological make-up and personality of the specific individual experiencing the illness and confronting the stressful life event. Only then can significant and meaningful predictions be made and the individual guided toward regaining control of himself and events.

Several factors affect the individual's responses to life events:

1. Cultural bias influences the individual's perception of both person and events. In the development of life-event scaling it is essential to consider social and cross-

cultural differences in assessing and weighing life events.
2. Life events are mediated by several variables including biologcial, psychological, social, physical characteristics of the individual and the environment.
3. The individual's personality is important to life events. Biological and intellectual variables limit adaptation (Lieberman, 1975). Costa and McCrae (1980) found that all events over which individuals had control were related to personality.
4. Timing and clustering of events affect life events. Events may be particularly difficult to deal with when they occur close together. Adults adapt well to given life events such as retirement, widowhood, departure of the last child from home, and illness (Palmore and Erdman, 1979) unless two or more such life events occur simultaneously, which can cause serious problems of adaptation.
5. Variables that affect life events include socioeconomic status, income, and interpersonal support systems including family and friends. Supportive interpersonal relationships may serve as resources for the individual to the degree to which they provide physical, psychological, or financial support (Adams and Lindemann, 1974). Miller, Wilson, and Dumas (1979) and more recently, Miller (1981) and Miller and Proudfoot (1981) have assessed the effects of communication style as a precipitator of relapse and developed a model of training family members and significant others in communicating with schizophrenics. The person's sociocultural world, including social structures (family social class and occupation and political affiliation), and historic events such as war and the economy; participation including specific roles, such as husband, friend, worker, and parent, and the life events related to those roles, such as marriage, birth of a child, promotion, and retirement; aspects of self including fantasies, moral values, talents,

and skills, all need to be considered as variables affecting life events (Levinson, 1978).

Future studies must (1) explore how life changes contribute to the etiology and the onset of illness; (2) assess the full range of psychological components that account for adjusted persons; (3) study the range of effects each stressful life event produces on a range of different types of people; (4) engage in a biosocial approach to understanding stress, life events, and the individual differences among human beings.

Recent large scale prospective studies do not support significant correlation among life events, stress, and illness (Andrews, 1978). From this perspective, significant relationships previously reported could be attributable to the accuracy/ inaccuracy of patient reporting or the sensitivity/insensitivity of the instruments used in collecting and classifying data.

Therefore, those who continue to explore the science of life events must be open to the possibility that stressful life events may be only extraneous variables. Moreover, if we continue to focus only on generating lists of life events and applying them to various samples, we will fail to recognize the important interchange between psychological and numerous genetic, metabolic, and biochemical variables. These adjacent areas are important in the larger scope of successfully assessing stressful life events. The state of the science of life events scaling remains in its infancy. However, the scientific community must appreciate efforts made so far to identify and analyze the impact of life events on psychological and physical adjustment.

References

Adams, J. E., & Lindemann, E. (1974), Coping with long-term disability. In: *Coping and Adaptation*, ed. G. V. Coelho. New York: Basic Books, pp. 127–138.

American Psychiatric Association (1980), *Diagnostic and Statistical Manual of*

Mental Disorders. 3rd ed. Washington, DC: American Psychiatric Association.

Andrews, G. C. (1978), Life events stress, social support, coping style, and risk of psychological impairment. *J. Nerv. & Ment. Dis.*, 166/5:307–316.

Antonovsky, A., & Kats, R. (1967), The life crisis history as a tool in epidemiological research. *J. Health & Soc. Behav.*, 8:15–21.

Brown, G. W., & Birley, J. L. (1968), Crisis and life changes and the onset of schizophrenia. *J. Health & Soc. Behav.*, 9:203–214.

Coddington, R. D. (1972), The significance of life events and etiologic factors in the disease of children. Part 1. A survey of professional workers. *J. Psychosom. Res.*, 16:7–18.

Costa, P. T., Jr., & McCrae, R. R. (1980), Still stable after all these years: Personality as a key to some issues in aging. In: *Life-Span Development and Behavior*, Vol. 3, ed. P. B. Baltes & O. G. Brim, Jr. New York: Academic Press, pp. 65–102.

Dohrenwend, B. S., Krasnoff, L., Askenasy, A. R., Dohrenwend, B. P. (1978), Exemplification of a method for scaling life events: The PERI Life Events Scale. *J. Health & Soc. Behav.*, 19:205–229.

—— Dohrenwend, B. P. (1978), Some issues on research in stressful life events. *J. Nerv. & Ment. Dis.* 153:207–234.

Elder, G. H., Jr. (1974), *Children of the Great Depression.* Chicago: University of Chicago Press.

Graffam, S. R. (1970), Nurse response to the patient in distress-development of an instrument. *Nurs. Res.*, 19:331–336.

—— (1969), A technique for the study of nurse response to adult patients' complaints of distress. New York: Teachers College, Columbia University. Unpublished doctoral dissertation.

Hawkins, N. G. (1957), Evidence of psychosocial factors in the development of pulmonary tuberculosis. *Amer. Rev. Tuber. & Pulmon. Dis.*, 75:768–780.

—— Davis, W. G., & Holmes, T. H. (1957), Evidence of psychosocial factors in the development of pulmonary tuberculosis. *Amer. Rev. Tuber. & Pulmon. Dis.* 75:768–780.

Holmes, T., & Masuda, M. (1974), Life change and illness susceptibility. In: *Stressful Life Events: Their Nature and Effects*, ed. B. S. Dohrenwend & B. P. Dohrenwend. New York: Basic Books, pp. 45–73.

—— Rahe, R. H. (1967), The Social Readjustment Rating Scale. *J. Psychosom. Res.*, 11:213–218.

Hough, R. L. (1980), Universal and group specific life change scales. Los Angeles: Life Change and Illness Research Project, University of California. Unpublished manuscript.

Hudgens, R. W. (1974), Personal catastrophe and depression. A consideration of the subject with respect to medically ill adolescents, and a requiem for retrospective life event studies. In: *Stressful Life Events: Their Nature and*

120   THOMAS W. MILLER

Effects, ed. B. S. Dohrenwend & B. P. Dohrenwend. New York: John Wiley, pp. 119–134.

Kreisman, D. E. (1979), Rejecting the patient: Preliminary validation of a self-report scale. *Schiz. Bull.*, 5/2:220–222.

Leff, J., & Vaughn, C. (1980), The interaction of life events and relatives expressed emotion in schizophrenia and depressive neurosis. *Brit. J. Psychiat.*, 136:146–153.

Lehman, J. (1975), Schizophrenia: Clinical features. In: *Comprehensive Textbook of Psychiatry*, Vol. 1, 2nd ed., ed. A. M. Freedman & H. I. Kaplan. Baltimore, MD: Williams & Wilkins, pp. 890–923.

Levinson, D. J. (1978), *The Seasons of a Man's Life*. New York: Alfred A. Knopf.

Lieberman, M. A. (1975), Adaptive processes in late life. In: *Life-Span Developmental Psychology: Normative Life Crisis*, ed. N. Datan & L. Ginsberg. New York: Academic Press.

Miller, T. W. (1979), Development and evaluation of social skills training for schizophrenic patients in remission. *J. Psychiat. Nurs.*, 17:42–46.

——— (1981), Training schizophrenics and their families to communicate: A cognitive behavioral model. *Hosp. & Comm. Psychiat.*, 32/12:870–871.

——— Proudfoot, C. A. (1981), Group sociotherapy: A psychoeducative model for patients with a schizophrenic disorder in remission. Colloquium Presentation: State University of New York, Buffalo, New York.

——— Wilson, G. C., & Dumas, M. A. (1979), Development and evaluation of social skills training for schizophrenic patients in remission. *J. Psychiat. Nurs.* 17/6:42–46.

Myers, J. K., Lindenthal, J., Pepper, M., & Ostrander, D. (1972), Life events and mental status: A longitudinal study. *J. Health & Soc. Behav.*, 152:149–157.

Palmore, E., & Erdman, J. (1979), Stress and adaptation in late life. *J. Gerontol.*, 34:841–851.

Paykel, E. S. (1974), Life stress and psychiatric disorder: Applications of the clinical approach. In: *Stressful Life Events: Their Nature and Effects*, ed. B. S. Dohrenwend & B. P. Dohrenwend. New York: John Wiley, pp. 135–149.

——— Prusoff, B. A., & Uhlenhuth, E. H. (1971), An Anglo-American comparison of the scaling of life events. *Brit. J. Med. Psychol.*, 49:237–247.

——— Uhlenhuth, E. H. (1972), Rating the magnitude of life stress. *Can. Psychol. Assoc. J.*, 17 Supp. 2:5593.

Rahe, R. H. (1974a), The pathway between subjects' recent life changes and their near-future reports: Representative results and methodological issues. In: *Stressful Life Events: Their Nature and Effects*, ed. B. S. Dohrenwend & B. P. Dohrenwend. New York: John Wiley, pp. 73–86.

——— (1974b), Predictions of near-future health change from subjects preceding life changes. *J. Psychosom. Res.*, 13:72–177.

—— Floistad, R. L., & Bergan, C. (1974), A model for life changes and illness research. Cross-cultural data from the Norwegian Navy. *Arch. Gen. Psychiat.*, 31:172–177.

—— Mahan, W. J., & Arthur, R. J. (1970), Prediction of near-future health change from subjects' preceding life changes. *J. Psychosom. Res.*, 13:401–405.

—— Romo, T., Bennett, J. W., & Siltanen, R. (1974), Recent life changes, myocardial infarction, and abrupt coronary death. Studies in Helsinki. *Arch. Intern. Med.*, 133:221–228.

Riegel, K. F. (1976), The dialectics of human development. *Amer. Psychol.*, 31:689–700.

Rubin, R. T., Gunderson, E. K. E., & Arthur, R. J. (1971), Life stress and illness patterns in the U.S. Navy—IV. Environmental and demographic variables in relation to illness onset in a battleship's crew. *J. Psychosom. Res.*, 15:221–227.

Skinner, H. A., & Lei, H. (1980), The multidimensional assessment of stressful life events. *J. Nerv. & Ment. Dis.*, 168:535–541.

Stevens, S. S. (1974), *Psychophysics: Introduction to Its Perceptual, Neutral and Social Prospects*. New York: John Wiley.

Vaughn, C. E., & Leff, J. F. (1976), The influence of family and social factors on the course of psychiatric illness. A comparison of schizophrenic and depressed neurotic patients. *Brit. J. Psychiat.*, 129:125–137.

Volicer, B. J. (1973), Perceived stress levels of events associated with the experience of hospitalization: Development and testing of a measurement tool. *Nurs. Res.*, 22:491–497.

—— Bohannon, M. W. (1975), A hospital stress rating scale. *Nurs. Res.*, 24:352–359.

Chapter 7
Reliability of Life-Event Ratings: An Independent Replication

GLENYS PARRY, M.R.C., S.S.R.C., DAVID A. SHAPIRO, M.R.C., S.S.R.C., AND LISA DAVIES, M.R.C., S.S.R.C.

Despite the recent proliferation of studies measuring life-event stress, there remain only two main methods of assessment. The first uses a standard checklist of events assigned a priori weightings derived from a rating sample (Holmes and Rahe, 1967). The second method, Brown's "London measure" (Brown and Harris, 1978), uses a semistructured interview to elicit information concerning life-event and circumstances. Trained interviewers also act as raters, assessing on four-point scales the degree of "threat" associated with each event. With knowledge of subjects' social context, but ignorant of their psychiatric or emotional reactions, each rater makes three judgments: the event's short-term threat, its long-term threat (at the end of a week) and its focus (for example, "subject" for "other"). Raters then meet to pool judgments, and a consensus is reached. Recently, an extensive "dictionary" of precedents has been compiled by Brown's group, to aid the rater in assigning "threat" scores.

Acknowledgment. This chapter was first published in the *British Journal of Clinical Psychology* (1981), 20:133–134, and it is reprinted with permission.

123

The checklist method is by far the more widely used, owing to its simplicity, availability and economy. However, it has been widely criticized for oversimplification of complex issues, and doubts have been raised about its validity, retest and interrater reliability (Tennant, Smith, Bebbington, and Hurry, 1979). Katschnig (1979) has shown that whilst the Holmes-Rahe and Brown measures yield comparable results using a simple correlation over grouped data, for individuals the two methods can give discrepant results, implying that the two methods are not interchangeable. Although it is relatively cumbersome and expensive, the London measure promises significant advantages in its thoroughness and subtlety. Brown and his colleagues have made their method available by training and supervising others in its use. Following this training, researchers work independently, and increasing numbers of studies using the measure are forthcoming. Levels of interrater agreement in these circumstances are unknown, and doubts have already been raised (Shapiro, 1979). Existing reliability data are sparse. Brown and Harris (1978) report their data incompletely in a footnote, using inappropriate product moment correlations. Tennant et al. (1979) showed very satisfactory agreement over a long period of research by independent groups with turnover of interviewing and rating personnel. These are the circumstances under which most data using the London measure are collected.

The present study reports interrater agreement data from a group researching employment, self-concept and depression in working-class mothers of young children. Data from 381 life events are reported, rated over a period of eight months. At any one time three raters made judgments of events, based on the interviewer's written account of the event and context, independently of each other but with access to the life-events dictionary. On two occasions an interviewer left the team and was replaced, so that five raters were involved in all. All five were social science graduates, and one a clinical psychologist. Four received a one-week initial training from Brown's group, who subsequently monitored their recorded interviews. The fifth was trained by the existing Sheffield group.

For short-term and long-term threat, agreement was calculated using Kendall's coefficient of concordance (W), which is suitable for ordinally scaled data, although taking no account of chance agreements. Over 381 events, Ws were 0.84 and 0.81 respectively. The nominally scaled focus data yielded an overall kappa of 0.78, using Fleiss's (1971) procedure.

W and kappa coefficients were calculated for threat and focus ratings, respectively, for each of nine overlapping blocks of 76 events (comprising events 1–76, 39–114, and so on). There was no evidence of decaying agreement; if anything, the reverse was true, with slightly rising trends interrupted only by temporary deterioration associated with the recruitment of a new rater. Thus, Ws for short- and long-term threat began at 0.83 and 0.78 respectively, reaching 0.88 and 0.84 respectively, before falling to 0.76 and 0.80 with the recruitment of a new rater, and recovering within some 50 events to reach 0.87 and 0.85 at the end of the series. Similarly, kappas for focus began at 0.73, fluctuating somewhat but rising to 0.81 before falling to 0.76 at the recruitment of a new rater, and recovering to 0.86 by the end of the series.

For all the events gathered by each of three interviewers, Spearman's rank order correlations were obtained between the three pairs of raters, and correlations involving the interviewer were compared with those between the non-interviewer pair. If the interviewer had been influenced by her subjective experience of the interview, not communicated in writing to the other raters, her ratings would tend to be discrepant. No trend of this kind was obtained, however, with correlations involving the interviewer sometimes higher and sometimes lower than those not involving the interviewer, and no differences approaching statistical significance.

Although these results are not directly comparable with those of Tennant et al. (1979), owing to differing statistical procedures, they are of a comparable level of significance. Short-term threat was slightly, but consistently, more reliably rated than was long-term threat. Agreement fluctuated somewhat more for focus than for the threat ratings.

Although the necessity or otherwise of initial training with Brown's group cannot be ascertained from the present data, we can conclude that the London measure of threatening life events can be used reliably by research groups working independently.

REFERENCES

Brown, G. W., & Harris, T. (1978), *Social Origins of Depression*. London: Tavistock.

Fleiss, J. L. (1971), Measuring nominal scale agreement among many raters. *Psychol. Bull.*, 76:378–382.

Holmes, T. H., & Rahe, R. H. (1967), The Social Readjustment Rating Scale. *J. Psychosom. Res.*, 11:219–255.

Katschnig, H. (1979), Measuring life stress: A comparison of two methods. In: *The Suicide Syndrome*, ed. R. Farmer & S. Hirsch. London: Croom Helm.

Shapiro, M. B. (1979), Review of *The Social Origins of Depression*, by G. W. Brown and T. Harris: Its methodological philosophy. *Behav. Res. & Ther.*, 17:597–604.

Tennant, C., Smith, A., Bebbington, P., & Hurry, J. (1979), The contextual threat of life events: The concept and its reliability. *Psychol. Med.*, 9:525–528.

Chapter 8
Reliability of Life-Event Interviews with Outpatient Schizophrenics

RICHARD NEUGEBAUER, PH.D., M.P.H.

The role of recent stressful experiences in psychological distress and in the onset or recurrence of discrete psychiatric disorders has been a major research area for several decades. Since the early 1960s numerous investigators have sought to measure subjects' exposure to stressors with life-event checklists. Currently, these life-event inventories enjoy a central place in the arsenal of stress research.

While substantive studies of life events and psychological as well as somatic morbidity have continued apace, investigation of the measurement properties of life-event inventories has been uneven. Item construction and scaling receive most attention. Methodologically exacting efforts are devoted to the creation of inventories, generation and cross-cultural comparison of magnitude ratings, and production of scoring schema to achieve the best predictive or construct validity. Instrument reliability has provoked less interest, especially in the psychiatric field, a surprising state of affairs given that validity presupposes reliability.

Acknowledgment. This chapter was first published in the *Archives of General Psychiatry* (1983), 40: 378–383, and it is reprinted by permission.

127

Among 18 studies of the reliability of life-event recall, seven employed psychiatric patients as subjects. Only one study used schizophrenic patients exclusively, despite the strong research interest in the association between recent life events and schizophrenic episodes. Although that study reported an impressive reliability estimate of .79, there are good a priori grounds for suspecting that patients with disorders of thought would prove reliable chroniclers of their recent experience.

To date, research on stress and episodes of schizophrenic illness has not consistently or persuasively demonstrated an association. Since measurement error attenuates the observed relationship between study variables, unreliability of event reports by schizophrenics may help explain the current fortunes of this research area. It should be noted in this connection that chronic schizophrenics, the quality of whose life-event reports might be particularly dubious, have composed a substantial proportion, sometimes even a majority, of the patients in several retrospective stress studies (Birley and Brown, 1970; Leff, Hirsch, and Gaind, 1973; Lahniers and White, 1976; Bech and Worthen, 1972; Schwartz and Myers, 1977). The present investigation aims to provide some further information on the reliability of life-event reports among this group of patients.

The selection of outpatient schizophrenics as study subjects was also influenced by recent calls for prospective stress studies (Birley and Brown, 1970; Schwartz and Myers, 1977; Bech and Worthen, 1972). The present investigation aims to provide some further information on the reliability of life-event reports among this group of patients.

The selection of outpatient schizophrenics as study subjects was also influenced by recent calls for prospective investigations of stress and the course of psychiatric illness (Dohrenwend and Dohrenwend, 1974). The relative rarity of most severe psychiatric conditions makes necessary the use of prospective studies.

In general, studies with psychiatric patients have assessed reliability by comparing patient recall with that of an informant, whereas studies with medical patients or nonpatient subjects have relied most often on test-retest formats. In addition, information about life events is usually elicited from psychiatric patients and their informants during personal interviews; other reliability studies depend on self-report methods of instrument administration. Nonetheless, few precautions have been taken to ensure that patient-informant pair members were seen to be different interviewers and did not discuss the checklist with each other until both had completed it. Nor were efforts made to establish whether informants were ignorant of certain events recalled by patients and therefore did not report them. In this study, reliability was measured only after controlling, through study design and data analysis, for these sources of data contamination and of underestimation of pair agreement.

METHODS

The primary subjects of the investigation, the psychiatric patients, were drawn from the case load of a bilingual (Spanish-English) psychiatrist practicing at a community mental health center in the Washington Heights area of Manhattan. All individuals over 17 years of age diagnosed as schizophrenic by means of a structured clinical interview (Wing, Cooper, and Sartorius, 1977) and with a history of at least two psychiatric hospitalizations were invited to participate after the nature of the study procedure had been fully explained. At recruitment, each eligible patient was asked for the name of the individual who would know most about his or her experiences during the preceding 12 months. Permission was sought to interview this potential informant.

The life-event interview for both patient and informant was the 102-item schedule developed by the Dohrenwend group (Dohrenwend, Krasnoff, Askenasy, and Dohrenwend, 1978) for the Psychiatric Epidemiology Research Interview (PERI). The inventory was constructed using events appearing on previous checklists, from the researchers' own experiences, and from two Washington Heights studies that asked respondents to name their last major event. This last source of many PERI items made the checklist particularly appropriate for the present study of Washington Heights residents.

Two female bilingual (Spanish-English) students from Columbia University School of Social Work, New York, were selected as interviewers. Both were of Puerto Rican ancestry, in their mid-20s, and planning careers in clinical social work. They were given two weeks' training on the administration of the life-event schedule, and their first five pairs of study interviews were monitored by means of audiotape recordings.

Initial patient recruitment was handled by the treating psychiatrist. The student interviewers then obtained the consent of the informant and scheduled further contacts. Eight informants refused participation and 11 patients reversed their earlier consent, thereby resulting in a study sample of 18 patient-informant pairs. (We suspect that the unanticipated absence of the recruiting psychiatrist, who was hospitalized for a prolonged period owing to an automobile accident, played a role in some patients' withdrawal of consent.) Data on age, sex, ethnicity, nativity, frequency of psychiatric hospitalizations, and marital and employment status of patients who refused (or whose informant refused) participation were available through chart reviews. Participating and nonparticipating patients were comparably distributed on each of these variables.

Interviewers were randomly assigned to the patients, with patient and informant seen by different people. Interviews with members of each pair were conducted separately, but in all but one case either simultaneously or at least on the same day. Pair members were asked not to discuss the interview with each other and were interviewed in the same language, either Spanish or English.

Subjects were asked to report events happening during the preceding 12 months to the patient or persons important to the patient. For each recalled event, interviewers requested the exact date, the person who was the central figure (that is, the primary person to whom the event occurred), and other major distinguishing details of the occurrence (e.g., where the event took place, the identity of other persons involved). If subjects could not provide an exact date for the event, they were asked to assign the event as best they could to a particular week, half-month period, month, or season. Probes used with patients asked whether the informant knew of the event. At the start of the interview, both patient and informant were asked whether the informant was the individual knowing most about the patient's recent life events. At the completion of the interview, subjects were rated as to whether they understood the life-event questions with "only brief instruction," "after repeated instruction only," or "never fully," or "completely misunderstood the task."

Several studies have found that special categories of events (e.g., losses) and sometimes quite specific events (e.g., death of pets) (Jacobs and Myers, 1976) are associated with elevated risk of subsequent psychiatric illness. Consequently, it was considered important to measure reliability in terms of agreement on individual events rather than in terms of the correlation of pair members' aggregated "stress" scores. Without data, however, on the number of events going unreported by both members of each pair, the use of many conventional measures of agreement is rendered infeasible (Steele, Henderson, and Duncan-Jones, 1980; Neugebauer, 1981). In the present study, reliability was estimated with an intrapair agreement statistic formed by dividing the number of events going unreported by both members of a pair by the number reported by at least one member. Paired-subject designs and some form of this intrapair agreement statistic have been used in previous studies of life-event reliability with psychiatric patients, including the one prior study of schizophrenic patients (Brown and Birley, 1968). Consequently, this statistic has the merit of comparability with earlier findings. The ability to calculate an intrapair agreement index for each pair individually adds to the appeal of this measure.

Before describing the reliability results, a distinction must be made between item agreement and event agreement. The reading of a given item may prompt the recall of one event by the patient and of an altogether different event by the informant. In response to the item "close friend died," the patient may mention the recent death of a friend at the mental health center whereas the informant may report the death a year ago of a neighbor. On the other hand, a major change in the patient's work status, involving both more responsibilities and more prestige, may be reported by the patient under the item "significant success at work" and by the informant under "increased work load." Consequently, reliability statistics that equate item endorsement with event agreement, irrespective of the specific events prompted by that item or prompted by other items, may overestimate or underestimate true agreement within pairs. In calculating intrapair (event) agreement, we considered the former example of item concordance to constitute event disagreement, and the latter instance of item discordance, event agreement.

Events reported by the patient but not recalled by the informant were excluded in calculating intrapair agreement if the patient indicated that the informant did not know of the event or if the patient was not sure whether the informant knew. Patients stated that informants did not know about 4 percent of the patients' events, and were "not sure" about an additional 2 percent. Of the 11 events in the former category, none was reported by informants; of the five events in the latter category, one was reported by an informant. (These results offer some indirect confirmation that patients nominated informants familiar with their recent experiences.)

Events reported by any given respondent tend to be interdependent (Goldberg and Comstock, 1980). (For example, the birth of a child might occasion a salary rise, a change in residence, and substantial purchases on installment plans. For a given individual, therefore, these four events would be linked occurrences.) As a result, subjecting intrapair agreement to tests of statistical significance has been explicitly discouraged (Steele et al., 1980) because the assumption of independence of observations is not met. This structure is not compelling when individual intrapair agreements are calculated separately for each pair and treated as the pair's agreement score. The obvious abnormality of these score distributions, however, prompted resort to nonparametric alternatives to the paired t-test. When within-pair comparisons of agreement scores on two different types of items or events were conducted, the Wilcoxon signed-rank test for paired comparisons was employed; the Friedman test for aligned ranks was used for comparisons of three within-pair agreement scores (Lehmann and D'Abrera, 1975). Analyses of differences in mean event frequencies were based on the t-test for equal sample variances. All probability values refer to two-tailed tests.

RESULTS

Informants were in all instances the first persons nominated by the patient as the individual who knew most about the patient's life events. The sociodemographic characteristics of the patients participating in the study and of their informants are presented in Table 8.1. In eight pairs, the informant was the patient's parent. In four of the remaining pairs, the informant was the spouse; in three, a sibling; and in the rest, a child. Most subjects were rated as understanding the instructions immediately, and all but one as understanding them after several clarifications.

Intrapair agreement across pairs ranged from 0 to .42, with a mean of .22. (When events reported only by the patients and classified by them as unknown to the informant were reintroduced into the data, the mean intrapair agreement dropped from .224 to .217.) These low levels of agreement for all pairs render moot a detailed analysis of the influence of subject characteristics on instrument reliability. While, however, pair reliability for all events combined is inadequate, certain subsets of events or of items might nonetheless enjoy respectable reliability levels. The time interval since the event (recency) and its degree of stressfulness (salience), the subjectivity of the material de-

Table 8.1
Sociodemographic Characteristics of
Schizophrenic Patients and Informants

Characteristic	Patients ($N = 18$)	Informants ($N = 18$)
Sex		
Female	9	10
Age, yr		
Mean ± SD	44 ± 9	53 ± 21
Range	30–59	15–83
Ethnicity		
White	4	4
Black[a]	3	3
Hispanic[a]	11	11
Nativity		
Europe	0	1
Latin America	13	9
United States	5	8
Education		
Grammar school only	5	5
Junior high–high school only	6	7
High school graduate	2	3
Some college	3	3
College graduate	2	0
Marital status		
Currently married	8	10
Never married	8	5
Employment status		
Full-time student	0	3
Employed	5	8
Government aid (other than retirement related)	13	2
Retired	0	5
Resides with		
Spouse	7	10
Parent	10	3
Sibling	1	2
Child	0	3

[a]Black individual born in a Spanish or Portuguese-speaking country in Latin America was classified as Hispanic.

noted by an item, and the clarity of item wording were examined next for their possible effect on intrapair agreement.

Intrapair agreements for all pairs combined for events occurring within three months of the interview date, between three and six months, and between six and 12 months are presented in Table 8.2. Recency did not have a substantial or even statistically significant influence on agreement levels, with pair agreement even on very recent events remaining unsatisfactory.

Table 8.2
Intrapair Agreement on Reports of Life
Events, by Event Characteristic

Event Characteristic	No. of Events Reported by Either Pair Member	Intrapair Agreements
Event recency[a]		
3 mo before interview	170	.24[b]
4 – 6 mo before interview	85	.25
7 – 12 mo before interview	114	.21
Event salience[c]		
All central figures		
Highly stressful	80	.26[d]
Moderate or little stress	289	.18
Patient as central figure		
Highly stressful	9	.20[e]
Moderate or little stress	96	.26

[a] If the patient and informant provided dates for a given event that fell into two different time periods, a contrived date was assigned to the event representing the calendar midpoint between the two discrepant dates. In cases where patient and informant were not interviewed on the same day, no events reported by both pair members fell on different sides of the 3 month or 6 month dividing point.

[b] For three months before interview versus 4–6 months versus 7–12 months, the Friedman test for aligned ranks was not significant.

[c] In no case where patient and informant were credited with event agreement but disagreed on the item was there a categorical difference in the stress rating of the two items.

[d] For all central figures, highly stressful versus moderate/little stress. Wilcoxon signed-rank test was not significant.

[e] For patient as central figure, highly stressful versus moderate/little stress. Wilcoxon signed-rank test was not significant.

The effect of salience on reliability was examined using item magnitude rating generated in a prior New York City study. Items belonging to the top quartile of magnitude ratings were classified as highly stressful; the remainder, as representing either moderate or little stress. Two analyses were conducted. First, agreement over highly stressful events was compared with agreement over events of moderate or little stress for all events combined, irrespective of the central figure of the event; second, the same comparison was performed, but restricting events to those in which the patient was the central figure (Table 8.2). Event salience did not emerge as an important or statistically significant factor in reliability levels.

The results of analyses by item characteristic are presented in Table 8.3. Items may be classified dichotomously as referring either to "objective" or "subjective" events. Objective items (e.g., "divorce," "retired," and "abortion") pertain to events in theory verifiable independently of the subject's account and whose reporting depends primarily on simple subject recall. Subjective items (e.g., "relations with spouse changed for the better") are less readily substantiated by external means since they depend more on a respondent's judgment and emotion. Items in the 102-item checklist were categorized as either objective (79 items) or subjective (ten items) by relying on previous classification of

Table 8.3
Intrapair Agreement on Reports of Life
Events, by Item Characteristic

Item Characteristic	No. of Events Reported by Either Pair Member	Intrapair Agreement
Objectivity		
Objective	292	.25[a]
Subjective	37	.04
Clarity		
Ambiguous	117	.19[b]
Clear	252	.25

[a]For objective versus subjective items, $p = .0024$, Wilcoxon signed-rank test.
[b]For ambiguous versus clear items, Wilcoxon signed-rank test was not significant.

this type (Dohrenwend, 1974; Hudgens, Robins, and DeLong, 1970; Brown, Sklair, and Harris, 1973). Items that eluded this classification scheme, such as "conditions at work got worse, other than demotion or trouble with the boss," were excluded from analysis since the unspecified conditions might be either subjective (e.g., improved relations with a colleague) or objective (e.g., better lighting). Intrapair agreement for objective items (25 percent) was significantly greater for the subjective items (4 percent). (Intrapair agreement for unclassifiable items was .26.)

Many items on the checklist contain evaluating or quantitative words or phrases that lead to the confounding of subject interpretation with simple recall. For example, the first item under schooling, "started school . . . after not going to school for a long time," requires the respondent both to recall whether someone had started school and to decide whether the time interval that had lapsed since the person's last being in school was "long." Similarly, a work-related item asks whether someone had taken "on a greatly increased work load." Respondents, even paired respondents, may not share a consensus about when an "increased" work load becomes a "greatly" increased work load. Since pair members can be expected to report the same event only when they agree on their understanding of an item, we anticipate pair disagreement to be greatest over these items with ambiguous or evaluative wording. Intrapair agreement for ambiguous items (31) was 19 percent; for unambiguous items (71), 25 percent (Table 8.3). This difference was not significant.

Precision and agreement on event dates, recall decrements, and interviewer effect on volume of elicited events were also investigated. Patients and informants separately were able to date one fourth of all events to a specific calendar day. Another 30 percent could be assigned to approximately a one-week period, while only 6 percent could not be located in a given month. (These results seem particularly impressive given that certain events are sometimes very gradual in nature, such as "conditions at work got worse," and therefore remain intrinsically difficult to date. Yet an analysis restricted to items such as "fired" and "abortion," which could be assigned calendar dates, improved dating precision only marginally.) Patients and informants, however, reported the same calendar dates for only 2 percent of agreed-on events. For 20 percent of events, patients and informants provided dates falling within approximately one week of each other, and for 40 percent within a half month. Analysis confined to events during the three months preceding the interview did not alter the distribution.

To examine whether patients reported a greater number of events during months closer in time to the interview date, the mean number of events during the two halves of the 12-month period of recall were compared. During the more distant half-year, patients reported an average of 4.2 events; during the more recent half-year, 9.2 ($p<.005$, $t=3.5$ $df=16$). The corresponding event means for informants were 3.1 and 8.4 ($p<.001$, $t=4.55$, $df+16$). (An analysis-of-variance approach to these sets of patient and informant data was judged inappropriate since informants engaged in a recall task different from that of the patients.)

One interviewer saw ten patients; the other, eight. The 18 patients reported a total of 241 events. There was a significant interviewer effect ($p<.05$), with the first interviewer eliciting on average a greater number of events (Table 8.4). The difference between the two analogous groups of informants was significant at the $p<.05$ level.

Table 8.4
Interviewer Effect on Event Recall

| Group | No. of Events (Means ± SE) | | Difference |
	First Interviewer	Second Interviewer	
Patient	10.50 ± 1.99	17.00 ± 2.19	6.50 ± 2.79*
Informant	8.88 ± 1.74	13.80 ± 1.74	4.92 ± 2.35**

*$p<.05$, $t=2.33$, $df=16$; t-test.
**$p<.055$, $t=2.09$, $df=16$; t-test.

COMMENT

Reliability levels as low as .60 are acceptable for research instruments under development (Nunnally, 1967). Despite certain psychometric anomalies in the intrapair agreement statistic and the paired-subject design, a level of .22 is clearly inadequate for an extensively piloted and deployed research tool. These results cannot be explained away as a consequence of the patients' deficits in mental function or the specific checklist, study design, or reliability statistic employed. Interviewer ratings in this study suggested adequate comprehension of the checklist task by most respondents, while numerous, widely varied reliability studies using nonpatients or medical patients as well as psychiatric patients have also reported low levels of reliability.

Among the seven reliability studies using psychiatric patients, all but one employed a patient-informant design (Yager, Grant, and Sweetwood, 1981; Horowitz, Schaefer, and Hiroto, 1977). The range of reliability values was from .35 to .81, with a mean of roughly .57. Five reported reliability levels at or below .60.

Both the remaining investigations were conducted by George Brown and his colleagues. One involved interviews with recently hospitalized male and female schizophrenic patients and close relatives (Brown and Birley, 1968); the other, depressed female inpatients and outpatients and informants (Brown et al., 1973). Intrapair agreement levels were .81 and .79, respectively.

Findings from studies with medical patients and with subjects not selected on the basis of patient status are no more auspicious. Eleven separate studies have appeared since 1967. Their reliability figures ranged from .07 to .81; only two exceeded .70. The mean of these variegated reliability estimates is .59. Included among the investigations reporting reliability figures below the mean are Jenkins and colleagues' (1979) test-retest study using air-traffic controllers (the majority of whom had some college education) and Yager and colleagues' paired-subjects design with Veterans Administration Hospital and

University of California, San Diego, campus employees and partners. The reported reliabilities in these two studies were a Pearson r value of .38 and a k value (averaged across all inventory items) of .39, respectively. In short, the results of the present study appear to reflect psychometric shortcomings of the life-event checklist rather than difficulties inherent in administering the instrument to schizophrenic patients.

Our efforts to identify events or checklist items with satisfactory reliability have proved largely unsuccessful. On commonsense grounds, we would expect recent or highly stressful experiences to be recalled more reliably by patients and close relatives than temporally distant or trivial occurrences. No effect of evident recency or salience was evident. Other studies have reported either meager or contradictory associations between event recency and recall reliability (McDonald, Pugh, and Gunderson, 1972; Rahe, Romo, and Bennett, 1974) and inconsistent results with regard to event salience (Jenkins, Hurst, and Rose, 1979; Casey, Masuda, and Holmes, 1967). While three studies reported lower reliability levels for ambiguous or vaguely worded checklist items (Thurlow, 1971), this relationship did not emerge in our data. These negative findings from the present study remain of limited value, however, owing to the low statistical power attending small sample sizes.

The one inventory characteristic to show a significant association with reliability was item objectivity. Objective items exhibited a pronounced and statistically significant advantage in recall reliability over subjective items. Three of five other studies showed similar results, although the superior performance of objective items was nowhere sizable (Schless and Mendels, 1978).

Prior reliability studies are laconic on the question of date agreement. Our pairs were unable to assign 60 percent of agreed-on events to the same half-month period. This level of unreliability in event chronology, if characteristic of research subjects generally, could create serious interpretive problems in studies where dating of the disease process is itself attended with difficulty or where the role of events as precipitants of illness episodes is under investigation. The generalizability of these findings needs to be explored in future investigation.

The generally poor reliability of event checklists demonstrated in numerous investigations casts some doubt on certain previous studies, irrespective of the direction of their findings. An unreliable index of stress cannot explain much variance in an outcome measure. Therefore, when retrospective studies, involving subjects who share the researchers' belief in the role of stress in illness episodes, report statistically significant associations between event frequencies and such episodes, the suspicion arises that those results may be owed partially to bias. On the other hand, an unreliable instrument would have difficulty disclosing an association even where one existed. Consequently, studies reporting no association between stress and illness remain inconclusive.

While prompting caution in drawing inferences about stress and illness from retrospective studies, the reliability investigations themselves are open to criticism. Since the items on these inventories produce recall of different and varying numbers of events for each subject, psychometric theory is strained when we assess checklist reliability as though the checklist measured subject attributes or represented a common and shared rating task. The intrapair agreement statistic, while serviceable and by now an established part of the life-event literature, relies on measurement assumptions that await clarification. Furthermore, studies examining agreement between patients and informants suffer from special shortcomings, in particular, the obvious difference in the vantage points from which the two pair members are asked to view and report events. Finally, the counterintuitive finding that recent and stressful events are not consistently characterized by greater recall reliability reinforces the belief that these study designs and statistics may not be measuring reliability properly.

A decrement in the volume of recalled events for time periods increasingly distant from the interview date is not a reliability issue, properly speaking. Nevertheless, we tested for such decrements because of the recent interest and debate on this question. Both patient and informants reported more than twice as many events during the second six months of the 12-month recall period than during the first six months. Since all subjects were interviewed in the same summer months, a season basis for this excess cannot be excluded. It is more plausible, however, to attribute this variation in event reports to decreasing completeness of recall in more distant time periods.

By and large, life-event researchers have treated the events prompted by checklist items as external phenomena whose recall, while possibly unreliable, was nonetheless largely impervious to interviewer effects and effects of differing methods and checklist administration generally. As a consequence, reliability and substantive studies using life-event inventories have not fastidiously reported their schemes for distributing interviewers between paired subjects or between cases and controls, respectively. In addition, some investigations have borrowed data on life-event frequencies for controls from prior studies while using their own interviewers to generate data on psychiatric cases (Jenkins et al., 1979).

On average, one of our interviewers elicited roughly 50 percent more events from patients and from informants. Monitoring of interviews with tape recordings indicated that these results were not achieved by some simple mechanism such as recording of questionable events. On the contrary, she promoted the production of more recollections in subjects perhaps through subtle processes linked to interpersonal rapport. It seems likely therefore, that in substantive case-control studies, interviewer endorsement of the general research hypothesis, namely, that patients experience more events than controls, could also affect the magnitude of event reporting. Where interviewers have not generally been blind to a subject's caseness status nor shielded from the research hypothesis, the considerable consistency across many studies of an event excess among cases as compared with controls may appear both predictable and dubious. On the other hand, perhaps our results reflect only the unique efficacy of one interviewer in eliciting events or the peculiar vulnerability of certain chronic psychiatric patients and their relatives to interviewer style. These findings remain suggestive, pending replications with sets of interviewers in studies using patient and nonpatient populations.

This interviewer effect has implications for the interpretation and computation of the intrapair agreement statistic. Within-pair differences in the volume of recalled events necessarily limit intrapair agreement. If one pair member reports five events and the other 25, their agreement cannot exceed .20. Therefore, when pair members are divided between two interviewers who differ in their ability to generate event recall, the observed intrapair agreement may well underestimate the subjects' true reliability.

To assess the possible magnitude of the damage of interviewer effect to intrapair agreement in this study, we calculated our statistic under least unfavorable assumptions. Within each pair, the number of disagreed-on events was equalized by subtraction while the number of agreed-on events was left unchanged. The resulting adjusted mean intrapair agreement figure was .43. Interviewer effect was not correlated either with item characteristics, such as objectivity, clarity, or degree of stress, or with event recency. Consequently, the pattern of findings described earlier concerning these events and item attributes was not overturned when reexamined using this adjusted intrapair statistic.

CONCLUSION

Intrapair agreement between patient and informant on a standard life-event checklist covering a 12-month period has proved inadequate for research purposes among a group of outpatient schizophrenics. Despite the probable cognitive and affectual deficits of these subjects, however, the reliability of their event recall fell well within the range of previously reported values, several of which derived from studies of nonpatient, often college-educated individuals. The generally low reliability of life-event checklists brings into question the findings, both positive and negative, of many retrospective investigations of life events and illness onset. Our additional finding of a pronounced interviewer effect, while requiring extensive replication with studies using multiple interviewers, suggests that particular caution must be exercised in interpreting the results of retrospective studies deriving data on life-event frequencies by means of interviewers.

Acceptance of these reliability findings does not necessarily preclude the possibility of investigating the role of life events in schizophrenic illness with a checklist. To permit a subdivision of the recall period into recent and distant intervals, we asked patients to report events occurring during the preceding 12 months. A prospective investigation of life events and schizophrenia might interview patients at four-week intervals demarcated by clinic visits. The reliability of recall for such brief periods is not addressed in this study and requires separate investigation.

Thucydides reported some early observations on the reliability of event recall. His notion that people disagree over events that they personally witness is supported by the majority of recent reliability studies. Only one group of investigators, Brown and his colleagues, have reported satisfactory reliability of life-event reports with psychiatric patients. A major challenge for future research in the reliability field must be to identify characteristics of Brown and colleagues' patients or their data collection methods that would explain his atypically encouraging results.

REFERENCES

Askenasy, A. R., Dohrenwend, B. P., & Dohrenwend, B. S. (1977), Some effects of social class and ethnic group membership on judgments of the magnitude of stressful life events: A research note. *J. Health & Soc. Behav.*, 18:432–439.
Bech, J., & Worthen, K. (1972), Precipitating stress, crisis theory and hos-

pitalization in schizophrenia and depression. *Arch. Gen. Psychiat.*, 26:123–129.

Birley, J. L., & Brown, G. (1970), Crises and life changes preceding the onset of relapse on acute schizophrenia. *Brit. J. Psychiat.*, 116:327–333.

Brown, G. W., & Birley, J. L. T. (1968), Crisis and life changes and the onset of schizophrenia. *J. Health & Soc. Behav.*, 9:203–214.

———— Sklair, F., & Harris, T. O. (1973), Life events and psychiatric disorders: I. Some methodological issues. *Psychosom. Med.*, 3:74–87.

Casey, R. L., Masuda, M., & Holmes, T. H. (1967), Quantitative study of recall of life events. *J. Psychosom. Res.*, 11:239–247.

Clancy, J., Crowe, R., & Winokur, G. (1973), The Iowa 500: Precipitating factors in schizophrenia and primary affective disorder. *Compr. Psychiat.*, 14:197–202.

Dohrenwend, B. P. (1974), Problems in defining and sampling the relevant population of stressful life events. In: *Stressful Life Events: Their Nature and Effects*, ed. B. S. Dohrenwend & B. P. Dohrenwend. New York: John Wiley, pp. 275–312.

———— Dohrenwend, B. P. (1974), Overview and prospects for research on stressful life events. In: *Stressful Life Events: Their Nature and Effects*, ed. B. S. Dohrenwend & B. P. Dohrenwend. New York: John Wiley, pp. 275–312.

Dohrenwend, B. S., Krasnoff, L., Askenasy, A. R., & Dohrenwend, B. P. (1978), Exemplification of a method of scaling life events: The PERI life event scale. *J. Health & Soc. Behav.*, 19:205–229.

Eisler, R., & Polak, P. (1971), Social stress and psychiatric disorder. *J. Nerv. & Ment. Dis.*, 153:227–233.

Goldberg, E. L., & Comstock, G. W. (1980), Epidemiology of life events: Frequency in general populations. *Amer. J. Epidemiol.*, 111:736–752.

Grant, I., Gerst, M., & Yager, J. (1976), Scaling of life events by psychiatric patients and normals. *J. Psychosom. Res.*, 20:141–149.

Harmon, D. K., Masuda, M., & Holmes, T. H. (1970), The social readjustment scale: A cross-cultural study of western Europeans and Americans. *J. Psychosom. Res.*, 12:391–400.

Horowitz, M., Schaefer, C., & Hiroto, D. (1977), Life event questionnaires for measuring presumptive stress. *Psychosom. Med.*, 6:413–431.

Hudgens, R. W., Robins, E., & DeLong, W. B. (1970), The reporting of recent stress in the lives of psychiatric patients. *Brit. J. Psychiat.*, 117:635–643.

Jacobs, S., & Myers, J. (1976), Recent life events and acute schizophrenic psychosis: A controlled study. *J. Nerv. & Ment. Dis.*, 162:75–87.

———— Prusoff, B., & Paykel, E. (1974), Recent life events in schizophrenia and depression. *Psychol. Med.*, 4:444–453.

Jenkins, C. D., Hurst, M. W., & Rose, R. M. (1979), Life changes: Do people really remember? *Arch. Gen. Psychiat.*, 36:379–384.

—— —— —— (1980), Recall and reporting of life events. *Arch. Gen. Psychiat.*, 37:485.

Komaroff, A. L., Masuda, M., & Holmes, T. H. (1968), The Social Readjustment Rating Scale: A comparative study of Negro, Mexican and white Americans. *J. Psychosom. Res.*, 12:121–128.

Lahniers, C., & White, K. (1976), Changes in environmental life events and their relationship to psychiatric hospital admissions. *J. Nerv. & Ment. Dis.*, 163:154–157.

Leff, J., Hirsch, S., & Gaind, R. (1973), Life events and maintenance therapy in schizophrenic relapse. *Brit. J. Psychiat.*, 123:659–660.

Lehmann, E. L., & D'Abrera, H. J. M. (1975), *Nonparametrics: Statistical Methods Based on Ranks*. New York: McGraw-Hill.

Lundberg, U., & Theorell, T. (1975), Life changes and myocardial infarction: Individual differences in life change scaling. *J. Psychosom. Res.*, 19:27–39.

McDonald, B. W., Pugh, W. M., Gunderson, E. K. (1972), Reliability of life change cluster scores. *Brit. J. Soc. Clin. Psychol.*, 11:407–409.

Mueller, D. P., Edwards, D. W., & Yarvis, R. M. (1977), Stressful life events and psychiatric symptomatology: Change or undesirability? *J. Health & Soc. Behav.*, 18:307–317.

Neugebauer, R. (1981), The reliability of life event reports. In: *Stressful Life Events and Their Context*, ed. B. S. Dohrenwend & B. P. Dohrenwend. New York: Prodist, pp. 85–107.

Nunnally, J. C. (1967), *Psychometric Theory*. New York: McGraw-Hill.

Paykel, E. S., Myers, J. K., & Dienelt, M. N. (1969), Life events and depression. *Arch. Gen. Psychiat.*, 21:753–760.

—— Prusoff, B. A., & Uhlenhuth, E. H. (1971), Scaling of life events. *Arch. Gen. Psychiat.*, 25:340–347.

—— (1980), Recall and reporting of life events. *Arch. Gen. Psychiat.*, 37:485.

Rabkin, J. G. (1980), Stressful life events and schizophrenia: A review of the research literature. *Psychol. Bull.*, 87:408–425.

Rahe, R. H., Romo, M., & Bennett, L. (1974), Recent life changes, myocardial infarction, and abrupt coronary death. *Intern. Med.*, 133:221–228.

Ross, C. E., & Mirowsky, J., II (1979), A comparison of life event-weighting schemes: Change, undesirability, and effect-proportional indices. *J. Health & Soc. Behav.*, 20:166–177.

Schless, A. P., & Mendels, J. (1978), The value of interviewing family and friends in assessing life stressors. *Arch. Gen. Psychiat.*, 35:565–567.

Schwartz, C. C., & Myers, J. K. (1977), Life events and schizophrenia: II. Impact of life events on symptom configuration. *Arch. Gen. Psychiat.*, 34:1242–1245.

Shrout, P. (1981), Scaling of stressful life events. In: *Stressful Life Events and Their Contexts*, ed. B. S. Dohrenwend & B. P. Dohrenwend. New York: Prodist, pp. 29–47.

Steele, G. P., Henderson, S., & Duncan-Jones, P. (1980), The reliability of reporting adverse experiences. *Psychol. Med.*, 10:301–306.

Thurlow, H. J. (1971), Illness in relation to life situation and sick role tendency. *J. Psychosom. Res.*, 15:73–88.

Wing, J. K., Cooper, J. E., & Sartorius, N. M. (1974), *Measurement and Classification of Psychiatric Symptoms: Instruction Manual for the PSE and Catego Program.* London: Cambridge University Press.

Yager, J., Grant, I., & Sweetwood, H. L. (1981), Life event reports by psychiatric patients, nonpatients, and their partners. *Arch. Gen. Psychiat.*, 38:343–347.

Chapter 9
Is There a Short-Cut? An Investigation into the Life-Event Interview

P. McC. Miller, B.Sc., Ph.D., and D. P. Salter, M.D.

Over the past two decades there have been an enormous num-ber of studies using life events, and considerable controversy over the best ways of gathering life-event data. The issues have been recently reviewed (Paykel, 1983) and need little elabora-tion here. There are two well-known methods of data collection, the first, the Schedule of Recent Experiences (SRE), introduced by Holmes and Rahe (1967); the second, the Bedford Life Events and Difficulty Schedule (LEDS) devised by Brown and Harris (1978). The SRE relies on normative weights and meas-ures the degree of social readjustment which each event would require. In its simplest form it is easy to administer, requiring only that the subject checks which events on a list have occurred to them personally during some specified time period. There have been many modifications to the technique (Paykel, Myers, Dienelt, Klerman, Lindenthal, and Pepper, 1969; Paykel, Pru-

---

Acknowledgment. This chapter was first published in *Acta Psychiatrica Scan-dinavia* (1984), 70:417–427, and it is reprinted by permission of the Journal and the publisher, Munksgaard International.

soff, and Uhleuhuth, 1970) and it has been subjected to some severe and basic criticism (Brown, 1974; Miller and Ingham, 1979). The LEDS is a semistructured interview in which the contextual threat of events and degree of long-term difficulties are the main entities measured (Cochrane and Robertson, 1973; Sarason, Johnson, and Siegel, 1978). The method requires careful training of interviewers and raters and the interviews can sometimes be very long.

Few direct comparisons of the two systems have been made, and those of which we are aware (Faravelli and Ambonetti, 1983) have relied on applying variations of both methods in their entirety to the same sample of people. Katschnig (1980) found that for an individual there was little correspondence between the SRE score and contextual threat. Faravelli and Ambonetti (1983) found a much greater degree of correspondence, but, unfortunately, measured "the contextual amount of readjustment required to withstand each event," rather than contextual threat.

The present study attempts to investigate whether all the context surrounding an event or difficulty really needs to be elicited in order for valid ratings of contextual threat to be made. An interview was designed, intended to reveal the context of each event or difficulty in carefully controlled stages. At each stage a rater trained in LEDS methodology, rated the situations (i.e., both events and difficulties) elicited on the information available up to that point, while being blind to the information contained in the next stage. The ratings were made on contextual threat (T) and on the five other dimensions described by Miller and Ingham (1983), namely choice of action (C), uncertainty of outcome (U), personal loss (L), hopeless situation (H), and anti-social act (A). For half the interviews the first stage was intended to correspond to the simplest possible SRE method of data gathering, and the last to the full LEDS interview. For the rest of the interviews an extra stage was added at the beginning (see below).

Method

A total of 100 male and female parasuicides were interviewed in the Regional Poisoning Treatment Centre of the Royal Infirmary, Edinburgh. However, five of these were later discounted, four because for various reasons the interviewer was unable to finish the interview, and one because of a coding error at a later stage. This left 42 men and 53 women. Subjects were recruited into the study when they were considered well enough to answer the questions, generally within 8 to 12 hours of admission. The sample was drawn randomly from consecutive admissions aged between 18 and 65, except those judged by the ward staff to be too confused to participate. There was one refusal and a few selected patients were not seen for other reasons—usually because of discharge before they could be approached.

The subject's cooperation was obtained by means of a standard introduction, during which the interviewer (D.P.S.) emphasized that the data to be collected would not be used to determine the subject's medical treatment or time of discharge. It was assumed that the subject would not distort the data in order to gain a rapid discharge from the ward. The time span covered in the life-event data was the six-month period immediately preceding the parasuicidal act. Any life events subsequently found to be outside the six-month period were discounted.

The study was designed to have two conditions. In both conditions the interview began with the collection of data concerning the subject's sex, age, marital status, occupation, close relatives, and confidants. Condition I consisted of three stages:

(1) The list. A list in the format of the SRE was completed by the subject. The list together with its instructions (Appendix I) was developed for use in a study carried out by Surtees and

Ingham (1980). It contained one section for life events and another for long-term difficulties.

(2) The probe stage. Each event or difficulty ticked was systematically probed as follows:

Events

(1) Who did this happen to?
(2) When did this happen?
(U) What is the situation now?
(H) Can you see any good coming out of the situation—In what way?
(C) After . . . was over did you have any important decisions to make?
(A) Were the police, courts, or official bodies involved?

Difficulties

(1) When did this difficulty start?
(T) Have you ever found this upsetting?
(C) Do you feel you have any important choices to make? If so, what?
(H) Do you see any chance of the situation improving in the next six months?
(U) Are you expecting the situation to change in the future?
(A) Have the police, courts, or other official bodies been involved in this difficulty?

The letters (U), (H), etc., indicate that the probe was intended to clarify the rating of uncertainty of outcome (U) or hopeless situation (H), etc. The probes were intended to provide the absolute minimum of information which, together with the list information, might allow ratings of presence or absence of CUHAL and T to be made, and also allow a provisional placement on the Bedford long-term threat (events) and objective severity (difficulties) scales.

(3) A final "free flow" interview was carried out to gain further contextual information surrounding the events and difficulties elicited in stage (2). This stage was terminated when

the interviewer was satisfied that he had sufficient contextual information for ratings to be made on the Bedford and Edinburgh Scales.

Condition II differed in that an extra stage, the "initial free flow" was added between the demographic data and the list. It began with a standard introduction: "Most people have situations occur in their lives that cause them worry or trouble. Have any situations arisen in the last six months that you would say have caused you any problems?" There then followed an unstructured interview concerned only with the problems elicited in response to this introduction. The stage was terminated when the subject was not forthcoming with further information about them, and the interviewer then proceeded with the list and the other stages as in Condition I. The main intention of this extra stage was to see whether with this minimal prompting the subjects would "spontaneously" reveal their worst difficulties and events. A second aim was to see whether the extra rapport established early in the interview had any important effects. In Condition II the initial free flow was timed to the nearest minute, and in both conditions, the times were recorded for the list plus probe stages together and for the final free flow.

Each interview was then rated after each of its stages by one of two independent raters, experienced in LEDS methods. In Condition I they began by rating the list according to a predetermined standard scheme. No attempt was made at this stage to establish whether each ticked situation would meet the LEDS criteria for inclusion as an event or difficulty, or to see whether the same situation would meet the LEDS criteria for inclusion as an event or difficulty, or to see whether the same situation had been included under more than one heading. The predetermined scheme contained nine ratings for each situation—i.e., whether or not CUHLA or T were present, the likely focus (4) of the situation and whether it would be an event or a difficulty. Thus for instance, if the subject had ticked "burglaries (only burglaries of your property)" this was automatically scored as an event, subject focused, with some Bedford threat and all else absent. In setting up the predetermined scoring we decided to assign the minimum scores that the situation was likely to have. There were two reasons for this. Firstly, we felt much more certain about these minimum ratings than about some rather nebulous "average" ratings, and, secondly, rating minimally should compensate somewhat for including many "situations" which would later turn out to be not worth inclusion.

Separate ratings of the same variables were made at the end of the probe section (blind to the final free flow) and again at the end of the final free flow. In both cases the raters used their best judgment on the information available up to that point in the interview. This procedure resulted in several situations ticked on the list being dropped from further consideration as it became clear that they did not qualify as events or difficulties. Occasionally, the opposite happened. Situations turned up, and were rated, which had not originally been found by the list.

Condition II was treated similarly except that the raters began by rating the first free flow stage using their best judgment. At the list stage they did their best to identify on the list those ticks which referred to situations already found in the first free flow. Having done so they left the ratings for these situations unchanged. Thus, if for example, during first free flow, the subject had described a traumatic separation event in which her husband had gone off with another woman and this had been scored as an event with CLHT all present, Bedford threat marked, subject focused, then this was the scoring assigned to "separation" ticked on the list, and not the predetermined minimal score of some Bedford threat other focused and all else absent. At the two later stages, however, it was permissible to change the ratings if new information seemed to make this desirable. This seldom, if ever, happened.

RESULTS

The first question to be investigated was whether or not there were any discernible differences between Conditions I and II.

In this analysis and throughout what follows four dependent variables were used. These were (1) the total number of situations elicited, (2) the number of situations containing T and/or L, (3) the total threat score, and (4) the total number of characteristics (C, U, L, H, A or T) present. Table 9.1, shows the mean values on these variables for the two conditions after the four interview stages.

The observed significant differences between the conditions after the administration of the list are entirely due to the rating procedure. In Condition II those situations discovered after the first free flow have been fully rated. These appear again, fully rated at the list stage so that Condition II is made up partly of fully rated and partly of minimally rated situations. These are set against the entirely minimally rated situations of Condition I. There are no other differences between the conditions and their means throughout the rest of the table are similar.

The scores on number of situations present both fall after the probe stage, due to the pinpointing of situations which do not meet the inclusion criteria and clarification of which checks on the list clearly refer to the same situation. Despite the removal of these spurious situations, the other three scores all rise as rating becomes more accurate.

The second question to be tackled is that of the completeness and accuracy of the information gained at each stage. To test this we used the final free flow stage as the criterion. Completeness of information at each stage can then be assessed on the basis of the mean scores at each stage, and the accuracy by the correlations between the final free flow scores and the scores at each stage.

Table 9.2 shows the correlations between scores at the final stage and at the various other stages. Conditions I and II have been pooled where possible.

Since the correlations are so high all the differences between scores at the probe stage and scores at the final stage are highly significant. (Using repeated measures t-tests for number of situations $t = 3.06$, p 0.01, for number with L or T, $t = 5.64$, p 0.001, for threat score, $t = 5.36$, $p < 0.001$, for number of

Table 9.1
Mean Values of Number of Situations Elicited, Number of Situations T or L, Threat Score, Number of Characteristics and Time Taken for the Two Conditions After the Four Interview Stages

	After first free flow		After list		After probes		After final free flow	
	Cond. I (n = 43)	Cond. II (n = 52)	Cond. I	Cond. II	Cond. I	Cond. II	Cond. I	Cond. II
No. situations	—	2.3	7.1	6.4	4.8	5.1	5.3	5.3
No. situations with L or T	—	1.8	.08[a]	2.3[a]	3.7	3.5	4.4	4.1
Threat score	—	4.1	5.7[a]	7.5[a]	8.6	8.4	9.9	9.4
No. characteristics (C, U, L, H, A, and T)	—	4.6	3.3[a]	6.6[a]	9.1	9.5	11.0	11.1
Average time taken (min)	—	8.9	—	—	17.8	27.3	32.7	40.0

[a] Condition I differs from Condition II. $p < 0.01$.

Table 9.2
Correlations of Scores After the Final Free Flow Stage with Scores at Other Stages

	After initial free flow	After list	After probes
No. situations	0.44	0.69	0.87
	$n = 52$	$n = 95$	$n = 95$
No. situations with L or T	0.53	0.39	0.88
	$n = 52$	$n = 95$	$n = 95$
Threat score	0.47	0.65	0.89
	$n = 52$	$n = 95$	$n = 95$
No. characteristics	0.55	0.55	0.88
(C,U,L,H,A, and T)	$n = 52$	$n = 95$	$n = 95$

characteristics, $t = 6.70$, $p < 0.001$). We did not consider it worthwhile to test other differences in the table.

These differences although significant are small. If one views the information gained as something that increases continually up to the end of the interview then for number of situations 4.94/5.29 or 93 percent has been obtained after the probe stage. For L or T situations the figure is 86 percent, for threat score 88 percent, and for number of characteristics 84 percent. However, it may be noted that in Condition II, had the interview been terminated after the first free flow stage, rather less than half the available information would have been obtained.

Thirdly, we were interested in the time taken to acquire the data. In Table 9.1 the last row shows the mean times taken (minutes) after the first free flow, the probe, and the final free flow stages. (The time after the list stage was not recorded.) For Condition I, 84–93 percent of the available data are gathered after (on average) approximately 18 minutes interviewing time. The remainder are gathered after a further 15 minutes. For Condition II the corresponding times are approximately 27.5 minutes and 12.5 minutes.

So far, we have considered the total scores for each subject. We turn now to the individual events and long-term difficulties, to investigate the changes that these underwent as the interviews proceeded. A life situation, once it had appeared, could either disappear again altogether (if found later not to meet the inclusion criteria), or it could have its ratings changed. Table 9.3 sets out the relevant data.

It may be seen that to use the list alone without further probing would be highly inaccurate. Only 20 percent of the situations there discovered remain unchanged as the interview progresses, and 32 percent are found not to meet the Bedford inclusion criteria. On the other hand, for Condition II only, stopping the interview after the first free flow stage would have left 83 percent of the situations correctly rated according to the final free flow criterion. Stopping the interview after the probe stage would have left 75 percent of the situations correct. This is the figure for the pooled total group. To find the figure for Condition I alone, i.e., the figure uninfluenced by the presence of a first free flow stage, one can simply subtract the figures in the top row from those in the third. The revised percentages then become 7 percent after final free flow, 24 percent changed after final free flow, and 72 percent unchanged.

DISCUSSION

In a study such as this, it would be desirable to be certain there was no interviewer bias and, particularly, to be sure that the information after the final stage was as complete and accurate as possible. In the current study one interviewer, only, performed all the interviews. His interview times are perhaps shorter than might be expected. The interview situation is not absolutely ideal—there are some time pressures in the ward and, in fact, four patients were lost because the interview was not fully completed. Nevertheless, we believe there is no very serious bias for two reasons. Firstly, we are dealing with a sample of very severe events and difficulties. For many of them it is immediately evident how serious they are, and the ratings are never in doubt. Hence, less time is needed in the free flow stages. Secondly, our results are similar to those of Katschnig

Table 9.3
Changes in Rating of Situations After the Various Interview Stages

	Removed completely after probe stage	Ratings changed after probe stage	Removed completely after final free flow stage	Ratings changed after final free flow stage	Remained unchanged through re-maining stages	Total
Situations present at end of the first free flow stage	0	12 (10%)	3 (2%)	6 (5%)	99 (83%)	120
Situations present after the list stage	205 (32%)	287 (45%)	8 (1%)	17 (3%)	126 (20%)	643
Situations present after the probe stage	—	—	26 (6%)	92 (19%)	353 (75%)	471
Situations present after the final free flow stage	—	—	—	—	503 (100%)	503

(1980). His sample, also drawn from the Edinburgh Regional Poisoning Treatment Centre, consisted of 11 men, mean age 34 years, and 31 women, mean age 27 years. Our sample had relatively more men and was slightly older—42 men, mean age 34, 53 women, mean age 35. Katschnig found that in the six months before interview "nearly 60 percent" of his sample had at least one markedly or moderately threatening life event. Our figure for the same statistic is 72/95, or 76 percent. Given the enormous rise in unemployment between 1975 and 1983 and the greater percentage of men in our sample we believe these figures to be comparable. Serious unemployment situations (e.g., redundancies or long-term unemployment of self or spouse) were in fact found in 33/95, or 35 percent of our subjects. Certainly, we are not underestimating the threats present.

The results seem to indicate that it is possible to obtain considerable accuracy of rating on very slight data—even though for the raters the experience can only be described as mildly harrowing. One is often making ratings, after the probe stage, without any clear idea of what is taking place. Whether the accuracy obtainable after the probe stage is sufficient for any given purpose must be left for the reader to judge. Our own belief is that, high though it is, it is not sufficient. Considering individual situations—nearly 30 percent of these would be misrated in some way if one had only the information from the probe stage, a proportion which might well be greater in samples of less traumatic situations. This could lead to large errors in inference about differences among samples. However, the solution might well lie in more detailed standard probing rather than in further free flow interviewing.

References

Brown, G. W. (1974), Meaning, measurement and stress of life events. In: *Stressful Life Events: Their Nature and Effects*, ed. B. S. Dohrenwend & B. P. Dohrenwend. New York: John Wiley, pp. 74–87.

—— Harris, T. (1978), *Social Origins of Depression: A Study of Psychiatric Disorder in Women.* London: Travistock.

Cochrane, R., & Robertson, A. (1973), The life events inventory: A measure of the relative severity of psycho-social stressors. *J. Psychosom. Res.,* 17:135–139.

Faravelli, D., & Ambonetti, A. (1983), Assessment of life events in depressive disorders. *Soc. Psychiat.,* 18:51–56.

Holmes, T. H., & Rahe, R. H. (1967), The Social Readjustment Rating Scale. *J. Psychosom. Res.,* 11:213–218.

Katschnig, H. (1980), Measuring life stress: A comparison of two methods. In: *The Suicide Syndrome,* ed. R. Farmer & S. Hirsch. London: Croom Helm.

Miller, P. McC., & Ingham, J. G. (1979), Reflections on the life-events-to-illness link with some preliminary findings. In: *Stress and Anxiety,* Vol. 6, ed. I. G. Sarason & C. D. Spielberger. New York: John Wiley.

—— —— (1983), Dimensions of experience. *Psychol. Med.,* 13:417–429.

Paykel, E. S. (1983), Methodological aspects of life event research. *J. Psychosom. Res.,* 27:341–352.

—— Myers, J. K., Dienelt, M. N., Klerman, G. L., Lindenthal, J. J., & Pepper, M. P. (1969), Life events and depression: A controlled study. *Arch. Gen. Psychiat.,* 21:753–760.

—— Prusoff, B. A., & Uhlenhuth, E. (1970), Scaling of life events. *Arch. Gen. Psychiat.,* 25:340–347.

Sarason, I. G., Johnson, J. H., & Siegel, J. M. (1978), Assessing the impact of life experiences survey. *J. Consult. Clin. Psychol.,* 46:932–946.

Surtees, P. G., & Ingham, J. G. (1980), Life stress and depressive outcome: application of a dissipation model to life events. *Soc. Psychiat.,* 15:21–31.

APPENDIX: THE LIFE SITUATION LIST

INSTRUCTIONS

"Here is a list of things that can happen to people. I want you to place a check in front of any of these things that have happened to you or to people close to you, in the past six months —that is back to (Date). By people close to you, I mean: (Spell out all the living people that are relevant. These are parents, siblings, husband [whether or not separated], fiancé, children, step-parents, step-siblings, adopted children, confidants not otherwise covered.)" "You may find that something that has happened falls into more than one category. If so, check it each time it occurs. This is just to start us off. When you have finished I will be asking you about these things in more detail."

When S reaches the end of the Events section say: "Now this is a list of aspects of life in which you may have been experiencing difficulty during the past six months. Once again, place a tick in front of any of these which have happened to you or to the people close to you."

EVENTS

Remember. Include things that have happened either to you personally or to the people close to you.

———— Loss of job or change of job

———— Time off work because of illness

———— Return to work after period away from it

———— Trouble at work (e.g., arguments with bosses or work-mates; strikes)

———— Promotion or change of responsibilities at work

———— Pregnancy

———— Birth

———— Starting or leaving school or university; starting a new course

———— Engagement (including also decision to get engaged as well as the formal or informal announcement)

———— Marriage (ceremony; setting the date of a wedding)

———— Divorce

———— Separation (including temporary separation)

———— Retirement

———— Illness (including nervous illness)

———— Admission to hospital

———— Discharge from hospital

———— Death (including also the deaths of friends and more distant relatives)

———— Miscarriage

—— Surgical operation
—— Contact with the police or the courts
—— Accidents (including witnessing an accident or being involved in the consequences of an accident)
—— Burglaries (only burglaries of your property)
—— Loss, damage or theft of your property
—— Examinations (including also hearing the results)
—— Crises or emergencies (e.g., emergencies involving the children, money, housing or marriage)
—— Receiving news (e.g., getting bad or surprising news about something or somebody)
—— Satisfactions and disappointments (including anything which has upset you or made you happy, e.g., substantial increase in income)
—— Making important decisions (e.g., buying a house, giving up work, etc.)

DIFFICULTIES

Remember. Include difficulties experienced both by you personally and by the people close to you.
—— Family relationship (e.g., problems with state of repair or decoration of house; size, privacy; problems with landlord, neighbors)
—— Work (e.g., lack of employment; insecurity of job; poor work conditions; problems getting on with workmates; difficult hours)
—— Money (e.g., problems with hire-purchase repayments; gambling; paying the rent or mortgage)
—— Health (including nervous illness, mental or physical handicaps, drugs, drinking problems, problems associated with the change of life, worries about aged relatives)
—— Children (including problems in looking after them, problems with schooling, behavior, discipline, and trouble with the police)
—— Personal relationships (including problems associated

164   P. McC. MILLER AND D. P. SALTER

with sex; problems concerning getting on with friends, neighbors)

——— Has anything else happened to you during this period which has not been covered in this list?

Chapter 10
Personal Assessments of Life-Event Stress and the Near Future Onset of Psychological Symptoms

D. G. BYRNE, PH.D.

Reports of statistical associations between distressing life events and psychological symptoms are abundant in the clinical literature (Masuda and Holmes, 1978; Goldberg and Comstock, 1980). So too are the critical challenges in this literature (Kellam, 1974; Andrews and Tennant, 1978). Two occur with particular consistency: associations are typically weak (Miller and Ingham, 1979) and arise largely from retrospective examinations of clinical groups, so that causal inferences cannot be drawn.

Acknowledgments. This chapter was first published in the *British Journal of Medical Psychology* (1984), 57:241–248, and it is reprinted by permission of the author and the British Psychological Society.

These data were collected as part of a study on neurosis and the social environment conducted by the Social Psychiatry Research Unit at the Australian National University. The author is grateful to Mr. Richard Craft for undertaking the computational tasks.

Request for reprints should be addressed to Dr. D. G. Byrne, Department of Psychology, Australian National University, GPO Box 4, Canberra, ACT 2601, Australia.

A handful of studies (Theorell, Lind, and Floderus, 1975; Eaton, 1978; Andrews, 1981) have examined life events and symptoms from a prospective viewpoint. Their evidence supports a significant association when measures of life events and of symptoms are separated by up to a year. Moreover, in the sense that Andrews's (1981) sample was chosen for psychological health at the time of life-event measurement, the evidence indicates that the influence of life events on symptom onset is uncontaminated by the effects of existing illness.

A prospective methodology, therefore, enhances the utility of research associating life events with psychological symptoms. The issue which remains to be more fully investigated, however, concerns the nature of the link between environmental occurrences and states of psychological disorder.

The quantification of life-event impact using magnitude estimation scales based initially on life change (Holmes and Rahe, 1967) and later on distress (Paykel, Prusoff, and Uhlenhuth, 1971) showed a recognition among investigators that not life events per se, but their immediate cognitive and affective sequelae, led to symptoms. This approach, however, while having much to recommend it, does not exploit the uniqueness of life events for individuals to whom they have occurred. Personal experience of life events certainly influences the ways in which impact is perceived and judged (Lundberg and Theorell, 1976). There is, moreover, good empirical evidence from the cognitive study of emotion that environmental experiences are not in themselves endowed with affective meaning, but acquire this only after a process of interpretation within the personal cognitive framework of the individual (Lazarus, 1966).

This reasoning is supported by recent evidence of a broad kind that the noxious quality of the social environment, insofar as it relates to psychological health and illness, is more determined by personal construction than by objective reality (Henderson, Byrne, and Duncan-Jones, 1981). With this in mind, the present study attempts a more complete description of the role of life events in the development of psychological symptoms. It advanced the hypothesis that symptom onset is more strongly a function of personal interpretations of the affective significance of life events than it is of life-event impact quantified in terms of group-based, consensual judgments (magnitude estimation scale weights). A prospective design is used to serially examine the influence of measures of life events on the future onset of symptoms.

METHOD

SAMPLE

This was drawn from a pool of 756 persons selected from the general population to participate in an epidemiological study of the community. This represented an 85 percent response rate in a random sample of the general population. Of these, a randomly chosen subset of 231 completed three follow-up interviews over a 12-month period. The cohort for the present study, 169 persons (68 men, X age = 36.72, X = 12.08; and 101 women, X age = 39.60, S = 14.96), were selected on the basis of having scored less than 4 on the General Health Questionnaire (Goldberg, 1972) at initial interview. Thus, the cohort was deliberately chosen to be symptom-free at the outset. A more detailed description of sampling may be found in Henderson et al. (1981).

PROCEDURE

All data were collected during household interviews by lay interviewers trained for the task by the author and colleagues. Data on life events and symptoms formed part of a lengthier interview, the details of which may be found in Henderson et al. (1981). Four closely similar interviews were conducted with each subject: an initial interview to collect life-event data (as the independent variable set) and data on psychological symptoms to establish cross-sectional correlations, followed by three subsequent interviews at intervals of four months to collect serial data on symptom onset. Thus, life events could be related to the serial onset of symptoms over a whole year. Life-event data were also collected at follow-up interviews, though they will not be considered in this communication to any extent.

MEASURES

(a) *Life-event data.* Reports of life-event experience were elicited by means of a 72-item inventory drawn from that developed by Tennant and Andrews (1976) for use in an Australian population, and expanded for the purposes of the present study. The rationale underlying its construction and a complete listing of items are given in Henderson et al. (1981). Life-event experience was sampled over the 12 months immediately prior to initial interview since this period seems standard for studies of this kind. Reported experiences were dated to ensure accuracy in this exercise. Interviewers were given detailed guide notes to assist in the collection of these data, and these notes have already been published (Henderson et al., 1981).

(b) *Quantification of life-event data.* Three separate indices of life-event experience and impact were calculated:

1. The frequency of life events reported in the year prior to initial interview, though with few exceptions (Grant, Sweetwood, Gerst, and Yager, 1978) this is no longer regarded as a satisfactory index of life events.
2. Cumulative distress scores, to represent the degree of affective distress arising from encountered life events and accumulating over a year's life-event experiences. Distress scores allocated to each life event were derived from magnitude estimation scales reported by Tennant and Andrews (1976) and revised for the present study (Henderson et al., 1981).
3. Cumulative scores based on visual analogue scales designed to assess personal interpretations of the impact of life events encountered and accumulating over a year. Visual an-

alogue scales, based on a 10 cm line and anchored at either end by statements of minimum and maximum impact, were constructed to assess personal interpretations along the dimensions of *emotional upset, disruption, adjustment, depression, anxiety, anger,* and *helplessness.* Each of the seven scales was completed for each reported experience, and subjects were instructed to refer their ratings not to current feelings but to those which existed at the time of life-event occurrence. Scoring simply involved measuring the linear distance of a subject's rating from the point of minimum impact. A more detailed description of scale construction and administration may be found in Byrne and Whyte (1980). The psychometric performance of these scales in the general population has been described by Henderson et al. (1981). While the accuracy of recall of life events over time has been challenged (Jenkins, Hurst, and Rose, 1979), reliability analyses of these measures (Steele, Henderson, and Duncan-Jones, 1980) indicate that this is unlikely to be a major source of difficulty for the present data.

(c) *The General Health Questionnaire (GHQ).* The 30-item GHQ (Goldberg, 1972) was administered on all four occasions to assess the presence of anxiety and associated neurotic symptoms. This instrument has had wide use in community studies (Goldberg and Huxley, 1980) and has been validated in an Australian population (Tennant, 1977).

(d) *The "Number of Symptoms" Index (NSYMP).* This state measure was devised for the present study to quantify less distinct complaints of psychological disturbance. It inquires whether, in the previous four weeks, the subject had suffered from any symptoms of anxiety, depression, nervousness or irritability, and was administered for each interview.

(e) *The Self-Rating Depression Scale (SDS).* This was developed by Zung (1965) to detect the presence of depression and associated symptoms. It has had extensive use (Blumenthal, 1975) and has been found suitable for Australian studies (Byrne, 1978, 1980).

It was administered at the initial interview and at 8 and 12 months.

RESULTS

All life-event measures used in the substantive analyses were collected at the beginning of the study and refer to experiences encountered in the year prior to initial interview. Thus, cross-sectional correlations refer to associations between life-event measures and symptoms assessed at the same point in time (the beginning of the study). Cross-lagged correlations refer to associations between life-event measures at the beginning of the study and symptoms evident 4, 8, and 12 months later. In addition to correlational analyses (product moment) life-event experiences prior to initial interview for subjects reporting symptoms at 4-, 8-, or 12-month follow-ups were compared with life-event experiences of subjects remaining symptom-free, using unrelated sample t-tests.

The choice of symptom-free subjects (GHQ 5) at the outset assumed that sufficient numbers would go on to experience symptoms sometime in the subsequent 12 months to ensure usable outcome variance. There are grounds for trusting this assumption (Duncan-Jones, 1981). In fact 38 subjects (22.5 percent) made this transition, though not all remained symptomatic for the entire follow-up period. Small numbers dictated against a finer, temporal examination of this process.

Personal interpretations of life-event impact, measured by means of the technique described above and made by subjects experiencing symptoms (GHQ 5) at some time during the 12-month follow-up were compared with measures of impact collected from those remaining symptom-free in this period. While differences were in the expected direction (those with symptoms interpreting the impact of life events as greater than those without symptoms) none reached statistical significance. When data were examined independently for each 4-month period, it was found that those reporting symptoms (GHQ 5) at 8 months had, at the time of the initial interview, also reported more significantly (on all seven scales) than had those remaining sympton-free. Significances at other follow-up interviews were marginal. Table 10.1 presents t values (unrelated samples) and significance levels for these breakdowns.

Cross-sectional correlations between life-event frequency and symptoms were significant in only one instance (SDS) and only barely. Cross-lagged correlations with GHQ and NSYMP were significant at 4 months (no SDS data) but for no symptom measure at 8 or 12 months. These data are shown in Table 10.2.

A similar pattern of associations emerged when cumulative distress weight was used as the life-event index. These data, too, are shown in Table 10.2. Strengths of associations appear to have been augmented by the added sophistication of the life-event measure, which now incorporated a measure of the immediate distress arising from life events, as a step between the environmental occurrence and the appearance of a neurotic state.

Cumulative scores based on personal interpretations of life-

Table 10.1

Differences (t-tests) in Cumulative Self-Report Scores of Life-Event Impact between Persons Reporting Symptoms in the Year After Initial Interview and Those Remaining Symtom-Free

Cumulative scale	Initial interview (t)	4-month follow-up (t)	8-month follow-up (t)	12-month follow-up (t)
Upset	− 1.45	− 1.40	− 4.80**	− 2.87**
Disruption	− 1.77	− 2.15*	− 3.34**	− 1.53
Adjustment	− 1.85	− 2.31	− 3.80**	− 1.69
Depression	− 0.92	− 1.79*	− 4.30	− 1.53
Anxiety	− 1.22	− 1.85	− 3.62*	− 2.52*
Anger	− 1.17	− 1.15	− 2.91	− 0.99
Helplessness	− 1.78	− 1.88	− 3.56**	− 2.60*

*$p<0.05$
**$p<0.01$

event impact produced three out of seven significant correlations with GHQ score on cross-sectional analysis. These associations strengthened further for symptoms (GHQ scores) evident at four months, but disappeared at 8- and 12-month intervals. Table 10.3 presents these data.

Correlations between cumulative scores on scales of personally interpreted life-event impact and SDS scores were all significant on cross-sectional analysis. No SDS data were available

Table 10.2
Retrospective and Prospective Correlations between Objective Life-Event Measures (Frequency and Distress Weights) and Psychological Symptom Measures

	Initial interview	4-month follow-up	8-month follow-up	12-month follow-up
Life-event frequency with:				
GHQ	0.05	0.20**	0.08	−0.02
SDS	0.14*	—	0.03	0.03
NSYMP	0.10	0.25	0.07	0.04
Cumulative distress weight with:				
CHQ	0.10	0.19**	0.09	−0.01
SDS	0.19**	—	0.05	0.10
NSYMP	0.18**	0.33**	0.14*	0.10

$*p < 0.05$
$**p < 0.01$

Table 10.3
Retrospective and Prospective Correlations between Cumulative Self-Report Scores of Life-Event Impact and GHQ Scores

Cumulative scale	Initial interview	4-month follow-up	8-month follow-up	12-month follow-up
Upset	0.09	0.25**	0.05	−0.01*
Disruption	0.10	0.25**	0.14*	0.09
Adjustment	0.17**	0.02**	0.09	0.06
Depression	0.06	0.17**	0.00	−0.02
Anxiety	0.17**	0.21**	0.07	0.06
Anger	0.18**	0.15*	0.05	−0.03
Helplessness	0.10	0.34**	0.09	0.03

$*p < 0.05$
$**p < 0.01$

at 4 months, and no correlations were significant at eight months. However, cumulative scores on four of the seven scales correlated with SDS scores at 12 months. These data are shown in Table 10.4.

Cross-sectional analysis revealed significant correlations between cumulative scores on all scales of personally interpreted life-event impact and NSYMP scores. These associations were strengthened by cross-lagged correlations using NSYMP scores at 4 months. Significance remained for three of seven scales at 8 months and four of seven scales at 12 months, though strengths of associations generally diminish with time. These data are shown in Table 10.5.

DISCUSSION

This exercise aimed to examine the sequential influence of various measures of life events, accumulating to one point in time, on the future development of neurotic symptoms among a cohort of initially symptom-free subjects. Interpretation of results demands the recognition that influences other than life events will, over time, account for portions of future symptom variance, and so correlations, where they emerge, should not be viewed as representing simple or univariate paths of influence.

Table 10.4
Retrospective and Prospective Correlations between Cumulative Self-Report Scores of Life-Event Impact and SDS Scores

Cumulative scale	Initial interview	4-month follow-up	8-month follow-up	12-month follow-up
Upset	0.16*	No data	0.07	0.12
Disruption	0.18**		0.11	0.11
Adjustment	0.16*		0.01	0.11
Depression	0.20**		0.06	0.16*
Anxiety	0.20**		0.03	0.16*
Anger	0.17**		0.06	0.18*
Helplessness	0.19**		0.07	0.21**

*$p<0.05$
**$p<0.01$

Table 10.5
Retrospective and Prospective Correlations between Cumulative Self-Report
Scores of Life-Event Impact and NSYMP Scores

Cumulative scale	Initial interview	4-month follow-up	8-month follow-up	12-month follow-up
Upset	0.30**	0.42*	0.23**	0.16*
Disruption	0.20**	0.39**	0.10	0.11
Adjustment	0.20**	0.40**	0.11	0.11
Depression	0.22**	0.40**	0.11	0.09
Anxiety	0.29**	0.41**	0.20**	0.19**
Anger	0.23**	0.30**	0.10	0.13*
Helplessness	0.24**	0.34**	0.20**	0.13*

*$p<0.05$
**$p<0.01$

RETROSPECTIVE DATA

These analyses showed correlations which were occasionally significant, always small and always consistent with the sizes of associations reported in other studies (Grant et al., 1978; Andrews, 1981). Correlations increased marginally when summated distress evoked by life events encountered a year prior to initial interview was quantified using a cumulative weighting score. Since this score was designed to take account of an interpretive stage between environmental circumstances and neurotic symptoms, the result was expected.

Cumulative scores based on scales of personally interpreted life-event impact generally strengthened correlations even further. It would seem, therefore, that where individuals are permitted to judge for themselves the distressing impact of personally experienced life events, the potential association between this aspect of the environment and neurotic symptoms is enhanced. Once more, this result was expected and in accord with previous findings (Byrne and Whyte, 1980).

However, while cross-sectional associations emerged in an expected manner, they remained modest in size and accounted for only the anticipated 10 percent or so of the variance (Miller and Ingham, 1979). The deliberate selection of the psycholog-

ically healthy cohort may have contributed to this by constrain-
ing the potential size of correlations.

PROSPECTIVE DATA

Even the simplest life-event measures (frequency and cumulative distress weights) yielded significant associations with
symptoms measured 4 months later. Since life-event measures
predated those of symptoms, resultant associations may be
causal. The use of personally interpreted measures of life-event
impact produced a more complete picture of associations between life events and neurotic symptoms.

Differences in cumulative indices of personally interpreted
life-event impact for the year prior to initial interview were not
marked when subjects who reported symptoms at 4- or 12-
month follow-up were compared with those remaining symptom-free at these times. At 8-month follow-up, however, those
who were not reporting neurotic symptoms (GHQ 5) had, in
the year prior to initial interview, also reported significantly
higher scores on scales of personally interpreted life-event impact than had those who were symptom-free at this time. The
finding must, of course, be treated cautiously since the distinction is only really evident at 8-month follow-up.

Cross-lagged correlations were also undertaken on the data
to examine prospective associations between measures of the
personal interpretation of life-event impact and the serial, future occurrence of neurotic symptoms. Correlations at 4-month
follow-up (for GHQ and NSYMP only) were stronger than was
evident on retrospective analysis. The tendency to attribute affective significance to life events accumulating to one point in
time might, therefore, be seen to predispose to the appearance
of neurotic symptoms at some time in the future. The disparity
between strengths of associations evident in prospective and
retrospective data must, however, be seen in the light of the
possibility that the deliberate choice of healthy subjects at the
outset limited the potential size of retrospective correlations.

Significant cross-lagged correlations were also apparent at

8- and 12-month follow-ups, and an interesting temporal patterning of associations emerged. For the GHQ, reflecting anxiety and concomitant neurotic symptoms, correlations were strongest at 4 months and diminished rapidly after that. Correlations with NSYMP were generally stronger, and while they diminished in size over time, significance occasionally persisted for up to 12 months after collection of initial life-event data. SDS data were not available at 4 months and no correlations were significant at 8 months. Cumulative scores on four of seven scales of personal interpretations of life-event impact did, however, correlate significantly with SDS scores obtained at 12-month follow-up. This suggests, though tenuously, that the temporal course of the link between personal interpretations of life-event impact and neurotic symptoms varies according to the nature of the symptoms being measured. While these observations remain tentative, they underscore the value of multiple, serial measures of neurotic symptoms in studies of this kind.

One final observation on these data is of interest. In broad terms, it is personal interpretations of life-event distress rather than those of life change which predominate among the significant correlations, and this is consistent with the previous findings on life events and illness (Mueller, Edwards, and Yarvis, 1977; Byrne and Whyte, 1980).

The evidence, as it stands, supports two conclusions. First, life events reported by healthy subjects correlate prospectively with the future appearance of neurotic symptoms. Secondly, the recognition of an affective interpretive phase between the occurrence of environmental events and the appearance of symptoms strengthens correlations both retrospectively and prospectively. Several possible challenges to these conclusions must, however, be given credence in the final consideration of the data.

Prospective correlations were generally stronger than retrospective ones, giving support to a "formative" notion of life events and symptoms. The choice of initially healthy subjects may, however, have constrained the size of cross-sectional associations. Thus, while healthy subjects were chosen to reduce contamination of life-event reports by existing symptoms (Brown, Sklair, Harris, and Birley, 1973), this methodological strategy may have given rise to an artifactual disparity between correlations.

Both Eaton (1978) and Andrews (1981) remarked on "chaining" of life events, where the occurrence of one event may foreshadow the future appearance of a chain of related events. Cumulative life-event measures for the period between initial interview and 4-month follow-up for those with symptoms at 4 months were not significantly higher than for those remaining symptom-free. Those with symptoms at 8 months did, however, report significantly more life events ($t = 3.89$, $p < 0.01$) and higher distress scores ($t = 4.83$, $p < 0.01$) in the 4 months between interviews than those symptom-free at 8-month follow-up. Similarly, those with symptoms at 12 months had accumulated a significantly higher distress score ($t = 2.62$, $p < 0.05$) for events occurring in the period between 8- and 12-month interviews than had those remaining symptom-free at 12-month follow-up. The possibility of life-event chaining as a prospective influence on symptom development cannot, therefore, be discounted.

In the sense that measures of life events predated measures of symptoms, the present study infers causal associations. The logic of causal inference is, however, sufficiently complex (Susser, 1973) that care must be exercised in concluding thus.

This technique of cross-lagged correlations, since it considered only one independent and one dependent variable, may be too unsophisticated to do justice to longitudinal data. More complex, multivariate techniques may have been more appropriate. However, confirmation of these simple analyses by other means would give added weight to the conclusions.

REFERENCES

Andrews J. G. (1981), A prospective study of life events and psychological symptoms. *Psychol. Med.*, 11:795–801.

—— Tennant, C. (1978), Life events, stress and psychiatric illnesses: A review. *Psychol. Med.*, 8:545–549.

Blumenthal, M. D. (1975), Measuring depressive symptomatology in a general population. *Arch. Gen. Psychiat.*, 32:971–978.

Brown, G. W., Sklair, F., Harris, T. O., & Birley, J. L. (1973), Life events and psychiatric disorders: Part 1. Some methodological issues. *Psychol. Med.*, 3:74–87.

Byrne, D. G. (1978), Cluster analysis applied to self-reported depressive symptomatology. *Acta Psychiat. Scand.*, 57:1–10.

—— (1980), The prevalence of symptoms of depression in an Australian general population. *Austral. & N.Z. J. Psychiat.*, 14:65–71.

—— Whyte, H. M. (1980), Life events and myocardial infarction revisited: The role of measures of individual impact. *Psychosom. Med.*, 42:1–10.

Duncan-Jones, P. (1981), The natural history of neurosis: Probability models. In: *What Is a Case? The Problems of Definition in Psychiatric Community Surveys*, ed. J. K. Wing, P. Bebbington, & L. N. Robins. London: Grant McIntyre.

Eaton, W. W. (1978), Life events, social supports and psychiatric symptoms: A re-analysis of the New Haven data. *J. Health & Soc. Behav.*, 19:230–234.

Goldberg, D. P. (1972), *The Detection of Psychiatric Illness by Questionnaire*. London: Oxford University Press.

—— Comstock, G. W. (1980), Epidemiology of life events: Frequency in general populations. *Amer. J. Epidem.*, 111:736–752.

—— Huxley, P. (1980), *Mental Illness in the Community*. London: Tavistock.

Grant, I., Sweetwood, H., Gerst, M. S., & Yager, J. (1978), Scaling procedures in life events research. *J. Psychosom. Res.*, 22:525–530.

Henderson, A. S., Byrne, D. G., & Duncan-Jones, P. (1981), *Neurosis and the Social Environment*. Sydney, Australia: Academic Press.

Holmes, T. H., & Rahe, R. H. (1967), The Social Readjustment Rating Scale. *J. Psychosom. Res.*, 11:213–218.

Jenkins, C. D., Hurst, M. W., & Rose, R. M. (1979), Life changes: Do people really remember? *Arch. Gen. Psychiat.*, 36:379–384.

Kellam, S. (1974), Stressful life events and illnesses: A research area in need of conceptual development. In: *Stressful Life Events: Their Nature and Effects*, ed. B. S. Dohrenwend & B. P. Dohrenwend. New York: John Wiley.

Lazarus, R. S. (1966), *Psychological Stress and the Coping Process*. New York: McGraw-Hill.

Lundberg, Y., & Theorell, T. (1976), Scaling of life events. Differences between three diagnostic groups and between recently experienced and non-experienced events. *J. Hum. Stress*, 2:7–17.

Masuda, M., & Holmes, T. H. (1978), Life events: Perceptions and frequencies. *Psychosom. Med.*, 40:236–261.

Miller, P., & Ingham, J. (1979), Must we be content with a non-directional 10% of the variance? Reflections on the life events to illness link with some preliminary findings. In: *Stress and Anxiety*, Vol. 6, ed. I. G. Sarason & C. D. Spielberg. New York: Hemisphere.

Mueller, D. P., Edwards, D. W., & Yarvis, R. M. (1977), Stressful life events and psychiatric symptomatology: Change or undesirability. *J. Health & Soc. Behav.*, 18:307–317.

Paykel, E. S., Prusoff, B. A., & Uhlenhuth, E. H. (1971), Scaling of life events. *Arch. Gen. Psychiat.*, 25:340–377.

Steele, G. P., Henderson, S., & Duncan-Jones, P. (1980), The reliability of reporting adverse experiences. *Psychol. Med.*, 10:301–306.

Susser, M. (1973), *Causal Thinking in the Health Sciences*. New York: Oxford University Press.

Tennant, C. (1977), The general health questionnaire: A valid index of psychological impairment in Australian populations. *Med. J. Austral.*, 2:392–394.

Theorell, T., Lind, E., & Floderus, B. (1975), The relationship of disturbing life changes and emotions to the early development of myocardial infarction and other serious illnesses. *Internat. J. Epidem.*, 4:281–293.

Chapter 11
The Stability of the State-Trait Anxiety Inventory Trait Anxiety Scale

MELISSA A. ELKIND, M.S., AND ANTHONY J. DEVITO, PH.D.

According to Spielberger (1983), "The twentieth century has been called the Age of Anxiety" (p. 1) and the influence of anxiety on people's lives has become increasingly apparent. Anxiety is a component of many psychiatric illnesses, such as the neuroses and schizophrenia, as well as a contributing factor to several medical and psychosomatic illnesses ranging from headaches and asthma to ulcers, hypertension, and coronary heart disease. In short, anxiety plays a major role in the mental and physical health of individuals.

Two types of anxiety, state and trait, have been distinguished by Cattell and Scheier (1961) and Spielberger (1966, 1983). State anxiety is defined as a transitory emotional condition with psychological and physiological components. The psychological component is characterized by subjective, conscious feelings of tension and apprehension, and the physiological component refers to the activation or arousal of the autonomic nervous

Acknowledgment. A briefer version of this chapter was presented at the meeting of the American Psychological Association, Los Angeles, California, August, 1985.

181

system. Trait anxiety, on the other hand, is viewed as a relatively stable personality characteristic indicating anxiety proneness and may reflect individual differences in the frequency and intensity of anxiety states. For example, an individual with high trait anxiety is likely to experience elevations in state anxiety in a wider variety of situations than an individual with low trait anxiety; in addition, the elevations in state anxiety of the highly trait anxious individual will be experienced as more intense. Spielberger (1983) also reports that individuals high in trait anxiety are likely to respond with greater increases in state anxiety in situations experienced as threatening to self-esteem (ego-threat) than in situations experienced as physically threatening. According to state-trait theory, trait anxiety measures should not change substantially over time or increase in stressful situations. There is, however, conflicting evidence regarding this issue.

Lamb (1969, 1973) administered the State-Trait Anxiety Inventory (STAI; Spielberger, Gorsuch, and Lushene, 1970) under four experimental conditions to investigate the effects of giving a speech (an ego-threat) on state and trait anxiety. STAI state anxiety scale scores were significantly higher under ego-threat conditions than under normal and physical threat conditions. On the other hand, no significant differences in trait anxiety were found under the various experimental conditions. Allen (1970) found an increase in state, but not trait, anxiety under examination stress conditions. Studies by Martuza and Kallstrom (1974), Newmark (1972), and Johnsen, Tracy, and Hohn (1983) also demonstrated the consistency of trait anxiety.

On the other hand, certain studies have brought into question the immutability of trait anxiety. Sachs and Diesenhaus (1969) found small, but significant, increases in trait anxiety between first (beginning of the term) and second (prior to final exam) testings. Tsushima (1957) also found changes in trait anxiety; students who were told they failed an examination obtained higher trait scores after this feedback. In one of a series of studies to evaluate the STAI, Kendall, Finch, Auerbach, Hooke, and Mikulka (1976) found trait anxiety scores to be reliable across stress and nonstress conditions. However, in another study in the same series, trait anxiety varied significantly across situations. To account for this variation, Kendall et al. speculated that the differences in trait anxiety scores may have occurred because the place of administration was different (classroom vs. home). "This finding provides evidence for the situational variability in the examination of A-trait [STAI Trait Anxiety] . . ." (p. 411).

Past research (Lazarus, 1966; Kasl and Cobb, 1979) has suggested that the anticipation of an event can be more stressful than the actual experience of an event. In support of this view, DeVito (1984) found that STAI state anxiety scores were higher under imagined examination-stress conditions than under actual examination-stress conditions. The imagined examination-stress condition was induced by altering the instructions of the STAI state anxiety scale. Subjects in the imagine condition were requested to respond according to how they *would* feel immediately before an exam. Subjects in the actual examination-stress condition were administered the STAI state anxiety scale with standard instructions ("indicate how you feel right now") immediately before an exam.

However, contrary to their own hypothesis, Bucky, Spielberger, and Bale (1975) found lower state and trait anxiety scale scores in aircraft flight students when tested under an imagined stressful situation ("respond as if you just made your first landing on an aircraft" [p. 276]) than when tested initially, without any intentionally induced anxiety. The authors attributed their findings to a "denial of anxiety" in order to "look good" in a situation in which the flight students believed their future may be at stake. Theoretically, imagined stress should affect state anxiety differentially depending on the intensity and consequences of the imagined situation, whereas imagined stress should not affect trait anxiety. The results of Allen (1970) support this view; state anxiety was higher under imagine than under normal conditions while trait anxiety remained relatively stable under both conditions.

This study examined the stability of trait anxiety using two approaches: (1) the analysis of mean differences in trait anxiety scores under actual stress, imagined stress, and nonstress conditions and (2) the correlation between trait anxiety scores of subjects tested twice, under both actual stress and nonstress conditions. Subjects in the nonstress condition were administered the STAI state anxiety scale with either standard or imagine instructions. If trait anxiety is a stable characteristic, there should be no significant differences in the means and there should be a high correlation between trait anxiety scores of subjects tested twice. Both approaches are necessary for determining the consistency of trait anxiety.

As an additional aspect of this research, the relationship between performance (academic achievement) and trait anxiety was investigated. Early work in the area resulted in the articulation of the Yerkes-Dodson Law which states that performance is best at moderate levels of anxiety rather than at high or low levels (Hebb, 1958). This relationship between anxiety and performance is commonly illustrated as an inverted-U shaped curve. Further investigation of this relationship distinguished test anxiety from other types of anxiety and found that it is the level of experienced test anxiety which is associated with performance (Alpert and Haber, 1960; Sarason, 1961). Spielberger (1980) defines test anxiety as individual differences in anxiety proneness in test situations, implying a correlation between test anxiety and trait anxiety. However, in the Test Anxiety Inventory (TAI) manual, Spielberger (1980) states that "on the basis of these correlations the TAI cannot be definitively classified as a measure of either trait or state anxiety" (p. 5). Hedl (1972) and Trent and Maxwell (1980) support the view of test anxiety as a trait while Sarason (1975) concludes that test anxiety is a form of trait anxiety but with statelike fluctuations.

Research indicates that the level of trait anxiety influences the intensity of state anxiety in situations which pose a threat to self-esteem (ego-threat) such as achievement or intelligence tests (Houston, Olson, and Botkin, 1972; Spielberger, 1983). Thus, much of the past research focused on the interactive relationship between trait and state anxiety and its effect on performance (O'Neil, Spielberger, and Hansen, 1969; Spielberger, O'Neil, and Hansen, 1972). The relatively few studies directly assessing the relationship between trait anxiety and performance are inconclusive (Anson, Bernstein, and Hobfoll, 1984; Heinrich, 1979; King, Heinrich, Stephenson, and Spielberger, 1976; Spielberger, 1958). Spielberger (1958) found no relationship between STAI trait anxiety scale scores and achievement while more recent research (Heinrich, 1979; King et al., 1976) found that STAI trait anxiety scores have a direct influence on academic achievement.

There is also conflicting evidence regarding sex differences in general or trait anxiety. In some studies females were found to be significantly higher than males in general anxiety (Castaneda, McCandless, and Palermo, 1956; Manley and Rosemier, 1972; Phillips, 1962) while in other studies no significant sex differences were found (Bendig, 1954; Lazowick, 1955; Spielberger et al., 1970; Lin and McKeachie, 1971). Because sex differences in anxiety are often reported, this study also investigated sex differences in the stability of trait anxiety.

METHOD

TEST INSTRUMENTS

The experimental design of this study required that the state and trait anxiety scales of the STAI be administered twice. But evidence (Bendig and Bruder, 1962; Windle, 1954) indicates that repeated administrations of the same form of a personality test result in changes in the positive direction. Spielberger (1983) suggests using a 10-item subscale when repeated measures are necessary. Thus, for purposes of this study, alternate, equivalent forms (A and B) of the STAI (DeVito and Kubis, 1983) were used.

186   MELISSA A. ELKIND AND ANTHONY J. DEVITO

SUBJECTS

Subjects (316 females and 186 males) were undergraduate students at the City University of New York (CUNY) enrolled in introductory psychology courses. The 502 subjects used in the study were those for whom complete data were available. The 502 subjects were assigned to performance groups depending upon whether they scored in the lowest, middle, or highest third on the examination in their class.

PROCEDURE

The experimental procedure is schematized in Table 11.1. At least two weeks into the semester, but at least a day before any hourly examinations had been given in the course, Form A (DeVito and Kubis, 1983) of the STAI (both state and trait scales) was administered. The state anxiety scale with either standard or imagine instructions was randomly distributed to

Table 11.1
Schematization of the Experimental Design

Feedback Group	Cell	At least 1 day before the exam	Cell	Immediately before the exam
E	1	State (Imagine) Trait	7	State (Standard) Trait
	2	State (Standard) Trait	8	State (Standard) Trait
B	3	State (Imagine) Trait		
	4	State (Standard) Trait		
A	5	State (Imagine) Trait		
	6	State (Standard) Trait		

Note. Either standard or imagine instructions for the STAI state anxiety scale are indicated within parentheses.

all subjects. Subjects given imagine instructions were told to respond according to how they believed they would feel immediately before their first full period course exam. Subjects given standard instructions were told to respond according to how they "feel right now." All subjects received the Form A of the STAI trait anxiety scale. (In this study, the trait anxiety scale was always administered with standard instructions.) Immediately before an hourly exam, approximately one third of the subjects (Group E) received Form B of the STAI (both state and trait anxiety scales with standard instructions). (School classes were randomly assigned to one of three "feedback" groups as part of the aspect of the research studying the effects of accurate feedback on the recollection of state anxiety under examination stress conditions. The three feedback groups were Group E, before an hourly exam; Group B, before feedback; and Group A, after feedback.) The identifying numbers within each cell of Table 11.1 are for future reference.

RESULTS

Means and standard deviations for Trait Anxiety scale scores are presented in Table 11.2. Cell numbers of Table 11.2 refer to the cells identified in Table 11.1. Time of testing refers to the class period in which the STAI was administered.

First, a $2 \times 2 \times 3 \times 3$ independent groups ANOVA was performed: (a) to determine the equality of the three groups (E, B, and A), (b) to compare trait anxiety scores of subjects administered the STAI state anxiety scale with imagine or standard instructions (cells 1, 3, 5 vs. 2, 4, 6 of Table 11.1), (c) to reveal relationships between trait anxiety and academic performance (low, medium, high), and (d) to determine sex differences. Thus, the independent variables for this analysis were group (E, B, or A), instructions (imagine or standard), performance level (high, medium, or low), and sex. The dependent

Table 11.2
Means and Standard Deviations for Trait Anxiety Scale Scores

Cell[a]	Time of Testing[b]	Instructions at first Testing[c]	Sex	Performance Group								
				Low			Medium			High		
				n	M	SD	n	M	SD	n	M	SD
1	1	I	M	10	22.9	5.0	16	21.2	5.2	12	20.6	6.3
			F	21	20.1	4.6	18	21.0	4.7	18	21.7	5.8
2	1	S	M	9	21.4	6.7	9	20.7	4.7	16	18.7	3.2
			F	20	20.4	4.2	20	20.8	4.2	14	18.4	3.1
3	1	I	M	14	17.6	3.0	6	20.0	6.2	6	19.3	3.6
			F	22	22.1	4.9	26	21.0	5.3	24	21.7	5.3
4	1	S	M	8	21.8	4.0	7	20.7	3.1	10	20.5	5.2
			F	20	20.5	4.1	23	22.5	3.6	20	19.5	4.0
5	1	I	M	7	22.6	5.4	7	19.1	6.9	15	22.2	5.4
			F	9	20.4	5.7	7	22.3	3.9	12	19.4	4.3
6	1	S	M	16	19.3	4.1	9	19.2	5.8	9	21.2	3.0
			F	12	21.8	5.7	18	20.5	4.0	12	20.8	5.3
7	2	I	M	10	21.4	4.2	16	21.1	5.4	12	20.3	8.0
			F	21	20.2	3.8	18	20.4	4.9	18	21.9	6.6
8	2	S	M	9	19.8	4.4	9	18.3	5.2	16	19.6	5.0
			F	20	19.3	4.2	20	20.5	3.2	14	18.9	4.3

[a]Cell numbers refer to cells identified in Table 11.1.
[b]Time of testing: 1 = At least one day before exam, 2 = Immediately before exam.
[c]Instructions on STAI State Anxiety Scale at first testing: I = Imagine, S = Standard.

variable was trait anxiety scale scores at first testing. None of the obtained F-values was significant.

Next, two analyses for mean differences in trait anxiety under normal and examination-stress conditions were performed. One analysis was a $2 \times 2 \times 3 \times 2$ ANOVA with repeated measures on one factor, time of testing (cells 1 and 2 vs. 7 and 8). The main effects were state anxiety scale instructions at first testing, examination stress condition (normal—at least one day before exam vs. examination-stress—immediately before exam), performance group, and sex. The dependent variable was STAI trait anxiety scores. Again, no significant F-values were obtained. However, the main effect of state anxiety scale instructions at first testing did approach significance [$F(1,171) = 3.55, p < .06$]. The mean trait anxiety scale scores for subjects administered the state anxiety scale with imagine or standard instructions at first testing were 21.0 and 19.8, respectively.

Another analysis, with the same main effects and dependent variable as the previous one, was a $2 \times 2 \times 3 \times 2$ independent groups ANOVA comparing cells 3, 4, 5, and 6 with cells 7 and 8. Because no group differences were found in trait anxiety scale scores at the time of first testing, cells 3 and 5 (both imagine instructions) were collapsed and cells 4 and 6 (both standard instructions) were collapsed for the purpose of this ANOVA. Based on the results of the preceding repeated measures ANOVA, one would not expect significant differences in the present analysis, and, indeed, no significant results were obtained. However, the main effect of state anxiety scale instructions at first testing did approach significance [$Fs(1, 478) = 2.87, p < .09$]. Mean trait anxiety scale scores for subjects administered the state anxiety scale with imagine or standard instructions at first testing were 20.9 and 19.9, respectively.

Pearson product-moment correlation coefficients between the two trait anxiety measures were computed for subjects tested under both normal and examination-stress conditions. For subjects administered the STAI state anxiety scale with imagine instructions at first testing (cells 1 and 7), the correlation coefficients computed were .871 ($df = 36, p < .001$) for males and .823 ($df = 55$, $p = .001$) for females. For subjects administered the STAI state anxiety scale with standard instructions at first testing (cells 2 and 8), the correlation coefficients computed were .663 ($df = 32$, $p < .001$) and .558 ($df = 52$, $p < .001$) for males and females respectively. The correlation coefficients computed for subjects administered the STAI state anxiety scale with imagine instructions at first testing appeared to be much greater than the correlation coefficients computed for subjects administered the STAI state anxiety scale with standard instructions at first testing. For this reason, tests for significant differences between the correlations were performed. The correlation coefficients were significantly higher for subjects receiving imagine instructions at first testing than for subjects receiving standard instructions at first testing; results were significant for both males ($p < .05$) and females ($p < .01$).

DISCUSSION

Mean trait anxiety measures were remarkably similar under normal and actual examination-stress conditions (cells 1 and 2 vs. 7 and 8; cells 3, 4, 5, and 6 vs. 7 and 8). The analyses of variance also showed virtually equal mean trait anxiety scores for subjects administered the STAI state anxiety scale with either imagine or standard instructions at the time of first testing (cells 1, 3, and 5 vs. 2, 4, and 6). These factorial findings support the aspect of state-trait theory asserting that trait anxiety is a relatively stable personality characteristic.

However, the results of the analyses of variance involving imagined examination stress and actual examination stress were not as clear cut. Although results were not statistically significant, there was a tendency for subjects to obtain higher trait anxiety scores under actual examination stress when receiving imagine, rather than standard, instructions on the state anxiety scale at first testing; this tendency was noted in the repeated measures ANOVA (cells 1 and 2 vs. 7 and 8) and in one of the independent groups ANOVAs (cells 3, 4, 5, and 6 vs. 7 and 8). It is possible that prior imagining of a stressful situation may later increase trait anxiety when experiencing the actual stress.

The correlational findings lend further support to the stability of trait anxiety. Trait anxiety scores of subjects tested under both normal and examination-stress conditions (with standard instructions on the STAI state anxiety scale at first testing) were highly and significantly correlated (cells 2 and 8; $p < .001$). Additionally, there was a significant ($p < .001$) correlation between trait anxiety scores of subjects administered the state anxiety scale with imagine instructions at first testing and trait scores of the same subjects administered the state anxiety scale with standard instructions immediately before an examination.

However, the significant differences in the correlations between trait anxiety scores of subjects who were tested twice indicate that imagining a stressful situation does have some effect on trait anxiety. One group of subjects (cells 1 and 7) received imagine examination-stress instructions at first testing and standard instructions under examination-stress conditions. Another group (cells 2 and 8) received standard instructions both at first testing and under examination-stress conditions. The correlation coefficients between trait anxiety scale scores for the first group (cells 1 and 7) were significantly higher than the correlation coefficients for the second group (cells 2 and 8). On the basis of the previously discussed analysis for mean differences (cells 1, 3, and 5 vs. cells 2, 4, and 6), it appears that imagine examination-stress instructions do not directly affect STAI trait anxiety scale scores. The significant differences in the correlations just mentioned, however, suggest that imagine instructions do affect the relationship between STAI trait anxiety scale scores under the two conditions studied. In short, there are no direct effects of imagined stress on trait anxiety, but there may be some subtle and complex effects as indicated by the significant differences in the correlation coefficients.

Other studies which found changes in trait anxiety (Tsushima, 1957) may be outdated since the measures available at that time were not as "pure" in their construction as the STAI. While in one study in the series by Kendall et al. (1976) there were no changes in STAI trait anxiety scale scores in stress and nonstress conditions, changes were found in another study in the same series in which the STAI was administered in different settings (classroom vs. home). Research to further clarify the concept of trait anxiety might explore the differential effects of settings, situations, and environments on trait anxiety.

Another goal of this research was the investigation of the relationship between trait anxiety measured by the STAI trait anxiety scale and performance measured by grades on a course examination. An analysis of variance showed no significant differences in trait anxiety for the three performance groups (low, medium, and high). These results did not support the Yerkes-Dodson Law showing enhanced performance at moderate levels of anxiety and lower performance at high and low levels of anxiety. Our inability to find support for the inverted-U relationship may be due to the restriction of the range of the population (only college students) in this study. It is possible that highly trait anxious individuals and poor performers in school tend to avoid going to college. They tend not to apply and tend not to be accepted even if they do apply. Thus, they are probably under-represented in this study. Also, the Yerkes-Dodson Law is stated in terms of individual performance and is usually not applied to groups. While graphs of the relationship between anxiety and performance may take the form of an inverted-U shaped curve for an individual, when large numbers of subjects (such as the 502 participants in this study) are averaged, any curvilinear relationship between trait anxiety and performance may appear as a straight line.

Another possibility is that there is no direct relationship between trait anxiety and achievement and it is truly an interaction between state and trait anxiety which affects performance (Spielberger, 1983). This explanation, however, disregards the findings of King et al. (1976) and Heinrich (1979) which showed a direct relationship between trait anxiety and academic achievement.

A final aspect of this research was concerned with sex differences in general or trait anxiety. There were no significant differences between males and females in STAI trait anxiety scale scores. These results lend support to some of the earlier research regarding sex differences (e.g., Spielberger et al., 1970). There were no differences in the nonstress (at least one day before exam) condition or in the examination-stress condition regardless of instructions or performance group. Thus, not only did males and females experience approximately equal amounts of anxiety under normal conditions (no apparent stress), but they did not respond differently when exposed to academic stress. Many of the studies which did find sex differences in general or trait anxiety (e.g., Phillips, 1962) used a different subject population (children and/or adolescents rather than college students) which may account for the discrepant findings in the various studies.

It is remarkable that there were so few significant results in this research, especially in view of the large number of subjects sampled and the fact that three four-way ANOVAs were performed. Only one factor of the repeated measures ANOVA and the same factor of the independent groups ANOVA (instructions on STAI state anxiety scale at first testing) even approached significance ($.05 < p < .10$). The virtual equality of STAI trait anxiety scale scores for all independent variables (instructions, time of testing, performance group, and sex) indicates the relative stability of trait anxiety as an individual characteristic.

These findings have important implications for the treatment of individuals suffering from stress and anxiety. The many techniques developed for reducing anxiety in individuals (e.g., biofeedback, relaxation training, and meditation) are directed primarily at anxiety states (Spielberger, 1979) and are usually used when a person is experiencing acute stress. It is also important to consider a person's level of trait anxiety or "anxiety proneness." Because trait anxiety is such an enduring characteristic, long-term approaches may be necessary to induce meaningful change. If a treatment approach successfully lowers trait anxiety, effects may be more permanent. One treatment strategy, for example, would be to apply one or more of the stress-reducing techniques to the many situations in which the highly trait anxious person experiences anxiety. By tackling the person's anxiety from several angles, a reduction in the level of trait anxiety may result.

REFERENCES

Allen, G. J. (1970), Effect of three conditions of administration on "trait" and "state" measures of anxiety. *J. Consult. & Clin. Psychol.* 34:355–359.

Alpert, R., & Haber, R. N. (1960), Anxiety in academic achievement situations. *J. Abnorm. & Soc. Psychol.*, 61:207–215.

Anson, O., Bernstein, J., & Hobfoll, S. E. (1984), Anxiety and performance in two ego threatening situations. *J. Personal. Assess.*, 48:168–172.

Bendig, A. W. (1954), Age, sex, and the Manifest Anxiety scale. *J. Consult. Psychol.*, 18:16–18.

——— Bruder, G. (1962), The effect of repeated testing on anxiety scale scores. *J. Consult. Psychol.*, 26:392–393.

Bucky, S. F., Spielberger, C. D., & Bale, R. M. (1975), Effects of instructions on measures of state and·trait anxiety in flight students. *J. Appl. Psychol.*, 56:275–276.

Castaneda, A., McCandless, B. R., & Palermo, D. S. (1956), The children's form of the Manifest Anxiety scale. *Child Develop.*, 27:317–326.

Cattell, R. B., & Scheier, I. H. (1961), *The Meaning and Measurement of Neuroticism and Anxiety.* New York: Ronald Press.

DeVito, A. J. (1984), The anticipation, experience, and recollection of text anxiety [summary]. *Proceedings and Abstracts of the Annual Meeting of the Eastern Psychological Association,* 55:9.

——— Kubis, J. F. (1983), Alternate forms of the State-Trait Anxiety Inventory. *Ed. & Psychol. Meas.* 43:729–734.

Hebb, D. O. (1958), *A Textbook of Psychology.* London: Saunders.

Hedl, J. J., Jr. (1972), Test anxiety: A state or trait concept? [Summary]. *Proceedings of the 80th Annual Convention of the American Psychological Association,* 7:503–504.

Heinrich, D. L. (1979), The causal influence of anxiety on academic achievement for students of differing intellectual ability. *Appl. Psychol. Meas.,* 3:351–359.

Houston, B. K., Olson, M., & Botkin, A. (1972), Trait anxiety and beliefs regarding danger and threat to self-esteem. *J. Consult. Clin. Psychol.*, 38:152–156.

Johnsen, E. P., Tracy, D. B., & Hohn, R. L. (1983), Induced response bias on the State-Trait Anxiety Inventory. *Soc. Behav. & Person.*, 11:113–117.

Kasl, S. V., & Cobb, S. (1979), Some mental health consequences of plant closing and job loss. In: *Mental Health and the Economy*, ed. L. A. Ferman & J. P. Gordus. Kalamazoo, MI: W. P. Upjohn Institute for Employment Research, pp. 255–300.

Kendall, P. C., Finch, A. J., Auerbach, S. M., Hooke, J. F., & Mikulka, P. J. (1976), The State-Trait Anxiety Inventory: A systematic evaluation. *J. Consult. & Clin. Psychol.* 44:406–412.

King, F. J., Heinrich, D. L., Stephenson, R. S., & Spielberger, C. D. (1976), An investigation of the causal influence of trait and state anxiety on academic achievement. *J. Ed. Psychol.* 68:330–334.

Lamb, D. H. (1969), *The Effects of Public Speaking on Self-report, Physiological, and Behavioral Measures of Anxiety.* Florida State University, Tallahassee, FL. Unpublished doctoral dissertation.

——— (1973), The effects of two stressors on state anxiety for students who differ in trait anxiety. *J. Res. Pers.*, 7:116–126.

Lazarus, R. (1966), *Psychological Stress and the Coping Process.* New York: McGraw-Hill.

Lazowick, L. M. (1955), On the nature of identification. *J. Abnorm. & Soc. Psychol.* 51:175–183.

Lin, Y., & McKeachie, W. J. (1971), Sex similarity in personality correlates of test anxiety. *Psychol. Rep.*, 29:515–520.

Manley, M. J., & Rosemier, R. A. (1972), Developmental trends in general and test anxiety among junior and senior high school students. *J. Genet. Psychol.*, 120:219–226.

Martuza, V. R., & Kallstrom, D. W. (1974), Validity of the State-Trait Anxiety Inventory in academic setting. *Psychol. Rep.*, 35:363–366.

Newmark, C. S. (1972), Stability of state and trait anxiety. *Psychol. Rep.*, 30:196–198.

O'Neil, H. F., Jr., Spielberger, C. D., & Hansen, D. N. (1969), The effects of state anxiety and task difficulty on computer-assisted learning. *J. Ed. Psychol.*, 60:343–350.

Phillips, B. N. (1962), Sex, social class, and anxiety as sources of variation in school achievement. *J. Ed. Psychol.*, 53:316–322.

Sachs, D. A., & Diesenhaus, H. (1969), *The Effects of Stress and Order of Administration on Measures of State and Trait Anxiety.* New Mexico State University, Las Crucas, NM. Unpublished manuscript.

Sarason, I. G. (1961), Test anxiety and the intellectual performance of college students. *J. Ed. Psychol.*, 52:201–206.

——— (1975), Test anxiety, attention, and the general problem of anxiety. In: *Stress and Anxiety*, Vol. 1, ed. C. D. Spielberger & I. G. Sarason. Washington, DC: Hemisphere.

Spielberger, C. D. (1958), On the relationship between manifest anxiety and intelligence. *J. Consult. Psychol.*, 22:220–224.

——— (1966), Theory and research on anxiety. In: *Anxiety and Behavior*, ed. C. D. Spielberger. New York: Academic Press, pp. 3–19.

——— (1979), *Understanding Stress and Anxiety*. New York: Harper & Row.

——— (1980), *Preliminary Professional Manual for the Test Anxiety Inventory*. Palo Alto, CA: Consulting Psychologists Press.

——— (1983), *Manual for the State-Trait Anxiety Inventory (Form Y)*. Palo Alto, CA: Consulting Psychologists Press.

——— Gorsuch, R. C., & Lushene, R. E. (1970), *STAI Manual*. Palo Alto, CA: Consulting Psychologist Press.

——— O'Neil, H. F., Jr., & Hansen, D. N. (1972), Anxiety drive theory and computer-assisted learning. In: *Progress in Experimental Personality Research*, ed. B. A. Maher. New York: Academic Press.

Trent, J. T., & Maxwell, W. A. (1980), State and trait components of test anxiety and their implications for treatment. *Psychol. Rep.*, 47:475–480.

Tsushima, U. (1957), *Failure Stress in Conditions Related to Anxiety Inventory Scores*. Unpublished master's thesis, University of Illinois, Urbana, IL.

Windle, C. (1954), Test-retest effect on personality questionnaires. *Ed. Psychol. Meas.*, 14:617–633.

Chapter 12
Stress as a Potential Barrier to the Search for Health

R. BARKER BAUSELL, PH.D., AND S. PETCHEL DAMROSCH, PH.D.

The effects of stress, especially when operationalized in terms of significant changes in life events, upon both the onset of physical illness (Dohrenwend and Dohrenwend, 1974; Kobasa, Maddi, and Kahn, 1982; Locke, 1982; Murphy and Brown, 1980; Rahe, 1968; Raye, Bennett, and Romo, 1972; Spilkin and Jacobs, 1971; Wyler, Masuda, and Holmes, 1971) and recovery therefrom has received considerable attention in the health literature. An equally important, and often overlooked, effect of stress, however, lies in its potential as an impediment to health seeking behavior, the absence of which can itself lead directly to illness (Belloc and Breslow, 1974; Metzner, Carman, and House, 1983).

The possibility of such an effect is at least tacitly hypothesized by the Health Belief Model [see Kasl and Cobb (1966), or Bausell (1986) for a more thorough description of the Health Belief Model as it relates to health behavior] which posits that the probability of adopting any given health seeking behavior is a function of the following factors:

Acknowledgments. This study was funded by the Prevention Research Center, Emmaus, PA. A version of this chapter, entitled "Health Seeking, Affective, and Demographic Correlates of Stress," was presented at the American Psychological Association Convention, Los Angeles, 1985.

197

1. perceived susceptibility to the illness in need of preventing,
2. perceived severity of the illness,
3. perceived efficacy of the behavior with respect to preventing the illness,
4. perceived control over one's future health [actually this variable is a latecomer to the Health Belief Model; see Langlie (1977) for an illustration of its use], and
5. personal and environmental barriers to engaging in the preventive behavior in question.

Stress, of course, is subsumed under this latter factor and can be visualized as either an environmental (i.e., in terms of life events that are considered universally stressful) or a personal (in the sense that large individual differences among people are possible with respect to their reactions to similar stressors) barrier to health seeking behavior.

The purpose of the present chapter is to explore this potential link between stress and preventive behavior. Toward this end, a random sample of the telephone owning population of the United States was interviewed both with respect to self-reported compliance with a number of discrete health seeking behaviors and their global perceptions of the frequency with which they felt under great personal stress. It was hypothesized, based upon the conceptualization of stress as a potential barrier to salutary health seeking action, that persons who perceived themselves as living under conditions of high stress would engage in relatively fewer health seeking behaviors than their less stressed counterparts in the general population. It was further hypothesized that this effect would be observed *after* those health belief (i.e., perceived efficacy and control over future health; perceived susceptibility and severity of the illnesses potentially prevented by the behaviors could not be employed since multiple conditions could be affected by the behaviors used) and demographic (i.e., sex, age, race, and education) variables traditionally related to health seeking behavior had been statistically controlled.

METHOD

SAMPLE

A telephone interview of 1254 adults 18 years of age or older was conducted using a random digit dialing procedure stratified by geographical region and metropolitan versus nonmetropolitan residence. This represented a 71 percent acceptance rate. Demographic characteristics of this relatively heterogenous sample are presented in Table 12.1.

HEALTH SEEKING BEHAVIORS

The present study defined health seeking behavior as a comprehensive attribute encompassing dietary, safety, life-style, and health monitoring components. In all, 20 such behaviors were employed. (See Table 12.2 for these behaviors and their compliance definitions.) Total health seeking scores were generated by summing the number of individual behaviors with which each respondent reported compliance.

Table 12.1
Demographic Characteristics of the Sample (N = 1254)

	% of Total
Sex	
males	46
females	54
Race	
white	84
nonwhite	16
Education	
non-high school graduate	19
high school graduate	35
some college	24
college graduate	21
Age	
18–29	30
30–49	32
50 & over	37

Table 12.2
Compliance Definitions for the 20 Behavioral Items

Item	Definition
1. How often do you have a blood pressure reading?	At least once a year.
2. How often do you go to the dentist for treatment or a checkup?	At least once a year.
Thinking about your personal diet and nutrition, do you try a lot, try a little, or don't you try at all to:	
3. Avoid eating too much salt or sodium	Try a lot.
4. Avoid eating too much fat.	Try a lot.
5. Eat enough fiber from whole grains, cereals, fruits, and vegetables.	Try a lot.
6. Avoid eating too many high-cholesterol foods, such as eggs, dairy products, and fatty meats.	Try a lot
7. Get enough vitamins and minerals in foods or in supplements.	Try a lot.
8. Avoid eating too much sugar and sweet food.	Try a lot.
9. In feet and inches, what is your height without shoes on? What is your present weight without clothes? What kind of body frame or bone structure would you say you have—small, medium, or large?	In range based upon Metropolitan Life Insurance tables.

10. How often do you exercise strenuously—that is, so you breathe heavily and your heart and pulse rate are accelerated for a period lasting at least twenty minutes?   At least 3 times a week.

11. Do you smoke cigarettes now or not?   Do not smoke.

12. How many hours do you *usually* sleep each 24-hour day in total?   7-8 Hours.

13. In general how often do you consume alcoholic beverages? On a day when you do drink alcoholic beverages, on average, how many drinks do you have? (By a "drink" we mean a drink with a shot of hard liquor, a can or bottle of beer, or a glass of wine.)   No more than 4 drinks per day for a total of no more than 15 per week.

14. How often do you wear a seatbelt when you are in the front seat of a car   Always.

15. How often do you drive above the speed limit?   Never does so.

16. How often do you drive after drinking alcoholic beverages?   Never does so.

17. Do you have a smoke detector in your home?   Yes, owns one.

18. Does anyone in your household ever smoke in bed?   No one does.

19. Do you take any special steps or precautions to avoid accidents in and around your home?   Yes, takes steps.

20. About how often do you socialize with close friends, relatives, or neighbors?   At least once a week.

202   R. BARKER BAUSELL AND S. PETCHEL DAMROSCH

HEALTH BELIEF VARIABLES

Perceived efficacy of the health seeking behaviors was measured by asking respondents to rate a subset of the behaviors employed with respect to their ability to help people maintain their health. A total score was generated by simply summing these responses.

Perceived control over future health was ascertained by asking respondents how much (i.e., a great deal, some, very little, or none at all) control they felt that they had over their future health.

STRESS

In the present study stress was measured by simply asking respondents how often (i.e., almost every day, several days a week, once or twice a week, or never) they felt themselves to be under *great* stress. As illustrated in Table 12.3, this question produced a relatively wide range of responses with approximately the same number of people reporting feeling under stress almost every day as reporting never feeling under stress at all.

Table 12.3
Distribution for the Stress Measure

	%
Never	16%
Less often than once a week	29%
Once or twice a week	27%
Several days a week	12%
Almost every day	16%
Not sure	1%[a]

[a]These respondents were not included in any of the reported analyses.

RESULTS

The data were analyzed in two basic ways. First, respondents were dichotomized as either compliant or noncompliant with respect to each individual behavior. The resulting compliant/noncompliant groups (the memberships of which differed for each individual behavior) were then contrasted with respect to the mean frequency with which respondents reported feeling under great stress. Following this analysis a stepwise multiple regression was performed using the stress item as the dependent variable and sex, age, education, race, perceived efficacy, and perceived control as the independent variables.

INDIVIDUAL BEHAVIORS

As indicated in Table 12.4, the mean stress levels for compliant respondents were lower than their noncompliant counterparts for 17 of the 20 behaviors employed. (Actually this trend was reversed only in the case of regular blood pressure checks, since the compliant/noncompliant means were identical for avoiding salt and consuming adequate fiber.) Six of these differences were statistically significant at the .05 level or beyond: three of these were related to safe driving behavior (i.e., wearing seatbelts, not speeding, and not driving after drinking) while two were smoking related (i.e., not smoking and not smoking in bed). The sixth statistically significant difference describes a scenario in which persons receiving recommended levels of sleep reported feeling under less stress than persons receiving either more or less sleep than normal.

TOTAL HEALTH SEEKING BEHAVIOR

As indicated in Table 12.5, the stepwise multiple regression employing stress as the dependent variable produced a statistically significant, although relatively small, Multiple R of .18

Table 12.4
Univariate Relationship Between Stress and 20 Individual Health
Seeking Behaviors

Behavior	Compliant[a]	Noncompliant	p
Regular Blood Pressure Checks	2.86	2.82	ns
Regular Dental Visits	2.83	2.89	ns
Avoid Salt	2.85	2.85	ns
Avoid Fat	2.82	2.89	ns
Consume Fiber	2.85	2.85	ns
Avoid Cholesterol	2.79	2.90	ns
Consume Vitamins/Minerals	2.83	2.89	ns
Avoid Sugar	2.83	2.88	ns
Control Weight	2.78	2.68	ns
Exercise Regularly	2.79	2.88	ns
Not Smoking	2.79	2.98	.02
7–8 Hours Sleep	2.79	2.96	.03
Moderate Alcohol Consumption	2.85	2.86	ns
Always Wear Seatbelts	2.71	2.88	.05
Drive Speed Limit	2.78	2.96	.02
Avoid Driving after Drinking	2.80	2.97	.03
Own Smoke Detector	2.85	2.86	ns
Avoid Smoking in Bed	2.81	3.13	.01
Avoid Home Accidents	2.83	2.90	ns
Socialize Regularly	2.83	2.96	ns

[a]Stress means are based on the following scale: 1 = never, 2 = less than once a week, 3 = once or twice a week, 4 = several days a week, 5 = almost every day.

Table 12.5
Multiple Regression Summary Table for
Stress as the Dependent Variable

Step	Variable	B Value	Contributions to R^2	R^2	F
1	Age	-.067	.0129**	.0129	15.0(1,1147)***
2	Control over Health	-.260	.0100**	.0229	13.5(2,1146)***
3	Education	.056	.0046*	.0275	10.8(3,1145)***
4	Health Seeking Behavior	-.028	.0041*	.0316	9.3(4,1144)***

*$p<.05$
**$p<.01$
***$p<.0001$

($p < .0001$). The variables making unique contributions to the overall R^2 were, in order of importance: age, perceived control over future health, education (which was negatively correlated indicating that persons with lower educational attainments perceived themselves to be under relatively *more* stress), and the total health seeking behavior measure. Of the other independent variables employed, both race (defined as white versus nonwhite) and perceived efficacy of the health seeking behaviors were significantly related to stress from a univariate perspective. Both relationships were quite weak, however, being .07 and .08, respectively.

DISCUSSION

Although this evidence must be considered preliminary given the correlational nature of the present study, these data do appear to lend support to the premise that stress may serve as a barrier to health seeking behavior. If this finding is eventually substantiated in prospective studies, it may require some compensatory alterations in our current thinking about the role of stress in causing physical illness. In other words, it may be that *one* of the reasons for the increased probability of illness among people operating under conditions of high stress resides in their decreased propensity to take effective actions in order to avoid contracting such illnesses.

Such a conclusion is certainly not inconsonant with current stress theory, but it does open intriguing avenues for future empirical research. Certainly the relationships observed were extremely weak, but this may be a function both of the probable unreliability of the single stress item employed and the relatively weak relationships found between illness and stress.

The weaknesses of these relationships should not be allowed to disguise their potential importance, however. It must be remembered that the present study employed a random sample of the United States population. The effects observed could be relatively more pronounced within higher risk groups. It is also important to note that of the six individual behaviors found to be related to stress, four (not smoking, not smoking in bed, wearing seatbelts, and not driving after drinking) were the highest rated health seeking behaviors among a survey of public health experts conducted by Louis Harris and Associates (Taylor and Kagay, 1983). If stress does impede compliance with these preventive acts, its overall effects upon health may be even greater than previously hypothesized. At the very least, the potentially complicated interactions among stress, health seeking, and health outcome variables deserve considerably more professional attention than they now receive.

REFERENCES

Bausell, R. B. (1986), The development and evaluation of a model to explain preventive behavior. *Eval. & Health Prof.*, 9:1–30.

Belloc, N. B., & Breslow, L. (1972), Relationship of physical health status and health practices. *Prev. Med.*, 1:409–421.

Dohrenwend, B. S., & Dohrenwend, B. P. (1974), *Stressful Life Events: Their Nature and Effects.* New York: John Wiley.

Kasl, S. V., & Cobb, S. (1966), Health behavior, illness behavior, and sick role behavior. *Arch. Envir. Health*, 12:246–268.

Kobasa, S. C., Maddi, S. R., & Kahn, S. (1982), Hardiness and health. *J. Pers. & Soc. Psychol.*, 42:168–177.

Langlie, J. D. (1977), Social networks, health beliefs, and preventive health behavior. *J. Health & Soc. Behav.*, 18:244–260.

Locke, S. E. (1982), Stress, adaptation and immunity: Studies in humans. *Gen. Hosp. Psychiat.*, 136:326–338.

Metzner, H. L., Carman, W. J., & House, J. (1983), Health practices, risk factors, and chronic disease in Tecumsen. *Prev. Med.*, 21:491–507.

Murphy, E., & Brown, G. W. (1980), Life events, psychiatric disturbance and illness. *Brit. J. Psychiat.*, 136:326–338.

Rahe, R. H. (1968). Life-change measurement as a predictor of illness. *Proc. R. Soc. Med.*, 61:1124–1126.

—— Bennett, L., & Romo, M. (1972), Subject's recent life change and coronary heart disease in Finland. *Amer. J. Psychiat.*, 130:1222–1226.

Rosenstock, I. M. (1974), Why people use health services. *Milbank Mem. Fund Quart.*, 44:94–123.

Spilkin, A. Z., & Jacobs, M. A. (1971), Prediction of illness behavior from

measures of life crisis, manifest distress, and maladaptive coping. *Psychosom. Med.*, 33:251–264.
Taylor, H., & Kagay, M. (1983), *Prevention in America: The Experts Rate 65 Steps to Better Health.* New York: Louis Harris.
Wyler, A. R., Masuda, M., Holmes, T. H. (1971), Magnitude of life events and seriousness of illness. *Psychosom. Med.*, 33:115–122.

Part III
Life Stress and Behavioral Medicine

The past three decades have witnessed substantial progress in better understanding and identifying risk factors related to coronary heart disease. Although clinical research specifically related to stress has become fashionable over the past years, the medical profession has been concerned about the ideology and treatment of stress for many centuries. Hippocrates, in his analysis of stress, divided suffering caused by disease from suffering involved in nondisease states. More recently Selye et al. have addressed stress as a stimulus that elicits a physiological response aimed at restoring physiological balance to the organism. After all, it can be argued that life is stress and stress is life. Selye et al. further confirmed that stress is a biophysiological condition and concluded that anxiety provoked experiences whether they come from within the individual or from external events can literally make an individual mimic or experience symptomatology associated with illness and disease. Many efforts have been attempted to quantify the medical risks of certain types of illness. Holmes and Rahe's work focused on stressful events rather than on measuring an actual response to an event while Lazarus' work emphasized the cognitive appraisal of an event and elaborated the viewpoint that an event can be stressful only if the individual perceives it to be so; thus, it is clear that stress leaves an unmistakable imprint on the lives of the individuals who experience it. Whether it be headaches or other types of stress related problems, including hypertension, heart disease, skin disorders, influenza or asthma or other medical maladies, life truly is a series of stressful experiences challenging the organisms to adapt and respond appropriately.

The suggestion that stressful life events are associated with coronary heart disease and other medical and physiological experiences has a long history but a very brief scientific past. Osler et al., have suggested that the high pressure under which human beings live and the habit of working the machine to its maximum capacity are certainly responsible for degeneration of the system and in this case the arterial generation and the likelihood that certain personality characteristics are linked closely to the probability that an individual may, in fact, experience a disease state as a result of the stress experienced.

Myocardial infarction as it may be affected by stress and stressful life events provides the initial two articles in this section. Cardiologists under the direction of Dr. G. Magni of the University of Padua, Padua, Italy, address the interaction between myocardial infarction and stressful life events reported to have occurred 12 months before the onset of the illness were compared in 55 inpatients matched for age, sex, marital status and social class and afflicted with acute abdomen, trauma, and multiple trauma. Results suggest that recent life events are correlated with the onset of first episode myocardial infarction.

In Chapter 14, Dr. D. G. Byrne draws data from several studies undertaken by the author to examine the idea that life events are associated with myocardial infarction. He further purports that life events are to some degree influenced by personal factors characteristic of the individual. Results suggest that persons with the type A behavior pattern were more likely to encounter life events than others, and patients with myocardial infarction were more likely than others to interpret encountered life events in an emotionally adverse way. These data were discussed in the light of research strategies linking life events with cardiovascular disease.

Eating disorders have long been associated with anxiety and stress. Perceptual and cognitive dysfunction related to ego identity issues have played a key role. The impact of stressful life events has led clinical researchers like Dr. Strober to address this topic within the realm of eating disorders. Dr. Strober examines the relation of life-event stress to the occurrence of bulimia in young anorexia nervosa patients. Life events recorded in the 18 months preceding symptomatic onset were analyzed in 25 anorexics with bulimia and a matched group of 25 anorexics characterized by strict dietary control (restricters). Scores were derived by summing life change unit values for events experienced during successive six-month time blocks and are subjected to repeated measures analysis of variance. Findings indicated that bulimics experienced significantly more life stress than restricters in each six-month period (all $ps < .001$) and experienced two and a half times the magnitude of life stress observed in normal adolescents (Coddington, 1972) for a comparable time period. Results are discussed with respect to biological, psychological, and cognitive processes of possible relevance to the genesis of binge eating in anorexic patients. Concepts drawn from developmental theory, attribution theory, and psychobiology are relevant to our understanding of the genesis and maintenance of deranged eating patterns in bulimic anorexic patients.

Dr. Zack Z. Cernovsky of St. Thomas Psychiatric Hospital, Ministry of Health, Ontario, Canada, provides keen insight and understanding to the role of stressful life events and their influence on sleep disorders. Scales to assess nightmare recall frequency and recall frequency of insomnia-related disorders were administered, together with the Social Readjustment Rating Scale of Holmes and Rahe and the Life-Events Inventory of Tennant and Andrews to results suggested that the relationships of different types of scores for life events (scores for change, for distress, for amount of control over events, weighted and unweighted scores for negative and positive events) to reports of sleep disorders were mostly weak and nonsignificant. Of all life-event measures, negative life events listed on the Readjustment Scale were the most closely associated with reports of sleep disorders; all 14 coefficients involving negative events were significant and in the clinically expected direction. Further research is needed to examine whether the size of correlations between events and sleep disorders is related to factors such as readiness to recall and report negative personal experiences.

The relationship between stress in life events and uterine bleeding is explored through the work of Dr. Fred Tudiver of the Family Practice Unit of Memorial University of Newfoundland, Canada. Dysfunctional uterine bleeding (DUB) that occurs between menarche and menopause is often described but poorly understood. Relatively few studies have tried to associate DUB with life change and stress. In this case-control study, questionnaires measuring life change events and self-scored life stress were administered to 26 patients with DUB and 31 control. The participants were matched for age, gavidity, and contraceptive use. The participants were all aged between 18 and 35 years, and none were perimenopausal.

Drs. Stodola and Miller discuss stressful life events and their relationship to end stage renal disease (ESRD). ESRD is irreversible kidney failure that causes disruption of a primary process for exchanging matter with the environment. Stressors and stress responses associated with ESRD and dialysis treatment are discussed after a biobehavioral model of health and illness. The biobehavioral model is inclusive of three definitions of stress: stress as a response, stress as interaction, and stress as a stimulus. Prigogine's concept of dissipative structures and Hill's model of family stress are used to anchor discussion of adjustment to dialysis. ESRD, dialysis treatment, uncertainty about survival, machine dependence, fluid and diet restrictions, time demands, reduced mobility, and other factors are addressed as critical factors. The relationship of stress in ESRD patients to such critical life issues as depression, fatigue, suicide, sexual problems, marital functioning, pain, and cognitive, motor and sensory deficits is explored. Finally research findings on the course of adjustment to ESRD and the quality of life of people with ESRD are summarized.

Psychosomatic medicine has focused on the relationship between stress and various dermatologic disorders. Dr. Giovanni Fava and her associates investigated a consecutive unselected series of 60 inpatients suffering from dermatologic disorders (psoriasis, chronic urticaria and fungal infections of the skin). Twenty patients with each illness were included. Stressful life events immediately before illness onset, levels of psychological distress, and alexithymic traits were investigated. Patients with psoriasis and chronic urticaria were exposed to stressful life situations before disease onset and suffered from psychological distress (anxiety, depression, inadequacy) significantly more than those with fungal infections. Implications for psychosomatic research and treatment are explored.

Finally, Dr. van Uitert and his research team identified stressors and psychosocial adjustment factors among wives of stroke victims. Seventy wives completed the research protocol questionnaires. Environmental, individual, cognitive and behavioral mediating variables were examined. Better adjustment ratings were related to the experience of more pleasant events, involvement in larger social support networks to which they felt committed, fewer day-to-day problems, lesser severity of husbands' disability, and less use of avoidance coping mechanisms. Results support Lazarus' transactional formulation of stress. A model for identification of, and intervention with wives at risk for poorer adjustment following onset of their husbands' disabilities is offered.

Chapter 13
Life Events and Myocardial Infarction

G. MAGNI, M.D., A. CORFINI, M.D., F. BERTO, M.D., R. RIZZARDO, M.D.,
S. BOMBARDELLI, M.D., AND G. MIRAGLIA, M.D.

Many studies have been carried out on the relationship between life events and the onset of myocardial infarction (MI) which has been recently reviewed (Theorell, 1982). Some investigators have found that patients with MI complained of a greater quantity of life stress before the illness than did controls (Theorell and Rahe, 1972, 1974; Theorell, 1974; Connoly, 1976), while others have found a difference only if the quantity of emotional distress caused by each event, and evaluated by the subject, was considered (Lundberg, Theorell, and Lind, 1975; Byrne and Whyte, 1980). Others have found no difference (Spittle and James, 1977).

Jenkins (1976) concludes that the results of these studies are "provocative but remain unconvincing because of the inconsistencies among them." It is suggested that careful use of control groups (e.g., composed of people who have survived a serious medical condition analogous to MI) might eliminate some possible sources of bias. Wilhelmsen (1980) has recently reviewed the difficulties in analyzing the association of stress

Acknowledgment. This chapter was first published in the *Australian and New Zealand Journal of Medicine* (1983), 13:257–260, and it is reprinted by permission.

215

and coronary heart disease. In most of the studies cited, the investigators have carried out essentially quantitative evaluations of stress, ignoring its qualitative aspects.

The retrospective study on the relationship between life events and myocardial infarction presented here used a control group as suggested by Jenkins (1976) and a life-event scale giving a qualitative as well as a quantitative evaluation.

MATERIALS AND METHODS

Fifty-five consecutive patients admitted to the Cardiology Department of the University Hospital, Padua, with a diagnosis of myocardial infarction were studied. Diagnosis was based on evidence from clinical examinations, electrocardiograms and enzyme analyses. Those patients who had had a previous myocardial infarction were disqualified from the study. All subjects were interviewed while in hospital or within one month of admission.

SAMPLE CHARACTERISTICS

Fifty-five patients (45 males and 10 females), age range = 23 to 67 years (average age = 52.9 and SD 10.2), 44 married, six single, two divorced and three widowers, 20 middle class and 35 working class. One patient refused to participate in the study.

CONTROLS

Controls were matched with patients for sex, age (within four years), marital status, and social class. The latter was evaluated using the occupation of the head of the family as the criterion (Goldthorpe and Hope, 1974), and adopting the modifications suggested by Brown, Harris, and Copeland (1977). The controls were patients admitted to Padua Hospital for the following reasons: acute abdomen, trauma, multiple trauma. They were interviewed when they were well enough to permit their collaboration. They had no memory disturbances. One control refused to participate.

Recording of Life Events. The life events were derived from Paykel's revised interview for Recent Life Events (Paykel, Emms, Fletcher, and Rassaby, 1980) in the validated Italian translation (Fava, Munari, Pavan, and Kellner, 1981). The scale covers 64 defined life events. It was administered as a semistructured research interview, with each event being inquired about unless it clearly did not apply, by two interviewers well trained in its use. The scale gives two sorts of evaluation, a quantitative one and a qualitative one. The former is given by the total number of events experienced by a person over a certain period of time, and there is a further evaluation of the "objective negative impact." The expected severity of the negative impact is marked on a five point scale taking into account the nature of the event and the particular circumstances surrounding it, and completely ignoring the patient's subjective reporting of his reaction. This evaluation was carried out by an external assessor, and was based on the history obtained in the interview. The assessor was unaware of whether the event had happened to a patient with myocardial infarction or to a control.

The events were qualitatively classified in three categories:

1. "Entrances and exits": Entrances, meaning the entrance of new persons (for example, marriage or the birth of a child) and exits, meaning the exit of a person (for example, divorce, death, etc.).
2. "Desirable and undesirable events": Socially desirable events (for example, promotion at work) and clearly undesirable events (for example, redundancy, serious illness, etc.).
3. "Controlled and uncontrolled events": Controlled events, that is to say events under the control and choice of the person, and uncontrolled events, that is events outside of the person's control or against his will. For both pa-

tients and controls, the period covered by the interview was the 12 months immediately preceding onset of the illness.

Statistical methods: For statistical analysis we used the Student t-test, the chi-square, the chi-square with Yates correction and the Spearman Rank Correlation test, when appropriate. Statistical significance was chosen as α + 0.01.

RESULTS

The patients with myocardial infarction reported a total of 138 events, 2.51 per person while the controls reported a total of 54 events, 0.98 per person ($p<$ 0.001). Of those who reported more than one event, 37 were myocardial infarction patients and 12 were controls ($p<$ 0.001). A second comparison was carried out for the objective negative impact. The patients with myocardial infarction reported 93 events, 1.69 per person, which had been classified as having a moderate, marked, or severe impact, while the controls reported 38, 0.69 per person ($p<$ 0.01). The third comparison concerns the qualitative comparison of the events (see Table 13.1).

The myocardial infarction group was found to have experienced significantly more undesirable ($p<$ 0.01) and uncontrolled ($p<$ 0.01) events than the control group. A fourth evaluation looked at the period during which the events occurred. The year was divided into two terms; among the myocardial infarction patients 54 events (39.1 percent) occurred during the first term (the most distant from the onset of the illness) and 84 (60.9 percent) in the second term. Among the controls 13 events (24 percent) occurred in the first six months and 41 (76 percent) in the second. No correlation was found between age and number of events either for myocardial infarction patients or for controls. Lastly, for the areas of activity in which the events are catalogued see Table 13.2.

Table 13.1
Life Events in MI Patients and Matched Controls
Number of Individuals Reporting at Least One Event in Any Category

Category	MI (55)	Controls (55)	Significance[a]
Entrances	2	1	N.S.
Exits	24	14	N.S.
Desirable events	13	3	N.S.
Undesirable events	43	24	$p < 0.01$
Controlled events	7	4	N.S.
Uncontrolled events	41	22	$p < 0.01$

[a]Chi-square and chi-square with Yates correction, when appropriate.

Table 13.2
Analysis of Categorized Events
Number of Subjects Experiencing at Least One Event

Event Category	MI	C
Work (events 1-10)	17	9
Education (events 11-15)	2	1
Financial (events 16-18)	15	4
Health (events 19-25)	18	6
Bereavement (events 26-30)	22	13
Moving house (events 31-33)	4	4
Courting (events 34-37)	2	2
Legal (events 38-41)	6	2
Family and social (events 42-54)	22	8
Marital (events 55-63)	12	2
Other (event 64)	4	0

DISCUSSION

One of the inherent risks of retrospective studies is that the association between life events and the illness is not due to a real connection between these two variables, but to biased recall. It might in fact be true, as Jenkins (1976) has pointed out, that the patients tend to explain their illness by reporting more events. The use of a control group which has lived through a dangerous illness has certainly, if not completely, eliminated this possible source of bias. It has been reported that during moments of crisis the patient and family tend to distort the meaning and magnitude of the events (Paykel et al., 1980) while when the patient's condition is improving they are more likely to report positive or favorable events (Lipman, Hammer, Bernardes, Park, and Cole, 1965). The fact that interviews were carried out at a certain distance of time from the episode for which the patients were admitted to hospital and thus during a period in which they were "out of danger," should also have led to a more accurate reporting of the events. Another potential source of error relates to the passage of time. The more chronic the disease, the less accurately will life events be reported and evaluated (Barnett, 1979). By studying patients during their first myocardial infarction, interviewing them shortly after the episode, and using Paykel's scale which contains rigorous definitions of the event itself, we feel errors due to passage of time have been minimized.

The results reported are not only concerned with the quantity of the events [already reported in other studies (Theorell, 1974; Theorell and Rahe, 1974)], but also with their quality.

Our data show a significantly higher incidence of undesired events and uncontrollable events in myocardial infarction patients than in the control group.

It can be supposed that these kinds of events are particularly distressing as demonstrated in studies carried out in the psychiatric field (Myers, Lindenthal, and Pepper, 1971; Gersten, Langer, Eisemberg, and Orzeck, 1974; Mueller, Edwards, and Yarvis, 1977; and Seligman, 1975).

Patients with myocardial infarction were subjected to more events than the controls in both the first and the second six months of the year preceding the onset of the disease. For both groups, the number of events in the second six months is higher than that in the first. We can suppose that the higher incidence of events in this period is linked to the greater facility of recall for recent events than for chronologically more distant ones. However, the difference between the first and the second six months is more marked in the control group. These data are difficult to interpret. It may be hypothesized that a prolonged series of stress events. One hundred and twenty-six healthy students were tested and it was found that life events seen as undesirable, unexpected, or ambiguous in terms of perceived control were positively correlated with increased distress for students with type A behavior pattern (Suls, Gastrof, and Witemberg, 1979). The mechanism through which life events are linked to myocardial infarction may be indirect (e.g., influencing cigarette consumption) or direct. Nevertheless, it seems reasonable to consider life events as possible risk factors in the genesis of acute myocardial infarction.

REFERENCES

Barrett, J. E. (1979), The relationship of life events to the onset of neurotic disorders. In: *Stress and Mental Disorder*, ed. J. E. Barret. New York: Raven Press, pp. 211–217.

Brown, G. W., Harris T., Copeland, J. R. (1977), Depression and loss. *Brit. J. Psychiat.*, 130:1–18.

Bryne, D. G., Whyte, M. M. (1980), Life events and myocardial infarction revisited: The role of measures of individual impact. *Psychosom. Med.*, 42:1–10.

Connoly, J. (1976), Life events before myocardial infarction. *J. Hum. Stress*, 4:3–17.

Fava, G. A., Munari, F., Pavan, L., Kellner, R. (1981), Life events and depression. A replication. *J. Affect. Dis.*, 3:159–165.

Gersten, J. C., Langer, T. S., Eisemberg, J. G., & Orzeck, C. (1974), Child behavior and life events; undesirable change or change per se? In: *Stressful Life Events: Their Nature and Effects*, ed. B. S. Dohrenwend & B. P. Dohrenwend. New York: John Wiley, pp. 36–43.

Goldthorpe, J. H., & Hope, K. (1974), *The Social Grading of Occupations*. Oxford: Oxford University Press.

Jenkins, C. D. (1976), Recent evidence supporting psychological and social risks factors for coronary disease. (Second of two parts.) *N. Engl. J. Med.*, 394:1033–1038.

Kaplan, H. B. (1970), Self derogation and adjustment to recent life experiences. *Arch. Gen. Psychiat.*, 22:324–331.

Lipman, R. S., Hammer, H. M., Bernardes, J. F., Park, L. E., & Cole, J. O. (1965), Patient report of significant life situation events. *Dis. Nerv. Sys.*, 26:586–590.

Lundberg, V., Theorell, T., Lind, E. (1975), Life changes and myocardial infarction: Individual differences in life change scaling. *J. Psychosom. Res.*, 19:27–32.

Mueller, D. P., Edwards, D. W., & Yarvis, R. M. (1977), Stressful life events and psychiatric sympomatology. *J. Health & Soc. Behav.*, 18:307–311.

Myers, J. K., Lindenthal, J. J., & Pepper, M. P. (1971), Life events and psychiatric impairment. *J. Nerv. & Ment. Dis.*, 152:149–154.

Paykel, E. S., Emms, E. M., Fletcher, J., & Rassaby, E. S. (1980), Life events and social support in puerperal depression. *Brit. J. Psychiat.*, 136:339–346.

Seligman, M. E. P. (1975), *Helpless: On Depression, Development, and Death.* San Francisco: Freeman.

Spittle, B., & James, B. (1977), Psychological factors and myocardial infarction. *Aust. & N. Zeal. J. Psych.*, 11:37–43.

Suls, J., Gastrof, J. W., & Witemberg, S. H. (1979), Life events, psychological distress and the type A coronary-prone behavior pattern. *J. Psychosom. Res.*, 23:315–319.

Theorell, T. (1974), Life events before and after the onset of a premature myocardial infarction. In: *Stressful Life Events: Their Nature and Effects*, ed. B. S. Dohrenwend & B. P. Dohrenwend. New York: John Wiley, pp. 346–361.

——— (1982), Review of research on life events and cardiovascular illness. *Adv. Cardiol.*, 29:140–147.

——— Rahe, R. H., (1972), Psychosocial factors and myocardial infarction. An in-patient study in Sweden. *J. Chronic Dis.*, 25:139–145.

——— ——— (1974), Psychosocial characteristics of subjects with myocardial infarction in Stockholm. In: *Life Stress and Illness*, ed. E. K. E. Gunderson & R. H. Rahe. Springfield, IL: Charles C Thomas.

Wilhelmsen, L. (1980), Stress and coronary heart disease. *Aust. & N. Zeal. J. Med.*, 10:135–138.

Chapter 14
Personal Determinants of Life-Event Stress and Myocardial Infarction

D. G. BYRNE, PH.D.

INTRODUCTION

Reports of significant associations between stressful life events and the onset of myocardial infarction (MI) are now routine in the psychosomatic literature. Moreover, with recent attention to the methodological pitfalls to which this area is subject (Byrne and Whyte, 1980) these reports have now accumulated into an acceptable body of credible, scientific evidence. However, useful as this work has been, it seems to have rested on two tacit and questionable assumptions.

Firstly, life events have been assumed to occur fortuitously. Recent evidence (Tennant and Andrews, 1978) challenges this assumption, and suggests instead, that persons may behave, albeit unwittingly, in ways which increase or decrease their chances of encountering life events. Thus, life events must be viewed within the context of ongoing human behavior.

Secondly, when life events occur, they have been assumed

Acknowledgment. This chapter was first published in *Psychotherapy Psychosomatics* (1983), 40:106–114, and it is reprinted with permission.

223

to be endowed with an intrinsic and invariant degree of emotional impact. This is at odds with contemporary views of stress (Lazarus, 1966; Byrne and Whyte, 1980) in which the emotional impact on the individual of an environmental occurrence is seen to be modulated by interpretive factors unique to the individual.

This chapter draws on data from several recent studies to explore these assumptions and the questions arising from them.

METHOD

Life-event data to be considered arose from two studies, the one to do with survivors of MI (Byrne and Whyte, 1978, 1980) and the other to do with the general population (Henderson, Byrne, and Duncan-Jones, 1981). Samples have, therefore, been described in detail elsewhere. In summary, these were: (a) MI sample—120 survivors of a first, unequivocal MI ($\times$ age = 52.36, SD = 7.92), interviewed within 14 days of admission to hospital. (b) Patient comparison sample—40 patients admitted to coronary care with chest pain but shortly discharged with a diagnosis neither of MI nor other serious illness ($\times$ age = 49.34, SD = 5.34) drawn from a larger, random sample of the community, so as to match the age distribution of the clinical samples.

MEASURES

Reports of life-event experience in the year prior to MI (hospitalization or interview for other samples) were collected using a life-event inventory developed by Tennant and Andrews (1976) and refined for these studies by Henderson et al. (1981). This inventory contained 71 items and was not dissimilar to the instrument of Holmes and Rahe (1967). Individual interpretations of the emotional impact of encountered life events was assessed by means of the seven scales of upset, disruption, adjustment, depression, anxiety, anger and helplessness, using the method described by Byrne and Whyte (1980).

Measures of independent variables (state anxiety, neuroticism, and type A behavior) will be noted when they are discussed in the Results section.

RESULTS AND DISCUSSION

Neither frequency of encountered life events nor cumulative scores based on magnitude estimation scales of event distress (Holmes and Rahe, 1967; Tennant and Andrews, 1976) distinguished patients with MI from the less seriously ill, hospitalized comparison group. The empirical substance of these results has been reported by Byrne and Whyte (1980). Patients with MI did report the occurrence of significantly greater numbers of life events in the 12-month sampling period than did an age-matched group of healthy subjects drawn from the general population, but cumulative distress scores based on magnitude estimation scales failed to distinguish between the two groups. These data are shown in Table 14.1.

These results are, by and large, at variance with the collective wisdom on life events and MI. This body of evidence would have us accept not only that MI is associated with a premorbid surfeit of life events, but that these life events are somehow endowed with an intrinsically greater degree of distressing impact than those events encountered by persons with no or less serious pathology (Theorell and Rahe, 1974). To be fair, persons in the general population sample did encounter significantly fewer life events than those in the MI sample, though few would now argue that frequency of life events, in the absence of indices of distress, is a useful predictor of illness risk (Grant, Sweetwood, Gerst, and Yager, 1978).

These data present a particular challenge to the notion that arbitrary, magnitude estimation scales of life-event distress allow a useful quantification of the emotional impact of life

Table 14.1
Measures of Life-Event Stress: MI versus General Population

Life-Event Measure	MI Sample (n = 120)		Population Sample (n = 209)		t
	$\bar{x}$	SD	$\bar{x}$	SD	
Event Frequency	4.37	2.41	3.41	2.29	3.42*
Cumulative Distress	40.81	35.49	43.75	38.87	0.70
Mean Upset	5.02	6.27	2.64	2.46	3.97*
Mean Disruption	3.65	2.63	2.29	2.38	4.69*
Mean Adjustment	3.30	2.45	2.25	2.18	3.87*
Mean Depression	3.86	3.12	1.74	2.32	6.66*
Mean Anxiety	4.35	2.83	2.48	2.45	6.06*
Mean Anger	2.73	2.53	1.37	2.04	5.04*
Mean Helplessness	3.67	3.12	1.92	2.30	5.39*

*$p < 0.01$

events. This bears, of course, on the more implicit assumption that life events carry with them an invariant degree of distressing impact which holds regardless of the individual experiencing those events.

When subjects were permitted to judge for themselves, the degree of emotional impact engendered by personally experienced life events, differences between MI and other groups became apparent. Patients with MI consistently ascribed significantly higher distress ratings to encountered life events than did either of the two comparison groups. Since there was some evidence that the MI group encountered more life events than those in the general population, ratings were corrected for individual event frequencies, and mean rather than cumulative scores on scales of emotional impact are considered.

Data comparing patients with MI, with less seriously ill patients revealed substantial differences in mean scores of life-event impact, and these have been presented in detail by Byrne and Whyte (1980). Group differences were even stronger when compared with the general population sample, and these data are presented in Table 14.1 as well.

This evidence is very much in line with the cognitive notions

of stress (Lazarus, 1966) which hold, inter alia, that environmental occurrences are not intrinsically noxious, but may become so if interpreted as such within personal, cognitive
frameworks. The evidence is consistent with the idea that the
emotional impact of life events is modulated by factors unique
to the individual, though it gives little hint as to whether these
factors are learned, dynamic or otherwise determined. The
present evidence throws some light (perhaps only dim) on the
postulated difference between distress ratings of experienced
and non-experienced life events (Lundberg and Theorell, 1976)
and provides some empirical confirmation to speculation on
the variability of interpretations of life-event stress (Dressler,
Donovan, and Geller, 1976). Most importantly, it generates the
prospective hypothesis that persons who are the potential victims of MI have within them the tendency to interpret their
own encountered life events in an emotionally adverse manner.

The present data were, of course, collected retrospectively,
and in any like study, the possibility exists that measures so
subjective as individual interpretations of life-event distress will
be as much influenced by the person's immediate affective state
as by the more enduring mechanisms of cognitive interpretation
operating at the time of life-event occurrence. In the present
context, one must concede that the data may be as much an
indication that patients with MI recall past events in an emotionally adverse light, as they are that those who will get MI
were to interpret immediate events adversely. Brown, Sklair,
Harris, and Birley (1973) recognized this as a general difficulty
in life-event research and termed the phenomenon "effort after
meaning."

Measures of the immediate anxiety surrounding MI were
in fact collected concurrently with life-event data, using scales
of state anxiety developed for this purpose by Byrne (1979).
Resulting correlations are presented in Table 14.2. While two
thirds of these were significant, they were without exception
very small, and accounted for even smaller percents of the
variance (r^2). Data arising from the general population have
hinted at similar results (Henderson et al., 1981) while a delib-

Table 14.2
Life-Event Measures (Reported Frequency and Recalled Affective Impact) with Immediate Affect

	Reported frequency	Upset	Disruption	Adjustment	Depression	Anxiety	Anger	Helplessness
Concern	+0.16* 3%	+0.01 0%	+0.21* 4%	+0.25** 6%	+0.18* 3%	+0.24** 6%	+0.20* 4%	+0.16* 3%
Fear	+0.20* 4%	+0.09 0%	+0.23** 5%	+0.27** 7%	+0.21* 4%	+0.21* 4%	+0.19* 4%	+0.20* 4%
Worry	+0.18* 3%	+0.09 0%	+0.26** 7%	+0.30** 9%	+0.28** 8%	+0.28** 8%	+0.20* 4%	+0.25** 6%
Anxiety	+0.12 1%	+0.09 0%	+0.35** 12%	+0.42** 17%	+0.33** 11%	+0.40** 16%	+0.30** 9%	+0.30** 9%
Tension	+0.09 0%	+0.09 0%	+0.17* 3%	+0.24** 6%	+0.21* 4%	+0.20* 4%	+0.23** 5%	+0.19* 4%

$*p < 0.05$
$**p < 0.01$

erate attempt to demonstrate the phenomenon in a laboratory analogue study (Siegel, Johnson, and Sarason, 1979) failed to provide convincing evidence of its power.

These results do not totally dispell the possibility that the affective sequelae of an illness may act on the recall of life events leading up to that illness. Nor do they detract from the overall superiority of prospective designs in life-event research. However, the collective body of evidence on the potential size of the contamination allows the present data to be accepted with a degree of confidence.

The amount of stress engendered by any given life event would, therefore, seem to arise at least in part from mechanisms of interpretation unique to the individual. The extent to which personal factors might also be called on to explain the actual occurrence of life events occur fortuitously, though recent challenges demand that this can no longer be readily accepted.

Tennant and Andrews (1978) asked subjects to consider each item on a life-event inventory and to allocate degrees of both "internal" and "external" cause for those items. Thus, some items (e.g., death of a spouse) were rarely seen as following from personal behavior while others (e.g., a prison sentence) were more often seen as a direct consequence of individual activity. Any psychological examination of life-style and social behavior could serve to indicate that some individuals will behave in ways which make the occurrence of life events almost inevitable.

With this in mind, patients from both the MI and non-MI groups were asked to consider their own reported life events and to estimate whether their own behavior caused it or whether it resulted from the behavior of some other person. There was no evidence to suggest that patients with MI considered themselves to be either more or less responsible for their own life-event encounters than patients in the comparison group. These data are presented in Table 14.3.

The issue of personal control and the state of helplessness which might result from this (Seligman, 1975) has been discussed elsewhere with regard to these data (Byrne, 1980). In

Table 14.3
Mean Differences Between Group A (MI) and Group B (No MI)
Measures of Attributed Responsibility

	Group A, $n = 120$		Group B, $n = 40$		
	$\bar{x}$	SD	$\bar{x}$	SD	t
Self-responsibility	3.12	2.54	3.50	2.83	-0.76
Other responsibility	4.18	2.58	3.99	2.69	0.39
Chance responsibility	3.11	2.62	2.64	2.45	1.11

the present context, they simply reflect the extent to which individuals agree that their own personal behavior or life-style has had some bearing on subsequent life-event encounters.

The personality dimension of neuroticism was also examined in relation to life events, since Eysenck's (1967) conceptualization of this as instability of personality would suggest that the more neurotic a person is, the more likely would that person be to behave so as to encourage the occurrence of life events. Life-event measures were, therefore, correlated with N scores on the Eysenck Personality Inventory (Eysenck and Eysenck, 1964) and resulting associations are presented in Table 14.4.

The emergence of very weak correlations suggests that neuroticism has little to do with either the occurrence or experience of life events. This is not entirely consistent with results arising from a general population study (Henderson et al., 1981) though the discrepancy may be partly accounted for by differences between samples. It has also been shown that patients with MI are not particularly characterized by high N scores (Byrne, 1979) and possible correlations may have been truncated by limited sample variance in neuroticism. Personality as a determinant of life-event occurrence and experience does seem to be a likely prospect, and further research would seem to be indicated.

One attribute of the individual which did relate systematically and consistently with life-event measures was that of type A behavior. Subjects in both the IM and non-MI groups were asked to complete a brief, self-report inventory of type A be-

Table 14.4

Life-Event Measures (Reported Frequency and Recalled Affective Impact) with Neuroticism

Neuroti-cism	Reported frequency	Upset	Disrup-tion	Adjust-ment	Depres-sion	Anxiety	Anger	Helpless-ness
r	0.01**	+0.05	+0.09	+0.15	+0.25**	+0.21*	+0.10	+0.11
r^2	0%	0%	0%	2%	6%	4%	1%	1%

*$p < 0.05$
**$p < 0.01$

havior (Vickers, 1973) at the same time life-event data were collected. Regrettably, this measure was not used in the general population sample. Correlations were only rarely significant for the non-MI group (Byrne, 1981), perhaps due to small sample sizes. Correlations were uniformly significant for the MI group and these are shown in Table 14.5.

This finding is particularly interesting since it links two risk factors for MI, life events and type A behavior, which had hitherto been thought to operate quite independently. The significant correlation between type A behavior and life-event frequency is not at all unusual, since current views of this behavior pattern (Byrne, 1981; Herman, Blumenthal, Black, and Chesney, 1981), insofar as they portray the type A person as hard-driving, competitive, ambitious, aggressive and time-urgent, would also countenance the notion that such a person lives life

Table 14.5
Correlations (Pearson r) between Type A Behavior and Measures of Life Events

Life-Event Measure	MI group ($n = 120$)
Frequency	-0.31**
Cumulative perceived distress	-0.29**
Mean perceived distress	-0.25**
Cumulative perceived life change	-0.32**
Mean perceived life change	-0.26**
Cumulative perceived upset	-0.35**
Mean perceived upset	-0.22*
Cumulative perceived disruption	-0.37**
Mean perceived disruption	-0.28**
Cumulative perceived adjustment	-0.35**
Mean perceived adjustment	-0.30**
Cumulative perceived depression	-0.41**
Mean perceived depression	-0.28**
Cumulative perceived anxiety	-0.33*
Mean perceived anxiety	-0.27**
Cumulative perceived anger	-0.41**
Mean perceived anger	-0.36**
Cumulative perceived helplessness	-0.39**
Mean perceived helplessness	-0.25**

*$p < 0.05$
**$p < 0.01$

in such a way as to facilitate the occurrence of life events. The correlations between type A behavior and the interpreted emotional impact of life events are somewhat more unexpected. Jenkins (1978) in a review of the measurement of type A behavior, quite explicitly denied the presence of any emotional involvement in the behavior pattern. Why this inconsistency has occurred is not clear, though the present results coincide nicely with those of Dimsdale, Hackett, Block, and Hutter (1978).

CONCLUSIONS

Two conclusions may be drawn from the data presented above. Firstly, life events associated with MI cannot be viewed independently of individual, premorbid behavior. Persons exhibiting the type A behavior pattern certainly appear to be behaving in ways which facilitate life-event occurrence, though the evidence on attributed responsibility for life events suggests that they may not recognize this. Secondly, it seems that some individuals are sensitized to interpreting the emotional impact of life events in a more distressing way than others, and it is the former group who go on to develop MI.

The methodological difficulties associated with investigations of the personal determinants of life-event stress are not insubstantial and must clearly be considered. The conceptual errors likely to arise by ignoring these aspects of life-event stress are, however, sufficiently great to necessitate their inclusion in any study of life events and MI.

REFERENCES

Brown, G. W., Sklair, F., Harris, T. O., & Birley, J. K. T. (1973), Life events and psychiatric disorders. *Psychol. Med.*, 3:74–87.
Byrne, D. G. (1979), Anxiety as state and trait following survived myocardial infarction. *Brit. J. Soc. Clin. Psychol.*, 18:417–423.

———— (1980), Attributed responsibility for life events in survivors of myocardial infarction. *Psychother. Psychosom.*, 33:7–13.
———— (1981), Type A behavior, life events and myocardial infarction: Independent or related risk factors? *Brit. J. Med. Psychol.*, 54:371–377.
———— Whyte, H. M. (1978), Dimensions of illness behavior in survivors of
myocardial infarction. *J. Psychosom. Res.*, 22:485–491.
———— ———— (1980), Life event and myocardial infarction revisited: The role
of measures of individual impact. *Psychosom. Med.*, 42:1–10.
Dimsdale, J. E., Hackett, T. P., Block, P. C., & Hutter, A. M. (1978), Emotional
correlates of type A behavior pattern. *Psychosom. Med.*, 40:580–583.
Dressler, D. M., Donovan, J. M., & Geller, R. A. (1976), Life stress and
emotional crisis; the idiosyncratic interpretations of life events. *Compr.
Psychiat.*, 17:549–558.
Eysenck, H. J. (1967), *The Biological Basis of Personality*. Springfield, IL: Charles
C Thomas.
———— Eysenck, S. B. G. (1964), *Manual of the Eysenck Personality Inventory*.
London: United Press.
Grant, I., Sweetwood, H., Gerst, M. S., & Yager, J. (1978), Scaling procedures
in life events research. *J. Psychosom. Res.*, 22:525–530.
Henderson, A. S., Byrne, D. G., & Duncan-Jones, P. (1981), *Neurosis and the
Social Environment*. Sydney: Academic Press.
Herman, S., Blumenthal, J. A., Black, G. M., & Chesney, M. (1981), Self-
ratings of type A (coronary prone) adults: Do type A's know they are
type A's? *Psychosom. Med.*, 43:405–413.
Holmes, T. H., & Rahe, R. H. (1967), The Social Readjustment Rating Scale.
J. Psychosom. Res., 11:213–218.
Jenkins, C. D. (1978), A comparative review of the interview and questionnaire
methods in the assessment of the coronary prone behavior pattern. In:
Coronary Prone Behavior, ed. T. M. Dembrowski et al. New York: Springer-
Verlag.
Lazarus, R. S. (1966), *Psychological Stress and the Coping Process*. New York:
McGraw-Hill.
Lundberg, D., & Theorell, T. (1976), Scaling of life events: Difference be-
tween three diagnostic groups and between experienced and nonexper-
ienced events. *J. Hum. Stress*, 2:7–17.
Seligman, M. E. P. (1975), *Helplessness: On Depression, Development and Death*.
San Francisco: Freeman.
Siegel, J. M., Johnson, J. H., & Sarason, I. G. (1979), Mood states and the
reporting of life changes. *J. Psychosom. Res.*, 23:103–108.
Tennant, C., & Andrews, J. G. (1976), A scale to measure the stress of life
events. *Aust. & N.Z. J. Psychiat.*, 10:27–33.
———— ———— (1978), The cause of life events in neurosis. *J. Psychosom. Res.*,
22:41–45.

Theorell, T., & Rahe, R. H. (1974), Psychosocial characteristics of subjects with myocardial infarction in Stockholm. In: *Life Stress and Illness*, ed. H. Gunderson & R. H. Rahe. Springfield, IL: Charles C Thomas.

Vickers, R. (1973), A short measure of the type A personality. University of Michigan, Institute of Social Research, Ann Arbor.

Chapter 15
Stressful Life Events Associated with Bulimia in Anorexia Nervosa: Empirical Findings and Theoretical Speculations

MICHAEL STROBER, PH.D.

Recent studies (Casper, Eckert, Halmi, Goldberg, and Davis, 1980; Garfinkel, Moldofsky, and Garner, 1980; Strober, 1981; Strober, Salkin, Burroughs, and Morrell, 1982; Vandereycken and Pierloot, 1982) have drawn attention to the fact that anorexia nervosa is a clinically heterogeneous syndrome with variability among patients in personality functioning and particular aberrations in eating behavior. Although a comprehensive, empirically conceived nosology of anorexia nervosa is still lacking, there is increasing evidence that anorexics who exhibit bouts of unrestrained and excessive food consumption ("bulimics") differ from anorexics who maintain a relatively sustained pat-

Acknowledgment. This chapter was first published in *International Journal of Eating Disorders*, 3/2:3–16 (1983), and it is reprinted by permission of John Wiley & Sons, Inc.

tern of dietary restraint ("restricters") in their greater susceptibility to mood and impulse disorders, premorbid history of obesity, and intensity of family conflict.

Yet another potential distinction between these subgroups concerns the presence and cumulative severity of stressful life events preceding illness onset. Although the role of life stress in the precipitation of anorexia nervosa has received comment (Yager, Rudnick, and Metzner, 1981), prior studies in this area have not demonstrated adequate regard for precision in the sampling or quantification of event occurrences, nor are there existing data on the frequency and temporal distribution of undesirable life events in clinically heterogeneous subgroups of anorexic patients. Regarding this latter point, a wide variety of experimental studies (see Robbins and Fray, 1980) have demonstrated that aversive or stress-inducing events potentiate significant increases in food consumption in both animals and man. Although one can fault the extrapolation of laboratory animal data to complex forms of human psychopathology, there are several especially intriguing parallels between the stress-induced hyperphagic response and peculiarities of eating behavior demonstrated by the bulimic anorexic; these include a selective preference for palatable foods high in carbohydrate, stereotypy and drivenness of ingestive behavior, and irritability, finickiness, and generally heightened arousal that precedes and accompanies consummatory bouts (Johnson and Larson, 1982; Mitchell, Pyle, and Eckert, 1981; Morley and Levine, 1980; Rowland and Antelman, 1976).

Based on these considerations, this study presents data, obtained from a sample of young women with anorexia nervosa, on stressful life events preceding illness. Its major purpose is to (1) investigate comparatively the frequency and temporal distribution of event occurrences in restricter and bulimia subgroups of patients and (2) to offer several theoretically speculative analyses of the relationship between stress and bulimia in the anorexia nervosa syndrome.

METHOD

SUBJECTS

Subjects who participated in this study were consecutive admissions to the adolescent service of a large university teaching hospital satisfying DSM-III (American Psychiatric Association, 1980) criteria for a first episode of anorexia nervosa. Subjects were classified dichotomously as (1) bulimic or (2) restricter. For the purpose of this study, patients with bulimia in the absence of anorexia nervosa were excluded. Bulimia was defined as recurrent episodes of uncontrolled, rapid ingestion of excessive amounts of food leading to marked physical discomfort; by contrast, anorexics who maintained a continuous pattern of compulsive dietary control were designated restricters. Subclassification was determined on the basis of all available information concerning the subject's illness-related dietary patterns and eating behavior.

Several exclusion criteria were adopted in screening prospective subjects. (1) The first was any ambiguity surrounding the subject's dietary and intake patterns which prevented assignment to one or the other subgroup. (2) The next was an inability to date onset of illness to within a period of one month. Precise dating of onset is, of course, a necessary prerequisite for evaluating a possible empirical association between illness and preceding life stress and is necessary to avoid recording of events that may be consequences rather than antecedents of illness behavior. We defined as the date of appearance of binge eating. (3) Only subjects who were in a relatively early stage of illness were studied (duration less than one year). This criterion was imposed since it is assumed that accuracy of a person's recall of event occurrences diminishes as remoteness of the time period being recalled increases. (4) Group composition was determined by as close a matching as possible on age; social class based on the Hollingshead (1965) two-factor index; duration of illness; and percentage of weight loss from the subject's average expected weight for age and height, as determined from pediatric growth charts.

With this screening procedure, a final sample of 50 matched subjects—25 bulimics and 25 restricters—was obtained. Sample-wide means on matching variables were as follows: age, 15.6; social class, 2.5; duration of illness, 7.8 months; percentage of weight loss from average, 23.1 percent. All between-group *t*-test comparisons on these matching variables were nonsignificant.

RECORDING OF LIFE EVENTS

A semistructured interview was used to obtain information on 42 life events experienced during the 18 months preceding illness onset. All events were drawn from the inventory devised by Coddington (1972) to measure the epidemiological and adaptive correlates of stressful life changes in children and adolescents. Each event has a weighted severity rating, expressed in life change units (LCU), which is a numerically scaled estimate of the degree of readjustment that is required to cope with or accommodate to the event. The LCU was derived by querying over 200 professionals working with children as to their judgment (expressed numerically) of the intensity and time necessary for an adolescent to accommodate to a particular event. These judgments were made in relation to a modulus event, "birth of a brother or sister," which had a preassigned LCU rating of 500. The final LCU score for an event was the geometric mean of these ratings. Normative LCU values for an event was the geometric mean of these ratings. Normative LCU values for children and adolescents may be found in Coddington (1972). Thus, use of this particular inventory allowed a comparison between the present patient sample and adolescent norms.

All interviews were conducted by a trained social worker who remained blind to the hypothesis of this study. The interview was explained to the subject and her parents as a routine intake procedure conducted on all patients and family members. Thus, no specific association between life events and the initiation of anorexia nervosa was directly implied. The semi-structured technique was designed to permit flexible probing as to the general circumstances, context, and timing of each event occurrence. If an event could not be timed precisely, the best approximation within one month was sought. The interview occurred in two stages. First, each parent and the subject was seen individually, reasoning that certain subjects might choose not to divulge certain personal experiences in the presence of their parents; the family was then seen as a unit. The average intrapain correlation of aggregated stress scores was 0.69 for bulimics and 0.73 for restricters. Twenty-four subjects—12 bulimics and 12 restricters—and their parents were reinterviewed two weeks later to check the temporal stability of these data. Reliability was calculated as the percentage of original events acknowledged in the second interview. Agreement was 0.90 for bulimics and 0.94 for restricters.

STATISTICAL ANALYSES

To statistically analyze characteristics of stress changes, event occurrences were partitioned into three continuous six-month blocks (e.g., 18–13 months, 12–7 months, and 6 months prior to onset). A total score was calculated by summing the LCU values for events experienced during each of the three time blocks. Differences between groups over time were tested using repeated measures analysis of variance (ANOVA). Since bulimics were hypothesized to experience a greater incidence and cumulative severity of stress, one-tailed probability levels were used to test significance.

RESULTS

Several analyses were conducted to determine whether the data violated statistical assumptions underlying the use of repeated measures univariate procedures. Following recommendations of Bargmann (1976), several tests for homogeneity of error variances were conducted. The Hartley F_{max} did not exceed the critical ratio, indicating that the hypothesis of homogeneity of population variances was confirmed [F_{max} (2,24) = 2.06, $p >$ .05]. Next, separate chi-square statistics were computed to test the hypotheses of equality and symmetry of the population variance-covariance matrices (Box, 1950). Both were nonsignificant, X^2 (6) = 10.48, $p >$ .05 and X^2 (4) = 7.79, $p >$ .05, respectively, indicating that the ANOVA paradigm is justified.

In regard to total event incidence, bulimics incurred a mean of 16.2 events during the 18-month period, compared to 7.8 events recorded for restricters, t (48) = 9.23, $p <$ .001. Figure 15.1 summarizes the mean total event scores (LCUs) of the two groups for the three time intervals. As Figure 15.1 illustrates, there is a substantial difference between the two groups: consistent with a priori predictions, a Group X Time ANOVA with repeated measures on the time factor showed a powerful main effect of Group, $F(1,48)$ = 142.87, $p <$ .025, indicating that bulimics experienced considerably more stressful life-event changes prior to illness onset than restricters did, and that the two groups differed with respect to the temporal pattern of LCU scores. Post hoc comparisons among scores performed using tests of simple main effects revealed that differences between bulimics and restricters were significant (all $ps <$ .001) for each 6-month time block. For bulimics, the simple main effect of time was not significant, indicating that stress scores did not vary across time intervals. For restricters, the variation in LCU scores across time blocks was statistically significant, F (2,96) = 4.62, $p <$ .025. An orthogonal trend analysis showed that differences in the linear trend of LCU scores contributed significantly to the Group X Time interaction, $F(1,48)$ = 29.82, $p <$ .001. Thus, as may be seen graphically in Figure 15.1, bulimics experience little change in the overall amount of life stresss impinging on them over the 18-month period, whereas, in restricters, event occurrences begin to peak in the 6-month period immediately preceding onset.

Since it is customarily assumed that events that are socially undesirable or negative are more evocative of stress and psy-

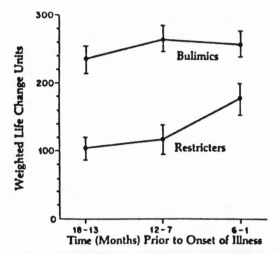

Figure 15.1.   Mean total life change unit scores (+ standard error) for bulimic and restrictor subgroups over successive six-month time blocks.

Table 15.1
**Percentage of Bulimics and Restricters Experiencing Undesirable
Life Events Preceding Illness Onset**

Event	Bulimics	Restricters	$p <$ [a]
Change in acceptance by peers	72	40	.05
Increase in number of arguments between parents	68	20	.005
Increase in arguments with parents	64	12	.001
Serious illness of parent	36	8	.05
Personal illness requiring hospitalization	28	4	.10
Not making extracurricular activity	28	8	.10
Increased father absence from home	36	8	.05
Becoming involved with drugs	20	0	.10

[a] Chi-square test, corrected for continuity; $df = 1$

chological disequilibrium, the incidence of this class of events was compared across groups. The most statistically differentiating contrasts are shown in Table 15.1. Events experienced more frequently by bulimics included alienation from peers;

marital discord; bickering with parents; personal illness requiring hospitalization; serious illness in a parent; involvement with drugs; increased absence of father from the home; and personal disappointment in the area of school activities. A further post hoc analysis showed that two or more of the events depicted in Table 15.1 were experienced by 68 percent of bulimics, compared with 24 percent of restricters ($p < .005$). This general trend was even more striking at the level of three or more events, which characterized 68 percent of bulimics but only 12 percent of restricters ($p < .001$). Thus, it is clear that bulimics experienced more life events of greater negative emotional impact than restricters did.

These contrasts gain in significance when viewed alongside normative data furnished by Coddington (1972). Coddington has reported that normal adolescent females of junior and senior high school age incur a total mean LCU score of approximately 218, based on life events recorded in a one-year time period. Tallying only those events occurring in the 12 months prior to onset yielded mean LCU scores of 522 for bulimics and 284 for restricters. Thus, using Coddington's data as a standard of reference, we see that the overall magnitude of life stress experienced by the bulimic subjects is nearly two and a half times greater than the average LCU value in a normal adolescent female cohort. It is acknowledged, however, that any use of Coddington's adolescent data for purposes of comparison poses methodologic and interpretive problems, and that a normal control group drawn from the same general community as the present cohort of anorexics could be more desirable.

Given support for the main hypothesis, one final line of analysis was pursued, based on the speculation that greater amounts of life stress would correlate with greater severity of bulimia in individual subjects. To evaluate this possibility, Pearson correlations were computed between total LCU score (tallying weighted scores for all events recorded during the 18 months) and a three-point severity rating of bulimia obtained on each bulimic subject at the time of intake. Total LCU score was also correlated with a four-point rating of the severity of depression in these subjects at intake, reasoning that the most highly stressed subjects would also exhibit increased signs of depressive affect, and that there might be significant interrelationships among stress, severity of the bulimic state, and affective change. Both of these severity ratings were made without knowledge of LCU scores, and each demonstrated high interrater reliability coefficients, $r = 0.81$ and 0.92 for bulimia and depression ratings, respectively.

Consistent with expectation, significant correlations were obtained between LCU score and severity of bulimia, r (23) $= .58$, $p < .01$; and between LCU score and depression, r (23) $= .52$, $p < .01$. It is of interest to note that severity of bulimia and depression also covaried significantly, r (23) $= .50$, $p < .01$; however, the relationship between LCU score and severity of bulimia remained even after variance attributed to depression was partialled, $r = .43$, t (22) $= 2.24$, $p < .025$.

DISCUSSION

METHODOLOGICAL LIMITATIONS

On balance, the objective findings of this study are consistent with anecdotal reports and autobiographic accounts linking stressful life events to the instigation, maintenance, and reinstatement of bulimic eating in anorexic patients. As a group, bulimics report approximately twice as many life change units as restricters do over the 18 months prior to illness onset and experience more events of an uncontrollable and undesirable nature. The time series analysis indicated that magnitude of life stress remains relatively constant for the bulimic group over 18 months, whereas in restricters life-event changes peak in the 6 months prior to onset.

The present data are preliminary and must be interpreted with caution, given the inherent problems of life-event measurement and the conceptualization of event-symptom associations. One of the problematic issues that surfaces in research of this type concerns the reliability and possible biasing of retrospective data supplied by the informants. For instance, at present we cannot be entirely certain whether or not the life-event accounts of bulimics and restricters reflect a systematic bias toward under- or over-reporting due to cohort differences in: (1) accuracy of recall and retrieval of past events; (2) cognitive style influences governing the perception, interpretation, and representation of event meaning; (3) the efficacy of coping strategies and emotional sensitivities that determine an individual's "distress threshold" and designation of an event as stressful versus benign; or, (4) degree of underlying psychopathology and persistent life strains that may dispose toward a general negatively biased perception of events as disruptive or stressful. In regard to these points, recent empirical accounts of differentiating patterns of individual psychopathology, family relationships and communicative style, genetic-risk for affective illness, and emotional expressiveness in bulimic and restricter anorexic subtypes (Casper et al., 1980; Garfinkel et al., 1980; Hudson, Pope, Jonas, and Yurgelun-Todd, 1983; Strober, 1981; Strober et al., 1982; Vandereycken and Pierloot, 1982) lead one to infer such biasing in the direction of over-reporting versus under-reporting in bulimics and restricters, respectively. On the other hand, there is no firm evidence that these confounds or measurement errors are not distributed randomly across the two subject samples. Moreover, these factors could not readily explain the greater incidence of certain undesirable events in bulimics, as was depicted in Table 15.1.

A second limitation that bears directly on interpretation of the results concerns the dating of illness onset; if unreliable, then certain purportedly antecedent events in bulimics may have actually developed as a result of disorder, thus producing a spuriously inflated event-illness association. Once again, however, this begs the question of how such a bias might operate selectively in bulimics. It seems unlikely that this is a serious flaw in the data, given that high levels of stress were already evident in bulimics as far back as 18 months prior to documented onset and that inability to fix date of onset with relative precision was grounds for exclusion from the study.

A third limitation concerns the generalizability of these findings to the anorexic population at large. Clearly, replication of the present findings with larger, more representative samples, using appropriate case-controls, is warranted before causal inferences are entertained and theoretical and clinical implications firmly established.

Lastly, even if measurement error and other potential sources of contamination prove to be inconsequential, the present study is correlational in nature and thus does not provide a clear-cut demonstration of causality. One cannot exclude the possibility that the association between increased stress and bulimia is spurious—that these stressors only mask or simply correlate with other susceptibility factors. By the same token, there may be pitfalls in using a purely quantitative score as a gauge of life stress if it is the case that only certain categories of events (e.g., undesirable, uncontrollable) rather than cumulative stress per se are relevant for onset or precipitation of eating binges. Thus, it may be more informative for future work in this area to make use of refined life inventories that divide events into these conceptually relevant categories (e.g., Dohrenwend, Krasnoff, Askenasy, and Dohrenwend, 1978). The present study is also hampered by the exclusive focus on antecedent events; the etiologic significance of concurrent events (i.e., occurring after onset of dieting and weight phobia but prior to bulimia onset), as well as the possible interactive or summative effects of stressors occurring at different time points during the course of illness in bulimic patients, remain to be elucidated by future work that involves consecutive longitudinal assessment (i.e., multitudinal assessment (i.e., multiple time point sampling) of life-event stressors (e.g., Monroe, Bellack, Hersen, and Himmelhoch, 1983).

THEORETICAL INFERENCES

The observed association between increased life stress and bulimia tempts one to make a number of interpretations of underlying mechanisms. These are clearly speculative, and it is recognized that focus on a single causative factor risks conclusions of limited generality, given the multidimensional nature of anexoria nervosa and bulimia. Thus, they are offered heuristically as a guide for future work.

One hypothesis is that bulimia is a secondary or ancillary effect of stress-precipitated deviations in monoamine, adrenocortical, or neuropeptide systems that normally organize and regulate feeding behavior (Lytle, 1977) and that are known to be activated by stressful stimulation. Supporting this hypothesis are experimental animal data showing that (1) norepinephrine administered in physiological doses directly into the medial hypothalamus induces a rapid and large feeding response directed selectively toward palatable foods which is present even in satiated rats (Leibowitz, 1980); (2) increases in food consumption associated with hypothalamic noradrenergic activation are significantly potentiated by increased adrenocortical steroid release (Leibowitz, 1980) thus suggesting possible stress-related interactions between these systems; and (3) hypothalamic administration of β-endorphin, which is known to be elevated simultaneously with plasma cortisol under stimulated conditions in animals and man (Guillemin, Vargo, Rossier, Minick, Ling, Riviser, Vale, and Bloom, 1977; Risch, Cohen, Janowsky, Kalin, and Murphy, 1980), produces large increases in food consumption which can be rapidly suppressed by opiate antagonists (Grandison and Guidotti, 1977; Morley and Levine, 1980). Other evidence (Leibowitz and Hor, 1982) indicates that this opiate-induced feeding response may be dependent on hypothalamic noradrenergic mechanisms regulating feeding behavior.

If there is some correspondence betwewen these stress-induced neurochemical deviations and bulimic eating, a theoretical question is then raised concerning the effects of chronic or repetitive stress on the auto-regulation and sensitivity of these mechanisms. In this regard, recent research on the phenomena of kindling and behavioral sensitization (Post, 1978) has demonstrated that animals and man show a potentiation of hyperactivity and stereotypy following the repeated administration of psychomotor stimulants. By extension, steadily increasing sensitization of neurochemical mechanisms regulating feeding behavior resulting from repeated stress might offer some explanation of why many patients experience their bulimic episodes to recur with increasing frequency following each successive bout, and why stressful experiences can so easily bring about the reappearance of episodes in patients who were previously abstinent.

Were one to hypothesize that stress-induced alterations in mechanisms governing feeding behavior come about in this fashion, then it may be fruitful to consider how such events interact with certain state-dependent biological concomitants of the anorexic's acute starvation and weight loss. One of the most thoroughly studied deviations is elevated rate of cortisol production (Walsh, 1980). This clinical observation bears some parallel to experimentally obtained evidence of increased adrenal steroid activity and enhanced turnover of norepinephrine in animals subjected to food deprivation (McArthur and Blundell, 1982; van der Gugten, de Kloet, Versteeg, and Slanger, 1977); it is of interest that these phenonema seem to be necessary for the normal appearance of compensatory feeding responses following states of prolonged deprivation (Leibowitz and Brown, 1980). Although the psychobiological significance of cortisol elevation in acutely disturbed anorexics has yet to be determined, if, as just noted, the adrenocortical steroids play a role in food ingestion, it may well be that more highly stressed (hence, biologically aroused) anorexics are particularly sensitive to further, malnutrition-relaxed activation of the hypothalamic-pituitary-adrenal axis and, therefore, are particularly susceptible to driven and extreme forms of compensatory feeding behavior. The strenuous physical exercise that anorexics commonly engage in is conceivably another potentiating factor since noradrenergic function is known to be elevated in states of increased physical activity (Goode, Dekirmenjian, Meltzer, and Maas, 1973). Overall, these ideas are congruent with Mawson's (1974) hypothesis that bulimic states in anorexia nervosa result from profound disruptions of the steady state noradrenergic-cholinergic regulation of feeding behavior. Whether these changes occur in anorexia nervosa is, of course, an open issue at the present time. Nonetheless, these speculations draw attention to the need for longitudinal, multivariate research designs that allow us to separate out the role of antecedent and concurrent stress in bulimia proneness and to delineate their tangled interactions with the emotional and physiological aberrations that are part of the overall clinical picture of anorexia nervosa.

A second alternative explanation of the present findings relates to the psychologically and cognitively debilitating consequences of stressful events. Laboratory and clinical studies with a variety of species (Garber, Miller, and Seaman, 1979; Maier and Seligman, 1976) have demonstrated that repeated exposure to uncontrollable aversive events results predictably in a negatively biased expectancy of diminished personal responsibility for stimulus-response outcomes. According to the theory of learned helplessness (Maier and Seligman, 1976), the causal chain that links stress to psychopathological functioning involves two central and interrelated dysfunctional processes: (1) cognitive deficit—the perception of noncontingency in response-outcome relations; and (2) motivational deficit—a reduced initiation of self-regulating or control behaviors. These deficits, it is interesting to note, do not appear to be limited to aversive experiences but have also been induced experimentally in animals exposed to noncontingent (i.e., uncontrollable appetitive events. That is, animals administered food in a random, noncontingent fashion become progressively impaired in their instrumental control and operant learning of feeding behavior (Welker, 1976; Wheatley, Welker, and Miles, 1977). Taken together, these findings support the contention that anorexics exposed to repeated stressors acquire cognitive and behavioral dispositions characterized by expectancies of lack of behavioral self-control, and that these expectancy and control deficits generalize to the regulation of consummatory behaviors. These anorexics view themselves with passive resignation and as personally helpless in the face of hunger and other appetitive stimuli that challenge their efforts at control—in short, as being capable of maintaining dietary restraint. This formulation receives some indirect support from studies (Hood, Moore, and Garner, 1982; Strober, 1982) showing that anorexics with external locus of control beliefs.

A related hypothesis views the causal chain between stress and deranged eating more simply in terms of response disinhibition and counterregulation. According to experimental studies of chronic dieters by Herman and Polivy (1975) and Polivy and Herman (1976), changes in emotionality and sympathetic arousal, such as those induced by stressful stimulation, naturally elicit behavior incompatible with the dieter's efforts to maintain restraint and, therefore, bring about eating binges as these restraints collapse to overcome the state of negative energy balance. Again, because the present study focused only on events preceding onset of abnormal dieting, the usefulness of this framework remains uncertain; however, inasmuch as control deficits produced by recurrent stress are often difficult to reverse once established (Garber et al., 1979), it seems plausible that these chronically stressed individuals become particularly susceptible to the restraint-interfering effects of stressors that impinge once pathological dieting and other anorexic symptoms have begun.

In a different vein, a Pavlovian learning interpretation of stress-induced overeating has been advanced by Robbins and Fray (1980). Noting the wide variety of stressful stimuli that can provoke feeding responses, these authors suggest that stressful stimulation, against the backdrop of prior learning and conditioning effects, induces a "general activational state which could elicit a variety of consummatory activities depending upon the goal-objects present, and the previous experience with those goal objects." This activational state is characterized by exaggerated reactivity to many different motivational cues and stimuli, of which food is particularly salient in the human environment—being found in a variety of emotional experiences. Robbins and Fray additionally maintain that once stress and increased food consumption are temporally related, secondary metabolic effects conditionally reinforce this association; thus, over time, stressful states spontaneously evoke increased reactivity to food-related stimuli and become potent signals for food seeking, regardless of the organism's energy needs at the moment. Although there is little convincing evidence that food ingestion actually reduces subjective experiences of discomfort, at least judging from studies of normal and obese individuals (Robbins and Fray, 1980), clinical impression and recent objective analysis of the binge-purge cycle in women with bulimia (Johnson and Larson, 1982) suggest that binging effectively distracts attention away from core dysphoric states relating to the bulimic's low self-esteem and ineffectiveness, and that completion of the binge-purge cycle brings considerable tension reduction. Hence, the overall emotional context in which this behavior evolves and the response-contingent attenuation of tension/dysphoric states may well maintain and further reinforce its occurrence.

CONCLUSION

This chapter sets forth a number of methodological and theoretical issues concerning the contributory role of stress in the etiology and maintenance of bulimia in anorexia nervosa patients. Several alternative speculations have been advanced. These are not assumed to be mutually exclusive and in many ways complement one another. For instance, a growing body of data (Depue, 1979) supports the idea that coping strategies, cognitive attributions, and social support mediate both the emotional and physiochemical impact of stressful events. And adding to this the hypothesized role of genetic factors in regulating metabolic responses to stressful stimulation (Stolk and Nisula, 1979), it would seem plausible that stress, biological activation, cognitive appraisal, restraint, and conditioning of feeding behavior are more meaningfully considered as interactive and interdependent phenomena. This fact once again reemphasized the possible far-reaching significance of heterogeneity in family psychiatric history, developmental background, and personality functioning among bulimic and restricter anorexics (Strober, 1983). The very complexity of anorexia nervosa and bulimia indicates the heuristic value of multicausation models of research.

To reiterate the caveats noted above, these interpretations are preliminary and rest in large measure on suggestive parallels between stress-induced eating in animals and bulimia in humans. Whether these formulations are also relevant for understanding the phenomenon of bulimia in normal-weight individuals remains an open question. It is hoped that future research will qualify, extend, or refute these propositions.

REFERENCES

American Psychiatric Association (1980), *Diagnostic and Statistical Manual of Mental Disorders*, 3rd ed. Washington, DC: American Psychiatric Association.

Bargmann, R. A. (1976), A study of dependence in multivariate normal analyses. Institute for Statistics Mimeograph.

Beumont, P. J. V., George, G. C. W., & Smart, D. E. (1976), "Dieters" and "vomiters and purgers" in anorexia nervosa. *Psychol. Med.*, 6:617–622.

Box, G. E. P. (1950), Problems in the analysis of growth and war curves. *Biometrics*, 6:362–389.

Casper, R. C., Eckert, E. D., Halmi, K. A., Goldberg, S. C., & Davis, J. M. (1980), Bulimia: Its incidence and clinical importance in patients with anorexia nervosa. *Arch. Gen. Psychiat.*, 37:1030–1035.

Coddington, R. D. (1972), The significance of life events as etiologic factors in the disease of children. I. A survey of professional workers. *J. Psychosom. Res.*, 16:7–18.

Depue, R. A. (1979), *The Psychobiology of the Depressive Disorders: Implications for the Effects of Stress*. New York: Academic Press.

Dohrenwend, B. S., Krasnoff, L., Askenasy, A. R., & Dohrenwend, B. P. (1978), Exemplification of a method for scaling life events: The PERI life events scale. *J. Health & Soc. Behav.*, 19:205–229.

Garber, J., Miller, W. R., & Seaman, S. F. (1979), Learned helplessness, stress, and depressive disorders. In: *Psychobiology of the Depressive Disorders: Implications for the Effects of Stress*, ed. R. A. Depue. New York: Academic Press, pp. 121–136.

Garfinkel, P. E., Moldofsky, H., & Garner, D. M. (1980), The heterogeneity of anorexia nervosa: Bulimia as a distinct subgroup. *Arch. Gen. Psychiat.*, 37:1036–1040.

Goode, D. J., Dekirmenjian, H., Meltzer, H. Y., & Maas, J. W. (1973), Relation of exercise to MHPG excretion in normal subjects. *Arch. Gen. Psychiat.*, 29:391–396.

Grandison, L., & Guidotti, A. (1977), Stimulation of food intake by muscimol and beta endorphin. *Neuropharmaco.*, 16:533–536.

Guillemin, R., Vargo, T., Rossier, J., Minick, S., Ling, N., Riviser, C., Vale, W., & Bloom, F. (1977), β-endorphin and adrenocorticotropin are secreted concomitantly by the pituitary gland. *Science*, 197:1367–1369.

Herman, C. P., & Polivy, J. (1975), Anxiety, restraint, and eating behavior. *J. Abnorm. Psychol.*, 84:666–672.

Hollingshead, A. B. (1965), Two factor index of social position. New Haven: Yale Station.

Hood, J., Moore T. E., & Garner, D. (1982), Locus of control as a measure of ineffectiveness in anorexia nervosa. *J. Consult. & Clin. Psychol.*, 50:3–13.

Hudson, J. I., Pope, H. G., Jonas, J. M., & Yurgelun-Todd, D. (1983), Family history study of anorexia nervosa and bulimia. *Brit. J. Psychiat.*, 142:133–138.

Johnson, C., & Larson, R. (1982), An analysis of moods and behavior. *Psychosom. Med.*, 44:341–352.

Leibowitz, S. F. (1980), Neurochemical systems of the hypothalamus: Control of feeding and drinking behavior and water-electrolyte excretion. In: *Handbook of the Hypothalamus*, Vol. 3A, ed. P. J. Morgane & J. Panksepp. New York: Marcel Dekker, pp. 286–294.

——— Brown, L. L. (1980), Analysis of behavioral deficits produced by lesions in the dorsal and ventral midbrain tegmentum. *Physiol. & Behav.*, 25:829–843.

——— Hor, L. (1982), Endorphinergic and a-noradrenergic systems in the paraventricular nucleus: Effects on eating behavior. *Peptides*, 3:421–428.

Lytle, L. D. (1977), Control of eating behavior. In: *Nutrition and the Brain*, ed. R. J. Wurtman & J. J. Wurtman. New York: Raven Press.

Maier, S. F., & Seligman, M. E. P. (1976), Learned helplessness: Theory and evidence. *J. Exp. Psychol.*, 105:3–46.

Mawson, A. R. (1974), Anorexia nervosa and the regulation of intake: A review. *Psychol. Med.*, 4:289–308.

McArthur, R. A., & Blundell, J. E. (1982), Effects of age and feeding regimen on protein and carbohydrate self-selection. *Appetite*, 3:153–162.

Mitchell, J. E., Pyle, R. L., & Eckert, E. D. (1981), Binge eating behavior in patients with bulimia. *Amer. J. Psychiat.*, 138:835–836.

Monroe, S. M., Bellack, A. S., Hersen, M., & Himmelhoch, J. M. (1983), Life events, symptoms course, and treatment outcome in unipolar depressed women. *J. Consult. & Clin. Psychol.*, 51:604–615.

Morley, J. E., & Levine, A. S. (1980), Stress-induced eating is mediated through endogenous opiates. *Science*, 209:1259–1260.

Polivy, J., & Herman, C. P. (1976), Clinical depression and weight change: A complex relation. *J. Abnorm. Psychol.*, 85:338–340.

Post, R. M. (1978), Frontiers in affective disorder research: New pharmacological agents and new methodologies. In: *Psychopharmacology: A Generation in Progress*, ed. M. A. Lipton, A. DiMascio, & K. F. Killam. New York: Raven Press, pp. 411–418.

Risch, S. S., Cohen, R. M., Janowsky, D. S., Kalin, N. H., & Murphy, D. L. (1980), Mood and behavioral effects of physostigmine on humans are accompanied by elevations in plasm β-endorphin and cortisol. *Science*, 209:1545–1546.

Robbins, T. W., & Fray, P. J. (1980), Stress-induced eating: Fact, fiction, or misunderstanding? *Appetite*, 1:103–133.

Rowland, N. W., & Antelman, S. M. (1976), Stress-induced hyperphagia and obesity in rats: A possible model for understanding human obesity. *Science*, 191:310–312.

Stolk, J. M., & Nisula, B. C. (1979), Genetic influences on catecholamine metabolism. In: *The Psychobiology of Depressive Disorders: Implications for the Effects of Stress*, ed. R. A. Depue. New York: Academic Press, pp. 67–73.

Strober, M. (1981), The significance of bulimia in juvenile anorexia nervosa: An exploration of possible etiologic factors. *Int. J. Eating Dis.*, 1:28–43.

———— (1982), Locus of control, psychopathology, and weight gain in juvenile anorexia nervosa. *J. Abnorm. Psychol.*, 10:97–106.

———— (1983), An empirically derived typology of anorexia nervosa. In: *Anorexia Nervosa: Recent Developments in Research*. New York: Alan R. Liss.

———— Salkin, B., Burroughs, J., & Morrell, W. (1982), Validity of the bulimia-restricter distinction in anorexia nervosa: Parental personality characteristics and family psychiatric morbidity. *J. Nerv. & Ment. Dis.*, 170:345–351.

Vandereycken, W., & Pierloot, R. (1982), The significance of subclassification in anorexia nervosa: A comparative study of clinical features in 141 patients. *Psychol. Med.*, 66/6:445–450.

van der Gugten, J., de Kloet, E. R., Versteeg, D. H. G., & Slanger, J. L. (1977), Regional hypothalamic catecholamine metabolism and food intake regulation in the rat. *Brain Res.*, 135:325–336.

Walsh, B. T. (1980), The endocrinology of anorexia nervosa. *Psychiat. Clin. N. Amer.*, 3:299–312.

Welker, R. L. (1976), Acquisition of a free-operant-appetitive response in pigeons as a function of prior experience with response-independent food. *Learn. & Motivation*, 7:394–405.

Wheatley, K. L., Welker, R. L., & Miles, R. C. (1977), Acquisition of bar pressing in rats following experience with response independent food. *Animal Learn. & Behav.*, 5:236–242.

Yager, J., Rudnick, F. D., & Metzner, R. J. (1981), Anorexia nervosa: A current perspective and new directions. In: *From Research to Practice: Biobehavioral Contributions*, ed. E. Serafetinides. New York: Grune & Stratton, pp. 118–129.

Chapter 16
Life Stress Measures and Reported Frequency of Sleep Disorders

ZACK ZDENEK CERNOVSKY, PH.D.

Experimental studies have shown that emotionally intensive presleep experiences alter sleep parameters (Goodenough, Witkin, Koulack, and Cohen, 1975; Witkin, 1969) and/or dream content (Breger, Hunter, and Lane, 1971; De Koninck and Koulack, 1975). Unplanned, highly aversive life events such as war, imprisonment, or accidents have been clinically observed to modify human sleep qualitatively in an aversive manner (Grinker and Spiegel, 1945; Oppenheim, 1889; Trautman, 1964). Recently, using a list of life events, Healey, Kales, Monroe, Bixler, Chamberlin, and Soldatos (1981) demonstrated that the onset of insomnia in chronic insomniacs was preceded by a greater number of stressful events than the number experienced by good sleepers during a time interval of the same length. Similarly, the goal of the present study was to estimate the size of association of sleep disorders, including insomnia, to two different questionnaire measures of life stress or change.

Acknowledgment. This chapter was first published in *Perceptual and Motor Skills* (1984), 58:39–49, and it is reprinted by permission of author and publisher.

257

The two questionnaires were the Social Readjustment Rating Scale (Holmes and Rahe, 1967), which was also used in the insomnia study by Healey et al., and the Life Events Inventory (Tennant and Andrews, 1976).

The Social Readjustment Rating Scale was chosen because it is widely used, which allows the comparisons of present findings to results published by other investigators such as correlations of the Readjustment Scale scores to symptoms other than sleep disorders [see an anthology by Dohrenwend and Dohrenwend (1974)]. The Life Events Inventory was selected because this list of events can be scored in several manners: for the extent of life change, amount of distress, and for the degree of control or choice over the incidence of the event. Although many investigators (Holmes and Masuda, 1974; Rahe, 1974; Wildman and Johnson, 1977) reported that their data indicated that the amount of life change per se rather than the desirability of the event is the decisive element in the illness-generating impact of life events, there is also evidence at present that undesirable events are more closely associated with the occurrence of pathology than are desirable events (Crandall and Lehman, 1977; Mueller, Edwards, and Yarvis, 1977; Paykel, 1974; Sarason, Johnson, and Siegel, 1978; Vinokur and Selzer, 1975). The Social Readjustment Rating Scale is not well suited for comparisons of the impact of any life change with the impact of negative life changes specifically. Although the inventory includes some clearly aversive events and their relationship to insomnia has already been documented elsewhere (Healey et al., 1981), the number of clearly negative events is smaller than the number of events scored for life change per se and might be too short to allow comparisons of the impact of undesirable life change with life change generally. This complication is avoided when measures of change and of distress of the Life Events Inventory are included in similar comparisons; both are based on an identical list of events. Another advantage of the Life Events Inventory, as mentioned earlier, is its scales for the degree of control over events. The degree of control has significantly differentiated between suicide attempters and normals, in respect to the type of events experienced by the two groups (Paykel, Prusoff, and Myers, 1975). The lack of control over life events was expected, in the present study, to be associated with an increased incidence of sleep disorders.

Many researchers have found that working with unweighted scores for life change (each event, regardless of importance, being assigned one point) leads to equally good (or superior) results as does differential weighting of events (Paykel et al., 1975). This stands in considerable contrast with the effort of others, e.g., the authors of the Readjustment Scale and Life Events Inventory, to weight the events. To provide more data on this controversial issue, effects of weighted and unweighted scores were compared in the present study. The use of both weighted and unweighted scores is likely to appear as clinically irrelevant to some readers, however, such comparisons are badly needed for advancing knowledge of event-illness associations [see a review of life events assessment by Monroe (1982)].

Many types of life-event scores were included in the computations, with the goal of evaluating their relationship to self-reported incidence of sleep disorders. The group of sleep disorders included nightmares (defined in questionnaire items as "any frightening dream"), difficulty falling asleep, waking up at night, unrefreshing sleep, and restless (not quiet) sleep.

METHOD

SUBJECTS

Sample A. One hundred and seventy part-time students enrolled in undergraduate psychology courses in U.S. military settings participated. They were members of the military or family members of military staff. Their ages ranged from 18 to 55 years; mean age was 27.4 years (SD = 7 years). Ninety-seven were men (mean age 27.7 years, SD = 7.4 years) and 73 were women (mean age 27.0 years, SD = 6.6 years). The majority

were married (117 persons); 50 were divorced, single, separated, or widowed, and the remaining three students did not
indicate their status.

Sample B. This group included 91 persons recruited from
the same settings as members of Sample A. Their ages ranged
from 18 to 45 years, and mean age was 26.0 years (SD = 6.3
years). Fifty-three were men (mean age 27.1 years, SD = 6.4
years) and 37 were women (mean age 24.4 years, SD = 5.8
years); gender information was not indicated by one student.
Fifty-two were married and 38 were single, divorced, or separated; this information was missing for one person.

PROCEDURE

The participants received questionnaires to be completed anon-
ymously on a volunteer basis. The questionnaire administered
to Sample A included the Social Readjustment Rating Scale, the
Lie Scale of the MMPI, a set of items dealing with incidence of
sleep disorders and with dream recall frequency. The following
events listed in the Readjustment Scale were counted as undesirable in subsequent analysis of data: death of spouse, divorce, marital separation, jail term, death of close family
member, personal injury or illness, fired at work, sex difficulties, death of close friend, mortgage over $10,000, foreclosure
of mortgage or loan, trouble with in-laws, trouble with boss,
mortgage or loan less than $10,000, and minor violations of the
law. No comparable score for desirable events was calculated
because too few events in the Readjustment Scale are clearly
positive. The added instructions indicated that every event
should be checked which has occurred within the last six
months; the same time span was delineated for the recall of
nightmares and other sleep disorders and of non-nightmare
dreams.

To indicate their nightmare recall frequency, the students
were to circle a number in the following row which would be
the closest to the number of nightmares they had in the last six
months: 0, 1, 2, 3, 4, 5, 6, 7, 8, 9, 10, 12, 15, 20, 30, 40, 50, or

to circle a statement "more than 59 times." The frequency of dream recall was assessed in an identical manner. Several additional questions dealt with dream and nightmare content.

Incidence of insomnia and related disorders was assessed by the following four items: How often did you have difficulties falling asleep?, How often have you awakened during your sleep time and had difficulties falling asleep again?, How often have you felt that your sleep did not refresh you as it usually does?, and How often have you felt that your sleep was not quiet, i.e., you were moving restlessly or feeling tense or speaking, etc., while asleep? It was emphasized that only disturbances not caused by extremes of climate, outside noise, thirst, etc., should be reported. The frequency of each disorder during the previous 6 months was to be indicated by choosing one of five answer possibilities: never (scored as 0), once or twice (scored as 1 point), nearly once a month (scored as 2), nearly once a week (score of 3), and more often (score of 4). The score value in parentheses indicates computational values assigned to answers in the analysis of the data.

The questionnaires administered to persons in Sample B differed only in that the Readjustment Scale was replaced by the Life Events Inventory and the Lie Scale of the MMPI was omitted because no pathological elevations on this scale were observed for Sample A and preliminary analyses of the data on Sample A (available prior to data collection on Sample B) showed no significant correlations of the LIE scores with life event and sleep disorder variables.

RESULTS

Mean number of reported events was similar for the Readjustment Scale ($M = 8.4$, SD $= 5.3$) and for the Life Events Inventory ($M = 7.8$, SD $= 3.4$). Average weighted score on the former was 193.6 (SD $= 120.4$). Average score for life change on the latter was 134.5 (SD $= 71.8$), and its average score for

distress was 72.5 (SD = 49.2). Mean number of reported nightmares was similar for Sample A (M = 2.7, SD = 3.6) and
Sample B (M = 3.4, SD = 6.8). Mean composite score for
insomniac disorders (sum of scores for difficulties falling asleep,
maintaining sleep, and unrefreshing sleep, and not quiet sleep)
was also closely comparable for Sample A (M = 6.6, SD = 4.0)
and Sample B (M = 6.9, SD = 4.). As explained earlier, all
reported frequencies of events or sleep disorders are for the
six-month period preceding the investigation.

Sixty percent in Sample B and 59.4 percent in Sample A
reported at least one nightmare. The proportions of those who
reported no difficulties falling asleep, sleep maintenance problems, unrefreshing sleep, and restless sleep were, in order, 12.4,
23.5, 12.4, and 21.8 percent for each variable in Sample A and
11.1, 20, 14.3, and 20 percent in Sample B. For all four variables
and some other variables in both samples, the distribution of
scores was positively skewed and the measures were not based
on interval scales. The basic assumptions for the use of Pearson
rs were violated. However, Havlicek and Peterson (1977) have
recently demonstrated that Pearson's coefficients are quite insensitive to similar violations of the basic assumptions of normality and the type of measurement. In the present study,
Pearson rs were used to evaluate the size of relationships.

The major concern was the relationship of scores based on
incidence of life events to scores dealing with sleep disorders.
The scattergrams of the relationships did not suggest any strong
curvilinear trends. The coefficients computed between the two
sets of variables are listed in Table 16.1 (see first seven columns
of coefficients, counting from left to right).

The relationships of sleep disorders to scores on the Readjustment Scale were weak and often nonsignificant, especially
the relationships based on life change rather than on aversive
life-change scores. It should, however, be noted that all relationships of negative events to variables of sleep disorders were
significant and contrast with those between life change and
sleep disorders. The use of unweighted as opposed to weighted

Table 16.1

Relationship of Scores on Social Readjustment Rating Scale and Life Events Inventory to Reports of Sleep Disorders and to Personality Variables ($n = 170$ for the Readjustment Scale and $n = 91$ for the Life-Events Inventory)

Sleep variables	Readjustment						Life-Event Inventory							
	All events		Negative events		Life change		Dis-tress	Negative events		Positive events		Difference index	
	W[a]	U/W[b]	W	U/W	W	U/W	W	W	U/W	W	U/W	W	U/W
All sleep disorders	.17*	.17*	.28**	.27**	.07	.06	.18**	.16	.19*	-.14	-.12	.22*	.24*
Nightmare frequency	.23**	.24**	.24**	.26**	.11	.18*	.14	.29**	-.13	.13	-.04	-.28**	.13
Insomniac disorders	.12	.11	.24**	.22**	.05	.02	.15	.11	.16	-.14	-.12	.19*	.22*
Falling asleep	.01	.02	.16*	.15*	-.06	-.06	.07	.07	.12	-.13	-.14	.14	.19
Waking up	.12	.13	.28**	.24**	.09	.03	.18*	.11	.19*	-.11	-.09	.16	.22*
Unfreshing sleep	.14	.12	.15*	.15*	.02	-.02	.04	.00	.04	-.17	-.13	.10	.12
Not quiet sleep	.12	.10	.19*	.19*	.08	.03	.10	.05	.09	-.08	-.05	.09	.10
Personality variables													
Age	-.34**	-.35**	-.17*	-.24**	.04	-.05	-.05	-.16	-.09	.01	.13	-.16	-.16
Sex	.00	.02	.10	.03	-.05	-.05	-.06	.02	-.06	-.06	-.02	.05	.04
Dream f	-.01	.04	.01	-.05**	-.02	.03	-.05	-.07	-.08	.04	.00	-.09	-.06

a Weighted. b Unweighted. *.05 (one-tailed). **.01 (one-tailed).
Note—Insomniac disorders is a variable formed by adding scores on difficulties falling asleep, waking during sleep time, nonrefreshing sleep, and not quiet sleep. All sleep disorders is a variable formed by the score for insomniac disorders to the frequency of nightmare recall. The weights assigned to the Readjustment Scale items are listed in Holms and Rahe (1967); the weights of Life-Event Inventory items are listed in Tennant and Andrews (1976).

life-event scores did not lead to marked differences in correlational patterns.

The Life Events Inventory measures were mostly unrelated to sleep disorder scores. It is possible that the inventory includes too many ambiguous events not sufficiently related to aversive life change. To examine this assumption, the listed events were evaluated in respect to their desirability and a group of 36 clearly negative events and a group of 14 clearly positive events were formed to serve as indices of negative life change and of positive life change, respectively. In addition to the two new measured, a difference index was calculated by subtracting the positive from the negative events index. The three indices were included in the analysis of data both with weighted and with unweighted score values and led to six new variables. Their relationship to sleep disorder measures was also estimated by means of Pearson rs; the coefficients are listed in Table 16.1 (see last six columns of coefficients on the right side of the table). Again, the relationships were weak and mostly non-significant, especially those between positive events and sleep disorders. Only the use of the weighted difference index resulted in a more marked increase in number of significant coefficients in the expected direction: The more extreme (in the undesirable direction) the balance between positive and negative events, the more frequent were the sleep disruptions.

Further analysis examined whether the relationships of scores on the Social Readjustment Rating Scale to insomnia measures were not confounded by other personality variables. In the present sample, age seemed to be such a potentially confounding variable with a depressing effect on rs computed between insomnia and Readjustment Scale scores for the following reason. As shown in Table 16.1, younger persons experienced both more life change and more negative events listed in the Scale. High scores in the present sample tended to be younger than low scorers. Insomnia has been observed to be more common in advanced age groups (Mendelson, Gillin, and Wyatt, 1977); however, in the present sample, older persons were more likely to experience less life change or stressful life change and so were perhaps more sheltered from the consequences of life stress such as insomnia. The interaction of these factors working in opposite directions along the age dimension could explain why, in the present sample, the correlations between age and insomnia variables were low (absolute value not exceeding .07) and nonsignificant. It is possible that high scores on the Readjustment Scale in the present sample would be more clearly related to insomnia if the sample were more homogeneous in respect to age, e.g., upon exclusion of older persons, i.e., of insomnia-prone but low Readjustment Scale scores. For this reason, the correlation matrix was recomputed for persons between 20 and 30 years of age ($N = 110$) without, however, finding the expected increase in size of coefficients. The lack of stronger relationships of negative events to insomnia variables did not primarily seem to result from an underlying relationship of age to insomniac disorders.

The effect of degree of control over events on the relationship of events to sleep disorders was examined by using three types of weights developed for each event in the Life Events Inventory by Tennant and Andrews (1977). The first indicates the degree of control a person usually has over the incidence of the event, the second the extent to which the incidence of the event is usually attributed to chance alone, and the third the extent to which the event is under the control of other people. The relationships of the three control measures to scores for sleep disorders were nonsignificant ($p > .05$, one-tailed) except the relationship of the nightmare recall frequency to scores for events controlled by chance alone ($r = .20$) and scores for events controlled by others ($r = .18$).

Some unanticipated trends in gender differences emerged, all of which involved only the Life Events Inventory but not the Readjustment Scale measures. Above all, the trends were present in the relationships of the nightmare recall frequency to both the number of negative events ($r = .48$ for women and .00 for men) and to scores for events controlled by chance alone ($r = .39$ for women and $- .04$ for men). Although the size of the differences when tested via Fisher's z transformation of rs appeared as significant with a criterion of a $p < .05$ (two-tailed), the difference did not reach $p < .01$ (two-tailed) which was adopted as a criterion in the present study because there were a very large number of possible similar differences, none of which was anticipated prior to computational analyses.

No comparable gender-linked trends in differences in correlational patterns were observed for other groups of rs. Similarly, when Pearson rs were computed to evaluate relationships of personality variables (age, sex, and marital status) to both sleep disorders and life-event measures, no significant ($p < .01$, two-tailed) coefficients were found except the relationship of age to Readjustment Scale scores (Table 16.1) mentioned earlier and a relationship of the nightmare recall frequency to gender found in Sample A ($r = .36$): Women reported more nightmares. This trend was not significant for Sample B ($r = .20$). Again, the criterion of significance was $p <$ to .01 (two-tailed) because there were a large number of coefficients and a lack of specific expectations in respect to the direction of relationships.

The events in Life Events Inventory are divided by Tennant and Andrews (1976) into eight categories according to their content: health, bereavement, family and social, friends and relatives, education, work, moving house, and financial and legal. To examine whether events in any of the categories were more clearly related to sleep disorders than were other categories of events, a correlation matrix was computed between scores for each category and all sleep-disorder variables. The data were computed three times, with each event being assigned one point (i.e., with unweighted scores for life change in the second and with weighted scores for amount of distress in the last series of computations). The number of coefficients was large ($N = 168$) but only eight reached $p < .05$ (one-tailed). Their size was small and two were in a direction opposite to that expected. The only relationship which would withstand attempts to eliminate chance findings by adopting a more stringent criterion of significance ($p < .01$, two-tailed) was between the nightmare recall frequency and weighted scores (weightings for life change) in the category health, i.e., a relationship which could be based on an association of nightmares with somatic dysfunctions generally rather than with the stress implied by theories of life change.

Finally, an attempt was made to examine whether any single event listed in the two inventories had, when considered alone, a noticeable impact on the sleep measures. To avoid unreliable findings, only events reported by at least 10 persons were included in the analysis. Pearson rs were computed for the relationships of all eligible events to the sleep-disorder variables but the search for any coefficients larger than .30 (an arbitrarily set criterion to avoid or minimize both chance level and weak findings on two samples of different size) led only to two rs: The nightmare recall frequency was related to reports of being separated from someone important to the person ($r = .34$) and to reports of moderate financial difficulties ($r = .31$).

DISCUSSION

Similarly to results of the recent insomnia study by Healey et al. (1981), a small subgroup of negative events of the Readjustment Scale emerged as the variable with the most clearly marked relationships to reports of sleep disorders. Even the largest coefficients, however, suggested that the relationships are weak and do not present any evidence for a causal relationship. A different study design, e.g., cross-lagged correlational studies (Kenny, 1975), would be more helpful in this latter respect. In fact, the weak association between reports of events and of sleep disorders could easily be accounted for by memory or attitudinal factors such as a readiness to recall and report negative personal experiences; both negative events and experiences of sleep disorders are negative personal experiences and the correlation between the two types of negative experiences could be spurious. If positive or neutral experiences were also involved, the rs computed between variables such as the dream recall frequency and scores for life events would be higher than in the present study (all 13 rs were low and nonsignificant, see Table 16.1). Research is needed on the influence of personality factors on key correlational findings in similar studies based exclusively on self-report data: The correlations could be spurious. Another problem arises from the large number of Pearson rs computed in the present study ($N = 1171$). Many of them may be significant by chance: the results should not be overinterpreted. Replications are needed.

To examine an opposite viewpoint, the failure to find stronger support for the clinical lore that aversive events do disrupt sleep could reflect several things. First, many highly personal negative life experiences are listed neither in the Readjustment Scale nor in the Life Events Inventory, e.g., subtle emotional problems in close relationships. Second, the inaccuracy of measures inherent in similar retrospective reports based not only on memory but also on other factors such as perceived social desirability could somewhat distort the results. Third, intervening social support (Dean and Lin, 1977) or personality variables which modify the effects of exposurer to life stress might minimize the size of coefficients computed to estimate the relationship of stress to symptoms; see a review by Johnson and Sarason (1979). Fourth, the effect of events on sleep disorders may have been delayed. A similar delayed effect has been clinically observed in war veterans (Horowitz and Solomon, 1975).

A further complication lies in the possibility that different types of stressful life events result in specifically different pathological symptoms. There is need to counteract an unthinking belief in widely used global measures of life change or distress. Listing which events or clusters of single events, from those included in global inventory measures, were significantly related to a specific symptom or syndrome could, at the least, provide some negative findings. For example, in the present study, many markedly negative events had occurred too infrequently for statistical analysis and the relationships of the remaining single events to sleep disorders were weak and often nonsignificant. It seems that in spite of many studies the hypothesized (and clinically assumed) relationship of events to symptoms still remains a largely unmapped territory in need of extensive research.

REFERENCES

Breger, L., Hunter, I., & Lane, R. W. (1971), *The Effects of Stress on Dreams*. *Psychol. Issues*, Monogr. 27. New York: International Universities Press.

Crandall, J. E., & Lehman, R. E. (1977), Relationship of stressful life events to social interest, locus of control, and psychological maladjustment. *J. Consult. & Clin. Psychol.*, 45:1208.

Dean, A., & Lin, N. (1977), The stress buffering role of social support. *J. Nerv. & Ment. Dis.*, 165:403–417.

De Koninck, J. M., & Koulack, D. (1975), Dream content and adaptation to stressful situation. *J. Abnorm. Psychol.*, 84:250–260.

Dohrenwend, B. S., & Dohrenwend, B. P. (1974), *Stressful Life Events: Their Nature and Effects*. New York: John Wiley.

Goodenough, D. R., Witkin, H. A., Koulack, D., & Cohen, H. (1975), The effects of stress films on dream affect and on respiration and eye movement activity during REM sleep. *Psychophys.*, 12:313–320.

Grinker, R. R., & Spiegel, J. P. (1945), *Men Under Stress*. Philadelphia: Blakiston.

Havlicek, L. L., & Peterson, N. L. (1977), Effect of the violation of assumptions upon significance levels of the Pearson r. *Psychol. Bull.*, 84:373–377.

Healey, E. S., Kales, A., Monroe, L. J., Bixler, E. O., Chamberlin, K., & Soldatos, C. R. (1981), Onset of insomnia: Role of life-stress events. *Psychosom. Med.*, 43:439–451.

Holmes, T. H., & Masuda, M. (1974), Life change and illness susceptibility. In: *Stressful Life Events: Their Nature and Effects*, ed. B. S. Dohrenwend & B. P. Dohrenwend. New York: John Wiley, pp. 45–72.

——— Rahe, R. H. (1967), The Social Readjustment Rating Scale. *J. Psychosom. Res.*, 11:213–218.

Horowitz, M. J., & Solomon, G. F. (1975), A prediction of delayed stress response syndromes in Vietnam veterans. *J. Soc. Issues*, 31:67–80.

Johnson, J. H., & Sarason, I. G. (1977), Recent developments in research on life stress. In: *Human Stress and Cognition*, ed. V. Hamilton & D. M. Warbuton. New York: Plenum, pp. 24–29.

Kenmy, K. A. (1975), Cross-lagged panel correlation: A test for spurious. *Psychol. Bull.*, 82:887–903.

Mendelson, W. B., Gillin, J. D., & Wyatt, R. J. (1977), *Human Sleep and Its Disorders.* New York: Plenum.

Monroe, S. M. (1982), Life events assessment: Current practices, emerging trends. *Clin. Psychol. Rev.,* 2:435–453.

Mueller, D. P., Edwards, D. W., & Yarvis, R. M. (1977), Stressful life events, and psychiatric symptomatology: Change or undesirability? *J. Health & Soc. Behav.,* 18:307–317.

Oppenheim, H. (1889), *Die traumatischen Neurosen.* Berlin: Hirschwald.

Paykel, E. S. (1974), Life stress and psychiatric disorders. In: *Stressful Life Events: Their Nature and Effects,* ed. B. S. Dohrenwend & B. P. Dohrenwend. New York: John Wiley, pp. 135–149.

Paykel, E. W., Prusoff, B. A., & Myers, J. K. (1975), Suicide attempts and recent life events. *Arch. Gen. Psychiat.,* 32:327–333.

Rahe, R. H. (1974), The pathway between subjects' recent life changes and their near future illness reports. In: *Stressful Life Events: Their Nature and Effects,* ed. B. S. Dohrenwend & B. P. Dohrenwend. New York: John Wiley, pp. 73–86.

Sarason, I. G., Johnson, J. H., & Siegel, J. M. (1978), Assessing the impact of life change. *J. Consult. & Clin. Psychol.,* 46:932–946.

Tennant, C., & Andrews, G. (1976), A scale to measure the stress of life events. *Aust. & N.Z. J. Psychiat.,* 10:27–32.

——— ——— (1977), A scale to measure the cause of life events. *Aust. & N.Z. J. Psychiat.,* 11:163–167.

Trautman, E. C. (1964), Fear and panic in Nazi concentration camps. *Inter. J. Soc. Psychiat.,* 10:134–141.

Vinokur, A., & Selzer, M. L. (1975), Desirable versus undesirable life events: Their relationship to stress and mental distress. *J. Person. & Soc. Psychol.,* 32:329–337.

Wildman, R. C., & Johnson, D. R. (1977), Life change and Langner's 22-item mental health index: Study and partial replication. *J. Health & Soc. Behav.,* 18:179–188.

Witkin, H. A. (1969), Influencing dream content. In: *Dream Psychology and the New Biology of Dreaming,* ed. M. Kramer. Springfield, IL: Charles C Thomas, pp. 285–359.

Chapter 17
Dysfunctional Uterine Bleeding and Prior Life Stress

FRED TUDIVER, M.D., C.C.F.P.

Dysfunctional uterine bleeding (DUB) with its various synonyms (e.g., functional uterine bleeding) is an often seen but poorly understood entity. It is usually defined as abnormal menstrual bleeding in which organic lesions cannot be detected by ordinary means. (Kistner, 1971; Chamberlain, 1981). Examples of DUB include problems of menstrual irregularity and bleeding difficulties (ranging from menorrhagia to secondary amenorrhea) in the absence of organic disease or pregnancy. DUB is commonly seen during the extremes of the fertile period —menarche and menopause. At these times it is often easily explained in terms of hormonal disequilibrium. The cause of DUB between those extremes, however, is usually not known.

The cause has been made for a psychoemotional cause of DUB. Secondary amenorrhea has been found to be related to the stress of being an inmate during war (Whitacre and Barrera, 1944; Drew, 1961), and to stresses such as entering college or awaiting execution (Sydenham, 1946; Osofsky and Fisher,

Acknowledgment. This chapter was first published in *Journal of Family Practice* (1983), 17/6:999–1003, and it is reprinted by permission.

1967; Singh, 1981). Other researchers found secondary amen-orrhea and dysmenorrhea more common in certain psychiatric patients (Kelly, Daniels, and Poe, 1954; Gregory, 1957; Dia-mond, Rubinstein, Dunner, and Fiere, 1976; Coppen, 1965). More recent stress-related research has used the Social Read-justment Scale (Holmes and Rahe, 1967) to relate life changes to illness (Theorell and Rahe, 1971; Perlman, Ferguson, and Bergum, 1975) as well as the Schedule of Recent Experiences (Rahe, 1975) which uses self-scored stress value estimates for experienced life changes. Using these new stress questionnaires, some researchers have found relationships between stress scores or life changes and dysmenorrhea (Wentz, 1976; Siegel, John-son, and Sarason, 1979).

Little, if any, research has taken a comprehensive look at DUB, examining its relationship to prior life changes and stress. Pepitone-Arreola-Rockwell, Sommer, and Sassenrath (1981) carefully defined DUB as six possible symptom or sign com-plexes of irregularity or secondary amenorrhea and tried to relate it to job stress only, but they failed to find a significant relationship.

Siegel et al. (1979) looked at the relationship between the accumulation of life changes (especially "negative" ones) and menstrual irregularity. No significant relationship was found. These studies and others (Coppen, 1965; Siegel et al., 1979) used retrospective records of self-recording to determine the diagnosis of DUB. In addition, several critics (Minter and Kem-ball, 1978; Rabkin and Struening, 1976; Gannon, 1981) have reported that very few studies in this area have had good ob-jective diagnostic criteria for DUB. The research in this area has also been criticized for having poor or no controls (Minter and Kemball, 1978). It has also been suggested that self-scoring of stress by the participant instead of the total count of life change events might more accurately take into account other important mediating variables, such as support systems, di-mensions of various life events, and coping mechanisms of the participants.

There are several studies linking some forms of dysfunctional uterine bleeding to extreme examples of stress. In addition, an inorganic menstrual symptom such as dysmenorrhea has been shown to be related to life changes and life stress. Based on these studies it seems reasonable to assume that there is a relationship between stress and DUB. Anecdotal evidence from the investigator's clinical practice also supports this hypothesis. However, there are no well-controlled studies of this hypothesis. The present study examines the relationship between carefully defined DUB (diagnosed prospectively) and recent life changes and self-scored stress scores of those changes that are experienced.

METHODS

The study was done at the Family Practice Unit of Memorial University in St. John's, Newfoundland, Canada. The unit comprises seven faculty and three to four residents at any one time. Approximately 22,000 patients are seen per year.

The participants were all those women aged 18 to 35 years who were attended by three of the faculty physicians at the Family Practice Unit and who came in for a regular checkup or suffered from dysfunctional uterine bleeding. The patients were asked to participate in a study looking at life changes. They were told that many of the women in the clinic were being included in this study.

The study (experimental) group consisted of those 26 participants newly diagnosed as suffering from dysfunctional uterine bleeding as defined below. The control group consisted of 31 participants seen consecutively by the same three physicians during the same time period for regular checkups and diagnosed as being well with no menstrual problems. The two groups were statistically matched for age, gravidity, and contraceptive use; no significant differences were found for these three indices (Table 17.1).

A version of the Recent Life Changes Questionnaire, tested

Table 17.1
Number, Age, Gravidity, and Contraception Uses of Participants

	Total Number	Mean Age (yr)	Gravidity (Mean)	Contraception Use		
				Oral Contraceptives	IUD	Other/ None
Study group	26	25.1	(0.5)	6	4	16
Control group	31	25.4	(0.5)	10	1	20

$x^2 = 2.83$, 2 df, $p = .24$

many times for validity and reliability by others (Rahe, 1975) was used. The questionnaire yielded a count of all experienced life changes for the previous year. In addition, subjective self-scores of stress for each life change experienced by the participant were calculated (stress score of 1 to 100 for each life change). Self-scored stress scores were calculated for the same 12-month period.

The procedure was a case-control format. During an office visit with a potential participant (study or control), the attending physician noted the women's birthdate, physician, chart number, presence and duration of DUB, gravidity (number of pregnancies), uses of specific contraception methods, and a detailed history (on a checklist) of the form(s) of DUB detected. The list of symptoms and reported signs was derived from Kistner (1971) and included all forms of irregularity or secondary amenorrhea collectively known as dysfunctional uterine bleeding.

All charts were examined three months after study entry to determine whether the diagnosis of DUB could still be made in retrospect. Three study participants were dropped from the study because an organic etiology for their DUB was subsequently detected. The study was terminated when an acceptable number of study subjects was reached. The minimum number of subjects in each group was judged to be 25 to 30 to obtain a 95 percent confidence level in the statistical analyses (t-test).

RESULTS

There were 26 study participants with dysfunctional uterine bleeding and 31 controls. Results of t-tests indicated there were no significant differences between the two groups in age, gravidity, or contraceptive use (Table 17.1).

The number of life changes (life change events) was determined for the 12-month period prior to study entry (Table 17.2). The range was 3 to 34 life change events for the study group and 0 to 14 for the control group. Results of the t test indicated that the differences between the two groups were highly significant ($p < .001$).

The total stress scores for all experienced life change events were determined for the same 12-month period (Table 17.2). The range was 205 to 2,800 for the study group and 3 to 1,179 for the control group. Results of the t-test indicated that these differences were also significant ($p < .001$) between the groups.

The use of various contraceptives was not statistically significantly different between the groups (Table 17.1), but there were more oral contraceptive users in the control group and more intrauterine device (IUD) users in the study group. For this reason t-tests were repeated three ways for life change events and stress scores: (1) dropping all IUD users from the

Table 17.2
Comparison of Life-Change Events and
Life Stress Scores (on a scale of 1 to 100) Between Groups (t-test)

	Life Change Events (all subjects)		Life Stress Score (all subjects)	
	Mean	SD	Mean	SD
Study group	18.4	6.7	87.4	57.5
Control group	11.6	6.1	42.1	26.5
	$t = 4.02$, 55 df, $p < .001$		$t = 3.92$, 55 df, $p < .001$	

analysis, (2) dropping all oral contraceptive users, and (3) dropping all IUD and oral contraceptive users. For each of these tests there were still significant differences between the two groups for the life change events and self-scored stress scores. For these six analyses all $p \leq .001$. None of the participants was taking estrogens or other replacement hormones for menopausal symptoms.

The Recent Life Changes Questionnaire is subdivided into five areas of life change: changes in health, job, family, personal-social, and financial areas of life. For each of the five areas t-tests were used of life. For each of the five areas t-tests were used to examine life change events and stress scores (Table 17.3). For self-scored stress scores there were significant differences between groups for all areas of life stress excluding the job area. For the life change events there were significant differences between the groups only for the health and personal-social areas. Stress and life change events in the health and personal-social areas seem to be the most sensitive predictors of DUB.

Table 17.3
Comparison of the Types of Life-Change Events and of the
Types of Life Stress Scores

	Life Events		Stress Scores	
	Study Group (Mean Number)	Control Group (Mean Number)	Study Group (Mean Number)	Control Group (Mean Number)
Health	2.7	1.2*	120	36*
Job	2.5	2.7 (NS)	147	101 (NS)
Family	3.6	2.4 (NS)	185	89**
Personal Social	7.4	4.2*	355	163*
Finance	1.6	1.2 (NS)	73	36**

*$p < .001$
**$p < .05$
NS = Not significant

DISCUSSION

The study group with dysfunctional uterine bleeding documented significantly more life change events in the year prior to study entry than did the control group of healthy women. In addition, the study group documented that the life changes have given them more stress in that year than did the control group. All these relationships among life change, stress, and DUB were independent of contraceptive use, which may sometimes be attributed to the life changes and stress experienced by the contraceptive user rather than to the contraceptive.

The health and personal-social types of life changes and stress scores seem to be the best predictors of dysfunctional uterine bleeding. The health differences may, however, just reflect the health stress of having DUB itself. A future prospective cohort study could examine this variable.

A potential explanation for this study's findings is that stress and significant emotional change can influence hypothalamic control in the brain by means of the cerebral cortex and limbic system (Check, 1978). Mild dysfunction in the hypothalamic-pituitary-ovarian axis can affect production levels of estrogen, which in turn can affect release of luteinizing hormone or follicle-stimulating hormone. Significant alterations in the levels of these two hormones can affect the menstrual cycle, often causing anovulatory cycles, which are one of the most common physiological events underlying dysfunctional uterine bleeding.

Stress from health problems may have shown up as a good predictor of DUB because many illnesses and medications used to treat those illnesses can affect the hypothalamic-pituitary-ovarian axis. A more detailed collection of data on the participants' health history would have to be done to clarify whether the illnesses or the stress from these illnesses were the crucial variables involved. Personal-social types of stress were also shown to be good predictors of DUB. A possible explanation is that this particular group of stresses (changes and stresses of social activities, friendships, accidents, major personal decisions, and education) may affect a woman (and her endocrine system) more directly because personal-social life changes usually provide the most intimate stresses of life.

Research that attempts to find relationships between stress and disease is open to problems of validity and bias. The problem of internal validity to address in this study is whether the differences found between the two groups of participants are due only to the presence or absence of DUB and not to some other confounding variable(s). The participants in this study were self-selected and did not necessarily represent a random sample. In particular, the control group comprised women who decided to see their physician for a checkup. Such women may come from less stressful backgrounds and perhaps DUB illness in itself may account for much of the perceived stress documented in this study. In addition, there may be a recall bias because the participants were asked to recall events that occurred up to 12 months prior to study entry. Self-selection bias and recall bias could be minimized by repeating the study as a long-term prospective cohort study of asymptomatic women using daily log diaries of stressful events and menstrual difficulties. Such a study would be able to examine whether stress preceded the onset of DUB.

The problem of external validity to address in this study is whether the findings can be expanded to the general population. This study did not examine certain demographic data of the population such as socioeconomic status. A future study as described above would have to include such data.

Another potential bias is the ascertainment bias of whether a participant has a valid diagnosis of DUB. One way to minimize this bias would be to consult a "blind" gynecologist for a diagnosis of exclusion of other organic disease, and no standard investigations are available to validate the diagnosis of DUB.

The personal-social and health stress elements of the questionnaire were so critical in this study that they should be looked at more closely in a future cohort study to discover the best predictors of DUB so that ways of preventing this problem may become available.

CONCLUSIONS

A statistically significant relationship was found between dysfunctional uterine bleeding and recent prior life changes and experienced stress from those changes. In particular, personal-social and health stresses showed the widest differences between the DUB sufferers and controls. These findings were independent of contraception use, even though there were more IUD users among the DUB sufferers and more oral contraceptive users among the controls. This study may thus help focus on a more specific cause of DUB.

REFERENCES

Chamberlain, G. (1981), Dysfunctional uterine bleeding. *Clin. Obstet. Gynecol.*, 8:93–104.

Check, J. H. (1978), Emotional aspects of menstrual dysfunction. *Psychosomatics*, 19:178–184.

Coppen, A. (1965), The prevalence of menstrual disorders in psychiatric patients. *Brit. J. Psychiat.*, 3:155–158.

Diamond, S. R., Rubinstein, A. A., Dunner, D. L., & Fiere, R. R. (1976), Menstrual problems in women with primary affective illness. *Compr. Psychiat.*, 17:541–546.

Drew, F. L. (1961), The epidemiology of secondary amenorrhea. *J. Chron. Dis.*, 14:396–398.

Gannon, L. (1981), Evidence for a psychological etiology of menstrual disorders: A critical review. *Psychol. Rep.*, 48:287.

Gregory, B. (1951), The menstrual cycle and its disorders in psychiatric patients. *J. Psychosom. Res.*, 2:199–206.

Holmes, T. H., & Rahe, R. H. (1967), The Social Readjustment Rating Scale. *J. Psychosom. Res.*, 11:213–218.

Kelly, K., Daniels, G. E., & Poe, J. (1954), Psychological correlations with secondary amenorrhea. *Psychosom. Med.*, 16:129–134.

Kistner, R. W. (1971), *Gynecology Principles and Practice*. Chicago, Year Book.

Minter, R. E., & Kemball, C. P. (1978), Life events and illness onset: A review. *Psychosomatics*, 19:334–344.

Osofsky, H. F., & Fisher, S. (1967), Psychological correlates of the development of amenorrhea in a stress situation. *Psychosom. Med.*, 29:15–19.

Pepitone-Arreola-Rockwell, F., Sommer, B., & Sassenrath, E. N. (1981), Job stress and health in working women. *J. Hum. Stress,* 7:19–26.

Perlman, L. V., Ferguson, S., & Bergum, K. (1975), Precipitation of congestive heart failure: Social and emotional factors. *Ann. Intern. Med.,* 75:1–19.

Rabkin, J. G., & Struening, E. L. (1976), Life events, stress, and illness. *Science,* 194:1013–1024.

Rahe, R. H. (1975), Epidemiological studies of life change and illness. *Int. J. Psychiat. Med.,* 6:133–144.

Siegel, J. M., Johnson, J. H., & Sarason, I. G. (1979), Life changes and menstrual discomfort. *J. Hum. Stress,* 5:41–47.

Singh, K. (1981), Menstrual disorders in college students. *Amer. J. Obstet. Gynecol.,* 140:299–306.

Sydenham, A. (1946), Amenorrhea at Stanley Camp, Hong Kong, during internment. *Brit. Med. J.,* 2:159–166.

Theorell, T., & Rahe, R. H. (1971), Psychosocial factors and sudden cardiac death: A pilot study. *J. Psychosom. Res.,* 15:19–24.

Wentz, A. C. (1976), Abnormal uterine bleeding. *Primary Care,* 3:9–15.

Whitacre, F., & Barrera, B. (1944), War amenorrhea. *J. Amer. Med. Assn.,* 124:399–407.

Chapter 18
End-Stage Renal Disease as a Stressful Life Event

EDWARD STODOLA, PH.D., AND THOMAS W. MILLER, PH.D., A.B.P.P.

INTRODUCTION

End-stage renal disease (ESRD) refers to irreversible failure of the excretory functions of the kidney. Two substitute-organ treatment procedures are available for ESRD: dialysis and transplantation. Two types of dialysis procedures are used: hemodialysis and peritoneal dialysis. The former entails circulating a patient's blood through a dialysis machine to remove fluids and metabolic endproducts. Peritoneal dialysis entails the removal of the same substances from the body by bathing the peritoneum of the abdominal cavity with a dialysate. Both hemodialysis and peritoneal dialysis may take place in a dialysis center or in the patient's home; the patient may be directly involved in administering the procedure or the patient may be passive while the procedure is administered by another trained person. Continuous ambulatory peritoneal dialysis (CAPD) is a "portable" form of peritoneal dialysis which minimally re-

Acknowledgment. This chapter reflects segments of the first author's Doctoral Dissertation, University of Kentucky, Department of Educational and Counseling Psychology, and the second author's clinical research with renal dialysis patients, VA and University of Kentucky Medical Centers.

281

stricts patient mobility. Organs for transplants are obtained from three sources: living nonrelative donor, living relative donor, and cadaver donor. Each of the dialysis and transplant treatments has advantages and disadvantages with respect to psychosocial variables.

Our purpose in this chapter is to discuss psychosocial aspects of stress associated with ESRD and its treatment. We will focus primarily on stress factors associated with dialysis treatment: stressors which precipitate stress responses, stress responses, course of adjustment, and the quality of life of people who receive dialysis treatment. In addition to findings reported in literature on psychosocial aspects ESRD, our ideas and discussion are anchored in the concepts of dissipative structures (Prigogine, 1971) and a biobehavioral model of illness conceived by Straus (1972).

STRESS DEFINED

The distinction between stress and factors which cause stress is neither simple nor clear. A simple model presents a stressor as an independent variable that leads to stress, the dependent variable. While this model may be useful for hypothesizing causal links, it does not account for the confounding of independent and dependent variables nor the influence of mediating variables that are often found with both psychological disorders and physical disease.

The confounding of stress and stressor is shown by an interactional model of depression (Coyne, 1976). According to this model, depression (stress response) is a result of a disruption (stressor) in the social field of the person. Once established, however, the depressive process presents symptoms that influence the social field in such a way that the process is maintained and difficult to abort. In short, the depressive process becomes, over time, a component of its own etiology. Similarly, a DSM-III diagnosis of schizophrenia implies behavioral impairment.

In turn, Miller (1981) has proposed that such impairments are prime components of vulnerability to schizophrenia.

The causes of ESRD are complex and cannot be linked to stress in any simple, linear fashion. However, it seems reasonable to at least hypothesize that stress factors may be directly associated with two of the major causes of ESRD, nephritis and hypertension. Stress factors may influence immunological responses anad therefore contribute to nephritis. The case of hypertension is more complex because renal failure may be both a cause and effect of hypertension; yet, the role of stress in the etiology of hypertension is well known. On another level, ESRD and its treatment may be viewed as stressors which perturb the lives of renal patients. To begin disentangling the stress-stressor confound associated with ESRD, it seems best to first look at the major ways in which stress has been defined for purposes of research and then add conceptual material that serves the purpose of this paper. Three major categories of definition appear in the contemporary stress literature.

STRESS AS A RESPONSE

Stress may be defined in terms of a disruption in biological or behavioral homeostatic functioning. Defined in this way, stress is assessed using measures of autonomic arousal, changes in endocrine function, reports of emotional distress, and changes in coping behavior. Conceiving stress in terms of homeostasis is grounded in thinking from the biological sciences; the classic response definition of stress is: A state manifested by a specific syndrome consisting of all nonspecifically induced changes within a biologic system (Selye, 1978).

Defining stress as a response has face validity with respect to colloquial usage. Autonomic nervous system activity (e.g., rapid heartrate, perspiration, dizziness, flushing, contracted muscles), feelings of emotional distress, and the experience of deterioration in performance are often construed as indicators that we are under stress. However, defining stress strictly in terms of responses has limited value for developing a complete picture of ESRD because of the problem of confounding stressor and stress. For example, neurapathy, which is often a consequence of ESRD, is also a stressor that provokes further deterioration in the daily functioning of renal patients. Labeling either the neurapathy or the further deterioration stress adds little to our understanding of ESRD.

STRESS AS AN INTERACTION BETWEEN STIMULUS AND MODERATING FACTORS

The interactional approach is derived from the social sciences and defines stress only in relation to the characteristics of the individual and his or her surrounding life context. Simply, a situation or an event is considered a stress if the individual responds to it as such or, if in the judgment of a rater, it presents demands for responses that exceed the available resources for coping. The central theme in the interactionist approach is that it is impossible to objectively define stress independent of the characteristics of the person and the life context on which it has impact. In this light, a life event such as ESRD is seen as controlled and moderated by idiosyncratic cognitive or perceptual structures of the individual (Mechanic, 1978; Lazarus, 1974), cultural qualities which influence the meaning of symptoms (Good and Delvecchio Good, 1981), and by the general environmental supports available to the individual (Brown, 1974). The general dialectical theme in the interactionist approach is summarized by Berger and Luckmann (1966) in their analysis of knowledge and reality: "This object is society as part of a human world, made by men, inhabited by men, and, in turn, making men, in an ongoing historical process" (p. 173). The interactionist definition is also supported by conventional wisdom: one person's stressor is another's challenge; a stressor in one culture is not a stressor in another culture; what is a stressor at one time is not a stressor at another time; and I'll be okay as soon as I get home. This approach makes excellent sense and, when used in combination with other definitional approaches, it can yield important findings. However, it has little utility to understanding relationships between stress and ESRD when used alone because of the overwhelming number of confounding intrapersonal and contextual variables that are presented. Nevertheless, it is essential to recognize that the ESRD patient is both the creator and the creation of ongoing historical processes.

STRESS AS A STIMULUS

A third way stress may be defined is in terms of stressors. Stressors are stimuli with objectively specifiable properties whose probability of occurrence is not determined by the characteristics of the individual on whom they have an impact. This is the definition of stress used in experimental research on stress wherein randomly assigned subjects are exposed to noxious physical (e.g., noise, heat, crowding) or psychological (e.g., failure, competition) stressors. Most stressful life-event studies also assume this definition of stress.

Two reservations must be considered with respect to defining stress in terms of stressors. First, the assumption that life events "assign themselves" randomly in the empirical world is at best tentative; the interactionists' claim that people at least in part create their reality and thereby influence their life events should not be dismissed. Second, differences exist within individuals as well as between individuals; life events may influence a person differently with respect to changes in time and place. The advantage of a definition based on stressors as stimuli is its suitability for drawing causal inferences. While the problem of confounding independent and dependent variables is set to the side when stress is defined in terms of objectively specified stressors, the objectivity associated with stress as a response and the more robust "empirical flesh" allowed by the interactionist definition are sacrificed when this approach is used alone. What is needed is a definitional framework that acknowledges both the objective and subjective components of stress along with the interactions between these components.

A Biobehavioral Model of Stress

Straus (1972) proposes an alternative to the biomedical model which emphasizes material and efficient causation to explaining behavior, health, and illness. His biobehavioral model offers a unifying concept of behavior by incorporating six sets of interacting and interdependent components or levels: biological, psychological, sociological, cultural, environmental, and temporal. Whereas the conceptions of stress as a response or a stimulus are linear, this biobehavioral model emphasizes that degrees of health, illness and adjustment to illness depend upon interaction among factors contained in the six levels. The temporal level, for example, is not isolated from the other levels but is instead seen as including each of the other levels: biological diurnal rhythms, psychological sense of urgency, role expectations, organization of environmental space, and cultural orientations to time. This interactive quality goes one step beyond saying that the whole is more than the sum of its parts by claiming that each part to some degree contains the whole and simultaneously influences the other parts, much like an individual to some degree contains a culture.

The more one becomes familiar with ESRD the more it becomes clear that the consequences of stress on one level become the causes of stress on another level. For this reason, we believe that the biobehavioral model has heuristic value both for guiding research on ESRD and for planning treatment. It incorporates the interactionist point of view while at the same time recognizing that stress can be seen both as a response and as a stimulus. It provides a framework for specifying and studying the many variables associated with ESRD plus a means for conceptualizing comprehensive treatment.

Dissipative Structures

Prigogine (1971) describes two types of structures in nature: equilibrium structures and dissipative structures. Equilibrium structures are closed systems that are maintained in a fixed state without exchanging energy or matter with the outside world. Dissipative structures, on the other hand, are maintained only through exchanges of matter and energy. A dissipative structure is an open system that is continuously adapting to maintain organization away from equilibrium.

A dissipative structure is conservative; that is, it maintains its organization unless it is perturbed by either an internal or external source of stress. So long as the matter-energy exchange is in sum convergent, the organization holds. When the organization is perturbed—that is, amplified in a divergent direction—it fluctuates. If the fluctuation is sufficient, the system either dies (entropy) or if sufficient "re-sources" are available, a new level of organization is created. The new level is maintained so long as energy and matter exchange is possible and it is not again sufficiently perturbed. The shift from one level to the next is non-linear: all parts of the open system are affected simultaneously. The theory of dissipative structures is a description of the transformation of structures.

All living organisms are dissipative structures (or sets of dissipative structures). The biobehavioral model constructed by Straus presents a picture of the human being as a dissipative structure. So long as the person is not sufficiently perturbed, the existing conservative system for exchanging matter and energy with the environment confirms itself. Once the established system is sufficiently perturbed, however, its capacity for conservation breaks down and a new system of organization with new limitations and potentialities is required. ESRD can be understood in this framework as a serious life event that perturbs the person and creates instability first on the biological level by destroying a primary capacity for exchanging matter with the environment. The instability is extended to the other levels.

The dialysis machine (or transplant) is a substitute organ that makes possible the continuation of life by returning the lost capacity to exchange matter. Because dialysis treatment does not efficiently replace all renal functions and because dialysis is itself a stressor, renewal of the former system is hardly possible, and a new level of organization is required. Adjustment to dialysis is therefore a struggle to achieve a new level of organization.

A Biobehavioral Definition of Stress

For purposes of this chapter stress is defined simply as any change that requires some degree of adjustment. Significant change, whether positive or negative, is never convenient and requires adaptation: it amplifies a system either convergently or divergently. In terms of the biobehavioral model and dissipative structures discussed above, a stressor is any influence that perturbs the existing open biobehavioral system. Stress then refers to fluctuations in that system that result from such perturbations and that require adjustments to either maintain the existing organization or to create a new level of organization. The interactionist perspective is also represented in this definition. Our attention now turns to stressors associated with dialysis treatment.

Stressors Associated with ESRD and Renal Dialysis

Devins (1981) has suggested that ESRD patients may be viewed as a "living stress laboratory" for the study of coping with chronic illness. People who receive dialysis treatment typically are faced with stressors that impact on all six levels included in the biobehavioral definition. ESRD is itself the primary stressor and, for the most part, other stressors are subsequent changes in the biobehavioral matrix which formerly supported the person. Binik (1983) classified the substantial number of stressors associated with ESRD and dialysis treatment into six categories.

Uncertainty About Survival

Perhaps the most important stressor is uncertainty about life expectancy. Patients we have interviewed rarely revealed definite ideas or plans for their future and were more willing to talk about their past. This observation is supported by Pozanski, Miller, Salguero, and Kelsh (1978) who found that ESRD patients do not project themselves into the future. In many ways, patient uncertainty regarding their survival appears realistic. A study by Hutchinson, Thomas, and MacGibbon (1982) found an average expected survival of approximately seven years for all ESRD patients. The increase in relative risk with every ten years of age is approximately the same for ESRD patients as for the general population but the baseline risk is approximately six times higher for the ESRD population. Three pretreatment characteristics—age, duration of diabetes, and left-sided heart failure—were found to significantly contribute to relative risk of death; some evidence also suggested that premorbid depression may also contribute to risk of death. Uncertainty is a stressor in another form for some patients because renal disease is often diagnosed in its very early stages and patients may have to contend with uncertainty regarding the pretreatment course of the disease for as long as fifteen years, knowing that at some time substitute-organ treatment will become necessary.

Machine Dependence

Survival for dialysis patients depends on a machine serving as a substitute for a vital organ. The patients' dependence extends to others who assist with dialysis: the professional renal staff in the case of in-center dialysis and to a key support person for home dialysis treatment. Changes in the professional staff or fluctuations in the relationship with the support person further accentuates the power of this stressor. The machine dependence often conflicts with other activities that require independence and that would serve as buffers to the effects of this stressor.

Severe Fluid and Diet Restrictions

All types of dialysis treatment require severe diet and fluid restrictions. Deviations from this regimen quickly result in discomfort, sometimes severe pain, to the patient. The regimen provides a constant reminder that choices once available cannot be made without risking survival. Given that food and drink are often part of social activities, patients' social lives are also affected by this stressor.

Time Demands of Treatment

Dialysis treatment demands a substantial portion of a patient's time. Dialysis patients typically spend 10–20 hours per week at a hospital and, depending on travel to and from a dialysis center and other demands of treatment, dialysis treatment may require as many as 40 hours per week. Several patients in our study in effect said of dialysis: "It's a job." Many patients need a recovery period of several hours after each dialysis treatment, which adds indirectly to the time demands of dialysis. An early study (Friedman, Goodwin, and Chaudhry, 1970) indicated that 31 percent of the patients' 120-hour Monday through Friday workweek was consumed by actual dialysis or activities necessitated by dialysis treatment, and an average of 28 days per year were spent in the hospital. With improved procedures, the time required for treatment has since been reduced. Nevertheless, in a society that is highly regulated by time schedules, the demands of dialysis treatment are an especially significant stressor, and time flexibility in the workplace becomes an important factor in rehabilitation.

Reduced Patient Mobility

Few patients are able to be as mobile and active as they were before ESRD. One reason for this is reduced physical strength for engaging in activities. A second reason is the necessity of remaining close to a dialysis treatment facility for the next treatment. Though arrangements can be made for treatment in other centers, this requires special advanced planning and dealing with an unknown dialysis staff and environment. When we ask patients what has changed most in their lives or what they miss most, they frequently mention being "tied down" and unable to participate in formerly satisfying activity. The loss of familiar activity is a significant stressor that is secondary to reduced mobility.

OTHER STRESSORS

Binik (1983) identified several additional factors that create stress for ESRD patients. These include income or job loss, general feelings of malaise, medication side-effects, reduced reproductive capacity and difficulty in finding stable mates, and disrupted family life and friendships. Each of these in some way removes elements of certainty or adds elements of uncertainty to the lives of the patients.

An additional stressor that bears further mention here has been termed "unphysiology" by Kjellstrand, Rosa, Shidman, Rodrigo, Davin, and Lynch (1978). Unphysiology refers not to actual chemical deficiencies or excessive fluid levels but to the oscillations in blood chemistries and fluid volumes associated with intermittent dialysis. These oscillations may be seen as a stressor because they are accompanied by oscillations in subjective feelings of psychological and physical well-being. Feelings of fatigue, mood changes and anxiety likewise oscillate with the treatment regimen. These effects may be reduced with CAPD which provides continuous instead of intermittent dialysis.

Meaning of Dialysis Treatment. Good and Delvecchio Good (1981) stress the importance of the meaning patients associate with illness. The dialysis treatment itself and the meaning patients associate with it may be seen as direct stressors that are presented at regular intervals. One patient with whom we have worked described hemodialysis treatment as both invasive and intrusive. The invasive quality refers to "being stuck" or, after becoming a home dialysis patient, "sticking yourself" to initiate treatment. The same patient was further distressed by the regular violation of his privacy. He described the dialysis process as one which intrudes, removes his blood, and then makes his blood visible to others. Uremia means literally urine in the blood. The purpose of dialysis treatment is simply the removal of urine from the blood. What this means is that a process that formerly occurred privately within the body has now become public. When we consider colloquial usages of the word blood—"It's in my blood," "She is a blood relative," etc.—we can begin to see how issues of existential meaning may bear upon the dialysis procedure. In addition, the meaning our patient associated with this process demonstrates how a cognitive factor can determine the degree to which an event becomes a stressor. Our sense is that few people who receive dialysis treatment see it only as a technical procedure void of other meaning.

Each of the stressors discussed here is likely to affect not just one area of a person's life but will likely cause stress in several areas. For example, reduced mobility may alter participation in familiar social roles, influence feelings of psychological and physical well-being, make time schedules difficult to meet, and generally reduce the person's capacity for extension into his or her physical environment.

Stress Associated with ESRD

ESRD patients selected for dialysis treatment have demonstrated a variety of psychological concerns that are tied to the stressors described above. While these are discussed here as examples of stress, they may also be seen as secondary stressors that further aggravate the stress experienced by patients.

Depression

Numerous investigators have identified depression as a primary complication associated with dialysis treatment (Cardenas and

Kutner, 1982; Levy, 1979b, 1981; and Cardenas, Kutner, and de Andrade, 1984) and of transplantation (Gulledge, Buszta, and Montague, 1983). Depression scores appear lower for employed persons, and white male homemakers were the only group to show clinical depression (Kutner and Gray, 1981). Long-term dialysis patients (3 + years) showed lower levels of depression than short-term patients (Kutner, 1983), suggesting that depression levels may diminish over time with adjustment to illness. Other findings suggest that depression should not be attributed directly to ESRD because a host of losses and other factors secondary to ESRD contribute to depression (Levy, 1979b). A second negative mood state related to ESRD is high anxiety (Levy, 1979b; Malmquist, 1973; Kutner and Gray, 1981; and Gulledge et al., 1985). Kutner (1983) also found that anxiety decreases with time on dialysis treatment, again suggesting a positive adjustment over time.

A review of recent literature (Binik, 1983) suggests that the frequency of clinical depression is not as high as early studies suggest, particularly those conducted in the 1960s. Taking information from a series of studies that controlled for other factors known to be involved in the etiology of depression, he concludes that we can no longer assume clinical depression is a primary problem among dialysis patients. If depression decreases over time as Kutner's findings indicate, we should then expect to find less depression now because more long-term patients are included in the dialysis population. High depression levels may represent acute rather than chronic depression, and any study of depression should control for length of time on dialysis treatment. Binik suggests research assessing nonclinical depression and other negative mood states.

FATIGUE

Fatigue among dialysis patients appears to be caused by psychological and physical stressors and correlates negatively with length of time since beginning dialysis treatment. Exercise appears to have an important role in renal rehabilitation generally and specifically with respect to the reduction of subjective fatigue (Cardenas and Kutner, 1982). However, there seems to be a subset of patients who experience severe fatigue; long-term patients are less likely to report fatigue, but long-term and short-term patients are equal with respect to severe fatigue (Kutner, 1980). Kutner (1983) also reports more feelings of physical fitness, improved upper body coordination, and less weight gain between dialysis treatments for long-term patients.

SUICIDE

The most definitive study of suicide among dialysis patients, conducted by Abram, Moore, and Westervelt (1971), showed that suicide among these patients is greater than for the general population. A more recent study (Haenel, Brunner, and Battegay, 1980) confirms this finding but reports a smaller difference compared to the general population. Binik (1983) points out that neither of these studies controlled for other factors that are known predictors of suicide (age, sex, etc.), suggesting that the high suicide rates may not be due only to renal failure and dialysis treatment. Nevertheless, it seems reasonable to claim that stress experienced by dialysis patients is to some degree expressed in a higher suicide rate. It is important to remember that non-compliance is always available as an effective means of suicide.

SEXUAL PROBLEMS

Rates of sexual dysfunction (impotency for men and decrease in frequency of orgasm for women) higher than that for the general population were reported in several studies (Levy, 1979a, 1981; Gulledge et al., 1983; and Cardenas et al., 1984). Sexual functioning also appears to become worse after the start of dialysis treatment, even though dialysis reduces uremia (Levy, 1981); these findings agree with reports from patients we have interviewed.

Marital Functioning

Mixed findings have been found in studies that look at the marital and family problems associated with ESRD and dialysis treatment (Binik, 1983). One study reviewed by Binik showed a strong negative correlation between individual psychological well-being and marital role strain, which is what one would expect. This correlation became stronger with dialysis treatment, suggesting that the dialysis patient leads an increasingly family-centered life. Our current research with dialysis patients confirms this finding: patients identify family support as the single most important factor in helping them cope with their renal failure (Stodola and Miller, 1985). At this point, it appears reasonable to assume that ESRD is a major stressor that significantly perturbs family homeostasis, requiring major adjustments.

Pain

Little research has been conducted on pain associated with ESRD. Kjellstrand et al. (1978) reported that cramps and headache often accompany and follow dialysis treatment along with other somatic complaints such as nausea. These are the types of pain most frequently reported by the patients with whom we have worked clinically; patients also report chest pains associated with excessive fluid levels. Binik (1983) reports that increased pain is associated with two factors: decreased perceived control over treatment and increased depression, both of which have been associated with chronic pain in general (Blumer and Heilbronn, 1982).

Cognitive, Motor and Sensory Deficits

Binik (1983) reports that a large number of deficits in these areas have been identified for dialysis patients but points out that they do not for the most part appear to be clinically significant. Patients scored within normal ranges on an intelligence estimate and on most assessments of cognitive/motor functioning, and long-term patients showed improved ability to readily process information (Kutner, 1980). Organic brain dysfunction was reported as a result of uremia in an early study (Ebra and Toth, 1972). Decreased mental acuity is identified as a common secondary symptom (Cardenas et al., 1984). These deficits may not be necessary consequences of renal failure but rather indicators of the adequacy of dialysis treatment. In this respect, they may be useful clinically for monitoring the treatment regimen. Edwards, Kopple, Miller, Fields, and Der (1977), for example, found that accuracy of time perception was inversely related to degree of uremic toxicity and improved with each hemodialysis treatment, which suggests that an easily administered measure of time perception may be useful in monitoring uremia.

ADJUSTMENT TO ESRD AND DIALYSIS TREATMENT

Adaptation to the stress of dialysis treatment for ESRD has become the focus of considerable study over the past two decades. Viederman (1975) suggests that for successful treatment a patient must have the capacity to adaptively regress to the state of dependence without conflict. The thrust of Viederman's claim is that regression of this nature allows acceptance of the machine and the diverse personalities of the treating staff, which in turn encourages an open willingness to follow a demanding dietary regimen. While these elements of increased dependence may be necessary parts of a constructive adjustment process, there seems to be more to adjustment to ESRD than regression. Regression implies a decremental developmental picture similar to that which has in the past characterized most research on aging, one in which an existing organization diminishes but new organization is not established.

A Stress-Transformation Model

The structure of Hill's A + B + C + =X family crisis framework (Hill, 1949), which continues to serve as a foundation for research in family stress, has utility for further understanding adjustment to ESRD, especially when placed alongside a biobehavioral conception of illness and the concept of dissipative structures. This framework may briefly be described first as a set of theoretical statements regarding crisis: A (the stressor) interacting with B (resources for meeting the crisis) interacting with C (the way the person construes the stressor) produce X (the crisis or stress). Hill's framework also offers a set of statements describing three overlapping stages of adjustment: (1) a period of disorganization, (2) an angle of recovery, and (3) a new level of organization.

A similar conception is discussed by Banton (1965) who borrowed findings from cultural anthropology to discuss role change as a three stage process: the first stage is separation from the old (disintegration); the second stage is a period of transition during which the person is unsettled; finally, the person enters the third stage which involves a new role and reintegration into a community. The developmental patterns of adjustment outlined by Hill and Banton describe a process of transformation that involves the decay of one system of organization and the growth of another within and across all levels of a biobehavioral system.

Course of Adjustment

The question that emerges here is whether ESRD patients who receive dialysis treatments are able to create satisfying new levels of organization. In other words, do Prigogine's concept of dissipative structures and Hill's family stress model hold up for ESRD dialysis patients?

Two descriptions of the course of successful adjustment to ESRD suggest that it may be best viewed as a developmental process that results in a new level of organization. One, developed by Abram (1969), consists of five stages—apathy, euphoria, anxiety, convalescence, and the struggle for normalcy. The second, developed by Reichsman and Levy (1972), consists of three stages—honeymoon, disenchantment and discouragement, and long-term adjustment. Both descriptions outline a pattern of early satisfaction followed by disturbance and ending with on-going adjustment. Healthy adjustment appears related to not letting the machine be in control; and differences between short-term and long-term patients, such as improved processing of information and reduced levels of depression and anxiety indicate that many patients successfully negotiate this adjustment process (Kutner, Baker, Bretches, Chyatte, Fair, Gray, and Wortham, 1980; Kutner, 1983).

On the other hand, Gutman, Stead, and Robinson (1981) gathered data from a representative sample of dialysis centers throughout the United States and found evidence to suggest that a large percentage of dialysis patients are severely debilitated and do not improve over time. A potential problem with Gutman's findings is that they are based on data collected from social workers instead of directly from patients. Interview data collected in our current research with ESRD dialysis patients suggest that some people who receive dialysis treatment do manage to create new levels of organization for their lives that are both satisfying and meaningful (Stodola and Miller, 1985). Two case descriptions drawn from our current research illustrate that successful adjustment is a developmental process that occurs over time.

Mr. A is a 56-year-old successful businessman, father, husband, and active community member who first learned of his ESRD disease in 1960, a time when effective treatment was not available. He began dialysis treatment in 1973 and received a transplant in 1977. The transplant was rejected after 15 months, and he then trained for home dialysis. In 1983 he again became an in-center dialysis patient because he wanted his home free of the stressors associated with dialysis treatment. At the present time, he is able to regulate his business and leisure activities effectively to the demands of treatment. Looking back, he now views his life, including his years as a person with ESRD, as a series of successfully negotiated and positive developmental stages. He reports that the most difficult time for him was the pre-dialysis period when he knew of his ESRD but did not know if treatment would be effective. During this time he "held in" his fears and anxiety. Looking back, he claims that the hope he found when dialysis treatment became available, after years of living without hope of treatment, has been a key to his adjustment.

Mr. B is a 60-year-old father, husband, grandfather, and ex-businessman. His life before dialysis was characterized by hard work, constant struggle to get ahead, and little time for family and leisure. The onset of his ESRD was sudden; he was taken to a hospital for emergency care and began dialysis treatment within days. He describes himself as depressed and without concern for survival during the first four years of dialysis treatment. Then, after four years "on the machine," the course of his adjustment changed radically. His depression diminished and he became interested in his family. His description of his present life and scores on standardized life satisfaction measures indicate highly satisfactory adjustment. Talking about the shift in his life, he says: "This machine made me stop and think about my life and what is important . . . now I can just be with my family." Listening to him, one gets the sense that the machine was "the Buddha" that presented the obstacle that required a transformation that permitted him new meaning.

The point made by these cases is that successful adjustment requires the action of time. In both cases a new level of organization was invented. For Mr. A this process occurred prior to beginning dialysis while for Mr. B it occurred during the first four years of dialysis. The inventive process suggested by these patient accounts seems to support what Bergson (1911, p. 11) said about time: "The more we study the nature of time, the more we shall comprehend that duration means invention, the creation of forms, the continual elaboration of the absolutely new." And this is what Prigogine, who refers to Bergson when explaining his work in physical chemistry, had in mind when he described an open system shifting to a new level of organization after being sufficiently perturbed. While there is evidence to suggest that some patients are able to invent a new level of organization, we should be careful to not think of the "typical" patient; our experience tells us that the "typical" patient is indeed "atypical." In this light, it is important to identify those factors that facilitate successful adjustment.

FACTORS ASSOCIATED WITH SUCCESSFUL ADJUSTMENT

A number of studies have identified specific psychosocial factors that help facilitate a positive course of adjustment to ESRD. Lundin and Lundin (1983) claim that degree of self-care is related to survival and rehabilitation; patients who actively engage and act on their world do better. A positive staff attitude toward dialysis fosters a patient attitude that leads to patient involvement in treatment. Kutner et al. (1980) identified six factors which promote adjustment—exercise, useful tasks or work, time flexibility at work, social support, not placed in sick role by others, following treatment regimen (especially diet). In the same study Kutner et al. found eight factors that undermine adjustment—time demands and schedule of treatment, insensitive staff, lack of information, employer prejudice, disincentives to work, medicare disincentives for home dialysis, cost of medication, and loss of mobility. The importance of useful work to adjustment is supported by evidence in a study by Calsyn, Sherrard, Hyerstay, and Freeman (1981). Several investigators support the importance of a sensitive and open dialysis staff (Gray and Kutner, 1983; Cramond, 1971; Kaplan-DeNour and Czaczkes, 1974). Close ties to a significant other is also viewed as important to overall adjustment (Kutner and Cardenas, 1981). It may be especially important to inform ESRD patients who are new to dialysis treatment that successful adjustment is a developmental process occurring over time. Knowledge of this process may also support the morale of professionals who work with dialysis patients.

EMPLOYABILITY AND REHABILITATION

Employment possibilities appear directly related to educational status because changes in physical capacities have stronger implications for patients without post-secondary education (Kutner, 1983). Regardless of sex or race, patients who have attended college were more likely to be employed. Generally, employment rates among ESRD patients compared favorably with rates for patients with other chronic disabilities. However, Gutman et al. (1981) found evidence to suggest that a large proportion of dialysis patients are severely debilitated; they found that only 25 percent of the patients worked outside the home. A problem with this analysis is that it reduces rehabilitation to employment outside the home. Nevertheless, employment was found to be an important source of self-esteem for both men and women (Kutner and Gray, 1981).

QUALITY OF LIFE ISSUES IN ESRD

Because a renal transplant is a possibility for many ESRD patients, it is important to consider the advantages and disadvantages of a transplant. Generally, it is true that dialysis presents a high probability of a low payoff while transplant treatment presents a low probability of a high payoff. The quality of life appears to be better for patients with successful transplants than it is for dialysis patients (Kutner, 1980, 1983; Johnson, McCauley, and Copley, 1982). This does not mean that transplantation is without its own negative psychosocial aspects, however. Interpersonal issues often develop between a live donor and the recipient. Donors become overprotective of their gift (Cramond, 1967), while recipients feel in debt to the donors. Recipients also experience weight gain, anxiety regarding the operation site, and loss of libido. Gulledge et al. (1983) claim that the physical and psychological well-being of both donor and recipient must be considered. Finally, the immunosuppressants used to prevent rejection of the graft are not without adverse side effects. Treatment choice depends, therefore, on a number of biomedical and psychosocial considerations.

Among dialysis patients, survival and quality of life is higher for home-dialysis than for in-center patients (Ebra and Toth, 1972; Kreis, 1978). Not all patients are in a position to dialyze at home, however. Limited care dialysis, defined as in-center treatment with minimal active patient involvement, is the best treatment for some patients (Hedenberg, 1980). Erichsen (1981) claims three advantages for CAPD—mobility, fewer dietary and fluid restrictions, and higher hemoglobin which results in greater strength, and a stronger subjective sense of physical fitness and well being. In one study of dialysis patients, men showed better adjustment to illness than women (Kaplan-DeNour, 1982). However, treatment alternatives associated with optimal outcome (e.g., home dialysis) and employment opportunities that would affect self-esteem may be less accessible to women (Kutner and Gray, 1981). Not surprisingly, quality of life is related to age. Patients aged 25–34 were found to have the best adjustment to dialysis treatment; older and younger patients were less likely to be in dialysis treatment after three years; borderline and clinical depression was more frequent among patients 55+ years old (Kutner and Cardenas, 1981). The study by Kaplan-DeNour (1982) showed that the 40–49 age group enjoyed the best overall adjustment while the 60+ group showed poorest adjustment. The differences in these findings result from differences in the age distributions within the samples.

Black patients tend to be older than white patients (Kutner and Gray, 1981). In some communities, blacks comprise a disproportionately high percentage of ESRD patients because hypertension, a leading cause of renal failure, is higher among the black population (Watkins, 1979). Vocational rehabilitation is higher among white male patients than among black male patients; however, these differences disappear when age and education are held constant (Gutman et al., 1981). Being black appears to be associated with etiology, treatment and adjustment factors that adversely affect outcomes (Kutner and Gray, 1981).

SUMMARY

Individual lives are grounded by six sets of anchors: biological, psychological, environmental, social, cultural, and temporal. End-stage renal disease along with hemodialysis is a serious life event that severely perturbs these anchors.

It is difficult to clearly separate factors which cause stress from responses to those factors. That which is at one time most clearly a response to ESRD (e.g., uncertainty about the future) is at another time better seen as a stressor or cause of stress. We have used a biobehavioral concept of illness and health proposed by Straus to (1) resolve this stress-stressor confound and (2) consider the interaction between stressors and the life context of the person.

Stressors involved in ESRD and hemodialysis may be grouped under six headings: uncertainty about survival, machine dependency, fluid and diet restrictions, time demands of treatment, reduced mobility, and other stressors including "unphysiology," job loss, and issues of personal privacy and meaning. We reviewed and discussed research findings that pertain to seven biobehavioral factors that may be considered effects of stressors: negative mood states, fatigue, suicide, sexual problems, marital and family problems, pain, and cognitive, motor and sensory deficits. While these are identified as effects of stressors, they may also function as stressors.

Hill's family stress model and Prigogine's concept of dissipative structures provide background for discussing the course of adjustment to ESRD. A key question emerges—are people who receive hemodialysis treatment able to invent satisfying new levels of organization for their lives. Research findings on the course of adjustment suggest that a significant number of patients are able to do so. Factors that contribute positively to adjustment and to quality of life among hemodialysis patients were identified. Knowledge of these should aid those who work or live with people who are dependent upon dialysis treatment for the essential exchange of matter with their environment.

REFERENCES

Abram, H. S. (1969), The psychiatrist, the treatment of chronic renal failure and the prolongation of life: II. *Amer. J. Psychiat.*, 124:157–167.

—— Moore, G. L., & Westervelt, F. B. (1971), Suicidal behavior in chronic dialysis patients. *Amer. J. Psychiat.*, 127:1199–1204.

Banton, M. (1965), *Roles: An Introduction to the Study of Social Relations.* New York: Basic Books.

Berger, P. L., & Luckmann, T. (1966), *The Social Construction of Reality.* Garden City, NY: Doubleday.

Bergson, H. (1911), *Creative Evolution*, trans. A. Mitchel. New York: Henry Holt.

Binik, Y. M. (1983), Coping with chronic life-threatening illness: Psychological perspectives on end stage renal disease. *Can. J. Behav. Sci.*, 15/4:373–391.

Blumer, D., & Heilbronn, M. (1982), Chronic pain as a variant of depressive disease: The pain-prone disorder. *J. Nerv. & Ment. Dis.*, 170:381–406.

Brown, G. W. (1974), Life events and psychiatric illness. *J. Psychosom. Res.*, 16:311–320.

Calsyn, D. A., Sherrard, D. J., Hyerstay, B. J., & Freeman, C. W. (1981), Vocational adjustment and survival on chronic hemodialysis. *Arch. Phys. Med. & Rehab.*, 62:483–487.

Cardenas, D. D., & Kutner, N. G. (1982), The problem of fatigue in dialysis patients. *Nephron.*, 30:336–340.

—————— de Andrade, J. R. (1984), Rehabilitation and the chronic renal disease patient. In: *Current Therapy in Psychiatry*, ed. A. P. Ruskin. Philadelphia: Saunders.

Coyne, J. (1976), Toward an interactional description of depression. *Psychiat.*, 39:29–40.

Cramond, W. A (1967), Homotransplantation: Some observations on recipients and donors. *Brit. J. Psychiat.*, 113:1223–1230.

—— (1971), Renal transplantations: Experiences with recipients and donors. *Seminars Psychiat.*, 3:116–132.

Devins, G. M. (1981), Helplessness, depression and mood in end stage renal disease. Unpublished dissertation. McGill University, Montreal.

Ebra, G., & Toth, J. C. (1972), Chronic hemodialysis: Some psychological and rehabilitative considerations. *Rehab. Lit.*, 33/1, part 1:2–10, 13.

Edwards, A. E., Kopple, J. D., Miller, J. M., Fields, L. G., & Der, D. (1977), Time perception and hemodialysis. *Nephron.* 19:140–145.

Erichsen, K. (1981), The disabled and the nurse: Continuous ambulatory peritoneal dialysis. *Lamp*, 38/10:53–54.

Friedman, E. A., Goodwin, N. J., & Chaudhry, L. (1970), Psychosocial adjustment to maintenance hemodialysis: I. *N.Y. State J. Med.*, 70:629–637.

Good, B., & Delvecchio Good, M. J. (1981), The meaning of symptoms: A cultural hermeneutic model for clinical practice. In: *The Relevance of Social Science for Medicine*, ed. L. Eiesenberg & A. Kleinman. Dordrecht, Holland: D. Riedel, pp. 165–196.

Gray, H., & Kutner, N. G. (1983), Spatial rearrangement: Its effect on social environment in a renal dialysis clinic. *Eval. Health Prof.*, 6:77–89.

Gulledge, A. D., Buszta, C., & Montague, D. K. (1983), Psychosocial aspects of renal transplantation. *Urol. Clin. N. Amer.*, 10:327–335.

Gutman, R. A., Stead, W. W., & Robinson, R. R. (1981), Physical activity and employment status of patients on maintenance dialysis. *N. Engl. J. Med.*, 304:309–313.

Haenel, T., Brunner, F., & Battegay, R. (1980), Renal dialysis and suicide: Occurrence in Switzerland and in Europe. *Compr. Psychiat.*, 21:140–145.

Hedenberg, A. D. (1980), Limited care hemodialysis—An appropriate treatment modality for end-stage renal disease. *J. Amer. Assn. Nephrol. Nurses & Technic.*, 7:243–244.

Hill, R. (1949), *Families Under Stress*. New York: Harper & Bros.

Hutchinson, T. A., Thomas, D. C., & MacGibbon, B. (1982), Predicting survival in adults with end stage renal disease: An age equivalence index. *Ann. Intern. Med.*, 96:417–426.

Johnson, J. P., McCauley, C. R., & Copley, J. B. (1982), The quality of life of hemodialysis and transplant patients. *Kidney Internat.*, 22:286–291.

Kaplan-DeNour, A. (1982), Psychosocial adjustment to illness scale (PAIS): A study of chronic hemodialysis patients. *J. Psychosom. Res.*, 26/1:11–22.

——— Czaczkes, J. W. (1974), Bias in assessment of patients on chronic dialysis. *J. Psychosom. Res.*, 18:217–221.

——— Poll, I. B. (1980), Locus of control and adjustment to chronic haemodialysis. *Psychol. Med.*, 10:153–157.

Kjellstrand, C. M., Rosa, A. A., Shidman, J. T., Rodrigo, F., Davin, T., & Lynch, R. R. (1978), Optimal dialysis frequency and duration: The "unphysiology hypothesis." *Kidney Internat.*, 13 Suppl. 8:120–124.

Kreis, H. (1978), Selection of hemodialysis versus cadaveric transplantation. *Kidney Internat.*, 13 Suppl. 8:91–94.

Kutner, N. G. (1980), Medical, psychosocial and vocational evaluation of kidney transplant and dialysis patients whose treatment began four or more years ago: Final report. Rehabilitation Research Monograph Series No. 2.

——— (1983), Predictive criteria in rehabilitation of ESRD patients: Perspectives from rehabilitation medicine. *Contemp. Dial.*, 4:34–39.

——— Baker, H., Bretches, P., Chyatte, H., Fair, P., Gray, H., & Wortham, C. (1980), Programs and treatments: Views of dialysis and transplant patients. *Dial. & Transplant.*, 9:1138, 1140–1142.

——— Cardenas, D. D. (1981), Rehabilitation status of chronic renal disease patients undergoing dialysis: Variations by age category. *Arch. Phys. Med. & Rehab.* 62:626–631.

—— Gray, H. L. (1981), Women and chronic renal failure: Some neglected issues. *J. Sociol. & Soc. Welf.*, 8:320–333.

Lazarus, R. S. (1974), *Patterns of Adjustment*, 3rd ed. New York: McGraw-Hill.

Levy, N. B. (1979a), The sexual rehabilitation of the hemodialysis patient. *Sexual. & Disab.*, 2:60–65.

—— (1979b), Psychological problems of the patient on hemodialysis and their treatment. *Psychother. & Psychosom.*, 31:260–266.

—— (1981), Psychological reactions to machine dependency: Hemodialysis. *Psychiat. Clin. N. A.*, 4:351–363.

Lundin, A. P., & Lundin, M. F. (1983), Some impediments to rehabilitation in dialysis patients. *Amer. Assn. Nephrol. & Transplant Nurses J.*, 10:29–31, 57.

Malmquist, A. (1973), A prospective study of patients in chronic hemodialysis: I. Method and characteristics of the patient group. *J. Psychosom. Res.* 17:333–337.

Mechanic, D. (1978), *Students under Stress: A Study in the Social Psychology of Adaptation.* Madison: University of Wisconsin Press.

Miller, T. W. (1981), A model for training schizophrenics and their families to communicate more effectively. *Hosp. & Commun. Psychiat.*, 32/12:870–871.

Poznanski, E. O., Miller, E., Salguero, C., & Kelsh, C. (1978), Quality of life for long-term survivors of end stage renal disease. *J. Amer. Med. Assn.* 239:2332–2347.

Prigogine, I. (1971), Unity of physical laws and levels of description. In: *Interpretations of Life and Mind*, ed. M. Grene. New York: Humanities Press, pp. 1–13.

Reichsman, F., & Levy, N. B. (1972), Problems in adaptation to hemodialysis: A four-year study of 25 patients. *Arch. Intern. Med.*, 130:859–865.

Selye, H. (1978), *The Stress of Life.* New York: McGraw-Hill.

Stodola, E., & Miller, T. (1985), Time perspective of dialysis patients. Unpublished data, University of Kentucky.

Straus, R. (1972), Hospital organization from the viewpoint of patient centered goals. In: *Organization Research on Health Institutions*, ed. B. S Georgopoulos. Ann Arbor, MI: Institute for Social Research of the University of Michigan, pp. 207–211, 218.

Viederman, G. E. (1975), Desirable versus undesirable life events: The relationship of mental distress to stress. *J. Pers. & Soc. Psychol.*, 32:329–337.

Watkins, V. B. (1979), Rehabilitation risks of E.S.R.D. *J. Rehab.*, 45:30–33.

Chapter 19
Life Events and Psychological Distress in Dermatologic Disorders: Psoriasis, Chronic Urticaria, and Fungal Infections

GIOVANNI A. FAVA, M.D., GIULIA I. PERINI, M.D., PAOLO SANTONASTASO, M.D., AND CLETO VELLER FORNASA, M.D.

Psoriasis and chronic urticaria are two skin conditions which have often been ascribed to stressful life situations and emotional disturbances.

Wittkower and Russel (1953) identified emotional stress as a cause of psoriasis in about 40 percent of 72 patients; Susskind and McGuire (1959) in 70 percent of 20 patients; and Farber,

Acknowledgments. We are deeply indebted to Drs. Robert Kellner and Eugene S. Paykel, for their supervision and encouragement through the work, to Drs. George L. Engel, George Molnar, and Peter E. Sifneos, for their invaluable criticism and comments, and to Dr. Jerome D. Frank, whose remarks on a previous work were helpful in the design of this study. Dr. Stella Agosti (Centro di Calcolo, University of Padua) performed the statistical analysis.

This chapter was first published in the *British Journal of Medical Psychology* (1980), 53:277–282, and it is reprinted with permission.

Bright, and Nall (1968) in 32–44 percent of more than 2,000 patients. Susskind and McGuire (1959) also attempted to define the degree of neuroticism in their sample by the MPI, but failed to obtain differences from the general population. Goldsmith, Fisher, and Wacks (1969) studied 13 patients with psoriasis and a similar group with other dermatoses through the MPI and the MMPI. Only differences in the scales of hysteria and psychasthenia of MMPI were reported. Baughman and Sobel (1971) using Cattell's 16 PF test could not observe any specific personality profile in their 252 patients. They also employed the SRSS elaborated by Holmes and Rahe (1967) for evaluating life events and concluded that stress was only a minor determinant of the severity of psoriasis in their population. Seville (1977) carried out a controlled study and recognized specific stress before the first attack in 39 percent of 132 patients, compared to 10 percent of the control group. A significantly better prognosis was observed in those patients assessed as having insight into stress.

As to chronic urticaria, Stokes, Kulchar, and Pillsbury (1935) detected significant stress in 83 to 100 patients; and Rees (1957) in 51 of 100 patients. Reinhold (1960) detected a significant stress in about 55 percent of 27 patients, who, however, were not entirely unselected. The same bias concerning selection was present also in the study by Kraft and Blumenthal (1959), who examined 22 patients with chronic urticaria. The MMPI used on 10 patients did not show any marked abnormality.

This literature suggests that emotional disturbances detectable on psychological testing do not seem to be present in psoriasis and chronic urticaria. Also, the above-mentioned studies dealing with stress, other than that of Baughman and Sobel (1971), have a serious flaw in that objective and standardized criteria of life events were not used. It is particularly difficult to evaluate subjective opinions in this area (Susskind and McGuire, 1959; Farber et al., 1968), since the validity of the patient's judgment about the course of his own illness has been questioned (Baughman and Sobel, 1970).

In our study we examined patients suffering from three

different dermatologic disorders: psoriasis, chronic urticaria, and fungal infections of the skin. Two of them (psoriasis and chronic urticaria)—as we previously discussed—are conditions frequently ascribed to emotional disturbances and stress, while in the other (fungal infections) psychological factors are not supposed to play a significant role (Rook, Wilkinson, and Ebling, 1972). Sainsbury (1960), however, in a survey of out-patients attending a general hospital, reported that patients with fungal infections associated with hyperhidrosis scored highly on neuroticism as measured by the MPI. A retrospective study of the occurrence of life events prior to illness onset is here associated with measures of psychological distress and al-exithymia. Alexithymia is a relatively new concept to describe the impoverished fantasy life of psychosomatic patients with a resulting utilitarian way of thinking and a characteristic inability to use appropriate words to describe their emotions (Nemiah, Freyberger, and Sifneos, 1976).

METHOD

A consecutive unselected series of 60 inpatients suffering from dermatologic disorders (psoriasis, chronic urticaria, and fungal infections of the skin) were studied, including 20 patients with each illness. All patients were hospitalized at the Institute of Dermatology of the University of Padua School of Medicine. All diagnoses were verified by a dermatologist (C.V.F.). The following criteria were employed. In the psoriasis group, clinical forms of nummular psoriasis with an irregular chronic course were included, but other forms such as pustular, exfoliative, and guttate psoriasis were excluded. Patients with a diagnosis of chronic urticaria were considered when this was certainly not allergic, exogenous, physical, symptomatic, or cholinergic and symptoms had been present for over three months. As to fungal infections of the skin, we examined chronic long-standing le-sions of tinea pedis, tinea cruris, and tinea circinata, with symptoms present for over 3 months and not associated with hyperhidrosis. The mean age of patients was 31.95 ($\pm$ 12.83) for psoriasis, 45.30 ($\pm$ 19.73) for uticaria, and 40.15 ($\pm$ 14.06) for fungal infections. Other demographic data are summarized in Table 19.1. Our measure of social class was based on Goldthorpe and Hope's (1974) social grading of occupations, with Brown, Harris, and Copeland's (1977) subdivision. Although no significant differences as to sex, marital status, social class and duration of illness, by chi square, are observed, one notes that the fungal infections group is the least chronic.

Each patient had a semistructured research interview covering stressful life events occurring in the six months immediately preceding the symptomatic onset of dermatologic illness, which was accurately determined. The life events recorded derived from the long scale of Paykel, including 61 events (Paykel, McGuiness, and Gomez, 1976). All patients, during their hospital stay, were given two questionnaires in an Italian form. One was the Kellner-Sheffield Symptom Rating Test (SRT), a 30-item self-rating scale of distress (Kellner and Sheffield,

Table 19.1
Demographic Data and Duration of Illness

	Psoriasis ($n = 20$)	Chronic Urticaria ($n = 20$)	Fungal Infections (n = 20)
Sex			
Male	13	11	9
Female	7	9	11
Marital Status			
Married	13	11	16
Single, divorced	4	9	3
Widowed	3	0	1
Social Class			
Working class	14	11	14
Middle class	6	9	6
Duration of Illness			
Less than 1 year	6	9	12
1–5 years	8	8	7
More than 5 years	6	3	1

1973). The SRT (here used in the original paper-and-pencil version) is designed to measure changes in the symptoms of neurotic patients participating in experiments in therapeutics such as drug trials. The test scores discriminate significantly between psychiatric patients and normals (Kellner and Sheffield, 1973). It includes four subscales: anxiety, depression, somatization, and inadequacy. These subscales have satisfactory correlations with other specific scales measuring these traits, like the Taylor MAS or the Zung Depression Self-Rating Scale (Kellner and Sheffield, 1973). The other questionnaire was a preliminary form of the Schalling-Sifneos Personality Scale (here used by kind permission of Dr. Sifneos), a 20-item self-rating questionnaire for evaluating alexithymic traits, whose definitive form and validation is in progress.

The statistical significance of differences among groups was evaluated through chi-square and t-tests, when appropriate.

RESULTS

The first comparison among these dermatologic patients concerns stressful life events. We found that 16 out of the 20 patients with psoriasis (80 percent), 18 of those with chronic urticaria (90 percent) and 10 of those with fungal infections (50 percent) reported at least one event listed in Paykel's scale before illness onset. The differences among groups were significant ($p < 0.05$) by chi-square test. Patients with psoriasis reported a total of 29 events (with a mean of 1.45 per patient), those with urticaria a total of 17 (with a mean of 0.85). Applying the American scaling of this scale of events (Paykel et al., 1976), there was a mean of 14.83 per patient in psoriasis, a mean of 25.22 in urticaria and of 8.67 in fungal infections.

A second comparison among the three illnesses involves the severity of psychological distress, as measured by SRT (Kellner and Sheffield, 1973). This scale, in the form here used, gives a total score of 49.82 (± 27.21) per patient for new neurotic outpatients in the United States, and a total score of 11.88 ($\pm$ 13.64) for normals. We obtained a mean total score per patient of 18.50 ($\pm$ 11.04) in psoriasis, 22.25 (11.75) in chronic urticaria and 11.00 ($\pm$ 6.92) in fungal infections. The differences by t-test are significant between psoriasis and fungal infections ($p < 0.01$). A one-way analysis of variance revealed statistically significant differences among groups in the subscales of anxiety ($F = 4.47$, $df = 2$, $p < 0.05$), depression ($F = 5.51$, $df = 2$, $p < 0.01$). Table 19.2 shows the mean score per item and per patient for each of the four subscales of SRT in the three groups.

The third and last comparison among groups involves alexithymia, as measured by the self-rating questionnaire. Analysis of the total scores per patient does not reveal significant differences by t-test among groups (Table 19.3). A one-way analysis of variance per item does so in two cases. Interestingly enough the two items are very similar. The first states: "I think

Table 19.2
Psychological Distress: Mean Scores per Item and Patient for SRT Subscales

Subscale	Psoriasis	Chronic Urticaria	Fungal Infections	p^a
Anxiety	0.76	0.91	0.48	$p < 0.05$
Depression	0.52	0.72	0.28	$p < 0.01$
Somatization	0.50	0.66	0.38	n.s.
Inadequacy	0.67	0.65	0.32	$p < 0.01$

[a]By one-way analysis of variance.

Table 19.3
Alexithymic Scores

Illness	$\bar{x}$	SD
Psoriasis	24.75	7.24
Chronic urticaria	25.65	5.82
Fungal infections	25.85	4.92

it is not worthwhile discussing how one feels. I prefer to act." Patients suffering from chronic urticaria report a higher score on this item than those with psoriasis and fungal infections ($F = 3.17$, $df = 2$, $p < 0.05$). The second item states: "I prefer taking action rather than thinking." Patients with urticaria again are differentiated ($F = 6.42$, $df = 2$, $p < 0.01$). These differences as to tendency to act (a characteristic alexithymic trait) may be due to chance. They would confirm however the observations made by Shoemaker (1963), who identified some kind of symptomatic activity (e.g., excessive physical work, premature acceptance of responsibilities, etc.) as the outstanding behavioral characteristics of people suffering from chronic urticaria.

DISCUSSION

The concept of psychogenesis of organic disease is no longer tenable (Engel, 1977). Psoriasis cannot be considered any more a psychodermatosis in the old sense, namely one in which we can clearly describe the psychogenesis of the disease (Musaph, 1976). It, as well as chronic urticaria and fungal infections, can be caused by several factors, one of which may be psychosocial (Whitlock, 1976). Many authorities—notably Engel (1977)—state in fact that social and psychological factors are codeterminants of health and illness and propose a biopsychosocial model of illness to provide room for the doctrine of multicausality of all disease. Moreover, Lipowski (1977) remarks that the relative contribution of psychosocial factors varies from disease to disease, from person to person, and from one episode to another of the same illness in the same person. It is one of the tasks of psychosomatic research—according to Lipowski (1977)—to try to determine the extent of this relative contribution in various disorders and in individual patients. This exactly clarifies the aims and the limits of this research.

Patients suffering from psoriasis and chronic urticaria seem to be more exposed to the kind of stressful life events listed in Paykel's scale (Paykel et al., 1976) in the six months immediately prior to illness onset than those with fungal infections. Although our groups were unselected and formed a consecutive series, the percentages of patients reporting at least one event (80 percent in psoriasis and 90 percent in urticaria) are higher than those found in previous reports. This is probably due to the fact that the investigation of stressful life events is more accurate with Paykel's semistructured research interview and scale than with other methods previously employed. One may question the accuracy with which people can be expected to remember precisely what happened before illness onset in distant retrospect. This may be true especially for those patients whose duration of illness is over five years (about 16 percent of the sample). If failures to recollect life events are to be expected, they should mainly concern, however, patients with psoriasis and chronic urticaria, since the fungal infections are the least chronic conditions. Incidence of life events prior to disease onset in psoriasis and urticaria thereby may have been underestimated.

As to psychological distress in the form of neurotic symptoms, this was present in a significantly higher grade in patients suffering from psoriasis and chronic urticaria than fungal infections. Previous investigations employing the MPI (Susskind and McGuire, 1959; Goldsmith et al., 1969), the Cattells' 16 PF (Baughman and Sobel, 1971) and the MMPI (Kraft and Blumenthal, 1959; Goldsmith et al., 1969) had failed to obtain significant and substantial differences between patients with psoriasis or chronic urticaria and control groups. The fact is not surprising because of SRT sensitivity, which, for instance, is reported to discriminate more accurately than the neuroticism scale of MPI (Kellner and Sheffield, 1973). It is worth mentioning that the differences in psychological distress here reported may be a consequence of the disabling form of illness examined and that all the patients have been hospitalized because of their dermatoses and thereby may not be representative of the larger group of patients with these diseases who are never hospitalized because of their skin lesions. Anyhow clinical management should reflect these differences. Two controlled studies (Lester, Wittkower, Kalz, and Azima, 1962; Sanger, 1970) reported good results with psychotropic drugs in a number of skin disorders. According to Lester et al. (1962), tranquillizers and antidepressants are more effective when the disorder of affect is conspicuous. Obviously the basis for drug selection lies in an understanding of the particular affect state of the patient involved. The SRT, because of its anxiety, depression, somatization and inadequacy subscales, is very suitable for this screening purpose. Its routine use in patients suffering from psoriasis and chronic urticaria is thereby strongly recommended.

REFERENCES

Baughman, R., & Sobel, R. (1970), Psoriasis: A measure of severity. *Arch. Dermatol.*, 101:390–395.

——— ——— (1971), Psoriasis, stress and strain. *Arch. Dermatol.*, 103:599–605.

Brown, G. W., Harris, T., & Copeland, J. R. (1977), Depression and loss. *Brit. J. Med. Psychiat.*, 130:1–18.

Engel, G. L. (1977), The need for a new medical model: A challenge for biomedicine. *Science*, 196:129–136.

Farber, E. M., Bright, R. D., & Nall, M. L. (1968), Psoriasis. *Arch. Dermatol.*, 98:248–259.

Goldsmith, L. A., Fisher, M., & Wacks, J. (1969), Psychological characteristics of psoriatics. *Arch. Dermatol.*, 100:674–676.

Goldthorpe, J. H., & Hope, K. (1974), *The Social Grading of Occupations*. London: Oxford University Press.

Holmes, T. H., & Rahe, R. H. (1967), The Social Readjustment Rating Scale. *J. Psychosom. Res.*, 11:213–218.

Kellner, R., & Sheffield, B. F. (1973), A self-rating scale of distress. *Psychol. Med.*, 3:88–100.

Kraft, B., & Blumenthal, D. L. (1959), Psychological components in chronic urticaria. *Acta Allergol.*, 13:469–475.

Lester, E. P., Wittkower, E. D., Kalz, F., & Azima, H. (1962), Phrenotropic drugs in psychosomatic disorders (skin). *Amer. J. Psychiat.*, 119:136–142.

Lipowski, Z. J. (1977), Psychosomatic medicine in the seventies. *Amer. J. Psychiat.*, 134:233–244.

Musaph, H. (1976), Psychodermatology. In: *Modern Trends in Psychosomatic Medicine*, Vol. 3, ed. O. W. Hill. London: Butterworth, pp. 46–62.

Nemiah, J. D., Freyberger, H., & Sifneos, P. E. (1976), Alexithymia. In: *Modern Trends in Psychosomatic Medicine*, Vol. 3, ed. O. W. Hill. London: Butterworths.

Paykel, E. S., McGuinness, B., & Gomez, J. (1976), An Anglo-American comparison of the scaling of life events. *Brit. J. Med. Psychol.*, 49:237–247.

Rees, L. (1957), An etiological study of chronic urticaria and angioedema. *J. Psychosom. Res.*, 2:172–189.

Reinhold, M. (1960), Relationship of stress to the development of symptoms in alopecia areata and chronic urticaria. *Brit. Med. J.*, 1:846–849.

Rook, A., Wilkinson, D. S., & Ebling, F. J. G. (1972), *Textbook of Dermatology*. Oxford: Blackwell.

Sainsbury, P. (1960), Psychosomatic disorders and neurosis in outpatients attending a general hospital. *J. Psychosom. Res.*, 4:261–273.

Sanger, M. D. (1970), Psychosomatic allergy. *Psychosom.*, 11:473–476.

Seville, R. H. (1977), Psoriasis and stress. *Brit. J. Dermatol.*, 97:297–302.

Shoemaker, R. J. (1963), A search for the affective determinants of chronic urticaria. *Psychosom.*, 4:125–132.

Stokes, J. H., Kulchar, G. V., & Pillsbury, D. M. (1935), Effect on the skin of emotional and nervous states. *Arch. Dermatol. & Syphilol.*, 31:470–499.

Susskind, W., & McGuire, R. J. (1959), The emotional factor in psoriasis. *Scottish Med. J.*, 4:503–507.

Whitlock, F. A. (1976), *Psychophysiological Aspects of Skin Disease*. London: Saunders.

Wittkower, E. D. (1953), Studies of the personality of patients suffering from urticaria. *Psychosom. Med.*, 15:116–126.

——— Russel, B. (1953), *Emotional Factors in Skin Disease*. New York: Hoeber.

Chapter 20
Stress and Coping of Wives Following Their Husbands' Strokes

DENNIS VAN UITERT, PH.D., RAINA EBERLY, PH.D.,
AND BRIAN ENGDAHL, PH.D.

INTRODUCTION

Stroke is a significant stressor, not just for the victim, but for family members as well. Because rehabilitation literature and practice focus primarily on the patient or only view family members as collaborators in the patient's rehabilitation process, systematically collected data about the adjustment of stroke patients' family members rarely have been reported (Van Uitert, 1984).

The present study examines this issue. It outlines a model which may permit the identification of wives at risk for poor adjustment following their husbands' strokes. Using the data, intervention strategies may be designed to help wives of stroke victims adjust to their situations more effectively. This study also is a test of Lazarus' Theory of Psychological Stress (Lazarus,

Acknowledgment. This chapter was first presented at the 93rd annual meeting of the American Psychological Association, Los Angeles, California, August, 1985.

1974) in which the transaction among environmental factors (e.g., problems, resources), characteristics of individuals interacting with an environment (e.g., age, sex, personality type), and those individuals' cognitive and behavioral mediating efforts (e.g., appraisal, intrapsychic coping, active behavioral coping) determine the amount of stress an individual will experience. This level of stress affects current behavior and subsequent adjustment.

Both the psychosocial adjustment of wives of stroke patients and variables that were hypothesized to be related to this adjustment were sampled at one point in time. Subjects were 70 wives of stroke victims whose husbands had been referred to the Behavioral Neurology Section of the Minneapolis VA Medical Center for neuropsychological evaluation.

RESEARCH INSTRUMENTS

A problem checklist developed by the first author asked wives to indicate whether they had experienced difficulties with a variety of situations and whether each difficulty had been resolved. This inventory was based on an extensive literature review and consultations with rehabilitation personnel and wives of stroke patients. A coping behavior inventory similar to those developed by Moos (Moos, Cronkite, Billings, and Finney, 1983) and Lazarus (Folkman and Lazarus, 1980) asked wives to indicate how frequently they had used a sample of specific coping behaviors and to indicate how helpful these coping behaviors had been. The questionnaire includes items about demographic variables, major life events, the wife's health, the wife's social support network, pleasant events, the wife's rating of the severity of her husband's disability, and the wife's rating of her own adjustment. The Beck Depression Inventory also was used.

The Social Adjustment Scale (Weissman and Paykel, 1974) was used to assess the wives' psychosocial adjustment through taped interviews (typically one-half to one hour in length). This scale allowed the rating of adjustment in six areas of functioning: work, social and leisure activities, extended family, marital, parental, and economic. An overall rating of psychosocial adjustment also was determined. Raters were staff psychologists at the Minneapolis VAMC. The raters achieved inter-judge agreement coefficients ranging from .78 to .93 for the subscales and .89 for the rating of overall adjustment.

DATA ANALYSIS AND DISCUSSION OF THE RESULTS

Descriptive data included demographics, health, social support, self-rating of adjustment, characteristics of the husband's stroke and disabilities, pleasant events, problems, coping, and outcome measures (see Table 20.1).

Correlations between variables of interest and the wives' overall ratings of adjustment yielded a nonsignificant but negative correlation between the number of major life events and adjustment. A significant negative correlation was found between the number of day-to-day problems and adjustment. A t-test for the difference between these correlations indicated that the number of day-to-day problems bore a stronger relationship to overall adjustment ratings than the number of life events. These findings have positive treatment implications since day-to-day problems often are more resolvable than problems due to major life events. Better adjustment was associated with a greater percentage of resolved day-to-day problems.

The number of people from whom the wife believed she could expect real help in times of trouble was the social support variable most strongly correlated with overall adjustment ratings.

The correlations between both the number of different pleasant events and the frequency of these events as measured by the pleasant events weighted score were highly significant. These results suggest that consideration of positive experiences

320   DENNIS VAN UITERT ET AL.

Table 20.1
Predictors of Positive Overall Adjustment

Variable	df	r
Major Life Events	68	-.147
Day-to-Day Problems	68	-.536***
Real Help from Friends and Family	60	.349**
Pleasant Events	68	.401***
Pleasant Events Weighted Score	64	.540***
Composite Disability Rating	63	-.513***
Husband's Ability to Get Along with Wife and Others	67	.578***
Husband's Activity Level	66	.328**
Husband's Ability to Help Around the Home	66	.387**
Avoidance Coping Use	61	-.430***
Total Coping Discrepancy Score	61	-.284*
Active Cognitive Coping Discrepancy Score	61	-.285*
Avoidance Coping Discrepancy Score	61	-.294*
Age	66	.092
Education	68	.065
Income	59	.084
Self-Rating of Adjustment	66	.404***
Depression Inventory	68	-.454***
Physical Symptoms	68	-.398***

*$p< .05$
**$p< .01$
***$p< .001$, two-tailed.

might be as important or even more important than consideration of just the dysfunctional aspects of a person's situation when attempts are being made to understand problems in coping.

The wife's composite rating of the severity of her husband's disability was significantly correlated with her overall adjustment. In addition, each of the following three disability subcategories was significantly correlated with the wife's adjustment by itself: Husband's ability to get along with wife and others, husband's activity level, and husband's ability to help around the home.

The only significant correlation between any of the coping

scale or subscale scores and adjustment was between the avoidance coping usage score and the wife's mean overall adjustment rating. Use of avoidance coping was associated with lower adjustment scores.

To reflect how much control the wife felt she had over her situation as a result of her coping efforts, a discrepancy score was calculated by subtracting the coping helpfulness score from the coping usage score. Three of the four correlations between these calculated discrepancy scores and overall adjustment ratings were of moderate significance. Considering both coping usage and perceived helpfulness ratings is therefore important.

As predicted, relationships among three demographic characteristics of these subjects (age, education, and income) and their overall adjustment rating were not significant. Time since the husband's first stroke did not significantly correlate with adjustment for this sample in which the minimum number of months since first stroke was six and the mean was 60.2.

The correlations among the interview-based overall adjustment ratings and three self-report outcome measures (self-rating of adjustment, number of physical symptoms, and depression inventory score) were all highly significant. These findings suggest that increased confidence in the accuracy of the other self-report data is warranted.

Consideration of environmental characteristics, individual characteristics, and cognitive and behavioral mediating efforts, singly and in combination, increases one's ability to understand, predict, and control stress and its effects. The role of the combined effects of these factors appears to be especially significant.

Results of a stepwise multiple regression analysis (Table 20.2) indicated that the combination of the pleasant events weighted score, the number of day-to-day problems, the wife's rating of the severity of her husband's disability, and the avoidance coping usage score was the best predictor of overall adjustment ratings, accounting for almost 50 percent of the criterion variance. These results also support a transactional formulation of stress since the best predictors of adjustment included variables that represent the joint effects of environ-

Table 20.2
Stepwise Multiple Regression Prediction of Adjustment
Using All Variables

Predictor	Regression Weight
Pleasant Events Weighted Score	.30
Number of Day-to-Day Problems	-.29
Overall Severity of Husband's Disability	-.24
Avoidance Coping Usage Score	-.20

Multiple $R = .70$, $R^2 = .49$

Table 20.3
Stepwise Multiple Regression Using Only Coping Variables

Predictor	Regression Weight
Avoidance Coping Usage	-.48
Active Cognitive Coping Helpfulness	.35

Multiple $R = .57$, $R^2 = .32$

mental characteristics, cognitive mediating efforts, and behavioral mediating efforts.

A second stepwise multiple regression analysis (Table 20.3) indicated that the best prediction of overall adjustment based exclusively on coping variables was provided by a combination of not using avoidance coping and of rating active cognitive coping as helpful. It accounted for over 32 percent of the criterion variance. These findings suggest that cognitive and behavioral mediating efforts bear a significant relationship to adjustment.

SUGGESTIONS FOR INTERVENTION PROGRAMS

Although a review of the literature indicated that family education and participation in counseling groups are the most common intervention programs, such programs are not always available. The effectiveness of those that exist rarely is reported. The level of participation in the present study (nearly 90 percent) suggests that the vast majority of these women were interested in understanding and adjusting to their situations. This study's results indicate that such people would benefit from counseling focused on resolution of day-to-day problems and which would help them learn how to experience more pleasant events. Facilitation of active involvement in and personal commitment to a social support network would be of benefit. Intervention strategies that help wives face their problems and that help them differentiate between situations they could change and those they must accept would help them adjust more effectively.

References

Folkman, S., & Lazarus, R. S. (1980), An analysis of coping in a middle-aged community sample. *J. Health & Soc. Behav.*, 21:219–239.

Lazarus, R. S. (1974), Psychological stress and coping in adaptation and illness. *Internat. J. Psychiat. Med.*, 5:321–333.

Moos, R., Cronkite, R. C., Billings, A. G., & Finney, J. W. (1983), *Health and Daily Living Form Manual*. Palo Alto, CA: Social Ecology Laboratory, Veterans Administration and Stanford University Medical Center.

Van Uitert, D. (1984), Factors related to the adjustment of wives following their husbands' strokes. Unpublished doctoral dissertation. University of Minnesota, Minneapolis.

Weissman, M. M., & Paykel, E. S. (1974), *The Depressed Woman*. Chicago: University of Chicago Press.

Part IV
Life Events and Mental Illness

Psychopathology, particularly anxiety and depressive related disorders have been at the forefront of both the clinical interest and research that has been done in the area of mental illness as it is related to stressful life events. Within the context of psychopathology, areas which address schizophrenia and thought disorders as well as major affective disorders and personality disorders are discussed within the context of social environmental factors that may affect the course and relapse process in these most serious of psychiatric anomalies.

Is stress a precipitator of schizophrenia? Professional opinions on the question have completed several full cycles over the course of the past century. Dr. Spring's chapter discusses definitional ambiguities in research on the role of stress in the etiology of schizophrenia. Implications of the change to DSM-III criteria are considered, as is the question of whether prior research samples have over-included acute schizophrenics. Dr. Spring suggests that the problem of defining schizophrenia's time of onset is one of the thorniest in this literature. Three different operational definitions of stress are examined. Stress may be considered a response involving disruption in homeostasis or a stimulus with objectively specifiable properties. Stress is also defined interactionally with reference to characteristics of the individual and the surrounding life context. Relative merits of three definitions are evaluated, and an attempt is made to clarify the differentiation between formative and triggering effects of stress.

Recognized for the significant contribution to the clinical research on stressful life events, Drs. Dohrenwend and Egri investigate in the next chapter in this section the causal significance of recent stressful life events in episodes of schizophrenia. As a result of their analyses of the case-control studies, the literature on extreme situations, and the cross-cultural findings, they conclude that the consensus that stressful life events play only a trivial role in causing schizophrenic episodes is premature.

The internationally recognized clinical research team of Drs. Leff and Vaughn address in the next manuscript the interaction of expressed emotionality and its role as a stressful life event on the relapse of patients with schizophrenia. A history of life events in the three months before onset of illness was taken in a group of schizophrenic and a group of depressed neurotic inpatients. The Expressed Emotion (EE) of the patients' key relatives was measured. There was no difference between the schizophrenic and depressed patients in the rate of events in the three-month period before onset or in the proportion of undesirable events. However, the two groups exhibited significantly different patterns of interactions between life events and relatives' EE. Schizophrenic patients living with high EE relatives had a low rate of life events compared with those living with low EE relatives, whereas depressives living with high criticism relatives had a high rate of events compared with those living with low criticism relatives. The implications of these findings are discussed in relation to schizophrenic and depressive patients' differential vulnerability to environmental stress.

Drs. Lukoff, Snyder, Ventura, and Neuchterlein address some of the socioenvironmental factors that seem to predict the onset of schizophrenic episodes in vulnerable persons. In particular, stressful life events have been found to cluster in the three- to four-week period preceding a schizophrenic episode in some patients. Many persons with a schizophrenic disorder also seem to contribute to additional stressful life change events—for example, by high geographic mobility—thereby playing an active role in precipitating the onset of illness episodes. Irregularities in the communication style of parents also predict the subsequent development of schizophrenia spectrum disorders among disturbed adolescents. Finally, any schizophrenic patients seem to be deficient in the coping skills required to remediate the losses brought on by life events or to deal effectively with stressful relatives. They may therefore experience greater and more prolonged stress than most others due partially to inadequate social and problem-solving skills and less supportive social networks.

The relationship between personality traits and stressful life events becomes the focus of clinical research by Drs. McKeon, Roa, and Mann who investigated 25 patients with obsessive-compulsive neurosis and matched controls had their life-event scores (Paykel's Life-Event Schedule) rated for the year prior to the onset of illness and the date of interview, respectively. The Standard Assessment of Personality Schedule, whose high inter-temporal and inter-informant reliability was confirmed, was used to rate the patients' premorbid personality. The obsessive-compulsive patients' mean life-event scores were significantly higher than those of the control subjects; and this excess spanned the six months prior to the onset of illness. Patients with abnormal personality traits (obsessional, anxious, and self-conscious) experienced significantly fewer life events than those without such traits.

Retaining the notion that personality characteristics are a core ingredient in the study of stressful life events, Dr. H. Perris, Department of Psychiatry, Umea University, Sweden, explores its relationship in depressed patients. Evidence from many sources supports the view that stressful life events might be relevant for the onset and development of depression, but their pathogenic role is still only poorly understood. One approach in trying to elucidate the role of life events in depression might be to study them from a multifactorial point of view, taking into account the vulnerability of the individual experiencing them. As part of such an investigation, 138 depressed patients with a mean age of 45 years have participated in a study of life events and personality traits. In particular, it was tested whether aspects of aggression had experienced more stressful events, and patients who scored high on inhibition of aggression had experienced fewer, but more negatively. It is concluded that a combined study of the occurrence of life events and the personality characteristics of the patients experiencing them might enhance our understanding of the pathogenic role of life events in depression.

Drs. Glassner and Haldipur discuss bipolar disorder patients. Their relatives and friends were interviewed in depth about life events preceding the first and the latest episode of the subjects' affective illness. Twenty years of age was the cutting point for dividing the sample into early- and late-onset groups. The late-onset group reported the occurrence of significantly more stressful life events before the first and before the latest episode of affective illness than did the early-onset group.

Cross-cultural exploration of life events and depression becomes the focus of the next investigation in the section. Drs. Ndetei and Vadher of the Departments of Psychiatry, Kenyatta National Hospital, Nairobi, Kenya, and Oxford University, Oxford, England, respectively, examined life events in depressed patients in Kenya and found that the rate of life events was higher in the depressed group in the 27 weeks preceding the onset of depression but with a sharp increase in the last six–nine weeks before onset. Furthermore, depressed patients continued to experience independent life events after the onset of depression and this was an incentive to seek help and, eventually, a psychiatric referral.

Chapter 21
Stress and Schizophrenia: Some Definitional Issues

BONNIE SPRING, PH.D.

Is stress a precursor of schizophrenia? Professional opinions on the question have completed several full cycles over the course of the past century. The fact is that stressful life events have been found to account for somewhat less than 10 percent of the onset of schizophrenia and depression (Andrews and Tennant, 1978). However, it has been suggested that problems of sample size (Rabkin and Struening, 1976) and sample selection (Dohrenwend and Egri, 1981) may have rendered this estimate overly conservative. This chapter suggests that conceptual issues in defining stress and dating illness onset have never been adequately resolved. Therefore, both the magnitude and the importance of the association between stress and schizophrenia may warrant reexamination.

DEFINING SCHIZOPHRENIA

For more than a century, psychopathologists have attempted to come to grips with the major problem of the schizophrenia

Acknowledgment. This chapter was first published in _Schizophrenia Bulletin_ (1981), 7/1:24–33, and it is reprinted by permission.

researcher: heterogeneity. Schizophrenics are a diverse group
in terms of their symptoms, premorbid social functioning, and
event precipitating circumstances. It has long been hoped that
if a core group of "true" schizophrenics could be isolated based
on homogeneity of these presenting features, a unitary etiology
might perhaps emerge. It may be worth questioning whether
such a fantasy bids fair to come true. If we carefully reduce the
schizophrenic populace into a nuclear, core, or process group,
and various other peripheral clusters (e.g., schizotypal, reactive,
schizoaffective), will we find a uniform causal pathway for the
nuclear group? Or will we continue to rediscover the historic
truth—that the schizophrenic clinical picture emerges as a final
common pathway along many different etiological highways.
If, in the final analysis, schizophrenics persist in arriving at their
illnesses by divergent routes, we would have to admit that the
question beginning this article is naive. Indeed, it might never
be possible to develop a formulation of the role of stress in
schizophrenia that applies with any validity to the majority of
schizophrenics. Stress might be a sufficient cause for some
schizophrenias, a necessary cause for others, and an irrelevant
factor for still others. Progress in explaining the role of stress
may only come by way of evaluating subgroups of schizophrenics who are homogeneous with respect to etiology as well as
presenting clinical features. The role of stress may truly be
different for each subgroup of schizophrenics who are homogeneous with respect to etiology as well as presenting clinical
features. The role of stress may truly be different for each
subgroup.

     Although we are faced with the possibility that the problem
of etiologic heterogeneity may be here to stay, we should consider what efforts have been made to arrive at clinically homogeneous schizophrenic groups. Interestingly, presence of a
precipitating stress has historically been a feature used to con-
traindicate the diagnosis of true schizophrenia, even though
typical psychotic features might be present. Thus, Langfeldt
(1956) distinguished between schizophrenia on the one hand
and the "emotion psychoses" or schizophreniform illness on the

other—the latter arising in response to exogenous factors but mimicking "endogenously produced" schizophrenia. Kety, Rosenthal, Wender, and Schulsinger (1968) and Pope and Lipinski (1978) continue the historic tradition that equates schizophrenia with biological causation, insidious onset, and chronicity. These researchers question whether "acute schizophrenias" of sudden onset and discernible precipitants should be regarded as schizophrenias at all. The chronicity element has now been incorporated into the nomenclature of the new DSM-III, wherein schizophrenia cannot be diagnosed unless signs of the illnesses of shorter duration are classified as "schizophreniform disorders," and those that appear transiently as a result of a psychosocial stressor are called "brief reactive psychoses." However, neither is considered a subtype of schizophrenia.

Ironically, constraint of experimental design may have led stress researchers to select as schizophrenic probands primarily those patients who would no longer qualify for schizophrenic diagnoses according to DSM-III. If one wishes to determine whether stressful life events precede the occurrence of schizophrenia, it is desirable that the illness onset can (1) be clearly dated and (2) have occurred recently so that surrounding life circumstances can be accurately remembered. However, the gain in precision that these selection criteria afford may be offset by the cost of having a sample population that is unrepresentative of schizophrenics in general. In searching for schizophrenic cases with recent, datable onset, Brown and Birley (1968) excluded 60 percent of a schizophrenic hospital population. By definition, first-break cases with recent onset—less than six months ago—would now be seen as "schizophreniform" rather than schizophrenic. However, it should be pointed out that there are disadvantages in attempting to do research on stressful precipitants of a "true" schizophrenia that is more than six months old, since Uhlenhuth, Huberman, Balter, and Lipman (1977) found that 5 percent of life events are forgotten per month over an 18-month period.

Clearly, we need to address the problem of defining illness onset. The onset of schizophrenia has in the past been most commonly dated by the appearance of psychotic symptoms. An implicit criterion is that the patient must seek care or somehow come to the attention of mental health or medical facilities, or we can never learn of the onset of his psychosis. As the revised version of DSM-III points out, prodromal features often antedate psychotic symptoms. It is, therefore, basically an arbitrary decision whether we define onset as the appearance of prodromal or psychotic symptoms. Logically, it would be best if we could define onset as the point when there is a veritable certainty that a schizophrenic psychosis will occur. When schizophrenia is already a foregone conclusion, we might say that it has, in essence, begun. But when has this point been reached? Some theorists might trace onset to the point at which a very high level of vulnerability beyond a certain threshold will inevitably translate into disorder. Only the timing of this occurrence remains uncertain. Brown, Harris, and Peto (1973) suggest such an approach. However, according to a different approach—the diathesis-stress model—vulnerability implies no such inevitability. All will depend on whether, not just when, a triggering event causes vulnerability to germinate into disorder. But what does a trigger initiate—the prodromal syndrome or the psychotic syndrome?

An analogy might be drawn to the following problem: When has an individual lost a job? Is it at the point at which his performance deteriorates to a totally unacceptable level? Some later time when this fact reaches the attention of his supervisor? The point at which the trusted supervisor informs the employer? The employer's memo to the personnel department asking that termination be initiated? The date of the notification sent to the employee? The time when the employee realizes he is leaving? Or the precise date when he cleans out his desk and goes? By analogy, we conventionally date the onset of schizophrenia to this last, desk-clearing behavior. We could for all practical purposes date it much earlier. Also by analogy, if we looked for the immediate precipitating cause of job loss defined as actually leaving one's post, we would identify the cause as receiving a notification from the personnel department. Actually, this mechanical cause is only the last in a sequence of causal events. The causal factors of greatest importance occurred much earlier.

In psychopathology research, the problem of dating schizophrenia's onset is often treated as a methodological pitfall to be circumvented by improving interrater agreement. In actuality, it is a conceptual problem. Schizophrenia is a disorder that often develops by gradual accretion. It is difficult to determine when behavioral eccentricities have passed the threshold into a paranoid or schizoid personality, when these have shaded into a prodromal syndrome, and when this, in turn, has met the criteria for frank psychosis. The issue is further complicated by the fact that not all schizophrenias progress through this sequence of manifestations. The "acute schizophrenias," appear to descend suddenly without warning signs, although, as discussed earlier, there is a question as to whether such an uncomplicated onset is compatible with a diagnosis of true schizophrenia.

Clearly, present procedures for defining onset are basically arbitrary. If we wish to maintain criteria that apply to acute schizophrenics as well as to other subtypes, then we must use psychotic symptoms as the benchmark since these are the only features manifested in common by all the subtypes. If we exclude cases that begin acutely, then it becomes possible to consider earlier markers of onset. However, we are on equally unsure footing when we propose alternative criteria. Logically, we could use the first manifestations that indicate with absolute certainty that a schizophrenic psychosis will ensure. Can we identify such markers? The appearance of a schizoid personality is clearly unsuitable since many individuals manifesting such traits never develop schizophrenia (Bleuler, 1978). We do not yet have adequate ways to assess the level of vulnerability quantitatively, and to test whether high vulnerability is the precursor of an inevitable episode of schizophrenia. The implications of the appearance of a prodromal syndrome are as yet untested.

Given the complexity of schizophenia's onset, perhaps the

best that could be done is to examine separately those factors immediately preceding the onset of the schizoid or paranoid personality, the schizophrenic prodromal state, and the schizophrenic psychosis. Only in this way is it possible to avoid the pitfall of mechanical and superficial causal inference described earlier in the job loss analogy, and to understand any sequence of causal factors that may bring about schizophrenia.

DEFINING STRESS

In order to investigate whether stress is causally related to schizophrenia, it is essential that stress be defined and measured independently of other factors related to the onset of schizophrenia. If the occurrence of the predictor/independent variable (stress) is influenced by the criterion/dependent variable (schizophrenia) or vice versa, our ability to draw inferences about causality is severely restricted. In offering any suggestions for disentangling measurement of stress and schizophrenia, it may be best to start at square one—with how stress is defined for the purposes of research. Three major categories of definition appear in the contemporary research literature.

STRESS AS A RESPONSE

Stress may be defined and measured by a disruption or alteration in biological, physiological, emotional, or behavioral homeostatic functioning. Measures of autonomic nervous system arousal, changes in endocrine function, reports of emotional distress, and disruptions in coping behavior have all been used as indices of stress. The tendency to define stress in terms of disruptions in homeostasis is rooted in modes of thinking from the biological sciences. The classic response definition of stress is: A state manifested by a specific syndrome consisting of all nonspecifically induced changes within a biologic system (Selye, 1956). Response definitions of stress have some face validity in terms of colloquial usage. We often conclude that we are under stress based on signs of autonomic nervous system activation (e.g., rapid heartrate, perspiration, dizziness, flushing), a feeling of emotional distress, or the fact of performance deterioration.

Unfortunately, response definitions of stress are of limited value for research on stress as a cause of schizophrenia, because the measurement of independent and dependent variables is severely confounded. If behavioral disruption or disordered coping is taken as the index of stress, it is likely to be confounded with the criteria for diagnosing schizophrenia's onset, as well as with early signs of prodromal features of the disorder. In the DSM-III diagnostic criteria for schizophrenia, one required sign is significant impairment in two or more areas of routine daily functioning—e.g., work, social relations, or self-care. Thus, the diagnosis of schizophrenia of necessity implies behavioral impairment. Moreover, Phillips (1968) has proposed that longstanding inefficiencies in social functioning are prime components of vulnerability to schizophrenia. Since the onset of psychotic symptoms often occurs against a backdrop of disordered coping, thereby provoking even further deterioration of daily functioning, labeling either the backdrop or the further plunge "stress" adds no new information and certainly no explanatory power.

If biological responses are used to index stress, similar problems are encountered. Patients in an episode of schizophrenia are characterized by a host of abnormalities in physiological arousal (Mednick, 1958; Venables, 1964; Broen and Storms, 1967; Kornetsky and Eliasson, 1969). If such signs are detected shortly before psychotic symptoms appear, the findings may merely signify that the episode has begun but not yet reached full clinical bloom. Moreover, since there is some evidence (Mednick and Schulsinger, 1968) that individuals at risk for schizophrenia show unusual patterns of arousal, the researcher who calls these signs of stress may be mistakenly examining stable components of the predisposition for schizophrenia.

Indexing stress by anxiety or subjective reports of distress cannot take us much further, particularly since a sense of panic and subjective discomfort is one of the first symptoms of encroaching schizophrenia (Docherty, Van Kammen, Siris, and Marder, 1978).

STRESS AS AN INTERACTION BETWEEN STIMULUS AND MODERATING FACTORS

An interactionist approach, based in social science modes of thought, defines stress only in relation to the characteristics of the individual and the surrounding life context. A situation or an event is considered to be a stress if it is perceived as such by the individual, or if in the judgment of a rater, it exceeds the available resources for coping. The common theme in the interactionist approach is that it is impossible to define stress objectively, without regard to the person or life context on which it has an impact. Thus, the effects of any life event are believed to be controlled and moderated by the idiosyncratic cognitive or perceptual structures of the individual (Mechanic, 1967; Lazarus, 1974), and by the general environmental supports available to the individual (Brown, 1974).

As is the case for the response definition of stress, the interactionist definition incorporates conventional wisdom. One person's stressor is another's challenge. This approach makes excellent common sense and splendid clinical sense. When used in combination with other definitional approaches, it can yield important findings. However, when used alone, no definition of stress is more pernicious to the goal of drawing a causal relationship between stress and schizophrenia.

If stress is defined by the perceptions or cognitive interpretations of the individual, then measurement of stress is hopelessly confounded by phenomena that may be symptoms or predisposing factors for schizophrenia. Cognitive idiosyncrasies are the most salient feature of schizophrenia, and the tendency to feel overwhelmed by many events may well be an early symptom of illness. Moreover, eccentricities in cognition or perception may predispose both to schizophrenia (Mednick and Schulsinger, 1968; Strauss, Harder, and Chandler, 1979) and to the tendency to construe life events in an unusual way. Any real relationship between life events and schizophrenia might be obscured by a predisposition on the part of the preschizophrenic individual either to overreact to minor events or to underreact to real danger. The direction of the bias in measurement could not even be specified with certainty. Brown differs from these theorists in emphasizing environmental resources and explicitly attempting to exclude subjective appraisals of stress (Spring and Coons, in press).

STRESS AS A STIMULUS

Finally, stress may be defined in terms of stressors, or stimuli whose properties are objectively specifiable, and whose probability of occurrence is independent of the actions or characteristics of the individual on whom they have an impact. This is the definitional framework used in laboratory experiments on stress wherein noxious physical (e.g., noise, heat, crowding) or psychological (e.g., failure, competition) stimuli are imposed on randomly assigned subjects. It is also the basic definitional approach used in most studies of stressful life events, although it must be acknowledged that there is some tentativeness to the assumption that life events "assign themselves" randomly across individuals. If there is any validity to this assumption for at least some types of events, then this is the only definition of stress suitable for drawing causal inferences, because it is the only one for which independent and dependent variables are likely to be unconfounded.

In life events research, there is controversy over whether events are most validly seen as falling into discontinuous categories or as falling along a continuous dimension of magnitude. In laboratory research, it's unlikely that heat and noise stressors would be conceptualized as falling along the same continuum. Similarly, in life-event research, there is some evidence that particular types of stressors may have specific causal impact for certain disorders—for example, exits from the social field and depression (Paykel, Myers, Dienelt, Klerman, Lindenthal, and Pepper, 1969). However, events are also commonly scaled along a continuum of magnitude.

What assumptions are made in attempting to specify objectively the properties of life events? Along what dimension should magnitude be scaled? Holmes and Rahe (1967) originally scaled life events in terms of the amount of readjustment they would require the average person to make. Paykel, Prusoff, and Uhlenhuth (1971) subsequently scaled events for the degree of upset they would normatively engender. The assumptions underlying such scaling procedures are borrowed from models of stress in the physical sciences. For example, in Hooke's law and Young's modulus of elasticity, a stressor (e.g., a weight) is quantified according to the load it places on an object (e.g., a string). The degree of distortion provoked in the object is assumed to be linearly related to the physical magnitude of the stressor. This assumed parallelism between stimulus and response dimensions provides the rationale for having subjects provide normative magnitude ratings of stimuli along a hypothetical response dimension. Even though life events are scaled along a putative response dimension, it is important to note that the weights were neither literally derived nor have they ever been successfully validated against direct measures of response disruption or symptoms. Indeed, the fact that correlations with most outcome variables are as high for simple counts of events as for summed magnitude scores (Rahe, 1974) suggests that the hypothetical magnitude dimension may lack validity. Although this is disappointing from the standpoint of the assumptions of the model, it also implies that stress scores are at least partially independent of symptoms and behavioral outcomes. Precisely such independence is required to test hypotheses about the causal relationship of stress to schizophrenia.

Using objectively specifiable life events to define stress is a first step in evaluating stress independently from schizophenia. At least this strategy attempts to disentangle the independent variable from the welter of disturbances in arousal, disruptions in coping, cognitive eccentricities, and peculiarities of lifestyle that are known to be associated with the dependent variable. Of course, it remains open to question whether the scaling procedures currently in use do yield anything resembling an objective metric for stressors. The rationale, derived from principles of magnitude estimation in psychophysics (Stevens and Galanter, 1957), is solid, but there is no corresponding physical metric that could be used to validate life-event scales.

Although I have argued that objective measures of stress are the ones primarily useful in investigating whether stress is a cause of schizophrenia, I would now like to suggest that for descriptive purposes it may be useful to make tandem use of subjective and objective stress rating. If subjective distress were the only measure of stress, then any link with symptomatic distress might be exlicable by response bias. However, if both subjective and objective scorings were used, then empirical support might be found for the clinical observation (Beck and Worthen, 1972; Donovan, Dressler, and Geller, 1975) that schizophrenia often follows subjectively traumatic but objectively trivial events.

Disentangling Measurement of Stress and Schizophrenia

Even if the definitional issue were to be resolved, the research problem of disentangling stress from other factors related to the emergence of schizophrenia can only be described as mind-boggling. Potential confounds exist at many levels: in the implicit or explicit use of information about stress to make a diagnosis of schizophrenia; in the fact that the schizophenic illness can provoke stress; in the fact that prodromal conditions may also provoke stress; and finally, in the possibility that aspects of vulnerability present long before the emergence of illness may also influence the occurrence of stress.

When information about stress is used in deciding whether a diagnosis of schizophrenia is warranted, a test of the hypothesis that stress causes schizophrenia can only lead to spurious results. The dominant belief in contemporary medicine is that schizophrenia is a biological disorder that arises endogenously. Hence, it is likely that some proportion of cases presenting typical schizophrenic symptomatology may be diagnosed nonschizophrenic, if there is evidence that the illness was preceded by stress. Therefore, to some unknown degree, prevailing contemporary theoretical beliefs about the etiology of schizophrenia impose such a selection bias that the presence of a stressful event leads diagnosticians to ignore the presence of schizophrenia. It might be argued that diagnostic criteria should legitimately include information other than symptoms (Feighner, Robins, Guze, Woodruff, Winokur, and Munoz, 1972; Pope and Lipinski, 1978), so that stress might be a justifiable parameter in the diagnostic process. If this premise is accepted, however, it must also be acknowledged that none of the parameters assessed in the diagnostic appraisal can be used to validate the diagnosis etiologically, concurrently, or predictively. Only by quintessential circularity can we test whether stress is an etiological factor in schizophrenia when diagnostic assignments are, in part, implicitly based on evidence of recent stress.

It is likely that information about stress is used implicitly rather than explicitly in determining whether a schizophrenic diagnosis is warranted. Therefore, the confounding is not really eliminated by the usual procedure of deleting stress from the list of explicit criteria for diagnosing schizophrenia or dating its onset. The only real solution may be to assure that diagnosticians are blind to information about recent life events. The counterpart strategy is to keep life events interviewers blind to diagnosis, but this is rarely feasible. These solutions are clearly not undone by the usual research design, in which the same clinician administers interviews about life events and symptoms, but is then asked to evaluate stress and diagnosis independently.

A second problem of nonindependence adheres in the fact that the schizophrenic's peculiar behavior during an episode is capable of provoking a storm of stressful occurrences. Since these stressors are consequences of the illness, we must find some way of separating them from earlier stressors that might have caused the episode. The strategies generally adopted to achieve this end are twofold: an attempt at carefully dating the onset of the episode and efforts to eliminate stressors that might have been brought on by unusual behavior signifying the onset of disorder (Brown and Birley, 1968).

However, the Brown and Birley solution may fall short of the mark of attaining independence for two reasons. One is the conceptual problem of dating onset. The other is that although the patients' preepisode behavior may not be grossly unusual, it may be influenced by the underlying vulnerability or by pro-dromal features in such a way that the behavior alters the prob-able incidence of stress. It would be difficult to say in this case that the stressors cause schizophrenia. Rather, they might be epiphenomena in a cycle whereby the vulnerability gives rise both to schizophrenia and to stress.

Since patients often "slide" toward illness by a very gradual process, it is important to recognize as possibly nonindependent any stressors whose occurrence is influenced by the developing features of the preschizophrenic on this gradual slide. Whether we perceive such events to be associated with the early symptoms of the onset of illness will basically be an arbitrary function of whether we choose early or late criteria for defining onset. If we define onset at the beginning of the slide, these events will seem to be secondary consequences of illness. If we define onset at the very end of the slide, with the appearance of psychotic symptoms, then such events may appear to be associated with the manifestations of high vulnerability.

It is now apparent that as far back as childhood, there may be certain behavioral features associated with preschizophrenic conditions. Watt, Stolorow, Lubensky, and McClelland (1970) found that a substantial proportion of preschizophrenic boys showed poor school performance, emotional instability, and aggressiveness. Many preschizophrenic girls appeared oversensitive and introverted. Each of these behavior patterns might be expected to enhance the occurrence of stress.

Fontana, Marcus, Noel, and Rakusin (1972) have noted that life events are often goal-directed; that is, they may be brought on by the individual to achieve certain ends. Some of the events immediately preceding the onset of schizophrenia may illustrate this principle. Leff (1976) has suggested that in the years immediately before illness, schizophrenics show an increasing tendency to withdraw from contact with individuals close to them. Instead of fatefully befalling the patients, some of the events in the period before onset may be willfully provoked in pursuit of social isolation. To a neutral third party with certain preconceptions about the value of social isolation, they may seem well worth the cost.

Leff (1976) reviews evidence that in the few years before a first schizophrenic attack the individual often leaves his family of origin in a small town or rural area and moves to a single-person household in the "transitional zone" of a city. Relocations or changes in residence have been found to be significantly more prevalent for first-episode preschizophrenics than for controls during a comparable time period (Jacobs and Myers, 1976). Events involving other people (Schwartz and Myers, 1977), and family-related events (Jacobs and Myers, 1976), also appear in significant excess during the time period immediately preceding a schizophrenic episode. Clearly, the preschizophrenic who becomes embroiled in interpersonal conflicts and changes in residence may experience stress and suffer a disruption of social supports. However, it may also be the case that these events are secondary consequences of preschizophrenic behaviors and goals.

THE NATURE AND TIMING OF THE
MAXIMUM STRESS EFFECT

In research on stress and schizophrenia, two intriguing questions remain unanswered. The first of these is when we might expect stress to have the greatest impact on the probability of schizophrenia's occurrence. Are the most momentous stressors those that are recent or those that are remote (i.e., occurring earlier in the individual's developmental history)? The best known studies of stress and schizophrenia have concerned events immediately (within two years) preceding the appearance of schizophrenic disorder (Brown and Birley, 1968; Brown et al., 1973; Jacobs and Myers, 1976). These studies have suggested that schizophenics report more recent stressful life events than normal controls, but fewer than depressives. Findings generally indicate that stress is frequently a precursor of schizophrenia, although it is not necessary in all cases. Results do suggest that recent stress might play a causal role in the initiation of schizophrenia. However, as has already been pointed out, this inference is limited by possible atypicalities in the schizophrenics who comprised the research samples, as well as by difficulties in pinpointing schizophrenia's onset.

An entirely separate question is whether remote stressors occurring early in the life span may also play a causal role in schizophrenia. There is an increasingly impressive body of evidence to suggest that preschizophrenics suffer more than the normal incidence of pregnancy and birth complications (McNeil and Kaij, 1978) as well as early parent loss (Wahl, 1956; Garmezy, 1974). Might such remote stressors be involved in schizophrenia's etiology, and if so, what might the mechanism be?

In the research literature, two types of stress effects have been postulated: triggering and formative. Most researchers of recent events see themselves as investigating a triggering rather than a formative effect of these events on schizophrenia. Conceptually, however, the distinction between the concepts of triggering and formative effects has never been very clear. The formative-triggering distinction is sometimes taken to mean that a factor with a formative effect is a necessary condition for the occurrence of schizophrenia (Rabkin, 1980). By contrast a factor with a triggering effect is not a necessary condition—i.e., not a causal factor. Rather, a trigger may influence some ancillary property of the disorder, such as its timing. Alternatively, based on the mathematical assumptions of their "brought forward time" index, Brown, Sklair, Harris, and Birley (1973) have argued that the distinction between formative and triggering factors can be made on the basis of which factors are most important etiologically. If life events are more important etiologically than predispositional factors (stable properties of the individual and his environment), then they have a formative effect. If they are not, then, by default, a triggering effect cannot be ruled out, although it cannot be directly confirmed either. As Dohrenwend and Egri (1981) point out, however, the inference that the "brought forward time" index can be used to judge the relative impact of stress versus predisposing factors remains untested, since life events and dispositional properties have never been measured and directly compared in the same study. Finally, the formative-triggering distinction has been defined with reference to whether life events advance the appearance of schizophrenia a lot or a little in time (Brown et al., 1973). Although this latter formulation is again mathematically clever, it is also somewhat teleological and not directly testable.

Quite clearly, the distinction between formative and triggering effects of stressful life events has remained unclear and open to multiple interpretations. It may, therefore, be fruitful to examine the theoretical model that differentiates between these two effects of stress. The distinction is best elaborated in the vulnerability (Zubin and Spring, 1977; Spring and Coons, 1982) or diathesis-stress (Meehl, 1962; Rosenthal, 1970) models of schizophrenia. First, it is postulated that some stressors contribute to the formation of the vulnerability or diathesis for schizophrenia. Vulnerability is described as a relatively stable trait of individual difference that mediates the risk or capacity to become schizophrenic. Generally, remote stressors early in life are thought to have the most pronounced formative effects, although it might also be possible that recent trauma could exert formative effects on vulnerability. The vulnerability model also postulates a second triggering or precipitating role of stress. The precipitating role of stress is qualitatively different from the formative effect that augments vulnerability. Vulnerability is postulated to remain latent until it is elicited by a precipitating or triggering event. The precipitant does not add to vulnerability, but rather causes vulnerability to become manifest. Stated differently, a "trigger" precipitates an episode but does not alter the threshold for future responses to new triggering events. An event with a formative effect changes vulnerability and modifies the response to future stressors. The effects of a trigger are reversible, whereas those of a formative event are relatively irreversible. Nonetheless, according to the theoretical model, a triggering event of some magnitude is always needed to bring about a schizophrenic episode, even if vulnerability is very high. Thus, triggering stressors influence not just the timing of schizophrenia, but its very probability of occurrence (Spring and Coons, 1982).

CONCLUSIONS

The purpose of this article has been to raise some new questions about the role of stress in the etiology of schizophrenia. Currently it appears that stress may play some causal role, but its impact is smaller than we might have wished and certainly less specific than the role of loss in depression. It has frequently been concluded that stress plays only a triggering role at best, rather than a formative role. However, the triggering-formative distinction has remained open to multiple interpretations. Before the nature of the effect of stress on schizophrenia can be clearly discerned, it seems important to pay more careful attention to several issues of timing. For instance, is the onset of schizophrenia defined as that point when the psychotic syndrome becomes manifest, or is it more reasonable to conceive of onset as occurring at some point in the prodromal syndrome? In addition to questions about the onset of illness, the role of remote events in the development of schizophrenia bears further investigation. The search for causal factors which have the potential to trigger episodes needs to be supplemented by greater attention to the effects of remote stressors on the formation of vulnerability to schizophrenic illness. This information should prove useful in our attempts to define the relationship between stress and schizophrenia.

REFERENCES

Andrews, G., & Tennant, C. (1978), Editorial, Life event stress and psychiatric illness. *Psychol. Med.*, 8:545–549.

Beck, J. C., & Worthen, K. (1972), Precipitating stress, crisis theory, and hospitalization in schizophrenia and depression. *Arch. Gen. Psychiat.*, 26:123–129.

Bleuler, M. (1978), *The Schizophrenic Disorder: Long-Term Patient and Family Studies.* New Haven, CT: Yale University Press.

Broen, W. W., & Storms, L. H. (1967), A theory of response interference in schizophrenia. In: *Progress in Experimental Personality Research*, Vol. 4, ed. B. Maher. New York: Academic Press, pp. 269–312.

Brown, G. W. (1974), Meaning, measurement and stress of life events. In: *Stressful Life Events: Their Nature and Effects*, ed. B. S. Dohrenwend & B. P. Dohrenwend. New York: John Wiley, pp. 217–243.

——— Birley, J. L. T. (1968), Crises and life changes and the onset of schizophrenia. *J. Health & Soc. Behav.*, 9:203–214.

——— Harris, T., & Peto, J. (1973), Life events and psychiatric disorders: Part II. Nature of the causal link. *Psychol. Med.*, 3:159–176.

——— Sklair, F., Harris, T. O., & Birley, J. L. T. (1973), Life events and psychiatric disorders: Some methodological issues. *Psychol. Med.*, 3:74–87.

Docherty, J. P., Van Kammen, D. P., Siris, S. G., & Marder, S. R. (1978), Stages of onset of schizophrenic psychosis. *Amer. J. Psychiat.*, 135:420–426.

Dohrenwend, B. P., & Egri, G. (1981), Recent stressful life events and episodes of schizophrenia. *Schiz. Bull.*, 7:12–23.

Donovan, J. M., Dressler, L. M., & Geller, R. A. (1975), Psychiatric crisis: A comparison of schizophrenic and nonschizophrenic patients. *J. Nerv. & Ment. Dis.*, 161:172–179.

Feighner, J. P., Robins, E., Guze, S. B., Woodruff, R. A., Winokur, G., & Munoz, R. (1972), Diagnostic criteria for use in psychiatric research. *Arch. Gen. Psychiat.*, 26:57–58.

Fontana, A., Marcus, J., Noel, B., & Rakusin, J. (1972), Prehospitalization coping styles of psychiatric patients: The goal-directedness of life events. *J. Nerv. & Ment. Dis.*, 155:311–321.

Garmezy, N. (1974), Children at risk: The search for the antecedents of schizophrenia. Part I. Conceptual models and research methods. *Schiz. Bull.*, 8:14–90.

Holmes, T. H., & Rahe, R. H. (1967), The Social Readjustment Rating Scale. *J. Psychosom. Res.*, 11:213–218.

Jacobs, S., & Myers, J. (1976), Recent life events and acute schizophrenic psychosis: A controlled study. *J. Nerv. & Ment. Dis.*, 162:75–87.

Jacobs, S. C., Prusoff, B. A., & Paykel, E. S. (1974), Recent life events and acute schizophrenia and depression. *Psychol. Med.*, 4:444–453.

Kety, S. S., Rosenthal, D., Wender, P. H., & Schulsinger, F. (1968), The types and prevalence of mental illness in the biological and adoptive families of adopted schizophrenics. In: *The Transmission of Schizophrenia*, ed. D. Rosenthal & S. S. Kety. New York: Pergamon Press, pp. 345–362.

Kornetsky, C., & Eliasson, M. (1969), Reticular stimulation and chlorpromazine: An animal model for schizophrenic overarousal. *Science*, 165:1273–1274.

Langfeldt, G. (1956), The prognosis in schizophrenia. *Acta Psychiat. Scand.* Suppl. 110:1–66.

Lazarus, R. S. (1974), Cognitive and coping processes in emotion. In: *Cognitive Views of Human Motivation*, ed. B. Weiner. New York: Academic Press, pp. 21–32.

Leff, J. P. (1976), Schizophrenia and sensitivity to the family environment. *Schiz. Bull.*, 2:566–574.

Mayer-Gross, W., Slater, E., & Roth, M., eds. (1969), *Clinical Psychiatry*, 3rd ed. Baltimore: Williams & Wilkins.

McNeil, T. F., & Kaij, L. (1978), Obstetric factors in the development of schizophrenia: Complications in the births of preschizophrenics and in reproductions by schizophrenic parents. In: *The Nature of Schizophrenia: New Approaches to Research and Treatment*, ed. L. C. Wynne, R. L. Cromwell, & S. Matthysse. New York: John Wiley, pp. 401–429.

Mechanic, D. (1967), Invited commentary on self, social environment and stress. In: *Psychological Stress*, ed. M. H. Appley & R. Trumbull. New York: Appleton-Century-Crofts, pp. 199–201.

Mednick, S. A. (1958), A learning theory approach to research in schizophrenia. *Psychol. Bull.*, 55:316–327.

———— Schulsinger, F. (1968), Some premorbid characteristics related to breakdown in children with schizophrenic mothers. In: *The Transmission of Schizophrenia*, ed. D. Rosenthal & S. S. Kety. New York: Pergamon Press, pp. 267–291.

Meehl, P. E. (1962), Schizoptxia, schizotypy, schizophrenia. *Amer. Psychol.*, 17:827–838.

Paykel, E. S., Myers, J. K., Dienelt, M. N., Klerman, G. L., Lindenthal, J. J.,

& Pepper, M. P. (1969), Life events and depression: A controlled study. *Arch. Gen. Psychiat.*, 21:753–760.

—— Prusoff, B. A., & Uhlenhuth, E. H. (1971), Scaling of life events. *Arch. Gen. Psychiat.*, 25:340–347.

Phillips, L. (1968), *Human Adaptation and Its Failures*. New York: Academic Press.

Pope, H. G., & Lipinski, J. F. (1978), Diagnosis in schizophrenia and manic-depressive illness. *Arch. Gen. Psychiat.*, 35:811–827.

Rabkin, J. (1980), Stressful life events and schizophrenia: A review of the research literature. *Psychol. Bull.*, 87:408–425.

—— Struening, E. (1976), Life events, stress and illness. *Science*, 194:1013–1020.

Rahe, R. H. (1974), The pathway between subjects' recent life changes and their near-future illness reports: Representative results and methodological issues. In: *Stressful Life Events: Their Nature and Effects*, ed. B. S. Dohrenwend & B. P. Dohrenwend. New York: John Wiley, pp. 73–86.

Rosenthal, D. (1970), *Genetic Theory and Abnormal Behavior*. New York: McGraw-Hill.

Schneider, K. (1959), *Clinical Psychopathology*. New York: Grune & Stratton.

Schwartz, C. D., & Myers, J. K. (1977), Life events and schizophrenia. I. Comparison of schizophrenics with a community sample. *Arch. Gen. Psychiat.*, 34:1238–1241.

Selye, H. (1956), *The Stress of Life*. New York: McGraw-Hill.

Spring, B., & Coons, H. (1982), Stress as a precursor of schizophrenia. In: *Psychological Stress and Psychopathology*, ed. R. W. J. Neufeld. New York: McGraw-Hill, pp. 386–411.

Stevens, S. S., & Galanter, E. H. (1957), Ratio scales and category scales for a dozen perceptual continua. *J. Exper. Psychol.*, 54:377–411.

Strauss, J. S., Harder, D. W., & Chandler, M. (1979), Egocentrism in children of parents with a history of psychotic disorders. *Arch. Gen. Psychiat.*, 36:191–200.

Uhlenhuth, E. H., Huberman, S. J., Balter, M. D., & Lipman, R. S. (1977), Remembering life events. In: *The Origins and Course of Psychopathology: Method of Longitudinal Research*, ed. J. S. Strauss, H. M. Babigian, & M. Roff. New York: Plenum Press, pp. 117–132.

Venables, P. H. (1964), Input dysfunction in schizophrenia. In: *Progress in Experimental Personality Research*, Vol. 1, ed. B. Maher. New York: Academic Press, pp. 1–47.

Wahl, C. W. (1956), Some antecedent factors in the family histories of 568 male schizophrenics of the United States Navy. *Amer. J. Psychiat.*, 113:201–210.

Watt, N. F., Stolorow, R. D., Lubensky, A. W., & McClelland, D. C. (1970),

School adjustment and behavior of children hospitalized for schizophrenia as adults. *Amer. J. Orthopsychiat.*, 40:637–657.

Zubin, J., & Spring, B. (1977), Vulnerability—A new view of schizophrenia as adults. *J. Abnorm. Psychol.*, 86:103–126.

Chapter 22
Recent Stressful Life Events and Episodes of Schizophrenia

BRUCE P. DOHRENWEND, M.D., AND GLADYS EGRI, M.D.

Schizophrenia is a ". . . descriptive entity without clear margins" (Gruenberg, 1974, p. 455). Historically, broader or narrower definitions of these margins have held sway depending on whether focus has been on chronically ill older patients who have made up the bulk of the patients in mental hospitals, or on cohorts of first admissions who have been followed up over time and show highly variable course and outcomes (Gruenberg, 1974). In this context, we shall sidestep such thorny issues as whether there is such a thing as a single disorder called "schizophrenia," or whether, in fact, we are dealing with a group disorder. Consistent with the nature of the available evidence, we shall be concerned with stressful life events and schizophrenic episodes. For purposes of this chapter, we will accept the operational definitions used by the various investigators as describing such episodes.

Among researchers concerned with the problem, there appears to be a growing consensus that stressful life events such

Acknowledgment. This chapter was first published in *Schizophrenia Bulletin* (1981), 7/1:12–23, and it is reprinted with permission.

as marriage, divorce, birth of a child, death of a loved one, and loss of a job play a role in onset and recurrence of schizophrenic episodes, but that this role is quite trivial (e.g., Brown, Harris, and Peto, 1973; Hudgens, 1974; Gottesman and Shields, 1976), Consider the conclusions of Hudgens on the one hand and Brown et al. on the other on the basis of their analyses of much of the most important research. Hudgens (1974) states:

Investigators have demonstrated a causal connection between stressful life events and subsequent worsening of conditions already underway, between life events and admission to psychiatric hospitals or clinics. . . . It does not seem to me that investigators have yet convincingly demonstrated that life stress can cause madness in a person previously sound of mind . . . [p. 120].

For their part, Brown et al. distinguish between two types of causal role that life events might lay: "formative" in contrast to "triggering" (Brown et al., 1973, p. 162). Events have a formative environmental effect when they are more important in the causation of a schizophrenic episode than dispositional factors such as "genetic and constitutional difference, early childhood experiences, and personality traits" together with "ongoing social difficulties and amount of current social support" (Brown et al., 1973, p. 159). By contrast, events have a triggering effect when such predispositional factors play the larger role. Brown and his colleagues conclude that life events are less important than dispositional factors for schizophrenic patients and that "in the majority of cases they trigger an onset that might well have occurred quite soon in any case" (Brown et al., 1973, p. 172).

According to Brown et al. (1973) the point of consensus, then, is that life events are judged unlikely to have a formative effect or, in Hudgens' (1974) vivid phrase, cause madness in a person previously sound of mind. Is such a consensus supported by the evidence? That is, do recent life events have a causal influence on onset and relapse? If so, is this effect formative or that of trigger? If the effect is to trigger, is it weak or strong when compared to the effects of various other endogenous and exogenous predispositional factors?

CASE-CONTROL STUDIES OF LIFE EVENTS AND SCHIZOPHRENIA

Given the rarity of diagnosed schizophrenia the general population (Cooper, 1978; Dohrenwend, Dohrenwend, Gould, Link, Neugebauer, and Wunsch-Hitzig, 1980), and the tremendous expense in both time and effort that long-term prospective research involves, the strategy for systematically investigating the role of life events has involved retrospective case-control designs. Both Brown and Hudgens have set forth criteria for adequate case-control studies of the problem. We have been influenced by them in developing the list shown in Table 22.1.

The criteria listed in Table 22.1 are probably essential if we are to have decisive findings; however, several of the criteria are extremely difficult to meet. For example, to obtain a representative sample of persons who develop schizophrenic episodes, we must be able to agree upon and identify the important characteristics of these episodes and draw a representative sample of those showing such characteristics—whether these individuals have been officially recognized (e.g., by admission to a mental hospital) or not. In analyses of results from epidemiological studies of true prevalence, Link and Dohrenwend (1980) have found that substantial minorities of the diagnosed schizophrenics in the general population have never been in inpatient or outpatient treatment. And while it is clear that some fateful events such as death of a loved one are very likely to occur independently of the individual's mental condition or behavior, and others such as being convicted of a crime are not, most events are between these extremes and require considerable additional information about the context in which they occur before such a determination can even begin to be made. More-

Table 22.1
Ideal Criteria for a Case-Control Study of Life
Events and Schizophrenic Episodes

- The cases should consist of a representative sample of individuals from the population being studied who have recently developed the schizophrenic episodes the first time.
- The procedures of collecting the symptom data and the rules for combining these data into diagnoses of cases should be explicit and replicable.
- The controls should consist of a representative sample of the demographic counterparts of the cases in the population being studied.
- There should be similarly selected comparison groups of cases with other types of symptomatology.
- Data on life events should be gathered systematically from the subjects and their informants on fully enumerated lists of events rather than from patient charts where recording of the relevant information tends to be fragmented.
- Both the occurrence of the events and the occurence of onsets and/or recurrences of the schizophrenic episodes should be dated accurately with respect to one another.
- Events that are likely to occur as consequences of the individual's mental state and behavior must be distinguished from events that occur independently of such personality factors.
- Data on alternative or complementary dispositional or risk factors should be secured.
- Repeated followups should be conducted at suitable intervals of time to test whether the circumstances preceding recurrence are the same as the circumstances preceding onset, and whether they can be made to differ in meaningful ways with the occurence of intervening factors such as type and duration of treatment.

over, data on the most firmly established risk factor, a high rate of the schizophrenic symptomatology in first-degree relatives, are extremely difficult and expensive to secure. It should not be surprising, therefore, that there is no single case-control study of life events and schizophrenia that meets all of the above criteria.

Two studies meet more of these criteria, however, than any of the others of which we are aware. Interestingly, they also come closest to satisfying the four criteria that constitute the irreducible minimum for providing useful results bearing on the problem of whether life events play a causal role—adequate controls, replicable diagnostic criteria, attention to assessing which events occur independently of the subjects' prior mental state, and careful dating of occurrence of the events in relation to the occurrence of the schizophrenic episodes. One of the two case-control studies was conducted in New Haven by Jacobs and Myers (1976); the other in London by Brown and Birley (1968) and Birley and Brown (1970).

THE NEW HAVEN STUDY

The 62 cases in the New Haven study were selected from all patients admitted to three hospitals over a 6-month period with a hospital "diagnosis or a diagnosis listed for exclusion of schizophrenia, schizoaffective illness, and delusions and hallucinations" (Jacobs and Myers, 1976, p. 76). To enter the study, the patient had to be a first admission and, on the basis of a personal interview by a psychiatrist 2–4 weeks after admission, to meet study diagnostic criteria for schizophrenia. These criteria consisted of the presence of two or more of the following symptoms: "ideas of influence, feelings of telepath, thought disorder, inappropriate or flat affect, catatonic disturbances, persecutory delusions, grandiose delusions, and other types of delusions and hallucinations that were not depressive in quality or secondary to drugs" (Jacobs and Myers, 1976, p. 77). The characteristics of the patients are summarized in the left hand portion of Table 22.2.

The 62 controls were systematically subsampled from a representative sample of 938 individuals from the general population of a mental health catchment area in New Haven. They were matched to the schizophrenic patients on the basis of age, sex, marital status, and socioeconomic status. The recent experience of this community sample with stressful life events had been previously studied by Myers, Lindenthal, and Pepper (1974). These investigators had developed a detailed list of life

Table 22.2
Description of Patients in New Haven and London Case-Control Studies

Patient Characteristics	New Haven (62 cases; 62 controls)	London (50 cases; 325 controls)
Socioeconomic Status	Median: Class IV	Not Identified
Diagnosis	"Definite. schizophrenia" ($n = 24$) "Probable schizophrenia" —i.e., schizophreniform state ($n = 26$)	45 schizophrenic 4 schizoaffective
Age	Average: 28	"Definite"—mean 38.2 "Probable"—younger mean 29.3
Diagnostic Criteria	Similar but not identical	
Type of Onset	Not described All patients were first admissions and very likely to be first episodes	Normal to schizophrenic: "Probable" = 75% (18/24) "Definite" = 42% (11/26) Normal to schizophrenic—29 patients Nonschizophrenic symptoms to schizophrenic—8 patients Exacerbation from mild to severely schizophrenic—13 patients

events for the purpose, based on their own research and that of others.

The same interview approach was used by Jacobs and Myers (1976) to obtain data on life events in the interviews with the patients 2–4 weeks after admission. The period covered by the interview was 1 year before onset. This interval was chosen to correspond with the 1-year period covered in the interviews with the controls.

THE LONDON STUDY

In the London study conducted by Brown and Birley, the 50 schizophrenic patients were selected by screening the case notes of all patients admitted to hospitals serving a catchment area in London. All who were judged to be possibly schizophrenic were interviewed with an early edition of the Present State Examination (Wing, Cooper, and Sartorius, 1974), and diagnosed by one of the two participating psychiatrists as showing at least one of the following four groups of symptoms (Birley and Brown, 1970, p. 328):

1. Subjective experience of disordered thought or body control.
2. Delusions of persecution or reference which were thought to be undeserved and not occurring in the context of severe depression.
3. Grandiose, religious, somatic, or bizarre delusions but not in a setting of severe depression or mania.
4. Consistent hallucinations, but not depressive in content and not symptomatic of alcohol addiction.

For about 40 percent of the schizophrenic patients, onset was dated as occurring at some time within 13 weeks before admission. The first 40 of these patients constituted the schizophrenic cases in this study, and their characteristics are summarized in the right hand portion of Table 22.2. Almost half of the patients were experiencing their first hospital admission and 30 percent were experiencing their "first ever" episode of schizophrenia (Birley and Brown, 1970, p. 329).

The controls were a random sample of 325 employees at six local firms. Most were clerical workers and semiskilled or unskilled factory workers. Both patients and controls were given the same, detailed interview about life events and the time and context in which they occurred. For the controls, the period covered was 13 weeks before the interview; for the patients, the period covered was the 13 weeks before onset. Coinformants from among the relatives or close acquaintances of the patients were also interviewed to check on the reliability of reported events, and the precise time was recorded of the occurrence of each event within the 13-week period covered by the reports.

Main Results From the London and New Haven Studies

The consistent finding from the two studies is that there was a significantly higher rate of life events for the patients in the reporting period of 3 months in the London study and 1 year in the New Haven study than for the controls. However, since this rate was based mainly on events that may be dependent on the patients' mental condition, the conclusion from these results alone might well be that the patients were more prone to get themselves into stressful situations than victims of such situations (Fontana, Marcus, Noel, and Rakusin, 1972). Consider, however, the additional finding from the London study of a higher rate of independent events in the 3-week period before onset for patients in their first episode or recurrence than for patients in subsequent episodes. Forty-six percent of patients had experienced at least one independent event in the 3-week period as compared with only 12 percent of the controls. Consequently, we have evidence of a causal role for life events. Fortunately, the Brown and Birley (1968) finding is not an isolated instance. In another study, Leff, Hirsch, Gaind, Rohde, and Stevens (1973) found similar increase of events in the period just before relapse in a sample of schizophrenics being treated with phenothiazines in the community. The Brown and Birley finding held, moreover, regardless of type of onset, first admission versus readmission status of the patient, and also among those experiencing first schizophrenic episodes versus those experiencing recurrences.

Let us assume that the main difference in the results of the New Haven and London studies stems from the fact that the New Haven researchers apparently did not date the occurrence of the events at weekly or monthly intervals within the year period and were, therefore, unable to determine whether there had been a significant increase in independent events just before the episode. The results then suggest that stressful life events do play a role in both onset and recurrence. What kind of role do they play, and how strong is it?

LIFE EVENTS IN SCHIZOPHRENIA AND DEPRESSION

Brown and his colleagues, as mentioned earlier, concluded that the role of life events in schizophrenic episodes is mainly that of trigger. Their argument, like that of the New Haven researchers, appears to be based largely on comparisons with patients with affective disorders. In these comparisons, the preponderance of evidence supports the conventional wisdom that stressful life events are more important in depression than in schizophrenia; for example, calculations of relative risk (Paykel, 1978) and "brought-forward time" (Brown et al., 1973) appear to support this view. The results do not, however, speak directly to the central theoretical question: Are life events more or less important than predispositional factors in the causation of the schizophrenic episode? There has been no attempt to measure the dispositional factors in the case-control studies of life events and schizophrenic episodes that would have prospective studies of subjects selected for high genetic risk of schizophrenia as yet begun to provide some of the relevant information on this matter that could come from such studies (Garmezy, 1974).

PSYCHIATRIC SYMPTOMATOLOGY IN EXTREME SITUATIONS

In the absence of a direct rest, let us consider what kinds of events should have taken place for us to be able to infer a formative instead of a triggering effect. Bleuler (1976), in a recent description of his view of the role of environmental influences in the development of schizophrenia, gives us an idea of what they should not be. He writes:

No known particular, "specific," enigmatic environmental influence is decisive in the development of schizophrenia; instead, the psychological stress that we discover in the life histories of schizophrenics emanates from a combination of worries, stress, and tensions that by their nature cannot clearly be distinguished from those that afflict all of us at times in one form or another [p. 356].

The implication is that, if life events are to have a formative effect, they must be clearly distinguishable either in type, combination, or frequency of occurrence from those that afflict all of us at times in one form or another. Most important would be the location of a set of recent events that had been shown, in Hudgens' apt phrase, to cause madness in a person previously sound of mind. Our best clues as to what these events might be come from the literature on extreme situations, especially the situation of combat during wartime, since such situations have indeed been found to produce severe psychopathology in previously normal persons (Dohrenwend, 1979).

A wide variety of symptoms have occurred under combat conditions. These have included psychotic symptoms. Were the psychotic symptoms caused by the extreme situations?

Paster (1948), in a remarkable study of the records of 1,500 psychotic patients and their relatives during World War II, found less evidence of individual predisposing factors among combat soldiers who became psychotic than among soldiers who developed psychotic disorders in less stressful circumstances. The large majority of the psychoses, over 70 percent, were judged to be schizophrenic. Discussing these results, Paster observed:

It is generally believed that the psychotic soldier is of a fundamentally weak make-up and is unable to withstand the stress and strain associated with military life. In this connection it is significant to note that 45% of soldiers in the non-overseas group succumbed within one year of service.

On the other hand, many soldiers who later broke down had succeeded in serving both overseas and in combat. In these less vulnerable individuals, tension, prolonged separation from home and exposure to combat undoubtedly played a significant role in finally precipitating the psychotic reactions. This is corroborated by the fact that among the combat participants the largest group affected was that composed of soldiers who had been in the Army the longest period of time. These soldiers who succumbed in combat had endured the battlefield for an average period of four months . . . [pp. 56–57].

Moreover, Wagner (1946), in a study of 5,203 neuropsychiatric casualties of the Normandy campaign, compared psychotic and nonpsychotic admissions to "exhaustion centers," finding that: "Compared with our nonpsychotic admissions, their military achievements, as judged by ratings and combat days, were equal if not superior to the neurotic casualties" (p. 365).

Wagner estimated that only about 3 percent of the patients at exhaustion centers were diagnosed as psychotic at time of discharge. He states that within the classification of psychosis: "More than half of these were placed in the category 'undiagnosed' usually out of reluctance to consider a patient schizophrenic after so limited a period of observation" (p. 355).

By all accounts, psychotic symptomatology was far more prevalent under combat conditions than such rates of reluctantly assigned final diagnoses at exhaustion centers would suggest. There are reports, for example, of "three day" psychoses (Kolb, 1973, p. 438), "five-day schizophrenia" (Kormos, 1978, p. 4), and "twilight states" (Schneider, 1959, p. 58) that would be omitted from such statistics.

The question can be raised, of course, as to whether these psychiatrists were seeing the same kinds of schizophrenic symptoms in the military setting that they observed with their patients in civilian life. For example, the prognosis for combat soldiers diagnosed as schizophrenic was far better than would have been expected on the basis of civilian experience (Wagner, 1946; Paster, 1948). Students of combat reactions, such as Paster and Wagner, however, have reported that symptomatology of schizophrenia observed in combat situations is indistinguishable from the symptoms of schizophrenia observed in patients from civilian populations. Kurt Schneider (1959), as Birley and Brown (1970) point out, holds that symptoms of "true" schizophrenia with a "somatic etiology" can be distinguished from "psychic reactions" caused by external events. Schneider would, therefore, be expected to be a harsh judge of the matter. Yet he wrote:

At the battlefront, it was often hard to make a differential diagnosis between psychogenic twilight state and schizophrenia . . . the accumulation of psychotic-like symptoms among men waiting at the base dressing-stations is naturally some contraindication for schizophrenia. Once I saw three such doubtful cases together, but in the isolated case it can be impossible for the most practiced eye not to be deceived at first [p. 58].

Combat is not the only situation in which such acute and transient symptomatology has been observed. Murphy (1968) has pointed out that in nonwesternized societies:

Acute short-lasting psychoses form a major part of all recognized mental disorder, and there is no agreement where these lie in our current diagnostic classifications. . . . Some psychiatrists include most such cases under schizophrenia on the grounds of their delusional or hallucinatory elements and of the fact that a few of these acute states, indistinguishable from the rest initially, develop into typically chronic schizophrenia later. Other workers, however, call them organic psychoses, incriminating one of the various infections or infestations which nearly every patient in these countries has. Still others regard them as something different from either. The relative number of such conditions is too high for us to treat them as we do borderline schizophrenias in North America, by pretending that they do not make a real difference one way or the other, and their short duration creates serious difficulties for field surveys, which are usually forced to deduce incidence on the basis of prevalence [p. 138].

Consider, moreover, the striking findings from the World Health Organization study of schizophrenia indicating that prognosis is also far better for patients actually diagnosed as schizophrenics in underdeveloped countries (Sartorius, Jablensky, and Shapiro, 1978). In this study, the investigators were using modern methods of diagnosis. Clearly, the nature of schizophrenic symptoms per se tells us little if anything about future course (Strauss and Carpenter, 1972, 1974; Hawk and Carpenter, 1975) in civilian as well as in military settings. There appears to be no way to distinguish between the symptomatology of schizophrenic episodes in civilian in contrast to military settings.

Let us consider, then, the circumstances under which combinations of more ordinary stressful life events might induce an approximation of the conditions involved in extreme situations such as prolonged exposure to heavy combat in wartime. Such extreme situations involve being faced with unanticipated negative events whose occurrences are outside the control of the individual experiencing them—in wartime, for example, they involve death of comrades, threat of one's own death or disablement, physical exhaustion, and being stripped of the social support of comrades as the casualty rate rises. Events in civil life such as loss of loved one, life-threatening physical illness or injury, events that disrupt social supports (e.g., a move to new community or change to new place of employment) may, if they occur in close proximity to one another, create conditions of environmentally induced stress resembling those of extreme situations. Hypothetically, we have a triad of events whose occurrence in close proximity to one another over a relatively brief period of time may induce psychopathology in previously normal persons in much the same way that extreme situations involved in natural or manmade disasters are known to do (Dohrenwend, 1979).

THE NATURE OF LIFE EVENTS DESCRIBED IN THE LONDON AND NEW HAVEN STUDIES

Is there evidence that such a pathogenic triad of recent events has preceded schizophrenic onset or recurrence among the patients in the New Haven and London studies? Fortunately, Brown and Birley (1968) provide information on the actual events experienced in the 13-week period before onset or relapse by the individuals diagnosed as schizophrenic in their study. It is clear from this material that no one of the cases experienced events from all three elements of our hypothesized pathogenic triad. However, Brown et al. (1973) have reported that about 16 percent experienced events that they judged to be markedly severe and that, moreover, this was three times the rate of such threatening events among the controls. This later finding led Brown et al. (1973) to speculate that there might be a formative effect of stressful events at least for a small minority of schizophrenics.

Looking over the case material that Brown and Birley (1968) provided in their earlier article, we could make our own judgments about the severity of stress that may well correspond to those made by Brown and his colleagues. Like them, one of us selected eight persons or 16 percent of the total number of schizophrenics as seeming to have experienced unusually severe objective stress. The other independently selected five of the same persons and added no one who was not previously selected. Based on Brown and Birley's material, Table 22.3 shows the independent events that one or both of us judged to be

Table 22.3
Markedly Severe "Independent" Events Experienced by Eight
Schizophrenic Patients in the London Study

- Birth of a child whom patient was told was "ill" with white asphyxia
- Husband admitted to hospital with a carcinoma
- Father with whom patient lived died
- Parents with whom patient lived had problems of severe physical illness: father developed pneumonia; mother an invalid, returned to hospital
- Patient required police protection around the clock because of threats about giving evidence in a criminal trial
- Mother with whom patient lived committed suicide
- Patient admitted to hospital with rapidly failing eyesight due to an eye infection
- Mother hospitalized for mental illness

---

markedly severe. We were also struck in going over this material by the fact that slightly over 40 percent of the patients experienced actual, or, in a few cases, impending residential changes and/or job changes that would seem highly likely to disrupt usual social supports. Such moves appear to be characteristic of schizophrenic patients (Odegard, 1932; Dunham, 1965, p. 162).

The data from the New Haven study (Jacobs and Myers, 1976) on the actual life events experienced are presented in more aggregated form than in the London study. We could not, therefore, do an analysis of the particular events experienced by each subject. It is intriguing to note, nevertheless, that, consistent with the London findings and the larger literature on schizophrenia, the New Haven patients moved from one neighborhood to another far more frequently than the community controls. However, there is again no evidence that two major elements of our hypothesized pathogenic triad—physical illness or injury and other severe loss events such as death of loved one—are more frequent among the patients than among the controls. Several studies suggest that both types of events may be more prominent among recent events experienced by depressed patients (Beck and Worthen, 1972; Jacobs, Prusoff, and Paykel, 1974; Lahniers and White, 1976). Also, it is disconcerting to find that only one of the events Jacobs and Myers defined as independent in the New Haven study showed a statistically significant difference between their schizophrenic patients and their controls; the event was "death of a pet" (Jacobs and Myers, 1976, p. 80). In fact, all six events that discriminated at the .05 levels or better between cases and controls in that study could have been confounded with the patient's disorders. This would be particularly relevant for events such as being arrested, court appearance, and disagreement or trouble with boss and, perhaps, for changes of residence as well (Jacobs and Myers, 1976, p. 80).

How, then, are we to interpret this information from the London and New Haven studies about the types of recent events experienced by schizophrenic patients? These events clearly fall short of our hypothesized pathogenic triad in approximating the conditions of extreme situations such as combat or natural disasters. On the other hand, they appear quite different from those that, as Bleuler (1976, p. 356) put it, ". . . by their nature cannot clearly be distinguished from those that afflict all of us at times in one form or another." Rather, when we see for each individual patient the specific event he or she experiences as Brown and Birley's (1968) case material permits us to do, it seems evident that these are not the kinds of events that afflict all of us at one time or another. For example, these patients are more likely to have mothers who are admitted to mental hospitals or commit suicide, to be themselves involved with the police and the courts, and to change their residences and their jobs frequently. These stressful circumstances do not seem objectively as severe as those created by the pathogenic triad, so we must infer that such schizophrenic patients are more vulnerable than most people. On the other hand, the patients are exposed not only to ordinary stressful events that most people experience, but also to events that appear peculiar to their biological and psychological status as schizophrenics and their social status as psychiatric patients. For example, since there is strong evidence of a genetic component in schizophrenia, pathology is likely to run in members of the families of these patients on whom they are dependent for social support, creating "binds in the family situation" (Clausen, 1979, p. 40). And since there is something about either the disorder and/or the way it is handled in modern Western societies that makes schizophrenics prone to some types of disruptive events, they must try to cope more than most people have to with losses of social supports stemming from moves from one region to another, from one residence to another, from one job to another, and disruptive contact with the law.

Brown et al. (1973) argue cogently that if events that can be shown to be independent of the individual's mental condition occur more frequently before onset or relapse in schizophrenics than controls, these events could play at least a minimal role in causation. We believe that a person who has first-degree relatives diagnosed as schizophrenic and/or suffering from possible related disorders (Kety, Rosenthal, Wender, and Schulsinger, 1976) is likely to experience stressful events as a direct result of his or her family situation—events that are more than such ordinary events as changes in job and residence. Brown and Birley (1968), for example, classified both the suicide of one schizophrenic patient's mother and the institutionalization of the mother of another as independent events. Moreover, those patients, with their unusual family situations, are likely to be just as vulnerable to more ordinary stressful events as the rest of us. Thus, the excess of events experienced by schizophrenic patients in these case-control studies has a certain plausibility as being both unusually severe and as including independent events that qualify for a causal role. What kinds of effect do they have?

Brown et al. (1973) suggest that the life events trigger the onset of florid symptoms in predisposed persons. Schwartz and Myers (1977), however, have reported findings suggesting that life events have a greater influence on nonpsychotic symptoms in a sample of posthospitalized schizophrenics living in the community. The kinds of symptoms they describe correspond closely to what we would, following Frank's (1973) conceptualization, describe as "demoralization," a syndrome of psychological distress that follows a wide variety of situations, including combat, in which individuals find themselves in circumstances with which they are unable to cope. It seems possible to us that situationally induced demoralization may be a forerunner of the schizophrenic episode in predisposed persons. If this is so, it would carry implications for prevention, since demoralization is thought to be extremely responsive to social support (Frank, 1973). Only closely monitored prospective research will tell if this is the case.

ONSET VERSUS RECURRENCE

It is remarkable that the main findings from the Brown and Birley study (Brown and Birley, 1968; Birley and Brown, 1970)—an increase of life events just before the onset of a schizophrenic episode or a relapse—held true for first admission cases and readmissions. The similar findings appear to have occurred despite the fact that many personal and social circumstances at relapse are likely to be different from those at onset. For example, medication is likely to affect the person's behavior; and having displayed psychiatric symptoms and/or been hospitalized is likely to affect the person's social role in society, with general social rejection occurring once a person has been officially labeled as "mentally ill" (Farina, Murray, and Groh, 1978).

Effective medication and other treatment modalities probably act as buffers against stress, thereby reducing vulnerability (Hogarty and Goldberg, 1973). The results from the study by Leff et al. (1973) provide direct evidence that this is the case. It is possible, therefore, that other more negative factors associated with hospitalization that would be expected to increase both the amount of stress experienced and personal vulnerability to such stress are offset by the treatment. This could explain why life events appear to play a similar role in both onset and recurrence of a schizophrenic episode. It is also possible that the distinction between onset and recurrence is blurred in these studies due to difficulty in establishing the presence or absence of previous schizophrenic episodes, and/or dating the present episode accurately with reference to the date of admission to hospital. The latter problem is especially important since it would suggest, as Hudgens (1974) implied, that life events are more important in leading to admission to treatment than in producing the schizophrenic episodes, which frequently precedes admission to treatment by several months (Brown and Birley, 1968; Jacobs and Myers, 1976). However, in the London study an effort was made to avoid this possibility by selecting patients whose schizophrenic episode the investigators believed could be accurately dated with reference to the occurrence of life events. And in the New Haven study, the claim is made that ". . . with few exceptions, the interviewer psychiatrist was satisfied that he could date acute illness onset to within a period of several days on the basis of occurrence or exacerbation of symptoms and marked change in social functioning" (Jacobs and Myers, 1976, p. 79). We are aware of controversy in the literature over what constitutes onset and relapse in schizophrenia. For purposes of this article, we accept the researchers' criteria for the onset of an acute schizophrenic episode. It is certain, however, that more information is needed about differences in the processes involved in first as against later episodes. Thus far, no retrospective case-control study of life events in first-break schizophrenics has included followups over time to examine the issues.

GENERALIZABILITY OF THE RESULTS OF THE LONDON AND NEW HAVEN STUDIES

Consider again the list of criteria presented in Table 22.1 for an adequate case-control study of the problem. We noted that the London and New Haven studies came closest to meeting these criteria. They did not, however, meet all of them. Among the criteria the London and New Haven studies did not meet was that of providing a representative sample of new cases showing schizophrenic symptoms for the first time.

Is this important? In defining schizophrenia solely by the presence of characteristic symptoms a particular time, the investigators may have used selection criteria that were too broad. From this point of view, duration of the disorder should have been added as a defining characteristic (American Psychiatric Association, 1980). The ground for this argument would include the fact that symptoms do not, as noted earlier, predict outcome. What does predict outcome is chronicity of the disorder before inclusion of the patient in the cohorts being investigated (Strauss and Carpenter, 1974). A serious problem with introducing such an additional criterion, however, is that duration of a schizophrenic episode is related to factors extraneous to the nature of the underlying disorder. Such extraneous factors include, for example, length of interval between onset and admission to treatment and the availability of effective treatments. Moreover, as Strauss and Carpenter (1974) point out:

Adding established chronicity as a diagnostic criterion . . . weakens seriously the diagnostic utility of characteristic symptoms to define a supposed disease process. Since established chronicity predicts chronicity for most psychiatric disorders, its addition as a diagnostic criterion also negates the utility of poor outcome as a validating criterion for the existence of a specific disease process [p. 433].

We suspect, therefore, that our chance to learn more about the precursors of onset and predictors of course will indeed depend on our ability to study and follow more representative samples of individuals who develop schizophrenic symptoms for the first time regardless of the duration of the episode. In addition, we would include the need to secure the kind of carefully selected community controls that were used in the New

Haven study, and at the same time also include carefully selected samples of patients of other diagnostic types. Such a retrospective case-control strategy with provision for frequent followup over time would be a major step forward. In combination with an examination of life events in contrast to other predisposing factors in more narrowly defined samples in high-risk studies using prospective designs, it should assist us in answering questions about the formative and triggering roles of recent stressful life events in the onset and course of schizophrenia.

CONCLUSIONS

A dozen years have passed since Brown and Birley (1968) published their important study, and it has been nearly five years since the valuable investigation by Jacobs and Myers (1976) appeared. There are many gaps to be filled in by future research. Meanwhile, on the basis of the preceding analyses of the existing evidence, it is possible to offer in summary some relatively firm and some fairly tentative conclusions about the role of recent stressful life events in the occurrence of schizophrenic episodes:

•Stressful life events whose occurrences are outside the control of the subject play a part in the causation of schizophrenic epidodes.

•Some of these fateful events occur to persons who develop schizophrenic episodes precisely because there is a hereditary component to this disorder. That is, what close relatives (some of them suffering from or disposed to psychopathology) do and what happens to them tend to create unusual events that affect the subject.

•The unusual fateful events can interact with or add to more ordinary fateful events that most of us experienced at one time or another; the net effect, other things being equal, is greater stress for those predisposed to schizophrenia.

•Both types of fateful events interact with events to which the predisposed subject is prone (e.g., moves, job changes) and produce additional stressful situations. Taken together, such "particular" and "specific" combinations of events may provide the kind of "enigmatic environmental influence" to which Bleuler referred.

•The stressful circumstances may lead to demoralization which precedes and/or coincides with the schizophrenic episode.

•The stressful situation before the schizophrenic episode rarely, however, approaches in severity our hypothesized pathogenic triad of events—at least in samples of subjects whose schizophrenic episodes resulted in hospitalization in the London and New Haven studies.

•Since recent life events have not been tested against predisposing factors, we do not know to what extent recent life events are formative for some types of subjects who develop schizophrenic episodes, are important triggers for other types, or are virtually irrelevant for still other types of subjects who develop schizophrenic episodes.

•While life events appear to play a role in both onset and recurrence of schizophrenic episodes, we know very little about how the processes differ in the different circumstances of onset and recurrence.

•On the basis of analysis of the epidemiological literature on true and treated rates, the literature on extreme situations, and results from the World Health Organization cross-national studies, we suspect that samples of subjects who are admitted to hospitals in modern Western societies after developing schizophrenic episodes are biased in the direction of underestimating the etiological importance of recent stressful life events.

•The consensus that recent life events have only a trivial impact on the onset and course of schizophrenia is premature. What is needed is further research on the nature of their "enigmatic environmental influence."

REFERENCES

American Psychiatric Association (1980), *Diagnostic and Statistical Manual of Mental Disorders*, 3rd ed. Washington, DC: American Psychiatric Association.

Beck, F. C., & Worthen, J. (1972), Precipitating stress, crisis theory, and hospitalization in schizophrenia and depression. *Arch. Gen. Psychiat.*, 26:123–129.

Birley, J. L. T., & Brown, G. W. (1970), Crises and life changes preceding the onset or relapse of acute schizophrenia: Clinical aspects. *Brit. J. Psychiat.*, 116:327–333.

Bleuler, M. (1976), An approach to a survey of research results on schizophrenia. *Schiz. Bull.*, 2:356–357.

Brown, G. W., & Birley, J. L. T. (1968), Crises and life changes and the onset of schizophrenia. *J. Health & Soc. Behav.*, 9:203–214.

——— Harris, T. O., & Peto, J. (1973), Life events and psychiatric disorders. Part 2: Nature of the causal link. *Psychol. Med.*, 3:159–176.

Clausen, J. A. (1979), Sociocultural features in the etiology of schizophrenia. In: *Progress in the Functional Psychoses*, ed. R. Cancro, L. E. Shapiro, & M. S. Kesselman. New York: Spectrum Publications, pp. 35–44.

Cooper, B. (1978), Epidemiology. In: *Schizophrenia: Towards a New Synthesis*, ed. J. K. Wing. New York: Grune & Stratton, pp. 31–51.

Dohrenwend, B. P. (1979), Stressful life events and psychopathology: Some issues of theory and method. In: *Stress and Mental Disorder*, ed. J. E. Barrett, R. M. Rose, & G. L. Klerman. New York: Raven Press, pp. 1–15.

——— Dohrenwend, B. S., Gould, M. S., Link, B., Neugebauer, R., & Wunsch-Hitzig, R. (1980), *Mental Illness in the United States: Epidemiological Estimates*. New York: Praeger.

Dunham, H. W. (1965), *Community and Schizophrenia: An Epidemiological Analysis*. Detroit, MI: Wayne State University Press.

Farina, A., Murray, P. J., & Groh, T. (1978), Sex and worker acceptance of a former mental patient. *J. Clin. & Consult. Psychol.*, 46:887–891.

Fontana, A. F., Marcus, J. L., Noel, B., & Rakusin, J. M. (1972), Prehospitalization coping styles of psychiatric patients: The goal-directedness of life events. *J. Nerv. & Ment. Dis.*, 155:311–331.

Frank, J. D. (1973), *Persuasion and Healing*. Baltimore, MD: Johns Hopkins University Press.

Garmezy, N. (1974), Children at risk: The search for the antecedents of schizophrenia. Part II: Ongoing research programs, issues, and intervention. *Schiz. Bull.*, 1/1:55–125.

Gottesman, I. I., & Shields, J. (1976), A critical review of recent adoption, twin, and family studies of schizophrenia: Behavioral genetics perspectives. *Schiz. Bull.*, 2:360–401.

Gruenberg, E. M. (1974), The epidemiology of schizophrenia. In: *American Handbook of Psychiatry*, Vol. 2, ed. G. Caplan. New York: Basic Books, pp. 448–463.

Hawk, A. B., & Carpenter, W. T. (1975), Diagnostic criteria and five-year outcome in schizophrenia. *Arch. Gen. Psychiat.*, 32:343–347.

Hogarty, G. E., & Goldberg, S. C. (1973), Drug and sociotherapy in the aftercare of schizophrenic patients: One year relapse rates. *Arch. Gen. Psychiat.*, 28:54–64.

Hudgens, R. W. (1974), Personal catastrophe and depression: A consideration of the subject with respect to medically ill adolescents, and a requiem for retrospective life event studies. In: *Stressful Life Events: Their Nature and Effects*, ed. B. S. Dohrenwend & B. P. Dohrenwend. New York: John Wiley, pp. 119–134.

Jacobs, S., & Myers, J. (1976), Recent life events and acute schizophrenic psychosis: A controlled study. *J. Nerv. & Ment. Dis.*, 162:75–87.

——— Prusoff, B. A., & Paykel, E. S. (1974), Recent life events in schizophrenia and depression. *Psychol. Med.*, 4:444–453.

Kety, S., Rosenthal, D., Wender, P. H., & Schulsinger, F. (1976), Studies based on a total sample of adopted individuals and their relatives: Why they were necessary, what they demonstrated and failed to demonstrate. *Schiz. Bull.*, 2:413–428.

Kolb, J. C. (1973), *Modern Clinical Psychiatry*. Philadelphia, PA: W. B. Saunders.

Kormos, H. R. (1978), The nature of combat stress. In: *Stress Disorders Among Vietnam Veterans: Theory, Research and Treatment*, ed. C. R. Figley. New York: Brunner/Mazel.

Lahniers, C. E., & White, K. (1976), Changes in environmental life events and their relationship to psychiatric hospital admission. *J. Nerv. & Ment. Dis.*, 163:154–158.

Leff, J. P., Hirsch, S. R., Gaind, R., Rohde, P. D., & Stevens, B. S. (1973), Life events and maintenance therapy in schizophrenic relapse. *Brit. J. Psychiat.*, 123:659–660.

Link, B., & Dohrenwend, B. P. (1980), Formulation of hypotheses about the ratio of untreated to treated cases in the true prevalence studies of functional psychiatric disorders in adults in the United States. In: *Mental Illness in the United States: Epidemiologic Estimates*, ed. B. P. Dohrenwend, B. S. Dohrenwend, M. S. Gould, B. Link, R. Neugebauer, & R. Wunsch-Hitzig. New York: Praeger, pp. 133–149.

Murphy, H. B. M. (1968), Cultural factors in the genesis of schizophenia. In: *The Transmission of Schizophrenia*, ed. D. Rosenthal & S. S. Kety. New York: Pergamon Press, pp. 137–153.

Myers, J., Lindenthal, J. J., & Pepper, M. P. (1974), Social class, life events and psychiatric symptoms: A longitudinal study. In: *Stressful Life Events: Their Nature and Effects*, ed. B. P. Dohrenwend & B. S. Dohrenwend. New York: John Wiley, pp. 191–205.

Odegard, O. (1932), Emigration and insanity. *Acta Psychiat. et Neurol.*, Suppl. 4:1–206.

Paster, S. (1948), Psychotic reactions among soldiers of World War II. *J. Nerv. & Ment. Dis.*, 108:54–66.

Paykel, E. S. (1978), Contribution of life events to causation of psychiatric illness. *Psychol. Med.*, 8:245–253.

Sartorius, N., Jablensky, A., & Shapiro, R. (1978), Cross-cultural differences in the short-term prognosis of schizophrenic psychoses. *Schiz. Bull.*, 4:102–113.

Schneider, K. (1959), *Clinical Psychopathology*. New York: Grune & Stratton.

Schwartz, C. C., & Myers, J. K. (1977), Life events and schizophrenia: II. Impact of life events on symptom configuration. *Arch. Gen. Psychiat.*, 34:1242–1245.

Strauss, J. S., & Carpenter, W. T., Jr. (1972), The prediction of outcome in schizophrenia. *Arch. Gen. Psychiat.*, 27:739–746.

————— ————— (1974), Characteristic symptoms and outcome in schizophrenia. *Arch. Gen. Psychiat.*, 30:429–434.

Wagner, P. S. (1946), Psychiatric activities during the Normandy offensive, June 20–August 20, 1944: An experience with 5,203 neuropsychiatric casualties. *Psychiatry*, 9:341–363.

Wing, J. K., Cooper, J. E., & Sartorius, N. (1974), *The Description and Classification of Psychiatric Symptoms: An Instructional Manual for the PSE and CATEGO System*. London: Cambridge University Press.

Chapter 23
The Interaction of Life Events and Relatives' Expressed Emotion in Schizophrenia and Depressive Neurosis

JULIAN LEFF, M.D., AND CHRISTINE VAUGHN, PH.D.

It has now been established that life events play a part in the precipitation of episodes of depression (Brown, Ni Bhrolchain, and Harris, 1975; Brown and Harris, 1978) and of schizophrenia (Birley and Brown, 1970; Brown and Birley, 1968; Leff, Hirsch, Gaind, Rohde, and Stevens, 1974). There is also good evidence that the emotional atmosphere in the home generated by the patient's key relatives exerts a significant influence on the recurrence of schizophrenia (Brown and Birley, 1968; Brown, Birley, and Wing, 1972; Vaugh and Leff, 1976a). The

Acknowledgments. This chapter was first published in the *British Journal of Psychiatry* (1980), 136:146–153, and it is reprinted with permission.

We gratefully acknowledge the help of the consultants at the Maudsley, Bethlehem, and St. Francis hospitals who gave permission for their patients to take part in this study. We are most grateful to Dr. C. Tennant for assigning the life events to the various categories.

JULIAN LEFF AND CHRISTINE VAUGHN

emotional atmosphere was assessed in these studies from individual interviews with the relative or relatives (usually a
spouse or parents) within a week or so of the patient's admission
to hospital with a first episode of recurrence of schizophrenia.
The crucial measures are of critical comments and emotional
overinvolvement, which are used to construct an index of Expressed Emotion (EE). About half the patients returning to high
EE relatives will suffer a relapse of schizophrenia within nine
months whereas no more than 15 percent of those returning
to low EE relatives will do so.

The role of EE in depressive neurosis has been explored in
only one study. Vaughn and Leff (1976a) compared a group
of inpatients with depressive neurosis with a group of schizophrenic inpatients. They found that when the relatives of the
depressed patients were divided into high and low EE on the
same basis as the relatives of the schizophrenics, there were no
differences between the two groups of depressives in relapse
rates. However, when the level of critical comments determining assignment to the high EE group was lowered from six to
two, a significant difference in the relapse rate of depressives
emerged. Patients returning to relatives in the new high criticism group had a relapse rate of 67 percent over nine months
compared to 22 percent in the low criticism group. Only one
relative of the 31 depressed patients scored on emotional overinvolvement and he was markedly critical as well. Therefore
critical comments alone were sufficient to assign the relatives
of depressed patients to high or low groups. This is largely due
to the fact that overinvolvement is much rarer in spouses than
in parents, and for 29 of the 31 depressed patients in our sample
the key relative was a spouse.

In addition to assessing relatives' EE in these two groups of
patients, a history of life events in the three months preceding
the onset of illness was taken on admission. It was thus possible
to look for any interaction between the effects of EE and life
events in the precipitation of episodes of illness. No work on
this has previously been published although Brown et al. (1975)

have looked at the interaction of life events and certain aspects of the emotional atmosphere in the homes of depressed women.

In this chapter we present data on the rate of occurrence of life events in the three months preceding an episode of schizophrenia or depressive neurosis. We further break down this material according to the level of EE shown by the relatives in each diagnostic group. Other factors possibly related to the onset or relapse of psychiatric illnesses are also examined, including whether the episode is a first or subsequent one, and the prescription of maintenance medication. The issue of the *quality* of life events has been tackled by various workers and we have adopted a relatively simple method of categorizing events as desirable or undesirable. We apply this to events reported by the schizophrenic and depressed patients. Finally, we compare the clinical picture of precipitated and unprecipitated depression in an attempt to illuminate the current obscurity surrounding the classification of depressive states.

METHODS

The identification and selection of patients are described in Vaughn and Leff (1976a). The Present State Examination (PSE) in conjunction with the Category program (Wing, Cooper, and Sartorius, 1974) was used to diagnose the patients as either schizophrenic or depressive in the absence of delusions and hallucinations. The key relative or relatives were interviewed with the modified form of the Camberwell Family Interview (Vaughn and Leff, 1976b; Brown and Rutter, 1966) and measures of EE were made from tape recordings of the interviews. Life events were detected by using Brown and Birley's (1968) schedule and were evaluated with their manual. Usually the patient alone was interviewed to obtain a life-event history, but where this was difficult because of the patient's mental state, the history was taken from a key relative. The onset of the patient's illness was determined from the case notes and from interviews with the patient and relative. There were usually no problems in pinpointing the onset of schizophrenic symptoms but depressive episodes often were not as clear-cut. In such cases the onset was pushed back in time as far as possible. Various items of past history were also collected including the prescription and taking of maintenance medication prior to admission.

RESULTS

LIFE-EVENT RATES

Data were collected on independent and possibly independent life events. The latter category of events occurred much less frequently than the former and since by their nature they carry a higher risk of tautologous associations with illness, they have been omitted from these analyses. Thus we only present data on independent events, which are those that could not possibly have been the result of the patient's disordered behavior (Brown and Birley, 1968).

The proportions of patients experiencing at least one independent event in the *three months* before onset of illness are shown in Table 23.1.

The figures are given for the schizophrenic group divided into those with high and low EE relatives and for the depressive group dealt with in the same way using identical cut-off points. Data are also given for the depressive group divided into high and low criticism relatives as explained above. It is only when the depressed patients are assigned to two groups on the basis of the lower cut-off point, which significantly predicted relapse, that a significant difference appears in the proportions experiencing life events. However, the pattern that emerges is the mirror image of that shown by the schizophrenic group. Schizophrenic patients living with high EE relatives have experienced few life events in the first three months before relapse whereas

Table 23.1
Proportions of Patients with at Least One Independent
Event in Three Months Before Onset

Patient group	High EE	Low EE	p^*	High criticism	Low criticism	p^*	Total
Schizo-phrenia	6/21 (28.6%)	11/16 (68.8%)	.0175				17/37 (46.0%)
Depressive neurosis	7/11 (63.6%)	12/19 (63.2%)	NS	16/21 (76.2%)	3/9 (33.3%)	.0355	19/30 (63.3%)

*Significance evaluated by Fisher's exact test.

depressed patients from high criticism homes have a high rate of events in the same period. In fact the difference between the two groups in the proportion of patients reporting life events is highly significant (exact $p = .0024$). On the other hand, a high proportion of schizophrenic patients living with low EE relatives have experienced a life event in the three-month period whereas the depressives from low criticism homes have a low rate of events. In this instance, however, the difference between the two diagnostic groups does not reach significance. It should be noted that the overall life-event rate is not significantly different for the schizophrenic and depressed patients. It is only when the groups are subdivided on the basis of relatives' emotional attitudes that significantly different patterns appear.

The data are also presented for the *three-week* period preceding onset of illness, since this was found by Brown and Birley (1968) to be the time interval during which significant differences in life-event rates appeared between their schizophrenic and normal samples. Unfortunately, it is not possible to compare our data directly with any published normal sample, since our patients were a selected group, all of them living with at least one relative, whereas a general population sample contains a substantial proportion of people living alone. It is probably that people living alone experience a lower rate of life events than those living with others.

Table 23.2 shows the proportion of patients in each diagnostic group with at least one independent life event in the three weeks before onset of illness.

It can be seen that the difference in event rates between high and low EE schizophrenics becomes even more pronounced compared with the three-month data, whereas the significant difference between high and low criticism depressives disappears. Nevertheless, the difference in event rates between high EE schizophrenics and high criticism depressives remains significant (exact $p = .01$).

EFFECT OF FIRST ADMISSION

The possible influence of first admission versus readmission was studied. Event rates were calculated for first admitted and readmitted patients in each of the subgroups of diagnoses and relatives' emotional attitudes. No significant differences emerged.

EVENTS DESIRABLE OR UNDESIRABLE?

The question was examined of whether life events preceding depressive episodes were more likely to be undesirable than

Table 23.2
Proportions of Patients with at Least One Independent
Event in Three Weeks Before Onset

Patient group	High EE	Low EE	p^*	High criticism	Low criticism	p^*	Total
Schizo-phrenia	1/21 (4.8%)	9/16 (56.3%)	.0007				10/37 (27.0%)
Depressive neurosis	3/11 (27.3%)	7/17 (36.8%)	NS	8/21 (38.1%)	2/9 (22.2%)	NS	10/30 (33.3%)

those preceding schizophrenic episodes. This issue stems from Brown and Birley's (1968) assumption "that schizophrenic patients are equally susceptible to positive and negative emotional arousal," and Brown and colleagues' (1975) demonstration of the importance of events threatening loss in the precipitation of depression. Brown's (1974) method of assessing contextual threat was not used as it was in a developmental stage at the time these data were collected. Instead each event was assigned on a common-sense basis to one of three categories: (1) undesirable, (2) desirable, (3) neutral, or impossible to assign to (1) or (2) in the absence of contextual information. This follows a categorization used by Jacobs, Prusoff, and Paykel (1974) in a comparison of life events in schizophrenic and depressed patients.

The list of events was also presented to an independent rater (Dr. C. Tennant) who was asked to assign them to the above three categories. He was given no information about the diagnoses of the patients concerned. Disagreement between the two raters (J. L. and C. T.) on the categorization of events amounted to only 8.6 percent on all events and 7.7 percent on undesirable events alone. A list of events on each diagnostic category with their desirability ratings (J. L.'s) is included in Table 23.3.

For the 13-week period preceding onset, 24 (66.7 percent) of the 36 events occurring to depressives were judged undesirable compared with 14 (63.6 percent) of the 22 events experienced by the schizophrenic patients. If only the three-week period preceding a schizophrenic episode is considered, the proportion of undesirable events rises to 76.9 percent (10 out of 13). This can be compared with the figure of 73.9 percent (17 out of 23) derived from data given by Brown and Birley (1968).

Having discovered that undesirable events were no more common in depressed than schizophrenic patients, the data for the two diagnostic groups were reanalyzed using the proportion of patients experiencing at least one undesirable event during the relevant time period. The patterns of distribution of events shown in the two tables remained unchanged and with one exception the significance levels were only slightly reduced. The exception was the event rate for schizophrenic patients over the three-month period. When undesirable events only were considered, the significant difference between patients from high and low EE homes shown in Table 23.1 disappeared.

Table 23.3
Desirability Ratings for Independent Life Events

Patient #	Desirability Rating	Nature of Event
	Schizophrenic Group	
5	+	Father obtained new job after three months unemployment.
6	±	Moved house.
10	−	Husband confessed to adultery.
18	+	Brother became engaged.
19	+	Brother became engaged.
24	−	Stepdaughter emigrated.
29	−	Son had car accident in which the car was badly damaged.
33	−	Son admitted to psychiatric hospital.
36	−	Mother died.
	−	Husband told he was to go into hospital for hemorrhoidectomy.
50	−	Patient told he had to go into hospital for cystoscopy.
53	+	Husband got new job.
	−	Patient got summons to appear in court for nonpayment of rates.
56	−	Sister left home.
60	−	Sister came to England to have treatment for disseminated sclerosis.
63	−	Father admitted to hospital.
72	−	Admitted to hospital for thyroidectomy.
	−	Involved in car crash.
73	−	Son taken from home by estranged husband.
76	±	Moved house.
	+	Started attending Open University.
	±	Mother-in-law came to stay.

Table 23.3 (Continued)

Patient #	Desirability Rating	Nature of Event
		Depressive Group
7	−	Heard about rejection for new town.
8	−	Mother admitted to hospital with pneumonia.
	−	Father found to have leukemia.
12	−	Shop burgled.
	+	Pet dog died.
20	+	Son married.
	−	Son moved away from home.
23	−	Witnessed fatal accident.
	−	Admitted to hospital with spontaneous pneumonthorax.
25	+	Patient promoted to manager.
	±	Husband took up job driving cars again.
	−	Father-in-law beaten and robbed.
27	−	Learned that mother had incurable cancer.
35	−	Heard about husband's infidelity.
	+	Brother got married.
38	−	Daughter developed paralysis.
44	−	Learned that sister-in-law was to have deep radium treatment.
	−	Learned that car had been stolen.
47	−	Fish tank stolen.
	−	Housing recommendation turned down.
52	+	Heard of sister's engagement.
55	+	Husband promoted.
	+	Baby born.
58	+	Heard about her own promotion.
61	−	Stepson moved away from home.
62	−	Mother-in-law died. Patient present at death after operation for cancer.
	−	Heard that mother was to be admitted for heart and ulcer surgery.
66	−	Police guard on flat called off.
	−	Judge ordered retrial of relatives due to accusation of bribery.
67	±	Mother came to stay.
	+	Heard of daughter's pregnancy—first grandchild.
	−	Appeared in court as a witness.
	−	Lost her dog—first pet ever.
68	+	Baby born.
	−	Parent sterilized.

EFFECT OF MAINTENANCE PHENOTHIAZINE THERAPY

In view of the interaction found by Leff et al. (1974) between life-event rates and regular phenothiazine therapy in schizophrenia, it was hoped that data from this study would allow further exploration of this area. Unfortunately, very few patients were found to be on regular maintenance therapy at the time of relapse of schizophrenia. In fact only six patients fell into this category, all of them living with high EE relatives. The number is too small to allow valid comparisons with other groups, but it is worth recording that none of these patients had experienced a life event in the three weeks before relapse of their illness.

PRECIPITATED VERSUS UNPRECIPITATED DEPRESSION

The majority (70 percent) of depressed neurotic patients in this study lived with high criticism relatives, and most of these (76 percent) had experienced at least one independent event in the three months before they fell ill. The patients living with low criticism relatives had a low rate of life events, and could be considered as suffering from unprecipitated depression. One could argue that other environmental factors not considered in this study were operating to produce depression. In particular we did not assess "long term difficulties" which Brown et al. (1975) identified as provoking agents acting in conjunction with life events. However, our measure of critical attitudes in the spouses of depressed patients would overlap with Brown's "long term difficulties" to some extent. Furthermore, even if "long term difficulties" other than those connected with a critical spouse were present in the low criticism groups they would not explain the development of depression in the patients because there was a low life-event rate, and it is the *conjunction* of those two features that Brown et al. postulate as precipitating depression.

Hence it was considered to be of interest to compare precipitated and unprecipitated depressives in terms of symptoms detected with the PSE. It must be emphasized that patients with depressive delusions and/or hallucinations were deliberately excluded from this study to provide the maximum contrast with the schizophrenic sample. Therefore the two groups of depressed patients were compared in terms of the 20 nonpsychotic syndromes derived from the PSE by the Catego program. Only one significant difference below the 5 percent level of probability emerged: the precipitated depressives were more likely to show irritability (71.4 percent) than the unprecipitated depressives (22.2 percent, exact p = .018). However, one further difference was of borderline significance: the precipitated depression group included one third of patients with phobic anxiety, whereas none of the unprecipitated depressives showed this symptom (exact p = .057).

DISCUSSION

Our findings indicate that there are indeed interactions between life events and relatives' emotional attitudes in the period before the onset of both depression and schizophrenia. However the patterns which emerge are different for the two diagnostic conditions. Episodes of schizophrenia in patients living with high EE relatives are not preceded by an excess of life events, whereas those in patients from low EE homes are. Thus the onset or relapse of schizophrenia is associated *either* with high EE *or* with an independent life event. For the patients with depressive neurosis, the pattern is the reverse. In most patients it is the conjunction of a critical relative and an independent life event that is associated with the onset of a depressive episode. This finding echoes the work of Brown et al. (1975) who identified one of the vulnerability factors rendering women susceptible to the depressive effect of a threatening event as lack of an intimate, usually sexual, relationship providing the woman with someone to confide in. It is likely that our measure of criticism in spouses is tapping another aspect of nonconfiding relationships. It remains to be demonstrated that the conjunction of a life event and an unsatisfactory marital relationship is indeed a *causal* constellation in depression. Since life events cannot readily be manipulated, the more practical strategy to investigate the issue of causality would be to attempt to improve unsatisfactory marriages in patients prone to depression and look for an effect on the course of the illness.

A feature of considerable interest in our data is the way in which the patterns of interaction between life events and relatives' emotional attitudes vary in clarity with the duration of time before the onset of illness. Thus the maximum difference in life events rates between high and low EE schizophrenic groups is found in the *three weeks* before onset, whereas for the depressive groups the maximum difference appears in the *three months* before onset. This is in accord with the findings of Brown and his colleagues, that in comparison with a normal population life events are concentrated in the three weeks before the onset of schizophrenia (Birley and Brown, 1968) and the three months before onset of depression (Brown et al., 1975).

In this study we attempted to assess the desirability of life events in the two diagnostic groups using a categorization introduced by Paykel and his colleagues (1971). The technique proved to have a high interrater reliability in our hands but our findings appear to conflict with those of Paykel's group (Jacobs et al., 1974). They compared life-event rates in 50 first admission schizophrenics and 50 depressives matched on age, sex, marital status, race and social class. They found that undesirable events, a type of event excluded in our study because we chose to concentrate on independent events only. It is quite likely that interpersonal arguments are brought about by increased irritability in the patients, representing a prodromal manifestation of illness. Hence the inclusion of interpersonal arguments carries a high risk of contamination of events by symptoms, leading to spurious associations between "events" and onset of illness. In the study by Jacobs et al. serious arguments with a fiancé or steady date or with a nonresident family member were the onset categories of events occurring significantly more often in depressives than schizophrenics. Interpersonal arguments as a general class of event occurred in 26 depressives and only nine schizophrenics ($p < .001$). Although the authors did not give the relevant figures, it appears that the excess of undesirable events in the depressed patients was largely accounted for by interpersonal arguments, and that if these were excluded the difference between depressives and schizophrenics would probably become nonsignificant. In this case there would be no inconsistency between the findings of Jacobs and his colleagues and our own data showing that undesirable events form as high a proportion of independent events preceding schizophrenia as they do in depression.

Our findings for undesirable events do not conflict with those reported by Brown and Harris (1978) for severely threatening events, since these two ways of categorizing events, though not unrelated, are by no means identical. Brown and Harris conclude that whereas events with a severe degree of threat are associated with the onset of depression events of little or no long-term threat are implicated in the onset of schizophrenia. The contextual ratings of threat for the schizophrenic material were made retrospectively using data not collected specifically for that purpose. Hence Brown and Harris warn that their results "cannot be any more than provisional" (p. 124), and the issue of the specificity of severely threatening events for depressive episodes remains open.

In the small group of depressed neurotics in our study who lived with noncritical relatives, few life events were found preceding the onset of illness. We have already referred to these illnesses as non-precipitated depressions. They differ clinically in two respects from the precipitated type: they show less irritability and, in this small sample, no phobic symptoms. It is difficult to compare this group with patients studied by others because of our exclusion of depressed patients with delusions and/or hallucinations. However, there are some similarities with the groups identified by Paykel (1971) from a cluster analysis of a sample of depressed inpatients and outpatients. He also included interviews for recent life events in his study although he used the technique of Holmes and Rahe (1967). Paykel found the best solution of the cluster analysis to be a division of four groups: a psychotic or endogenous group, a predominantly anxious group, a predominantly hostile group, and a group of young depressives with personality disorder. The highest scores on Holmes and Rahe's life stress scale were achieved by the latter two groups but the endogenous group scored higher than the anxious group. One can tentatively suggest that our group of precipitated depressions is a mixture of Paykel's anxious, hostile and personality-disordered groups since it is character- ized by evironmental stress. However, Paykel's endogenous group differs from our unprecipitated depressions in having a high life stress score. Although it was not our original inten- tion to tackle the thorny problems involved in the classification of depressed patients, our findings suggest a useful technique for attempting to validate the reactive-endogenous dichotomy. The methods we used would need to be applied to a much larger sample which also included patients with depressive de- lusions and/or hallucinations. A more valid clinical comparison could then be made between precipitated and unprecipitated depressions.

CONCLUSION

The simultaneous measurement of two forms of environmental stress, life events and relatives' Expressed Emotion, has proven valuable in a number of respects. It has demonstrated signifi- cantly different patterns of interaction for schizophrenia and depressive neurosis, and it has suggested a useful strategy for the further exploration of the nosology of depressive illnesses. Our approach may seem complex enough but the fabric of this type of study needs to be further enriched, particularly where schizophrenia is concerned, by the interweaving of carefully collected data on preventive medicine.

REFERENCES

Birley, J. L. T., & Brown, G. W. (1970), Crises and life changes preceding the onset or relapse of acute schizophrenia: Clinical aspects. *Brit. J. Psychiat.*, 116:327–333.

Brown, G. W. (1974), Meaning, measurement and stress of life events. In: *Stressful Life Events: Their Nature and Effects*, ed. B. S. Dohrenwend & B. P. Dohrenwend. New York: John Wiley, pp. 108–114.

—— Birley, J. L. T. (1968), Crises and life changes and the onset of schizophrenia. *J. Health & Soc. Behav.*, 9:203–214.

—— —— Wing, J. K. (1972), Influence of family life on the course of schizophrenic disorders: A replication. *Brit. J. Psychiat.*, 121:241–258.

—— Harris, T. (1978), *Social Origins of Depression: A Study of Psychiatric Disorder in Women*. London: Tavistock.

—— Ni Bhrolchain, M., & Harris, T. (1975). Social class and psychiatric disturbance among women in an urban population. *Sociol.*, 9:225–254.

—— Rutter, M. (1966), The measurement of family activities and relationships: A methodological study. *Human Relations*, 19:241–263.

Holmes, T. H., & Rahe, R. H. (1967), The Social Readjustment Rating Scale. *J. Psychosom. Res.*, 11:213–218.

Jacobs, S. C., Prusoff, B. A., & Paykel, E. S. (1974), Recent life events in schizophrenia and depression. *Psychol. Med.*, 4:444–453.

Leff, J. P., Hirsch, S. R., Gaind, R., Rohde, P. D., & Stevens, B. C. (1973), Life events and maintenance therapy in schizophrenic relapse. *Brit. J. Psychiat.*, 123:659–660.

Paykel, E. S. (1971), Classification of depressed patients: A cluster analysis derived grouping. *Brit. J. Psychiat.*, 118:275–288.

Vaughn, C. E., & Leff, J. P. (1976a), The influence of family and social factors on the course of psychiatric illness. *Brit. J. Psychiat.*, 129:125–137.

—— —— (1976b), The measurement of expressed emotion in the families of psychiatric patients. *Brit. J. Soc. Clin. Psychol.*, 14:157–165.

Wing, J. K., Cooper, J. E., & Sartorius, N. (1974), *The Measurement and Classification of Psychiatric Symptoms*. London: Cambridge University Press.

Chapter 24
Life Events, Familial Stress, and Coping in the Developmental Course of Schizophrenia

DAVID LUKOFF, PH.D., KAREN SNYDER, M.A., JOSEPH VENTURA, M.A., AND
KEITH H. NEUCHTERLEIN, PH.D.

While many early theorists, such as Kraepelin (1919), regarded schizophrenia as a biological disorder of entirely endogenous origin, research over the past 30 years has documented several socioenvironmental factors that affect the course of the illness. Genetic predisposition has been clearly determined to be a major contributing factor in the development of schizophrenia (Gottesman and Shields, 1976; Kessler, 1980). Yet the concordance rate for schizophrenia among identical twins has been found to be only about 50 percent, suggesting that genetic factors, while very important, are not sufficient causes (Shields and Gottesman, 1972; Gottesman and Shields, 1976). Furthermore, the waxing and waning of psychotic symptoms that characterizes the course of schizophrenia in many patients is unlikely to be due totally to genetic influences (Zubin and Spring, 1977;

Acknowledgment. This chapter was first published in *Schizophrenia Bulletin* (1984), 10/2:258–292, and it is reprinted with permission.

M. Bleuler, 1972). A more complete understanding of the development and course of schizophrenic disorder has been sought in studies of various intrafamilial, interpersonal, and sociocultural factors as well as in studies of intrauterine, nutritional, and other biological factors. This chapter reviews the principal findings concerning the impact of life events and familial stress on the course of schizophrenic disorder. These are stressors which, when they occur to individuals with a sufficient vulnerability to schizophrenia, seem to be capable of triggering a schizophrenic episode. The chapter also reviews selected research with normal individuals and patients with other disorders that has revealed an intervening factor which plays a major role in determining the stress level resulting from exposure to stressors; the person's coping response to the stressor. Investigators in the life events and familial stress areas have begun to examine the mediating effect of coping responses and social support on stress and on the likelihood of developing pathology after being exposed to stressors.

The findings on life events, familial stress, and coping responses are reviewed in the three separate sections and are presented within the framework of a vulnerability/stress model of the course of schizophrenic disorder (Rosenthal, 1970; Zubin and Spring, 1977). In addition to reviewing studies bearing on the relationship between stress and schizophrenia, this examination of the literature highlights the broadened understanding of schizophrenic disorder generated by these more narrowly focused inquiries.

BACKGROUND OF RESEARCH ON LIFE EVENTS AND SCHIZOPHRENIC EPISODES

The hypothesis that emotional conflicts related to external events can precipitate mental illnesses was first formally suggested by Heinroth in 1818 in his designation of the term "psychosomatic." However, during the late 19th and early 20th centuries when schizophrenia was being delineated from other mental illnesses, medicine was dominated by Virchow and Pasteur's theory of the "specific cause of disease." Schizophrenia was considered to be solely a brain disease, and the etiology was sought in brain dissections to uncover anatomical abnormalities and in laboratory assays to isolate pathogens. Social and psychological factors were largely ignored. Modern sessions of this perspective are represented by Langfeldt (1956), Schneider (1959), and Mayer-Gross, Slater, and Roth (1969), who maintain that external factors such as stress do not play a causal role in "true" schizophrenia.

Jung (1907) was one of the earliest proponents of the "psychogenesis of mental disease," and Bleuler (1911) also considered life situations and emotional conflicts as causal factors in the onset of at least some cases of schizophrenia. Adolf Meyer's (1951) technique of life charts promoted the linking of life events and illness onset by tracking each on separate time lines which could be overlaid and examined. Situations he considered important to note included: "the changes of habitat, of school entrance, graduations or changes, or failures; the various 'jobs'; the dates of possibly important births and deaths in the family; and other fundamentally important environmental incidents" (Meyer, 1951, p. 53). Rather than bizarre or catastrophic events, these are events to which everyone is exposed over the course of a lifetime. Meyer argued that even such ordinary events can contribute to the development of a pathological condition.

In the early 1960s, Rahe and Holmes began developing a life-event schedule based upon findings from over 5,000 of Meyer's "life charts" taken on patients at the University of Washington. Each item selected for their Schedule of Recent Experience was included because it was found to have occurred in a large number of patients preceding the onset of their illness. Holmes and Rahe (1967) also developed the Social Readjustment Rating Scale by assigning weights for events of different judged severity from the Schedule of Recent Experience. Elevated scores on the Social Readjustment Rating Scale have been associated with the onset of numerous medical disorders including diabetes mellitus, rheumatoid arthritis, pregnancy complications, cardiovascular disease, stroke, and hospitalization for any medical reason (Rahe and Arthur, 1978). It has also been used extensively in studies of the onset of psychiatric disorder including schizophrenia, depression, and suicide attempts.

Spring and Coons (1982) have described aptly the advantage of using an objective metric for the assessment of stressors in research on schizophrenic disorder:

Defining stress in terms of objectively specifiable life events is a first step in operationalizing stress independently from schizophrenia. At least this strategy *attempts* to disentangle the independent variable from the welter of disturbances in arousal, disruptions in coping, cognitive eccentricities and peculiarities of lifestyle that are known to be associated with the dependent variable [p. 36].

However, despite the advance represented by the development of life-event scales, there are still many methodological difficulties inherent in investigating the relationship of life events to the onset of illness. An in-depth discussion of the unique conceptual and methodological problems encountered in life-events research on schizophrenia has recently been presented by Spring and Coons (1982). Furthermore, Rabkin's (1980) review of all of the controlled studies on life events and schizophrenia focuses on research design issues such as diagnostic rigor, definition and measurement procedures for life events, and choice of comparison groups. The methodology of each study is individually critiqued. Because of the availability of these two thorough critiques, methodological questions are addressed only indirectly in this article. This section on life events examines the published controlled studies on life events and the onset of schizophrenic episodes. The relevance of these findings to the vulnerability/stress model of schizophrenic relapse is also discussed.

STUDIES OF LIFE EVENTS AND
SCHIZOPHRENIC DISORDER

The research examining the relationship between life events and the onset of schizophrenic episodes can be divided into three groups. Type I: Some studies have found a significant increase in "independent" life events preceding the onset of psychotic symptoms, suggesting that they may play a *major triggering role for episodes*. Type II: Other studies have found an increase in life events before onset, but the occurrence of the life events was not independent of the influence of the patient's behavior. Nonindependent life events such as being fired from a job may reflect the prodromal period of the illness or an ongoing schizophrenic process. Zubin and Spring (1977) have labeled the processes by which schizophrenic patients often bring an excess of life events upon themselves as *"stress-prone patterns of living."* Type III: The third set of studies in the literature report *no relationship between life events and the onset of schizophrenic episodes*. The existing research on life events and schizophrenia is reviewed within the framework of these three patterns with an emphasis on the characteristics of the circumstances and patient subgroups to which these three patterns seem to apply.

TYPE I: MAJOR TRIGGERING ROLE

Of the three types of relationships between life events and schizophrenic episodes, the pattern of an increase in independent life events preceding the onset of a schizophrenic episode provides the most substantial support for the vulnerability/stress model. Although the issues of "independence" of life events and personal behavior are thorny ones (to be discussed further) and the criteria for establishing such independence have varied across studies, all of the studies reviewed in this section have attempted to isolate events which are not confounded with the onset of a schizophrenic episode.

Brown, Harris, and Peto (1973) introduced the term "formative" to describe situations in which "events play an important formative role and the onset is either substantially advanced in time by the event or brought about by it altogether" (p. 162). The study that is most often cited to illustrate that life events can have such a formative role in a schizophrenic episode is that of Brown and Birley (1968). The authors conducted extensive retrospective interviews with patients hospitalized for a schizophrenic episode and with their relatives to elicit life events in the 13 weeks before the onset of illness. Independent life events were defined as ones not brought on by the "unusual" behavior of the patient or planned by the patient at least 3 months ahead. Brown and Birley found that 46 percent of the schizophrenic patients experienced at least one independent life event in the 3-week period before symptom onset, while only 14 percent of the normal community comparison subjects experienced such an event in the 3 weeks before the interview. The number of independent life events during the full 13-week period did not differ significantly between the two groups. Thus, schizophrenic patients showed a significant increase in independent life events clustering the 3-week period before symptom onset.

Brown and Birley eliminated from the study 60 percent of the schizophrenic patients admitted to the hospital because the onset of their symptoms could not be dated within 1 week. Therefore, these findings can only be generalized to the segment of the schizophrenic population whose course of illness is characterized by the acute appearance of symptoms. Even within this subgroup among whom a statistically significant relationship between independent life events and onset was found, Brown, Harris et al. (1973) argue that ongoing difficulties and tense situations at home or at work or in a key relationship also played a major role in episode onset in most cases. They introduced the term that we have adopted here, *triggering*, to identify situations in which "events are seen as precipitating an illness that would probably have occurred before long for other reasons" (p. 159). However, when events in the Brown and Birley study were rated on a four-point scale of severity of threatening implications, 16 percent of schizophrenic patients experienced a markedly threatening event in the 12 weeks before onset, which was three times the incidence for the controls. This finding suggests that for at least a minority of datable-onset schizophrenic patients (16 percent of the 40 percent of schizophrenic hospital admissions who were included in the study) "events may be sufficiently traumatic to bring about onset without the experience of such [ongoing difficult] situations" (Brown et al., 1973, p. 169).

Maintenance antipsychotic medication appears to influence the likelihood that a schizophrenic patient will have a triggering life event before relapse. Leff, Hirsch, Gaind, Rohde, and Stevens (1973) found that independent life events preceded relapse significantly more often among patients on maintenance phenothiazines than among patients on placebo. The rate of independent life events in the 5-week period before relapse was 44 percent for the on-drug relapsed group as compared to 21 percent for the placebo relapsed group. Leff et al. (1973) interpreted their findings as follows: "Outpatients on maintenance therapy are protected against the stress implicit in uneventful social intercourse, and are unlikely to relapse unless exposed to some additional stress in the form of one or other life event" (p. 660). Birley and Brown (1970) reported similar suggestive findings regarding the relationship between medication status and life events among their sample of schizophrenic patients. Although the difference was not statistically significant, 60 percent (3 of 5) of the patients on medication reported an independent life event before onset, whereas only 31 percent (4 of 13) of the patients who were not on medication reported an event. The interpretation of Birley and Brown's (1970) results is restricted by the small sample size and by a self-selection bias regarding medication status. However, the Leff et al. (1973) study included 116 patients, controlled for medication status by random assignment, and did demonstrate a significantly different rate of prerelapse life events for on-drug and placebo cases. Thus, these two studies identify a subgroup—namely, patients on maintenance antipsychotic medication—among whom life events seem to play a triggering role in the onset of a schizophrenic episode.

Another factor that influences the likelihood of independent life events being associated with relapse emerged from the British research on expressed emotion (EE) in families of schizophrenic patients. Leff and Vaughn (1980) found that recently hospitalized schizophrenic patients from low EE families were significantly more likely to have experienced an independent life event in the 3 weeks preceding illness onset (56 percent) than were the patients from high EE families (5 percent). High EE families seem to produce stress sufficient to obviate the need for additional stressful life events in the generation of a relapse. However, among patients living in low EE environments, life events do seem to play a triggering role in the onset of episodes. This research is reviewed in detail in the Familial Stress section of this chapter.

Another strategy for investigating the relationship between a significant change in psychosocial environment and the onset of schizophrenic episodes has been to examine the effect of a particularly stressful life event occurring for an entire population. An inadvertently stressful life event was created for a group of schizophrenic outpatients by Goldberg, Schooler, Hogarty, and Roper (1977) during their study on major role therapy (MRT) in aftercare treatment. MRT was designed to help the patient become established in some societal role such as student, worker, or housewife. The assignment to MRT treatment can be considered an independent life event since it was outside of the patient's control. To the researchers' surprise, when they examined the interaction between relapse and level of symptomatology, they found that "inpatients at the 'good' pole of the [symptom] scale, MRT forestalls relapse, but for patients at the 'bad' pole, MRT surprisingly hastens relapse" (Goldberg et al., 1977, p. 178). The authors hypothesized that "symptomatic patients getting MRT are encouraged to perform at a level beyond their capacity, resulting in social failure, a flight to the sick role, and psychotic exacerbation" (Goldberg et al., 1977, p. 184). This same process of symptomatic exacerbation in response to treatment had been observed by George Brown and his colleagues in an earlier study: "Too enthusiastic attempts at reactivating unprepared long stay patient have been shown to lead to sudden relapse of symptoms that had not been present for years" (Brown, Birley, and Wing, 1972, p. 256).

In another study examining the effects of a stressful event common to an entire population, Steinberg and Durell (1968) checked the service records of every uncommissioned soldier in the U.S. Army who was hospitalized for schizophrenia from 1956 to 1960. They found that the rate of hospitalization during the early months of military service was significantly higher than during the second year. During the first month, the rate of hospitalization was six times that of the second year. Army enlistment would reflect individual choice, but induction into the Army of draftees is a stressful event clearly independent of the individual's behavior. Among draftees, the differential rate of hospitalization during the first month was even higher: eight times that of the second year. A review of the case records indicated the following:

Early detection of chronic cases probably accounts for only a very small part of the differential rate, and . . . the findings therefore represent a genuine increase in the rate of onset of acute schizophrenic symptoms during the early months of service [Steinberg and Durell, 1968, p. 1104].

Some of the cases in this study would probably meet DSM-III criteria for schizophreniform disorder rather than schizophrenic disorder (American Psychiatric Association, 1980). However, it is unlikely that schizophreniform disorders account for all of the relationship.

Wagner's (1946) figures for the population at risk during the 2 months of heavy fighting at Normandy indicated an elevated incidence of cases of psychosis and cases diagnosed as schizophrenia during the combat period. It is noteworthy that Swank (1949) maintains that soldiers selected for combat duty, such as the Normandy campaign that served as the stressor for this study, had shown themselves to be of better than average stability. They had passed training tests including induction, overseas assignment, battle simulation, and had participated in prior combat situations. The description of war by Grinker and Spiegel (1963) as a "laboratory which manufactures psychological dysfunction" (p. vii) in previously normal persons seems apt as a description of the findings of these studies. Although differences in diagostic criteria used 30–40 years ago diminish the interpretability of these combat studies, there was a general awareness of the transient nature of "3-day psychoses" (Kolb, 1973). The diagnosis of schizophrenia was not routinely assigned to cases with psychotic symptoms. Only 3 percent of patients admitted to exhaustion centers as neuropsychiatric casualties were diagnosed as psychotic at time of discharge (Wagner, 1946).

Dohrenwend (1976) reviewed the relationship between psychotic episodes and stressful events such as combat and natural or manmade disasters, which he termed "extreme situations." He concluded as follows: "Studies in which persons exposed to these extraordinary events have been examined years later have repeatedly found some individuals with more or less severe pathology that apparently began at the time the stressful experience began" (p. 4). Although not conclusively related to narrowly defined schizophrenia, these findings represent another methodological window for examining the relationship between life events outside of the individual's control and the onset of symptoms considered characteristic of schizophrenia.

Harder, Strauss, Kokes, Ritzler, and Gift (1980) measured life events that occurred to 217 first-admission psychiatric patients. Only 35 patients in their sample received a DSM-II diagnosis of schizophrenia (American Psychiatric Association, 1968). They used a version of the Social Readjustment Rating Scale (Holmes and Rahe, 1967) containing independent events only and assessed events over five time periods before admission: an entire year, 7–12 months, 3–6 months, 0–3 months, and 1 month. In their sample, level of stress was not related to severity of psychotic symptomatology, but "more severe levels of schizophrenic and general psychotic symptoms were associated with increases in life-event stress in the 12 weeks before admission" (Harder et al., 1980, p. 176). While the inclusion of patients with differing diagnoses limits the applicability of these findings to schizophrenic disorders, the results of this study point to an important issue in unraveling the relationship between life events and schizophrenic episodes. The Harder et al. (1980) study and other studies (Schwartz and Myers, 1977; Uhlenhuth and Paykel, 1973) have found that *level of stress* has its strongest impact on nonpsychotic symptoms such as anxiety and depression. However, psychotic symptoms may be particularly affected by *increases in stress level* shortly before exacerbation. With the exception of the Brown and Birley (1968) study, which also found an increase in life events immediately preceding onset, most life-event studies have not been designed to detect changes in the level of stress in the weeks immediately preceding the development of a schizophrenic episode. The results of the Brown and Birley (1968) and Harder et al. (1980) studies, however, suggest that increases in life-event stress level during the preceding few weeks rather than overall level of stress may be the most important triggering factor.

SUMMARY

This group of studies has shown that independent life events are associated with the onset of schizophrenic episodes among selected subgroups of schizophrenic patients. This relationship has been documented particularly for patients on antipsychotic medication and patients from low expressed emotion families. Large-scale studies of "naturalistic stressors" have shown that highly stressful life events such as induction into the Army and combat also seem capable of producing an increased incidence of schizophrenic episodes in the exposed population.

Studies finding that life events play a triggering role in schizophrenic episodes fit a simple version of the vulnerability/stress model. In this model, independent life events function as external stressors which raise a person's stress level. If the level of stress exceeds the threshold for schizophrenic episodes associated with the person's vulnerability level, an episode of psychotic symptoms is precipitated. However, the studies reviewed in this section represent a minority of the studies conducted on this topic. The other two types of relationship between life events and schizophrenic episodes have somewhat different implications for the vulnerability/stress model.

TYPE II: STRESS-PRONE PATTERNS OF LIVING

Many studies have found an increase in life events preceding the onset of schizophrenia illness, but the events are not clearly independent from the influence of the illness. As virtually all life-event researchers have pointed out, the finding of an increase in life events before an illness does not necessarily indicate a causal role for the life events. Several characteristics of schizophrenic disorders may contribute to the clustering of events around the time of onset. Both the symptoms of schizophrenia and the unusual goals and life-styles of persons with schizophrenia can contribute to the occurrence of life events, which may, in turn, exacerbate the psychopathology. In addition, schizophrenic patients may be more frequent victims of both independent and nonindependent life events than the average person due to hereditary and socioeconomic factors. Studies that have found this Type II relationship between life events and schizophrenic episodes are reviewed first, followed by studies that have depicted specific aspects of the stress-prone life-style of schizophrenic patients.

LIFE-EVENT STUDIES

Studies which have compared the frequency of occurrence of stressful life events among schizophrenic patients before a hospitalization with that of community controls and with that of nonhospitalized schizophrenic patients have consistently found a greater incidence of life events for the hospitalized patients.

In the Brown and Birley (1968) study reviewed earlier which found an increase in independent life events in the 3-week period before symptom onset, patients also reported nearly twice as many total events (independent and nonindependent) as community controls during the previous 13-week period: 1.74 vs. 0.96. Similarly, Jacobs and Myers (1976), in their interview of 62 first-admission patients and 62 community control subjects matched for age, sex, marital status, race, and social class, found significantly more total life events for the previous year among the patients: 3.2 vs. 2.1. However, Jacobs and Myers did not find a significant difference between the patients and control subjects when only independent life events were considered. As mentioned in the discussion of the Harder et al. (1980) study in the previous section, the use of a time period of 1 year may overlook increases which cluster in the few weeks preceding onset of a schizophrenic episode.

In two studies, schizophrenic patients who relapsed reported significantly more total life events before hospitalization than schizophrenic patients who survived in the community. Using a prospective design, Michaux, Gansereit, McCabe, and Kurland (1967) compared the 1-month period before hospitalization for patients who received a functional psychiatric diagnosis, mainly schizophrenia, with that of matched community controls. They found that the relapsed patients reported significantly more "difficulties" in the six areas of functioning assessed: interpersonal, marital and sexual, economic and domestic, occupational, recreational, and health. The Specific Stress Index interview focused on the occurrence of discrete events (e.g., "Has anything happened on your job or with the people you work with?") rather than on ongoing difficulties, thereby making these results relevant to this review of life-event research.

Leff et al. (1973) found that patients in the active drug condition also conformed to this pattern. The patients with a relapse were significantly more likely to have experienced a stressful life event (independent or nonindependent) in the 5 weeks preceding hospitalization than the patients without a relapse: 89 vs. 27 percent. As with the Brown and Birley (1968) study, the patients with a relapse also had a significantly higher incidence of independent life events, but at a lower rate: 44 vs. 13 percent.

Dohrenwend (1974) compared life events among five groups, including psychiatric inpatients, a representative community sample, and a group of community leaders. Life events were categorized into eight types ranging from "direct manifestations of psychiatric or emotional disturbance" to "objective loss events . . . whose occurrence is likely to be outside of the respondent's control" (pp. 18–19). The patients showed a significantly higher rate of loss events for which they may have been responsible than the community samples. Dohrenwend also found that psychiatrists' ratings on an index of severity of disorder were positively related to the likelihood that events reported were consequences of the subject's psychiatric condition. In a later article reviewing this study, Dohrenwend and Dohrenwend (1980) commented: "It seems clear from these results that, to some extent, the stressful events accompanying psychopathology are a function of this proneness of the individual involved" (p. 191).

Fontana, Marcus, Noel, and Rakusin (1972) distinguished whether the life events which occurred to a sample of hospitalized psychiatric patients and community controls were contingent (nonindependent) or noncontingent (independent). These investigators also found that during the previous year, "patients had significantly more events of the type they had a part in bringing about than controls had in total" (Fontana et al., 1972, p. 118). The number of noncontingent events did not differ from the controls. Again, the use of a 1-year time period may have obscured any increases in independent life events in the weeks preceding a relapse (Harder et al., 1980).

The applicability of the Dohrenwend (1974) and the Fontana et al. (1972) findings to schizophrenic disorder is unclear, unfortunately, due to a lack of diagnostic specification in both studies. The diagnoses of the inpatients in Dohrenwend's (1974) study are not reported, and Fontana et al. (1972) recruited their sample from consecutive admissions to a hospital including an unreported mixture of DSM-II psychotic, neurotic, and personality disorder diagnoses.

A novel research strategy has recently been used by Falloon, Pederson, Shirin, and Moss (1981) in their prospective study of the relationship between fluctuations in patient's level of symptomatology and the occurrence of life events. Both life events and symptom data were collected every 2 weeks over a 1- to 2-year period of 23 schizophrenic patients who were in outpatient treatment. Data on the occurrence of events were collected from relatives using a semistructured interview and the events were then assigned Social Readjustment Rating Scale scores (Holmes and Rahe, 1967). The period of highest and lowest symptomatology for each patient was compared to determine whether there was a significant difference in life event scores during the preceding 3-month interval. Somewhat higher Social Readjustment scores were found in each of the 3 months preceding the point of highest symptomatology, particularly in the month closest to exacerbation (15.0 vs. 11.6). Although preliminary analyses of the as yet unpublished data suggest that this trend may not be statistically significant, more definitive analyses, using the scoring methodology of Brown and Birley (1968), are under way.

Thus, both prospective and retrospective studies have shown that an increase in life events is associated with the onset of schizophrenic episodes. Comparisons of patients with a recent episode to community controls, nonhospitalized schizophrenia patients, and to themselves at a point of nonexacerbation argue strongly that the course of schizophrenia is associated with the frequency of occurrence of life events. However, since the studies reviewed in this section involve life events which are not clearly independent of the patient's behavior, this association cannot be considered to demonstrate a simple causal link. Other factors which have been found to affect the nature of the relationship between life events and schizophrenic episodes are discussed next.

STRESS-PRONE FACTORS

Prodromal and Residual Symptoms

Many of the life events included on the popularly used scales
can be manifestations of the early phase of a schizophrenic
episode rather than events which fatefully befall a person. For
example, the Holmes and Rahe (1967) Schedule of Recent Experience includes items such as "major changes in number of
arguments with spouse," major changes in sleeping habits,"
"divorce," and "being fired from work," which are difficult to
disentangle from the onset of schizophrenic symptoms. In the
Jacobs and Myers (1976) study, most of the six events which
discriminated patients from normals at the .05 level of statistical
significance could have been confounded with the onset of the
schizophrenic episode, i.e., being arrested, court appearance,
trouble with boss, and changes of residence. Similarly, in the
Brown and Birley (1968) study, 40 percent of the schizophrenic
patients were involved in legal proceedings, made moves from
one region to another, or changed jobs within the 13-week
period preceding the episode. Such stressful events expose patients to loss of social support, but they could also be secondary
consequences of the early phase of symptomatic exacerbation.
As noted earlier, one strategy used by Brown and Birley (1968)
to avoid confounding symptoms with the occurrence of life
events was to restrict their sample to patients for whom the
onset of the psychotic symptoms could be dated within a 1-week
period. However, the resulting elimination of 60 percent of
their sample of consecutive admissions indicates that this technique may entail a reduction in the extent to which the findings
generalize to the schizophrenic population as a whole.

    This difficulty is not merely a function of methodological
problems that could be overcome with more precise dating procedures. Schizophrenia has classically been associated with "insidious onset" (Kraepelin, 1919). In a recent study of first-
admission schizophrenic patients, only 28 percent had psychotic
symptoms for less than 1 week before hospitalization. Twenty-

nine percent had experienced some psychotic symptoms for more than 6 months (Gift, Strauss, Harder, Kokes, and Ritzler, 1981). When psychotic symptoms do not appear acutely, defining onset is basically arbitrary. Definite markers of the beginning of schizophrenic episodes do not exist, and patients can waver between prodromal and psychotic symptoms for long periods. Many of the prodromal and residual symptoms listed as part of the DSM-III duration criterion for the diagnosis of schizophrenia, such as markedly peculiar behavior, bizarre ideation, and perceptual abnormalities, are difficult to distinguish clinically from more florid psychotic symptoms such as delusions and hallucinations which characterize a schizophrenic episode. As Spring and Coons (1982) have pointed out:

In psychopathology research, the problem of dating onset of schizophrenia is often treated as a methodological pitfall to be circumvented by improving interrater agreement. In actuality, it is a conceptual problem. Schizophrenia is a disorder which may develop by gradual accretion. It is difficult to determine when behavioral eccentricities have passed the threshold into a paranoid or schizoid personality, when these have shaded into a prodromal syndrome, and when this in turn has met the criteria for frank psychosis [pp. 29–39].

In addition to the difficulties of dating the onset of psychosis, there are also formidable methodological and conceptual problems in determining whether the occurrence of life events is independent of the influence of the illness. For example, Brown and Birley (1968) eliminated events brought on by the unusual behavior of the individual. Yet events which are not influenced by behavior that is grossly unusual can still be influenced by underlying vulnerability or prodromal symptoms. Jacobs and Myers (1976) used the criterion that "fateful" events be "independent of the person's ability to influence them" (p. 78). Harder et al. (1980) eliminated eight events which they judged as very likely to be consequences of psychiatric disorder from the 43-item Schedule of Recent Experience (Holmes and Rahe, 1967) and also probed for the circumstances surrounding events to determine if they were the result of the patient's pathological condition. Yet, when Spring and Coons (1982) compared the lists of events which the studies of Dohrenwend, Krasnoff, Askenasy, and Dohrenwend (1978), Dohrenwend (1974), Jacobs and Myers (1976), and Schwartz and Myers (1977) designated as independent, they found that the only events the researchers agreed upon were those concerning deaths. Zubin and Spring (1977) have pointed out that the domain of independent events is actually quite small: "With the exception of such natural calamities as earthquakes, it may be that a person's choice of lifestyle contributes to his likelihood of encountering stressful events" (p. 119). Dohrenwend (1974) found that many psychiatric patients, when asked about the last major event that changed their activities, reported events specifically related to their psychiatric illness or treatment.

There is evidence that, as early as in infancy and childhood, persons who later develop schizophrenia engage disproportionately in behavior patterns which might enhance the occurrence of stressful life events. For example, in a prospective longitudinal study of children of schizophrenic mothers, differences between individuals diagnosed as exhibiting "schizophrenia spectrum" disorders versus those not showing signs of any mental disorder were detectable before the age of two (Parnas, Schulsinger, Schulzinger, Mednick, and Teasdale, 1982). The future schizophrenia spectrum babies were more passive and had poorer attention span at play. During the school years, they were described as having had more interpersonal difficulties, as exhibiting difficult, unusual behavior, and as being disciplinary problems. In two retrospective studies using school records, a significantly larger proportion of preschizophrenic boys than controls showed poor school performance, emotional instability, and disagreeableness. The preschizophrenic girls in the study were rated as emotionally unstable, introverted, and passive (Watt, Stolorow, Lubensky, and McClelland, 1970; Watt, 1978). Thus, aspects of the vulnerability to schizophrenia may be associated with behaviors which increase the likelihood of stressful interpersonal difficulties on an ongoing basis. As with dating onset, the difficulties in separating life events from manifestations of the illness point to an important aspect of the relationship between stress and the onset of schizophrenic episodes rather than a methodological difficulty to be surmounted.

Goal-Directed Pursuit of Life Events and Hospitalization

Some researchers have emphasized the active and willful participation of schizophrenics in creating life events. For example, Leff (1976), in his review of geographic mobility among schizophrenics before their first episode, highlighted the goal-directedness of life events connected with changes in residence. He concluded that the pursuit of social isolation was the major motivating factor in such relocations. Jacobs and Myers (1976) found more relocations among schizophrenic patients in the year preceding a relapse than among controls. Schwartz and Myers (1977) also found a higher incidence of exits among schizophrenic ex-patients living in the community than among controls, suggesting that the pursuit of social isolation is a continuing component of schizophrenic behavior. These findings point to the participation of schizophrenic patients in creating the disruptions in their social support systems that are considered a core aspect of the stressfulness of many life events.

In the Fontana et al. (1972) study of hospitalized patients, the authors viewed contingent (nonindependent) events preceding hospitalization, such as changing residence, angry outburst, being arrested, withdrawing, and hospitalization itself, as "attempts to negotiate changes in others' expectations" (p. 311). Such events may serve to recruit physical support and psychological gratification, enable the patient to flee an unpleasant situation by ensuring hospitalization, or publicly demonstrate that pressures have precipitated a "nervous breakdown." Even when the behavior is not consciously planned and appears grossly disordered, Fontana et al. (1972) maintain that "adopting an instrumental view of the behavior and of hospitalization will increase our understanding of both" (p. 311).

In another study addressing the motivational dimension of illness behavior, Lewis and Hugi (1981) examined the changes in utilization of mental hospitals by patients during the last 20 years of deinstitutionalization. Before the 1960s, psychiatric patients typically spent long periods of time confined to hospitals. However, the authors maintain that:

The contemporary world of the mental patient, we believe, looks and feels very different than it did a generation ago. . . . The present system is a mosaic of services and funding modalities which emphasize the voluntary nature of assuming the mental patient role [Lewis and Hugi, 1981, p. 208].

Lewis and Hugi found that most of their sample of 18 chronically treated patients (no diagnoses reported) lacked jobs, families, and adequate income. Hospitalization was one of the resources that they had available in their limited social network to replace or supplement families, friends, and jobs. From their interviews with these 18 patients, the authors concluded: "The continued use of inpatient facilities reflects . . . purposeful behavior of resources-poor citizens who can avail themselves of these situations when they feel it is necessary . . . a weekend retreat for those who have few other places to go" (p. 218). For example, one patient in their study stated: "It's like a vacation. I like it" (Lewis and Hugi, 1981, p. 216).

The use of psychiatric hospitals to recruit basic material and social resources instead of as treatment centers for relieving psychopathology is a possible confounding factor in the basic paradigm being used by researchers in the life-event area. It raises the possibility that the life events preceding the onset of a schizophrenic episode might have been motivated by the desire to gain access to the hospital. Unfortunately, none of the studies adopting this perspective have provided data indicating what proportion of life events or hospitalizations is attributable to motivated behavior. By restricting their research to case examples and not subjecting their model to empirical verification by operationally defining "purposive" and "instrumental" behavior, the proponents of this position overgeneralize the social perspective. Validation of their approach will require a stronger empirical foundation. Thus, the relevance of goal-directed life events to the onset of schizophrenic episodes awaits clarification.

Another manner in which some patients may actively contribute to an increase in stressful life events and psychotic symptoms has been isolated by Van Putten, Crumpton, and Yale (1976). They identified a group of schizophrenic patients who "seem to prefer psychosis to a drug-induced normality" (p. 1443). Their study compared a group of habitual drug refusers, who invariably discontinued antipsychotic medication and were repeatedly hospitalized afterward, with a group of drug compliers. While many factors associated with drug compliance have been identified—e.g., side effects, complexity of regimens, insight into illness, and severity of illness,—these did not account for the difference in rate of drug compliance between the two groups. The variable that provided the most powerful discrimination of the two groups was the Brief Psychiatric Rating Scale score for grandiosity. Patients who habitually refused medication experienced a resurgence of grandiose psychotic symptoms shortly after stopping their medication, while the drug compliers had decompensations characterized by anxiety and depression. While on medication, many of the drug refusers seemed to experience an increase in reality contact including awareness of their schizophrenic illness, status as a patient, loneliness, and lack of any life accomplishments. The investigators postulated that "some patients stop medication precisely because they prefer a schizophrenic existence" (p. 1444). Hogarty, Goldberg, and the Collaborative Study Group (1973) came to the same conclusion in explaining their finding that 40 percent of the patients in their study stopped medication within the first year after discharge.

While these findings are limited to the issue of medication compliance, they also suggest that schizophrenic episodes may sometimes result from the active pursuit of the illness state. Discontinuing medication and other life events, e.g., quitting a job, might at times be purposeful actions taken by the patient to initiate the onset of a schizophrenic episode, rather than events that precipitate psychotic symptomatology independent of patient control.

Exposure to Life Events

Although the previous two sections reviewed studies indicating that schizophrenic patients probably generate surplus life events as a result of their prodromal onset symptoms as well as their lifestyle and goals, there is also evidence that schizophrenic patients are exposed to life events beyond their control in greater numbers than nonpatients. Schwartz and Myers (1977) compared the incidence of life events occurring to schizophrenic patients living in the community 2–3 years after hospitalization with that in community controls. The discharged patients experienced significantly more "uncontrolled" (independent) events during the 6-month period studied than did the controls (.85 versus .42), indicating that individuals with schizophrenia are exposed to more independent life events than the average person while living in the community. When non-independent life events were considered, the difference was even greater (2.40 versus 1.09).

Dohrenwend and Egri (1981) have pointed out that, given the strong evidence for a genetic component in schizophrenia, schizophrenic patients are more likely to be exposed to psychopathology and problem situations in their immediate families than most people. In the Brown and Birley (1968) study, for example, the psychiatric hospitalization of one patient's mother and the suicide of another were considered independent life events since they were clearly outside the patient's direct control. Yet such events probably occur more frequently to individuals living in families with a genetic loading for schizophrenia, so they cannot be considered totally independent of the patient's disorder. In addition, Dohrenwend and Egri (1981) maintain that "patients are exposed not only to ordinary stressful events that most people experience, but also to events that appear peculiar to their biological and psychological status as psychiatric patients" (p. 20). Dohrenwend (1974) found that many patients reported major life events connected with their social role as psychiatric patients such as changes in their treatment programs. While difficult to document, the socialization in dependency, the side effects of medication, and the stigma of being a psychiatric patient—factors which are often part of the treatment process—may also expose the schizophrenic patient to additional life events.

SUMMARY

These findings concerning the contribution of patients' symptoms and personal choices to the occurrence of life events and psychotic episodes are at odds with the paradigm most investigators in the life-event field have been using. The central questions researchers have pursued is whether the occurrence of life events beyond the patients' control results in stress which, in turn, exacerbates pathology. However, this section highlighted findings on stress-prone factors which seem important in understanding the relationship between life events and the course of schizophrenic disorder, yet were not considered in the original life-event/illness paradigm based on physical illness (Holmes and Rahe, 1967). Although the studies showing a Type II relationship between life events and schizophrenic episodes do not provide support for the classic vulnerability/stress model of the course for schizophrenic illness, neither do they disconfirm it. Rather, they point to additional factors which a vulnerability/stress model needs to incorporate to account for these findings. A later section discusses some of these factors in the context of coping mechanisms.

TYPE III: NO RELATIONSHIP
BETWEEN LIFE EVENTS AND THE
ONSET OF SCHIZOPHRENIC EPISODES

Findings of no relationship between these two variables can be explained in two basic ways: (1) aspects of the research procedures have obscured the relationship or measurement procedures have missed the essential dimensions, or (2) the variable are not causally related in the situation being studied. First, the relevant life-event studies are reviewed. Then methodological and theoretical issues which might be involved in findings of a Type III relationship between life events and schizophrenic episodes are examined.

LIFE-EVENT STUDIES

All studies investigating the role of life events have found some patients who develop schizophrenic episodes in the absence of life events. Leff et al. (1973) identified two specific subgroups of schizophrenic patients for whom life events did not play a major role in onset. Leff and his colleagues found that patients randomly assigned to a placebo medication did not report a surplus of major life events in the 5 weeks before relapse: "Schizophrenic patients living in the community and not taking drugs seem to relapse as a result of the disturbing effect of everyday social interactions" (p. 660). Relapses for patients on medication, however, were associated with the occurrence of life events. Leff and Vaughn (1980) found that relapses among patients living in high EE fa..nilies also were not preceded by an increase in life events, whereas relapses from low EE families were associated with life events. It should be noted that Vaughn and Leff (1976a) found that schizophrenic patients who lived in high EE families, had more than 35 hours a week of contact with their families, and were not on antipsychotic medication had a 92 percent likelihood of relapsing within 9 months of discharge, thereby leaving virtually no room for other significant predictive factors to operate.

Studies which have compared schizophrenic patients with other psychiatric patients are difficult to place within the classificatory schema of this review. Of the five studies using this design, three found that schizophrenic patients reported significantly fewer events than depressives before an illness episode (Beck and Worthen, 1972; Clancy, Crowe, Winokur, and Morrison, 1973; Jacobs, Prusoff, and Paykel, 1974). However, Lahniers and White (1976) found no differences in the number of life events preceding onset among schizophrenic, neurotic, depressive, and alcoholic patients. Eisler and Polak (1971) also found no differences in the number of social areas in which stressors were reported among DSM-II schizophrenic, depressive, personality disorder, and transient situational reaction patients.

These five studies suggest that schizophrenic patients do not report more life events preceding illness onset than patients in other psychiatric diagnostic groups. They may experience fewer events than depressives before an episode. However, the implications of these findings for understanding the causal relationship between life events and schizophrenic episodes are ambiguous. Life events could play a greater contributory role in the onset of depression, but be important in the onset of schizophrenic episodes as well. The studies are discussed in this third category because they do not support a specific relationship between life events and schizophrenic illness. However, due to the nature of their design—comparing patients with patients—they cannot be considered to present evidence that life events are unrelated to the onset of schizophrenic episodes. For example, Beck and Worthen (1972) found precipitating events for the episode onset of 95 percent of depressives in their study compared to 53 percent of the schizophrenic patients. Similarly, Jacobs et al. (1974) found that depressives reported 50 percent more life events than did the schizophrenic patients. It is clear that neither of these results precludes a contributory role for life events in schizophrenic episode onset.

Although most of the studies failing to find a relationship between life events and schizophrenic episode onset seem to have used psychiatric comparison groups and are subject to be interpretive ambiguity just noted, the following methodological and conceptual issues suggest other possible contributing factors.

FACTORS ACCOUNTING FOR THE LACK OF AN OBSERVED RELATIONSHIP

Measurement Issues

One possibility is that major life events occurring before onset were overlooked. The studies are oriented toward married, working people, not the typical isolated, single, unemployed schizophrenic patient. Thus, stressful life events which occur commonly to schizophrenic patients—e.g., change in a patient's therapist at the community mental health center, notice to appear for an interview to review eligibility for SSI benefits, and rejection by acquaintances who learn that the patient is a "mental case"—are not adequately covered by these schedules. As mentioned earlier, a large proportion of psychiatric patients specifically mentioned these types of events, ones which were related to their psychiatric illness or its treatment, when they were asked what recent event had changed their activities (Dohrenwend, 1974).

A subtle diagnostic bias may also diminish the association between life events and onset. One lingering effect of theories which have viewed schizophrenia disorder is that "the presence of stressful life event leads diagnosticians to ignore the presence of schizophrenia" (Spring and Coons, 1982, p. 31). To an unknown degree, some cases meeting diagnostic criteria for schizophrenia may have been diagnosed as nonschizophrenic if the illness seemed to be preceded by a stressful event.

Elsewhere in this issue, Falloon (1984) discusses other reasons why hospitalization is an unreliable criterion for episode onset. Even studies which use independent criteria to establish the presence of a schizophrenic episode depend upon the hospital as the intake point for recruiting their samples. Yet, Link and Dohrenwend's (1980) epidemiological study found that a substantial minority of persons with diagnosable schizophrenia in the general population have never been in inpatient or outpatient treatment. The effects of limiting life-event studies to samples of identified patients are difficult to determine, but Dohrenwend and Egri (1981) maintain the following:

On the basis of analysis of the epidemiological literature on true and treat rates, the literature on extreme situations, and the World Health Organization cross-national studies, were suspect that samples of subjects who are admitted to hospitals in modern Western societies after developing schizophrenic episodes are biased in the direction of underestimating the etiological importance of recent stressful life events [p. 22].

Some technical methodological procedures may also diminish the observed link between life events and the onset of illness. Rabkin and Struening (1976) argue that sample size deficiencies may have minimized this relationship. The results of the Harder et al. (1980) study suggest that a measure of change in level of stress preceding onset rather than level of stress per se might show a more powerful relationship between life events and the development of schizophrenic episodes. Another implication from the Harder et al. (1980) study, as well as that of Brown and Birley (1968), is that events in the few weeks just before onset play an especially significant role in triggering episodes. Most life-event studies have not been designed to evaluate changes in level of stress before onset and have used time periods substantially longer than the 3–12 weeks used by these two studies that produced significant positive findings. Reliability of many life-event scales may also hamper the uncovering of significant relationships between life events and onset of episodes. Neugebauer (1983) found the main intrapair agreement between schizophrenic patients and informants for the 102-item PERI life-event checklist (Dohrenwend et al., 1978) among 18 patient/informant pairs was only .22.

In summary, deficiencies in measurement instruments, sample bias, sample size, and methodological inadequacies may all contribute to weakening the findings of relationship between life events and schizophrenic episodes. Although it is always possible to attribute negative findings to methodological problems, the nature of life events and the nature of schizophrenia seem to interact, making it particularly difficult to research the impact of one or the other.

High Vulnerability

Another possible factor in producing negative results is that minor, idiosyncratic events may be sufficient to precipitate symptom exacerbation in some cases. In fact, within the vulnerability/stress model, a highly vulnerable person is predicted to be "one for whom numerous contingencies encountered in daily living are sufficient to elicit an episode" (Zubin and Spring, 1977, p. 109). Such minor life events could easily escape detection by the standard life-event assessment procedures. Lewinsohn and Talkington (1979) have pioneered the use of "micro-events" in studies on depression, but to date, their procedure has not been used with schizophrenic patients. Examples of groups that may be particularly vulnerable include patients without antipsychotic medication (Hogarty and Ulrich, 1977) and patients with a strong family history of schizophrenic disorder.

High Prevailing Stress

Highly stressful environments might also obviate the need for major life events to occur to produce onsets of schizophrenic episodes. Brown et al. (1972) have described a process whereby a relapse could be precipitated by ongoing interactions with a high EE relative without additional major life events: "In the presence of a socially intrusive relative . . . [the patient] is unable to withdraw, and any residual or latent thought disorder will become manifest as expressed delusions or odd behavior"

(p. 256). In the case of patients from high EE homes who have more than 35 hours per week of face-to-face contact (high prevailing stress) and are also off-medication (high vulnerability), the need for a precipitating life event would seem to be virtually eliminated. As mentioned earlier, these patients have been found to have a 92 percent likelihood of relapsing within 9 months (Vaughn and Leff, 1976a).

Using a different methodology, Serban (1975) examined the prevailing stress levels of acute and chronic schizophrenic patients. On a 130-item scale he developed to cover areas of daily living, chronic patients reported the highest level of stress, normals the lowest, and acute patients an intermediate level. Serban described the chronic schizophrenic patient as highly stressed by the demands of daily living: "The surrounding world is a source of turmoil; almost everything creates anxiety and discomfort. . . . Everything appears to represent either an insurmountable demand which society places on them or worry induced by frustrated expectations" (p. 405). When hospitalized, only 38 percent of the schizophrenic patients could identify one of 21 categories of major life stressors as a contributing factor. Serban concluded that the most important factor in frequent readmissions was the continuously high level of stress. He argued that life events, even when present, "contribute to admission in the majority of cases . . . only by increasing the already existing high global stress in the life of schizophrenics" (p. 405). Brown et al. (1973) also mentioned that consideration must be given to the "total environmental effect," including ongoing difficulties and "long-term social problems not the result of a life event in the period studied" (p. 171).

Psychological and Biological Fluctuation

Although life-event research has focused on the role of high external stimulation, Wing (1978) and others have also pointed out the dangers of understimulating environments. Some early theorists such as Kahn and Kretschmer emphasized the role of isolation in precipitating delusions even without external precipitating events. These findings were based on their observations of psychiatric patients and the occurrence of delusions in life situations involving isolation such as deafness and incarceration in prison (Arthur, 1964). Research on sensorily deprived environments has also shown that psychotic symptoms including hallucinations and delusions can occur in situations of prolonged sensory deprivation (Lilly, 1956). The proclivity of schizophrenic patients toward isolation is well known, and in extreme cases where patients withdraw from social and other sources of stimulation for long periods of time, they might inadvertently or advertently stimulate sensorily deprived environments. In this manner the complete absence of major and minor life events could potentially exacerbate psychotic symptoms. However, understimulating environments are usually thought to contribute more to the development of negative symptoms such as poverty of speech and blunted affect than to the development of the positive symptoms of hallucinations and delusions that characterize an acute schizophrenic episode (Wing, 1978). Although isolation and withdrawal seem frequently to precede onset of schizophrenic episodes, their role has not been clarified. Van Putten et al. (1976) have identified a group of patients who seem to actively seek a delusional state of mind, and who may learn ways to cultivate psychotic states by discontinuing their medication and focusing on internal processes. Thus, in some cases of relapse characterized by increasing preoccupation with enjoyed hallucinations and delusions, external events may play only a minor role.

Some episodes may be triggered by fluctuations in biochemical factors or neurophysiological states that are not initiated by external stressors (Bowers, 1980). While acknowledging that the biochemistry of psychotic symptoms is not well understood, Zubin and Spring (1977) also mention that variations in internal chemistry could produce exacerbation of symptoms in the absence of external stressors. The possibly very important neurophysiological variability in producing or initiating relapse must await a more precise understanding of the biochemical pathways that contribute to psychotic symptoms. The brevity of our discussion of such factors reflects the focus of this chapter rather than the level of importance that biochemical and neurophysiological variables might have in influencing relapse.

SUMMARY

This review of possible factors leading in some studies to the absence of an observed relationship between major life events and schizophrenic episodes indicates that a vulnerability/stress model needs to recognize individual variability in the causal pathways for schizophrenic episodes. Variations in premorbid vulnerability and prevailing environmental stress need to be incorporated into the model and are likely to affect whether a major life event is needed to precipitate a relapse. As Spring and Coons (1982) have pointed out:

Stress might be a sufficient cause for some schizophrenias, a necessary cause for others, and an irrelevant factor for still others. Progress in explaining the role of stress may come only by way of evaluating subgroups of schizophrenics who are homogeneous with respect to etiology, underpinnings of vulnerability, and premorbid degree of vulnerability [pp. 28–29].

In addition, preexisting vulnerability may be potentiated differently among different individuals, with some people being more affected by external events involving their social support system such as the death of a relative, and others by blows to their self-esteem such as failing a test at school or being fired from a job. An adequate model of schizophrenic relapse also needs to cover situations in which the patient willfully courts the illness state or hospitalization. Thus, the role of stress in precipitating onsets of schizophrenic episodes may vary considerably among different subgroups of schizophrenic patients.

The final section of this chapter considers the coping responses schizophrenic patients make in response to stressful events and situations. These also have a role in understanding the relationship between stress and illness because coping responses have been shown to amplify or diminish the inherent stressfulness of major life events. But, first, research on family atmosphere, which was introduced here as a type of prevailing stress that interacted with life events in predicting the onset of schizophrenic episodes is reviewed.

FAMILIAL STRESS: HISTORICAL BACKGROUND

In 1927 Sullivan suggested that disturbed family relationships might be linked to subsequent schizophrenic illness, and in 1934, Kasanin, Knight, and Sage made the first systematic attempt to study the environmental effects of parents in the pathogenesis of schizophrenia (Hirsch and Leff, 1975). Since that time a number of well-known theories and studies, rich in clinical detail and notional phrases, have been advanced describing the role of the parental family in the development of schizophrenia. Among the prominent, psychoanalytically derived, etiological hypotheses are the following: Fromm-Reichmann's (1948) description of the "schizophrenogenic mother"; Lidz, Cornelison, Fleck, and Terry's (1957) delineation of "marital skew" and "marital schism" in parents of schizophrenic patients; Bateson, Jackson, Haley, and Weakland's (1956) "double-bind" hypothesis; Wynne and his colleagues' (Wynne, Ryckoff, Day, and Mirsch, 1958; Wynne and Singer, 1963a) theory of "pseudomutuality" in the communication patterns of families with schizophrenic offspring; and Laing's (1972) essay dealing with intrafamilial, interfamilial, and extrafamilial relations and networks.

Two other research tactics have recently been pursued which involve the prediction of an individual's schizophrenic symptoms from certain measurable characteristics of the social or familial environment. We review here familial factors that have predicted relapse in an existing schizophrenic illness in various patient samples and factors that have predicted the onset of schizophrenia spectrum disorders in a sample of disturbed teen-agers. This research has provided empirical validation that measurable aspects of the social environment are associated with the course of schizophrenia.

EXPRESSED EMOTION AND RELAPSE

Research on social factors in the community that might be related to the relapse and readmission of schizophrenic patients began in the 1950s as investigators both in London and the United States recognized the changing pattern of hospital care brought about by advances in psychopharmacology. Shorter hospitalization, frequently followed by later patient relapse and readmission, generally replaced long-term hospital care. Thus, investigations of social factors in the community might be related to patient relapse and readmission were undertaken. In the United States, Simmons (Freeman and Simmons, 1963) launched a project to uncover factors that affected the adaptation of patients discharged from mental hospitals, and concurrently, in London, George Brown and his colleagues began the first in a series of studies of social factors in the community which affected patients' hospital readmissions.

Freeman and Simmons (1963) set out to predict community performance levels and symptomatic behavior of discharged patients from social and cultural variables including relatives' attributes. Personality characteristics of patients' relatives were assessed in several ways: Srole's personality scales for anomie, authoritarianism, frustration, rigidity, and withdrawal; Brim and associates' personality scales; and clinical social workers' ratings on Borgatta's scales for 14 personality characteristics. Freeman and Simmons reported some relationships between patients' community performance level and relatives' personality traits, but found no differences on any personality scales between relatives of patients who remained in the community and relatives of patients who were rehospitalized. In addition, they found no association between family type, social class, values, or expectations and patients' symptomatic behavior. The authors concluded that "the course of the illness itself may not be related primarily to the setting the patient returns to after hospitalization or to [personality] characteristics of his family associates" (Freeman and Simmons, 1963, p. 200).

Brown and his colleagues (Brown, Carstairs, and Topping, 1958; Brown, 1959), like Freeman and Simmons, initially found that patients discharged to homes of spouses and parents did not have different relapse rates; however, Brown (1959) found that patients discharged to homes of spouses and parents or to hostels relapsed at a significantly higher rate than those discharged to live with their siblings or in "lodgings." Brown, Monck, Carstairs, and Wing (1962) then proceeded to the first of a series of studies in which patients' family environments were assessed by focusing on the interpersonal relationships of the relatives and patient rather than on relatives' personalities. Families were rated either high or low on emotional involvement with the patient, and these ratings proved to be associated with the return or exacerbation of patients' schizophrenic symptoms during the followup period. Fifty-six percent of patients living with families rated high on emotional involvement relapsed, in contrast to 21 percent of patients living with families rated low on emotional involvement.

Following the 1962 study, family assessment methods were standardized. A semistructured interview, the Camberwell Family Interview (CFI), and a reliable system for rating emotional expression during the interview were developed (Brown and Rutter, 1966; Rutter and Brown, 1966) to assess the quality of enduring interpersonal relationships within the family. More specifically, measurement of the quality of family relationships were operationalized by scales measuring the number of critical and positive remarks made by the relative about the patient, the presence or absence of hostility, and the extent of warmth, overprotectiveness, or emotional overinvolvement, along with more than a dozen other scales. In subsequent research, the Camberwell Family Interview has usually been administered to each relative living with the patient. The tape-recorded interview has then been scored for the scales just noted. An index of expressed emotion (EE) has been empirically derived to maximize the prediction of schizophrenic relapse. Family members are rated high on expressed emotion if they score high on the scales measuring critical comments, emotional overinvolvement, or hostility. If any family member is rated high on expressed emotion, the family environment is also considered to be high. For a detailed review of the concept of expressed emotion, see Kuipers (1979). Family members who might be assessed are not limited to biological parents, but include the spouse, siblings, and other relatives or significant others who have enduring relationships with the patient.

Using the standardized Camberwell Family Interview to measure expressed emotion, and the semistructured Present State Examination (Wing, Cooper, and Sartorius, 1974) to determine diagnoses and relapse, Brown et al. (1972) repeated the early study. In addition to family and psychiatric measures, measures of patient behavior including work impairment, disturbed behavior, and social withdrawal were collected. Measures of expressed emotion taken from patients' relatives at the time of hospital admission significantly predicted patients' symptomatic relapse over the 9-month followup period. Relapse was defined as a return or exacerbation of schizophrenic symptoms elicited by the Present State Examination. More than three times as many patients from high EE families relapsed (58 percent) as patients from low EE families (16 percent).

Two replications of Brown's work have been carried out. Vaughn and Leff (1976a), using the same EE scales and diagnostic procedures with a shortened family interview (Vaughn and Leff, 1976b), found strikingly similar results. In addition to replicating the main result that patients living in high EE homes had a higher relapse rate, they also found that the relapse rate for high EE patients varied according to whether patients had high (over 35 hours) weekly contact with relatives and whether they took antipsychotic medication regularly. Low contact with relatives and regular medication acted as protective factors for high EE patients. Relapse rates of low EE patients, on the other hand, did not interact with high or low relative contact or medication compliance during the 9-month followup period.

In a 2-year followup of the Vaughn and Leff sample (Leff and Vaughn, 1981), the proportion of relapses in the high and low groups remained virtually unchanged. However, it became obvious that even the low EE patients were, in fact, protected from relapse during the 2-year followup period if they continued to take antipsychotic medication regularly.

Vaughn and Leff's study was subsequently replicated by Vaughn, Snyder, Jones, Freeman, and Falloon (1982; in press) in the United States at the UCLA Mental Health Clinical Research Center for the Study of Schizophrenia. Once again, the EE index, that is, criticism or overinvolvement expressed by a key relative about a patient at the time of admission, proved to be the best single predictor of symptomatic relapse in the 9 months after discharge from the hospital. As in the British studies, the association among relatives' expressed emotion and patient's relapse was independent of all other variables investigated, including behavior disturbance, schizophrenic symptoms at admission and discharge, and work impairment. Two differences between the California and London samples are noteworthy. First, in the London study more than half of the families assessed were rated low on EE, whereas in the California sample only a third of the families were low on EE. Second, significantly more of the California patients had a poor clinical outcome at 9-month followup. Table 24.1 gives relapse rates from the three studies.

These studies have established that the familial environment is a strong predictor of the relapse rate of schizophrenic patients. Along with the life events findings, they constitute the most important known socioenvironmental factors that appear to affect the course of schizophrenic disorders. However, a critical question concerns the nature of the underlying mechanisms that are tapped by the EE measures.

In an effort to clarify the meaning of the EE index, two lines of investigation have been pursued—behavioral observa-

Table 24.1
Relapse Rate as a Function of Familial Expressed Emotion

Studies	n	High EE relapsed	Low EE relapsed	Level of Statistical Significance
Brown, Birley, & Wing (1972) — London	91	58%	16%	.001
Vaughn & Leff (1976) — London	37	48%	6%	.007
Vaughn et al. (1981) — U.S.	54	56%	17%	.015

tions of relative and patient interactions, and psychophysiological indexes of patient arousal in the presence of a relative. First, the studies employing physiological measures are reviewed.

It has been hypothesized that high levels of criticism and emotional overinvolvement by relatives may contribute to higher levels of physiological arousal in the patient, thereby precipitating a return of an individual's schizophrenic symptoms (Brown et al., 1972). This hypothesis has been tested in two studies which measured autonomic arousal while patients interacted with their high or low EE family members. In both studies, the principal measure of autonomic arousal was the rate of spontaneous electrodermal responses, i.e., responses that occur in the absence of known eliciting stimuli.

In the first study, Tarrier, Vaughn, Lader, and Leff (1979) collected measures of spontaneous electrodermal responses, heart rate, and blood pressure for a sample of remitted schizophrenic patients with either high or low EE relatives, first during 15 minutes with the experimenter only, and then for 15 minutes in the presence of the key relative. Results of this study showed that:

During the 15 minutes of recording of sweat gland activity, when the relative was absent, the low and high EE patient groups were similar in level of arousal. However, during the second 15 minutes, with the relative present, a significantly ($p < .01$) greater amount of spontaneous activity occurred in high EE patients. High EE patients also showed an increase in diastolic blood pressure in the presence of the relative compared to the decrease in low EE patients ($p < .002$) [pp. 312–313].

In a subsequent experiment, Sturgeon, Kuipers, Berkowitz, Turpin, and Leff (1981) found a significant reduction in the rate of spontaneous fluctuations of skin conductance responses when the relatives were present among patients with low EE relatives, but not among patients with high EE relatives. This finding is consistent with the results of Tarrier et al. (1979). Whereas measures were taken in the homes of 52 patients who were in relative remission in the earlier study, measures were taken from acutely ill patients in a laboratory setting in the Sturgeon et al. (1981) study. These findings, using different samples of schizophrenic patients evaluated in different settings, offer concurrent validation for the hypothesis that high autonomic arousal in a schizophrenic patient is associated with social stimulation by a high EE family member.

Elevated arousal has often been presented as the defining characteristic of stress, and prolonged elevated arousal has been found to be associated with the development of a variety of physiological disorders (Selye, 1956). The finding of elevated autonomic arousal among schizophrenic patients when a high EE relative is present provides a link between social and biological variables in understanding how familial environment can affect the course of a schizophrenic patient's illness.

The second line of investigation into the mechanisms underlying the EE measure has focused on behavioral dimensions of the relationship between the patient and the relative. Brown et al. (1972) have hypothesized as follows: "A high degree of expressed emotion on one occasion is a measure of a relative's propensity to react in that way to that particular patient, even though other factors may be needed to precipitate this" (p. 241). Thus, expressed emotion is thought to represent an enduring potential characteristic of the relative's behavior toward the patient.

The behavioral characteristics of interactions between relatives and patients have been investigated by Kuipers, Sturgeon, Berkowitz, and Leff (1980) and by Doane et al. (as reported by Falloon, Pederson, Shirin, and Moss, 1981). The sample studied by Kuipers et al. consisted of 20 patients and their relatives/ parents, spouses, and siblings. They examined differences between low and high EE relatives' behavior during the joint interview with patient, relative, and interviewer. Their preliminary results suggest that the high EE relative's reaction to a schizophrenic family member during an interview by a third person was to spend a considerable amount of time talking (55 percent) and less time (36 percent) looking at (listening to) the patient. Percentage of time spent speaking was not related to the total interview length or the amount of time the interviewer spent talking, but was related to the relative's EE level. Low EE relatives showed the reverse of this pattern. They spent more time listening and allowed silences, giving ill patients more chance to participate and express themselves. Kuipers et al. concluded that the differential reaction of relatives to an acutely ill schizophrenic patient provides preliminary evidence that high EE relatives are behaviorally distinguishable from low EE relatives during such interactions.

In another attempt to discover whether relatives' high EE status indicates discriminable, characteristic negative and/or intrusive interpersonal modes of relating to the patient that are evidence in their interactions, Doane, Pederson, Shirin, and Moss (1981) applied a direct interaction measure of parental affective style to patient/relative triads. This interaction measure, termed affective style (AS), is coded from a typed verbatim transcript of a directly observed family interaction task. The task, also called the confrontation, is a modification of Strodbeck's (1954) revealed-differences technique. It involves a series of procedures which result in a triadic family discussion of problems or issues relevant to the given family. The primary negative codes of affective style include two kinds of criticism—guilt inducement and intrusiveness. Certain AS codes seem to be interpersonal analogs of some of the EE constructs and may represent behavioral counterparts of the interview-based index of expressed emotion.

In preliminary pilot work, Doane and her colleagues, as reported by Falloon, Boyd, McGill, Razani, Moss, and Gilderman (1982), have found that high EE relatives with an excess number of critical comments on the Camberwell Family Interview (CFI) also made significantly more critical remarks during the direct interaction task than did relatives rated low on the EE scale of criticism. Those relatives designated as high EE because of overinvolved rather than critical statements during the CFI displayed less criticism but significantly more intrusive remarks during the direct interaction task, such as telling the patient how he or she thinks or feels. Thus, this pilot work suggests not only that verbal behavioral differences exist between high and low EE relatives, but also that there are subgroup differences within the high EE group related to scores on the different EE scales.

SUMMARY

The EE research is consistent with a vulnerability/stress model of schizophrenic relapse. This model predicts that persons vulnerable to schizophrenic episodes will have a lowered likelihood of relapse if their exposure to stressful events and situations is reduced. Patients who had less than 35 hours a week of contact with high EE relatives were found to have a lower relapse rate than patients who had more than 35 hours a week of contact with a high EE relative. Similarly, the reduced relapse rate found among patients on antipsychotic medication also conforms to predictions of a vulnerability/stress model. In addition, the findings that patients exposed to high EE relatives have a significantly higher relapse rate than patients interacting with low EE relatives and that patient autonomic arousal is elevated in the presence of a high EE relative support the conceptualization of high EE as a potent familial stressor for schizophrenic patients.

FAMILY STUDIES PREDICTING ONSET OF ILLNESS

While a body of research has developed over the last 20 to 30 years focusing on the influence of the family on the course of an established schizophrenic illness, studies of family circumstances that antedate a first episode of schizophrenia are scarce. A major difficulty has been the selection of criteria by which appropriate families could be isolated for study. Goldstein and Rodnick of the UCLA Department of Psychology Family Project (Goldstein, Rodnick, Evans, May, and Steinberg, 1978a) have successfully conducted a longitudinal prospective study of the development of schizophrenia spectrum disorders by examining disturbed nonpsychotic adolescents and their families. Their research has focused on reciprocal family interaction patterns between parents and their adolescent children. Their "ultimate aim was to determine whether there are observable and consistent styles of coping that exist among family members which relate to the patterns of psychopathology manifested (at a later date) by an adolescent" (Goldstein, Judd, Rodnick, Alkire, and Gould, 1968, p. 233).

One of the primary family variables under study was a Singer-Wynne measure of communication deviance (CD) among the adolescents' parents. The original communication deviance studies of Wynne and his colleagues (1958) grew in part from their observations of communication and role structure in a sample of four families, each with a schizophrenic offspring. Wynne and Singer hypothesized that the form and structure of family-wide transactions might influence the cognitive development of the offspring and facilitate the development of the schizophrenic patient's thought disorder (Wynne et al., 1958; Wynne and Singer, 1963a, b). The family variable under study, which is generally referred to as "intrafamilial relationships," was specifically operationalized using speech patterns of schizophrenic patients' biological parents. Projective test materials, usually Rorschach or Thematic Apperception Test

(TAT) cards, have been used as standardized stimuli to elicit speech samples from individual parents and sometimes from family members together. Types of communication deviances scored on the CD codes include lack of commitment to ideas or percepts, unclear or idiosyncratic communication of themes or ideas, language anomalies, disruptive speech, and closure problems. Measures of CD have been summarized, using standardized procedures, as total amount of CD (Singer and Wynne, 1966) and also as factor score reflecting different styles of CD (Jones, 1977). Wynne and Singer (1963a, b) used the total CD measure to differentiate parental families with schizophrenic offspring from other families. Hirsch and Leff (1975) have reviewed those studies and reported mixed results in their attempt to replicate the specificity of CD to families with schizophrenic offspring.

Goldstein et al. (1978a) were the first to use the CD measure to predict onset of schizophrenia spectrum disorders. The subjects selected for their high-risk study were nonpsychotic, disturbed adolescents seen at an outpatient clinic for emotional difficulties. This high-risk sample differs from most other high-risk samples because it was not selected on the basis of parental schizophrenic disorder. Two measures of risk for these adolescents were used: (1) their presenting behavior problems and (2) a parental CD measure. Adolescents were deemed at high risk for the development of schizophrenia spectrum disorder if they were withdrawn and socially isolated or if they were engaged in active family conflict. In addition, adolescents were considered at high risk if their parents scored in a specified high range of the CD measures.

Doane et al. (1981) reported that a recent analysis of the complete Family Project sample of high-risk adolescents at 5-year followup showed statistically significant relationships between both parental CD and parental AS with outcome. The AS and CD variables were also combined to predict outcomes, resulting in the most precise prediction of subsequent schizophrenia spectrum disorder in offspring.

In addition to the responses to TAT cards from which CD

measures were scored, a wealth of other material was collected from these families (Goldstein et al., 1968), including a standardized family interview, two simulated interaction sequences followed by direct interaction tasks, and skin resistance measures of parents and adolescents. In an effort to determine the interrelationships of communication deviance and other aspects of familial interaction patterns and attitudes, UCLA Family Project researchers have recently compared CD scores and direct interaction patterns (Lewis, Rodnick, and Goldstein, 1981); scored Family Project Interviews for expressed emotion (Norton, 1982); and compared affective style and expressed emotion scores (Valone, Norton, Goldstein, and Doane, in press). Most recently, these investigators have compared parental and adolescent electrodermal measures with EE scores from Family Project interviews in an attempt to extend the network EE correlates (Valone, Goldstein, and Norton, submitted for publication). These additional analyses of the Family Project data base have resulted in interesting hypotheses concerning the relationships and meanings of various measures.

Lewis et al. (1981) found significant associations between CD and the degree of disruption of communication focus in triadic family discussions. Thus, the CD that was scored from TAT responses was manifested in direct family interactions. Furthermore, high CD families had significantly fewer father-central role structures.

Norton (1982) was able to rate the Family Project interviews from expressed emotion. Her work represents the first instance of rating other than the CFI. She reported that when both parents were defined as high EE, 90.9 percent (10 of 11) of the adolescents received followup diagnoses of schizophrenia or hypothesized related disorders such as probable schizophrenia and borderline or schizoid personality disorders. In families in which both parents had been rated low on EE, only 9.5 percent (2 of 21) of the adolescent subjects received these diagnoses, while with a pattern of one low and one high EE parent, 25 percent (5 of 20) received such diagnoses at followup.

Valone et al. (in press) compared Norton's EE ratings with

the Doane et al. (1981) ratings of affective style. Doane et al. (1981) had hypothesized that affective style ratings of direct interaction sequences might be the interpersonal analogues of EE interview ratings. Indeed, Valone et al. found that when both parents were high EE, they expressed high levels of both mild and harsh criticisms in direct interactions with their offspring. When both parents were low EE, they manifested few mild or harsh criticisms in direct interactions.

In a recent analysis of parental and adolescent electrodermal measures, Valone, Goldstein, and Norton (submitted) obtained preliminary results which suggest that adolescents interacting with a high EE parent show greater autonomic reactivity than adolescents interacting with a low EE parent. Furthermore, high EE parents themselves appear to have higher levels of autonomic reactivity during these discussions than do low EE parents.

In addition to generating hypotheses concerning family factors that precede the onset of schizophrenia spectrum disorders, the UCLA Family Project researchers have sought to clarify the relationships among various measures of familial communication and environment. These studies offer preliminary indications that interactions in high CD families differ from those in low CD families. Furthermore, while both CD and AS are significantly predictive of outcome, a combination of the two measures is the most precise predictor of the onset of schizophrenia spectrum disorders. In this sample, it also appears that EE ratings of critical attitudes in parents are reflective of parental criticism of their adolescent offspring during a direct interaction task summarized as AS. Finally, at 5-year followup, adolescents who had two high EE parents were much more likely than adolescents who had two low EE parents to obtain diagnoses of schizophrenia, probable schizophrenia, or borderline or schizoid personality disorders.

The findings of the UCLA Family Project researchers from the longitudinal study of high-risk, nonpsychotic but disturbed adolescents indicate a conceptual transition in the CD measure. Wynne and colleagues first theorized that CD was highly characteristic of parents of schizophrenic patients, and its presence in the parental family was a necessary antecedent to the offspring's development of schizophrenia. Results of the UCLA Family Project research (Doane et al., 1981) indicate that parental CD was present in the vast majority of cases in which the offspring developed subsequent schizophrenia spectrum disorders (9 of 10). However, a number of high CD families did not have schizophrenia spectrum disorders in key offspring (7 of 16). Thus, at this point, parental CD does not appear to be a sufficient condition for development of schizophrenia spectrum disorders among offspring, although longer term followup of these individuals is still in progress.

SUMMARY

The results of the ongoing UCLA Family Project indicate that certain types of affective style are often present in parents of disturbed adolescents who develop schizophrenia spectrum disorders, and that these patterns exist before onset. As Doane, Goldstein, and their colleagues have shown, the AS index, which includes directly observed critical, guilt-inducing, and intrusive statements made by parents of their offspring, can be construed as an interpersonal analogue of the EE construct developed from parental attitude measures. High EE has been clearly associated with higher rates of relapse, and its impact on course of illness is modified by other variables such as medication compliance and degree of exposure to relatives, while negative AS has been related to high scores of EE and the onset of schizophrenia spectrum disorders. Thus, high EE and negative AS can be conceptualized as types of stressors (perhaps similar or at least overlapping) that operate within the family environment. As such, EE and AS variables are readily interpretable within the vulnerability/stress model.

The CD findings allow for at least four differing interpretations, which need not be mutually exclusive. Disruptions, language anomalies, and lack of clarity and closure in parental interactions could function, in a manner similar to overinvolved and overly critical attitudes in high EE relatives, by directly inducing stress. [Perhaps a study along the lines of that by Tarrier et al. (1979), or Valone et al. (submitted), regarding EE could clarify whether interactions with parents high on CD are associated with elevated autonomic arousal in the patient.] A second possible interpretation is that the underlying mechanism in CD may involve direct parental influence of the cognitive development of their schizophrenic offspring, as Wynne et al. (1958) theorized. From an early age, the child may learn a faulty style of communication that could facilitate the development of thought disorders similar in style to the CD being modeled in the family. Another alternative is that CD reflects a subclinical level of thought and communication disorder that is genetically transmitted and that expresses itself as clinical schizophrenia in only some family members. The fourth possibility is that high levels of CD among parents may result from rearing disturbed offspring. Although CD was present before the onset of schizophrenia spectrum disorders, the UCLA Family Project selected families with adolescents who were already disturbed although not in treatment at the time of initial assessment. Elevated CD has also been found in parents of retardates, suggesting that CD may not be specific to parents of schizophrenia spectrum offspring and might be partially reactive to the offspring's disturbance (Wender, Rosenthal, Ramer, Greenhill, and Sarlin, 1977). These possibilities need not be mutually exclusive.

Whether CD is genetically transmitted, directly stress-inducing, reactive, and/or a modeling influence has yet to be determined. However, it does appear that EE, AS, and CD are familial variables that help to predict the onset of schizophrenia spectrum disorders in a sample of disturbed, nonpsychotic adolescents, and that at least EE helps to predict the likelihood of relapse following an episode of a schizophrenic psychosis.

Coping Responses and Schizophrenic Episodes

While the previous two sections reviewed the impact of socioenvironmental stressors on the course of schizophrenic disorder, this section highlights the individual's ability to modify the stressfulness of such situations. Rahe and Arthur (1978), two of the key contributors to our understanding of the relationship between socioenvironmental stressor and illness onset, have warned against oversimplifying this connection into a deterministic causal relationship or, alternatively, of abandoning the untangling of this relationship due to "weak" or sometimes nonsignificant findings:

As the life change and illness concept has become popularized, a certain imprecision of thought has become apparent. It has seemed to some as if there is as close and immediate relationship between life change and illness as is the relationship between staphylococci endotoxin and acute dysentery. This kind of conceptualization is simplistic. There are several intervening steps which exist between subjects' recent life change experience and their subsequent near-future illness symptoms and reports. It is necessary to think in terms of a model which embraces the whole series of intervening variables [Rahe and Arthur, 1978, p. 12].

Although the association between EE and relapse is more robust, half of the patients living in high EE families have been found to avoid relapse during the period studied. An overly simplified model will not be sufficient to explain the complex family environment/illness interrelationships observed here either.

It is clear from numerous laboratory studies in which animals have been exposed to stressful stimuli that environmental factors can produce increase arousal and changes in hormonal and immunological competence which, when prolonged, culminate in physical and even psychiatric ("learned helplessness") illnesses (Selye, 1956; Seligman, 1975). Although the same mechanisms linking environmental stimuli and physiological responses exist in humans, "the human ability to recruit social support, defend intra-psychically and cope environmentally may limit arousal to nonpathogenic levels" (Andrews and Tenant, 1978, p. 545).

Pearlin and Schooler (1978) have defined this ability of persons to modulate the impact of stressors as coping: "Coping refers to behavior that protects people from being psychologically harmed by problematic social experience" (p. 2). In this review, coping responses will be broadly defined to include the three areas mentioned by Andrews and Tenant (1978) as intervening variables: (1) cognitive coping abilities which allow the person to neutralize the perception of stressor as problematic through subjective appraisal mechanisms and cognitive control strategies; (2) behavioral coping abilities which enable the individual to act directly to resolve the environmental stressor; and (3) social support recruitment which provides the person with emotional support to buffer the impact of stressors. These are factors that have been found to mediate the impact of stressors during laboratory studies conducted with normals and in studies of nonschizophrenic disorders. Unfortuantely, little research has been conducted specifically on the coping responses of schizophrenic patients. However, findings from other studies on different aspects of schizophrenic disorder provide some evidence about probable deficiencies in the coping abilities of schizophrenic patients. For example, documented deficits in areas such as social and problem-solving skills could diminish the ability of schizophrenic patients to cope effectively with stressful situations generated by life events and familial tension. Therefore, we now review research which suggests that the usual level of stressfulness that follows from life events and ongoing difficulty situations is amplified for patients with schizophrenia because of their pervasive cognitive and social impairments.

COGNITIVE COPING

Cognitive coping includes the appraisal process and cognitive control strategies, both of which have been shown to regulate emotional arousal in the face of stressors. Although appraisal and cognitive control strategies overlap because both may involve the use of language ("self-talk") that is similar in content, they are temporally and functionally distinct from one another. Appraisal refers to an almost instantaneous perceptual process by which people determine whether an event or situation has positive, negative, or benign implications toward their well-being. Cognitive control is an active process aimed at reducing stress by reinterpreting the meaning or reevaluating the threatening implications of the event. Thus, cognitive control strategies occur after the appraisal process and are only used if the event or situation is appraised as threatening.

COGNITIVE APPRAISAL

This section considers empirical evidence and theoretical formulations which suggest that an individual's cognitive appraisal of a socioenvironmental stressor mediates the amount of stress generated by that event or situation. One useful model has been proposed by Rahe and Arthur (1978) who emphasize the interaction of a life event, the cognitive appraisal of its threatening implications, the individual's response, and the illness behavior. The first step in their model, the perception of the stressor, is presented as a "polarizing filter" that can magnify or diminish the stressfulness of an event. The notion that the quality and intensity of emotional reactions to events are determined by cognitive appraisal and are alterable by reappraisal has been a consistent finding of Lazarus and his co-workers since the early 1960s. A series of studies reviewed in Lazarus, Averill, and Opton (1970) showed that differing cognitive appraisals used by subjects while viewing stressful films affected the level of stress induced by the films as measured by heart rate and self-report.

However, the initial research on life events and stress ignored subjective ratings of the stressfulness of events and focused solely on the amount of social readjustment demanded by an event (Holmes and Rahe, 1967). Beginning in the 1970s (Paykel, Prusoff, and Uhlenhuth, 1971), researchers added the measure of subjective appraisal and found that groups differed in the perceived amount of stressfulness associated with life events. Lundberg and Theorell (1976) reported that a group of myocardial infarction patients gave significantly higher ratings than a control group on ratings of the perceived "upset" versus degree of "adjustment" that would result from life events. These studies suggest that subgroups of individuals may appraise stressors in idiosyncratic ways and that perceived stressfulness is an important mediator of the relationship between life events and stress.

Unfortunately, very little research has been conducted directly on the cognitive appraisal process among schizophrenic patients. However, there are many anecdotal accounts and a few studies in the literature on schizophrenic disorder which suggest that cognitive appraisal processes in schizophrenic patients may tend to magnify the stressfulness of events and situations. For example, Grant, Gerst, and Yager (1976) found that a psychiatric patient group (21 percent DSM-II schizophrenic patients) generally assigned greater social readjustment weights to life events than normals. Thus, they anticipated more stress from a life event than did the controls. One event, "marital separation," although ranked fourth by both groups, was perceived by patients as 35 percent more stressful. However, the patient group was quite unstable in their item ratings. The authors hypothesized that the instability of ratings could have reflected fluctuations in symptomatic state resulting in greater ratings of required readjustment in response to stressors when the patient felt distressed.

Psychoanalytic and information-processing theories of schizophrenic thought patterns also suggest that reliance on idiosyncratic meanings and interpretations of events increases with the severity of disturbance (Shean, 1982). Heightened sensitivity to stimuli coupled with increasingly bizarre idiosyncratic thinking, e.g., referential meanings and persecutory ideas, could lead schizophrenic patients in the direction of overreacting to perceived or existing threats, thereby contributing to increased levels of stress. Although much of what has been written is anecdotal, a typical clinical observation follows:

Those who have worked extensively with schizophrenics know that these patients are extremely sensitive. They are very easily haunted by even slightly aggressive or rejecting behavior by others—behavior that, in most cases, would hardly be noticed by a person of normal sensitivity or, if noticed, certainly would not lead to traumatic experiences [Lehmann, 1980, p. 1154].

As reported in the earlier section on life events, some studies of events preceding hospitalization of depressed and schizophrenic patients have found that many schizophrenic patients decompensated in the context of life situation with no clear or identifiable life-event stressor (Beck and Worthen, 1972). In a study by Shean and Faia (1975), patients were asked to imagine fear-arousing situations. The process-nonparanoid patients used ordinary daily occurrences such as crossing the street on the hospital grounds, taking a trip to the local shopping center, and a thunderstorm.

Thus, the studies reviewed above suggest that schizophrenic patients may show greater variation over time than other populations in their cognitive appraisal of the stressfulness of events. During periods of symptomatic exacerbation they may be particularly prone to view events and situations that are independently judged as nonhazardous to be subjectively threatening. The overevaluation of the threatening implications of the major and minor life events and difficult interpersonal situations could enhance the inherent stressfulness of such occurrences.

COGNITIVE CONTROL STRATEGIES

The processes that people use to modulate their stress level by actively reinterpreting the meaning of the difficulty have been termed cognitive control strategies. In laboratory studies on stress, Lazarus and Alfert (1964) found that when the cognitive control strategies of "denial" and "intellectualization" were used during the viewing of a stressful film by subjects trained in these techniques, their arousal level was significantly lower than in untrained subjects. Denial can be viewed as a conscious effort to remove from awareness certain fear-arousing elements and characteristics of an event or situation to minimize emotional distress. Hackett and Cassem (1973) found that denial decreased anxiety among myocardial infarction patients in an acute coronary care unit. However, other studies have found that cardiac patients who used denial also tended to delay seeking treatment and later failed to comply with medical regimens, which Krantz (1980) considered as further manifestations of their use of denial as a cognitive coping strategy. Ultimately, such noncompliance decreases the probability of a successful long-term recovery.

A phenomenon similar to denial, that of "sealing over," refers to a style of coping with an initial schizophrenic episode (McGlashan, Levy, and Carpenter, 1975). Schizophrenic patients who were considered to have "sealed over" the occurrence of their illness retained a magical quality to their thinking and denied that anything important had happened. Patients who were considered "integrators" tended to accept their vulnerability to schizophrenic illness and attempted to understand the causes of their psychotic episode. Thus, "sealing over" may represent a cognitive coping strategy similar to denial which some schizophrenic patients use to manage the acute stress of having had an episode of a major mental disorder. Followup data by McGlashan and Carpenter (1981) did not show a relationship between these two styles of perceiving psychotic episodes and outcome. However, they found that a "realistic" attitude toward the illness and the future predicted a good outcome better than did either unrealistically negative or overly positive distortions. Thus, a cognitive control strategy which involves approaching the illness as a significant event without overdramatizing its positive or negative consequences may enable the patient to cope with the stressfulness of the illness and facilitate long-term recovery better than denial. These results parallel the finding of Van Putten et al. (1976) that the patients who refused medication and required more frequent hospitalization were rated higher on grandiosity. Denial of illness is often part of the clinical picture of grandiose patients. As with the myocardial infarction patients, reliance on denial as a dominant cognitive coping strategy may lead to noncompliance with medical regimens and, hence, poorer outcome.

Another factor that has been found to be associated with effective coping is the individual's self-concept in areas such as locus of control, sense of mastery, self-esteem, and personal efficacy (Moos and Billings, 1982). Pearlin and Schooler (1978) found that freedom from self-denigration, a sense of control over impinging forces and favorable attitudes toward self ameliorated the impact of emotional strain from perceived marital, parental, financial, and occupational stress. Among cancer patients, ego strength was found to be related to both psychosocial adaptation (lowered feelings of vulnerability and disturbance of mood) and use of effective coping strategies (seeking information, redefining problems, and avoidance of blaming) (Worden and Sobel, 1978).

Fitts (1972) found that the Tennessee Self-Concept Scale profiles of DSM-I schizophrenic patients indicated low self-esteem and poor self-concept integration. The schizophrenic patients perceived themselves as persons of little worth or social desirability. The mean Total P score, which reflects overall self-esteem level, of "schizophrenic reaction, simple type" patients fell near the 8th percentile of standardized group norms. Eighty-four percent of this group scored below the standardized mean. Although there are many alternative formulations, Mechanic (1974) has defined stress as the individual's perceived inability to meet life demands. With the possible exception of paranoid subtype patients, most schizophrenic patients have been found to have a lower level of self-esteem, a finding which suggests that they would more readily perceive themselves as inadequate to handle the demands generated by life events and ongoing stressful situations.

SUMMARY

Several factors contribute to the hypothesized inadequate cognitive coping strategies of schizophrenic patients. They may overevaluate the threatening potential of both major life events and daily hassles. Low self-esteem could contribute to schizo-phrenic patients perceiving themselves as less capable of re-solving problematic situations. Overappraising the external demands and underappraising their internal resources could add to the level of stress that schizophrenic patients experience following life events and familial difficulties. In addition, many schizophrenic patients seem to rely on a very limited number of cognitive coping strategies, particularly denial. These strat-egies may be useful in the short-term management of anxiety, but are probably unproductive for the long-term resolution of stressful situations such as marital difficulties or recovery from a psychotic illness. Although possibly amenable to retraining, the cognitive coping strategies that are often used by schizo-phrenic patients seem likely to render them more vulnerable than most people to the impact of stressors.

BEHAVIORAL COPING

Behavioral coping entails the application of cognitively gener-ated problem-solving options in behavioral action aimed at modifying, resolving, or eliminating the source of the stressful experience (Gal and Lazarus, 1975; Zubin and Spring, 1977; Pearlin and Schooler, 1978; Ilfeld, 1980). Behavioral coping can be viewed as a two-step problem-solving task. First, per-ceptual and cognitive abilities are required for the "receiving" and subsequent "processing" of relevant interpersonal stimuli in order to generate and select alternatives. Second, social skills are required for the "sending" of appropriate messages during the implementation of solutions. This section reviews basic cog-nitive problem-solving skills required to generate effective al-ternatives, and then the social skills necessary to implement solutions. Each review highlights studies in which schizophrenic patients have been shown to exhibit deficiencies that affect their ability to use effectively both the cognitive and social skills re-quired in behavioral coping.

Generating Alternatives

Spivack, Platt, and Shure (1976) identified six cognitive abilities required for solving interpersonal difficulties: problem recognition, generating options, means-ends thinking, causal thinking, perspective taking, and considering consequences. Other researchers agree with the importance of the cognitive components in problem solving and list similar skills (D'Zurilla and Goldfried, 1971; Trower, Bryant, and Argyle, 1978). In a series of studies, Platt and coworkers administered the means-ends problem-solving task to large populations of psychiatric patients, many of whom were schizophrenic. Patients were found to be deficient in most of the cognitive skills necessary for problem solving in comparison with normals. Patients generated fewer alternatives, less effective alternatives, and a lower ratio of relevant to total alternatives (Spivack et al., 1976). One study by Platt, Siegal, and Spivack (1975) found that psychiatric patients were less able to provide a valid reason for choosing a particular alternative, and were less able to generate and evaluate the consequences of an alternative. Deficiencies in problem-solving skills have been found to be associated with both a poor premorbid history (Platt and Spivack, 1972) and with elevated scores on the Pa, Sc, and F scales, and the Goldberg Index (a measure of risk factors for psychosis) on the Minnesota Multiphasic Personality Inventory (MMPI) (Platt and Siegal, 1976). Unfortunately, none of these studies were conducted with a population consisting exclusively of schizophrenic patients, nor have there been any rigorous prospective studies that examined the relationship between problem-solving skills and the prediction of outcome. Nevertheless, they constitute suggestive evidence that schizophrenic patients are generally deficient in cognitive problem-solving skills, and that such skills may be related to outcome among schizophrenic patients.

In addition to these specific problem-solving skill deficits, there are other well-documented basic disturbances in the attentional, perceptual, memory, and thinking processes of schizophrenic patients. Common deficiencies observed among schizophrenic patients include difficulty with sustaining focused attention over time, slowed processing of simple stimuli, overloading of information when stimuli are complex, distractibility during effortful processing, and ineffective use of active mnemonic strategies (reviewed briefly by Liberman, Nuechterlein, and Wallace [1982], and more extensively by Nuechterlein and Dawson [1984b], this issue). The combination of specific problem-solving skill deficits with more basic impairments in cognitive functioning has the potential to create a severe decrement in the problem-solving ability of schizophrenic patients.

Most life events result in problematic situations such as a loss in social support or material resources. The research of Platt and coworkers indicates that many schizophrenic patients begin the task of resolving stressful situations with deficient problem-solving skills. In addition, the stress induced by life events or ongoing familial tension might create sensory and information overload, thereby further impairing their problem-solving skills just when the application of problem solving is needed most. Given schizophrenic patients' impaired ability to generate effective behavioral alternatives, the stressful situation is likely to persist or even worsen.

IMPLEMENTING ALTERNATIVES

Once a behavioral alternative has been generated and decided upon, the second phase of behavioral coping begins and involves the application of social skills in order to implement the solution. Wallace (1982) has identified "sending" skills that are necessary for the implementation of goal-oriented problem solving (e.g., asking for a raise or renting an apartment) and for the resolution of interpersonal problems (e.g., expressing anger appropriately). In this implementation phase of behavioral coping, schizophrenic patients show both specific nonverbal and verbal sending skill deficits as well as other general social skill deficiencies that could impair instrumental functioning and the resolution of interpersonal stress. Wallace (1984) has reviewed the literature pertaining to the sending skills deficits of schizophrenic patients. In spite of the lack of consensus on what constitutes socially skilled behavior, it is generally acknowledged that paralinguistic elements of speech (e.g., eye contact, voice volume, and fluency) are important in communicating the meaning of messages (Bellack, 1979). Schizophrenic patients have been found to show deficient or excessive levels on these nonverbal dimensions in comparison to normal subjects (Eisler, Hersen, Miller, and Blanchard, 1975; Hersen, Bellack, and Turner, 1978). In addition, numerous studies have revealed inadequacies in the quantity and quality of speech of schizophrenic patients that are not due to their inability to understand or use the rules of speech. Instead they appear to be due to information-processing deficits, e.g., failure to self-edit and eliminate inappropriate verbalizations, impaired ability to produce associations to arrive at a correct verbalization, and failure to take account of the listener's cognitive context (Cohen, 1978). This results in the production of clauses with ambiguous referents that are confusing for listeners (Rochester, 1978). Therefore, the overall understandability of schizophrenic speech is impaired. Schizophrenic patients with impaired ability to communicate would be more prone to have difficulty during the implementation phase of problem solving, because that phase usually involves interpersonal interaction.

Schizophrenic patients may also be deficient in the ability to recognize basic emotions, another social skill that Wallace (1982) has hypothesized to be critical in problem solving. In addition, the timing and appropriateness of self-disclosing statements may be disturbed among schizophrenic patients (Levy, 1976). Thus, schizophrenic patients seem to show impairments in basic sending skills as well as higher level social skills that are necessary for effective social interaction.

Wallace (1984) notes that a number of studies have found a lower rate of social interaction among schizophrenic patients compared with nonschizophrenic populations, with the rate of chronic patients being particularly low. In fact, the preferred rate of interaction among schizophrenic patients may be lower than among most people. Yet, social interaction seems to play an essential role in resolving interpersonal stressors and attaining instrumental goals. Pearlin and Schooler (1978) have found that remaining committed and involved in interpersonal relationships when problems arise is a critical component of effective coping. Mechanic (1974) has maintained that developing competency in behavioral coping requires practice and experience in applying the composite skills. Thus, even social skills that were once part of a schizophrenic patient's repertoire might drop out due to nonuse (Liberman, 1982). A lowered rate of social interaction and lowered preferences for affiliation could retard the development, practice, and use of social skills, thereby reducing the behavioral coping competency of schizophrenic patients.

SUMMARY

Rectifying the changes and losses brought on by life events and resolving the sources of familial tension usually require the development of behavioral "plans of action" and the use of skilled social interactions to implement the cognitively generated solutions. Behavioral coping deficiencies among schizophrenic patients seem to occur during both stages of this problem-solving process. In the first phase, the processing of behavioral alternatives may be hampered by deficits in cognitive and information-processing abilities. During the second phase, the implementation of solutions may also be impaired by specific "sending" skills deficits and other basic social skill deficits. As reviewed in the previous section, when faced with stressors, schizophrenic patients may be less able to cope cognitively to control the perceived stressfulness of the situation. The research reviewed in this section suggests that many schizophrenic patients are also less competent than nonschizophrenic persons at coping behaviorally to alter the stressful conditions directly. This combination of coping inadequacies may result in a situation in which the impact of stressors is experienced more intensely and persists longer for many schizophrenic patients than for the typical individual.

SOCIAL SUPPORT RECRUITMENT

While life events are viewed as environmental factors that can negatively affect the course of schizophrenic disorder, social support is a positive environmental factor that may serve as a buffer for stressful life events and situations, thereby attenuating the likelihood of schizophrenic relapse. Social support has been variously defined. In an extensive review of studies of social support, Cobb (1976) defined it as "information leading the subject to believe that he is cared for and loved, esteemed, and a member of a network of mutual obligations" (p. 300). Caplan (1981) defined social support as a form of cognitive guidance:

Psychological stress may increase an individual's vulnerability to mental and physical illness; this may be prevented if the individual receives social support in mastering the stressful situation in the form of cognitive guidance. Cognitive guidance compensates for the reduction in the individual's problem-solving capacity caused by stress-reduced emotional arousal [p. 414].

Beels (1981), on the other hand, gave a much broader definition of social support for schizophrenic patients, e.g., "whatever factors there are in the environment that promote a favorable course of the illness" (p. 60).

A substantial body of evidence does indicate that in many life situations social support functions do mediate life events. Cobb (1976), Pilisuk and Froland (1978), and Caplan (1981) have reviewed studies of the role of social support and life stress in complications of pregnancy, hospitalization, psychiatric symptoms, recovery from illness, unemployment, bereavement, and aging. Studies in these areas generally support the hypothesis that social support protects against increased vulnerability to illness associated with high stress.

Only a few studies have been completed which describe the social support systems of schizophrenic patients or answer the specific question of whether social support affects the course of schizophrenic illness. The existing studies generally show that schizophrenic patients have smaller social networks than normal comparisons (Pattison, deFrancisco, Wood, Frazier, and Crowder, 1975). In a study of residents of single-room-occupancy hotels in New York City, Sokolovsky, Cohen, Berger, and Geiger (1978) reported smaller networks for schizophrenic patients with moderate to severe residual symptoms than for nonschizophrenic residents in the same hotels, but no difference between schizophrenic patients with minimal or no residual symptoms and the nonschizophrenic residents. The authors also found that the likelihood of rehospitalization for the schizophrenic patients was related to the size of their social networks for the patients with minimal or no residual symptoms. This study, although the only one of its kind and in need of replication, suggests that the smaller social networks found among many schizophrenic patients could negatively affect the course of their illness.

In addition to the size of the network, a second issue in understanding the social support systems of schizophrenic patients concerns the composition and quality of relationships in their networks. Several studies have shown that the social networks of schizophrenic patients usually contain a significantly higher proportion of relatives (Tolsdorf, 1976; Garrison, 1978; Randolph and Escobar, 1982). Yet, these same studies indicate that reliance on relatives may not offer as much protection during stressful events as a more broadly constituted social network. The schizophrenic inpatients in Tolsdorf's (1976) study reported significantly less confidence in the ability of their networks, which contained a high proportion of relatives, to help them in times of crisis than did the comparison group of medical inpatients. Garrison (1978) studied social support systems of Puerto Rican female schizophrenic patients with varying degrees of emotional disturbance. She concluded that "the salient finding of this analysis is that there is greater reliance upon neighbors, friends, and other non-kin than upon family among the schizophrenic women who lead their lives relatively successfully within the community" (p. 594). An ongoing study by Randolph and Escobar (1982) is focusing on social networks and social supports of Anglo and Hispanic male schizophrenic individuals under the age of 42 in Los Angeles. Preliminary results indicate that for both Anglos and Hispanics, the larger the ratio of friends to kin in the network, the better the individual's adjustment. They also report that large networks dominated by kin may actually be more dysfunctional than relatively smaller networks dominated by friends. Their preliminary findings concerning the benefits of a high proportion of friends within the social network are consistent with Garrison's description of networks of Puerto Rican schizophrenic women in New York.

A related hypothesis by Hammer (1981) concerns the finding that less than 35 hours a week of contact with intrusive, overstimulating relatives (high EE relatives) reduces schizophrenic relapse rates (Vaughn and Leff, 1976a; Vaughn et al., 1982). Hammer suggests that this may represent not only time not spent with these relatives, but additionally, time spent with friends in networks available for social support. These findings suggest that the high proportion of relatives comprising the social support networks of many schizophrenic patients may diminish the overall effectiveness of their social support systems in coping with stressful events. In addition, the constricted range of social outlets does not help a schizophrenic patient to cope with any ongoing familial tension because the patient may lack outside alternatives for social contact.

Beels (1981) notes that it may be difficult to apply certain useful concepts of social supports to schizophrenia, such as the idea of the "confidant": "A confiding relationship, especially with a spouse, has been shown to be a protective social support in a variety of conditions, from depression (Brown and Harris, 1978) to heart disease (Medalie and Goldbourt, 1976). But a confidant may be a very problematic person for a schizoprenic" (p. 61). Indeed, the investigations of schizophrenic patients' social networks by Lehmann (1980) and Lipton, Cohen, Fisher, and Katz (1981) showed positive correlations between ex-patients' favorable social functioning and casual rather than intimate relationships. On the basis of these results, Liberman (1982) has hypothesized that a quiet, undemanding, somewhat isolated social experience may be a supportive one for chronic schizophrenic outpatients.

SUMMARY

The evidence available indicates that many schizophrenic patients rely on smaller networks consisting of a higher proportion of relatives than typical nonschizophrenic persons. Both of these characteristics have been found to be associated with greater likelihood of rehospitalization. Although many schizophrenic patients may benefit from expanding the size and variety of their social networks, one should not immediately assume that the goal for this population would be to expand their social networks greatly and increase the intimacy of their relationships. Casual friendships seem to have a more positive effect on the course of schizophrenic illness.

The recruitment of social networks is being considered a coping response in this chapter because it is within the patient's control and it mediates the impact of stressors. Yet, as a coping response, it has some distinct qualities. Since cognitive and behavioral coping both involve responding directly to and during the stressful situation, they are vulnerable to what Zubin and Spring (1977) have termed "coping breakdown." Some patients who seem to possess adquate coping skills during periods of remission lose these skills just as stress mounts and the use of coping responses is most critical. A type of spiraling may ensue with increasing arousal, attention fractionation, and symptom exacerbation, which in turn can contribute to the creation of stressful events and tension in relationships. Such a pattern with feedback loops is hypothesized to precede the development of many relapses (Dawson, Nuechterlein, and Liberman, 1983; Nuechterlein and Dawson, 1984a).

However, a social network, once in place, may function even during times of "coping breakdown." Thus, schizophrenic patients whose social skills are impaired by the onset of symptoms but who possess adequate skills and have used them to recruit a social network during periods of remission might be able to create a protective buffer between themselves and relapse. This would make recruitment of a social network a particularly critical coping response for schizophrenic patients prone to periods of coping breakdown."

CONCLUSIONS

The studies reviewed in the first two parts provide strong empirical support for a vulnerability/stress model of the course of schizophrenic disorder. When persons who are vulnerable to schizophrenic disorder are exposed to socioenvironmental stressors in the form of independent and nonindependent life events that cluster in the span of a few weeks, the likelihood that they will develop a schizophrenic episode seems to be increased. Schizophrenic patients living in "stressful" families that are characterized by high criticalness, intrusiveness, and overinvolvement also have a greater likelihood of relapsing. Finally, communication deviance measured in parents predicts and might be involved in the onset of schizophrenia spectrum disorders.

However, the fact that life events and family atmosphere may play a role in triggering the onset of schizophrenic episodes tells us very little that is unique about the nature of schizophrenic disorders. An elevated incidence of life events has been found to precede the onset of virtually all medical and psychiatric disorders studied (Rahe and Arthur, 1978). Nor do the types of life events which precede the onset of schizophrenic episodes seem qualitatively different from those reported by other psychiatric patients (Rabkin, 1980). The findings regarding family atmosphere and course of illness are not specific to schizophrenia either. Elevated CD scores have been found in parents of mentally retarded children (Wender et al., 1977), and high EE in the family has also been found to be related to the onset of depression (Vaughn and Leff, 1976a). Stress seems to act as a general precipitant which results in varying symptomatology depending upon genetic and acquired vulnerability.

Yet, this review of the research on life events and familial stress as well as the coping response literature has uncovered some aspects of the relationship between stress and the course of illness that seem specifically characteristic of schizophrenia. First, schizophrenic patients seem to be highly stress-prone. Their vulnerability to schizophrenic disorder, residual persisting symptoms, prodromal early onset symptoms, lifestyle, goals, hereditary links to other persons with schizophrenic disorders, socioeconomic status as psychiatric patients, and the treatments they receive for their illness, all seem to predispose schizophrenic patients to a higher incidence of life events than persons without this disorder. In addition, the family atmosphere of many schizophrenic patients is characterized by criticalness and intrusiveness. Faulty communication patterns in many of their families may also contribute to ongoing tension.

Second, when faced with the occurrence of life events or residing in a stressful family atmosphere, schizophrenic patients seem less adept than most persons at coping skillfully to resolve the environmental threat through behavioral coping techniques, to reduce their resulting stress level through cognitive coping techniques, or to recruit social support during times of crisis. From these findings, two implications will be drawn—one regarding future research, and the other regarding the treatment of patients with schizophrenic disorders.

FUTURE RESEARCH

The studies conducted to date on familial factors have opened several promising new avenues for understanding psychosocial dimensions that influence the course of schizophrenic disorders. Several different instruments and indexes have been used in this research, and therefore it is important to clarify the relationships among the various family measures. This could be accomplished by administering multiple family measures to the same subject samples. The development of abbreviated, clinically oriented versions of the key family assessment instruments that are relatively easy to administer would also aid the process of conducting research with families.

Another key question requiring study concerns the specificity of parental EE and AS to the patient. Brown et al. (1972) have made the following suggestion: "The same relative would not necessarily respond to other people in the same way . . . the measure reflects a quality of relationship with a particular person (the patient), not a general tendency to react to everyone in a similar way" (p. 241). Research designs that included assessment of parents' attitudes and behavior toward the patient as well as toward sibling would help to address this specificity issue.

If this specificity to the patient-relative were to be empirically demonstrated, research on EE might also profitably search for patient characteristics that may play a role in eliciting high EE from relatives. The possibility that high EE develops through a transactional process between patient and parent deserves further exploration. To date, EE researchers have shown that some patient variables do not play a strong mediating role, such as an index measuring level of behavioral disturbance (Brown et al., 1972). However, this should not limit the search for other intervening variables.

Similarly, because EE research has shown that the amount of face-to-face contact with high EE relatives and the presence of antipsychotic medication serve as moderating variables in predicting the outcome of EE, additional consideration should be given to patient variables that might be related to medication compliance and contact with relatives. For example, a high level of residual disability might help to stimulate high relative contact. The EE research to date has relied on naturalistic observations without manipulation of these key moderating variables. The use of experimental designs would help to clarify whether patient variables interact with EE to predict outcome.

A related design question concerns the possible reactivity of CD to certain disturbances in the patient offspring. As mentioned earlier, Wender et al. (1977) found elevated CD among patients of mentally retarded individuals. The project by Gold-stein and his colleagues selected as subjects adolescents who had not experienced psychosis but who were showing some emotional or behavioral disturbance. Because not all the parents of these disturbed adolescents showed high CD, it appears that disturbances in offspring at least do not universally elicit these communication anomalies. It would be a very useful additional study (although tactically demanding) to demonstrate that parental CD, measured in a sample of well-functioning offspring relatively early in their lives, has predictive value for schizophrenia spectrum disorders. The last three of these suggestions would lead research on familial atmosphere and behavior into a more transactionally oriented direction with increased attention to patient variables that might play a role in eliciting high EE or CD from relatives and/or in mediating their effects on the patients.

Another promising strategy for clarifying casual relationships among EE, AS, and CD and the course of schizophrenic disorders is to evaluate the effect of illness course of interventions that are aimed at changing these parental attitudes and behaviors. Increased interest in family education and other family interventions may dovetail with the need to evaluate further the causal networks that underlie the predictive relationships that we have reviewed here.

A major weakness of life-event research has been its limitation to a two-variable design. Life events are recorded (usually retrospectively) and subjects are rated on the presence or absence of the onset of the illness. This narrow methodological focus is not unique to studies on schizophrenia, but has been the primary approach adopted by researchers in the life-event field. Two of the originators of this paradigm have recently argued that it is time for a change:

We believe that further studies of an epidemiological character which correlate life events and illness will be redundant. Instead, the enormously difficult task awaits us of filling in the crucial steps of an all-encompassing model which takes into account not only environmental variables but the sociological, psychological, and physiological characteristics of the individual [Rahe and Arthur, 1978, p. 13].

In schizophrenic disorders, the need to understand the mediating variables is especially important because the relationship between life events and psychotic symptoms, although measurable and usually statistically significant, is not very powerful. Schwartz and Myers (1977) found that in their sample of 132 posthospitalized schizophrenic patients, life events exerted their greatest impact on nonpsychotic symptoms such as anxiety and depression. Life events explained only 10 percent of the variance in the schizophrenia score, which included symptoms such as grandiosity, delusions, and looseness of association. When only independent life events were considered, they accounted for merely 4 percent of the variance. Similarly, Harder et al. (1980) found life-event variables explained only 3–7 percent of the variance in symptom measures among their sample of first-admission patients. Other studies have suggested that the impact of life events on the course of illness may, in fact, be less for schizophrenia than for other types of psychiatric disorders. Using the concept of relative risk, Paykel (1978) reviewed many of the published studies on depression, schizophrenia, and suicide attempts for which the risk of illness associated with the occurrence of life events could be computed. He concluded:

The occurrence of any of the spectrum of events included in these studies increases the risk of developing a schizophrenic illness in the next 6 months by something of the order by 2 or 3 times; of depression by 2–5, and of a suicide attempt by about 6 times. . . . There is some consistency between studies that the effect is greater for depression than schizophrenia [p. 251].

The many methodological problems that might affect the statistical association between life events and the onset of schizophrenic episodes were reviewed in a previous section of this chapter, and many of them are unique to schizophrenic disorders. However, a study by Tausig (1982) indicates that focusing primarily on resolving methodological obstacles may not improve the magnitude of the relationship between life events and schizophrenic episodes. He investigated the impact of a variety of methodological issues often cited as hampering findings of the etiologic role of life events on illness: scope of item content, multidimensional structure, confoundedness with dependent variable, objective-subjective scoring, and desirability. After examining the effect of each of these factors on the relationship between life events and depressive symptomatology, he concluded that "even when different ways of evaluating life events are considered, the relatively small relationship to depressive symptoms cannot be improved substantially" (p. 52).

The implication we draw from Tausig's findings corroborates Rahe and Arthur's (1978) point that future research should be directed toward uncovering the intervening variables that mediate the effect of life events on the onset of schizophrenic episodes. This article reviewed coping responses as one avenue that shows promise for exploration. Other articles in this issue focus on psychophysiological and cognitive processing factors which also seem to be variables that are likely to intervene between the occurrence of socioenvironmental stressors and the development of schizophrenic episodes.

CLINICAL INTERVENTIONS

The treatment implications that can be drawn from this review involve the remediation of coping skill deficiencies that were delineated in the third section of the article, as well as the reduction of particularly toxic socioenvironmental stressors uncovered in the first and second sections. To use an analogy to physical illness, coping responses are similar in function to an organism's "host resistance"—the natural or acquired immunity to an infectious disease that enables the organism to withstand an infectious challenge. Cognitive and behavioral coping and social support recruitment are the counterparts at the psychological level to the organism's resistance. They enable a person to withstand socioenvironmental challenges. The interventions that have been found promising in preventing relapse among schizophrenic patients can be viewed as programs that train patients to improve their coping response skills, e.g., social skills training (Wallace, 1984), and problem-solving (Falloon et al., 1982). Thus, to carry the analogy further, successful social skills and problem-solving skill training are comparable to the vaccinations that medicine uses to improve an organism's resistance to infectious agents.

Liberman, Falloon, and Aitchison (submitted), in their review of the family therapy intervention conducted at Camarillo State Hospital, demonstrated that when families are trained in problem-solving and communication skills, high EE can be reduced. Patients from families that participated in the family therapy program had a lower relapse rate, which might be partly attributable to the reduction in the stressfulness of the family environment. Based on the findings from the life events and familial stress research, environmental interventions for schizophrenic disorders should be aimed at (1) reducing the stressfulness of the patient's family through family therapy focused on problem-solving and communication skills, and (2) creating for schizophrenic patients or helping them to create stable residential environments outside of the family that avoid the extremes of understimulation and overstimulation, both of which seem to have detrimental effects on the course of schizophrenic disorders.

Studies conducted during the 25 years on life events, familial stress, and coping responses have uncovered some major socioenvironmental factors and some crucial skills deficits which seem to affect the course of schizophrenic disorders. Using these findings to guide empirically the development of psychosocial interventions can aid efforts to improve the quality of life and outcome of patients with this illness.

REFERENCES

American Psychiatric Association (1968), *The Diagnostic and Statistical Manual of Mental Disorders*, 2nd ed. Washington, DC: American Psychiatric Association.

—— (1980), *The Diagnostic and Statistical Manual of Mental Disorders*, 3rd ed. Washington, DC: American Psychiatric Association.

Andrews, G., & Tenant, C. (1978), Life event stress and psychiatric illness. *Psychol. Med.*, 8:545–549.

Arthur, A. Z. (1964), Theories and explanations of delusions: A review. *Amer. J. Psychiat.*, 121:105–115.

Bateson, G., Jackson, D. D., Haley, J., & Weakland, J. H. (1956), Toward a theory of schizophrenia. *Behav. Sci.*, 1:251–264.

Beck, J., & Worthen, K. (1972), Precipitating stress, crisis theory, and hospitalization in schizophrenia and depression. *Arch. Gen. Psychiat.*, 26:123–129.

Beels, C. (1981), Social support and schizophrenia. *Schiz. Bull.*, 7/1:58–72.

Bellack, A. S. (1979), A critical appraisal of strategies for assessing social skills. *Behav. Assess.*, 1:156–176.

Birley, J. L., & Brown, G. W. (1970), Crises and life changes preceding the onset or relapse of acute schizophrenia: Clinical aspects. *Brit. J. Psychiat.*, 116:327–333.

Bleuler, D. (1911), *Dementia Praecox or the Group of Schizophrenias*, trans. J. Zinkin. New York: International Universities Press, 1950.

Bleuler, M. (1972), *The Schizophrenic Disorders: Long-term Patient and Family Studies*, trans. S. M. Clemens. New Haven, CT: Yale University Press, 1978.

Bowers, M. B. (1980), Biochemical processes in schizophrenia: An update. *Schiz. Bull.*, 6:393–403.

Brown, G. W. (1959), Experiences of discharged chronic schizophrenic mental hospital patients in various types of living group. *Millbank Mem. Fund Quart.*, 37:105–131.

—— Birley, J. L. (1968), Crises and life changes and the onset of schizophrenia. *J. Health & Soc. Behav.*, 9:203–214.

—— —— Wing, J. K. (1972), Influence of family life on the course of schizophrenic disorders: A replication. *Brit. J. Psychiat.*, 121:242–258.

—— Carstairs, G. M., & Topping, G. D. (1958), The post hospital adjustment of chronic mental patients. *Lancet*, 2:685–689.

—— Harris, T. (1978), *Social Origins of Depression: A Study of Psychiatric Disorders in Women*. London: Tavistock.

—— —— Peto, J. (1973), Life events and psychiatric disorders: Part II. Nature of the causal link. *Psychol. Med.*, 3:159–176.

—— Monck, E. M., Carstairs, G. M., & Wing, J. K. (1962), The influence of family life on the course of schizophrenic illness. *Brit. J. Prevent. Soc. Med.*, 16:55–68.

—— Rutter, M. L. (1966), The measurement of family activities and relationships. *Human Rel.*, 19:241–263.

Caplan, G. (1981), Mastery of stress: Psychosocial aspects. *Amer. J. Psychiat.*, 138:413–420.

Clancy, J., Crowe, R., Winokur, G., & Morrison, J. (1973), The Iowa 500: Precipitating factors in schizophrenia and primary affective disorder. *Compr. Psychiat.*, 14:197–202.

Cobb, S. (1976), Social support as a moderator of life stress. *Psychosom. Med.*, 38:300–314.

Cohen, B. D. (1978), Self-editing deficits in schizophrenia. In: *The Nature of Schizophrenia*, ed. L. C. Wynne, R. L. Cromwell, & S. Matthysse. New York: John Wiley, pp. 313–319.

Dawson, M., & Nuechterlein, K. (1984), Psychophysiological dysfunctions in the developmental course of schizophrenic disorders. *Schiz. Bull.*, 10:204–232.

—————— Liberman, R. (1983), Relapse in schizophrenic disorders: Possible contributing factors and implications for behavior therapy. In: *Perspectives on Behavior Therapy in the Eighties*, ed. M. Rosenbaum, C. Frank, & Y. Jaffe. New York: Springer, pp. 265–286.

Doane, J., West, K., Goldstein, M., Rodnick, E., & Jones, J. (1981), Parental communication deviance and affective style: Predictors of subsequent schizophrenia spectrum disorders in vulnerable adolescents. *Arch. Gen. Psychiat.*, 38:679–685.

Dohrenwend, B. P. (1970), Stressful life events and psychopathology: Some issues of theory and method. In: *Stress and Mental Disorder*, ed. J. E. Barrett, R. M. Rose, & G. L. Klerman. New York: Raven Press, pp. 1–15.

—————— (1974), Problems in defining and sampling the relevant population of stressful life events. In: *Stressful Life Events: Their Nature and Effects*, ed. B. P. Dohrenwend & B. S. Dohrenwend. New York: John Wiley, pp. 275–310.

—————— Dohrenwend, B. S. (1980), Psychiatric disorders and susceptibility to stress. In: *The Social Consequences of Psychiatric Illness*, ed. L. N. Robins, P. J. Clayton, & J. K. Wing. New York: Brunner/Mazel, pp. 183–197.

—————— Egri, G. (1981), Recent stressful life events and episodes of schizophrenia. *Schiz. Bull.*, 7:12–23.

—————— Krasnoff, L., Askenasy, A. R., & Dohrenwend, B. P. (1978), Exemplification of a method for scaling life events: The PERI Life Events Scale. *J. Health & Soc. Behav.*, 19:205–229.

D'Zurilla, T. J., & Goldfried, M. R. (1971), Problem solving and behavior modification. *J. Abnorm. Psychol.*, 78:107–126.

Eisler, R. M., Hersen, M., Miller, P. M., & Blanchard, E. B. (1975), Situational determinants of assertive behaviors. *J. Consult. & Clin. Psychol.*, 43:330–340.

—————— Polak, P. (1971), Social stress and psychiatric disorder. *J. Nerv. & Ment. Dis.*, 153:227–233.

Falloon, I. R. H. (1984), Relapse: A reappraisal of assessment of outcome in schizophrenia. *Schiz. Bull.*, 10:293–299.

———— Boyd, J. L., McGill, C. W., Razani, J., Moss, H. B., & Gilderman, A. M. (1982), Family management of the prevention of exacerbations of schizophrenia: A controlled study. *N. Eng. J. Med.*, 306:1437–1440.

———— Pederson, J., Shirin, K., & Moss, R. (1981), Life events in schizophrenia: Measuring the effects and modifying the impact. Presented at the NIMH Workshop on Preventive Intervention Programs for Stress-Related Disorders, San Francisco, CA, December.

Fitts, W. H. (1972), *The Self Concept and Psychopathology*. Dede Wallace Center Monograph IV. Nashville, TN: Counselor Recordings and Tests, pp. 24–44.

Fontana, A. F., Marcus, J. L., Noel, B., & Rakusin, J. M. (1972), Prehospitalization coping styles of psychiatric patients: The goal-directedness of life events. *J. Nerv. & Ment. Dis.*, 155:311–331.

Freeman, D., & Simmons, O. (1963), *The Mental Patient Comes Home*. New York: John Wiley.

Fromm-Reichmann, F. (1948), Notes on the development of treatment of schizophrenics by psychoanalytic psychotherapy. *Psychiat.*, 2:263–273.

Gal, R., & Lazarus, R. (1975), The role of activity in anticipating and confronting stressful situations. *J. Hum. Stress*, 1:4–20.

Garrison, V. (1978), Support systems of schizophrenic and nonschizophrenic Puerto Rican migrant women in New York City. *Schiz. Bull.*, 4:561–596.

Gift, T. E., Strauss, J. S., Harder, D. W., Kokes, R. F., & Ritzler, B. A. (1981), Established chronicity of psychotic symptoms in first-admission schizophrenic patients. *Amer. J. Psychiat.*, 138:779–784.

Goldberg, S., Schooler, N. R., Hogarty, G., & Roper, M. (1977), Prediction of relapse in schizophrenic outpatients treated by drug and sociotherapy. *Arch. Gen. Psychiat.*, 34:171–184.

Goldstein, M., Judd, L., Rodnick, E., Alkire, A., & Gould, E. (1968), A method for studying social influences and coping patterns within families of disturbed adolescents. *J. Nerv. & Ment. Dis.*, 147:233–151.

———— Rodnick, E. H., Evans, J. R., May, P. R. A., & Steinberg, M. R. (1978a), Drug and family therapy in the aftercare of acute schizophrenics. *Arch. Gen. Psychiat.*, 35:1169–1177.

———— ———— Jones, T., McPherson, S., & West, K. (1978b), Familial precursors of schizophrenia spectrum disorders. In: *New Approaches to Research and Treatment*, ed. L. C. Wynne, R. L. Cromwell, & S. Matthysse. New York: John Wiley, pp. 487–498.

Gottesman, I. I., & Shields, J. (1976), A critical review of recent adoption, twin, and family studies of schizophrenia: Behavioral genetics perspectives. *Schiz. Bull.*, 2:360–401.

Grant, I., Gerst, M., & Yager, J. (1976), Scaling of life events by psychiatric patients and normals. *J. Psychosom. Res.*, 20:141–149.

Grinker, R., & Spiegel, J. (1963), *Men Under Stress.* New York: McGraw-Hill.

Hackett, T. P., & Cassem, N. H. (1973), Psychological adaption of convalescence in myocardial infarction patients. In: *Exercise Testing and Exercise Training in Coronary Heart Disease*, ed. J. P. Naughton, H. K. Hellerstein, & I. Mohler. New York: Academic Press, pp. 253–262.

Hammer, M. (1981), Social support, social networks, and schizophrenia. *Schiz. Bull.*, 7:45–57.

Harder, D., Strauss, J., Kokes, R., Ritzler, B., & Gift, T. (1980), Life events and psychopathology severity among first psychiatric admissions. *J. Abnorm. Psychol.*, 89:165–180.

Hersen, M., Bellack, A. S., & Turner, S. M. (1978), Assessment of assertiveness in female psychiatric patients: Motor and autonomic measures. *J. Behav. Ther. & Exper. Psychiat.*, 9:11–16.

Hirsch, S. R. (1976), Interacting social and biological factors determining prognosis in the rehabilitation and management of persons with schizophrenia. In: *Annual Review of the Schizophrenic Syndrome*, Vol. 4, ed. R. Cancro. New York: Brunner/Mazel, pp. 453–467.

—— Leff, J. (1975), *Abnormalities in Parents of Schizophrenics. A Review of the Literature and an Investigation of Communication Defects and Deviances.* London: Oxford University Press.

Hogarty, G. E., Goldberg, S. C., & the Collaborative Study Group (1973), Drug and sociotherapy in the aftercare of schizophrenic patients. *Arch. Gen. Psychiat.*, 28:54–63.

—— Ulrich, R. F. (1977), Temporal effects of drug and placebo in delaying relapse in schizophrenic outpatients. *Arch. Gen. Psychiat.*, 34:297–301.

Holmes, T. H., & Rahe, R. H. (1967), The Social Readjustment Rating Scale. *J. Psychosom. Res.*, 2:213–218.

Ilfeld, F. (1980), Coping styles of Chicago adults: Effectiveness. *Arch. Gen. Psychiat.*, 37:1239–1243.

Jacobs, S., & Myers, J. (1976), Recent life events and acute schizophrenic psychosis: A controlled study. *J. Nerv. & Ment. Dis.*, 162:75–87.

—— Prusoff, B., & Paykel, E. (1974), Recent life events in schizophrenia and depression. *Psychol. Med.*, 4:444–453.

Jung, C. G. (1907), *Uber die psychologie der Dementia Praecox.* Marhold: Halle/Saale.

Kasanin, J., Knight, E., & Sage, P. (1934), The parent-child relationship in schizophrenia. *J. Nerv. & Ment. Dis.*, 79:249–263.

Kessler, S. (1980), The genetics of schizophrenia: A review. *Schiz. Bull.*, 6:404–416.

Kolb, L. C. (1973), *Modern Clinical Psychiatry.* Philadelphia: W. B. Saunders.

Kraepelin, E. (1919), *Dementia Praecox*, trans. R. Barclay. Edinburgh: E. S. Livingston.

Krantz, D. S. (1980), Cognitive processes and recovery from heart attack. A review and theoretical analysis. *J. Hum. Stress*, 6:27–38.

Kuipers, L. (1979), Expressed emotion: A review. *Brit. J. Soc. & Clin. Psychiat.*, 18:237–243.

―――― Sturgeon, D., Berkowitz, R., & Leff, J. (1980), *Behavioral Indices of Expressed Emotion: Some Preliminary Evidence for Construct Validity*. London: MRC Social Psychiatry Unit, Institute of Psychiatry.

Lahniers, C., & White, K. (1976), Changes on environmental life events and their relationships to psychiatric hospital admissions. *J. Nerv. & Ment. Dis.*, 163:154–157.

Laing, R. D. (1972), *The Politics of the Family*. New York: Vintage Books.

Langfeldt, G. (1956), The prognosis in schizophrenia. *Acta Psychiat. Scand.*, Suppl. 110:1–66.

Lazarus, R. S., & Alfert, E. (1964), Short-circuiting of threat by experimentally altering cognitive appraisal. *J. Abnorm. & Soc. Psychol.*, 69:195–205.

―――― Averill, J. R., & Opton, E. M., Jr. (1970), Toward a cognitive theory of emotions. In: *Feelings and Emotions*, ed. M. Arnold. New York: Academic Press, pp. 207–232.

Leff, J. P. (1976), Schizophrenia and sensitivity to the family environment. *Schiz. Bull.*, 2:566–574.

―――― Hirsch, S. R., Gaind, R., Rohde, P. D., & Stevens, B. S. (1973), Life events and maintenance therapy in schizophrenic relapse. *Brit. J. Psychiat.*, 123:659–660.

―――― Vaughn, C. (1980), The interaction of life events and relatives' expressed emotion in relapse of schizophrenia and depression neurosis. *Brit. J. Psychiat.*, 136:146–153.

―――― ―――― (1981), The role of maintenance therapy and relatives' expressed emotion in relapse of schizophrenia: A two-year followup. *Brit. J. Psychiat.*, 139:102–104.

Lehmann, H. (1980), Schizophrenia: Clinical features. In: *Comprehensive Textbook of Psychiatry*, Vol. 2, 3rd ed. A. Freeman, H. Kaplan, & B. Sadock. Baltimore: Williams & Wilkins, pp. 1153–1192.

Lehmann, S. (1980), The social ecology of natural support. In: *Community Mental Health: A Behavior Ecological Perspective*, ed. A. Jeger & R. W. Slotnick. New York: Plenum Press.

Levy, S. M. (1976), Schizophrenic symptomatology: Reaction or strategy? *J. Abnorm. Psychol.*, 85:435–445.

Lewinsohn, P. M., & Talkington, J. (1979), Studies on the measurement of unpleasant events and relations with depression. *Appl. Psychol. Meas.*, 3:83–101.

Lewis, D. A., & Hugi, R. (1981), Therapeutic stations and the chronically treated mentally ill. *Soc. Serv. Preview*, 55:206–220.

Lewis, J., Rodnick, E., & Goldstein, M. (1981), Intrafamilial interactive behavior, parental communication deviance, and risk for schizophrenia. *J. Abnorm. Psychol.*, 90:448–457.

Liberman, R. P. (1982), Social factors in schizophrenia. In: *The American Psychiatric Association Annual Review*, ed. L. Grinspoon. Washington, DC: American Psychiatric Press, pp. 207–232.

—— Falloon, I., & Aitchison, R. (submitted), Multiple family therapy for schizophrenia: A behavioral, problem-solving approach. Clinical working paper.

—— Nuechterlein, K. H., & Wallace, C. J. (1982), Social skills training and the nature of schizophrenia. In: *Social Skills Training: A Practical Handbook for Assessment and Treatment*, ed. J. P. Curran & P. M. Monti. New York: Guilford Press, pp. 5–56.

Lidz, T., Cornelison, A. R., Fleck, S., & Terry, D. (1957), The intrafamilial environment of the schizophrenic patient, II: Marital schism and marital skew. *Amer. J. Psychiat.*, 114:241–248.

Lilly, J. C. (1956), Mental effects of reduction or ordinary levels of physical stimuli on intact, healthy persons. *Psychiatric Research Reports*, No. 5. Washington, DC: American Psychiatric Association, pp. 1–9.

Link, B., & Dohrenwend, B. P. (1980), Formulation of hypotheses about the ratio of untreated to treated cases in the true prevalence studies of functional psychiatric disorders in adults in the United States. In: *Mental Illness in the United States: Epidemiologic Estimates*, ed. B. P. Dohrenwend, B. S. Dohrenwend, M. S. Gould, B. Link, R. Neugebauer, & R. Wunsch-Hitzig. New York: Praeger, pp. 133–149.

Lipton, F., Cohen, C., Fisher, E., & Katz, S. (1981), Schizophrenia: A network crisis. *Schiz. Bull.*, 7:144–151.

Lundberg, U., & Theorell, T. (1976), Scaling of life changes: Differences between three diagnostic groups and between recently experienced and non-experienced events. *J. Hum. Stress*, 2:7–17.

Mayer-Gross, W., Slater, E., & Roth, M., eds. (1969), *Clinical Psychiatry*, 3rd ed. Baltimore: Williams & Wilkins.

McGlashan, T. H., & Carpenter, W. T., Jr. (1981), Does attitude toward psychoses relate to outcome? *Amer. J. Psychiat.*, 138:797–801.

—— Levy, S. T., & Carpenter, W. T., Jr. (1975), Integration and sealing over: Distinct recovery styles from schizophrenia. *Arch. Gen. Psychiat.*, 32:1269–1272.

Mechanic, D. (1974), Social structure and personal adaptation. Some neglected dimensions. In: *Coping and Adaptation*, ed. G. Coelho, D. H. Hamburg, & J. E. Adams. New York: Basic Books, pp. 32–44.

Medalie, J., & Goldbourt, U. (1976), Angina pectoris among 10,000 men, II:

Psychosocial and other risk factors as evidenced by a multivariate analysis of a five-year incidence study. *Amer. J. Med.*, 60:910–921.

Meyer, A. (1951), The life chart and the obligation of specifying positive data in psychopathological diagnosis. In: *The Collected Papers of Adolf Meyer*, Vol. 3, ed. E. Winters. Baltimore: Johns Hopkins University Press, pp. 52–56.

Michaux, W., Gansereit, K., McCabe, O., & Kurland, A. (1967), The psychopathology and measurement of environmental stress. *Commun. Ment. Health J.*, 3:358–371.

Moos, R. H., & Billings, A. G. (1982), Conceptualizing and measuring coping resources and processes. In: *Handbook of Stress: Theoretical and Clinical Aspects*, ed. J. Goldberger & S. Breznitz. New York: Free Press, pp. 212–230.

Neugebauer, R. (1983), Reliability of life-event interviews with outpatient schizophrenics. *Arch. Gen. Psychiat.*, 40:378–383.

Norton, J. P. (1982), Expressed emotion, affective style, voice tone and communication deviance as patterns of offspring schizophrenia spectrum disorders. Unpublished doctoral dissertation. University of California, Los Angeles.

Nuechterlein, K. H., & Dawson, M. E. (1984a), A heuristic vulnerability/stress model of schizophrenic episodes. *Schiz. Bull.*, 10:300–312.

——— ——— (1984b), Information processing and attentional functioning in the developmental course of schizophrenic disorders. *Schiz. Bull.*, 10:160–203.

Parnas, J., Schulsinger, F., Schulzinger, H., Mednick, S., & Teasdale, T. (1982), Behavioral precursors of schizophrenia spectrum: A prospective study. *Arch. Gen. Psychiat.*, 139:658–664.

Paykel, E. S. (1978), Contribution of life events to causation of psychiatric illness. *Psychol. Med.*, 8:245–253.

——— Prusoff, B. A., & Uhlenhuth, E. H. (1971), Scaling of life events. *Arch. Gen. Psychiat.*, 25:340–347.

Pattison, E. M., deFrancisco, D., Wood, P., Frazier, H., & Crowder, J. (1975), A psychosocial kinship model for family therapy. *Amer. J. Psychiat.*, 132:1246–1251.

Pearlin, L. I., & Schooler, C. (1978), The structure of coping. *J. Health & Soc. Behav.*, 19:2–21.

Pilisuk, M., & Froland, C. (1978), Kinship, social networks, social support, and health. *Soc. Sci. & Med.*, 1213:273–280.

Platt, J. J., & Siegel, J. (1976), MMPI characteristics of good and poor social problem-solvers among psychiatric patients. *J. Psychol.*, 94:245–251.

——— Siegel, J., & Spivack, G. (1975), Do psychiatric patients and normals see the same solutions as effective in solving interpersonal problems? *J. Consult. & Clin. Psychol.*, 43:279–286.

———— Spivack, G. (1972), Problem-solving thinking of psychiatric patients. *J. Consult. & Clin. Psychol.*, 39:148–151.

Rabkin, J. G. (1980), Stressful life events and schizophrenia: A review of the research literature. *Psychol. Bull.*, 87:408–425.

———— Struening, E. (1976), Life events, stress and illness. *Science*, 194:1013–1020.

Rahe, R. H., & Arthur, R. J. (1978), Life change and illness studies: Past history and future directions. *J. Hum. Stress*, 4:3–15.

Randolph, E., & Escobar, J. (1982), Social network factors in schizophrenic relapse: A longitudinal study. Presented at the Annual Meeting of the American Association of Behavior Therapy, Los Angeles, November.

Rochester, S. R. (1978), Are language processing deficits in acute schizophrenia actually information-processing problems? In: *The Nature of Schizophrenia: New Approaches to Research and Treatment*, ed. L. C. Wynne, R. L. Cromwell, & S. Matthysse. New York: John Wiley, pp. 320–328.

Rosenthal, D. (1970), *Genetic Theory and Abnormal Behavior*. New York: McGraw-Hill, pp. 193–199.

Rutter, M., & Brown, G. W. (1966), The reliability and validity of measures of family life and relationships in families containing a psychiatric patient. *Soc. Psychiat.*, 1:38–53.

Schneider, K. (1959), *Clinical Psychopathology*. New York: Grune & Stratton.

Schwartz, C. C., & Myers, J. K. (1977), Life events and schizophrenia: II. Impact of life events on symptom formation. *Arch. Gen. Psychiat.*, 34:1242–1245.

Seligman, M. E. (1975), *Helplessness: On Depression, Development, and Death*. San Francisco: W. H. Freeman.

Selye, H. (1956), *The Stress of Life*. Toronto: McGraw-Hill.

Serban, G. (1975), Stress in normals and schizophrenics. *Brit. J. Psychiat.*, 126:397–407.

Shean, G. (1982), Cognition, emotion, and schizophrenia. In: *Psychological Stress and Psychopathology*, ed. R. W. J. Neufeld. New York: McGraw-Hill, pp. 55–66.

———— Faia, C. (1975), Autonomic control, selective attention and schizophrenic subtype. *J. Nerv. & Ment. Dis.*, 160:176–181.

Shields, J., & Gottesman, I. I. (1972), Cross-national diagnosis of schizophrenia in twins. *Arch. Gen. Psychiat.*, 27:725–730.

Singer, M., & Wynne, L. (1966), Principles for scoring communication defects and deviances in parents of schizophrenics: Rorschach and TAT scoring manuals. *Psychiatry*, 29:260–288.

Sokolovsky, J., Cohen, C., Berger, D., & Geiger, J. (1978), Personal networks of ex-mental patients in a Manhattan S.R.O. hotel. *Hum. Organ.*, 37:5–15.

Spivack, G., Platt, J. J., & Shure, M. B. (1976), *The Problem-Solving Approach to Adjustment*. San Francisco: Jossey-Bass.

Spring, B., & Coons, H. (1982), Stress as a precursor of schizophrenia. In: *Psychological Stress and Psychopathology*, ed. R. Neufeld. New York: Mc-Graw-Hill, pp. 13–53.

Steinberg, H., & Durell, J. (1968), A stressful social situation as a precipitant of schizophrenic symptoms: An epidemiological study. *Brit. J. Psychiat.*, 114:1097–1105.

Strodbeck, F. L. (1954), The family as a three-person group. *Amer. Sociol. Rev.*, 19:23–29.

Sturgeon, D., Kuipers, L., Berkowitz, R., Turpin, G., & Leff, J. (1981), Psychophysiological responses of schizophrenic patients to high and low expressed emotion relatives. *Brit. J. Psychiat.*, 138:40–45.

Sullivan, H. S. (1927), The onset of schizophrenia. *Amer. J. Psychiat.*, 1:105–134.

Swank, R. (1949), Combat exhaustion. *J. Nerv. & Ment. Dis.*, 109:475–508.

Tarrier, N., Vaughn, C., Lader, M. H., & Leff, J. P. (1979), Bodily reactions to people and events in schizophrenia. *Arch. Gen. Psychiat.*, 36:311–315.

Tausig, M. (1982), Measuring life events. *J. Health & Soc. Behav.*, 23:52–64.

Tolsdorf, C. C. (1976), Social networks, support and coping: An exploratory study. *Fam. Proc.*, 15:407–418.

Trower, P., Bryant, B., & Argyle, M. (1978), *Social Skills and Mental Health*. Pittsburgh: University of Pittsburgh Press.

Uhlenhuth, E. H., & Paykel, E. S. (1973), Symptom configuration and life events. *Arch. Gen. Psychiat.*, 28:744–748.

Valone, K., Goldstein, M., & Norton, J. (submitted), Parental expressed emotion and psychophysiological reactivity in an adolescent sample at risk for schizophrenia spectrum disorders.

——— Norton, J., Goldstein, M., & Doane, J. (in press), Parental expressed emotion and affective style in an adolescent sample at risk for schizophrenia spectrum disorders. *J. Abnorm. Psychol.*

Van Putten, T., Crumpton, E., & Yale, C. (1976), Drug refusal and the wish to be crazy. *Arch. Gen. Psychiat.*, 33:1443–1446.

Vaughn, C., & Leff, J. (1976a), The influence of family and social factors on the course of psychiatric illness: A comparison of schizophrenic and depressed neurotic patients. *Brit. J. Psychiat.*, 129:125–137.

——— ——— (1976b), The measurement of expressed emotion in the families of psychiatric patients. *Brit. J. Gen. Psychiat.*, 15:157–165.

——— Snyder, K., Jones, S., Freeman, W., & Falloon, I. (1982), Family factors in schizophrenic relapse: A replication. *Schiz. Bull.*, 8/2:425–426.

——— ——— ——— ——— ——— (in press), Family factors in schizophrenic relapse: A California replication of the British research on expressed emotion. *Arch. Gen. Psychiat.*

Wagner, P. S. (1946), Psychiatric activities during the Normandy offensive,

June 20–August 20, 1944: An experience with 5,203 neuropsychiatric casualties. *Psychiatry*, 9:341–363.

Wallace, C. W. (1982), The social skills training project of the Mental Health Clinical Research Center for the Study of Schizophrenia. In: *Social Skills Training: A Practical Handbook for Assessment and Treatment*, ed. J. P. Curran & P. M. Monti. New York: Guilford Press, pp. 57–89.

────── (1984), Community and interpersonal functioning in the course of schizophrenic disorders. *Schiz. Bull.*, 10:233–257.

Watt, N. F. (1978), Patterns of childhood social development in adult schizophrenics. *Arch. Gen. Psychiat.*, 35:160–165.

────── Stolorow, R. D., Lubensky, A. W., & McClelland, D. C. (1970), School adjustment and behavior of children hospitalized for schizophrenia as adults. *Amer. J. Orthopsychiat.*, 40:647–657.

Wender, P. H., Rosenthal, D., Ramer, J. D., Greenhill, L., & Sarlin, B. (1977), Schizophrenics' adopting parents. *Arch. Gen. Psychiat.*, 34:777–784.

Wing, J. K. (1978), Social influences on the course of schizophenia. In: *The Nature of Schizophrenia: New Approaches to Research and Treatment*, ed. L. C. Wynne, R. L. Crowmwell, & S. Matthysse. New York: John Wiley, pp. 599–616.

────── Cooper, J. E., & Sartorius, N. (1974), *The Description and Classification of Psychiatric Symptoms: An Instruction Manual for PSE and CATEGO System*. London: Cambridge University Press.

Worden, J. W., & Sobel, H. J. (1978), Ego strength and psychosocial adaptation to cancer. *Psychosom. Med.*, 40:585–592.

Wynne, L., & Singer, M. T. (1963a), Thought disorder and family relations of schizophenics: I. A research strategy. *Arch. Gen. Psychiat.*, 9:191–198.

────── ────── (1963b), Thought disorder and family relations of schizophrenics: II. A classification of forms of thinking. *Arch. Gen. Psychiat.*, 9:199–206.

────── Ryckoff, I., Day, J., & Mirsch, S. (1958), Pseudo-mutuality in the family reactions of schizophrenics. *Psychiatry*, 21:205–220.

Zubin, J., & Spring, B. (1977), Vulnerability—A new view of schizophrenia. *J. Abnorm. Psychol.*, 86:103–126.

Chapter 25
Life Events and Personality Traits in Obsessive-Compulsive Neurosis

JOSEPH MCKEON, M.B., M.R.C.P.I., M.R.C.Psych., BRIDGET ROA, B.Sc., AND ANTHONY MANN, M.B., M.R.C.P., M.R.C.Psych.

Several investigators have reported an excess of precipitating life events in obsessional neurosis (Rudin, 1953; Pollitt, 1957; Ingram, 1961; Lo, 1967; Bridges, Goktepe, and Maratos, 1973). However, it is difficult to interpret the significance of these studies because of the absence of well-defined event criteria, the use of different premorbid study periods and the absence of reliability and normal control data. More recently, reliable and valid life-event schedules have been devised and used in a variety of psychiatric syndromes (Brown, Sklair, Harris, and Birley, 1973; Paykel, 1974; Paykel, Prusoff and Myers, 1975). Their application in obsessive-compulsive neurosis has, unfortunately, been hampered by the paucity of cases of recent onset who seek medical attention (Black, 1974).

Acknowledgments. This research was funded by a grant from St. Patrick's Hospital, Dublin. We wish to thank Professor Isaac Marks for allowing access to his patients, Dr. Robin Murray for his helpful comments, and Dr. Anthony Unwin for his statistical advice. Finally, to the patients and relatives who have given so generously of their time we express our sincere appreciation.

This chapter was first published in the *British Journal of Psychiatry* (1984), 144:185–189, and it is reprinted by permission.

473

Despite such methodological difficulties, an attempt has been made to investigate, in a case-controlled study, the number and type of life events that occur prior to the onset of obsessive-compulsive neurosis, and to examine the role of premorbid personality traits in the relationship between events and the onset of illness.

METHODS

PATIENTS

The patients studied were consecutive attenders at the Maudsley Hospital Behaviour Therapy Unit who had received a primary diagnosis of obsessive-compulsive neurosis (300.3 on the 8th Revision of the International Classification of Diseases) from their psychiatrist, and who also met the operational definition of the Research Diagnostic Criteria for obsessive-compulsive disorder (Spitzer, Endicott, and Robins, 1978). Only those patients whose illness had developed within the past ten years and who had consented to have a close relative (parent, spouse, or sibling) interviewed were included.

COMPARISON GROUP

A normal comparison group was drawn from randomly selected housing units in a south London borough, from which one person per household was selected for interview. Subjects were included in the sample if they could be matched with a patient for sex, age at the time of onset (within three years), marital and socioeconomic status (within one SEC group), race, religion, and immediate family size (spouse and first-degree relatives). Subjects were excluded if they were considered to have had a psychiatric disorder at any time in the twelve months before interview which was sufficient to be classified as a case, as defined by the Research Diagnostic Criteria.

INTERVIEWS

1. Life events: Paykel's schedule for life events, which covers 64 defined life events, was administered in a semistructured interview, with each event inquired for unless it clearly did not apply (Paykel, 1974). Detailed further questioning was then carried out to determine the exact time and nature of each reported event, its objective negative impact, and the degree of control the subject had over the occurrence of the event.

Onset was defined as a change from normality and non-obsessive-compulsive symptoms to obsessive-compulsive symptoms. For the patients, the inquiry covered the twelve months prior to the onset of the illness, and for the control subjects the twelve months before the date of the interview. In addition, a close relative of each patient had an audio-recorded interview, using this schedule. As with events, an attempt was made to date onset to a 2-week period, but if there was uncertainty a range was plotted and its midpoint was used in the analysis.

2. Premorbid personality: This was rated using the Standard Assessment of Personality (SAP) which has been shown to be a valid and reliable measuring instrument (Mann, Jenkins, Cutting, and Cowen, 1981). It consists of a standardized interview with a close relative, or friend who has sufficient knowledge to describe the patient's personality characteristics before the onset of their illness. The schedule covers six personality categories, based on the International Classification of Diseases, Personality Section (ICD 301), with two other categories not listed in the ICD, called self-conscious and anxious personalities. Each personality category is rated as follows: Grade 0—no features present; Grade 1—features present; and Grade 2—features pronounced or abnormal personality. The informants in this study were close relatives of the patients.

The SAP inter-informant and inter-temporal reliability was assessed for the obsessive-compulsive patients.

INTERVIEWERS AND RATERS

All interviews were conducted by one interviewer (J. P. M.). Since a pilot study had shown that patients were not forthcoming about unpleasant and embarrassing events when the interview was being tape-recorded, only life-event and SAP interviews with informants could be tape-recorded for the purposes of inter-rater reliability. The patient and comparison group life-event scripts were rated blindly by one author (B. R.), while the informant relative's life-event interview was rated independently by another (J. P. M.). All SAP scripts and tapes were rated independently and blindly (A. H. M.).

POPULATION

Of 83 consecutive patients meeting the diagnostic criteria, 28 (33.7 percent) had their onset of illness within the specific time limit, but three (12 percent) of these declined to have a relative interviewed. Comparing the 25 patients participating in the study with the 58 who did not meet the selection criteria for age, sex, marital and socioeconomic status, race and religion shows that they did not differ significantly on these demographic features, apart from age; the mean age for those included was 25.2 years, and 34.7 years for those excluded. In addition, the age of onset of obsessive-compulsive symptoms was comparable in both groups. The mean time from onset of illness to study date was 4.5 years.

AGREEMENT AND RELIABILITY

1. *Dating Onset:* Twenty-two of the 25 (87 percent) patients and their relatives described the same onset, while the three remaining patients had a private onset, in that they concealed their symptoms, their relatives describing a later exacerbation. In those pairs describing the same onset, 19 (82.6 percent) dated the onset within one month of each other. Where there was disagreement between patients and relatives for dating onset, a median date was selected, based on their reports; this gave life-event scores comparable to those when either the latest or earliest date of onset was used, thus minimizing the unreliability of uncertain dates.

2. *Occurrence and Nature of Events*: The interinformant reliability was calculated, using Goodman's and Kruskal's G (Kendall and Stuart, 1966) and was found to be $+0.93$ for the obsessional category, $+0.96$ for the anxious and $+0.88$ for the self-conscious category ($p < 0.01$). Inter-temporal reliability (two interviews conducted one year apart) using the same statistical test was $+0.76$ ($p < 0.01$), $+0.96$, and $+0.96$ for the obsessional, anxious and self-conscious categories respectively.

RESULTS

LIFE EVENTS

1. *Occurrence of events:* Obsessive-compulsive patients reported a mean of 1.60 events per person over one year before onset, and the matched comparison group a mean of 0.76 events for their period of enquiry; the differences were significant at $p < 0.01$ (one-way analysis of variance).

The month of occurrence of each event was coded for both groups and their distribution is shown in Figure 25.1. Initially, both groups have a similar frequency, but for the six months prior to onset, the patient group has a higher rate, with a peak at one month.

2. *Type of events:* Serious illness in the subject and their close relatives, arguments, and birth of a child were reported most frequently, but their occurrence was too infrequent to test for significance. An unexpected finding was that three of the patient group described having head injuries in the week prior to the onset of their obsessional illness. Two of these qualified as events under the heading of serious personal illness, while the third did not meet event criteria.

As the frequencies of individual events were too low for useful analysis, they were categorized, using Paykel et al.'s (1975) classification into four alternative but partly overlapping

478   JOSEPH McKEON ET AL.

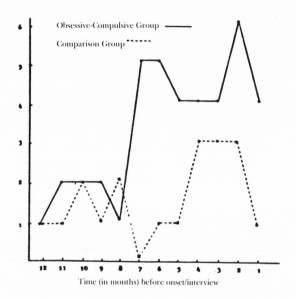

Figure 25.1. Timing of life events for the 12 months prior to onset (patients) and interview (comparison group).

groups (Table 25.1): the social desirability of the event, whether it was an entrance or exit (introduction or departure of person from subject's life), its objective negative impact, and the degree of control the subject had in initiating the event.

For each of these categories, the patient group scored higher than the comparison group; the difference between the two was statistically significant for objective negative impact, both moderate to severe and mild to none, and for the subcategory of moderate to complete degree of control.

LIFE EVENTS AND PREMORBID PERSONALITY

Premorbid personality assessment with the SAP in the patient group showed a high frequency of obsessional, anxious, and

Table 25.1
Mean Occurence in Life-Event Categories

Category	Obsessive-compulsive group ($n = 25$)	Comparison group ($n = 25$)	Significance by f test
Undesirable	0.44	0.28	NS
Desirable	0.08	0.04	NS
Objective negative impact			
Moderate to severe	1.00	0.48	$p < 0.01$
Mild or none	0.60	0.28	$p < 0.01$
Degree of control			
Moderate to complete	0.76	0.24	$p < 0.01$
Some of none	0.84	0.52	NS
Exit	0.08	0.04	NS
Entrance	0.12	0.04	NS

self-conscious categories. Informant relatives did not describe any other personality category, and there were six patients (24 percent) without any abnormal personality traits.

The "overall" personality grade refers to the rating irrespective of the personality type (Figure 25.2). Patients designated Grade 2 personality category had at least one score of Grade 2 on any of the three frequently occurring personality categories, while those designated Grade 1 had no abnormal personality traits. The correlation between the life event score and the "overall" personality grade was -0.62 ($p < 0.05$) using Goodman's and Kruskal's G (Kendall and Stuart, 1966). Also, the relationship between the obsessional, anxious, and self-conscious personality traits and the mean life event score showed a negative association, which was most marked for self-conscious personality traits (Figure 25.2).

DISCUSSION

The results of this study show a significant excess of life events in patients who develop an obsessive-compulsive neurosis, in the 12 months prior to its onset, compared with a matched

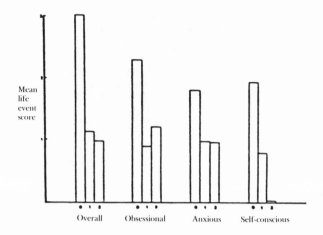

Mean life event score

Overall   Obsessional   Anxious   Self-conscious

Figure 25.2. Mean life-event score for four SAP categories.

comparison group. In addition, a negative correlation was found between premorbid personality traits and life events prior to onset within the obsessive-compulsive group; those with abnormal personality traits had significantly fewer life events than those without abnormal personality traits.

Despite having access to patients attending a busy behavior therapy unit, it was not possible to get a sufficiently large sample of cases of obsessive-compulsive neurosis with an onset within 12 months of the study date. Using a ten-year prestudy period within which the onset could occur, an adequate number of cases was obtained and these were representative of all attenders, in that they differed from those excluded only by the criterion of their mean age being younger. A high level of agreement was found between patients and their relatives for dating onset of symptoms and reporting life events, thus validating the former's accounts. Their accurate recall of events occurring on average four and a half years previously is possibly related to their perfectionistic attention to details such as dates and the orientating effect that the onset of an illness would have. As such, controls, who would be asked to recall distant events, would be disadvantaged, and for this reason, they were requested to report events for the year prior to the interview.

Mann et al. (1981), Tyler and Alexander (1979), and Walton and Presley (1973) concerned themselves with the recognition of abnormal personality types, and found that a relative's account of personality can be rated reliably by psychiatrists, and is consistent over time. The present study confirmed the satisfactory inter-informant and inter-temporal reliability of the SAP for a sample of obsessive-compulsive patients. Despite widely varying criteria for defining obsessional traits, most previous reports have indicated that appoximately two-thirds of obsessive-compulsive patients have such a personality type (Pollitt, 1960; Tyler, Alexander, Cicchetti, Cohen, and Remington, 1979; Ingram, 1961; Kringlen, 1965; McKeon and McColl, 1982), and a similar proportion was found in this study.

Life events occur more frequently than expected prior to the onset of obsessive-compulsive neurosis, but the rate was less than that reported for similar periods before the onset of acute schizophrenia (Brown and Birley, 1968) and depression (Paykel, Myers, Dienelt, Klerman, Lindenthal, and Pepper, 1969; Brown and Harris, 1979). The results of this investigation suggest that the role of life events in the pathogenesis of obsessive-compulsive symptoms without experiencing an excess of stressful life events, but those with normal premorbid personalities require a significant excess of events before developing such symptoms. These observations may have prognostic implications.

A further interesting result of this study is the delay between peak time of occurrence of events and the onset of the illness. In this respect, it differs from the relative recency of life events in studies of depression and schizophrenia (Paykel et al., 1969; Brown and Birley, 1968; Presley and Walton, 1973). This delayed impact of life events probably implies that a certain level of emotional arousal is necessary before obsessions supervene. Each of the 25 patients reported experiencing either anxiety or agitation before the onset of the obsessions, irrespective of whether they had an identifiable life event. The interaction between personality traits and the severity and number of life events appears to determine the onset and degree of emotional arousal, which in turn influences the onset of obsessions. This stress diathesis was first proposed by Eliot Slater in 1943 (Slater, 1943; Slater and Cowie, 1971), and the results of this study support his hypothesis.

Although patients experienced events over which they were rated as having moderate to complete control, their relative indecisiveness, submissiveness, and anxious personality traits may have limited the influence of this control, possibly resulting in the occurrence of associated secondary events and increased emotional arousal.

Finally, it is worth noting that as the comparison group had an advantage for life-event recall, the difference between the two groups provides a minimal estimate of the importance of environmental factors in this condition.

References

Black, A. (1974), The natural history of obsessional neurosis. In: *Obsessional States*, ed. H. R. Beech. London: Methuen.

Bridges, P., Goktepe, E., & Maratos, J. (1973), A comparative review of patients with obsessional neurosis and with depression treated by psychosurgery. *Brit. J. Psychiat.*, 123:663–674.

Brown, G. W., & Birley, J. L. T. (1968), Crises and life changes and the onset of schizophrenia. *J. Health & Soc. Behav.*, 9:203–214.

——— Sklair, F., Harris, T. O., & Birley, J. L. T. (1973), Life events and psychiatric disorder. 1. Some methodological issues. *Psychol. Med.*, 3:74–87.

——— Harris, T. (1979), *Social Origins of Depression*. London: Tavistock.

Ingram. I. M. (1961), Obsessional illness in mental hospital patients. *J. Ment. Sci.*, 197:382–402.

H.M.S.O. (1965), *International Classification of Diseases: A Glossary of Mental Disorders*, 8th ed. London: Her Majesty's Stationery Office.

Kendall, M. G., & Stuart, A. (1966), *Advanced Theory of Statistics*, Vol. 3. London: Griffin.

Kringlen, E. (1965), Obsessional neurotics: A long-term follow-up. *Brit. J. Psychiat.*, 111:709–722.

Lo, W. H. (1967), A follow-up study of obsessional neurotics in Hong Kong Chinese. *Brit. J. Psychiat.*, 113:823–832.

McKeon, J. P., & McColl, D. (1982), ABO blood groups in obsessional illness—State and trait. *Acta Psychiat. Scand.*, 65:74–78.

Mann, A. H., Jenkins, R., Cutting, J. C., & Cowen, P. J. (1981), The development and use of standardised assessment of abnormal personality. *Psychol. Med.*, 11:839–847.

Paykel, E. S. (1974), Recent life events and clinical depression. In: *Stress and Illness*, ed. E. K. Gunderson & R. H. Rahl. Springfield, IL: Charles C Thomas.

―――― Myers, J. K., Dienelt, M. N., Klerman, G. L., Lindenthal, J. J., & Pepper, M. P. (1969), Life events and depression: A controlled study. *Arch. Gen. Psychiat.*, 21:753–760.

―――― Prusoff, B. A., & Myers, J. K. (1975), Suicide attempts and recent life events: A controlled comparison. *Arch. Gen. Psychiat.*, 32:327–333.

Pollitt, J. (1957), Natural history of obsessional states. *Brit. Med. J.*, i:194–198.

―――― (1960), Natural history studies in mental illness: A discussion based on a pilot study of obsessional states. *J. Ment. Sci.*, 106:93–113.

Presley, A. S., & Walton, H. J. (1973), Dimensions of abnormal personality. *Brit. J. Psychiat.*, 122:269–276.

Rudin, E. (1953), Ein Beitrag zur Frage Zwangskrankgeit. *Arch. Psychiat. und Nervenkrankheit.*, 191:14–54.

Slater, E. (1943), The neurotic constitution. *J. Neurol. Neurosurg. & Psychiat.*, 6:1–8.

―――― Cowie, V. (1971), *The Genetics of Mental Disorders.* London: Oxford University Press.

Spitzer, R., Endicott, J., & Robins, E. (1978), Research diagnostic criteria. *Arch. Gen. Psychiat.*, 35:773–782.

Tyler, P., & Alexander, J. (1979), Classification of personality disorder. *Brit. J. Psychiat.*, 135:163–167.

―――― Alexander, M. S., Cicchetti, D., Cohen, M. S., & Remington, M. (1979), Reliability of a schedule for rating personality disorders. *Brit. J. Psychiat.*, 135:168–174.

Walton, H. J., & Presley, A. S. (1973), Use of a category system in the diagnosis of abnormal personality. *Brit. J. Psychiat.*, 122:259–268.

Chapter 26
Life Events and Personality Characteristics in Depression

H. PERRIS, M.D.

This investigation is part of a large multifactorial study on the possible impact of stressful life events on the onset and development of a depressive disorder (Perris, 1982), and deals with a possible relationship between life events and the personality make-up of the individual experiencing them.

Among the factors which might enhance an individual's vulnerability to affective disorders, considerable attention has been given personality characteristics, since Kraepelin (1913) emphasized the importance of habitual mental traits in the causation of manic-depressive insanity (MDI).

An aspect of the personality structure of depression-prone individuals which is relevant to the study reported in this article concerns the concept of aggression. Abraham (1916, 1924, 1927) and Freud (1957) first suggested that depression was caused by the introduction of aggressive impulses previously directed externally. Since that time, as Kendell (1973) puts it,

Acknowledgment. This chapter was first published in _Acta Psychiatrica Scandinavia_ (1984), 69:350–358, and it is reprinted by permission of the copyright holder, Munksgaard.

"the idea that aggression plays a fundamental role in the development of depression has been woven into the fabric of psychiatric thinking." Kendell (1973) has made an attempt to reformulate the hypothesis in a testable way as follows: "Depression is caused by the inhibition of aggressive response to frustration." The implications of this simplified hypothesis are that "the incidence of depression should be high in situations where aggression is aroused, but its expression prevented, and low in situations where relatively unrestricted outlets for aggression are available." In his paper Kendell reviews several findings from epidemiological studies of depression, and concludes that the results of most of them, even if not strong enough to establish the hypothesis in question, are sufficiently suggestive to make the hypothesis worthy of serious consideration.

Taking into account Kendell's hypothesis, it may be assumed that the perception of and the reaction to external stressful events are modulated by the personality structure of the person experiencing the event (cf. the concept of "resistance resources" used by Antonovsky (1974) and by Garrity, Somes, and Marx (1977) and the broader concept of "coping style" used in life-event research by Andrews, Tennant, Hewson, and Vaillant (1978). Paykel (1979) has taken into account personality characteristics in his model about the pathogenetic significance of life events for depression, and many others have stressed the relevance of personality factors in studies of life events. However, more extensive investigations of possible relationships between personality characteristics and life events in depressed patients have not yet been published.

Within the frame of a multifactorial study of life events and depression (H. Perris, 1981, 1983a, b, c; Perris, von Knorring, and Perris, 1982; von Knorring, Jacobson, Perris, and Perris, 1980; Perris, von Knorring, Oreland, and Perris, 1983) a separate investigation has also been planned in which the occurrence and experience of life events in a series of depressed patients have been studied in relation to personality characteristics.

In particular, inspired by the hypothesis advanced by Kendell (1973), we wanted to investigate possible relationships between life events and different aspects of aggression in the personality structure of our patients. To the extent that various components of aggression might influence an individual's vulnerability to depression it was assumed that patients characterized by inhibition of aggression would require less stressful events to develop a depressive syndrome than patients characterized by manifest aggression.

PATIENTS AND METHODS

THE SERIES

Patients suffering from any kind of primary depression consecutively admitted to the Department of Psychiatry, Umea University, in the years 1977–1980 have participated in the study if they did so agree.

A detailed composition of the patients comprised in the studies of life events has been presented in an earlier article (Perris, 1983a) together with their distribution into diagnostic subgroups according to different systems of classification [ICD-9, DSM-III, Feighner's criteria (Feighner, Robins, Guze, Woodruff, Winokur, and Munoz, 1972)] in comparison with the classification used in the present study. Diagnostic assignment to the subgroups in the different systems was made by two experienced psychiatrists (L. von Knorring and C. Perris) who worked independently of each other, and who were blind to the results concerning life events and personality characteristics. In the few instances when independent diagnoses did not correspond, the case was jointly discussed until agreement was reached.

Patients participated in the interview for the assessment of life events and self-assessment of personality traits by using a questionnaire when they had recovered from their depressive episode. One hundred thirty-eight patients entered the study.

Their mean age was 45.2 ± 1.2 SEM. Their distribution according to sex and diagnosis is presented in Table 26.1.

DIAGNOSTIC SUBDIVISION

The patients have been classified according to the Umea Classification of affective disorders, detailed definitions of which have been published in earlier papers (C. Perris, 1973; d'Elia, von Knorring, and Perris, 1974). The groups considered are: "bipolar depressed," meaning those patients who have suffered from at least one episode of mania and one of depression; "unipolar patients," meaning those patients who have suffered from at least three separate episodes of a severe depressive disorder with a free interval in-between; and patients suffering from "reactive-neurotic depression," implying the occurrence of a depressive breakdown closely related to a psychologically understandable traumatic event, or people with a life-long pronounced proneness to acute depressive reactions. Finally, an "unspecified" group comprised those patients who could not be classified in any of the above-mentioned subgroups. About 94 percent of the total series fulfilled Kendell's criteria for depression (Brockington and Leff, 1979), those few who did not were patients admitted for special investigations who were not currently depressed.

As we have found that bipolar patients do not differ significantly from unipolar patients on the variables covered by the KSP, the series has been treated as a whole without any further division into diagnostic subgroups.

Table 26.1
Distribution of the Series According to Sex and Diagnosis

	Unipolar	Bipolar	Neurotic-Reactive	Unspecified	Total
Male	18	6	18	13	56
Female	25	7	27	24	83
Total	43	13	45	37	138

Chi-square 0.63; p = n.s.

Assessment of Life Events

In separate interviews with each patient after recovery from depression, the occurrence of life events 12 to 4 months before and within 3 months of the onset of the disorder was assessed by the use of a 56-item life events inventory specially constructed as a guideline for semistructured interviews. Details about the life-event inventory are given elsewhere (Perris, 1983a). Briefly, the inventory covers events similar to those included by other authors in other life-event inventories. Apart from recording the occurrence of each event in the periods considered, the patient is asked to assess how the event is experienced (according to a 5-point scale from "very positively" = 1, to "very negatively" = 5). In addition, the patient is asked whether or not the event was expected and whether or not it was controllable. Finally, information is also obtained about any difficulty in adjusting to an experienced event (Tables 26.2 and 26.3).

In the further analysis the different subgroupings of the various events were considered, similar to those used in other studies of life events and depression (Paykel, 1974; Myers, Lindenthal, Pepper, Ostrander, 1972), e.g., "entrance" and "exit" to and from the social field, "object loss," and "conflicts in interpersonal relations." A subscale comprised of 32 events, logically unrelated to depression or to somatic health, was also used to study the "independent" events whose occurrence could not be confounded by the depressive symptomatology.

It is not always the case that the other events in the inventory might be influenced by depression, thus making it difficult to decide, retrospectively, whether they were a consequence of the patient's depression rather than a contributing factor, as the reverse is also possible. For this reason, it has been decided to retain all the events covered by the inventory, but to treat them separately (Schalling, 1978).

Table 26.2
Correlation Between Number of Events and
KSP Scores (Whole Period) (138 Patients)

Somatic anxiety	0.04	Aggression indirect	0.18**
Psychic anxiety	-0.08	Aggression verbal	0.19*
Muscular tension	0.06	Irritability	0.16**
Social desirability	-0.03	Suspicion	-0.03
Impulsivity	0.05	Guilt	0.01
Monotony avoidance	0.06	Inhibition of aggression	0.02
Detachment	-0.20*	Aggression factor	0.18**
Psychasthenia	0.02	Hostility factor	-0.00
Socialization	-0.15***		

*$p < .01$
**$p < .02$
***$p < .05$

Table 26.3
Correlation Between Patient's Scoring of the Experience of Life Events
and the Subscale of the KSP

Somatic anxiety	0.04	Indirect aggression	0.08
Psychic anxiety	0.11	Verbal aggression	-0.03
Muscular tension	0.06	Irritability	0.06
Social desirability	-0.02	Suspicion	0.16*
Impulsivity	-0.07	Guilt	0.08
Monotony avoidance	-0.08	Inhibition of aggression	-0.06
Detachment	0.10	Aggression factor	0.05
Psychasthenia	0.13	Hostility factor	0.14*
Socialization	-0.14*		

*$p < .05$

ASSESSMENT OF PERSONALITY
CHARACTERISTICS

The assessment of personality characteristics was made by means of a self-rating instrument—the KSP developed by Shall-ing and her "social desirability" and either the number or scored experience of life events. Had positive correlations been found it might have been suspected that the patients were less reliable and had tried to rationalize their depression by blaming the impact on negative external events.

In a previous study (Perris, Eisemann, Eriksson, Jacobsson, von Knorring, and Perris, 1979) we showed that the subscales referring to somatic and psychic anxiety, muscular tension, and social desirability were probably state-dependent. As we wanted to reduce the amount of data, these subscales have been disregarded in further analyses. The aggression variables have also been condensed into factors and the items will not be studied separately in the further analyses.

Tables 26.4–26.7 present the mean values of the life events grouped in relation to the personality traits. As expected, patients who scored high had experienced significantly more events than patients who scored low on the aggression factor. Conversely, patients scoring low on the variable, inhibition of aggression, had experienced significantly more life events than those scoring high on the same variable. Also, patients who scored high (Table 26.4).

When only the events classified as independent of the depressive syndrome were considered, the results still had the same trend regarding the relationship to components of aggression (Table 26.5).

Table 26.6 presents a separate analysis of the events classified as "conflicts" in a social relation. The figures in the table are low and should be treated with caution. "Conflicts" in a social relation could be a consequence of an already existing depressive disorder. However, all the statistically significant differences seem to be related to aggression and impulsiveness, thus suggesting a possible interaction between life events and personality characteristics.

Finally, in Table 26.7 the mean values are reported for the

Table 26.4
Occurrence of Life Events of Any Kind in Patients Classified, According to Their KSP Scores, into Those with Scores Above and Below the Median

KSP subscale	12–4 months before onset		Within 3 months	
	Mean number of events		Mean number of events	
	Below median	Above median	Below median	Above median
Impulsivity	3.2 1.8	3.1 2.2	1.4 0.18	1.5 1.5
Monotony avoidance	2.9 1.9	3.5 2.0	1.4 1.7	1.6 1.7
Detachment	3.3 2.0	2.8 1.9	1.6 0.18	1.3 1.6
Psychasthenia	3.1 1.9	3.2 2.0	1.5 1.6	1.4 1.8
Socialization	3.2 2.0	3.1 1.9	1.9 1.9	1.0 1.3
Aggression factor	2.9 1.9	3.4 2.0	1.0 1.4	2.0 2.0
Hostility factor	3.1 1.9	3.2 2.1	1.4 1.6	1.6 1.9
Inhibition of aggression	3.1 1.8	3.2 2.1	1.8 1.9	1.0 1.4

Table 26.5
Distribution of "Independent" ("Fateful") Events in Patients Classified According to Their KSP Scores
(Mean Number of Events and SD)

KSP subscale	12-4 months prior to onset		p	Within 3 months	
	Mean number of events			Mean number of events	
	Below median	Above median		Below median	Above median
Social desirability	1.6 (1.5)	1.8 (1.5)		0.6 (0.9)	0.9 (0.9)
Impulsivity	1.7 (1.5)	1.6 (1.5)		0.7 (1.0)	0.7 (0.8)
Monotony avoidance	1.6 (1.6)	1.8 (1.4)		0.7 (0.9)	0.8 (1.0)
Detachment	1.7 (1.5)	1.5 (1.5)		0.8 (0.9)	0.6 (0.9)
Psychasthenia	1.5 (1.3)	1.8 (1.7)		0.8 (0.9)	0.6 (0.9)
Socialization	1.6 (1.6)	1.7 (1.4)		0.8 (0.9)	0.7 (0.9)
Aggression factor	1.4 (1.2)	2.0 (1.8)	<0.05	0.6 (0.9)	0.8 (0.9)
Hostility factor	1.5 (1.3)	1.8 (1.8)		0.8 (1.0)	0.6 (0.8)
Inhibition of aggression	1.6 (1.5)	1.7 (1.6)		0.9 (1.0)	0.5 (0.8)

Table 26.6
Occurrence of "Conflict"Events in Patients Classified According to Their
KSP Scores. Events Occurred Within 3 Months Prior
to Onset of Depression

KSP subscale	Mean number of events				
	Below median	SD	Above median	SD	p
Impulsivity	0.1	0.3	0.5	0.8	0.005
Monotony avoidance	0.1	0.3	0.4	0.8	0.025
Detachment	0.2	0.6	0.3	0.5	
Psychasthenia	0.2	0.5	0.3	0.7	
Socialization	0.4	0.7	0.1	0.4	0.025
Aggression factor	0.1	0.2	0.5	0.8	0.001
Hostility factor	0.1	0.4	0.4	0.8	0.056
Inhibition of aggression	0.3	0.6	0.2	0.6	

events experienced by the patients "negatively" or "very negatively" showing a pattern similar to that in the previous tables.

DISCUSSION

The results of the present study should be interpreted with
caution as the correlations found are all very low and could be
due to chance. They seem, however, to support the general
hypothesis suggested by Kendell (1973) that aspects of aggression might be relevant for the occurrence of depression in an
interaction with external factors. Two relationships, in keeping
with the essential hypothesis of this study, have emerged: a
weak negative between life events and inhibition of aggression.
That an event might be a consequence of the patient's depression is not necessarily evidential as the opposite sequence might
equally be true. Clarity on this issue can be obtained only in
prospective studies in which both the mental status of the subjects and the occurrence of life events are consistently monitored on the same occasion.

Table 26.7
Occurrence of Events Perceived Negatively or Very Negatively by the Patients Classified According to Their KSP Scores

| | During the whole year prior to onset | | | | | Within 3 months | | | | |
| | Mean number of events | | | | p | Mean number of events | | | | p |
KSP subscale	Below median		Above median			Below median		Above median		
Impulsivity	1.9	1.4	1.7	1.3		0.7	0.9	1.0	1.1	
Monotony avoidance	1.7	1.4	2.0	1.4		0.8	1.0	0.9	1.0	
Detachment	1.9	1.4	1.7	1.3		0.9	1.0	0.7	0.9	
Psychasthenia	1.8	1.5	1.9	1.3		0.9	0.9	0.8	1.1	
Socialization	2.0	1.6	1.7	1.2		1.0	1.1	0.6	0.8	
Aggression factor	1.7	1.3	2.0	1.5		0.6	0.7	1.2	1.2	
Hostility factor	1.8	1.4	2.0	1.3		0.8	0.9	0.9	1.1	
Inhibition of aggression	1.9	1.4	1.8	1.4		1.0	1.0	0.6	0.9	<0.10

If the results of the correlations reported here are accepted as expressing a weak but significant relationship between personality characteristics and reactivity to external events, it would seem that the more vulnerable, inhibited patients require fewer external events to become depressed than the less vulnerable persons characterized by manifest aggression, who have the capacity of acting out their frustration.

In addition, the findings of this study show that the occurrence of particular events, for example the deterioration of a social relationship, might be related to such personality characteristics as aggression and impulsiveness. Patients who scored high on socialization, and who can be assumed to be more dependent on the support of social relationships, reported fewer events than those who scored low on the same variable. This finding is in keeping with expectations from psychodynamic theories.

Unfortunately, the KSP is not the most suitable instrument for investigating aspects of dependency. One instrument, specially constructed to investigate psychogenic needs, is the CMPS which was used by us in earlier studies (Perris and Strandman, 1979). Research, combining the assessment of life events with the use of the CMPS, would greatly further our understanding of the impact of stressful events in individuals with pronounced psychogenic needs in their personality make-up. One such study is now in progress.

REFERENCES

Abraham, K. (1927), Notes on the psycho-analytic investigation and treatment of manic-depressive insanity and allied conditions. In: *Selected Papers on Psychoanalysis*. London: Hogarth Press, pp. 137–156.

———— (1916), The first pregenital stage of libido. In: *Selected Papers on Psychoanalyses*. London: Hogarth Press, pp. 248–279.

———— (1924), A short study of the development of the libido viewed in the light of mental disorders. In: *Selected Papers on Psychoanalyses*. London: Hogarth Press, pp. 418–502.

Andrews, G., Tennant, C., Hewson, D. M., & Vaillant, G. E. (1978), Life events stress, social support, coping style and risk of psychological impairment. *J. Nerv. & Ment. Dis.*, 166:307–316.

Antonovsky, A. (1974), Conceptual and methodological problems in the study of resistance resources and stressful life events. In: *Stressful Life Events: Their Nature and Effects*, ed. B. S. Dohrenwend & B. P. Dohrenwend. New York: John Wiley, pp. 245–258.

Brockington, I. F., & Leff, J. P. (1979), Schizo-affective psychosis: Definitions and incidence. *Psychol. Med.*, 8:91–99.

d'Elia, G., von Knorring, E., & Perris, C. (1974), Non-psychotic depressive disorders: A ten-year follow-up. *Acta. Psychiat. Scand.*, Suppl. 255:173–186.

Feighner, J. P., Robins, E., Guze, B., Woodruff, R. A., Winokur, G., Munoz, R. (1972), Diagnostic criteria for use in psychiatric research. *Arch. Gen. Psychiat.*, 26:57–63.

Freud, S. (1917), Mourning and melancholia. *Standard Edition*, 14:243–258. London: Hogarth Press, 1957.

Garrity, I. F., Somes, G. W., & Marx, M. B. (1977), Personality factors in resistance to illness after recent life changes. *J. Psychosom. Res.*, 21:23–32.

Kendell, R. E. (1973), The relationship between aggression and depression. An appraisal of epidemiological evidence. In: *World Psychiat. Assoc.*, ed. M. Lader & R. Garcia.

Kraepelin, E. (1913), *Psychiatrie*, 8th ed. Leipzig: Barth.

Myers, J. K., Lindenthal, J. J., Pepper, M. P., & Ostrander, D. R. (1972), Life events and mental status: A longitudinal study. *J. Health & Soc. Behav.*, 13:398–306.

Paykel, E. S. (1979), Causal relationship between clinical depression and life events. In: *Stress and Mental Disorder*, ed. J. Barrett. New York: Raven Press, pp. 71–85.

———— (1974), Life stress and psychiatric disorder: Application of the clinical approach. In: *Stressful Life Events: Their Nature and Effects*, ed. B. S. Dohrenwend & B. P. Dohrenwend. New York: John Wiley, pp. 135–149.

Perris, C. (1973), The heuristic value of a distinction between bipolar and unipolar affective disorders. In: *Classification and Prediction of Outcome of Depression*, ed. J. Angst. Stuttgart: Schattauer, pp. 75–84.

———— Eisemann, M., Eriksson, U., Jacobsson, J., von Knorring, L., & Perris, H. (1979), Variations in self-assessment of personality characteristics in depressed patients, with special reference to aspects of aggression. *Psychiat. Clin.*, 12:209–215.

Perris, H. (1981), Livshandelser och depression. Res. Rep. Department Psychiatry Umea University, Umea, Sweden, 4:268–720.

———— (1982), A multifactorial study of life events in depressed patients. Umea University Medical Dissertations, New Series, 78.

——— (1983a), Life events and depression. I. Effect of age, sex and civil status. *J. Affect. Dis.*, 83:214–240.

——— (1983b), Life events and depression. II. Results in diagnostic subgroups and in relation to the recurrence of depression. *J. Affect. Dis.*, 83:225–310.

——— (1983c), Life events and depression. III. Relation to severity of the depressive syndrome. *J. Affect. Dis.*, 83:232–238.

——— Strandman, E. (1979), Psychogenic needs in depression. *Arch. Psychiat. Nervenkr.*, 227:97–107.

——— von Knorring, L., & Perris, C. (1982), Genetic vulnerability for depression and life events. *Neuropsychobiol.*, 8:241–243.

——— ——— Oreland, L., & Perris, C. (1983), Life events and biological vulnerability. A study of life events and platelet monoamine oxicase (MAO) activity in depressed patients. *Psychiat. Res.*, 243–245.

Schalling, D. (1978), Psychopathy-related personality variables and the psychophysiology of socialization. In: *Approaches to Research*, ed. R. D. Hare & D. Schalling. London: John Wiley.

von Knorring, L., Jacobsson, L., Perris, C., & Perris, H. (1980), Reactivity to incoming stimuli and the experience of life events. *Neuropsychobiol.*, 6:297–303.

Chapter 27
Life Events and Early and Late Onset of Bipolar Disorder

Barry Glassner, Ph.D., and C. V. Haldipur, M.D.

Research in several areas has suggested that bipolar affective disorder may be a heterogeneous condition. For instance, Hays (1976) speculated that hereditary factors operate in one subgroup of the disorder and organic factors in the other. Taylor and Abrams (1973, 1981) have presented data in support of multifactorial and polygenic etiology for the disorder and, unlike James (1977), who felt that age at onset was not helpful in elucidating genetic transmission, they have suggested that the transmitted factors are expressed in early onset and more bipolar relatives. In this chapter, we present a serendipitous observation that stressful life events may play different etiological roles in early- and late-onset bipolar disorders.

METHOD

To develop a diverse sample, we collected the names of patients diagnosed as manic-depressive from a state-funded community

Acknowledgment. This chapter was first published in the *American Journal of Psychiatry* (1983), 142/2:215–217, and it is reprinted by permission of the copyright holder, the American Psychiatric Association.

mental health center, a general hospital psychiatric unit, a private psychiatric hospital, and outpatients under the care of private psychiatrists in a city in New York State that is generally considered to represent a "mean demographics profile" of the United States. Of these 240 patients, only 53 met the criteria for admission to the study: compliance with standard diagnostic criteria (Feighner, Robins, and Guze, 1972), diagnosis of bipolar illness made by at least two independent psychiatrists, and documented history of cycles of acute mania and depression. There were no unipolar manic subjects in the sample. Although the subjects were screened prior to the publication of DSM-III, the criteria adopted for inclusion in the study make us reasonably confident that there were no atypical bipolar patients in the sample. Five subjects dropped out of the study (four could not be relocated after the initial interview, and one subject, in her 70s, proved unwilling or unable to be interviewed). Children and mentally retarded persons were excluded from the study.

We interviewed each subject in depth several times in order to obtain a life history. All available family members and friends were questioned. The format consisted of open-ended discussion with scheduled probes concerning precise circumstances and stressful life events during childhood and just prior to, during, and after episodes of affective illness. All interviews were transcribed verbatim, and hospital records were obtained or clinical staff interviewed for all subjects.

The method used in this study had limitations, however. The case history technique does not permit sophisticated quantitative analysis, and sample size was limited because the approach required the researchers to spend many hours investigating each case (in several instances, we followed subjects for up to 4 years). The study depended primarily upon retrospective data, which presents two major difficulties: people may experience events as a result of their disorders but may speak of them as preceding the disorders, and there may be inaccuracy of recall (Paykel, 1974). To reduce these threats to validity, we located as many additional informants as possible (in each case including at least one well-informed person), usu-

ally family members or long-time friends, who were also interviewed in depth. In 64 percent of the cases two or more
informants were interviewed, and in several cases we were able
to include four or five informants. There were no differences
between the numbers of informants interviewed for the early-
and the late-onset groups. Findings are reported only in cases
where all informants gave the same report. There may be a risk
that the onset of mania generates new interpretations of events,
and thus we considered these extensive efforts to obtain detailed
interview data and judgments of independence to be warranted.
Often the informants felt anger toward, or a distrust of, the
subjects and were quite willing to contradict reports that interviewers had gotten from the subjects. Portions of transcribed
interviews and other data have been published elsewhere (Glassner and Halipur, 1976).

We divided the subjects into an early-onset group and a late-
onset group, using the age of 20 years as the cutting point (those
with onset at age 20 were placed in the early-onset group). At
the time of data collection and coding we did not expect to find
differences between early- and late-onset probands.

We used the Holmes and Rahe (1967) scoring procedures
to obtain a stress score for each subject.

RESULTS

As summarized in Table 27.1, there were clear differences between the stress scores of the early- and the late-onset subjects.
In the year before the first episode, 23 percent of the early-
onset subjects and 64 percent of the late-onset subjects experienced stressful life events. The mean stress score during that
year for early-onset subjects was 20, and for late-onset subjects
it was 52. This difference approached statistical significance by
a two-tailed independent-samples t-test ($t = 1.96$, $df = 44$, $p < .10$). In addition, the late-onset subjects as a group noted

Table 27.1
Stress Patterns in Manic-Depressive Patients According to Age at Onset of Illness

Group[a]	Percentage of Subjects With Stress in Year Before Onset	Individual Stress Scores			Total Group Stress Score[b]
		Mean	SD	Median	
Early-onset subjects					
First episode (N = 13)	23	20	43	0	372
Latest episode (N = 13)	23	13	4	0	269
Late-onset subjects					
First episode (N = 33)	64	52	52	80	1007
Latest episode (N = 28)[c]	61	42	45	73	840

[a] The cutting point between early-onset and late-onset groups was 20 years of age. Information is given for the 46 patients whose informants confirmed their reports.
[b] Computed by summing individuals stress scores and standardizing as if N = 20 in each cell.
[c] Five late-onset subjects were continuous (rapid) cyclers and thus were excluded from this tabulation.

approximately two and a half times as much stress before the first onset of their illness as the early-onset group.

For the subjects' latest episode the results were quite similar. During the year before their latest episode, 23 percent of the early-onset subjects and 61 percent of the late-onset subjects reportedly suffered stressful life events (mean stress scores = 13 and 42, respectively; $t = 2.11$, $df = 39$, $p < .05$), and the late-onset group again reported about two and a half times as much stress as the early-onset group.

When the more conventional cutoff age of 30 years was used to define early and late onset, the results for both the first and latest episodes remained significantly different ($t = 1.85$, $df = 44$, $p < .10$, and $t = 2.14$, $df = 39$, $p < .05$, respectively). We did not compare differences within the sample by sex, since there were only four male subjects in the early-onset group.

DISCUSSION

These results suggest that there may be etiological differences between early- and late-onset bipolar disorders. Any cutoff age for early and late onset is arbitrary. Rather than base it on mean age at onset; indeed, as many as one-fifth of the subjects showed evidence of the disorder in adolescence (Lovanger and Levine, 1978). Unipolar disorder (major depressive illness) begins later and evenly throughout adult life (Wolpert, 1980). Further, for researchers interested in the role of life events in the etiology of affective disorder, this postadolescent period constitutes an important developmental milestone—a transition from dependence on family to autonomy, which for many in our culture is the first stressful life event.

It might be argued that young people typically do not experience as many stressful events as older persons and that the finding can therefore be explained by the age difference. This criticism, if valid, does not militate against our basic conclusion that stress was implicated in the onset history of one group (late-onset subjects) and not the other (early-onset subjects). Indeed, the differences remained at the time of the latest episode, when the mean age of the early-onset subjects was 30 years and many of the most stressful life events from the scale were prevalent in their lives (e.g., marital separation, job loss, gain of a family member, death of a family member, work changes).

Another possible limitation of the study is our use of the Holmes and Rahe scoring procedures. We adopted these because they are widely used in the literature and have been found to measure stressful events as well as other scales do (Dohrenwend, Krasnoff, Askenasy, and Dohrenwend, 1978; Ross and Mirowdoky, 1979). Although the scale has been criticized (Hudgens, 1974; Holmes and Masuda, 1978; Hough, Fairbanks, and Garcia, 1976; Ruch, 1977), none of the problems noted by these authors obviate its use in assigning crude weights to the events uncovered through our qualitative data-gathering procedures.

We speculate that lowering the cutoff age to 20 years may reveal equally significant genetic and prognostic differences and differences in patients' responsiveness to lithium. For instance, younger bipolar patients may be more responsive to lithium than older ones, if indeed this group characteristically experiences fewer life stresses before the onset of illness. Our research design did not permit us to examine these differences but suggests a more modest conclusion: that late-onset bipolar disorder may have in common with unipolar disorder (major depressive illness) a more important role played by life events (Lloyd, 1980). Early-onset bipolar disorder probands may have more relatives with bipolar illness (Taylor and Abrams, 1973, 1981) and fewer precipitating life events. This seems, however, to contradict the results of a study by Dunner, Patrick, and Fieve (1979), who reported that "positive family history occurred equally often among patients who reported life events and those who did not discuss whether they found differences in history of stress for patients of different ages at onset."

In summary, these results indicate that stressful life events play a more significant etiological role in late-onset than in early-onset bipolar disorder, thus lending further support to the notion that bipolar disorder may be a heterogeneous condition.

REFERENCES

Clayton, P. J. (1981), The epidemiology of bipolar affective disorder. *Compr. Psychiat.*, 22:31–41.

Dohrenwend, B. P. (1974), Problems in defining and sampling the relevant population of stressful life events. In: *Stressful Life Events: Their Nature and Effects*, ed. B. S. Dohrenwend & B. P. Dohrenwend. New York: John Wiley, pp. 275–312.

Dohrenwend, B. S., Krasnoff, L., Askenasy, A. R., & Dohrenwend, B. P. (1978), Exemplifications of a method for scaling life events. *J. Health & Soc. Behav.*, 19:205–299.

Dunner, D. L., Patrick, V., & Fieve, R. R. (1979), Life events at the onset of bipolar affective illness. *Amer. J. Psychiat.*, 136:508–511.

Feighner, J. P., Robins, E., & Guze, B. B. (1972), Diagnostic criteria for use in psychiatric research. *Arch. Gen. Psychiat.*, 26:57–63.

Glasner, B., Haldipur, C. V., & Dessauersmith, J. (1979), Role loss and working-class manic depression. *J. Nerv. & Ment. Dis.*, 167:530–541.

Hays, P. (1976), Etiological factors in manic-depressive psychoses. *Arch. Gen. Psychiat.*, 33:1187–1188.

Holmes, T. H., & Masuda, M. (1974), Life change and illness susceptibility. In: *Stressful Life Events: Their Nature and Effects*, ed. B. S. Dohrenwend & B. P. Dohrenwend. New York: John Wiley, pp. 45–73.

———— Rahe, R. H. (1967), The Social Readjustment Rating Scale. *J. Psychosom. Res.*, 11:213–218.

Hough, R. L., Fairbank, D. T., & Garcia, A. M. (1976), Problems in the ratio measurement of life stress. *J. Health & Soc. Behav.*, 17:76–82.

Hudgens, R. W. (1974), Personal catastrophe and depression. In: *Stressful Life Events: Their Nature and Effects*, ed. B. S. Dohrenwend & B. P. Dohrenwend. New York: John Wiley, pp. 119–134.

James, N. M. (1977), Early- and late-onset bipolar affective disorder. *Arch. Gen. Psychiat.*, 34:715–717.

Lloyd, C. (1980), Life events and depressive disorder reviewed, II. *Arch. Gen. Psychiat.*, 37:544–548.

Loranger, A. Q., & Levine, P. M. (1978), Age of onset of bipolar affective illnes. *Arch. Gen Psychiat.*, 35:1345–1348.

Paykel, E. S. (1974), Life stress and psychiatric disorder: Applications of the clinical approach. In: *Stressful Life Events: Their Nature and Effects*, ed. B. S. Dohrenwend & B. P. Dohrenwend. New York: John Wiley, pp. 135–149.

Ross, C. E., & Mirowdky, J. (1979), A comparison of life-event–weighting schemes: Change, undesirability, and effect-proportional indices. *J. Health & Soc. Behav.*, 20:166–177.

Ruch, L. P. (1977), Multidimensional analysis of the concept of life change. *J. Health & Soc. Behav.*, 18:71–83.

Taylor, M., & Abrams, R. (1973), Manic states: A genetic study of early and late onset affective disorders. *Arch. Gen. Psychiat.*, 28:656–658.

———————— (1981), Early- and late-onset bipolar illness. *Arch. Gen. Psychiat.*, 38:58–61.

Wolpert, E. A. (1980), Major affective disorders. In: *Comprehensive Textbook of Psychiatry*, 3rd ed., ed. A. M. Freedman, H. I. Kaplan, & B. J. Sadock. Baltimore: Williams & Wilkins.

Chapter 28
Life Events Occurring Before and After Onset of Depression in a Kenyan Setting—Any Significance?

D. M. NDETEI, M.D., AND A. VADHER, M.D.

There are two major methodological approaches to the study of life events in relation to the onset of psychiatric illness. The older of these two is the Weighted Life Events Inventories (Rahe and Holmes, 1967; Paykel, Prusoff, and Uhlenhuth, 1971; Paykel, McGuinness, and Gomez, 1976). Weighted Life Events have several shortcomings: they are based on a consensus of hypothetical expected threat by normal individuals who did not nec-

Acknowledgments. This chapter was first published in *Acta Psychiatria Scandinavia* (1981), 64:97–122, and it is reprinted with permission of the copyright holder, Munksgaard.

We would like to thank Profs. G. Brown and Tirril Harris of Bedford College, University of London, for help given; Nanita Contractor of the Institute of Psychiatry, University of London, for help with data analysis; the late Prof. Muhangi for allowing us to study his patients and introducing me (D. M. N.) to the joy of psychiatry and research; and Rodah Mulandi for secretarial assistance. It is with much regret that we announce the untimely death of Prof. Muhangi. His clinical, teaching, and academic excellence were a source of inspiration to his students.

essarily experience the event (Ndetei and Vadher, 1981); they do not take into account interrelation of life events, i.e., life events leading to other life events, and therefore spurious additive weightings may give false high scores (Brown and Harris, 1978). Depressed subjects may overreport events "in search for the meaning" and normal subjects may underreport events and lastly their test-retest (Mendels and Weinstein, 1972) and interrater reliability (Masuda and Holmes, 1967) are doubtful.

The more recent approach to the study of the relationship between life events and the onset of psychiatric illness is that developed by Brown and Harris (1978). It attempts to overcome most of the shortcomings of the Weighted Life Events Inventories by an interview technique which systematically and flexibly probes for the life events, their onset (to within a week), their timing in relation to each other and the onset of the illness, and whether they did not occur as a result of the illness (independent life events). Although the Brown and Harris (1978) method has its shortcomings it is still the most objective and scientifically viable method to date.

Until recently the Brown and Harris method had been tried mainly in Western settings, but a more recent trial in Kenya, a developing country with different cultural norms, produced results strongly similar to those obtained in London (Ndetei and Vadher, 1981; Vadher and Ndetei, 1981) in that life events were important in the causation of depression.

This chapter is an attempt to take the investigation further in order to ascertain whether independent life events not only lead to onset of depression but also whether they continue afterward and the possible effect of this continued occurrence of events. This kind of information is particularly desirable in a developing country where psychiatric services are meager (Ndetei, 1980) and the tendency therefore is to treat those who are already severely psychiatrically disturbed. This information may be useful in identifying potential cases at an early stage, and through health education and other preventive measures help to reduce the heavy burden on the limited resources. Nde-

tei and Vadher (1982b) have described elsewhere the types of
life events associated with depression in a Kenyan setting.

METHODS

Thirty consecutive first-ever referrals to the University Psychiatric Unit at Kenyatta National Hospital and the Mathari Psychiatric Hospital, Nairobi, who presented with depression
severe enough to require chemotherapy and whose depressive
illness was not complicated by physical or any other psychiatric
illness were included in the study group. They were divided
into two groups—15 who needed inpatient care (2 males and
13 females) and 15 (7 males and 8 females) who were receiving
chemotherapy on an outpatient basis. They were all seen by the
same professional team. Informed consent to participate in the
research was obtained from all patients.

The control group was selected by randomly approaching
people in and around Nairobi with the help of a social worker
and a medical student fluent in both English and Swahili (the
national langauge of Kenya) who interpreted. Each person approached was explained the purpose of the exercise and informed consent was obtained. All except one happily consented
and fully cooperated.

The following information was elicited from those in the
community who were approached in order to match the study
group: sex, age, race (only black Kenyans), occupation, level of
education and place or residence. Fifty-eight people were selected this way. They were then interviewed for depression
using a Present State Examination (PSE) (Wing, Cooper, and
Sartorius, 1974) and taking into account the local cultural variation in the presentation of depression (Ndetei and Muhangi,
1979). Eighteen (all females) had at least one symptom of
depression and were excluded from the study. The remaining
40 (28 females and 12 males) who had not suffered from

depression in the preceding 12 months were included in the control group.

The 70 people included in the study were interviewed for social-demographic information using a structured interview. They were then given the Brown and Harris (1978) life events interview which is able to date to within 1 week the onset of a life event, the onset of depression, and the nature of the relationship between the life event and the depression. For those who were depressed the onset of depression was dated to within 1 week. They were then probed for life events occurring in the 12 months preceding the onset of the depression and also for life events occurring between the onset and the interview. The time of onset and duration of the depression was determined according to Brown and Harris (1978). For the non-depressed group the interview for life events covered the 12 months prior to the interview. The whole exercise lasted 2–3 hours with each subject, a substantial part of the time being devoted to establishing a rapport with the subject.

The interviews with the patients were tape-recorded, with the controls extensive notes were made. G. Brown and T. Harris (Bedford College, University of London), on the basis of the information provided and without previous knowledge of the subjects' status as patient or control, made an independent decision as to:

1. The date of onset of each event and that of the depression (in the study group).

2. Whether the events were independent of or dependent on the depression (in the study group).

A t-test was done of the difference between the number of definitely independent life events in the patient group and the control group. Also the rate of events per 3 weeks per 100 patients/controls were calculated at 3-week intervals over a period of 52 weeks before the control and patient groups were interviewed and also before the onset of depression, thus also giving an impression of the duration of the depression.

RESULTS

Table 28.1 shows that independent life events continued to occur after the onset of depression although at half the rate of that before the onset. The same was true, although at a slower rate, for the possibly independent life events. The inpatient group had slightly more, though not significantly, dependent life events. The inpatient group had overall more, although not significantly, life events than the outpatient group. Overall the patient group had significantly more life events than the control group.

Figure 28.1 shows that the depressed group had a consistently higher rate of events than the control group in the 12 months preceding the interviews (curves B and A) but with a sharp rise in the 12 weeks (between the first and fourth 3-week interval) before the interview. However, there is no difference in the rate of events in the control and study groups before the onset of depression in the 27 weeks (the ninth 3-week interval) before the actual onset of depression. There is a further sharp rise in the rate of events in the last 9 weeks, particularly in the weeks before the actual onset of depression curve C, which shows the rate of events in the 12 months preceding the onset

Table 28.1
Independent and Nonindependent Life Events and Their Time Relation with the Onset of Depression

Subject group	Definite independent events		Possible independent events		
	Before	After	Before	After	Independent
Inpatient ($n = 15$)	27	14	9	2	9
Outpatient ($n = 15$)	28	14	6	2	3
Control ($n = 40$)	56	independent events at the time of interview[a]			

[a]There were more events in the study group than in the control group ($p < 0.001$) but the difference is accounted mainly by events occurring before onset of depression in the study group.

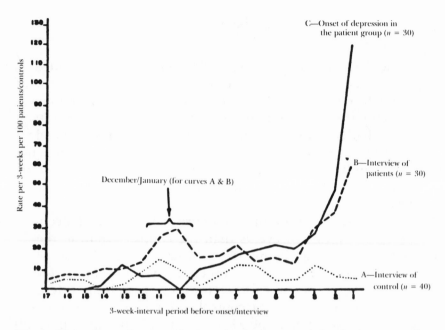

Figure 28.1. Rate of onset of events in 17 three-week intervals, onset of depression, and interview of patients and control.

of depression and not at the time of interview. Therefore, whereas curves A and B have the same time sequence curve C has its own time sequence which started before that of A and B.

Curves B and A show a peak at 30–36 weeks before the interview. As the interviews were done mainly in August this peak occurred in the months of December and January.

DISCUSSION

Although not the primary intention of this report these findings support the growing opinion that life events have an important relationship with psychiatric illness. However, there are important dissimilarities between the findings obtained in this study and those of Brown and Harris (1978), who found that although the depressed group had significantly more life events than the controls in the preceding 12 months this difference was mainly accounted for by more events occurring in the depressed group in the 27 weeks before the interview, whereas in this study the difference was mainly accounted for by a sharp rise in life events in the 12 months preceding referral/interview. Another difference between the two studies is that Brown and Harris found the high rate of events in the depressed group spanned the whole of the 12 months before the onset of depression, whereas in this study the higher rate was found only in the 27 weeks prior to onset, with a sharp rise again in the last 6 weeks.

There is a further observation unique to this study and which can be understood in terms of the local events in Kenya. The curves of both the patient and control groups show peaks in the months of December and January. In these two months important school examinations take place and children start their schooling or change schools. Ndetei and Vadher (1982a) have found that events to do with education are extremely important in the Kenyan lifestyle. A surprising finding in this study, however, is that independent life events continue to occur after the onset of the depression, although at roughly half the rate of that before onset.

Brown and Harris (1978) have advanced the hypothesis of vulnerability to psychiatric illness to explain why some people responded to life events with clinical depression whereas others did not, and some indeed seemed to be protected from the effects of life events. They identified four such vulnerability factors—low intimacy, loss of mother before the age of 11, three or more children before the age of 14, and lack of employment. They had no comment on the significance of independent life events continuing to occur after the onset of the depression. While some of their vulnerability factors have been found to be true in a Kenyan setting (Ndetei and Vadher, 1982a), it would appear that events, whether independent or dependent, occurring after the onset of the depression have the effect of worsening the distress of the depression so that the patient not only seeks help, but also the distress is more obvious to the referring agencies. Whether the patient's depression is considered severe enough for him to require inpatient care is highly dependent on multiple factors, such as the availability of resources, and admission policy, but it is noteworthy that those who required admission had more events, although dependent, than those who did not. These dependent events were not related to the actual process of admission since they were studied before the decision to admit was taken.

If it is likely, as these findings seem to suggest, that events occurring after the onset of depression—whether independent or dependent—are crucial for a psychiatric referral and possible admission, the implication is that crisis centers in the African setting, with psychotherapeutic intervention, are just as desirable, if not more so, as in Western settings. These centers will not only help to prevent the escalation of the distress but will also lighten the burden of the few psychiatrists who are overworked, have limited resources and are dealing mainly with major psychological disturbances. There is need for research from other centers to ascertain the significance of independent and dependent life events occurring after the onset of a psychiatric illness.

CONCLUSION

The frequency of life events occurring before and after the onset of depression in Kenyan patients has been examined. It is argued that although events occurring before the onset of the depression may have an important causal role, those occurring after onset have some significant influence on the illness already present.

REFERENCES

Brown, G. W., & Harris, T. (1978), *Social Origin of Depression. A Study of Psychiatric Disorders in Women.* London: Tavistock.

Holmes, T. H., & Rahe, R. H. (1967), The Social Readjustment Rating Scale. *J. Psychosom. Res.*, 11:213–218.

Masuda, M., & Holmes, T. H. (1967), Magnitude estimations of social readjustments. *J. Psychosom. Res.*, 11:219–225.

Mendels, J., & Weinstein, N. (1972), The schedule of recent experiences: A reliability study. *Psychosom. Med.*, 34:527–531.

Ndetei, D. M. (1980), Psychiatry in Kenya: Yesterday, today, and tomorrow. An overview. *Acta. Psychiat. Scand.*, 62:210–211.

——— Muhangi, J. (1979), The prevalence and clinical presentation of psychiatric illness in a rural setting in Kenya. *Brit. J. Psychiat.*, 135:269–272.

——— Vadher, A. (1981), The relationship between contextual and reported threat due to life events—A controlled study. *Brit. J. Psychiat.*, 139:540–544.

——— ——— (1982a), A study of some psycho-social factors in depressed and non-depressed subjects in Kenyan setting. *Brit. J. Med. Psychol.*, 55:235–239.

——— ——— (1982b), Types of life events associated with depression in Kenyan setting. *Acta Psychiat. Scand.*, 66:208–215.

Paykel, E. S., Prusoff, B. A., Uhlenhuth, E. H. (1971), Scaling of life events. *Arch. Gen. Psychiat.*, 25:340–347.

——— McGuiness, B., & Gomez, J. (1976), An Anglo-American comparison of the scaling of life events. *Brit. J. Med. Psychol.*, 49:237–247.

Vadher, A., & Ndetei, D. M. (1981), Life events and depression in a Kenyan setting. *Brit. J. Psychiat.*, 139:134–137.

Wing, J. K., Cooper, J., & Sartorious, N. (1974), *The Description and Classification of Psychiatric Symptoms: An Instruction Manual for the Present State Examination and the Category System.* London: Cambridge University Press.

Part V
Posttraumatic Stress: The Vietnam Experience

Much has been written on posttraumatic stress disorder, a DSM-III diagnosis. Drs. Silsby and Jones of the United States Marine Corps address the etiologies of posttraumatic stress noting that over the past several years, there has been increased interest in what has sometimes been seen as another victimized group—the Vietnam veterans. Their investigation suggests that the symptoms being diagnosed as posttraumatic stress disorder in many Vietnam veterans are believed not to be the result of severe combat trauma, but unresolved issues the soldiers took to the war coupled with ongoing environmental stress.

Drs. Penk, Robinowitz, Dorsett, and Black along with Mr. Bell examine cultural differences in the lingering effects of combat participation and posttraumatic stress in Vietnam veterans. For male substance abusers seeking treatment, two contradictory hypotheses have been advanced about cultural differences in lingering effects of combat participation upon subsequent personality adjustment: one is a "racial prejudice" hypothesis predicting comparatively more maladjustment among blacks while the second is a "limited opportunity structure" hypothesis predicting more maladjustment among whites. The validity of each notion was compared with the testing of three corollary hypotheses derived from Parsons' interpretation that premilitary racial prejudice interacts differentially with degrees of combat experience, producing greater stress residuals among minorities. Results are discussed by the authors in terms of (1) the etiological contributions given by combat participation to addiction disorders; (2) diagnosis and treatment implications

517

of cultural differences in the experience of stress; and (3) problems in the use of the Minnesota Multiphasic Personality Inventory (MMPI) for studies of ethnic status and personality adjustment.

In the next chapter, Drs. Miller and Feibelman of the Department of Psychiatry, College of Medicine, University of Kentucky and VA Medical Centers, examine a variety of clinical issues in the diagnosis and treatment of posttraumatic stress disorder. Difficulties and complexities in understanding and diagnosing PTSD in veterans presenting symptomatic complaints associated with this disorder are explored. Data collected on 25 Vietnam veterans complaining of PTSD and diagnosed by DSM-III criteria revealed MMPI clinical profiles appropriate for clinical application. Comparative data between combat and noncombat veterans complaining of PTSD and adjustment-related significant life stressors are discussed. Import on clinical strategies with diagnosed patients suggest other behavioral and psychopharmaceutical approaches to treatment are desirable.

With issues and questions emerging related to this controversial diagnosis, Drs. Edward Lynn and Mark Belza examine the potential for factitious posttraumatic stress disorder in Vietnam veterans. The authors present seven cases of factitious PTSD, a classic example of clinical deception found among veterans who were never in combat and, in some cases, were never in Vietnam. Drs. Lynn and Belza discuss the etiologies of the disorder and the underlying psychopathology, which suggests either factitious syndromes, such as Munchausen's, or malingering and conclude with recommendations for diagnosis and treatment. Finally, Dr. Ingram Walker examines chemotherapy as a treatment option with posttraumatic stress disorder.

Chapter 29
The Etiologies of Vietnam Posttraumatic Stress Syndrome

HARRY D. SILSBY, M.C., AND FRANKLIN D. JONES, M.C.

Over the past several years, there has been increased interest in what has sometimes been seen as another victimized group—the Vietnam veterans. Programs have been developed specifically for Vietnam veterans who are suffering delayed psychiatric disorders related to psychological trauma incurred while serving in Vietnam. The extent of such disorders has been estimated by members of the Veterans Administration (Morganthau, Shabad, and Lord) as high as 700,000 men and women, or approximately one fourth of those who served in Vietnam.

A number of authors (Atkinson, Henderson, Sparr, and Deale, 1982; Borus, 1974; Walker, 1981) have reported extensively on what is now being referred to as the posttraumatic stress disorder (PTSD) of the *Diagnostic and Statistical Manual of Mental Disorders*, Third Edition (DSM-III). Figley (1978) described the syndrome among college veterans in 1978, and Horowitz (1974) viewed the disorder as a group of symptoms which result as part of a general response syndrome in anyone exposed to a traumatic event.

Acknowledgment. This chapter was first published in *Military Medicine* (1985), 150:6–7, and it is reprinted with permission.

The DSM-III criteria for the diagnosis of PTSD include the existence of a "recognizable stressor that would evoke significant symptoms of distress in almost everyone," as well as the "reexperiencing of the trauma," and "numbing of responsiveness," along with two of a list of symptoms not present before the trauma.

CASE HISTORY

Sergeant A was a 38-year-old, married Caucasian male with 19 years of active duty, approaching the immediate stress of retirement. His father and mother were divorced when he was three and he was raised by his maternal grandmother until age six. His father remarried and he went to live with him until the age of 16. He described his childhood as "rough" in that his father was a perfectionist and he was unable to satisfy his expectations. His father had been a naval aviator during World War II and had been decorated for valor in the South Pacific. Sergeant A's school record was reportedly average. He left home at age 16 after having a fist fight with his father and lived with friends until he finished school. After completing high school, he joined the Army and had been on active duty ever since. He was married at age 18, divorced after five years, and remarried at age 26. His military history included two tours in the Republic of Vietnam.

History of present illness revealed complaints of irritability, insomnia, suicidal and homicidal ideation, and social isolation. He reported frequent fugue states during which he would find himself in the mountains, torn, scratched, disheveled, and frequently smeared with blood and surrounded by eviscerated animal carcasses. He stated that the onset of these symptoms had been approximately 9 years following his last Vietnam tour, and he felt that they were related to his Vietnam experiences. He went to great lengths to describe himself as a "super soldier." He stated that during both tours in Vietnam he was assigned to secret units with the mission of penetrating enemy lines; assassinating military, political, and occasionally allied leaders. He reported working alone for the most part, becoming known to the Vietnamese and Vietcong as "the assassin." He reported at first killing with a sniper scope, later using only a knife, and stated that he enjoyed killing.

Psychological testing confirmed mild depression, but was essentially within normal limits. Therapy was usually terminated following little improvement. The therapy was focused primarily on here-and-now issues. Reiteration of war stories was not encouraged and they became less frequent. The patient was observed to be well controlled in social settings, but was unable to get a job. Over the course of therapy, it became obvious that he had not been involved in or experienced the combat situations he related. This discrepancy was confirmed by a thorough scrutiny of his personnel records. It became obvious that his retreats to the mountains were also fantasy.

DISCUSSION

Figley (1978) separated Vietnam era veterans into those who experienced "combat" in Vietnam and those who saw military service but were not in the Republic of Vietnam. He refers to these as combatants and noncombatants respectively. The nature of the "combat" experience of those who served in Vietnam varied. It may have ranged from a situation of minimal danger to frequent exposure to death. Jones (1967) reported that the vast majority of soldiers were in support roles and did not kill anyone and were not themselves exposed to danger of death.

Hoiberg (1980) in studying post-Vietnam adjustment of Navy men who enlisted in 1966 (92, 203) and were followed until 1977 for hospitalizations, found that the group not exposed to combat had the highest hospitalization rates for stress-related disorders. Starr (1973), an investigative reporter for Ralph Nader's Center for Study of Responsive Law, found no

significant evidence of increased violence among veterans compared with their nonveteran cohorts.

Atkinson et al. (1982) have also recently reported difficulty
in diagnosing PTSD in Vietnam veterans, and enumerate 12
pitfalls in diagnosis such as lack of corroborative data as to
nature of the combat experience, exaggeration and falsification
of data, and intercurrent civilian stress.

It is our opinion that, although the symptoms we are seeing
in many of the Vietnam veterans are real, the initial stressor
was not an actual traumatic combat experience. We feel that
these individuals did not live up to their own expectations of
what they envisioned of themselves as "combat veterans." They
also were very often individuals who needed to identify with
the hyper-masculine role of the combat veteran for their own
unconscious reasons.

We believe that what the soldier took to the war (in the form
of personality, family, marital, or other problems), coupled with
social neglect and dissatisfaction; compounded with current
ongoing environmental stress to produce the clinical syndrome
we are seeing and often diagnosing as PTSD.

Treatment for these individuals, in our experience, should
be primarily directed toward here-and-now issues, and compensation contingent on symptoms production should be regarded as countertherapeutic. This is not to imply that the
Vietnam veterans' need for support is not legitimate, but rather
that this support should not be predicated on an implication
of mental disability. Such an expectancy becomes a self-fulfilling
prophecy. The support should instead be in the direction of
health: improved educational and job opportunities and public
recognition of the sacrifices and valor of having to fight an
unpopular war. Let us not palliate the symptoms but rather
treat the causes of the post-Vietnam syndrome.

REFERENCES

Atkinson, B., Henderson, J. M., Sparr, B. W., & Deale, R. (1982), Assessment
    of Vietnam veterans for post-traumatic stress disorder in veterans admin-
    istration disability claims. *Amer. J. Psychiat.*, 139:9.

Borus, J. F. (1974), Incidence of maladjustment in Vietnam returnees. *Arch. Gen. Psychiat.*, 30:554–557.

Figley, C. R. (1978), Symptoms of delayed combat stress among a college sample of Vietnam veterans. *Mil. Med.*, 143.

Hassener, P. W., & McCary, R. W. A. (1974), A comparative study of attitudes of veterans and non-veterans at the University of Northern Colorado. *Colorado J. Ed. Res.*, 14:11–18.

Hoiberg, A. (1980), Military effectiveness of navy men during and after Vietnam. *Armed Forces & Society*, 6/2:232–246.

Horowitz, M. J. (1974), Stress response syndromes. *Arch. Gen. Psychiat.*, 31:768–781.

Jones, F. D. (1967), Experiences of a division psychiatrist in Vietnam. *Mil. Med.*, 132/12:1003–1008.

Morganthau, T., Shabad, S., & Lord, M. (1981), The troubled Vietnam vet. *Newsweek*, March 30:24–29.

Starr, R. (1973), *The Discarded Army: Veterans After Vietnam*. New York: Charterhouse.

Walker, J. I. (1981), Vietnam combat veterans with legal difficulties: A psychiatric problem? *Amer. J. Psychiat.*, 138:1384–1385.

Chapter 30
Posttraumatic Stress Disorder: Psychometric Assessment and Race

WALTER PENK, Ph.D., RALPH ROBINOWITZ, Ph.D., DOVALEE DORSETT, Ph.D., WILLIAM BELL, M.S., AND JOHN BLACK, Ph.D.

Do ethnic groups differ in adjustment following their exposure to, and participation in, life-threatening experiences? Aspects of this question bearing on cultural differences in coping with stress were investigated by comparing measures of current adjustment of Vietnam combat veterans seeking treatment for substance abuse.

There are two seemingly contradictory thoughts when the

Acknowledgments. This chapter was first presented at the American Psychological Association Convention, Los Angeles, August 1985.

Funds for this research were furnished from the General Medical Research Service of the Veterans Administration.

The authors wish to express their deep appreciation to the many friends and colleagues who assisted at various times in a variety of capacities and functions: Frank Harris, a volunteer at the VAMC, Dallas; Howard Shattner, formerly employed in the Research Service of the VAMC, Dallas, now of the Dallas County Child Abuse Section, and John Skinner, UTHSC, Dallas; and Harriett Warren and James Ferguson of the VA Data Processing Center, Austin, Texas, whose help and consultation in data reduction and data processing was and continues to be invaluable. Appreciation is also extended to Penny Perkins for her patience and expertise in preparing this manuscript.

525

issue is tested in the form of the question, "Among substance abusers, do black Vietnam combat veterans differ from white Vietnam combat veterans on measures of personality adjustment such as the Minnesota Multiphasic Personality Inventory (MMPI)?" Each of these two hypotheses has important implications for theories of understanding stress and its interactions with culture which in turn then relate to differences in structuring treatment programming for stress disorders.

HYPOTHESIS ONE:
ENDURING EFFECTS OF RACIAL PREJUDICE PRODUCES GREATER MALADJUSTMENT AMONG BLACK COMBAT VETERANS

First, there is a "racial prejudice" hypothesis (e.g., Parsons, 1985; Adebimpe, Gigandet, and Harris, 1979; Egendorf, 1983). According to this notion, blacks are said to be more maladjusted than whites because blacks endured more racial prejudice. A variation of this hypothesis is the assertion that psychological tests in and of themselves contain biases in norms and inappropriate items which exaggerate psychopathology among samples of blacks.

Generalizing from blacks-in-general to black Vietnam combat veterans in particular, Parsons (1985) has hypothesized that blacks evidence greater stress disturbances than their white Vietnam combat veteran counterparts. Racial prejudice was seen as interfering with integrity of psychological identity among blacks which in turn rendered many blacks without the emotional and social resources with which to cope with the onslaughts of life-threatening events and anxieties. Merely being in the theater of war was sufficient to produce stronger stress residuals for blacks than for whites, according to Parsons' hypothesis: the more intense was the combat, the more severe are combat-related posttraumatic stress disorder (PTSD) symptoms among blacks. Parsons, in fact, estimates that as many as 70 percent of blacks, contrasted with only 20 percent of whites, will meet criteria for PTSD among Vietnam combat veterans.

Moreover, PTSD symptoms are likely to be of greater intensity and persist longer for blacks than for whites (1) because blacks experienced greater stress from racial prejudice before they went to war; (2) because blacks experienced greater conflict in fighting war against Asian minorities with whom they identified more than did whites; and (3) because black veterans experienced more prejudice once they returned to civilian life (Figley and Leventman, 1978).

Indirect empirical support for these speculations can be found in several large-scale, epidemiological studies of non-treatment-seeking populations (cf. Kadushin, Boulanger, and Martin, 1981; Card, 1983). Ethnic differences, however, have rarely been studied as an independent factor among treatment-seeking samples; race usually is accorded status only as a co-variate or nuisance variable (e.g., Nace, O'Brien, Mintz, Ream, and Meyers, 1978). The clearest support for the racial prejudice hypothesis can be found in the seminal work by Laufer and his associates (based upon stratified samples of nontreatment-seeking combat veterans in the nationwide study, *Legacies of Vietnam*). Participation in abusive war violence was associated with higher rates of self-reported post-combat psychiatric symptoms among blacks than among whites equivalent in combat intensity (Laufer, Gallops, and Frey-Wouters, 1984). Although the findings did not specify causes of greater psychopathology among blacks reporting abusive Vietnam war violence, nevertheless the results are consonant with predictions that blacks would evidence higher degrees of maladjustment.

HYPOTHESIS TWO:
LIMITED ECONOMIC AND SOCIAL OPPORTUNITIES LEADS TO A HIGHER NUMBER OF BETTER ADJUSTED BLACKS PARTICIPATING IN DEVIANT BEHAVIORS SUCH AS DRUG ABUSE

Another line of speculation (Lukoff, 1980) about ethnic differences in adjustment among substance abusers leads to an opposite prediction—namely, that blacks are better adjusted than whites. This alternate hypothesis may be restricted to substance abusers, where evidence accumulating over the last decade has indicated that black substance abusers in general are comparatively better adjusted than white substance abusers in general (Penk and Robinowitz, 1974; Penk, Woodward, Robinowitz, and Hess, 1978; Penk, Robinowitz, Roberts, Dolan, and Atkins, 1981; Penk, Roberts, Robinowitz, Dolan, Atkins, and Woodward, 1982; Patterson, Charles, Woodward, Roberts, and Penk, 1981). There is sufficient evidence to conclude that similar differences would not be found when comparing psychiatric samples or normals, where there are trends in contrasted-group differences studies showing that on some occasions blacks will report more psychopathology than will whites [cf. Dahlstrom and Gynther (1986) for a comprehensive review of this literature].

This second line of speculation, also based upon notions about long-term effects of racial prejudice, has been formulated from theories describing American society as a caste-like system in which certain minority group members are limited in their opportunities to economically and socially prosper outside their class structure [cf. the "limited opportunity" hypothesis of Merton (1957); Cloward and Ohlin (1960)]. Such hypotheses predict better adjustment among black drug abusers for the following reasons.

It is hypothesized that the American society has operated differentially so as to block (or at least impede) the actualization of aspirations among minority group members such as blacks: Blacks, as minority group members, are said to have less accessibility to legitimate jobs, which usually are first taken by majority members of the culture (i.e., whites). Because more blacks are blocked from legitimate opportunities, more blacks—including a greater proportion of better adjusted blacks—are said to be more likely to participate in such deviant behaviors as substance abuse. Since a disproportionate number of blacks are susceptible to deviant behaviors, by reason of lowered economic and social opportunities, then a higher number of better adjusted blacks are predicted to be involved in drug misuse. There being a higher incidence of better adjusted black substance abusers, it is also likely that a higher proportion of better adjusted blacks then seek treatment. This "limited opportunity structure" hypothesis, recently reformulated by Lukoff (1980), predicts a result for black-white personality adjustment differences that is opposite to that hypothesized by Parsons (1985) for combat veterans—at least among substance abusers seeking treatment: Since disproportionately more black substance abusers who are better adjusted will seek treatment, then it also follows that blacks will be better adjusted than whites when Vietnam veterans are compared. There is some empirical support for this line of speculation in findings where black substance abusers are better adjusted than white substance abusers whereas sometimes black psychiatric patients are found to be less well adjusted than white psychiatric patients (Gynther, 1979; Dahlstrom and Gynther, 1986).

Unfortunately, neither hypothesis has been empirically compared, despite the fact that policy decisions about treatment programming are made as if either one or the other line of speculation had some validity. For example, there is a groundswell of opinion, more clinically sensed than empirically supported, urging that different kinds of treatment be developed for blacks. Korman (1974) has questioned whether middle class criteria for mental health can be ethically extended to evaluating needs of ethnic clients. The assumption that different minority groups in a pluralistic society have different symptom-complexes varying in intensity and frequency of psychopathological indicators is gaining some currency in talks about making treatment culture specific. Such calls for individualizing psychotherapy are appearing under the rubric of "transcultural" therapy or transracially oriented therapy in which it is said that a therapist or a treatment program cannot cross over into the experiential realm or domain of a client who is racially foreign to the therapist's cultural background (cf. Acosta, Yamamoto, and Evans, 1982).

Instead of speculating about causes of black-white adjustment differences, the purposes of this study were more narrow—that is, "Can it be demonstrated that such differences exist in the first place?" Rather than assume that a minority client is less well adjusted simply because that client has sought treatment, the purposes of this study were to compare the relative merits of the two hypotheses by testing the basic question, "Are minority group members, black Vietnam combat veterans seeking treatment for substance abuse, really less well adjusted than their white counterparts?" Which hypothesis is more readily supported? Are black substance abusers more disturbed than whites, as Parsons has argued and Laufer and his associates have demonstrated among nontreatment-seeking samples? Or, are black substance abusers really less disturbed than whites, as Lukoff has reasoned and as Penk and his associates have found?

These questions were addressed by examining three hypotheses drawn from Parsons' paper (1985). First, we tested the general notion that black Vietnam combat veterans were more disturbed than white Vietnam combat veterans. Second, we tested the corollary of this general hypothesis, the notion that just being in the theater of war was enough to stress blacks more than whites: this second hypothesis was tested by comparing adjustment levels of blacks and whites who experienced lesser degrees of combat (i.e., light combat). Third, we tested the hypothesis that as the degree of combat intensity and frequency increased so the degree of postmilitary maladjustment is higher among blacks: this third hypothesis was tested by comparing only those blacks and whites who reported high levels of combat exposure. Variations of differential ethnic reactivity to combat stress were analyzed in subsequent analysis by comparing black and white noncombat veterans seeking treatment for substance abuse and by comparing black light with black heavy combat veterans and white light with white heavy combat veterans.

METHOD

SUBJECTS

Subjects were 618 Vietnam era male veterans seeking treatment for substance abuse. Subjects were tested on a consecutive-admissions basis: 2 percent attrition rates in testing occurred but rates did not differ by race. Assessment took place at a Drug Dependence Treatment Program (DDTP) and an Alcohol Dependence Treatment Program (ADTP) in a Veterans Administration (VA) Medical Center located in a large, Southwestern metropolitan complex: subjects were evaluated for personality adjustment within a week after entering treatment.

Six contrasted-group comparisons were made to test the three hypotheses drawn from Parsons' (1985) predictions that black combat veterans are more disturbed than white combat veterans: the data pool of 618 subjects was divided into subgroups according to questions targeted for study. First, 125 black Vietnam era *non*combat veterans were compared with 235 white Vietnam era *non*combat veterans (i.e., these noncombat subjects served in the military at the same time, as did the combat veterans of this study of the Vietnam era, 1964–1975). The purpose of first comparing noncombat Vietnam era veterans was to determine whether the expected pattern in which World War II and Korean War blacks had scored as better adjusted than did whites would hold for Vietnam veterans as well (Penk and Robinowitz, 1974).

Next, to test Parsons' general hypothesis about Vietnam combat veterans, 80 black and 171 white Vietnam *combat* veterans were compared on MMPI scores. Subjects were then divided into subgroups for within-combat group comparisons. The third contrasted-group comparison tested the hyothesis that merely being in the theater of war stressed blacks more than whites: only those veterans who reported "light" combat participation were compared—43 blacks and 89 whites. Thirty-seven blacks and 82 whites were compared in the fourth subgrouping, "heavy" combat, testing Parsons' third hypothesis which predicts that, as combat exposure increases, so stress increases, and blacks are differentially more disturbed than are whites. Supplementary analyses were performed in the fifth and sixth comparisons to pursue this point about differential susceptibility to stress as a function of ethnicity: black light were compared with black heavy combat veterans and white light were compared with white heavy combat veterans.

INSTRUMENTS

Comprehensive assessment was needed to insure that any observed adjustment differences were not attributable to dispositional or situational features irrelevant to ethnicity. This point is especially relevant for Minnesota Multiphasic Personality Inventory (MMPI) measures, which are readily sensitive to extraneous variations in sample characteristics (cf. Dahlstrom, Welsh, and Dahlstrom, 1975).

There are at least four major classes of sample bias which must be evaluated in a study of this nature. (1) Group differences in premilitary adjustment: subjects comprising any two samples under comparison might have been differentially disturbed before combat exposure. We addressed the question of differential premilitary adjustment by comparing retrospective ratings of family social climates, using the Family Environment Scales (FES) (Moos, Insel, and Humphries, 1974). Black combat veterans rated their childhood family adjustment as less disturbed than did white combat veterans (see Table 30.1), but analysis of covariance procedures did not reveal any significant effects by past FES scores on MMPI measures.

(2) Subject background factors possibly could interact dif-

ferentially by race and by combat. Some MMPI scale elevations are responsive to age, education, and socioeconomic differences. As shown in Table 30.1, samples were homogeneous in demographic characteristics, except in the case of education where comparisons containing white-light combat exposure demonstrated some differences. But again, covarying education did not change MMPI black-white comparisons.

(3) Groups might have differed in combat experience. We examined the groups for variations in combat intensity and frequency, using the Combat Experience Scale from the work of Figley and Stretch (1980) entitled the Vietnam Veteran Questionnaire. This scale consists of eleven items each rated on a five-point rating scale (e.g., How often did you fire your weapon at the enemy? 1. Never, 2. Rarely, 3. Occasionally, 4. Often, or 5. Very Often). These ratings were used in two ways: first, to insure that relevant groups did not differ in degree of combat participation, and, second, when the experimental design so dictated, to select groups on the basis of degree of combat participation. Subgroupings were made for this latter purpose to test Parsons' second and third hypotheses which require that samples be grouped on the basis of degree of combat experience—whether "heavy" or "light." "Heavy" combat participation was operationally defined as scoring 35 points or higher on the eleven-item, five-point rating scaled Combat Experience Scale; and "light" combat participation consisted of subjects scoring 34 points or less. Race groups did not differ in combat exposure when Combat Experience Scale scores were not controlled. Of course, the very definition of the "heavy" and "light" combat groups using 35 as a cutting score for group assignment resulted in significant group differences (in comparison 5 and 6 of Table 30.1).

(4) Samples might have differed in self-reported drug use, thereby confounding results on the dependent measures (i.e., MMPI scores). To check out this possible bias, samples were compared on the Chemical Use Questionnaire (Penk et al., 1981) where ratings of drug use are made on seven-point scales for each of 34 licit and illicit drugs. Again, samples were found

Table 30.1
Demographic, Chemical Use Patterns, and Family Environment of Black-White
Vietnam Veterans Seeking Treatment for Substance Abuse[a]

Measures		Vietnam Era (noncombat) Black (n=131)	White (n=242)	Combat Black (n=32)	White (n=175)	Light Combat Black (n=44)	White (n=90)	Heavy Combat Black (n=38)	White (n=85)	Blacks Heavy (n=38)	Light (n=44)	Whites Heavy (n=85)	Light (n=90)
Demographics													
Age	M	29.91	30.37	33.74	33.94	34.41	34.39	32.97	33.47	32.97	34.41	33.47	34.39
	SD	5.13	5.84	5.20	5.81	5.90	6.63	4.19	4.79	4.19	5.90	4.79	6.63
SES	M	4.08	3.63*	4.00	3.76	3.95	3.90	4.07	3.63	4.07	3.95	3.63	3.90
	SD	1.37	1.31	1.57	1.12	1.81	1.01	1.20	1.20	1.20	1.81	1.20	1.01
Education	M	12.69	11.76***	12.69	12.01*	12.76	11.63**	12.61	12.40	12.61	12.76*	12.40	11.63
	SD	1.49	2.48	1.71	2.23	1.33	2.15	2.12	2.26	2.12	1.33	2.26	2.15
Combat Scale	M	XXXX	XXXX	33.25	33.68	24.96	24.56	43.08	43.22***	43.08	24.16***	43.22***	24.56
	SD	XXXX	XXXX	10.96	11.20	6.13	6.59	6.20	5.70	6.20	6.13	5.70	6.59
Chemical Use Questionnaire													
Marijuana	M	3.77	4.12	4.58	4.12	4.71	4.12	4.41	4.13	4.41	4.71	4.13	4.12
	SD	2.37	2.46	2.69	2.31	2.63	2.16	2.82	2.47	2.82	2.63	2.47	2.16
Hard Liquor	M	3.77	4.18	4.36	4.32	4.73	4.56	3.86	4.06	3.86	4.73	4.06	4.56
	SD	2.48	2.30	2.51	2.36	2.41	2.37	2.60	3.34	2.60	2.41	2.34	2.37
Beer	M	3.35	3.56	3.75	3.72	3.97	3.72	3.47	3.72	3.47	3.97	3.72	3.72
	SD	2.31	2.60	2.51	2.70	2.39	2.66	2.67	2.76	2.67	2.39	2.76	2.66

Barbiturates	M	5.07	5.16	5.08	5.43	4.80	5.01	4.80	5.43	5.08	5.01	5.14
	SD	2.52	2.61	2.36	2.55	2.68	2.33	2.68	2.55	2.36	2.33	2.41
Amphetamines	M	4.52	4.78	5.16*	4.61	4.10	5.42	4.10	4.61	5.16*	5.42	4.93*
	SD	2.61	2.31	2.50	2.80	2.55	2.42	2.55	2.80	2.50	2.42	2.55
LSD	M	5.77	5.79	5.72	5.72	5.45	6.04	5.45	5.72	5.72	6.04	5.41
	SD	2.28	2.25	2.28	2.43	2.63	2.16	2.63	2.43	2.28	2.16	2.36
Opiates	M	4.97	4.75	4.86	4.41	4.96	4.76	4.96	4.41	4.86	4.76	4.96
	SD	2.64	2.63	2.62	2.85	2.53	2.56	2.53	2.85	2.62	2.56	2.69
Cocaine	M	3.89	4.45*	4.43	4.68	4.48	4.33	4.48	4.68	4.43	4.33	4.53
	SD	2.38	2.33	2.28	2.58	2.63	2.26	2.63	2.58	2.28	2.26	2.32

Family Environment Scales (Past)

Cohesion	M	51.69	43.90*	50.65	46.23	50.52	50.76	45.89	50.76	50.52	45.89	46.49
	SD	10.55	14.35	12.40	15.86	10.76	13.86	16.33	13.86	10.76	16.33	15.60
Expression	M	41.91	37.91*	41.04	39.28	41.76	40.41	37.44	40.41	41.76	37.44	40.70
	SD	10.69	13.56	9.70	13.85	9.92	9.63	12.65	9.63	9.92	12.65	14.63
Conflict	M	45.66	49.33	44.93	48.47	44.12	45.62	47.84	45.62	44.12	47.84	48.95
	SD	10.78	13.66	10.88	13.47	10.28	11.50	13.99	11.50	10.28	13.99	13.13
Independence	M	45.56	49.33*	44.50	43.21	46.56	42.72	44.93	42.72	46.56	44.93	41.89
	SD	10.78	13.66	13.45	16.21	12.70	14.05	14.41	14.05	12.70	14.41	17.45
Achieve Solution	M	57.94	55.71	57.67	56.26	58.48	56.97	56.74	56.97	58.48	56.74	55.89
	SD	8.43	11.38	7.85	11.05	8.47	7.36	11.32	7.36	8.47	11.32	10.90
Intellectual Cultural	M	45.28	36.29***	44.83	35.41***	43.80	45.72	36.28***	45.72	43.80	36.28	34.74**
	SD	10.62	11.53	10.99	11.76	11.32	10.80	11.14	10.80	11.32	11.14	12.24

Table 30.1 (Continued)

Measures		Vietnam Era (noncombat) Black ($n=131$)	White ($n=242$)	Combat Black ($n=32$)	White ($n=175$)	Light Combat Black ($n=44$)	White ($n=90$)	Heavy Combat Black ($n=38$)	White ($n=85$)	Blacks Heavy ($n=38$)	Light ($n=44$)	White Heavy ($n=85$)	Light ($n=90$)
Active Recreational	M	44.19	39.05***	45.00	38.17	43.72	37.77	46.10	38.68*	46.10	43.72	38.68	37.77
	SD	10.65	14.28	13.29	15.89	13.78	16.12	12.99	15.70	12.99	13.78	15.70	16.12
Moral Religious	M	62.38	56.54***	61.63	56.49	62.68***	56.95*	60.72	55.89*	60.72	62.68	55.89	56.95
	SD	7.37	10.65	8.09	10.08	6.59	9.51	9.21	10.84	9.21	6.59	10.84	9.51
Organization	M	59.15	54.17***	58.19	54.44	58.92*	53.77*	57.55	55.32	57.55	58.92	55.32	53.77
	SD	8.33	11.34	7.67	11.79	7.22	11.53	8.11	12.15	8.11	7.22	12.15	11.53
Control	M	57.99	58.69	56.87	58.17	57.28	57.31	56.52	59.28	56.52	57.28	59.28	57.31
	SD	8.99	11.21	10.31	10.82	11.64	11.61	9.21	9.68	9.21	11.64	9.68	11.61

a Heavy and light combat grouping is determined by a cutoff score derived from the Figley Vietnam Veterans Survey (1979) Combat experience section: self-report questionnaire.

*$p<.05$
**$p<.01$
***$p<.001$

to be comparatively homogeneous, as mean ratings for major classes of drugs show in Table 30.1.

MMPI scores served as dependent variables for assessing Parsons' hypothesis. Selection of MMPI scores is justified for the following reasons. Parsons has hypothesized that blacks will be more disturbed than whites for adjustment in general as well as for PTSD symptoms in particular: for this report, we tested the more general formulation of Parsons' racial-prejudice hypothesis with the more general measure of adjustment, the MMPI. Even though combat veterans and PTSD symptoms were not included in the original construction and validation of the MMPI, nevertheless, the MMPI has empirically yielded useful Vietnam combat-noncombat differences among psychiatric samples (Fairbank, Malloy, and Keane, 1983; Foy, Sipprelle, Rueger, and Carroll, 1984; Fairbank, Malloy, and Keane, 1983) and among substance abusers (Penk et al., 1981).

Parenthetically, it should be noted that the current study concerns the first DSM-III criterion for diagnosing combat-related posttraumatic stress disorders (PTSD); namely, "Existence of a recognizable stressor that would evoke significant symptoms of distress in almost everyone." We confined the focus of this research to defining groups based upon Vietnam combat exposure, rather than comparing groups defined by the more ambiguous cluster of subjective PTSD symptoms. We proceeded on this basis because we felt findings would be more compelling if the criterion for group definition was more specific. This precaution did not prove necessary, for, as it turns out, results were comparable when additional analyses were performed with samples defined by the full range of PTSD diagnostic criteria (this latter analysis is not reported here).

STATISTICAL ANALYSIS

Data were analyzed in the form of a criterion group distinction pre-experimental design (Campbell and Stanley, 1963) where clinical and validity scales of the MMPI were dependent variables and Race and Combat (or Noncombat) conditions, separately considered, were independent variables. Analyses of variance were performed for the following criterion group distinctions: black vs. white noncombat Vietnam era veterans, to check Lukoff's hypothesis as extended from World War II and Korean veteran substance abusers (Penk and Robinowitz, 1974) to Vietnam veteran substance abusers; then black Vietnam combat veterans were compared with white Vietnam combat veterans (Parsons' first hypothesis), followed by a comparison of black and white light Vietnam combat veterans (Parsons' second hypothesis) and black with white heavy Vietnam combat veterans (Parsons' third hypothesis); finally, to place the above findings into the perspective of between-combat degree, within-race comparisons, two supplementary analyses were performed comparing black light with black heavy combat veterans and white light with white heavy combat veterans.

RESULTS

Before testing Parsons' three hypotheses, representativeness of the current sampling was checked among Vietnam era (non-combat) veterans to see if blacks turned out to be better adjusted than whites, as had been found earlier among Wold War II and Korean War veterans seeking treatment for substance abuse (Penk and Robinowitz, 1974). As shown in Table 30.2 below, black Vietnam era *non*combat veterans reported appreciably less disturbance on the MMPI than did white Vietnam era *non*combat veterans. Blacks score significantly lower on scales *2* (Depression), *3* (Hysteria), *4* (Psychopathic deviate), *5* (Masculinity-femininity), *7* (Psychasthenia), and *0* (Social introversion), and significantly higher on scales *L* and *9* (Hypomania). Such results replicate earlier findings (e.g., Penk and Robinowitz, 1974; Penk et al., 1978; Penk et al., 1981; Patterson et al., 1981) and lend support to Lukoff's notions that black substance abusers seeking treatment are better adjusted than white substance abusers. Trends in black-white differences for World

War II and Korean War veteran substance abusers (Penk and Robinowitz, 1974) hold for Vietnam era veterans as well with the exception that black Vietnam veterans scored higher on scale 9 (Hypomania), a finding which may be attributable to the comparatively younger age of the Vietnam era sample.

PARSONS' HYPOTHESIS ONE:
BLACK VIETNAM COMBAT VETERANS
ARE MORE DISTURBED THAN WHITE
VIETNAM COMBAT VETERANS

Results do not decisively support Parsons' first hypothesis. Although black Vietnam veterans score significantly higher on scales 6 (Paranoia) and 9 (Hypomania), white Vietnam veterans score higher on scale 2 (Depression). Groups do not differ on scales 1 (Hypochondriasis), 3 (Hysteria), 4 (Psychopathic deviate), 5 (Masculinity-femininity), 7 (Psychasthenia), 8 (Schizophrenia), or 0 (Social introversion). Nor did groups differ on the validity scales L (Lie), F (Infrequency), or K (Defensiveness), obviating the need for controlling validity scales in the analysis. The results confirm expectations that substance abusers are maladjusted. And, the findings indicate that maladjustment is differentially expressed along ethnic lines—blacks reporting greater estrangement and distantiation from others (higher Paranoia) and more restlessness and irritation (higher Mania) contrasted with whites who register a more pessimistic outlook on life (higher Depression). It is noteworthy that in the combat comparison, blacks differed from whites by less than five T-score points, less than in other studies about ethnic differences (Gynther, 1979; Gynther and Green, 1980). Moreover, in psychiatric and normal sample comparisons, traditionally blacks have scored higher on Depression and whites have scored higher on Paranoia. The results coincide with most previous research, however, by finding that blacks score significantly

Table 30.2

MMPI Scale Scores of Black–White Vietnam Veterans Seeking Treatment for Substance Abuse

MMPI Scales		Noncombat		Combat		Light Combat		Heavy Combat		Blacks		Whites	
		Black (n = 125)	White (n = 235)	Black (n = 80)	White (n = 171)	Black (n = 43)	White (n = 89)	Black (n = 37)	White (n = 82)	Heavy (n = 37)	Light (n = 43)	Heavy (n = 82)	Light (n = 89)
L	M	49.32	47.40*	48.36	46.99	47.93	46.82	48.86	47.18	48.86	47.93	47.18	46.82
	SD	8.99	6.90	8.17	7.19	7.79	6.62	8.68	7.81	8.68	7.79	7.81	6.62
F	M	70.56	69.85	75.69	71.98	69.86	69.49	82.46	74.68*	82.46	69.86**	74.68	69.49*
	SD	18.81	16.75	18.99	16.46	16.77	14.08	19.39	18.42	19.39	16.77	18.42	14.08
K	M	48.34	48.33	47.18	46.68	47.95	47.06	46.27	46.28	46.27	47.95	46.28	47.06
	SD	8.90	8.96	7.85	8.47	7.03	7.73	8.72	9.24	8.72	7.03	9.24	7.23
1	M	67.03	66.87	71.75	68.68	65.95	66.84	78.51	70.67*	78.51	65.95**	70.67	66.84
	SD	16.93	15.64	19.16	17.21	17.84	17.88	18.64	16.33	18.64	17.84	16.33	17.88
2	M	71.25	76.58**	72.94	76.84*	67.05	77.92***	79.78	75.66	79.78	67.05***	75.66	77.92
	SD	15.80	15.36	17.62	16.59	14.94	15.87	18.20	17.36	18.20	14.94	17.36	15.87
3	M	65.21	67.55	66.13	66.66	61.81	66.28*	71.14	67.07**	71.13	61.81	67.07	66.28
	SD	12.65	10.99	13.85	11.76	12.58	11.71	13.73	11.88	13.73	12.58	11.88	11.71

		1	2	3	4	5	6	7	8	9	10	11	12
4	M	75.72	79.37*	76.94	77.94	73.44	78.67*	81.00	77.13	81.00	73.44*	77.13	78.67*
	SD	13.79	11.96	12.74	12.3	12.16	11.33	12.34	13.29	12.34	12.16	13.29	11.33
5	M	60.16	62.85*	60.59	60.70	59.40	60.91	61.97	60.48	61.97	59.40	60.48	60.91
	SD	10.64	10.87	10.52	9.28	9.40	9.66	11.66	8.90	11.66	9.40	8.90	9.66
6	M	65.81	66.66	71.53	66.95*	66.26	64.51	77.65	69.60*	77.65	66.26**	69.60	64.51*
	SD	16.59	13.13	17.43	13.75	15.50	12.33	17.73	14.76	17.73	15.50	14.76	12.33
7	M	70.62	74.79*	74.09	74.63	68.65	74.16*	80.41	75.15	80.41	68.65***	75.15	74.16
	SD	15.86	14.54	16.82	15.48	16.23	15.28	15.41	15.78	15.41	16.23	15.78	15.28
8	M	75.51	76.64	31.56	77.73	73.12	74.24	91.38	81.51*	91.38	73.12***	81.51	74.24*
	SD	23.05	20.59	25.99	21.91	23.85	20.37	25.21	23.00	25.21	23.85	23.00	20.37
9	M	72.63	70.14	74.25	70.89*	72.56	68.57*	76.22	73.41	76.22	72.56	73.41	68.57*
	SD	13.94	11.84	10.85	12.82	9.75	12.08	11.82	13.12	11.82	9.75	13.20	12.08
0	M	53.88	57.28**	57.25	58.26	55.12	58.93*	59.73	57.54	59.73	55.12*	57.54	58.93
	SD	9.01	10.84	9.81	11.27	9.40	11.29	9.82	11.28	9.82	9.40	11.28	11.29

*p < .05
**p < .01
***p < .001

higher on scale *9* than do whites (agreeing with 28 of the 52 black-white studies in the literature).

In sum, there is but little question that black-white substance abuser MMPI profiles differ as a function of whether or not the person was exposed to combat.

PARSONS' HYPOTHESIS TWO: BLACK LIGHT COMBAT VIETNAM VETERANS ARE MORE DISTURBED THAN WHITE LIGHT COMBAT VIETNAM VETERANS

"Merely being in the theatre of war was sufficient to produce stress-related problems in Black veterans" (Parsons, 1985, p. 12).

This hypothesis was tested by comparing only those substance abusers who experienced light degrees of combat. The second hypothesis also not confirmed. In fact, results fall into the opposite direction. Blacks score *lower* on scales *2* (Depression), *3* (Hysteria), *4* (Psychopathic deviate), *7* (Psychasthenia), and *0* (Social introversion) replicating previous findings (Penk and Robinowitz, 1974) and coinciding with Lukoff's (1980) predictions (see Table 30.2, comparing black light with white light combat veterans). Only on scale *9* do blacks score higher: this is a consistent finding across 52 black-white comparison studies (Gynther and Green, 1980) and certainly recommends itself by its ubiquity as a finding meriting a comprehensive search for behavioral correlates.

The results do not support Parsons' hypothesis that mild combat stress is more overwhelming for blacks than for whites (Egendorf, 1983). However, considering that black and white combat group MMPI profiles were similar, whereas black and white light combat MMPI profiles are dissimilar, now leads one to expect that something quite different will be found among heavy combat experienced veterans.

PARSONS' HYPOTHESIS THREE:
BLACK HEAVY COMBAT VIETNAM VETERANS
ARE MORE DISTURBED THAN WHITE
HEAVY COMBAT VIETNAM VETERANS

". . . . being in heavy combat was the most crucial factor in severe forms of post-trauma stress reactions and symptoms . . ." (Parsons, 1985, p. 12).

Parsons' (1985) hypothesis is supported. Black heavy combat veterans score significantly higher on scales F (Infrequency), 1 (Hypochondriasis), 6 (Paranoia), and 8 (Schizophrenia), and score near-significance higher on scale 7 (Psychasthenia). These findings are opposite to results for noncombat and light combat group comparisons. The findings are atypical (in the opposite direction) of all black-white substance abuser comparison studies published to date (Hill, Haertzen, and Glasser, 1960; Sutker, Archer, and Allain, 1978; Patalano, 1978; Sutker, Brantley, and Allain, 1980). The findings do not coincide with results previously found in this treatment setting (Penk and Robinowitz, 1974; Penk et al., 1978; Penk et al., 1981a, b; Patterson et al., 1981). The findings from heavy combat veterans seeking treatment do not support Lukoff's expectation that blacks are better adjusted than whites.

The finding indicates that theorizing about ethnicity and combat stress is far more complicated than what originally might have been expected—at least among clinical samples of substance abusers. The findings underscore the importance of identifying the contributions of antecedent conditions (such as trauma) to psychopathology before drawing rigidly fixed conclusions about ethnic comparison studies.

Black differences as a function of combat experiences are clearly delineated when effects of combat are compared within each race separately considered (see MMPI differences of black heavy combat versus black light combat veterans, compared with white heavy combat versus white light combat veterans, comparisons 5 and 6 in Table 30.2). Moderately significant differences are found in the white light and heavy comparisons, the white heavy Vietnam combat veteran scoring significantly higher on scales F (Infrequency), 6 (Parnaoia), 8 (Schizophrenia), and 9 (Hypomania). This comparison certainly substantiates what other investigators have found among psychiatric samples (e.g., Foy et al., 1984; Keane et al., 1985) where relative percentages of racial composition in the samples were not specified), namely that combat exposure is associated with greater psychopathology. However, white light-heavy combat comparisons yield far less magnitude of differences than that observed in the black light-heavy comparisons, where black heavy combat veterans score significantly higher on eight of ten clinical scales. These within race comparisons (systematically varying degree of combat) highlight the validity of Parsons' predictions that whereas white combat veterans are expected to evidence some maladjustment, black combat veterans are predicted to demonstrate even higher degrees of disturbance.

SUPPLEMENTARY ANALYSIS

The authors are well aware that the data might also have been analyzed in a race (black, white) by combat (no combat, light combat, heavy combat) model. This form of analysis yielded comparable results. As a consequence, it was decided to present the data in the form of a univariate model that approximated Parsons' (1985) formulation of his hypotheses. Alternate statistical approaches were performed, results of which do not alter in any way conclusions drawn about hypotheses advanced by Lukoff and Parsons.

In addition, multivariate analysis was performed to establish overall p values of error protection. The thirteen MMPI (including L, F, and K) measurements were the multivariate vector of dependent measurements. These were analyzed vis-à-vis two different factor structures. The first consisted of race, combat/noncombat, and the race by combat/noncombat interaction. The second analysis considered factors of race, heavy/light combat, and the interaction.

The MANOVAs gave overall p values of less than .03 for all the main effects which supports the univariate analysis. The two interaction terms were not significant. This appears inconsistent with the univariate analysis of the heavy/light by race interaction where more than 40 percent of the thirteen measurements were significant. (The multivariate analysis showed a p value of .16.) Explanation of this apparent inconsistency may be due to near multicolliniarities which appear among the dependent variables resulting in a nearly singular response matrix.

DISCUSSION

This study, then, provides empirical support for Parsons' hypothesis, but his predictions are limited to the heavy combat experience condition. Among noncombat Vietnam era male veterans, support was given Lukoff's prediction that black substance abusers are likely to be comparatively better adjusted than white substance abusers. However, there are limits to this hypothesis, limits imposed by finding that degree of combat participation interacts differentially among substance abusers as a function of ethnicity and combat intensity. For, by finding that black heavy combat veterans were more maladjusted than white heavy combat veterans, whereas black light combat veterans were less maladjusted than white light combat veterans, limits were placed on the generality of Lukoff's 1980 hypothesis at the extremes of combat intensity where Parsons' 1985 hypothesis began to hold sway.

Finding opposite results varying by combat intensity now highlights the need to reconcile the two hypotheses and the conflicting findings. Until those factors which account for black-white adjustment differences can be more fully specified, these findings have advanced our understanding about the role of ethnicity in personality adjustment of substance abusers seeking treatment only to the extent that it can be said: (1) blacks are more likely to be better adjusted than whites as long as back-ground history with trauma is negligible or mild; and (2) blacks are more likely to be less well adjusted than whites if extreme trauma has been experienced. The pivotal point for such dis-parate findings is the extent of life-threatening experiences in the history of the male substance abuser.

What these conflicting findings then establish is the differ-ential interaction of degree of combat and ethnicity. Studies of clinical samples of blacks and whites have been so focused upon questions about differences in current maladjustment that in-vestigators have neglected to ask whether samples have differed in background on such potentially explanatory variables as non-combat trauma. As a consequence, we know little about the traumatogenic dimension and its contribution to cultural dif-ferences in psychopathology, other than the fact that traumatic experiences are more prevalent among lower socioeconomic groups which contain a higher proportion of ethnic, minority groups (Dohrenwend and Dohrenwend, 1974), and that trauma in one's life history is acknowledged as playing an important role in the development of addiction disorders (Rounsaville, Weissman, Wilbur, and Kleber, 1982). The importance of these findings, then, is that they empirically establish the necessity for delineating the interaction of trauma and ethnicity on per-sonality adjustment, at least among male substance abusers seeking treatment.

These results may clarify why combat-noncombat MMPI differences were less striking among substance abusers (Penk et al., 1981) than observed among samples of psychiatric pop-ulations (e.g., Foy et al., 1984; Keane and Kaloupek, 1983): the proportion of blacks is higher in clinical samples of substance abusers than in psychiatric populations. These results also ex-tend prior findings by Laufer and his associates from nontreat-ment-seeking samples to treatment-seeking samples, and in so doing raise questions in several domains of research—theories about combat, substance abuse, as well as questions about prac-tical issues in testing ethnic groups with the MMPI.

First, it should be very clear, even to those resisting the

notion that there are noticeable long-term effects of combat, that combat effects are readily detectable even under very stringent test. For in this study, as in previous research (Penk et al., 1981), we have once again shown for both black and white substance abusers that combat veterans register more disturbance in adjustment than do noncombat veterans. We have shown this under conditions where the clinical samples are not seeking compensation for combat participation (only 5 percent of the 258 Vietnam combat substance abusers of this sample were service-connected or had applied for a service-connected disability: in this respect, male substance abusers are quite different from their psychiatric patient counterparts for whom the range of service-connected disability may reach as high as 50 percent in studies of combat-related posttraumatic stress disorders). Certainly, allegations that secondary gains increased reports about frequency and intensity of psychological symptoms could not be raised in this current study of substance abusers since combat and noncombat groups did not differ on MMPI validity scale scores. Significant differences in adjustment as a function of combat were demonstrated among clinical samples who were homogeneous in premilitary adjustment, socioeconomic status, and in type of presenting symptoms. Just by focusing upon the first criterion for PTSD alone (i.e., experiencing a life-threatening stressor), and not risking confounding our study by the introduction of the more subjectively determined other criteria for PTSD (such as reports of nightmares, startle responses, emotional numbing, etc.), we have demonstrated greater psychopathology among those who have been exposed to combat. We have replicated those aspects of our earlier study concerning effects of combat on adjustment of substance abusers (Penk et al., 1981).

Second, we have now empirically demonstrated something new—namely that there are important individual differences, along ethnic lines, in reaction to stressful experiences. Although we do not fully understand why more intense combat would be more difficult for blacks than for whites, nevertheless we at least have validated this clinical observation (Parsons, 1985;

Egendorf, 1983; Korman, 1974). The groundwork has been built for now exploring the characteristics which account for black-white differences: subsequent research must now go beyond the surrogate variables of "blacks" and "whites" and identify those features of being black and being white which produce differential responsivity to stressful experiences. It should be added that comparisons with Hispanic substance-abusing combat-noncombat veterans should be performed, as we are now doing. We have shown that the same degree of stress is associated with different degrees of maladjustment. The extent to which a stressor is stressful varies, then, not only as a function of the stress but also as a function of the person who has been stressed. Whereas a drift in the rising tide of PTSD research has been toward operationalizing the stressor, implications of the current results in which mildly stressed whites are more adjusted whereas severely stressed blacks are found to be less well adjusted than severely stressed whites leads to the inescapable conclusion that we must know more about the subject who has experienced stress in these studies of person-by-event interactions.

These findings have implications for studies of ethnic differences using the MMPI as measures of adjustment. The argument has been advanced that the MMPI, having not been standardized with black subjects, is biased in the direction of overestimating psychopathology. Considering that Gynther and Green (1980) have estimated the extent of ethnic bias in the MMPI to be no more than 5 points per scale we would still conclude that black light combat veterans were less disturbed than white light combat veterans and that black heavy combat veterans were more disturbed than white heavy combat veterans.

But what we have empirically observed in this current study is that the same test has documented different results, results in opposite directions even; e.g., black light combat veterans being better adjusted than white light combat veterans and black heavy combat veterans being more maladjusted than white heavy combat veterans. Such findings suggest that the MMPI is sensitively registering wide differences in ethnic comparisons. It is difficult to maintain that a test is biased when you consistently find that blacks do not evidence greater psychopathology than whites (not at least under conditions where noncombat and light combat groups are compared) and when you find, as expected in within racial group comparisons, that black heavy combat veterans are much more maladjusted than black light combat veterans. The MMPI has functioned sufficiently well in racial comparisons that it has registered significant differences as sample characteristics were systematically varied.

Regarding the treatment of substance abusers, the implications of the findings are relatively straightforward: as Rounsaville et al. (1982) have shown, substance abusers are heterogeneous as a diagnostic entity and one significant parameter contributing to subtypes among substance abusers is the influential role of trauma (in the case of this study, Vietnam combat trauma). The results indicate that combat veterans are more maladjusted than noncombat veterans and that blacks who have experienced intense combat are the more maladjusted. Combat experience as one of many etiological factors in the diagnosis of Substance Use Disorders awaits further study. But, at the moment, one can readily conclude that therapists should carefully examine a substance abuser's life history for traumatic events.

In summary, then, the major question of this study, "Can it be demonstrated that black Vietnam combat veterans are more disturbed than white Vietnam veterans?" was answered in the affirmative. The major goal for subsequent research is to specify those dispositional and situational variables which account for such black-white differences.

REFERENCES

Acosta, F. X., Yamamoto, J., & Evans, L. A. (1982), *Effective Psychotherapy for Low-Income and Minority Patients*. New York: Plenum Press.

Adebimpe, V. R., Gigandet, J., & Harris, E. (1979), MMPI diagnosis of black psychiatric patients. *Amer. J. Psychiat.*, 136:85–87.

Campbell, D. T., & Stanley, J. C. (1963), *Experimental and Quasi-experimental Designs for Research.* Chicago: Rand McNally.

Card, J. J. (1983), *Lives After Vietnam.* Lexington, MA: Lexington Books.

Cloward, R. A., & Ohlin, L. E. (1960), *Delinquency and Opportunity: A Theory of Delinquent Gangs.* Glencoe, IL: Free Press.

Dahlstrom, W. G., & Gynther, M. D. (1986), Previous MMPI research on black Americans. In: *MMPI Patterns of American Minorities*, ed. W. G. Dahlstrom, D. Lachar, & L. E. Dahlstrom. Minneapolis: University of Minnesota Press.

―――― Welsh, G. S., & Dahlstrom, L. E. (1975), *An MMPI Handbook*, Vol. 2. Minneapolis: University of Minnesota Press.

Dohrenwend, B. S., & Dohrenwend, B. P., eds., (1974), *Stressful Life Events: Their Nature and Effects.* New York: John Wiley.

Egendorf, A. (1983), The postwar healing of Vietnam veterans. *J. Hosp. & Commun. Psychiat.*, 33:901–912.

Fairbank, J. A., Malloy, P. F., & Keane, T. M. (1983), Validation of a multi-method assessment of posttraumatic stress disorders in Vietnam veterans. *J. Consult. & Clin. Psychol.*, 51:488–494.

Figley, C. R., & Leventman, S. A. (1978), *Strangers at Home.* New York: Brunner/Mazel.

―――― Stretch, R. H. (1980), Vietnam veterans questionnaire. Paper prepared for the Veterans Administration under contract V101 (134C) P-693, January 1980 (available from C. R. Figley, Family Research Institute, Purdue University, West Lafayette, IN, 47906).

Foy, D. W., Sipprelle, R. C., Rueger, D. B., & Carroll, E. M. (1984), Etiology of posttraumatic stress disorders in Vietnam veterans: Analysis of pre-military, military, and combat exposure influences. *J. Consult. & Clin. Psychol.*, 52:79–87.

Gynther, M. D. (1979), Ethnicity and personality: An update. In: *New Developments in the Use of the MMPI*, ed. J. N. Butcher. Minneapolis: University of Minnesota Press.

―――― Green, S. B. (1980), Accuracy may make a difference, but does a difference make for accuracy? A response to Pritchard and Rosenblatt. *J. Consult. & Clin. Psychol.*, 48:268–272.

Hill, H. E., Haertzen, C. A., & Glaser, R. (1960), Personality characteristics of narcotic addicts as indicated by the MMPI. *J. Gen. Psychol.*, 62:127–139.

Kadushin, C., Boulanger, G., & Martin, J. (1981), *Legacies of Vietnam: Comparative Adjustment of Veterans and Their Peers*, Vol. 4. Washington, DC: U.S. Government Printing Office.

Keane, T. M., & Kaloupek, D. G. (1980), Behavioral analysis and treatment of Vietnam stress syndrome. Paper presented at the annual meeting of the American Psychological Association, Montreal, Canada.

────── Zimering, R. T., & Addell, J. M. (1985), A behavioral formulation of posttraumatic stress disorder in Vietnam veterans. *Behav. Ther.*, 8:9–12.

Korman, M. (1974), National conference of levels and patterns of professional training in psychology. *Amer. Psychol.*, 29:441–449.

Laufer, R. S., Yager, T., Frey-Wouters, E., Donnellan, J., Gallops, M., & Stenbeck, K. (1981), *Legacies of Vietnam: Comparative Adjustment of Veterans and Their Peers*, Vol. 3. Washington, DC: U.S. Government Printing Office.

────── Gallops, M. S., & Frey-Wouters, E. (1984), War stress and trauma: The Vietnam veteran experience. *J. Health & Soc. Behav.*, 18:236–244.

Lukoff, I. (1980), Limited opportunity structure explanations of drug abuse. In: *Theories on Drug Abuse*, ed. D. Lettieri & H. Plemmons. Washington, DC: NIDA Research Monographs, U.S. Government Printing Office.

Merton, R. K. (1957), *Social Theory and Social Structure*. Glencoe, IL: Free Press.

Moos, R., Insel, P. M., & Humphries, H. (1974), *Preliminary Manual for the Family Environment Scales (FES)*. Palo Alto, CA: Consulting Psychologist Press.

Nace, E. P., O'Brien, C. P., Mintz, J., Ream. N., & Meyers, A. L. (1978), Adjustment among Vietnam veteran drug users two years postservice. In: *Stress Disorders Among Vietnam Veterans*, ed. C. R. Figley. New York: Brunner/Mazel, pp. 71–128.

Parsons, E. (1985), The intercultural setting: Encountering the psychological readjustment needs of black Americans who served in Vietnam. In: *Trauma: Its Consequences and Aftermath*, ed. C. R. Figley. New York: Brunner/Mazel, pp. 314–337.

Patterson, E. T., Charles, H. L., Woodward, W. A., Roberts, W. R., & Penk, W. E. (1981), Differences in measures of personality and family environments among black and white alcoholics. *J. Consult. & Clin. Psychol.*, 49:1–9.

Penk, W. E., Roberts, W. R., Robinowitz, R., Dolan, M. P., Atkins, H. G., Woodward, W. A. (1982), MMPI differences of black and white male polydrug drug abusers seeking treatment. *J. Consult. & Clin. Psychol.*, 50:463–465.

────── Robinowitz, R. (1974), MMPI differences of black and white drug abusers. *JSAS Catalog of Selected Documents in Psychol.*, 4:50.

────── ────── Roberts, W. R., Dolan, M. P., & Atkins, H. G. (1981), MMPI differences of male Hispanic-American, black, and white heroin addicts. *J. Consult. & Clin. Psychol.*, 49:488–490.

────── ────── ────── Patterson, E. T., Dolan, M. P., & Atkins, H. G. (1981),

Adjustment differences among male substance abusers varying in degrees of combat experience in Vietnam. *J. Consult. & Clin. Psychol.*, 49:426–437.

——— Woodward, W. A., Robinowitz, R., & Hess, J. L. (1978), Differences in MMPI scores of black and white compulsive heroin users. *J. Consult. & Clin. Psychol.*, 87:505–513.

Rounsaville, B. J., Weissman, M. M., Wilbur, C. H., & Kleber, J. D. (1982), Pathways to opiate addiction: An evaluation of different antecedents. *Brit. J. Psychiat.*, 141:437–446.

Sutker, P. B., Archer, R. P., & Allain, A. N. (1978), Drug abuser patterns, personality characteristics, and relationships with sex, race, and sensation seeking. *J. Consult. & Clin. Psychol.*, 46:1374–1378.

——— Brantley, P. J., & Allain, A. N. (1980), MMPI response patterns and alcohol consumption in DUI offenders. *J. Consult. & Clin. Psychol.*, 48:350–355.

Chapter 31
Traumatic Stresss Disorder: Diagnostic and Clinical Issues in Psychiatry

THOMAS W. MILLER, PH.D., A.B.P.P., AND N. DONALD FEIBELMAN, M.D.

Clinical issues in the diagnosis and treatment of posttraumatic stress disorder patients continues to be the focus of consultation liaison in psychiatry (Fleming, 1985; Penk, 1981; Williams, 1980). Horowitz and Solomon (1978) suggest that some Vietnam veterans have suffered long-term adaptive disability complicated by memories of the guilt and anxiety that resulted from atrocities of both a military and civilian nature. Polner (1968) cites numerous cases in which combat experiences disturbed individuals after they returned to civilian life. In most instances, the difficulties appear to center around guilt feelings over the process of having to kill. Strange and Brown (1970) compared combat and non-combat veterans who were experiencing emotional difficulties and concluded that the combat group showed a higher incidence of depression and of conflicts in close interpersonal relationships as well as aggressive tendencies and suicidal threats. DeFazio, Rustin, and Diamond (1975) found

Acknowledgment. This chapter was originally presented in the Colloquium Series of the Department of Psychiatry, College of Medicine, University of Kentucky, April 18, 1986, Lexington, Kentucky, and it is reprinted with permission.

553

that combat-related veterans reported certain symptoms twice as often as noncombat veterans. Most prominent among the symptomatology were frequent nightmares and recurring thoughts of combat experiences in the Vietnam era.

This chapter purports to address the difficulties and complexities in understanding and diagnosing the psychiatric syndrome of posttraumatic stress disorder in veterans presenting symptomatic complaints associated with this disorder. While the clear majority of posttraumatic stress disorder cases reported in the literature are related to veterans exposed to combat experience the presentation of information and normative data may have applicability to other patient populations experiencing stress.

THE DSM-III AND POSTTRAUMATIC STRESS

Current strategies of assessing posttraumatic stress disorder in Vietnam veterans focuses on both the DSM-III criteria for diagnosing what is now called "posttraumatic stress disorder" and empirical data bearing on the validity of the DSM-III delineation of that syndrome. The theoretical formulations of Freud, Kardiner, and Horowitz have significant impact on our understanding of posttraumatic stress. There is, however, a new and hitherto unconsidered formulation bearing on the understanding and treatment of traumatic stress disorders which may bear significance in our understanding of the process of a stress disorder.

Until the publication of the *Diagnostic and Statistical Manual of Mental Disorders* (American Psychiatric Association, 1980), clinicians attempting to diagnose traumatic war neuroses in Vietnam veterans had been frustrated by the multiplicity of symptoms enumerated and the lack of consensus as to what constitutes the syndrome. Disconcerting to many concerned professionals was that the DSM-II did not include traumatic war neurosis, possibly because of political/economic reasons. The gap generated the impression that there was no such entity as traumatic war neurosis. The result was clinicians could not understand, empathize with, and treat veterans who presented with symptoms they claimed were brought on by their involvement in the Vietnam War. One will undoubtedly accept that it would be difficult to successfully treat a fictitious disease.

The DSM-III not only incorporates the diagnostic entity of posttraumatic stress disorder, but also specifies which symptoms are necessary and/or sufficient for differential diagnosis. The four criteria for diagnosing posttraumatic stress disorder are: (1) harsh, recognizable stressor, the traumatic experience, (2) some evidence of a re-experiencing of the trauma (e.g., combat nightmares), (3) some evidence of numbed responsiveness to or reduced involvement with the external world (e.g., constricted affect or loss of interest in being active in the world), and (4) two of a list of six other symptoms not present before the trauma, such as hyperalertness, survival guilt, and difficulty concentrating. The chronic or delayed version of the disorder of the diagnosis is reserved for persons reporting symptoms that have manifested for longer than six months. Note that diagnosis is not established on the basis of particular individual symptoms, but rather is dependent upon evidence of symptoms reflective of fairly broad categories. Thus, some structure has been provided, but unrealistically excessive specificity has been avoided.

A clinical difficulty with the aforementioned schema is that diagnosis requires symptoms that to some extent are mutually exclusive, are not likely to co-occur, though admittedly each may appear sequentially. Symptoms representative of category 4, "numbed responsiveness to reduce involvement with the external world," labeled the "numbing-denial" tendency by Horowitz and Solomon, deserve closer examination. Clinical experience and research efforts suggest that in certain instances one of the two tendencies may be missing. It seems overly prohibitive to rule out the diagnosis of posttraumatic stress disorder for patients presenting with all but, for example, the symptoms associated with criterion 3, i.e., reduced involvement with the external world. Though the diagnosis of posttraumatic stress disorder has been incorporated into DSM-III, careful validational research needs to be carried out. It should not be *assumed* that an entity exists without empirically testing the currently acceptable model.

Some research findings bearing on the DSM-III *taxonomic* model are relevant (Miller and Buchbinder, 1980; Brende and Parsons, 1985). Within both psychiatric and "normal" populations, Vietnam combat veterans when compared with noncombat veteran peers, scored significantly ($p < .05$) higher on the following symptom scales of the Vietnam Experiences Questionnaire (VEQ): sleep disturbances, hypersensitivity to sound, psychotic-like manifestations (such as dissociative states) and perceived capacity of violence. Combat veterans do *not* score higher on scales measuring disturbances, such as loss of interest. Thus, it appears that numbed responsiveness to the external world may not be a key criterion of posttraumatic stress disorder. This is supported by data indicating significant combat/noncombat group differences on a scale measuring increased emotionality, but no significant difference on a scale measuring emotional anesthesia or numbing.

Also, there is *no* evidence that Vietnam combat veterans as opposed to any other comparison group of veterans are most beset by guilt, anxiety, or depression. Furthermore, though the media projects the perception that Vietnam veterans are more violent than other types of Americans, research data indicate that Vietnam veterans are not in actuality more violent (Archer and Garner, 1976). However, these veterans are more likely to fear that they could act-out violently.

To improve upon our current criteria for diagosing posttraumatic stress disorder, researchers must try to uncover symptoms that: (a) are more likely to appear to traumatic war neuroses than in any other diagnostic group, and (b) are manifest in a reasonably non-miniscule percentage of the relevant population of combat veterans. There are four symptoms that meet these two criteria: (1) combat nightmares and other sleeping disturbances, (2) hypersensitiveness to sound, (3) perceived capacity for violence, and (4) psychotic-like manifestations. These symptoms should be most practically useful in screening for traumatic war neurosis. They significantly differentiate Vietnam combat veterans from Vietnam era, noncombat veteran peers. In addition, it appears that the base rates for these symptoms are neither too high nor too low.

Several researchers have strongly claimed that the Vietnam War was markedly different from previous wars. Others have equally vociferously maintained that the Vietnam situation was not particularly different. It would appear that there is the likelihood that situational circumstances associated with each war vary to some extent and that the symptom picture may correspondingly differ. If the traumatic war syndrome has taken on a slightly new guise in veterans of the latest U.S. war involvement, what might the specific variant look like? It appears that two symptoms—perceived capacity for violence and psychotic-like manifestations—are more significantly seen in Vietnam veterans. Though the two symptoms manifest to some extent in World War II combat veterans (Kardiner, 1959), they seem to manifest even more intensely in Vietnam veterans.

As the world is in a constant state of flux, changes in society as a whole would be expected to color the presentation of persons exposed to trauma. Societal changes, the changing etiologies and purposes of war and non-war trauma, and the multitude of individual personality structures involved all contribute to problems in diagnosing sequelae of trauma. The magnitude and multitude of factors involved leads to confusion in the recognition of symptoms secondary to trauma vs. symptoms secondary to other etiologies. Also "clean" symptoms, those secondary only to traumatic stress, are almost impossible to identify. Recognizing these factors helps one to understand how posttraumatic stress disorder may become an inadvertently abused or improperly used diagnosis. Avoiding misuse of the diagnosis by selecting proper criteria has proven to be a difficult task. With this difficulty in mind the following study was conducted.

METHOD

Subjects were 25 veteran patients admitted to the VA Medical Center, Lexington, Kentucky, with a DSM-III medical diagnosis of post-traumatic stress disorder. Psychological testing along with chart review and screening measures relevant to specific aspects of the lives of these patients were recorded in an attempt to identify a life-style profile or pattern particular to persons who appear susceptible to posttraumatic stress disorder. Critical factors addressed include age, educational background, family background, military rank and type of discharge, years in service, combat versus noncombat, and psychiatric history.

The data revealed some interesting trends which display individual and environmental factors that may predispose individuals to limited adaptational resources and thus increase the potential for developing posttraumatic stress disorder. These critical factors include biological, psychological, and sociocultural aspects of life.

RESULTS

1. LEVEL OF INVOLVEMENT

Vietnam War veterans made up 80 percent of the veterans reviewed; World War II veterans, 12 percent; Korean War veterans, 4 percent, and 4 percent served in a non-combat arena. Table 31.1 includes demographic findings in tabular summary.

2. AGES

During the time of this study, 1983–1984, the ages of patients reveal a wide range with obvious cluster toward the younger Vietnam War veterans. At the time of the review, 28 percent were 33 years old, 16 percent were 32 years old, 12 percent

Table 31.1
Demographic Characteristics of Patients with Posttraumatic
Stress Disorder (Reported in Percentage)

	Combat Veterans	Noncombat Veterans
Age in years	37.1	39.4
Race		
White	83.7	100.0
Non-White	16.3	00.0
Education		
Substance Abuse		
None	24.4	17.4
Alcohol Only	41.6	50.0
Drugs and Alcohol	33.0	16.3
Drugs Only	0.0	16.3

were 34 years old, 8 percent were 31 years old, and 8 percent were 29 years old. Next we have an increase in the age range with two veterans at 56 years, and one each at 36 years, 40 years, 43 years, 50 years, plus the oldest, at 62 years.

3. MILITARY

The branches of service represented in this group are not surprising. Seventy-two percent were in the army, 20 percent were in the marines, and 8 percent were in the air force.

4. RACE AND RANK

Twenty-four of the 25 (96 percent) are white, Caucasian males; one is a black male. As to rank 25 (100 percent) were enlisted men; none were officers.

5. EDUCATION

Education revealed another enlightening element. Seven of the twenty-five (28 percent) have not completed the ninth grade; six (24 percent) have not completed the twelfth grade, four prior to service and two after service through the GED program; 16 percent have not completed the tenth grade; 12 percent have not completed the eleventh grade; one each has not completed the eighth, sixth, fifth, fourth and third grades. No college graduates were found in this group. In other studies of Vietnam POWs the conclusion was that an increase in formal education had an increasingly protective emotional value (Corcoran, 1982).

6. SUBSTANCE ABUSE

Alcohol and drug abuse were frequent characteristics of persons with the diagnosis of posttraumatic stress disorder. In the study group, 35 percent had a history of alcohol abuse prior to entering the service. Prior to entering service, two patients had a history of both alcohol and drug abuse and one a history of drug abuse only, for a total of 48 percent. This 48 percent represents abuse prior to entering the service.

During service or active duty, 16 percent developed alcohol and drug abuse, and two more developed alcohol abuse only. This yielded a total of 18 (72 percent) with drug or alcohol abuse or both. Following service discharge another two patients developed alcohol abuse. A grand total of 82.6 percent with drug and/or alcohol abuse is therefore realized. Also in this group, three patients during active duty added drug abuse to their pre-existing alcohol abuse. Of interest here is the large percentage of persons with PTSD with a history of substance abuse prior to military service.

DIAGNOSTIC VARIABLES

At the time of diagnosis of post-traumatic stress disorder utilizing DSM-III diagnostic criteria, the Minnesota Multiphasic Personality Inventory (MMPI) was administered to the patients for a confirmation of diagnosis. Table 31.2 indicates the results

Table 31.2
**MMPI Clinical Scales for Patients Diagnosed
as Posttraumatic Stress Disorder (N = 25)**

MMPI Clinical Scale	Mean	S.D.	Clinical Interpretation
L (Lie)	45.47	6.71	Honest in responding to items
F (Infrequency)	82.71	14.13	Moody, exaggerated symptoms, restless
K (Defensiveness)	46.49	8.63	Somewhat defensive, may lack insight
Hs (Hypochondriasis)	72.81	16.25	Somatic concerns, narcissistic, pessimistic
D (Depression)	81.85	18.11	Depressed, overcontrolled, irritable
Hy (Hysteria)	67.55	11.65	Some physical symptoms of a functional nature
Pd (Psychopathic Deviate)	78.42	11.05	Antisocial, impulsive, rebellious, aggressive
Mf (Masculinity, Femininity)	64.13	8.91	Somewhat unsure in identity role
Pa (Paranoia)	74.21	14.82	Sensitive, rationalize, suspicious, rigid
Pt (Psychasthemia)	81.75	16.02	Tense, anxious, obsessive, insecure
Sc (Schizophrenia)	90.11	27.39	Withdrawn, alienation, thought disturbance
Ma (Mania)	61.69	9.20	Impulsive, low frustration tolerance

obtained on the MMPI clinical scales for patients included in the study. The elevated scales from this psychological data suggest a DSM-III Axis II diagnosis of a personality disorder in most cases. A general interpretation of the results is included in tabular form. The personality disorders which are most salient include: borderline personality disorder, passive-aggressive personality disorder, obsessive-compulsive personality disorder, and passive-dependent personality disorder. MMPI psychological data also reveal elevated depression scales in close to 70 percent of the patients tested. Both the major affective disorder finding and the personality disorders noted are consistent with recently reported research results assessing posttraumatic stress disorder patients (Miller, 1984; Keane, Caddell, and Zimering, 1984).

OTHER DIAGNOSES

As a sequel to MMPI studies, the other diagnoses these patients carry represent a composite of information on each patient including MMPI, projective testing, multiple psychiatric interviews, and extended observation. The most frequent other diagnosis is major depression, 18 of 25, or 72 percent. This is followed by a three-way tie between borderline personality disorder, antisocial personality disorder, and passive-aggressive personality disorder (Table 31.3).

These patients have a variety of problem areas and selecting those patients with posttraumatic stress is an arduous task. Numerous criteria have been screened to select those which are not specific for posttraumatic stress disorder.

Overwhelming anxiety is considered a hallmark of the etiologic factors and ensuing symptoms of PTSD. Anxiety is a frequently discussed and poorly understood entity. Beck (1971) in his article, "Cognition, Affect, and Psychopathology," discusses the arousal of anxiety. Beck describes the etiology of anxiety as the perception of a threat to one's domain. The most frequently perceived threats are the danger of psychological or physical injuries to the person. Beck does expound on his belief to explain that one's domain may include family, friends, school, county, state, home, etc.

Anxiety, by Beck's definition, may be enhanced by: (1) appraisal that the individual cannot cope with or neutralize the threatening object, (2) the immediacy of the perceived danger, (3) unpredictability of when or where the actual damage will occur, (4) high (possibly increasing) probability attached to the occurrence of the noxious event (Beck, 1971).

Table 31.3
DSM-III Primary Diagnosis Reported in
Percentages of PTSD Patients Assessed[a]

Diagnosis	Percentages of Cases
Major Affective Disorder	72.1%
Borderline, Antisocial	26.7%
and Passive-Aggressive	
Personality Disorder	
Dependent, Histrionic	10.5%
Mixed Personality Disorder	
Schizophrenic Disturbance	17.0%
Borderline Retarded	
Explosive Disorder	
Seizure Gran Mal	
Intermittent Psychosis	
Gastric Cancer with Metastatic Disease	
Atypical Seizures	
Hepatitis	
Conversion Hysteria	
Schizotypal	
Undifferentiated Schizophrenia	

[a] Percentages reflect multiple diagnoses of some patients and therefore do not equal 100%.

Comparability studies of combat veterans, noncombat veterans and general populations with or without a history of psychiatric illness have also been addressed. In the past studies have consistently demonstrated disability of a greater severity for prisoners of war than that of veterans who served in the same combat theater and were not prisoners of war (Corcoran, 1982). Percentage of psychiatric impairment was high for all World War II and Korean POWs. This POW population did generate a significant correlation with high hospital admission rates, more frequent VA disability awards, and more frequent reported symptoms of medical concerns. Despite ominous predictions prior to their release, Vietnam air force POWs have done amazingly well. This is not to say that there have not been residual effects from their captivity but the large majority appear to show no severe effects of their traumatic prisoner of war experience. In repatriation, only 6 percent of air force POWs were given a psychiatric diagnosis—typically that of neurotic illness. This may reflect the higher educational level of air force pilots and suggests the realization that better educated and higher ranking officers tend to withstand the pressures of a prisoner of war situation more effectively. Recent screening studies suggest combat veterans do *not* score higher on scales measuring disturbances in interpersonal relations (Buchbinder, 1978). Vietnam combat veterans are compared to noncombat veterans and score higher on symptoms scales of sleep disturbance, hypersensitivity to sound, psychotic-like manifestations, and perceived capacity for violence. What is very interesting is that a majority of the patients in this study did have marked difficulty with interpersonal relationships. Their histories over and over again point to major personality disorders, some with multiple personality disorders. Their histories reveal multiple marriages, and multiple jobs, most patients unable to get along with wives and employers. The majority of these people come from chaotic childhoods and disrupted, abusive families of origin. The question is raised, is their limited ability to cope with stress and anxiety warranting a specific diagnosis such as post-traumatic stress disorder or is this actually another factor in their limited personality development? Should this be so, then we are actually dealing with personality disorders, recognizing these disorders, and treating them will be paramount to patient improvement, especially in the face of future trauma.

The deep-seated, inexplicable personality and life-style transformations undergone by Vietnam veterans may best be explained by "catastrophe theory model" (Buchbinder, 1980). This model attempts to describe and explain sudden or discontinuous transformations brought on by information "too varied, too new and foreign, (and) experiences for which the brain has no previously established or related patterns" (p. 185). The theory posits that information overload causes the mind to "snap," to become disjointed, unguarded, and scattered, leading one to withdraw from the outside world and if possible try to suppress disturbing thoughts and emotions. In order to restore the altered psyche, deprogramming becomes the treatment of choice. This process, carried out by sincere and sensitive individuals, aims to either suddenly or gradually snap the person back to their normal, pre-trauma functioning. This model may explain the snapping experienced by Vietnam combat soldiers who experienced a markedly different reality than that which they had previously known. They were then incapable of cognitively and emotionally integrating their experiences into their self-system. As apparent in the anti-cult work, traditional therapeutic approaches may not be as successful as specially devised deprogramming approaches. Thus, new treatment approaches may have to be formulated to deal with Vietnam veterans who have suffered protracted impairment of consciousness, affect, and behavior. It would seem that cognitively based treatment strategies are the interventions of choice. Also consistent with effective treatment of ex-cult members, clinically trained professionals and para-professionals may be able to provide psychotherapeutic intervention to traumatized Vietnam veterans suffering posttraumatic stress.

ADJUSTMENT RELATED TO SIGNIFICANT LIFE STRESSORS

There are a variety of sources from which adjustive demands and stressors emerge including biological, psychological, and sociocultural conditions. A clear emphasis on psychological conditions are relevant to the stressors faced by some Vietnam combat veterans is most apparent. The first of these is frustration which occurs when an individual's strivings are thwarted either by perceived of anticipated obstruction in progress toward a goal. These soldiers were not given the opportunity for a complete victory. There are clear indications that during the Vietnam conflict many veterans experienced this particular type of frustration creating both environmental (external) and internal frustration. Response to frustrations that individuals face depends heavily on factors such as personality characteristics, age, and maturity. In addition, the Vietnam situation presented frustrations which arose out of psychological barriers including ethical and moral restraints. The Vietnam people were ambivalent about the presence of American soldiers in their country.

Frustration, secondary to an adjustive demand or psychological stressor, may also lead to conflict. Stress may result when there are two simultaneously occurring incompatible needs or drives. For example, the drive to commit oneself to his country by combat in war, but the same person finds that the plan may not involve winning the war and massive economic abuse of the war is taking place.

Penk (1981) has addressed the adjustment differences among male substance abusers who have faced varying degrees of combat experiences. Adjustment to combat stress has also been addressed by others. Figley (1980) suggests that there are five stages of adjustment that the individual faces in the combat situation. The first phase is a stage of emergency or outcry, and in this particular phase, the individual feels very vulnerable, helpless and exhausted, and recognizes the life-threatening situation. Stage two is a phase involving relief, but also confusion. It can last from a few days to many months, perhaps years, wherein shock and disorientation may occur. Also noted are anger, frustration and disbelief, and the constant push toward revisiting the emergency or traumatic situation. At the third level, the individual experiences a psychic numbing, an emotional constriction, a narrowing in focus. In this state, an attempt toward adaptation is realized, but preoccupation with war presses the individual into a state of obsessive ideation concerning the meaning of the war and its events. This may later lead to recurring thoughts and nightmares, flashbacks, and other intrusive thoughts of war experiences. Later efforts are made to move again toward revisiting the traumatic experience with the person frequently slipping back into a stage of denial and avoidance. The fourth stage is basically of reconsideration in which the individual initiates a more personal perspective and rationale for the events which occurred. Coping and ego defense styles emerge and the individual employs more constructive and positive modes of adjustment to past trauma, allowing this person to work and relate to others. There is a return to prior stages but this occurs less frequently than in the other three stages. The final stage is a stage in which the individual shows a sense of adjustment, ego-synthesis, and experiences a restoration to a sense of continuity with respect to ego identity. Coping strategies at this stage allow the individual to prepare for, confront, cope, and self-reinforce any intrusive thoughts which may be of disturbing nature.

CLINICAL STRATEGIES WITH POSTTRAUMATIC STRESS

There are numerous descriptions of clinical cases with respect to posttraumatic stress disorder resulting from combat experiences in the literature. A growing awareness of posttraumatic stress presents the realization that there is wide variability and symptomatology (Figley and Southerly, 1980). Some patients report chronic anxiety, recurring thoughts, sleep disturbance, and multiple substance abuse, while others present agoraphobic or claustrophobic or anxiety-mediated types of behaviors. It is essential from the clinical perspective to examine and carefully explore the multiplicity of problems including marital, vocational, and interpersonal difficulties.

In order to assess the presence of posttraumatic stress disorder, 96 veterans who complained of post-Vietnam syndrome were administered the Veterans Experience Questionnaire (VEQ) (Buchbinder, 1978). Forty-five of these Vietnam veterans participated in combat experiences, while 51 were in support facilities indicating that they had never experienced direct contact with the enemy. Results indicated that the first hypothesis which addressed symptoms expected to be especially marked in Vietnam veterans was confirmed for one symptom only; namely, the perceived capacity for violence. Vietnam veterans, whether combat or noncombat, showed significant higher ratings on this particular dimension. A second hypothesis focused on symptoms which were expected to be especially apparent in combat-experienced veterans and was confirmed again for only one symptom: sleep disturbance. Only on this symptom did combat veterans score significantly higher than veterans with no combat experience. Three significant main effects for age were realized. Excessive rumination about service experiences, guilt, and psychotic-like symptoms seemed to be more apparent in younger veterans than in older veterans.

The data provided little suport for the existence of a post-Vietnam syndrome comprised of a specific group of symptoms, especially associated with Vietnam combat. It confirms earlier research (Miller and Buchbinder, 1980; Keane and Kaloupek, 1980) which failed to realize a symptoms cluster unique to the Vietnam veteran.

There certainly is present within the clinical cases assessed and treated a cluster which includes anxiety, depression, guilt, alienation, multiple drug abuse, eating disturbance, and low self-esteem. These are symptoms manifested by many Vietnam veterans, but which appear in many other psychiatric disorders and, therefore, are not considered particularly associated with the combat experience. The symptoms which are associated with the combat experience and the stresses of combat in any war and would seem to be especially correlated with service in Vietnam include startle reaction, sleep disturbance, irritability, guilt, psychosomatic symptoms, and psychotic-like symptoms. Added to this is the clear and definitive perceived capacity for violence since our data show that the perceived capacity for violence is more prominent in the younger Vietnam era veterans. Could it be related to the training in guerilla warfare that they received and the anticipatory anxiety created by the fact that several of these veterans were trained in guerilla tactics when they might not have otherwise been acceptable for inclusion in special forces training? Training in guerilla-type warfare takes a unique type of individual qualities which may not be found in individuals suitable for conventional warfare training.

The treatment interventions for the obsessive thought disturbances noted in delayed stress syndrome have been treated with mixed results. The tricyclic agent clomipramine has realized some attention in the treatment of obsessive-compulsive disorders. A number of uncontrolled studies have reported that significant improvement in obsessive-compulsive behavior after treatment with clomipramine (Marshall and Micev, 1975; Waxman, 1975) displayed the lack of controlled groups and other methodological concerns. The patients in these studies were severe chronic obsessive-compulsive patients and there is increasing evidence that the efficacy of clomipramine in obsessive-compulsive disorders may be advantageous in treating the obsessive-compulsive features of delayed stress.

The process of employing a strategy of systematic response prevention and the use of imaginal procedures in the treatment of obsessive-compulsive symptoms in a veteran experiencing extremely high levels of anxiety related to combat trauma and delayed stress reactions has been found to be effective over a 48-week period. The inclusion of spouse participation in the process seems to be an extremely important and effective measure and should be considered as a key strategy toward the resolution of the stressful life event. While there is a limited body of research that supports the use of flooding-response prevention, this certainly seems to be an essential direction for further research efforts. The techniques employed rely heavily upon the assumption that anxiety-eliciting properties of specific stimuli or traumatic life events may be extinguished if the anxiety is elicited and the anticipated outcome does not occur while avoidance behavior is also prevented. There is clinical evidence (Keane and Kaloupek, 1980) which does, in fact, suggest this mechanism has realized a level of effectiveness with specific application to posttraumatic stress disorders. Certainly it warrants more research. The increasing number of successfully applied anxiety-inducing techniques suggests it may be reasonable to conclude that anxiety-inducing strategies may provide a valid set of procedures for the treatment of anxiety-related disorders. The clinician is cautioned to carefully review the variety of behavioral techniques which might be applied because there is little evidence that suggests systematic desensitization is any less effective and there is certainly some evidence that will suggest that it is more effective and that it may be the preferred strategy to anxiety-inducing techniques because of the aversive reactions characteristics that response prevention employs.

REFERENCES

American Psychiatric Association (1980), *The Diagnostic and Statistical Manual of Mental Disorders*, 3rd ed. Washington, DC.

Archer, D., & Gartner, R. (1976), Violent acts and violent times: A comparative approach to post-war homicide rates, *Amer. Sociologic. Rev.*, 41/6:937–963.

Beck, A. T. (1971), Cognition, affect, and psychopathology. *Arch. Gen. Psychiat.*, 24:495–500.

Brende, J. O., & Parsons, E. R. (1985), *Vietnam Veterans: The Road to Recovery*. New York: Plenum Press.

Buchbinder, J. T. (1978), The Vietnam experience questionnaire: An experimental measure to assess post Vietnam syndrome. Unpublished manuscript, State University of New York, Buffalo.

——— (1980), Self-report assessment of the hypothesized post Vietnam syndrome. Unpublished doctoral dissertation, State University of New York, Buffalo.

Collins, G. (1973), The use of parenteral and oral clomipramine in the treatment of depressive states. *Brit. J. Psychiat.*, 122:189–190.

Corcoran, J. F. T. (1982), The concentration camp syndrome and USAF Vietnam prisoners of war. *Psychiat. Annu.*, 12/11:991–994.

DeFazio, S., Rustin, S., and Diamond, A. (1975), Symptom development in Vietnam era veterans. *Amer. J. Orthopsychiat.*, 45:258–263.

Figley, C. R. (1980), Combat as disaster: Treating combat veterans as survivors. Paper presentation at the Annual Meeting of the American Psychiatric Association, Chicago, IL.

——— Southerly, W. T. (1980), Stumbling block on stepping stone: Path analysis in family studies. *J. Marr. & Fam.*, 42/2:251–262.

Fleming, R. H. (1985), Post Vietnam syndrome: Neurosis or sociosis? *Psychiat.*, 48:122–139.

Horowitz, M. J., & Solomon, G. F. (1978), Delayed stress response in Vietnam veterans. In: *Stress Disorders Among Vietnam Veterans*, ed. C. R. Figley. New York: Brunner/Mazel, pp. 268–280.

Kardiner, A. (1959), Traumatic neurosis of war. In: *American Handbook of Psychiatry*, Vol. 1, ed. S. Arieti. New York: Basic Books, pp. 330–346.

Keane, T. M., Caddell, J. L., & Zimering, R. T. (1984), Multi-trait, multi-method assessment of combat-related post-traumatic stress shock disorder. Paper Presented at the Ninety-second Annual Convention of the American Psychological Association, Toronto, Ontario, Canada.

———— Kaloupek, D. G. (1980), Behavioral analysis and treatment of Vietnam stress syndrome. Paper Presented at the Annual Meeting of the American Psychological Association, Montreal, Canada.

Marshall, W., & Micev, V. (1975), The role of intravenous chlorimipramine in the treatment of obsessional and phobic disorders. *Scot. Med. J.*, Suppl. 20:49–53.

Miller, T. W. (1984), Lingering effects to threat to life in Vietnam veterans. Symposium Presentation at the Ninety-second Annual Convention of the American Psychological Association, Toronto, Canada.

———— Buchbinder, J. T. (1980), Clinical effect of cognitive-behavior therapy with post-traumatic stress disorder Vietnam veterans. Paper Presented at the American Association of Advancement of Behavior Therapy, New York.

Penk, W. E. (1981), Adjustment differences among male substance abusers varying in degree of combat experience in Vietnam. *J. Consult. Clinic. Psychol.*, 49:426–437.

Polner, M. (1968), Vietnam War stories. *Transaction*, 6/1:8–20.

Strange, R. E., & Brown, D. E., Jr. (1970), Home from the wars. *Amer. J. Psychiat.*, 127/4:488–492.

Waxman, D. (1975), A general practitioner trial of chlorimipramine in obsessions and phobias. *J. Internat. Med. Res.*, Suppl. 3:94–100.

Williams, T. (1980), *Post Traumatic Stress Disorders of the Vietnam Veteran*. Cincinnati: Disabled American Veterans.

Chapter 32
Factitious Posttraumatic Stress Disorder: The Veteran Who Never Got to Vietnam

EDWARD J. LYNN, M.D., AND MARK BELZA, M.D.

For the United States, the Vietnam conflict ended in 1972 after more than 2 million people served in the historically unique war. For many combatants, however, the onset of posttraumatic stress disorder (PTSD), with its terrifying nightmares, flashbacks, and numbing affective responsiveness, meant that the war was continuing on a personal level. The dysfunction of Vietnam veterans became so common that the United States government initiated Operation Outreach in 1979 to handle readjustment and psychiatric problems that had risen as a consequence of the conflict (Friedman, 1981; Walker, 1981; Silver, 1982).

With so many veterans suffering from PTSD, the media detailing their plight (Morganthau and Shabad, 1981; Santoli, 1981), and vet centers documenting their significant readjustment problems (Williams, 1980), the symptoms and character-

Acknowledgment. This chapter was first published in *Hospital and Community Psychiatry* (1984), 35/7:697–701, and it is reprinted with permission.

istics of PTSD became widely publicized. A related group of veterans, heretofore unrecognized in most psychiatric circles, consists of individuals who present with PTSD symptoms but who did not participate actively in actual hostilities and, indeed, who generally had never been stationed in Vietnam. These veterans present at Veterans Administration medical centers (VAMCs) with simulated symptoms of PTSD or what we have since diagnosed as factitious PTSD. In doing so, they pose yet another form of clinical deception to experienced as well as unwary clinicians.

We present here the cases of seven men who were admitted to the Reno VAMC claiming PTSD symptomatology despite never having been involved in combat or having been to Vietnam. While it is sometimes difficult to differentiate between clinical entities in our series, underlying psychopathology is invariably involved, suggesting either factitious syndromes, such as Munchausen's, or malingering. After presenting the cases, we will discuss the etiologies of factitious PTSD and propose recommendations for clinicians on how to appropriately diagnose and treat patients presenting with its symptoms.

CASE REPORTS

The Reno VA Medical Center has a 20-bed psychiatric unit and a significant interest in Vietnam-era veterans suffering from PTSD. We have an intimate relationship with the Reno Vet Center, an outreach program staffed by former Vietnam combat veterans. We obtain an automatic consultation from the vet center on every Vietnam veteran admitted to the psychiatry service. The seven cases presented here were admitted to the unit between November 1982 and March 1983.

Case 1 (PT). A 32-year-old unemployed man who claimed to be a Vietnam combat veteran with a master's degree in psychology presented as a paraplegic confined to a wheelchair. PT claimed that he had been informed that his reported symptoms were attributable either to an astrocytoma or to multiple sclerosis. He claimed to have been treated for these symptoms at several East Coast VAMCs. Furthermore, PT complained of nightmares and flashbacks as a result of his combat experience. His self-reported medical history included a head injury and a subsequent seizure disorder. PT alleged that the injury was the result of being shot out of a tree by a sniper in Vietnam. Staff at the Reno Vet Center were thoroughly convinced of the authenticity of his reported Vietnam experiences.

PT's hospital course included an extensive neurological workup, which was negative. The patient also underwent one surgical procedure consisting of irrigation and drainage of one of several abscesses of unknown etiology on his buttocks. He continuously presented staff with a myriad of somatic complaints, few of which could be verified medically.

While on the ward PT manipulated the staff and other patients. Suspicions as to his history were raised when the chief of the psychiatry service suggested that his intellectual ability was incompatible with his claim to have earned a master's degree in psychology at a major university. When the results of the Wechsler Adult Intelligence Scale revealed PT to have low-normal intelligence, we confronted him with our suspicions, and he admitted that he did not have a master's degree.

This was only the first of many confrontations and disclosures. We also obtained a copy of his military discharge records, which clearly refuted any Vietnam experience. When confronted with this evidence, PT admitted to fabricating much of his story and revealed that he had been discharged from the Coast Guard after only two months of service. He also admitted to 21 previous hospitalizations in VAMCs all over the United States.

During PT's previous admissions to neurological wards in VAMCs, he learned to mimic other patients' legitimate complaints of PTSD. PT also pointed out that whenever he was down and out, his factitious PTSD symptomatology became his hospital admission ticket for room and board. Three days after our final confrontation with PT, he was walking normally, and soon after discharge he found a job. He later left the Reno area.

PT's fabrications were perfect. The apparent authenticity of his combat experience and PTSD convinced an outreach program to hire him as a vet center counselor. From our discussions with him, it was clear that PT was trying to compete with a more successful older brother for his father's approval. His status as a Vietnam veteran was the only sense of worth that he had had for several years. We have been advised that since discharge he has twice again been admitted to California VAMC neurology services despite a nationwide telefax alert warning of his propensity for fabrication. PT's most recent hospitalization has been in the VAMC in Portland, where he is claimed to have said, "I have Munchausen's syndrome."

Case 2 (RK). A 29-year-old married, unemployed veteran with a reported history of chronic low back pain and alcohol abuse was admitted to the Reno VAMC in an inebriated state. RK complained of crying spells, nightmares, and flashbacks of experiences suffered during his reported Vietnam combat duty. He felt he was losing control and feared that he might harm others. With a great deal of catatonic-like posturing, fist clenching, and tears, he related many experiences from his tour of duty in Vietnam. He also described periodic episodes of sudden and complete lower body paralysis secondary to a work-related back injury. The episodes had continued despite a recent neurosurgical intervention.

Complete physical and laboratory evaluations contributed nothing to the etiology of the paralysis. During an interview the patient experienced what he claimed was a typical episode of lower body paralysis. Immediate neurological examination revealed subjective paraplegia. Intact anal sphincter, cremasteric reflexes, and lower abdominal reflexes supported the diagnosis of functional paralysis or malingering. Indeed, soon after the episode, the patient was observed walking around the ward with a normal gait.

Direct and precise questioning by a vet center staff member conclusively demonstrated that RK's combat story was a complete fabrication. When confronted with his lies, RK initially vehemently denied them, but then admitted that he had never been in Vietnam. Interestingly, he denied any embarrassment or anger at these revelations. He and his wife remained completely resistant to the suggestion that his paralytic episodes were not physiologic reactions to the alleged work injury.

Later during the hospitalization, we learned that RK was involved in litigation against the state industrial commission for workman's compensation. He was discharged and referred to an outpatient clinic but failed to appear for his scheduled appointments.

Case 3 (DC). A 34-year-old man claimed to be a Vietnam veteran who had retired from the military with a 100 percent service-connected disability. He had so convinced the staff at another VAMC of the authenticity of his PTSD that they begged us to admit him as a transfer because of our experience in treating the disorder. The patient claimed that his PTSD symptoms of nightmares, flashbacks, insomnia, and impulsivity had increased with the recent loss of his first wife and his son in an auto accident.

During the course of DC's hospital stay, we could not obtain any objective data confirming his history. When various staff members compared notes, DC's story began to show further discrepancies suggesting fabrication. When confronted with our suspicions, DC requested an earlier-than-planned discharge. Just before his departure from the hospital, he admitted to fabricating much of his story. He had never been to Vietnam, was not retired from the military, and had actually been married three times. DC offered no explanation for his fabrications nor could we pinpoint a basis for his behavior. He did not follow through with aftercare referrals.

Case 4 (DA). A 32-year-old twice-married man who claimed to be a Vietnam veteran was admitted for increasing episodes of uncontrollable violence, especially toward his wife. DA claimed that he had been a Ranger in Vietnam from 1971 to 1972 and had killed many times without sustaining any wounds. Although he was reluctant to talk about his combat experiences, he stated that during his second tour in Vietnam he injured his knee and was removed from combat duty but remained in the service another four years. According to DA, his problems with violence began after his combat duty. He also claimed to have had nightmares and flashbacks since Vietnam.

DA said that he couldn't take his wife's rejection, which was manifested through infidelity, sexual unavailability, and a desire to leave, and could "swear her face was turning 'gook.'" He reported a history of alcohol abuse, multiple job losses, and intolerance of being alone. He often experienced alienation, depression, and explosive outbursts.

On admission DA had no apparent psychiatric disturbance. During DA's hospital course, our suspicions of the veracity of his statements began to rise when staff realized they had been given discrepant military details.

Confrontation revealed that DA was not a Vietnam combatant. He finally confessed that enroute to Vietnam he became frightened in Okinawa and claimed "sole surviving son" status. DA admitted feeling guilty about not going to Vietnam, especially since he had buddies who had been killed there. He linked his guilt to the fabrication of his combat status. He soon found a job and was discharged and referred to an outpatient clinic.

DA did not follow through with outpatient treatment. A few months after discharge he apparently embezzled some money from a local veterans' organization and left town. He was also reported to have been drinking abusively.

Case 5 (MM). A 28-year-old unemployed veteran was admitted with complaints of difficulty in thinking, auditory hallucinations, confusion, and delusions of persecution. MM claimed that he had been well until his reported Vietnam service, during which he said he was a sergeant major in the Green Berets. He reported spending six years (1972 to 1978) in heavy combat with resulting PTSD. MM allegedly suffered a concussion in 1977 with the subsequent development of sporadic episodes of what he called "anascopic amnesia." He lived with his parents until 1981 when he became a drifter.

Initially, MM was vague and obviously guarded. Soon after

admission his behavior appeared inappropriate, and he admitted having constant auditory hallucinations. His associations became increasingly loose. He improved somewhat with perphenazine and benztropine but remained delusional about his belief of having served in Vietnam even after being confronted about never having been there. An eligibility check revealed that MM had enlisted on May 5, 1973, just two days before the pullout of troops from Vietnam. Evidently he did not serve in a combat position. He was discharged on neuroleptics with the diagnosis of schizophrenia, chronic undifferentiated type, and did not follow through with aftercare plans.

Case 6 (DM). A 31-year-old divorced and unemployed veteran with a service-connected disability was admitted for suicidal ideation. DM reported a medical history significant for petit mal seizures, which he claimed had begun following neurosurgery for wounds sustained during combat duty in Vietnam. Since the reported surgery DM claimed to have suffered from impulsivity and auditory and visual hallucinations, He alleged that he had received a bachelor's degree in child psychology, but when questioned he demonstrated little knowledge of the field. For several years before his admission, DM led a hobo existence following the alleged death of his family in an auto accident.

Although previous medical charts were never received to document his service record, when confronted about his history in group session he tearfully admitted to never having been in Vietnam. DM was discharged and did not follow through with aftercare after leaving the state.

Case 7 (DB). A 38-year-old unmarried, unemployed man who claimed to be a Vietnam veteran was admitted to the neurosurgery service with chief complaints of headaches and weakness. Various other somatic complaints included blurred vision, diplopia, difficulty walking, stiff neck, dysuria, coughing, rhinorrhea, and diarrhea. DB's self-reported medical history included childhood poliomyelitis resulting in a shortened right leg, and an occipital injury sustained during the Vietnam conflict, which he claimed had been treated surgically with a plate.

DB also stated that because of his combat experience he was suffering from posttraumatic stress disorder manifested by flashbacks, frequent nightmares, and crying spells.

Workup on the neurology service revealed inconsistent findings, and a CAT scan and skull films failed to demonstrate any pathology. Based on the patient's behavior and the lack of objective evidence to corroborate his complaints, he was transferred to the psychiatric unit for further evaluation.

DB's physical exam revealed that he was 5'2", with a very muscular build, a bravado-macho appearance, and a shortened right leg. Mental status exam revealed a querulous, sad, and helpless individual. DB was logical and coherent; his intellectual capacity was average but his judgment immature. He exhibited significant rage toward his father, whom he felt did not accept him.

DB's behavior during hospitalization was consistent with a dependent personality. His mood continued to be depressed and he expressed persistent feelings of hopelessness and helplessness.

When we called the several Vietnam outreach programs that DB said he had been involved in, they verified that he had been active in veterans' demonstrations and marches in the late 1970s. It was well known by the outreach program staffs that he had not served in Vietnam, but his personality at that time was so gregarious and helpful that the protest organizers accepted him as a "kind of mascot." DB was confronted with this information and admitted that it was true. Subsequent therapy sessions were of some benefit, and he was eventually discharged home.

DISCUSSION

In the history of warfare, some men have aggrandized their feats to receive further recognition or praise. Some individuals who do not have combat experience feel a need for the so-called advantage of warrior status or combat experience. These individuals have had to fabricate tales to gain the admiration of their peers or of the society in which they live. Some perpetrate falsehoods to augment their self-esteem or to hide personal inadequacies.

Factitious PTSD, heretofore undocumented, is a not-uncommon entity that arose as a consequence of the Vietnam conflict. Though unrecognized in DSM-III, it probably has been in existence as long as PTSD itself. It presents another form of a clinical deception for which the unsuspecting clinician must develop an index or degree of suspicion. So adept are factitious PTSD patients at their deception that even the most experienced physicians can find themselves fooled by the presenting complaints.

In analyzing the cases presented, one common denominator of factitious PTSD becomes apparent. Each patient had obviously acquired sufficient knowledge of PTSD to develop a tale best suited to his needs. The motives, however, varied in each case. PT, the patient in Case 1, had an obvious adjustment reaction to a broken home, a nonsupportive father, and a highly motivated and revered brother. The patient's efforts to match his father's adoration of his brother led to a lifetime of fabrication. A Munchausen existence evolved in turn. The only personal success PT experienced for a time was easily perpetuated through the VA system. There PT was not only offered compassionate treatment, but was even acknowledged as a hero and a person with counseling skills.

Clearly, in Case 2, secondary gain was the stimulus for RK's paralytic conversion reactions and factitious tales. Apparent dependency issues with his spouse contributed to his denial system and continuation of symptoms. The result was self-aggrandizement and a cover-up of significant personal inadequacies. The prospect of a workman's compensation settlement was doubtlessly another factor affecting his behavior. Of note is that RK and his wife were so blindly interdependent that their perspectives remained immutable even after they were presented with the reality of the patient's illness.

Case 3 exemplifies the problems that can be encountered when patients have a short hospital stay and staff lack immediate access to previous medical records. The discrepancies in DC's story enabled us to reach a diagnosis of factitious PTSD. Had time permitted, an indepth evaluation of the patient's past (as was done in Case 1) might have elucidated factors explaining his behavior. However, as is the case with so many patients with factitious disorders, discharge was requested before we could conduct a complete workup.

Case 4 represents a classic problem of noncombatant guilt. Competitive peer pressure combined with the actual fear of combat disrupted DA's ability to cope with military service and led to a fabricated history with face-saving behavior.

In Case 5 factitious PTSD even surfaces through the diagnosis of schizophrenia, chronic undifferentiated type. However, the patient in Case 5 is somewhat different than the other patients because his claims were purely delusional.

Like the patients in Cases 1, 2, and 7, the patient in Case 6 reported neurological symptoms. And, as in Case 3, the patient reported loss of family members in an auto accident.

Case 7 was interesting inasmuch as DB shared a similar background with the patient in Case 1: both had had an unsupportive father. Again a desire to be recognized, albeit through medical complaints and alleged combat experience, was the driving force behind DB's behavior. DB was very much at home as the adopted mascot of actual Vietnam veterans, whom he perceived as heroes. His involvement with the outreach program did much to alleviate his feelings of inadequacy.

The patients' knowledge of PTSD came from a variety of sources. As mentioned earlier, the media is replete with articles on the disorder. Interaction with legitimate veterans at vet centers and VAMCs around the country provided patients with additional opportunities to become aware of the symptoms and to learn to mimic them.

With the advent of the DSM-III classification system, the question at hand is how these cases might best be classified. The common element to all cases was the appearance and development of factitious PTSD. With the exception of the schizophrenic patient in Case 5, whose fabrications were part of a delusional system, all cases demonstrated subcomponents of Munchausen's syndrome or malingering. The patient in Case 2 exhibited symptoms of both.

There have been several recent articles on factitious illness especially those with psychiatric presentation (Pankratz, 1981; Cheng and Hummel, 1978; Gelenberg, 1977; Sale, Burvill, and Kalucy, 1979). Patients with Munchausen's syndrome usually present with a feigned illness of a dramatic or emergent nature, the symptoms of which may be corroborated during a physical examination. Common characteristics include evidence of previous hospital procedures; aggressive and manipulative behavior such as leaving the hospital against medical advice; multiple admissions in hospitals throughout the country; and pathologic lying and exaggeration. Patients are aware of the factitious nature of their symptoms, but often the motivation for such behavior is subconscious (Pop, Jonas, and Jones, 1982).

Individuals with the syndrome often have childhoods seriously lacking in parental affection. They are experts at clinical deception. Frequently they leave hospital before their previous records arrive and their deception is discovered. Although confrontation is the therapeutic approach of choice, the prognosis is inevitably poor. The patient in Case 1 was clearly lucky to have escaped with only an incision and drainage of a buttock abscess (possibly self-induced). He invited a host of invasive diagnostic procedures, with their inherent risks, to document evidence of his fabrications. Indeed, on a previous admission, he was given heparin therapy for a suspected pulmonary embolism and developed a venogram complication from which he is permanently scarred.

In contrast to Munchausen's syndrome, where motivation is often subconscious, malingering is described as a willfull and deliberate imitation or exaggeration of an illness, with a conscious intent to deceive observers for a specific purpose. Patients will usually be evasive during the history and physical, and quite histrionic on the ward. They often have had a model for the symptomatology they exhibit. If observed long enough, these patients might well be observed without the symptoms, or their symptoms may contradict the behavior and symptomatology of syndromes they actually have (Sparr and Pankratz, 1983).

As illustrated by the patient in Case 2, secondary gain is a common driving force in determining the behavior of malingerers. Symptoms rarely disappear before the gain is achieved. As in Case 7, malingering can often coexist with other physical or psychological pathology. It can also arise as an expression of an underlying schizophrenic process, as illustrated by the patient in Case 5.

CONCLUSION

During the five months when these cases were collected, our 20-bed unit treated a total of 125 patients and had an average daily census of only 14. Seven cases of factitious PTSD were discovered. Clinicians must be aware of the possibility of the disorder, and become suspicious when staff obtain contradictory data from patients. Further awareness of the disorder can be acquired by reading any of a number of recently published books and articles on Vietnam and PTSD (Santoli, 1982; Herr, 1978; Fitzgerald, 1973). The veteran's discharge papers (Form DD214) will indicate dates of service and also whether the veteran served overseas. The DD214 will also note if the veteran has the campaign and service medals universally awarded to servicemen who were in Vietnam. Lack of any of this documentation is strong evidence for not having served in Vietnam.

Vet center consultation provides the quickest and most accurate indirect determination of authenticity. Vet center counselors are well versed in the war's timetable of events and in the geography and culture of Vietnam. Few imitators, having never stepped on East Asian soil, can fool them. There are exceptions to this, however, as indicated by Case 1, which underscores the need for clinicians to take a multifaceted approach using several of the recommendations just discussed. Only then can clinicians avoid succumbing to the heart-rending tall tales of an accomplished storyteller and begin working on the issue at hand—the evaluation and therapeutic treatment of the patient's underlying psychopathology. Clearly, our first responsibility is to develop an awareness of factitious PTSD, malingering, and Munchausen's syndrome, for until we do, patients with such disorders will not receive appropriate care.

REFERENCES

Cheng, L., & Hummel, L. (1978), The Munchausen syndrome as a psychiatric condition. *Brit. J. Psychiat.*, 133:20–21.

Fitzgerald, R. (1973), *Fire in the Lake*. New York: Vintage.

Friedman, M. M. (1981), Post-Vietnam syndrome: Recognition and management. *Psychosom.*, 22:931–943.

Gelenberg, A. J. (1977), Munchausen's syndrome with a psychiatric presentation. *Dis. Nerv. Syst.*, 38:378–380.

Herr, M. (1978), *Dispatches*. New York: Avon.

Morganthau, T., & Shabad, S. (1981), The troubled Vietnam vet. *Newsweek*, March 30, p. 87.

Pankratz, L. (1981), A review of the Munchausen syndrome. *Clin. Psychol. Rev.*, 1:65–78.

Pop, H. G., Jonas, J. M., & Jones, B. (1982), Factitious psychosis: Phenomenology, family history, and long-term outcome of nine patients. *Amer. J. Psychiat.*, 139:1480–1483.

Sale, I., Burvill, J., & Kalucy, R. (1979), Munchausen syndrome in a psychiatric setting: Three case reports. *Austral. & N.Z. J. Psychiat.*, 13:133–138.

Santoli, A. (1981), After Vietnam: The long battle to readjust. *Family Weekly*, July 5, p. 6.

——— (1982), *Everything We Had*. New York: Ballantine Books.

Silver, S. (1982), PTSD in Vietnam veterans: An addendum to Fairbank. *Profess. Psychol.*, 13:4.

Sparr, L., & Pankratz, L. D. (1983), Factitious post-traumatic stress disorder. *Amer. J. Psychiat.*, 140:1016–1019.

Walker, J. I. (1981), The psychological problems of Vietnam veterans. *J. Amer. Med. Assn.*, 246:781–782.

Williams, T., ed. (1980), *PTSD of the Vietnam Veteran*. Cincinnati: Disabled American Veterans.

Chapter 33
Chemotherapy of
Traumatic War Stress

J. INGRAM WALKER, M.D.

The psychological conflicts of war have existed throughout history (Cavenar and Nash, 1976). Hammond (1883) examined the psychological reactions to Civil War combat; World War I was instrumental in Freud's (1955) development of the dual instinct theory; Grinker and Spiegel (1963) extensively studied World War II combatants. The Vietnam War has again led to the study of traumatic war stress (Walker, 1981a). Despite the extensive literature on war-related stress, no definitive treatment modality has proved completely successful. This chapter will discuss chemotherapy as an adjunct to treatment of traumatic war stress.

SYMPTOMS OF POSTTRAUMATIC
STRESS DISORDER

Symptoms of posttraumatic stress disorders include recurrent dreams of the war, mental flashbacks of the war, intense memories of the traumatic event, or a sudden feeling that the trau-

Acknowledgment. This chapter was first published in *Military Medicine* (1982), 147:1029–1033, and it is reprinted with permission.

587

matic events were recurring. Also necessary for the diagnosis of posttraumatic stress disorder is a numbing of experience, as demonstrated by constricted affect, diminished interest in activities, and feelings of alienation. At least two of the following symptoms that were not present before the war must exist: sleep disturbance, exaggerated startle responses, survival guilt, difficulty in concentrating, and avoidance of activities that arouse recollection of the traumatic event (American Psychiatric Association, 1980).

The stress disorder may develop from single or repeated traumatic war events (Kardiner, 1947). Acute traumatic stress will show a dramatic clinical picture of mental confusion, massive anxiety, and repetitive, intrusive memories and dreams of the event (Walker, 1982). Chronic traumatic stress may continue for decades (Archibald and Tuddenham, 1965) and years later the acute phase of this disorder can be reactivated by an event similar to the one that stimulated the original trauma (Christenson, Walker, Ross, and Maltbie, 1981).

Although symptoms of posttraumatic stress disorder are well defined, the diagnosis of traumatic war stress may be difficult (Walker and Nash, 1981a). The veteran may fail to volunteer information about combat; furthermore, the veteran may suppress the symptoms with alcohol or drugs. Because the veteran may conceal material about the war, the clinician must ask specifically about combat experience to avoid misdiagnosing alcoholism, depression, psychosis, antisocial personality, or drug abuse (Walker and Nash, 1981b).

CHEMOTHERAPY

Although no well-controlled studies have been done on chemotherapeutic agents in the treatment of traumatic war stress, several psychopharmacological agents have been suggested (Walker and Canevar, 1982). The uses, indications, and contraindications of these medications will be discussed.

SODIUM AMYTAL

Horsley (1936) employed the use of intravenous sodium amytal in combination with hypnosis, coining the phrase "narcoanalysis" for the method of interviewing the patient while under the influence of barbiturates. During World War II, Grinker and his associates used narcoanalysis extensively to aid combat veterans with stress disorders. Both sodium amytal and sodium pentothal were used extensively during World War II to produce an altered state of consciousness, which would allow the individual to talk more readily concerning the combat experiences (Canevar and Nash, 1977). Sodium amytal is reported to have a wider range between therapeutic effects and narcotic effects; amytal is longer acting than sodium pentothal and the patient may sleep for several hours after the treatment session. Sodium pentothal, on the other hand, has a faster onset of action and a shorter duration, so that the patient is unlikely to sleep after the interview session.

Whichever drug one chooses, the basic technique is similar. The patient, while in a recumbent position, receives a 5 or 10 percent solution of pentothal or amytal in the anticubital vein. The drug, given at a rate of no more than one grain per minute, is discontinued when the patient begins to demonstrate slurred speech and nystagmus. The patient can then be questioned directly about the traumatic combat events.

Narcoanalysis is a useful diagnostic aid. If, after an extensive interview, the diagnosis remains unclear, narcoanalysis may be of great value. Narcoanalysis may be utilized to distinguish a traumatic stress disorder from latent schizophrenic symptoms. During a sodium amytal interview, the schizophrenic individual will lose contact with reality; hallucinations, delusions, or paranoid ideation will be elicited. In contrast, the individual with stress disorder will talk about the events of war in an organized, although sometimes terrified, manner. Narcoanalysis may also be of benefit in distinguishing depression from stress disorder in a mute, noncooperative patient. With a small amount of barbiturate, the depressed patient will describe severe depressive symptoms without psychotic content. Likewise, patients with a conversion reaction will reveal unconscious psychological conflicts during a sodium amytal interview. Those individuals with a mild organic brain syndrome will demonstrate an exacerbation of the organicity during an amytal interview.

Although a useful diagnostic aid and, because of its cathartic effects, a useful method in offering temporary relief from the traumatic event, narcoanalysis should not be conceptualized as a definitive treatment. Many patients require several years of remembering, reexperiencing, and placing of the trauma into perspective before complete mastery of the trauma can be achieved (Walker and Nash, 1981a). Grinker and associates reported that simple abreaction of the feelings was insufficient for complete treatment; and in nearly every case subsequent interviews without medication were necessary, to allow working through of the traumatic material. Walker and Nash (1981b) reported four cases in which the patients initially gained relief of their symptomatology from narcoanalysis, but later relapsed with a reexperiencing of traumatic dreams, guilt feelings, startle reactions, and ruminations about the war. These individuals improved with group therapy (Walker and Nash, 1981a).

MONOAMINE OXIDASE INHIBITORS

Recently Hogben and Cornfield (1981) described the use of phenelzine (Nardil[R]) in the treatment of traumatic war stress. These patients had failed to respond to multiple previous trials with antipsychotics, tricyclic antidepressants, and psychotherapy. With phenelzine, traumatic dreams, flashbacks of the traumatic event, startle reactions, and violent outbursts ceased. The patients reported feeling calmer. In addition, Hogben and Cornfield reported that phenelzine appeared to enhance psychotherapy with these patients by stimulating an intense abreaction: all five patients had a period of emotional outpouring beginning approximately four days after starting phenelzine treatment and lasting for several weeks. The primary emotion was rage, followed by depression and, finally, by a brief period of elation. Memories consisted of traumatic war events and recollections of conflict with authority. Three of the five patients were gradually able to discontinue the phenelzine treatment after three to six months of therapy; these patients maintained their improved conditions for as long as 18 months. One of the patients continued to do well taking 30 mg of phenelzine daily. The fifth patient was lost to follow-up.

Traumatic dreams ceased in all five patients while they were taking phenelzine. When phenelzine was discontinued the traumatic dreams recurred. Phenelzine, a powerful inhibitor of REM sleep, abolishes dream activity in doses of 60 mg or more (Fisher, 1978; Dunleavy and Oswald, 1973).

Four of the five patients stopped having flashbacks completely during phenelzine therapy, while the fifth had less frequent daytime visualizations. Because evidence has been accumulating that the sleep-dream cycle is part of a continuing 24-hour biorhythm cycle, Hogben and Cornfield (1981) postulated that suppression of flashback activity with phenelzine therapy may have resulted from the inhibition of an awake REM state.

In our clinic, three patients placed on 60 mg of phenelzine reported less frequent traumatic dreams and flashbacks, but continued to have irritability, emotional numbness, and difficulties in interpersonal relationships. Two other patients placed on phenelzine had to discontinue the medication secondary to side effects.

Monoamine oxidase is a complex enzyme system widely distributed throughout the body, and is responsible for the metabolic decomposition of biogenic amines, thus terminating their activity. Drugs which inhibit this enzyme system, specifically monoamine oxidase inhibitors (MAOIs) cause an increase in the concentration of endogenous epinephrine, norepinephrine, and serotonin in storage sites throughout the nervous system (Baldessarini, 1977). It is believed that the increase in the concentration of monoamines in the central nervous system is the basis for the therapeutic effects of the MAOIs.

Indications for MAOIs in patients with traumatic war stress

would include those with a concomitant atypical depression (patients with pananxiety, phobias, hypersomnolence, and hypochondriacal complaints associated with depression) (Klein, Gittelman, Quitman, and Rifkin, 1980). In addition, those patients with traumatic war stress who have excessive nightmares and flashbacks may benefit from a trial with the MAOIs.

There are two classes of MAOIs available in the United States, the hydrazine-phenelzine (Nardil[R]) and isocarboxazide (Marplan[R]), and the nonhydrazine-tranylcypromine (Parnate[R]). Another nonhydrazine, pargyline (Eutonyl[R]), has been approved only as an antihypertensive. Because phenelzine has been more extensively studied and appears to be safer and more effective than the other MAOIs, it could be considered the MAOI of choice in traumatic war stress.

Ravaris, Nies, and Robinson (1976) studied the inhibition of platelet MAO as an index of brain MAO inhibition. They found that approximately 85 percent inhibition of brain MAO is needed before increases in platelet monoamines occur. They suggest that at least 60 mg of phenelzine a day is required to achieve 85 percent of MAO inhibition. In the combat veteran, the starting dose of phenelzine is 15 mg three times daily, gradually increased to 60 mg a day. Ninety mg of phenelzine daily may be necessary for a complete response.

Both minor and serious side effects can be encountered from MAOI therapy. Common adverse reactions include orthostatic hypotension, disturbances in cardiac rhythm, dizziness, vertigo, constipation, headache, hyperreflexia, tremors and muscle twitching, mania, hypomania, jitteriness, confusion and memory impairment, dry mouth, blurred vision, and hyperhidrosis. Most MAOIs reduce the amounts of intestinal MAO, thus allowing increased concentrations of tyramine and other sympathomimetics to be absorbed. This mechanism is believed to contribute to the pathogenesis of hypotensive crises (Klein et al, 1980). Patients taking MAOIs should avoid tyramine-containing foods such as cheese, wine, beer, yogurt, broad beans, unfresh meats, yeast, and pickled products. Any sympathomimetic agent, including nonprescription "cold" preparations, should be avoided. It is estimated that only 2 percent of patients being treated with MAOIs will develop headaches, 0.3–0.5 percent hypertensive crises, and less than 0.001 percent death (Klein et al., 1980). The death rate of MAOI treated patients is approximately one per 100,000.

If a patient is being switched from a tricyclic, there should be a delay of at least seven to ten days before beginning a MAOI, to prevent severe interactions (Walker and Brodie, 1980). Combined tricyclic and MAOI therapy requires further investigation before it can be recommended for use in traumatic war stress.

TRICYCLIC ANTIDEPRESSANTS

The combat veteran with traumatic war stress who has a secondary depression with biological signs, including initial and terminal sleep disturbance, decreased appetite, decreased libido, and decreased energy, may benefit from tricyclic antidepressant medication as an adjunct to psychotherapy. In prescribing these medications, it is important that the patient also receive some form of individual or group psychotherapy in conjunction with the antidepressant. Bielski and Friedel (1976) studied depressed patients without traumatic war stress. They reported that predictors of positive response to tricyclics include upper socioeconomic class, insidious onset, anorexia, weight loss, middle and late insomnia, and psychomotor disturbance. They also reported that predictors of poor response to tricyclics included hypochondriasis, hysterical traits, multiple episodes, and delusions.

The choice of tricyclic is empirical. The clinician can keep in mind that minor changes in the central ring and the side chain of the tricyclic result in difference in their clinical effects. Thus, amitriptyline has the most anticholinergic and sedative properties, while desipramine, nortriptyline, and protriptyline are the least sedative tricyclics. The onset of action of the newest tricyclic, amoxapine (which may prove to be the least cardiotoxic of the tricyclics), appears to be somewhat faster, with clinical response seen in some patients after four to seven days of therapy (Ayd, 1980).

Table 33.1 gives the dose range of the tricyclic antidepressants. A good rule of thumb in initiating therapy, if there are no extenuating precautions, is to begin with a dose estimated to be one-fourth to one-third the expected therapeutic dose, increased every four to seven days until the desired response is achieved. Because there is a lag period before the onset of antidepressant effect, the therapeutic trial period may be as long as three weeks (Walker, 1981b). Once the symptoms of depression have remitted, the patient is usually maintained on medication for at least six months. To prevent withdrawal symptoms, the drug can be gradually reduced at a rate of 25–50 mg every week. If a patient has a history of short intervals between recurrent depressive episodes, maintenance therapy may be indicated. The usual dose for maintenance therapy is approximately half the therapeutic dose, although as little as 25 mg may be sufficient to prevent relapse in some patients.

The most common side effects of tricyclics are caused by their anticholinergic properties, and include dry mouth, sweating, blurred vision, urinary retention, and paralytic ileus. Confusional states resembling atropine poisoning have been reported. Various skin reactions occasionally occur and sometimes an allergic, obstructive type jaundice or agranulocytosis occurs with tricyclic administration. In addition, the seizure threshold is lowered by tricyclics (Baldessarini, 1977).

Signs and symptoms of tricyclic overdose include cardiac arrhythmias, hypotension, confusion, mydriasis, ataxia, seizures, respiratory depression, and cardiac arrest. Because of extensive protein binding of tricyclics, overdoses do not respond to dialysis. Overdosage and subsequent toxicity may be significantly curtailed by limiting prescriptions to 1.25 mg of amitriptyline or its equivalent (Walker and Brodie, 1980).

A high percentage of patients in our clinic who meet the DSM-III criteria for posttraumatic stress disorder also meet the criteria for a major depression. These patients benefit from

Table 33.1
Tricyclic Antidepressant Dosage Information

Drug	Adult Starting Dose (mg/day)	Initial Adult Target Dosage (mg/day)	Adult Therapeutic Dosage Range (mg/day)	Plasma Half Life (hours)
Amitriptyline	25-50	150	75-300	10-50
Amoxapine	100-150	200-300	200-600	—
Desipramine	25-50	150	75-300	7-76
Doxepin	25-50	150	75-300	6-8
Imipramine	25-50	150	75-300	8-16
Nortriptyline	25	75	40-100	16-90
Protriptyline	10	30	10-40	54-198
Trimipramine	75	200	200	—

tricyclic antidepressant medication, prescribed in therapeutic doses in conjunction with group psychotherapy. Clearly, more detailed studies are needed to evaluate the incidence of depression in traumatic war stress, and psychopharmacological interventions need to be thoroughly investigated.

ANTIPSYCHOTICS

Low doses of antipsychotics may be useful to control severe flashback episodes and severe agitation in patients with traumatic war stress. Although no well-controlled studies have been done, the following criteria may be indications for antipsychotic use in this group of patients:

1. The occurrence of aggressive psychotic symptoms, frequently of a paranoid quality which are stress related, reversible, and transient.
2. An affective state characterized by the prominence of anger plus varying degrees of prolonged anxiety.
3. Self-destructive behavior such as self-mutilation, addiction, or repeated suicidal gestures.

4. Frequent "flashback" episodes characterized by visual or auditory hallucinations or traumatic events.

Antipsychotic medication should be used in low doses, for a brief period of time, and in conjunction with psychotherapy. The higher potency antipsychotics such as thiothixene (Narvane[R]), trifluoperazine (Stelazine[R]), fluphenazine (Prolixin[R]), and haloperidol (Haldol[R]) may be the antipsychotics of choice, because they are minimally sedating and have lower anticholinergic side effects. Dosage should be in the range of one to two mg of haloperidol or its equivalent given once or twice daily. As soon as the patient becomes stabilized, the medication should be discontinued.

The most common side effect of high potency antipsychotic medication is an acute dystonic reaction, characterized by spasms of the truncal, nuchal, buccal, and oculomotor muscle groups. These reactions usually occur within the first hour to five days of the onset of treatment with antipsychotics. Benztropine (Cogentin[R]) 0.5–2.0 mg intravenously or 25–50 mg of intravenous diphenhydramine (Benadryl[R]) can dramatically reverse acute dystonia.

Akathisia, motor restlessness with an inability to sit still, usually develops within the first few weeks of treatment. Akathisia can be misdiagnosed as agitation, causing the clinician to erroneously increase the dose of antipsychotic medication. This increased dosage will result in more restlessness or lead to sedation and rigidity. Benzotropine (Cogentin[R]) 0.5–2.0 mg orally daily, or trihexyphenadyl (Artane[R]) two to eight mg orally, given in daily divided doses, will generally reduce the symptoms of akathisia.

Anticholinergic medication should be given only when extrapyramidal symptoms develop for the following reasons (Walker and Brodie, 1980): (1) Anticholinergic medications decrease antipsychotic blood levels; (2) anticholinergic drugs slow intestinal mobility and decrease the absorption of antipsychotics; (3) anticholinergic medications exacerbate tardive dyskinesia, presumably by antagonizing the dopamine system;

and (4) the anticholinergic drug may produce side effects such as a toxic delirium, constipation, urinary retention, blurred vision, prostatic hypertrophy, cardiac arrhythmias, or aggravation of glaucoma.

Antipsychotic medications should be given only for a brief period of time to avoid the development of tardive dyskinesia, a neurological condition consisting of abnormal motor movements of the face. The typical facial movements include grimacing, involuntary protrusion of the tongue, pushing out of the cheeks, chewing movements, and licking of the lips. Since there is no effective treatment for tardive dyskinesia, every effort should be made to achieve therapeutic benefits of the antipsychotic with the least dosage administered for the shortest period of time.

PROPRANOLOL

Propranolol (Inderal[R]) is a beta-adrenergic blocking agent that can effectively control the somatic symtoms of anxiety, although it has not been aproved by the Federal Drug Administration for this use. Suzman (1976) studied 72 patients with anxiety marked by tremor, palpitations, headache, hyperventilation, and muscular weakness. Therapy was initiated with 40–80 mg of propranolol daily in four divided doses, and the dosage was gradually increased to control symptoms. Generally, 80–230 mg of propranolol was needed to control the somatic symptoms of anxiety. Again, although no well-controlled studies have been done, we have found propranolol useful as an adjunct to psychotherapy, to treat those combat veterans who manifest the autonomic symptoms of anxiety such as sweating, palpitations, dizziness, irregular heart beat and tremors.

Contraindications to propranolol include obstructive pulmonary disease, asthma, congestive heart failure, heart block, and allergic rhinitis. Depression is a common psychiatric complication of propranolol treatment.

BENZODIAZEPINES

With the possible exception of flurazepam (Dalmane[R]) or temazepam (Restoril[R]), the benzodiazepines are contraindicated in the treatment of traumatic war stress. The benzodiazepines interfere with normal adaptive functions necessary to cope successfully with problems (Walker, 1981b). In addition, paradoxical rage reactions have been reported with the benzodiazepines (Baldessarini, 1977). Withdrawl from large doses of benzodiazepines can produce shakiness, anxiety, insomnia, nightmares, and, if the benzodiazepines have been taken in large doses for prolonged period of time, seizures (Baldessarini, 1977).

Rarely, flurazepam (Dalmane[R]) or temazepam (Restoril[R]), 15–30 mg at bedtime, can be used for transient sleep disturbances. Because these medications lose their effectiveness after a few weeks (Walker and Cavenar, 1985), they should never be prescribed for more than a week.

SEDATIVE-HYPNOTICS

The barbiturates and the propanediols (meprobamate-like drugs) have no place in modern drug therapy. These medications have a potential to produce mental confusion and oversedation. In addition, they have a high abuse potential. Lethal overdosage is not uncommon.

OTHER SOPORIFICS

The antihistamines, diphenhydramine (Benadryl[R]) 25–50 mg at bedtime, and hydroxyzine (Atarax[R]) 10–25 mg at bedtime, have sedative properties; these drugs, however, can cause acute toxic delusions secondary to their anticholinergic properties. Chloral hydrate, in doses of 500 mg to 1 gm has sedative effects but can produce gastric irritation. Chloral hydrate also potentiates the effects of Coumadin and some studies suggest that it depresses REM sleep (Walker and Brodie, 1980).

LITHIUM

Although lithium has proved effective in treating patients with antisocial and explosive characteristics in uncontrolled studies (Walker and Brodie, 1978), no studies have been reported in the use of lithium in the treatment of traumatic war stress. We have not used lithium in our mental hygiene clinic to treat combat veterans with stress disorder.

SUMMARY

It is estimated that from 500,000 to 700,000 Vietnam combat veterans suffer from a posttraumatic stress disorder (Walker, 1981a). Countless other World War II and Korean War veterans continue to have symptoms of traumatic war stress. Unfortunately, no well-controlled studies have been done concerning the pharmacological treatment of this disorder. Clearly, a well-controlled, longitudinal study comparing variety of treatment modalities is needed.

REFERENCES

American Psychiatric Association (1980), *The Diagnostic and Statistical Manual of Mental Disorders*, 3rd ed. Washington, DC: American Psychiatric Association.

Archibald, H. C., & Tuddenham, R. D. (1965), Persistent stress reactions after combat. *Arch. Gen. Psychiat.*, 12:475–481.

Ayd, F. J. (1980), Amoxapine: A new tricyclic antidepressant. *Internat. Drug Ther. News.*, 10/9,10.

Baldessarini, R. J. (1977), *Chemotherapy and Psychiatry*. Cambridge, MA: Harvard University Press.

Bielski, R. J., & Friedel, R. D. (1976), Predictions of tricyclic antidepressant response. *Arch. Gen. Psychiat.*, 33/1:479–489.

Cavenar, J. O., & Nash. J. L. (1976), The effects of combat on the normal personality: War neurosis in Vietnam returnees. *Compr. Psychiat.*, 17:647–653.

———— ———— (1977), Narcoanalysis: The forgotten diagnostic aid. *Milit. Med.*, 142:553–555.

Christenson, R. N., Walker, J. I., Ross, D. R., & Maltbie, A. A. (1981), Reactivation of traumatic conflicts. *Amer. J. Psychiat.*, 138:984–985.

Dunleavy, D. L. F., & Oswald, I. (1973), Phenelzine mood response and sleep. *Arch. Gen. Psychiat.*, 28:353–356.

Fisher, C. (1978), Experimental and clinical approaches to the mind-body problem through recent research in sleep and dreaming. In: *Psychopharmacology and psychotherapy: Synthesis or Antithesis?* ed. N. Rosenzweig & H. Griscom. New York: Human Sciences Press, pp. 61–69.

Freud, S. (1916–1917), Introductory lectures. *Standard Edition*, 16:264–275. London: Hogarth, 1955.

Grinker, R. P., & Spiegel, J. P. (1963), *Men Under Stress*. New York: McGraw-Hill.

Hammond, W. A. (1883), *A Treatise on Insanity and Its Medical Relations*. London: H. K. Lewis.

Hogben, G. L., & Cornfield, R. B. (1981), Treatment of traumatic war neurosis with phenelzine. *Arch. Gen. Psychiat.*, 38:440–445.

Horsley, J. S. (1936), Narcoanalysis. *J. Ment. Sci.*, 82:416–422.

Kardiner, A. (1947), *War Stress and Neurotic Illness*. New York: Paul B. Hober.

Klein, D. F., Gittelman, R., Quitkin, F., & Rifkin, A. (1980), *Diagnosis and Drug Treatment of Psychiatric Disorders: Adults and Children*, 2nd ed. Baltimore: Williams & Wilkins.

Ravaris, C. L., Nies, A., Robinson, D. S., et al. (1976), A multiple dose controlled study of phenelzine in depression-anxiety states. *Arch. Gen. Psychiat.*, 33:347–350.

Suzman, N. M. (1976), Propranolol in the treatment of anxiety. *Postgrad. Med. J.*, 52:168–174.

Waal, H. J. (1967), Propranolol induced depression. *Brit. Med. J.*, 2:50–56.

Walker, J. I. (1981a), Psychological problems in Vietnam veterans. *J. Amer. Med. Assn.*, 346:781–782.

———— (1981b), *Clinical Psychiatry in Primary Care*. Menlo Park, CA: Addison-Wesley.

———— (1982), Post-traumatic stress disorder after a car accident. *Post-grad. Med.*, 69:82–86.

———— Brodie, H. K. H. (1978), Current Concepts of Lithium Treatment and Prophylaxis. *J. Cont. Educ. Psychiat.*, 39:19–30.

———— ———— (1980), Neuropharmacology of aging. In: *Handbook of Geriatric Psychiatry*, ed. E. W. Busse & D. G. Blazer. New York: Van Nostrand Reinhold.

———— Cavenar, J. O. (1982), Forgotten warriors: Continuing problems of Vietnam veterans. In: *Critical Issues in Psychiatry*, ed. J. O. Cavenar & H. K. H. Brodie. Philadelphia: Lippincott.

————— ————— (1985), Sleep disorders. In: *Signs and Symptoms in Psychiatry*, ed. J. O. Cavenar & H. K. H. Brodie. Philadelphia: Lippincott.

————— Nash, J. L. (1981a), Post-traumatic stress disorder in combat veterans: Diagnosis and treatment. *J. Psychiat. Treat. Eval.*, 3:247–250.

————— (1981b), Group therapy in the treatment of Vietnam combat veterans. *Internat. J. Group Psychother.*, 31:379–389.

Wyatt, R. J., Kupfer, D. J., & Snyder, F. (1971), Total prolonged drug induced REM sleep suppression in anxious depressed patients. *Arch. Gen. Psychiat.*, 24:145–155.

Part VI
Family and Life Span Development: Issues in Stressful Life Events

The family is an essential part of our life and just as individuals make the family, families have endured the stressors of life events from the very beginning of time. Societal, cultural, and psychological support have been ever present in our understanding of the family and its dealing with stressful life events. The family has been the single most important resource in dealing with stress. There are, as we have come to understand, a number of theoretical perspectives from which to view the family and to understand the interface the family experiences with stressful life events. McCubbin and Patterson (1982) have advanced the theory that the family crisis results from imbalances of family functioning—member to member and/or family to community relationships. It is the process of adaptation to these crises that reflects the efforts on the part of family members to achieve balance within these relationships.

There is growing interest in theory building and in hypothesis testing relating to stress related disorders within the family structure but because this area of family stress is relatively recent, research has not clearly defined all the issues and implications relevant to understanding and treating stress related disorders within family structure. With theory building as an important goal of family stress clinical research, however, there is an increasing likelihood that collaboration among scientists will result in new breakthroughs and yield valuable clinical in-

603

formation on the prevention and effective management of stress, both for the individual and the family. Until such realization occurs, however, it is imperative that we explore and understand multiplicity of stressors and the effective measures which can be utilized in coping with anxiety, stress, and tension in family structure.

The chapters which follow reflect the work of 16 scholars from five separate disciplines discussing a variety of issues appropriate to family life and its interface with stressful life events. The initial chapter in this section is by Drs. Fergusson, Horwood, and Shannon. Examined is the relationship between maternal reports of child-rearing problems, family life events, and maternal depressive symptoms studied in a birth cohort of children in New Zealand. Rates of child-rearing problems showed a steady increase with both increasing levels of family life events and maternal depressive symptoms. Log-linear modeling of the results suggested that the apparent correlation between family life events and reports of child-rearing problems was mediated by the effects of maternal depression, so that some who were subject to large numbers of adverse life events suffered increased rates of depression and in turn reported higher rates of problem behavior in their children. There was no significant correlation between family life and events and reports of child-rearing problems when the effects of maternal depressive symptoms were taken into account. The findings tend to suggest that the previously reported association between family life events and child-rearing problems arises because life events provoke depressive symptoms in women and in turn this alters the way in which they perceive or evaluate their children's behavior.

Further study from the Child Development Study, Christchurch, New Zealand, and the team of clinical researchers headed by Dr. D. M. Fergusson explores the relationship among variables that include family life events, maternal depression, and teacher and maternal ratings of child behavior. Analysis of variance and multiple regression analysis showed that for maternal ratings of child behavior, both maternal depression and family life events made significant independent contributions. For teacher ratings of children's behavior, the only significant predictor was family life events. These results persisted when appropriate controls for family social, economic, and demographic characteristics were taken into account. The theoretical implications of these findings are discussed. Drs. John Greene, Lynn Walker, Gerald Hickson, and Juliette Thompson examine the complexity of somatic complaints and their relationship to stressful life events in adolescents. While life stress has been associated with recurrent pain in children and adolescents, level of stress has not previously been found useful in differentiating patients with functional pain from those in whom other conditions are diagnosed. In this study the authors used a standard measure of stressful life events systematically administered to adolescents seen for the first time at an outpatient adolescent clinic. Patients with recurrent pain for which no organic etiology could be identified reported significantly higher life stress than patients being seen for routine checkup, acute minor illness, stable chronic illness, or pain with clinically diagnosed organic cause. Furthermore, patients referred for behavior problems indicated significantly higher life stress than all other patient groups. It is suggested that a measure of stressful life events may be a useful adjunct to the clinical interview and is of particular value in identifying specific stressors and planning treatment to address them.

Bush, Melamed, and Cockrell examine the relationship of self-reported maternal anxiety, coping, and parenting style, with observed parenting behaviors in a stressful pediatric clinic setting. Reliable observational ratings revealed that parenting behaviors were weakly predicted by questionnaires. Mothers who reported using punishment in common child fear situations tended to ignore their children's sociable-affiliative behaviors, and had children who showed more distress. Mothers who reported using positive reinforcement were more likely to distract and less likely to ignore child sociable-affiliative behavior, which appeared to inhibit child distress.

Lane Veltkamp and Dr. Thomas W. Miller address contested cases of child custody within the divorcing process of stressful life events. Recent efforts have been made to develop a model for family mediation and subsequent clinical strategies that can attempt to address the stressors involved in divorce and perhaps resolve through mediation aimed at the post-trauma stress experienced by both spouses and children. This chapter reviews the literature on the impact of separation and divorce on families and the use of family mediation to resolve disputes. It further addresses psychological factors involved in the mediation process and the possible effects of mediation on divorce. An established family mediation model for treatment is presented in detail as are clinical issues often addressed in the family mediation process.

Drs. Robert Harrington and Judith Burry and Dennis Pelsma, in the next chapter, examine factors contributing to teacher stress. Explored are the numerous job-related pressures endured by teachers in the school setting. The association between job stress and job satisfaction is addressed, as is the validity and reliability of measures developed to assess quality of teacher work life. Based on the data presented, stressed teachers are more likely to experience more difficulty with students and parents, and have problems related to time management, activity management, and relating to people in general. Future research areas are explored.

Drs. Elaine Anderson and Leigh Leslie studied three categories of working families—the dual-career, dual-income, and traditional breadwinner/homemaker—and its impact as their life stressors. In particular, the relationship between the number of changes experienced by a family, their level of coping, and their marital and life satisfaction was explored in each type of working family. Various aspects of work and family roles and how they affect family functioning are discussed as factors which may assist families in coping with the two-worker lifestyles.

Next, Shirley Campbell explores midlife stress with respect

to women. Explored and examined are the impact potential of widowhood, divorce, poverty, interpersonal strains, and other midlife stressors. Discussion reveals a variety of coping strategies that have been found effective for some women in the face of the stressors of midlife crises.

The Southeastern Regional Medical Education Conference on Geriatric Stressors considered the multifactor stressors in life change. Dr. Miller and Louis Jay address the variety of disturbances in life that can cause stress in the geriatric population. Concerns related to the physical environment, social and interpersonal relations, one's perception of various aspects of daily life, and issues related to relocation and dependence have all been shown to be critical stressors for the geriatric patient. Examined are a multiplicity of factors which have been recognized through clinical research as relevant to the geriatric patient. Specific issues related to life change events, its applicability to personality theory and recent clinical research are explored. The relevance of current measures of stressful life events and some suggested revisions are offered as are strategies for treatment which utilize cognitive and behavioral skills and stress management techniques appropriate for the geriatric patient.

Finally, Drs. Stein, Linn, and Stein, and Elisa Slater of the University of Miami School of Medicine explore future concerns and recent life events of our geriatric population. Elderly community residents completed a 37-item inventory that measured their level of concern about potentially stressful events or emotions. Later, they indicated whether selected life events had actually occurred in the last six months. All data were intercorrelated to determine if there were relationships between total scores, personal characteristics, and recent life events. Results showed elderly persons in this sample to be most worried about immediate economic survival and disability. Implications for those with poorer health and for the geriatric population are explored by the authors.

REFERENCE

McCubbin, H. I., & Patterson, J. M. (1982), Family adaptation in crisis. In: *Family Stress, Coping and Social Support*, ed. H. McCubbin, E. Cauble, & J. Patterson. Springfield, IL: Charles C Thomas, pp. 26–54.

Chapter 34
Relationship of Family Life Events, Maternal Depression, and Child-Rearing Problems

D. M. FERGUSSON, B.A. Hons., L. J. HORWOOD, B.A., B.Sc., AND F. T. SHANNON, F.R.C.P., F.R.A.C.P.

Beautrais, Fergusson, and Shannon (1982b) have examined the relationship between measures of family life events and maternal reports of child-rearing problems in a birth cohort of four-year-old children in New Zealand. It was found that rates of reported child-rearing problems showed a clear and general tendency to increase with measures of family life events: mothers reporting five or more life events in a given year reported more than two and a half times as many problem behaviors in their children as mothers who reported no life events. This association persisted when the effects of a series of potentially confounding factors relating to family and social background were taken into account.

These findings were consistent with at least two major explanatory hypotheses. The first and most direct is that "stress"

Acknowledgment. This chapter was first published in *Pediatrics* (1984), 73/6:773–776, and it is reprinted by permission of *Pediatrics.*

in the family has adverse effects on the child which may result in problem behavior. The alternative explanation is that stressful life events alter maternal mood and the way in which the mother perceives her child so that mothers facing stressful conditions tend to see their children as being more troublesome.

This chapter reports a further study of the cohort described by Beautrais et al. (1982b) and looks at the role of maternal mood on the apparent correlation between life events and reports of behavior problems. In particular, it has been well documented that adverse life events are associated with significant increases in rates of depressive symptoms in women (Brown and Harris, 1978; Stewart and Salt, 1981; Thompson and Hendrie, 1972; Andrews, 1981; Benjaminsen, 1981). It is, therefore, possible that the association between life-event measures and maternal reports of child-rearing problems is mediated by the intervening variable of depression so that women experiencing stressful life events tend to become depressed and this alters the way in which their child's behavior is perceived or evaluated.

METHOD

The data were collected during the seventh phase of the Christchurch Child Development Study. In this study, a birth cohort of 1,265 children born in the Christchurch (New Zealand) urban region has been studied at birth, four months, and annual intervals to the age of five years. At each point, information concerning the health, social background, and family conditions experienced by the child has been collected by a structured interview with the child's mother supplemented by information from hospital records, general practitioner records, and a diary record kept by the child's mother. The general methods of data collection and quality control of the data have been described previously (Beautrais et al., 1982a, b).

From the data base of the study the following measures were abstracted for analysis.

CHILD-REARING PROBLEMS DURING CHILD'S FIFTH YEAR

When the children were five years old, mothers were asked whether their child displayed any of the following behaviors: (1) difficulty in management or control (including disobedience, willfulness, stubbornness); (2) temper tantrums or breath-holding episodes; (3) eating or feeding problems (including finicky eating, picking at food, refusal to eat unless assisted); (4) aggressive behavior (e.g., bullying other children); and (5) tension, irritability, or nervousness.

These five problem areas were shown in a previous study to have significant correlations with life-event measures and following the methods used in this study, they are combined to produce a simple index based on a count of the number of problems cited by the child's mother. (It should be stressed that because we have been unable to conduct an independent behavioral assessment of the children in the study, this index should be interpreted as the frequency of maternal reports of child-rearing problems.)

FAMILY LIFE EVENTS SCORE

The family life events score was based on a reduced version of the Holmes and Rahe (1967) Social Readjustment Rating Scale and comprised 20 items. These items were selected on the basis that they were the most substantial in the scale and were least likely to be subject to errors of reminiscence. A description of the items is given in Beautrais et al. (1982a). The life events score was created by summing the number of life events reported by the mother as our earlier findings had indicated that a weighted sum of events was highly correlated with a simple unweighted sum.

MATERNAL DEPRESSION SCORE

Symptoms of depression were measured using a modified version of the Levine-Pilowsky questionnaire (Pilowsky, Levine,

and Boulton, 1969; Pilowsky and Boulton, 1970). This questionnaire was selected because it had been developed for an
Australasian population and thus might be more suitable for
a New Zealand sample than measures developed in the United
States or Europe. The questionnaire was modified in two ways:
(1) Because it had been developed on a clinically depressed
population, it contained a number of items that presumed the
respondent was depressed (e.g., "Do you think you will get
better?"). As these items were clearly inappropriate for a general population sample they were eliminated from the questionnaire. (2) The questionnaire also contained a number of
nonsymptomatic measures of life events ("Have you any serious
money worries?"). As these items were clearly correlates of
depression rather than symptoms of depression, they were not
included in the modified questionnaire.

The modified questionnaire comprised 37 items which were
subject to both factor analysis and cluster analysis. Both analyses
suggested that the scale measured a single common factor, reflecting the severity of the depressive responses reported by the
women. A scale score corresponding to this factor was constructed from a simple sum of the number of depressive symptoms reported by the woman and the resulting index showed
good reliability having a Kuder Richardson 20 reliability coefficient of .91.

FAMILY AND SOCIAL BACKGROUND VARIABLES

The following variables were used in the analysis for purposes
of statistical control: (1) maternal age when the child was five
years old; (2) maternal ethnic status (white vs. nonwhite); (3)
maternal educational level scored in three levels as: no formal
educational qualifications, secondary school qualifications, tertiary or technical qualifications; (4) family size; (5) family type:
one-parent family vs. two-parent family; (6) family living standards based on an interviewer's rating of the family's material

standard of living, standards were scored on a five-point scale from "very good" to "very poor."

These control variables were selected on the basis of preliminary multiple regression analysis as being the only measures sharing common variance with family life events, maternal depression score, and the child-rearing problems measures.

The sample obtained at five years comprised 1,123 children. This represented 89 percent of the original cohort and 96 percent of cohort members still alive and residing in New Zealand. Comparison of the sample obtained at five years with the characteristics of the 1,265 children who entered the study showed no significant biases in the five-year sample with respect to maternal age, education, ethnic status, the nuptial status of the birth, the child's sex, or perinatal characteristics.

RESULTS

Rates of maternal reports of child-rearing problems per 100 children aged four to five years related to the life events scores and maternal scores on the Levine-Pilowsky questionnaire are shown in Table 34.1. There is a general tendency for rates of reported problems to increase both with life events scores and with depression scores: (1) Women who reported five or more life events in the previous year cited child-rearing problems at a rate of 119.05 per 100 children in contrast to the rate of 57.71 per 100 children for those mothers who reported no life events. (2) Women reporting a total of 11 or more symptoms of depression of the Levine-Pilowsky questionnaire cited a rate of 113.85 child-rearing problems per 100 children in contrast to the rate of 35.50 child-rearing problems per 100 children for those mothers who reported no symptoms. At the same time, it is clearly shown in Table 34.1 that there is a general tendency for the scores on the life events and depression measures to be correlated (the Pearson product moment correlation between the two scores was .37; $p < .0001$).

Table 34.1

Rates (per 100 Children Aged 4 to 5 Years) of Maternal Reports of
Child-Rearing Problems by Life-Event Score and Maternal Depression Score

No. of Life Events	No. of Depressive Symptoms				
	0	1–5	6–10	11 +	Total
0	33.33	67.92	116.67	75.00	57.71
	(111)[a]	(106)	(24)	(12)	(253)
1 or 2	31.28	76.92	102.63	114.29	67.69
	(195)	(234)	(76)	(49)	(554)
3 or 4	42.59	82.52	102.50	97.14	78.88
	(54)	(103)	(40)	(35)	(232)
5 +	111.11	96.15	106.67	144.12	119.05
	(9)	(26)	(15)	(34)	(84)
Total	35.50	77.19	105.16	113.85	71.59
	(369)	(469)	(155)	(130)	(1,123)

[a] Number of children is shown in parentheses.

Table 34.2

Log-Linear Model Fitted to Results in Table 34.1

Effect	G^2	df	p
Zero-order effects			
Depression score (A) ⎫			
Life-event score (B) ⎬	777.75	7	< .0001
Child-rearing problems (C) ⎭			
1st-order effects			
AB	51.56	4	< .0001
AC	87.14	6	< .0001
BC	11.00	6	> .0500
Residual	13.15	12	> .3500

To examine the structure of the results in Table 34.1 in greater detail, the results were analyzed using log-linear modeling methods (Dixon, Brown, and Engelman, 1981). A summary of the analysis showing the log-likelihood x^2 (G^2) statistics is given in Table 34.2. However, the results may be explained more readily using the pictorial methods described by Freeman and Jekyl (1980). The results are depicted in Figure 34.1; significant associations between variables are indicated by a dashed line. The implications of the figure are fairly clear:

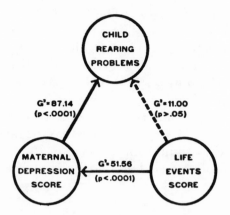

Figure 34.1. Fitted log-linear model of family life events, maternal depression score, and maternal reports of child-rearing problems.

1. The depression and life events scores are significatly associated ($G^2 = 51.56$; $df = 4$; $p < .0001$), indicating the general tendency for rates of maternal depression to increase with increasing life events scores.

2. The depression score is significantly associated with maternal reports of child-rearing problems ($G^2 = 87.14$; $df = 6$; $p < .0001$), indicating a general tendency for rates of reported child-rearing problems to increase with increasing maternal depression scores.

3. There is no significant association between family life events and child-rearing problems ($G^2 = 11.00$; $df = 6$; $p < .05$). That is, the apparent correlation between family life events and the behavior problem scores may be explained by the fact that family life events are related to maternal depression which is in turn related to reported child behavior problems.

To determine whether the structure of relationships in the figure was influenced by the effects of other family and social factors, the data were reanalyzed using multiple regression methods in which a series of control factors were introduced into the regression equation. The results are summarized in Table 34.3, which shows the bivariate correlation between each independent variable and rates of child-rearing problems, the corresponding standardized regression coefficient (B weight) and the F test of significance. It is clear that the conclusions of this analysis are essentially the same as the results in Figure 34.1: maternal depression is significantly related to child-rearing problems ($B = .23; p < .0001$) whereas the family life events measure shows no significant association ($B = .04; p < .05$) once the effects of maternal depression are taken into account.

DISCUSSION

The findings of this study of five-year-old children extend the findings for the birth cohort of four-year-olds described previously (Beautrais et al., 1982b). It is clear from the analysis that the apparent correlations between family life events and maternal reports of child-rearing problems can be almost entirely explained by the mediating effects of maternal depression. Women who reported significant numbers of life events also reported increased rates of depressive symptoms and child-

Table 34.3
Multiple Regression Analysis of Behavior Problems Score on Maternal Depression Score, Life-Event Score, and Control Factors*

Variable	r	B	F	p
Depression score	.28	.23	54.59	< .0001
Life events score	.14	.04	1.94	NS
Maternal age	-.10	-.03	1.19	NS
Maternal education	-.16	-.09	12.81	< .0010
Maternal ethnic status				
Family type	-.14	-.06	2.16	NS
Family size	-.08	-.07	3.97	< .0500
Standard of living	.18	.10	6.28	< .0500

* Multiple R = .34; p < .0001

rearing problems. These associations persisted when the effects of a range of family and social characteristics were taken into account. The findings are amenable to a number of different interpretations.

First, it is possible that maternal depression produces an increase in actual child-rearing problems so that children whose mothers are depressed or depressive respond to maternal behavior and mood by developing an increased number of behavior problems. If this is the case, the associations among family life events, maternal depression, and child-rearing problems is likely to conform to a causal chain model in which life events provoke maternal depression and maternal depression provokes child-rearing problems.

Alternatively, it is possible that maternal depression does not produce objective changes in a child's behavior but rather alters the way in which the woman perceives and evaluates her child's behavior so that stressed, depressed women see their children as being more troublesome. On the basis of the present data, it is not possible to distinguish between these explanations as the measurement of life events, maternal depression, and child-rearing problems were all based on maternal report.

However, in the next phase of this ongoing longitudinal study, it is proposed to study this cohort at age six years, collecting information on both parent and teacher perceptions of a child's behavior, using the home and school versions of the Rutter Child Behaviour Questionnaire (Rutter, Tizard, and Whitmore, 1970). This study will provide an opportunity to test the extent to which both family life events and maternal depression are related to a child's behavior problems, which are not measured solely on the basis of maternal report. The study should also shed light on the issue of whether biases in maternal reporting behavior influence the apparent correlation between family life events and behavior problems in children.

REFERENCES

Andrews, G. (1981), A prospective study of life events and psychological symptoms. *Psychol. Med.*, 11:795–798.

Beautrais, A. L., Fergusson, D. M., & Shannon, F. T. (1982a), Life events and childhood morbidity: A prospective study. *Pediatrics*, 70:935–939.

———— ———— ———— (1982b), Family life events and behavioral problems in preschool-aged children. *Pediatrics*, 70:774–778.

Benjaminsen, S. (1981), Stressful life events preceding the onset of neurotic depression. *Psychol. Med.*, 11:369–374.

Brown, G. W., & Harris, T. (1978), *The Social Origins of Depression*. London: Tavistock.

Dixon, W. J., Brown, M. B., & Engelman, L., eds. (1981), *BMDP Statistical Software*. Berkeley, CA: University of California Press.

Freeman, D. H., & Jekyl, J. F. (1980), Table selection and log linear models. *J. Chronic Dis.*, 33:513–518.

Holmes, T. H., & Rahe, R. H. (1967), The Social Readjustment Rating Scale. *J. Psychosom. Res.*, 11:213–218.

Pilowsky, I., & Boulton, D. M. (1970), Development of a questionnaire-based decision rule for classifying depressed patients. *Brit. J. Psychiat.*, 116:647–656.

———— Levine, S., & Boulton, D. M. (1969), The classification of depression by numerical taxonomy. *Brit. J. Psychiat.*, 115:937–939.

Rutter, M., Tizard, J., & Whitmore, K. (1970), *Education, Health and Behavior*. London: Wiley.

Stewart, A. J., & Salt, P. (1981), Life stress, life-styles, depression and illness in adult women. *J. Pers. Soc. Psychol.*, 40:1063–1068.

Thomson, K. C., & Hendrie, H. C. (1972), Environmental stress in primary depressive illness. *Arch. Gen. Psychiat.*, 26:130–133.

Chapter 35
Family Life Events, Maternal Depression, and Maternal and Teacher Descriptions of Child Behavior

D. M. Fergusson, B.A. Hons., L. J. Horwood, B.A., B.Sc., M. E. Gretton, B.Sc., and F. T. Shannon, F.R.C.P., F.R.A.C.P.

Beautrais, Fergusson, and Shannon (1982a) and Fergusson, Harwood, and Shannon (1984, see chapter 34, this volume) have examined the relationship between family life events, as measured by a modified version of the Holmes and Rahe (1967) Social Readjustment Rating Scale and behavior problems in a birth cohort of New Zealand children. These studies have reported consistent correlations between measures of family life events and maternal reports of child-rearing problems with preschool children. This association appears to be mediated by the effects of maternal mood as it was found that when the

Acknowledgments. This chapter was first published in *Pediatrics* (1985), 75:30–35, and it is reprinted by permission of *Pediatrics*.

This research was funded by grants from the Medical Research Council of New Zealand and the National Children's Health Research Foundation.

effects of maternal depression were taken into account, family life events made no independent contribution to the variability in maternal reports of child-rearing problems. Fergusson et al. (1984) suggested that the results conformed to a causal chain model in which family life events provoked increased levels of maternal depression which, in turn, led to increased rates of reported child-rearing problems.

These findings are consistent with at least two explanatory hypotheses. First, it may be argued that stress and maternal depression directly affect child behavior so that children in families under stress or suffering difficulties react by developing problem behaviors. Alternatively, it may be that the effects of stress and depression are an alteration of the way in which women perceive and evaluate their children's behavior so that stressed, depressed mothers see normally occurring childhood behaviors as being more troublesome. Unfortunately, in previous studies it was not possible to examine these alternative hypotheses because measures of child-rearing problems and child behavior were based solely on maternal report.

This chapter reports the results of a further study of the birth cohort described previously. In this study, we examined the extent to which family life events and maternal depression were related to both teacher and maternal reports of child behavior. The major aim of the research was to determine the extent to which the apparent correlations between family life events and maternal reports of child behavior could be ascribed to variations in maternal mood or to actual changes in behavior of the children.

In addition, in previous papers, we have examined the relationship between what may be called "short-term life events" and child behavior without examining the effects of the long-term history of life events throughout early childhood. In particular, it may be that while short-term family crisis has relatively little effect on child behavior, it is possible that children whose families are subject to consistent and chronic levels of financial, social, or emotional stress are more markedly influenced by their family situation. A further aim of this study was to examine the relationship between the history of life events throughout the child's preschool years and measures of child behavior based on both maternal and teacher reports.

MATERIALS AND METHODS

The data were collected during the first eight stages of the Christchurch Child Development Study (Beautrais et al., 1982a, b; Fergusson et al., 1984a, b). In this study a birth cohort of 1,265 New Zealand children has been studied at birth, four months, and at annual intervals to the age of six years using a combination of a home-based interview with the child's mother supplemented by information from hospital records, family doctors, the child's classroom teacher, and other documentary sources. The methods of data collection and quality control of the data have been described previously (Beautrais et al., 1982a, b; Fergusson et al., 1984a, b). The following measures were used in the present analysis.

MEASURES OF CHILD BEHAVIOR

These were based on the Rutter Child Behaviour Questionnaire (Rutter, Tizard, and Whitmore, 1970). This instrument is available in two comparable versions: one is suitable for completion by the child's mother and the other by the child's classroom teacher. (In all cases, the teacher's descriptions of the child's behavior were obtained only after the signed consent of the child's parent had been obtained.)

From the completed questionnaires two scores were constructed:

1. *Maternal Child Behavior Score.* This was based on a total of 30 items that described the child's behavior at home. The total score ranged from 0 for the child with no problem behavior to a maximum of 60 for the child with every possible behavior problem. The reliability of the questionnaire was

measured using coefficient α (Cronbach, 1951) and was found to be .71 which is similar to the test/retest reliability of .74 reported by Rutter et al. (1970).

2. *Teacher Behavior Score.* This was based on a sum of 26 items describing the child's behavior at school. The scores were a minimum of 0 for the child with no behavioral problems and a maximum of 52 for the child with all possible behavior problems. Coefficient α for the teacher rating was .79. It should, perhaps, be observed that maternal and teacher ratings of child behavior were not highly correlated ($r = +.27; p < .0001$), and this fact has been commented on by Rutter et al. (1970). However, this lack of correlation is perhaps not surprising because mothers and teachers describe child behavior occurring in quite different situations which are governed by quite different rules and expectations.

MEASURES OF LIFE EVENTS

These were based on the reduced 20-item version of the Social Readjustment Rating Scale (Holmes and Rahe, 1967) used in previous studies of this cohort. Two life events scores were constructed: (1) a short-term life events score based on a simple sum of the number of life events that the child's mother reported during the child's sixth year, and (2) a long-term life events score based on the total number of life events that the child's mother had reported since the child was one year of age.

For both scores, a simple unweighted sum of life events items was used because previous analysis (Beautrais et al., 1982a) had suggested that an unweighted sum of life events was very highly correlated with a weighted sum of events.

To examine whether the use of a predetermined checklist of life events had any influence on the results, at six years of age an alternative method of measuring life events was used. This alternative measure used a method of open-ended questioning in which the mother was asked to describe any events that had upset her. She was then asked to rate the extent of distress caused by each event on a four-point scale ranging from "very upset" to "only a little upset." An alternative life events measure was constructed by summing the ratings made by the mother. This alternative measure was highly correlated ($r =$ .77; $p < .0001$) with the number of life events reported by the mother during the year and furthermore showed an almost identical pattern of correlations with measures of child behavior and other variables as the simple unweighted sum of life events.

MATERNAL DEPRESSION

Maternal depression was based on the Pilowsky, Levine, and Boulton (1969) depression inventory administered when the children were six years of age. As described previously (Fergusson et al., 1984), a depression score was constructed by summing the number of symptoms reported by the child's mother. The resulting score was highly reliable (coefficient = .91).

CONTROL FACTORS

To take account of the effects of family social circumstances on the results, the following control factors were used in the analysis: (1) maternal age in years; (2) maternal education coded as, mother lacked formal educational qualifications, mother had secondary qualifications (i.e., New Zealand school certificated, university entrance), or mother had tertiary qualifications (i.e., university degree, tertiary professional qualifications); (3) maternal ethnic status (white or Polynesian); (4) family gross income in $NZ; (5) child's family placement at birth including the type of family situation that the child entered at birth coded as adoptive family, natural two-parent family, or single-parent family; (6) family living standards measured using a simple interviewer rating that measured the material conditions of the family on a five-point scale ranging from "very good, obviously affluent" to "very poor, family obviously in poverty"; and (7) birth order of child.

SAMPLE SIZES

The analysis is based on the sample of children for whom complete data on all variables in the analysis were available. Variations in sample size are indicated in the Tables 35.1–35.6 and in all cases, the sample was at least 1,046 children. This reduced sample represented 82 percent of the original cohort and 90 percent of those cohort members who were still alive and residing in New Zealand. As reported previously, no significant biases in the sample as a result of losses to follow-up were detected.

RESULTS

SHORT-TERM LIFE EVENTS, MATERNAL DEPRESSION, AND CHILD BEHAVIOR

The relationship among mean scores on the maternal version of the Rutter Behaviour Questionnaire, the maternal depression score, and the number of family life events occurring during the child's sixth year are shown in Table 35.1. It is clear that mean behavior problem scores tend to increase both with increasing symptoms of maternal depression and increasing numbers of life events occurring to the child's family. However, the life events and depression measures were significantly correlated ($r = +.35$; $p < .0001$), and to take account of this the results in Table 35.1 were analyzed using a nonorthogonal analysis of variance based on a regression partitioning of the sum of the squares. The results of this analysis showed a highly significant ($p < .0001$) tendency for maternal reports of child behavior problems to vary with maternal depressive symptoms, and a slight but statistically significant ($p < .05$) tendency for maternal reports of child behavior problems to vary with the measure of short-term life events. There was no significant interaction between maternal depression, short-term life events, and mean behavior scores.

Table 35.1
Mean Maternal Behavior Rating Scores by Short-Term Life-Event
Score and Maternal Symptoms of Depression[a]

No. of Depressive Symptoms	No. of Life Events (5–6 yr)				Total
	0	1 or 2	3 or 4	5 +	
0	5.02	4.94	5.24	8.87	5.11
	(111)	(144)	(29)	(8)	(292)
1–4	6.17	6.25	6.90	8.86	6.43
	(123)	(193)	(67)	(14)	(397)
5–8	7.45	8.08	8.19	9.06	8.09
	(31)	(75)	(36)	(18)	(160)
9–12	9.06	8.59	10.35	10.27	9.35
	(17)	(41)	(26)	(11)	(95)
13 +	12.64	8.70	10.50	8.96	9.71
	(11)	(46)	(40)	(23)	(120)
Total	6.28	6.57	8.07	9.15	6.95
	(293)	(499)	(198)	(74)	(1,064)

[a] Number of scores studied is shown in parentheses.

Mean teacher ratings of child behavior related to the family life events and maternal depression scores are shown in Table 35.2. Although there is less variability in this table, there is still a tendency for mean teacher ratings of child behavior problems to increase with the family life event score, but there is little association between maternal depressive symptoms and teacher ratings of child behavior.

These impressions were confirmed by two-way analysis of variance of Table 35.2 which showed the presence of a small but statistically significant association between the short-term family life events measure and teacher ratings of child behavior ($p < .05$) but no significant association between maternal depression scores and teacher ratings of child behavior ($p > .05$).

Table 35.2

Mean Teacher Behavior Rating Scores by Short-Term Life- Event
Score and Maternal Symptoms of Depression[a]

No. of Depressive Symptoms	No. of Life Events (5-6 yr)				
	0	1 or 2	3 or 4	5 +	Total
0	3.78	4.08	5.18	6.13	4.13
	(108)	(143)	(28)	(8)	(287)
1-4	4.07	3.92	4.42	4.64	4.07
	(120)	(193)	(67)	(14)	(394)
5-8	5.17	3.79	5.43	5.39	4.61
	(30)	(73)	(35)	(18)	(156)
9-12	4.65	3.85	6.62	5.91	5.00
	(17)	(40)	(26)	(11)	(94)
13 +	4.30	4.76	6.00	5.48	5.27
	(10)	(45)	(39)	(23)	(117)
Total	4.12	4.02	5.32	5.43	4.39
	(285)	(494)	(195)	(74)	(1,048)

[a] Number of scores studied is shown in parentheses.

LONG-TERM LIFE EVENTS, MATERNAL DEPRESSION, AND CHILD BEHAVIOR PROBLEMS

The relationship between teacher and maternal ratings of child behavior, measures of long-term family life events, and maternal ratings of child behavior, measures of long-term family life events, and maternal depression are shown in Tables 35.3 and 35.4. In general terms, the results are similar to those in Tables 35.1 and 35.2, but the association between family life events and child behavior appears to be stronger. These impressions were confirmed by two-way analysis of variance of the tables. The analysis showed: (1) For maternal ratings of child behavior, there were highly significant associations ($p < .0001$) with maternal depression and long-term family life events. (2) For teacher ratings of child behavior, there was a highly significant association ($p < .001$) between long-term life events and child behavior that reflected a tendency for child behavior problems to increase with increasing reports of life events, but there was

Table 35.3
Mean Maternal Behavior Rating Scores by Long-Term Life-Event
Score and Maternal Symptoms of Depression[a]

No. of Depressive Symptoms	No. of Life Events (2–6 yr)					
	0–5	6–10	11–15	16–20	21 +	Total
0	4.91	5.00	5.43	5.86	10.33	5.11
	(124)	(116)	(35)	(14)	(3)	(292)
1–4	5.38	6.38	7.25	7.47	7.88	6.43
	(108)	(157)	(92)	(32)	(8)	(397)
5–8	7.96	6.92	9.02	9.30	7.67	8.09
	(24)	(52)	(46)	(23)	(15)	(160)
9–12	8.08	7.10	10.70	10.39	13.00	9.35
	(13)	(31)	(23)	(18)	(10)	(95)
13 +	8.83	7.93	9.14	11.18	10.79	9.71
	(6)	(29)	(28)	(28)	(29)	(120)
Total	5.60	6.21	7.92	9.00	10.03	6.95
	(275)	(385)	(224)	(115)	(65)	(1,064)

[a] Number of scores studied is shown in parentheses.

Table 35.4
Mean Teacher Behavior Rating Scores by Long-Term Life-Events
Score and Maternal Symptoms of Depression[a]

No. of Depressive Symptoms	No. of Life Events (2–6 yr)					
	0–5	6–10	11–15	16–20	21 +	Total
0	3.09	4.72	5.29	5.36	4.67	4.13
	(121)	(115)	(34)	(14)	(3)	(287)
1–4	3.91	3.80	3.90	5.31	8.50	4.07
	(105)	(156)	(93)	(32)	(8)	(394)
5–8	3.78	4.06	5.04	5.13	5.71	4.61
	(23)	(51)	(45)	(23)	(14)	(156)
9–12	4.31	4.10	5.96	4.89	6.60	5.00
	(13)	(30)	(23)	(18)	(10)	(94)
13 +	2.60	4.52	4.65	5.89	6.45	5.27
	(5)	(29)	(26)	(28)	(29)	(117)
Total	3.52	4.19	4.65	5.36	6.48	4.39
	(267)	(381)	(221)	(115)	(64)	(1,048)

[a] Number of scores studied is shown in parentheses.

no significant ($p > .05$) association between maternal depression scores and teacher ratings of child behavior problems.

EFFECTS OF FAMILY SOCIAL AND ECONOMIC BACKGROUND

The analyses above show the associations between family life events, maternal depression, and behavior problems without taking into account the effects of other confounding social and economic factors that may be correlated with these measures. To examine this issue the results were reanalyzed using multiple regression methods to take into account the confounding effects of maternal age, education, ethnic status, the child's placement at birth, birth order, family income, and family living standards. The analysis of short-term life events, maternal depression, and child behavior problems is shown in Table 35.5. The bivariate correlations between short-term life events, maternal depression, and teacher and maternal ratings of child behavior and the corresponding standardized regression coefficients (B weights) adjusted for the effects of family social and economic circumstances are shown in Table 35.5. The conclusions are as follows: (1) For maternal ratings of child behavior, there was a small association with short-term life events (B = .06; $p < .05$) and a larger association with maternal depression (B = .27; $p < .0001$). (2) For teacher ratings, there are only slight associations with both short-term life events and maternal depression. Both standardized regression coefficients failed to reach statistical significance although the coefficient for short-term life events was of marginal significance ($p < .10$).

A parallel analysis using long-term family life events as an explanatory variable is shown in Table 35.6. The results show that: (1) For maternal ratings of child behavior, both maternal depression and long-term family life events made highly statistically significant ($p < .0001$) contributions. (2) For teacher ratings, there was a significant association between long-term family life events and the child behavior rating ($p < .0001$), but

Table 35.5

Multiple Regression Anaylsis of Short-Term Family Life Events, Maternal Depression, and Child Behavior Taking into Account Family Social and Economic Background

Variable	Maternal Rating			Teacher Rating		
	Bivariate Correlation	Standardized Regression Coefficient	p	Bivariate Correlation	Standardized Regression Coefficient	p
Short-term life events	.19	.06	.0500	.12	.06	.10
Maternal depression	.31	.27	.0001	.09	.05	NS

Table 35.6

Multiple Regression Analysis of Long-Term Family Life Events, Maternal Depression, and Child Behavior Taking Into Account Family Social and Economic Background

Variable	Maternal Rating			Teacher Rating		
	Bivariate Correlation	Standardized Regression Coefficient	p	Bivariate Correlation	Standardized Regression Coefficient	P
Long-term life events	.29	.16	.0001	.18	.17	.0001
Maternal depression	.31	.27	.0001	.08	.01	NS

there was not a significant association ($p > .05$) with maternal depression.

Finally, it should be noted that whereas the analysis showed the presence of statistically significant associations between family life events, maternal depression, and measures of child behavior, these associations were not large, and the results show quite clearly that a considerable amount of the variability in child behavior cannot be explained by variations in either maternal depression or family life events. It is clear, however, that measures of long-term family life events were consistently better predictors of child behavior than measures of short-term family life events.

DISCUSSION

The findings of this five-year longitudinal study serve to clarify some of the issues raised in our previous research into family life events and behavior problems in preschool children (Beautrais et al., 1982a). In particular, it seems likely that the apparent correlations between family life events and maternal report of child behavior reflect two distinct components. It would seem that family life events increase rates of maternal depression with the result that stressed, depressed women tend to see their children in a more negative light. However, independent of this, family life events make a small but independent contribution to the variability in child behavior. Evidence for this conclusion can be drawn from two sets of findings.

First, in this study and a previous paper (Fergusson et al., 1984a) it has been shown that a substantial component of the apparent correlation between family life events and child behavior is mediated by maternal mood so that increasing numbers of life events are associated with increased tendency for mothers to report more problem behavior in their children. However, in the present study (but not the previous study), family life events also make a small but nonetheless statistically significant independent contribution to the variability in child behavior, and this contribution is more marked for measures of life events that summarize the child's preschool family life history.

At the same time, maternal depression unrelated to teacher ratings of child behavior suggesting that maternal mood makes little contribution to actual child behavior although it appears to color maternal reports of the child's behavior. However, family life events make a small but statistically significant contribution to teacher reports of child behavior. These results were not substantially influenced by the introduction of statistical controls for the effects of the child's family and social background.

In summary, it would appear that the apparent correlation between family life events and maternal reports of child behavior reflects both the effects of maternal mood on the reporting of child behavior and the effects of family life events on actual child behavior.

The study also raises a number of other issues. In particular, whereas we have been able to demonstrate associations between family life events and both maternal and teacher reports of child behavior, these associations are not large, and family life events account for only a small portion of the variability in child behavior. This finding poses a strong challenge to popular lay and professional opinion that problems in the family often or usually lead to problem behavior in children; rather it would seem that there is a slight trend for child behavior problems to increase with increasing levels of adversity in the family.

At the same time, the findings do suggest an interesting trend: the association between measures of family life events throughout the child's preschool years and child behavior was far stronger than the association between measures of life events taken during the year in which child behavior was measured. This suggests that whereas short-term family crisis may have little impact on child behavior, the effect of a consistent history of adversity in the child's family may be more marked. In turn this leads to the speculation that whereas we have only been

632   D. M. FERGUSSON ET AL.

able to show small associations between family life events and behavior problems in six-year-old children, it may be that in later years these correlations will increase as the cumulative effects of family life events on child behavior and adjustment become more manifest.

REFERENCES

Beautrais, A. L., Fergusson, D. M., & Shannon, F. T. (1982a), Family life events and behavioral problems in preschool-aged children. *Pediatrics*, 70:774–778.
—— —— (1982), Life events and child morbidity: A prospective study. *Pediatrics*, 70:935–939.
Cronbach, L. J. (1951), Coefficient alpha and the internal structure of tests. *Psychometrika*, 16:297–306.
Fergusson, D. M., Horwood, L. J., & Shannon, F. T. (1981), Birth placement and childhood disadvantage. *Soc. Sci. Med.*, 15E:315–319.
—— —— —— (1983), Parental asthma, parental eczema and asthma and eczema in early childhood. *J. Chronic. Dis.*, 36:517–519.
—— —— —— (1984a), Relationship of family life events, maternal depression, and child-rearing problems. *Pediatrics*, 73:773–779.
—— —— —— (1984b), Domestic swimming pool accidents to preschool children. *N. Z. Med. J.*, 96:725–735.
Holmes, T. H., & Rahe, R. H. (1967), The Social Readjustment Rating Scale. *J. Psychosom. Res.*, 73:773–779.
Pilowsky, I., & Boulton, D. M. (1970), Development of a questionnaire based decision rule for classifying depressed patients. *Brit. J. Psychiat.*, 116:647–652.
—— Levine, S., & Boulton, D. M. (1969), The classification of depression by numerical taxonomy. *Brit. J. Psychiat.*, 115:937–949.
Rutter, M., Tizard, J. S., & Whitmore, K. (1970), *Education, Health and Behaviour*. London: Longman Group.

Chapter 36
Stressful Life Events and Somatic Complaints in Adolescents

JOHN W. GREENE, M.D., LYNN S. WALKER, PH.D., GERALD HICKSON, M.D., AND JULIETTE THOMPSON, F.N.C.

Adolescents with recurrent somatic complaints are often encountered by practitioners providing care to this age group. In a survey of primary care facilities, Starfield, Gross, and Wood (1980) found that children and adolescents with a psychosomatic diagnosis accounted for between 5.7 percent and 10.8 percent of all pediatric patients. The prevalence of recurrent pain may be considerably higher in the general population of children and adolescents (Oster, 1972). Complaints most frequently cited are abdominal pain, chest pain, and headaches (Cagahn, McGrath, and Morrow, 1978). Although many of these patients undergo extensive medical evaluations, organic pathologic causes are rarely found. Unfortunately, these extensive and often costly evaluations usually define only those conditions which are not present. Frequently it is only after organic lesions are "ruled out" that the role of psychological factors in precipitating or maintaining the complaints is examined.

Acknowledgment. This chapter was first published in *Pediatrics* (1985), 75:19–22, and it is reprinted by permission of *Pediatrics*.

Various authors have noted a relationship between psychological stress and recurrent pain in children and adolescents (Beautrais, Fergusson, and Shannon, 1982; Fine, 1980; Lesse, 1981). A major weakness in most of this literature is the absence of a systematic method of assessing stress among these patients. Without such a standard method, it is difficult to compare the level of stress across various diagnostic groups (Asnes, Santulli, and Bemporad, 1981). Thus, it is not surprising that there is at present no empirical evidence that level of stress is useful in differentiating patients with functional pain from those with other diagnoses. The purpose of this study was to determine whether a standard measure of stressful life events would distinguish adolescents with functional pain from the various other patients who were seen at an adolescent clinic.

METHODS

SAMPLE

Subjects were 172 adolescents, ranging in age from 11 to 19 years, who were attending Vanderbilt University Medical Center Adolescent Clinic. This clinic provides both primary care and referral evaluation services for the community and medical center. Approximately one-half of all patients are referred for comprehensive evaluations, and the other half are seen for routine health care visits. Data were collected over 6 consecutive months. All new patients, regardless of the reason for their clinic visit, were asked to complete a life-event questionnaire while waiting to be seen. The questionnaire was presented to subjects by individuals not involved in the clinical evaluation process. Verbal consent was obtained from subjects and their parents; only two patients chose not to participate. The average time needed to complete the questionnaire was 14 minutes. Completed questionnaires were not available to clinical examiners until after a tentative diagnosis and treatment plan had been formulated.

The majority of subjects were either self-referrals or were referred by outside physicians. Eight had been evaluated by a pediatric gastroenterologist, cardiologist, or neurologist and then referred to the Adolescent Clinic after these specialists failed to identify organic illness.

A structured history was obtained from all patients and a physical examination was performed by one of the clinical investigators. Laboratory evaluation was selective and obtained only for specific indicators in the history or physical examination that suggested organic illness.

As shown in Table 36.1, subjects were classified into six groups based on provisional diagnosis made after complete history, physical examination, and initial laboratory findings, but without the results of the questionnaire. These diagnostic groups included: (1) routine physical examination or checkup, (2) acute minor illness (excluding chest or abdominal pain), (3)

Table 36.1
Mean Life Change Scores and Ages for Diagnostic Groups

Group	N	Mean Age	Mean Positive Life Change Score[a]	Mean Negative Life Change Score[b]
1. Routine examination	33	14.8	5.4	3.7
2. Acute minor illness	24	14.8	4.6	3.5
3. Acute abdominal or chest pain; organic cause diagnosed	27	14.9	4.8	3.7
4. Recurrent abdominal/ chest pain	40	14.6	5.9	13.2
5. Behavioral problems	26	15.0	6.1	22.5
6. Stable chronic illness	22	15.1	5.6	4.1
	172			

[a] Analysis of variance showed no differences among the groups on Positive Life Change score ($F = .38$, $df = 5/166$)
[b] Analysis of variance showed significant differences among the groups on Negative Life Change score ($F = 85.78$, $df = 5/166$, $p < .0001$). Post hoc analysis (Duncan's multiple range test) showed that groups 4 and 5 had significantly higher Negative Life Change scores than the other groups.

abdominal pain, chest pain, or headache with clinically diagnosed organic cause, (4) recurrent abdominal and/or chest pain and/or headache without identifiable organic cause, (5) behavioral problems including acting-out and depression, and (6) stable chronic illness not associated with major limitations, e.g., hypertension.

All subjects with recurrent symptoms received minimal laboratory evaluations in addition to a complete history and physical examination. Individuals with abdominal pain had a complete blood count with differential and sedimentation rate, urinalysis and culture, and stool examination for occult blood. Those with chest pain had complete blood counts with differential and sedimentation rate, chest radiograph, and electrocardiogram. Five subjects with recurrent complaints were also evaluated by subspecialists and two were hospitalized for evaluation. Neither of these subjects had identifiable organic illness.

THE QUESTIONNAIRE

A modified version of Johnson and McCutcheon's Life Events Checklist (Johnson and McCutcheon, 1980) for older children and adolescents was used to measure stressful life events. This checklist consists of 46 events that adolescents may experience including moves, school changes, peer and family relationship problems, family events, and so on. Pilot testing had indicated that nine of the events were uncommon in our population so only 37 events were listed for this study.

The questionnaire calls for subjects to indicate (1) events which they have experienced during the past year, (2) their perception of the events as "good" or "bad," and (3) the degree to which the event had an impact on their lives. Impact ratings are on a four-point scale (0 = no effect, 1 = some effect, 2 = moderate effect, 3 = great effect). The impact ratings of events judged to be good are summed to yield a Positive Life Change score. The impact ratings of events judged to be bad are summed to yield a Negative Life Change score. Thus, for each subject two dependent measures were obtained: Positive Life Change score and Negative Life Change score.

RESULTS

The six diagnostic groups were compared on the two dependent variables, Positive Life Change score and Negative Life Change score, using analysis of variance. There was no significant difference among the groups with respect to Positive Life Change scores ($F = .38$, $df = 5/166$). There was, however, a significant difference among groups with respect to Negative Life Change scores ($F = 85.78$, $df = 5/166$, $p < .0001$). Patients in group 4 (recurrent abdominal and chest pain) and group 5 (behavioral problems) reported significantly higher Negative Life Change scores than the other diagnostic groups (Table 36.1). Group 5 had significantly higher Negative Life Change scores than group 4, although both groups scored significantly higher than the remaining four groups. Specific types of events were similar for all diagnostic groups. The events most frequently checked by all subjects are listed in Table 36.2.

To examine the degree of overlap among individual scores for subjects in each group, a scatter diagram was constructed (Figure 36.1). As noted, individual Negative Life Change scores were higher for groups 4 and 5 and overlap with other groups was minimal.

The data were also examined for age and sex differences among the diagnostic groups. Analysis of variance revealed no significant differences among the groups with respect to age. The mean age of the sample was 14.8 years. The majority of subjects (67 percent) were girls. A series of t-tests indicated no significant differences between boys and girls on the dependent variables.

Table 36.2
Negative Events Most Commonly Experienced by All Subjects

Event	% of All Subjects
1. Making failing grades on report card	33.9
2. Increased arguments between parents	28.3
3. Serious family illness	27.8
4. Broke up with boyfriend/girlfriend	23.6
5. Death in family	21.7
6. Problems with siblings	21.1
7. Increased arguments with parents	20.6
8. Failed grade	19.4
9. Loss of close friend	17.2
10. Personal illness or injury	15.6
11. Change in family financial status	15.5
12. Problems with classmates	14.4
13. Changed to new school	14.4
14. Teacher problems	13.9
15. Parents divorced	12.8
16. Mother/father lost job	12.2
17. Friend experienced serious illness	11.1
18. Brother/sister leaves home	11.1
19. Moved to new home	11.1
20. Death of close friend	10.6

DISCUSSION

The study shows that a standard measure of stressful life events, administered systematically to the patients of an adolescent clinic, can differentiate patients with recurrent pain for which no organic etiology could be identified had significantly higher Negative Life Change scores than patients seen for routine checkup, acute minor illness, stable chronic illness, or pain with clinically diagnosed organic cause. Furthermore, Negative Life Change scores differentiated patients referred for behavioral problems from all other patient groups. Thus, the data suggest that this measure is a useful adjunct to the clinical interview.

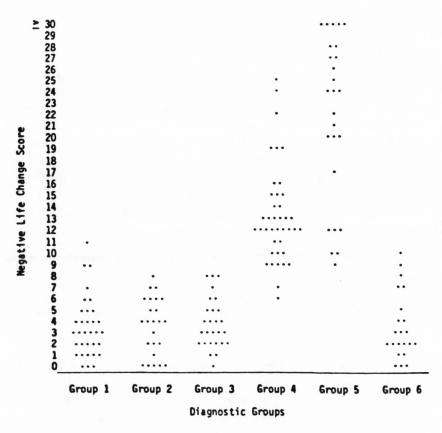

Figure 36.1. Scatter diagram of negative life change scores for each diagnostic group.

In the only other study that systematically compared the life stress of adolescents with idiopathic pain with those whose pain had an organic cause, Pantell and Goodman (1983) found that stressful life events were reported with equal frequency by adolescents in each of the diagnostic categories. The discrepancy between their findings and ours may in part be explained by the difference in measures. The Pantell and Goodman (1983) study used the Coddington Life Event Record which was designed for a broad range of children, whereas our study used the Johnson and McCutcheon Life Events Checklist which was designed specifically for adolescents. It may be that the Coddington measure failed to identify events that are particular to adolescents and that would have differentiated the diagostic groups (Stone and Barbero, 1970; Johnson and McCutcheon, 1980).

Although reported life stress was associated with recurrent pain and behavioral problems in our sample of adolescents, a causal relationship cannot be assumed. Even without the demonstration of a causal relationship, however, the findings yield practical implications for the practitioner. First, several authors have suggested that the exploration of physical and psychological bases for adolescents' symptoms should proceed concurrently (Brenner and Berman, 1983; Friedman, 1973). If the initial focus is on organic cause alone, the patient and family may assume that psychological factors are unlikely and unimportant. This belief may serve to fix the symptom in their minds and to heighten resistance to a later focus on psychological factors. Thus, the Life Events Checklist may be useful as an implicit message to the patient and family that psychological factors will not be excluded in the search for an etiology. Its use creates the opportunity for the adolescent and the family to reveal relevant information that they might not otherwise have considered worthy of mention.

Second, the Checklist is of value in that it provides hard data for parents who are reluctant to consider stress as a possible factor in their teenagers' symptoms. It has been our experience that parents presented with these data more readily accept the potential role of stress in the production or maintenance of complaints.

Finally, whether or not an organic basis for the symptoms is identified, information on the Life Events Checklist may suggest a target of intervention to alleviate stress. For example, a teenager who has indicated concern about the event "serious illness of a family member" may benefit from more information about the illness, or from a discussion of his fears. Similarly, identification of the event "increased arguments between parents" might suggest the need for family counseling. Thus, the Life Events Checklist represents an efficient, low-cost tool to aid the practitioner in dealing with the broad range of problems seen in adolescents.

SUMMARY

Recurrent somatic complaints of unknown origin are often seen in adolescents. Clinical observations have frequently suggested a relationship between these complaints and recent stressful events. This study shows that a standard measure of life events is useful in differentiating patients with recurrent pain from other patient groups. In addition, the measure is of value in identifying specific stressors and planning treatment to address the stressors identified.

REFERENCES

Asnes, R. S., Santulli, R., & Bemporad, J. R. (1981), Psychogenic chest pain in children. *Clin. Pediatr.*, 20:788–791.

Beautrais, A. L., Fergusson, D. M., & Shannon, F. T. (1982), Life events and childhood morbidity: A prospective study. *Pediatrics*, 70:935–940.

Boyce, W. T., Jensen, E. W., & Cassell, J. C., et al. (1977), Influence of life events and family routines on childhood respiratory tract illness. *Pediatrics*, 60:609–615.

Brenner, J. I., & Berman, M. A. (1983), Chest pain in childhood and adolescence. *J. Adolesc. Health*, 3:271–276.

Cagahn, S. B., McGrath, M. M., & Borrow, M. G., et al. (1978), When adolescents complain of pain. *Nurse Pract.*, 37/4:19–22.

Fine, S. (1980), Changing stresses and recurrent somatic symptoms in adolescents. *Psychiat. J. Univ. Ottawa*, 5:109–112.

Friedman, S. B. (1973), Conversion symptoms in adolescents. *Pediat. Clin. North Amer.*, 20:873–882.

Johnson, J. H., & McCutcheon, S. (1980), Assessing life stress in older children and adolescents: Preliminary findings with the life events checklist. In:

Stress and Anxiety, Vol. 7, ed. I. G. Sarason & C. D. Spielberger. Washington, DC: Hemisphere, pp. 111–125.

Lesse, S. (1981), Hypochondriacal and psychosomatic disorders masking depression in adolescents. *Amer. J. Psychother.*, 35:356–367.

Oster, J. (1972), Recurrent abdominal pain, headache and limb pains in children and adolescents. *Pediatrics*, 50:429–436.

Pantell, R. H., & Goodman, B. W. (1983), Adolescent chest pain: A prospective study. *Pediatrics*, 71:881–887.

Starfield, B., Gross, E., & Wood, M., et al. (1980), Psychosocial and psychosomatic diagnoses in primary care of children. *Pediatrics*, 66:159–167.

Stone, R. T., & Barbero, G. I. (1970), Recurrent abdominal pain in childhood. *Pediatrics*, 45:732–738.

Chapter 37
Parenting Children in a Stressful Medical Situation

JOSEPH P. BUSH, PH.D., BARBARA G. MELAMED, PH.D., AND CAROLYN S.
COCKRELL, PH.D.

INTRODUCTION

Visiting the dentist or pediatrician is often stressful for children
and their parents, and may contribute to the development of
dysfunctional health-care attitudes as well as psychological disturbances in the child. This problem points to a significant
deficiency in the delivery of health care services, as shown by
research which has estimated that, for example, 12 million
Americans avoid needed dental treatment each year because
of fears which may have been learned in childhood (Gale and
Ayer, 1969). However, these experiences may be altered in
accordance with the findings of psychological research (Mel-

Acknowledgments. This chapter was adapted from a presentation with the
same title at the American Psychological Association Annual Convention,
August 1985, Los Angeles, California.

Special thanks are due to Robyn Ridley-Johnson, Ph.D., for assistance in
data management.

This research was supported in part by a Faculty Grant-in-Aid to the first
author, awarded by Virginia Commonwealth University, and by grant number
DE05305 from the National Institute of Dental Research, awarded to Dr.
Melamed.

643

amed and Bush, 1985), reducing their potential negative effects, and may even benefit the child by providing opportunities for developing adaptive attitudes and coping skills. This endeavor has recently come to represent a major thrust in pediatric psychology (Peterson and Ridley-Johnson, 1980).

One promising approach to helping children in medical situations involves modifying parenting behaviors. Preliminary research suggests that this approach may be more effective and economical than child-focused interventions (Peterson and Shigetomi, 1981). Unfortunately, researchers have largely failed to examine actual parent behaviors in the setting of interest, relying instead on a variety of questionnaire measures of parental anxiety, health care attitudes, parenting style, etc. The purpose of the current study was to evaluate the relationship of questionnaire measures of anxiety, coping styles, and parenting styles with observed parent and child behaviors in a stressful medical setting.

It was hypothesized that there would be a direct correspondence between parents' self-reported parenting style and observed parenting behaviors. It was further hypothesized, however, that this correspondence would be incomplete and that some domains of parenting behavior would be predicted considerably more strongly than others. Situational anxiety was expected to have a disorganizing influence on parenting behavior, and therefore to be associated with greater parental use of ignoring of the child as well as with more observed parental agitation. Finally, it was hypothesized that parents whose self-report indicated greater use of problem-focused coping would be observed engaging in more parenting behaviors which would be expected to facilitate the child's coping efforts (e.g., information provision, distraction, and reassurance). On the other hand, parents who reported using more emotion-focused coping were expected to be observed engaging in more behaviors oriented toward their own efforts at affective modulation (e.g., manifest agitation, ignoring the child, and reassurance).

METHOD

SUBJECTS

Fifty children between four and 10 years of age who were seen as outpatients in the Pediatric Clinics at Shands Teaching Hospital at the University of Florida's J. Hillis Miller Health Center were videotaped along with their mothers while waiting for the physician in clinic examining rooms. These children had been referred for specialized diagnostic or therapeutic attention or postsurgical follow-up. Children with severe chronic disabilities were excluded. The sample was well-balanced with respect to age and sex. Demographic and diagnostic characteristics of the sample are given in Table 37.1.

PROCEDURES

Potential subjects were approached in the clinic's general waiting area, where informed consent was obtained from mother and child. Questionnaire measures were then administered, following which the dyad was called into an examining room equipped with a videotape camera. The videotaped observation period lasted from the moment the dyad entered the examining room, until the physician arrived. An observer was present in the room to operate the video camera and during the physician's examination. Observers attempted to remain inconspicuous and to appear preoccupied with monitoring the video equipment. They politely deferred any attempts by subjects to interact with them until after the examination.

MEASURES

An observational scale of parent-child interactions, the Dyadic Prestressor Interaction Scale (DPIS) was used to rate the vid-

Table 37.1
Sample Characteristics: Demographic and Medical Status

Age			Clinic Attended	
4-6	16		Gastroenterology	1
6-8	16		Urology	16
8-10	18		Surgery	23
			Diseases (Medical)	10
Sex				
Male	30			
Female	20			

Previous Medical Experience	Yes	No
Surgical experience	34	16
Hospitalization	40	10
Shands Clinic	42	8
Other Outpatient	38	12

Severity of Diagnosis

Least severe 1	2	3	4	5	6	7	8	9	10 Most Severe
0	7	9	7	4	5	5	5	1	1

eotapes. This scale has been described in detail elsewhere (Bush, Melamed, Sheras, and Greenbaum, 1986; Melamed and Bush, 1985). Parent behavior categories correspond to dimensions of parenting behavior indicated by past research as relevant to children's adjustment to stressful medical procedures: ignoring, reassuring, distracting, restraining, agitation, and informing (Bush, 1983). Child behavior categories were adapted from the four functional systems of child behavior which have been identified and replicated in studies of infants and young children in a strange situation (Bretherton and Ainsworth, 1974; Greenberg and Marvin, 1982): attachment, distress, exploration, and (nonmedical) prosocial behaviors. Operational definitions of these behaviors are given in Table 37.2.

Instantaneous scan ratings (Altman, 1974) of each behavior were made every 5 seconds. Ratings were made on all subject dyads for whom at least 5 minutes of videotaped interaction

Table 37.2
Dyadic Prestressor Interaction Scale: Functional Definitions

Child Behavior Categories

Attachment
Look at Parent:	Child looking at parent
Approach Parent:	Child motorically approaching parent
Touch Parent:	Child physically touching parent
Verbal Concern:	Child verbalizing concern with the parent's continuing presence throughout the procedures

Distress
Crying:	Child's eyes watering and/or (s)he is making crying sounds
Diffuse Motor:	Child running around, pacing, flailing arms, kicking, arching, engaging in repetitive fine motor activity, etc.
Verbal Unease:	Child verbalizing fear, distress, anger, anxiety, etc.
Withdrawal:	Child silent and immobile, no eye contact with parent, in curled-up position

Exploration
Motoric Exploration:	Child locomoting around room, visually examining
Physical Manipulation:	Child handling objects in room
Questions Parent:	Child asking parent a question related to doctors, hospitals, etc.
Interaction with Observer:	Child attempting to engage in verbal or other interaction with observer

Prosocial
Look at Book:	Child is quietly reading a book or magazine unrelated to medicine or looking at its pictures
Other Verbal Interaction:	Child is verbally interacting with parent on topic unrelated to medicine
Other Play:	Child playing with parent, not involving medical objects or topics
Solitary Play:	Child playing alone with object brought into room, unrelated to medicine

Parent Behavior Categories

Ingoring
Eyes Shut:	Parent sleeping or has eyes shut
Reads to Self:	Parent reading quietly
Sitting Quietly:	Parent sitting quietly, not making eye contact with child
Other Noninteractive:	Parent engaging in other medically unrelated solitary activity

Reassuring
    Verbal Reassurance: Parent telling child not to worry, that (s)he can tolerate the procedures, that it will not be so bad, etc.
    Verbal Empathy: Parent telling child (s)he understands his/her feelings, thoughts, situations; questions child for feelings
    Verbal Praise: Parent telling child (s)he is mature, strong, brave, capable, doing fine, etc.
    Physical Stroking: Parent petting, stroking, rubbing, hugging, kissing child

Distracting
    Nonrelated Conversation: Parent engaging in conversation with child on unrelated topic
    Nonrelated Play: Parent engaging in play interaction with child unrelated to medicine
    Visual Redirection: Parent attempting to attract child's attention away from medically related object(s) in the room
    Verbal Exhortation: Parent telling child not to think about or pay attention to medically related concerns or objects

Restraining
    Physical Pulling: Parent physically pulling child away from an object in the room
    Verbal Order: Parent verbally ordering child to change his/her current activity
    Reprimand, Glare, Swat: Parent verbally chastising, glaring at, and/or physically striking child
    Physically Holds: Parent physically holding child in place, despite resistance

Agitating
    Gross Motor: Parent pacing, flailing arms, pounding fists, stomping feet, etc.
    Fine Motor: Parent drumming fingers, tapping foot, chewing fingers, etc.
    Verbal Anger: Parent verbally expressing anger, dismay, fear, unease, etc.
    Crying: Parent's eyes watering, verbal whimpering, sobbing, wailing

Informing
    Answers Questions: Parent attempting to answer child's medically relevant/situationally relevant questions
    Joint Exploration: Parent joining with child in exploring the room
    Gives Information: Parent attempting to impart information, unsolicited by child, relevant to medicine/the current situation, to the child
    Prescribes Behavior: Parent attempting to describe to the child; appropriate behaviors for the examination session

were obtained, up to a maximum of 10 minutes. Interrater reliability coefficients for each behavior category ranged from .80 to .98 (see Table 37.3), with the exception of restraining ($r = .52$), which was a very low-frequency behavior. Previous analyses (Bush, 1983; Melamed and Bush, 1985; Bush et al., 1986) revealed patterns of mother-child interaction related to parenting and crisis theory models, and identified age trends in interactive behaviors (Bush and Melamed, 1983; Bush and Smith, 1983). In order to evaluate the reactivity of DPIS behaviors to questionnaires, an additional 15 subjects were videotaped who were not administered any questionnaires (other than an informed consent blank). No significant differences were found between these subjects and the 50 subjects who did complete the questionnaires on any of the ten DPIS behaviors, or on the multivariate composite of all ten behavior categories.

The questionnaires administered prior to videotaping included the State-Trait Anxiety Inventory (Spielberger, Gorusch, and Lushene, 1970), the Coping Questionnaire (Billings

Table 37.3
DPIS Interrater Reliability Coefficients

	Optimized Coefficient[a]	Nonoptimized Coefficient[b]	Estimated Reliability[c]
Child Behavior Categories			
Attachment	.97	.94	.82
Distress	.77	.80	.57
Exploring	.91	.92	.79
Prosocial	.95	.94	.82
Parent Behavior Categories			
Ignoring	.99	.97	.91
Reassuring	.93	.96	.89
Distracting	.92	.96	.89
Restraining	.60	.34	.89
Agitation	.95	.96	.04

[a]Based on 3 raters showing greatest agreement for each subject dyad.
[b]Based on 3 randomly selected raters for each subject dyad.
[c]Spearman-Brown correction formula.

and Moos, 1981), and the Child Development Questionnaire (CDQ)—a measure of self-reported parenting responses in a variety of common child fear situations (Zabin and Melamed, 1980).

DATA ANALYSES

Correlations were computed between questionnaire measures and DPIS behaviors. DPIS behaviors were quantified in three ways. First, the number of times a given behavior was rated as occurring (number of scored scanpoints) was divided by the number of observed scanpoints, yielding an index of the proportion of the observational period during which each behavior occurred. Second, some parent behaviors were expressed in terms of the conditional probability of their occurrence following certain child behaviors. Third, the differential use of certain parent behaviors was calculated as the conditional minus the unconditional probability of their emission. Conditional probabilities were calculated for each statistically significant child-parent behavior correlation. The conditional probability of the parent behavior following its correlate child behavior was obtained as follows: the number of times each occurrence of the child behavior was followed by one or more occurrences of the parent behavior over three scanpoints (15 seconds) was divided by the total number of occurrences of the child behavior.

RESULTS

Mean frequencies with which mothers and children were observed engaging in each of the ten DPIS behaviors are given in Table 37.4. Except for distress, child behaviors were mostly independent of one another. Distress was inversely associated with exploration ($r = -.28$, $p < .05$) and prosocial behavior ($r = -.34$, $p < .01$). Among the parenting behaviors, ignoring was inversely correlated with reassuring ($r = -.30$, $p < .05$),

Table 37.4
Means, Standard Deviations, and Ranges for DPIS Behaviors

	M	SD	Range
Child Behaviors			
Attachment	39.21	26.59	4.2–100
Distress	32.78	24.76	0–94.60
Exploring	12.27	13.55	0–63.57
Prosocial	25.82	25.07	0–7.53
Parent Behaviors			
Ignoring	33.80	31.84	0–100
Reassuring	8.63	18.65	0–95.77
Distracting	20.85	22.33	0–95.10
Restraining	2.18	3.40	0–15.87
Informing	11.05	14.91	0–57.83
Agitation	21.07	26.64	0–95.13

Note: DPIS scores represent proportional frequencies of occurence relative to number of scanpoints observed for each dyad.

distracting ($r = -.59, p < .0001$), restraining ($r = -.39, p < .01$), and informing ($r = .34, p < .05$), and was positively correlated with agitating ($r = .31, p < .05$). Agitated mothers also informed their children less ($r = -.28, p < .05$)

Significant associations between mother and child DPIS behaviors are shown in Table 37.5. Conditional probabilities of the maternal behavior consequating the child behavior are also given, for each significant correlation. It was found that mothers were more likely to use reassurance following the child's emission of attachment behavior, than they were to use reassurance in general, $t (49) = 3.82, p < .001$. Similarly, mothers were more likely to provide information following child exploration, $t (49) = 5.52, p < .001$. Mothers were more likely to distract, $t (49) = 8.12, p < .0001$, and were less likely to ignore, $t (49) = -2.11, p < .05$, their children who had just engaged in prosocial behavior. Finally, when children showed signs of distress, their mothers became more likely to ignore them, $t (49) = 5.31, p < .001$, as well as becoming more likely to themselves

Table 37.5
Correlations Between DPIS Parent and Child Behavior Categories

Parent	Child Categories			
Categories	Attachment	Distress	Exploration	Prosocial
Ignoring	−.17	.24	−.30* (.2957)	−.46** (.2417)
Reassuring	.56*** (.1365)	.39** (.0932)	−.21	−.17
Distracting	−.06	−.31* (.2408)	−.05	.77*** (.4934)
Restraining	−.21	−.20	.20	.21
Informing	−.12	−.05	.57*** (.2879)	−.11
Agitation	−.26	.32* (.2924)	−.02	0.07

Note: Conditional probabilities of parent behaviors following child behaviors are given in parentheses for each correlation significant at $p < .05$.

*$p < .05$
**$p < .01$
***$p < .001$

become agitated, $t(49) = 2.29$, $p < .05$. Maternal use of reassurance showed no conditional association with child distress, nor was maternal ignoring conditionally associated with child exploring.

As hypothesized, some limited relationships were found between maternal self-report and observed parenting behaviors. Mothers who reported relying more on modeling and reassurance, in response to the child fear situations on the Child Development Questionnaire (CDQ), were in fact observed to engage in more reassuring behaviors on the DPIS ($r = .32$, $p < .05$). Mothers who reported a greater reliance on positive reinforcement were observed using more distraction ($r = .39$, $p < .01$), and restraining ($r = .31$, $p < .05$). These mothers were also more likely to use distraction following child prosocial behaviors ($r = .33$, $p < .05$), and child distress ($r = .53$, $p <

.0001). In addition to distracting their distressed children, mothers high in self-reported use of positive reinforcement became less likely to ignore when their children showed distress ($r = -.29$, $p < .05$). Conversely, mothers whose CDQ scores indicated high self-reported use of punishment were likely to increase their use of ignoring following child prosocial behaviors ($r = .37$, $p < .01$), and their children were more likely to show distress ($r = .29$, $p < .05$). Contrary to hypotheses, CDQ modeling and reassurance was not associated with DPIS informing, nor was CDQ force associated with DPIS restraining.

Maternal coping style was not found to show the hypothesized predictive relationships with DPIS behaviors. Problem-focused coping was found to be positively correlated with observed maternal use of reassurance ($r = .34$, $p < .05$), and these mothers were more likely to report using modeling and reassurance on the CDQ ($r = .29$, $p < .05$).

Self-reported maternal anxiety, as measured on the State-Trait Anxiety Inventory (STAI) also showed little association with observed parenting behavior. While it was predicted that situational anxiety would be associated with observed maternal use of ignoring, it was found, rather, that trait anxiety predicted this behavior ($r = .37$, $p < .01$). Situational (state) anxiety showed none of the hypothesized predictive relationships, but was found to be inversely associated with maternal reassuring. Mothers who reported higher levels of situational anxiety used less reassuring ($r = -.28$, $p < .05$) and used less reassurance following child attachment than less state-anxious mothers ($r = -.36$, $p < .01$). In addition, state-anxious mothers were less likely to show differential use of reassurance (conditional minus unconditional probability) following child distress ($r = -.34$, $p < .05$).

DISCUSSION

Results strongly support the importance of utilizing direct observational measures in research on parenting children in a stressful medical setting. A number of complex patterns of parental responses consequating child distress and coping behaviors were identified, few of which were predicted by self-report measures which were expected to be relevant to parental functioning in this situation. This may be due to limitations in the questionnaires employed (e.g., social desirability response set), to the complexity of the determinants of parenting behavior, to the selection of which parental behaviors to observe, or to an actual lack of relationship between self-report of "disposition" and behavior. The ready availability of videotape equipment and the proliferation of observational techniques make this a realistic, and no longer just an idealistic alternative.

In this study, as hypothesized, some limited relationships were found between questionnaire measures and observed parental behaviors. While the breadth and magnitude of these relationships was not sufficient to justify an exclusive reliance on questionnaires as an index of parent behavior, some interesting patterns did emerge that may have important implications. While this general hypothesis was supported, specific hypotheses regarding the disorganizing influence of self-reported state anxiety and congruence between self-reported coping style and manifest parental behavior were not supported. The specific hypotheses regarding self-reported parenting responses to a variety of child fear situations did receive some support, however. Mothers who reported using modeling and reassurance were observed reassuring their children more often while waiting for the pediatrician than mothers who reported less use of these parenting strategies.

It was also found that mothers who reported punishing (or threatening to punish) their children in a variety of common child fear situations had children who showed more distress just prior to their examinations. These mothers were likely to ignore their children following child prosocial behavior. Prosocial behavior was found in this study, as well as in research on younger children in a strange situation (Greenberg and Marvin, 1982; Bretherton and Ainsworth, 1974), to be negatively related to distress. It may be speculated that these mothers were exhibiting a deficit in parenting solutions, on the Child Development Questionnaire and in their failure to support a generally effective child coping behavior in the pediatric examining room, which may be related to a lack of skill in recognizing and reinforcing positive child responses.

On the other hand, mothers who reported using positive reinforcement on the CDQ were observed engaging in what appeared to be a more effective pattern of parenting responses. These mothers were more likely to distract their children in response to child prosocial behavior, a response which often appeared to reciprocate the child behavior (i.e., interaction or dialogue unrelated to the medical situation) and therefore likely to sustain it. These mothers were also unlikely to ignore prosocial behavior. In addition, these mothers were more likely to use distraction in general, and distraction was negatively correlated with child distress.

Finally, it was found that trait anxiety predicted maternal ignoring, while state anxiety predicted a reluctance or failure to use reassuring. These findings suggest that ignoring may be a relatively stable parenting behavior, i.e., one that is associated with a relatively permanent personality variable. On the other hand, reassurance may be the parenting behavior most likely to be inhibited when mothers consider themselves to be situationally anxious. While self-reported state anxiety showed only this relationship, observed maternal agitation was negatively related to informing and positively correlated with child distress. Thus, mothers who were manifestly agitated were clearly more likely to have upset children, to ignore them and to fail to support positive coping efforts by their children. These mothers were not identified by self-report.

These results must be interpreted with caution due to the correlational nature of the research. The questions of causal direction, and of bidirectional influences between the dyadic interactants, were not examined in this study. Further research, employing sequential analytic techniques and experimental designs, will be necessary in order to establish the causal patterns underlying dyadic adjustment to medical stressors. This study does suggest, however, that interactive sequences, such as child distress followed by maternal reassurance, may be appropriate units of analysis for future research.

Also uninvestigated at this time are the generalizability of these findings to other settings, and the relationships of observed interactive patterns to child behavior during the examination as well as to more long-term learning and attitude development. It is believed, however, that the area of interpersonal impact and interaction in medical contexts is likely to be a fruitful one for future research on adjustment and learning relative to health care experiences. Results of the current study suggest some interactive patterns which may be elemental in such a program of investigation.

REFERENCES

Altman, J. (1974), Observational study of behavior: Sampling methods. *Behaviour*, 49:227–267.

Billings, A. G., & Moos, R. H. (1981), The role of coping responses and social resources in attenuating the stress of life events. *J. Behav. Med.*, 4/2:139–157.

Bretherton, I., & Ainsworth, M. (1974), Responses of one-year-olds to a stranger in a strange situation. In: *The Origins of Fear*, ed. M. Lewis & L. A. Rosenblum. New York: John Wiley, pp. 131–164.

Bush, J. P. (1983), An observational study of mother-child interactions in a stressful medical setting. *Dissertation Abstracts International*, 15/7:2303–2313.

———— Melamed, B. G. (1983), Mother-child interactions during medical examinations. Paper presented at American Association for Advancement of Behavior Therapy convention. December, Washington, DC.

———— ———— Sheras, P. L., & Greenbaum, P. (1986), Mother-child patterns of coping with anticipatory medical stress. *Health Psychol.*, 5/2:137–157.

———— Smith, A. (1983), Observational study of mother-child interactions in a pediatric clinic: Age trends. Paper presented at Virginia Forum for Developmental Research, November, Richmond, VA.

Gale, E. N., & Ayer, W. A. (1969), Treatment of dental phobias. *J. Amer. Dent. Assn.*, 73/6:1304–1307.

Greenberg, M. T., & Marvin, R. S. (1982), Reactions of preschool children to an adult stranger: A behavioral systems approach. *Child Develop.*, 53:481–490.

Melamed, B. G., & Bush, J. P. (1985), Family factors in children with acute illness. In: *Health, Illness and Families: A Life-span Perspective*, ed. D. C. Turk & R. D. Kerns. New York: John Wiley, pp. 183–219.

Peterson, L., & Ridley-Johnson, R. (1980), Pediatric hospital response to a survey on prehospitalization preparation for children. *J. Pediat. Psychol.*, 5/1:1–7.

——— Shigetomi, C. (1981), Use of coping techniques to reduce anxiety in hospitalized children. *Behav. Ther.*, 12:1–14.

Spielberger, C. D., Gorusch, R. L., & Lushene, R. (1970), *State-Trait Anxiety Inventory*. Palo Alto, CA: Consulting Psychologists Press.

Zabin, M. A., & Melamed, B. G. (1980), Relationship between parental discipline and children's ability to cope with stress. *J. Behav. Assess.*, 2/1:17–38.

Chapter 38
Contested Child Custody as a Stressful Life Event

Lane Veltkamp, M.S.W., and
Thomas W. Miller, Ph.D., A.B.P.P.

The process of separation and divorce dramatically alters one's lifestyle. Its impact is realized in a variety of ways, including a variation in parental responsibility, an assumption of new roles, a change in socioeconomic status (Hetherington, Cox, and Cox, 1978; Berman and Turk, 1981). Both males and females who have experienced conventional role responsibilities may find considerable difficulty in adjusting to the process of separation. Likewise, the children of divorce find themselves in a unique and devastating position, necessitating considerable understanding and support from both the health service delivery system and the legal profession. The purpose of this chapter is to address: (1) through a literary review the impact of separation and divorce on families, (2) a concept of family mediation in the separation and divorce process, and (3) the psychological variables that are important to consider in the course of family mediation. In addition, a unique model for treating the victims of separation and divorce has been designed and implemented at the University of Kentucky, Department

Acknowledgment. This chapter is adapted from a colloquium presentation by both authors through the Department of Psychiatry, College of Medicine, University of Kentucky (1986), Lexington, Kentucky.

of Psychiatry, Child Psychiatry Outpatient Clinic. The model is outlined and defined, as are the issues and implications of the separation and divorce process through family mediation.

The Impact of Separation and Divorce on Families

The impact of separation and divorce on families and children is the focus of much recent concern. The total number of children under 18 involved in divorce has tripled since 1955 and an estimated 30–40 percent of all families with children may be affected by separation or divorce in the next decade (Bane, 1976). In general, children who live in families where there is a high conflict between parents compared to those in low-conflict families, show poor adjustment, difficulty in peer relationships, greater aggressiveness and dependency, higher levels of stress, and disruptions in academic and intellectual functioning (Hess and Camara, 1979; Hetherington et al., 1978; Rutter, 1971; Wallerstein and Kelly, 1977). This pattern holds true for both divorced and non-divorced families. The ability of the child to maintain warm, close relationships with both parents also appears to play an important role in predicting children's adjustment. Hess and Camara's study of 9- to 11-year-old children compared family type and family process (parent conflict, warmth, and closeness of parent-child relationship) on measures of child's school performance, social relationship with peers, aggression and level of stress. The children's relationship with each parent proved to be a stronger predictor of all child outcomes than was interparental conflict. In addition, Hetherington, Cox, and Cox's 1979 study concluded that parental harmony was an important factor in children's adjustments. The effect of the divorce was less extreme in adults, when adults "supported each other in child-rearing tactics and disciplinary tactics." In addition, Hetherington et al. (1978) found that during the first year following divorce, parents made maturity demands, communicated less well, and tended to be less affectionate with their children than were parents of nuclear households. Of 400 children referred for outpatient evaluations, Kalter (1977) reported that children of divorced parents appeared at nearly twice the rate of their occurrence in the general population. Children of divorced, single-parent homes and stepparent homes exhibited more overt aggression and sexual behavior problems than children from intact families. Particularly at risk were boys ages 7 to 11 and girls 12 years and above. In a widely cited collection of studies, Wallerstein and Kelly (1974, 1975, 1976) interviewed 60 families with 131 children in a northern California suburb. The youngest preschool children, ages 2 to 3½, reacted with regression, cognitive bewilderment, and neediness. In the older preschool children, ages 3½ to 4½, fantasy was more prominent. In early latency-age children (ages 6 to 8), sadness was a pervasive response. In children ages 9 through 12, anger and aggressive behavior were most common. Nearly one-half of the 30 older latency-age children also suffered noticeable deterioration in school performance and peer relationships. In addition, in Hetherington, Cox, and Cox's two-year follow-up study (1976) in behavior observation of parent-child interaction, divorced parents made fewer maturity demands on their children, communicated less well with them, were less affectionate, and showed marked inconsistency in discipline. Poor parenting seemed most marked one year after the divorce.

FAMILY MEDIATION IN SEPARATION AND DIVORCE

Family mediation in its present form is a relatively new and innovative technique aimed at several variables affecting marital discord. The mediation process has been frequently endorsed since Congress signed into law the Dispute Resolution Act (PL-96190) in February 1980. The mediation process essentially aims to provide assistance to those individuals involved in the dispute and facilitating constructive solutions to controversial issues. Programs aimed at mediation have found a variety of endorsements (Mnoonkinn and Kornhauser, 1979; Ebel, 1980; Bahr, 1981). It is the purpose and intent of the mediator to facilitate communication and conflict resolution to define and establish norms for rational interaction to encourage exploration of all alternatives and utilize workable compromise. Deutsch (1973) defines this process in a series of stages which include: (1) communication, (2) development of norms for rational interaction, (3) generate alternatives, (4) determine when workable and mutually acceptable agreements have been determined and reached. More recently, Herman, McKenry, and Weber (1979) have addressed the issue of the mediation process and have identified three key variables which lead to successful conflict resolution and mediation. The three variables are: (1) commitment, (2) communication, and (3) power. It is the mediator who serves as the facilitator to encourage each of these variables and that these variables reach their maximum benefit in the course of evaluation. Herman et al. further addressed the fact that the success of the negotiation process can only occur when both parties experience equal control and power in the negotiation process.

Kochen and Jick (1978) have been instrumental in developing a model of the mediation process. The key to the success of the model involves four independent variables which include: (1) the nature of the conflict, (2) the situational stress factors involved, (3) the strategies to be utilized by the mediator, and (4) the personality characteristics of the mediator. Efforts to assess the effectiveness of the mediation process yielded results which would suggest that the experience of the mediator is positively correlated with the mediator's effectiveness level. Furthermore, the severity of the impasse was found to be inversely correlated with the success of the mediation efforts. Kressel, Jaffe, Tuchman, Watson, and Deutsch (1980) found further support for this, noting that most conflicted couples appeared to wish to use the litigation process as a means of punishing the spouse; furthermore, they also found that the greater the conflict, the less likely the success of the mediation resolution. Finally, they suggest that there are several advantages over court-arbitrated resolution of divorce, including the fact that it provides an improved opportunity for the needs of both parties to be fully heard, that it increases the spouse's feelings of competence by circumventing forced dependence on a lawyer or judge to arrive at a just resolution and that mediation is less costly and usually facilitated in a shorter period of time than are repeated sessions through court system. Kressel et al. (1980) and Ebel (1980) confirmed that mediated settlements tend to be of a more stable nature because they have been reached through a cooperative mediated process rather than a unilateral dictum of the courts. Research conducted by the Toronto-based Conciliation Counseling Service (Bahr, 1981) suggests that the contribution of the mediation process to post-divorce compliance demonstrates considerable improvement over unilaterally imposed court decisions. Bahr (1981) cites a 2-year follow-up of individuals receiving divorces wherein only 10 percent of the mediated couples returned to the court with problems related to custody or visitation compared to 26 percent of the traditional custody study couples. Bahr further notes that couples who were able to resolve their conflicts through the mediation process were three times as likely to report improved post-divorce relations between the divorced spouses than were other couples who had not received the mediation process.

Pearson and Thoennes (1982) conducted a 3-year mediation evaluation project with the support of the Colorado Bar Association and the Piton Foundation. Results from this study suggest that 60 percent of the mediation couples were able to reach agreement with respect to conflict disputes. Those couples who were unable to reach agreement through the mediation process were, however, supportive to the experience and reported improved cooperation and communication as a result of the mediation process even though it had not resolved the conflict. Sixty-one percent of the couples were unable to resolve disputes during mediation but did succeed in negotiating compromises prior to their court-appointed hearings and thus reduced the need for a custody study. Finally, 70 percent of the mediated couples agreed to joint custody, compared to only 14 percent of the control group.

Assessing Psychological Factors in the Mediation Process

The psychological impact of marital dissolution and the process of divorce had been addressed in a number of studies. Glenn (1975) and Wallerstein and Kelly (1980) view marital dysfunction as a consequence of divorce while Briscoe, Smith, Robins, Marten, and Gaskin (1973) view it more as a causal factor. It is clear that in addressing the ambiguity, the level of stress and the context within which the stressful life events occur become an important ingredient in considering the impact of mediation on the divorce program.

The Diagnostic and Statistical Manual of Mental Disorders (DSM-III) (American Psychiatric Association, 1980) views the process of divorce as a "single" life event. Within the context, however, the divorce process constitutes a major psychosocial transition and can be associated with a variety of stressful life events and psychological stressors (Chiriboga, 1979; Bloom and Hodges, 1980). Research assessing the complexity of such events as marital dissolution and divorce must clearly focus on a multidimensionality of stressors (Chiriboga and Dean, 1978; Rahe, 1979). The way in which the stressful life events are appraised (Lazarus, 1980; Baum, 1981), and finally, the relative impact of both positive and negative life changes on each of the family members within the complex of the family affected by the dissolution and divorce (Baum et al., 1981; Grant, Sweetwood, Yager, and Gerst, in press).

The process of marital dissolution and divorce has been associated with a variety of psychological cues and symptoms which relate directly to psychological dysfunction. When contrasted with other marital classifications, Bachrach (1975) and Briscoe et al. (1973) have found that separated and divorced individuals manifest a higher rate of admission into both public and private psychiatric facilities. Jacobsen and Portuges (1976) suggest that separated and divorced individuals also show a higher rate for suicidal ideation and intent as well as homicidal tendencies, and Nada (1971) and Wechsler, Thum, Demone, and Dwinnell (1972) suggest significantly higher rates of alcoholism and substance abuse among individuals experiencing dissolution and divorce than the normal population. All these issues focus on the psychological impact and potential dysfunction experienced by family members in the process of marital dissolution and divorce.

EFFECTS OF MEDIATION IN THE DIVORCE PROCESS

Considerable attention has addressed the variety of psychological problems experienced in marital separation (Bachrach, 1975; Bloom, 1975; Briscoe et al., 1973). The literature is consistently unclear as to the etiology and process variables which are addressed in the process of family dissolution, marital separation, and the mediation process. Efforts to assess the major psychosocial transition associated with this process have been carefully explored by Chiriboga (1979), Baum et al. (1981), Lazarus (1980), and Rahe (1979). The anxiety and frustration of the divorce process are frequently exacerbated by the legal process. Efforts to develop a mediation approach to marital dysfunction have provided a model which may be of some assistance in addressing these issues.

There are a number of issues to consider when one utilizes the mediation process as a significant factor in the resolution of disputed divorce proceedings. The research efforts of Kressel et al. (1980), Bahr (1981), and Pearson and Thoennes (1982) suggest that the following conclusions can be drawn:

1. Successfully mediated couples report a lower rate of problems and greater compliance with their litigated agreements than control group couples.
2. Successfully mediated couples report a higher level of satisfaction with the mediated agreements and perceive them as more fair than couples in the control group.
3. Successfully mediated couples report better relationships with their ex-spouse than do non-mediated couples.
4. Successfully mediated couples are able to realize a lower schedule of fees and expenses as a result of the mediation process than are couples in the control group.

FAMILY MEDIATION: A MODEL FOR TREATMENT

Disruption of the family unit due to separation and divorce is a highly stressful event for all family members, often leading to an increase in conflict and to significant pathology in the individual experiencing disruption, both adults and children. The Child Psychiatric Outpatient Clinic at the University of Kentucky Medical Center has received increasing numbers of referrals from circuit courts in central Kentucky requesting mediation and evaluation services. Because of the increasing number of referrals in recent years, a subspecialty clinic was established in the Child Psychiatry Outpatient Clinic to evaluate these families. The goals and procedures of this clinic are as follows:

1. To establish a clinical procedure useful in the mediation and evaluation of child litigation cases.

2. As advocates for the child in child litigation cases, our initial strategy is to attempt to see if reconciliation of the family is possible. Maintaining the family structure, if possible, is an ideal solution for the children involved. We begin by seeing the parents jointly to cut down on distortion and to clarify issues.

3. When reconciliation is not possible, mediation is used to help parents develop a custody and visitation plan that is in the best psychological interest of their children. Parents are seen jointly during this phase. The goals in mediation include: (a) reducing the conflict between the parents, (b) developing a plan where the children have frequent contact with each parent, (c) maintaining the psychological attachment between the child and significant adults including parents, siblings, and grandparents, (d) maintaining continuity of place, routine, and peer relationships.

4. When the parents remain polarized and mediation breaks down, we evaluate the family which includes a series of joint and individual sessions with parents and children. The goal is to develop an opinion regarding the custodial and visitation plan which will maintain the relationships the child has with each parent, maintain continuity of school experience, and maintain peer relationships. In addition, it is determined where the child feels most comfortable and what plan would best meet their needs in their current developmental stage. This is done through indirect evaluation strategies such as the kinetic family drawing, other case-specific drawings, and various structured and unstructured play therapy techniques.

5. After the evaluation is complete, we meet the parents individually stressing advantages of agreeing on an outcome and cutting down on the conflict and adversarial nature of their relationship. We specify the advantages to the children in the sense that the less external conflict the children experience, the less internal conflict they will experience, and the less chance there is of symptoms. These symptoms may vary depending on the child's developmental stage and may take the form of physical, behavioral, or emotional symptoms.

6. If mediation remains impossible, we dictate a rough draft of a report to the court using specific criteria outlined above. A suggested form for this rough draft of the court report includes:

(a) Paragraph one: "In response to the court's request for an initial evaluation in this contested custody case . . ." In this initial paragraph state who was seen, when they were seen, the one or two specific questions that you attempt to answer in the course of the evaluation.

(b) Paragraph two: "The history reveals. . . ." In this paragraph we spell out important dates and other information that is pertinent in the history.

(c) Paragraph three: "The current situation reveals . . ." Spell out important aspects of the current situation.

(d) Paragraph four: "The following themes emerged in the course of this evaluation." These themes include specific criteria and other issues that are relevant in helping develop the conclusions regarding the best custodial arrangement and visitation plan.

(e) Paragraph five: "Based on this evaluation I make the following recommendations for the court's consideration." Go back to the one or two questions outlined in paragraph one and state short, specific recommendations free of psychological jargon and easy for the court to understand.

7. Meet with the parents jointly and share the rough draft of the court report. This is important for a number of reasons as it helps cut out inaccurate statements, gives the parents the opportunity to discuss the report with you, helps clarify the issues before going to court, and gives them a final opportunity to agree on a decision.

The results of a two-year study at the University of Kentucky (Veltkamp and Miller, 1984), utilizing the family mediation model with 70 cases referred for court ordered family mediation, resulted in 47 percent of those cases being successfully mediated. Couples who were unable to reach agreement were, however, generally supportive of the mediation experience. In addition, communication skills and social skills training were found to be beneficial to couples requiring court ordered mediation. In 53 percent of the cases, a recommendation was made to the court which involved a plan for custody and a resolution to the dispute wherein the psychological interests of the child or children were considered as extremely important.

A number of clinical issues emerged in assessing the family

mediation process, including one's acceptance of the divorce process, relationships between ex-spouses, the impact of divorce on the social support system of all parties involved, both adults and children, and the perception of failure that exists among both adults and children when a family is dissolved through divorce.

CLINICAL ISSUES IN FAMILY MEDIATION

THE INDIVIDUAL'S ACCEPTANCE OF THE DIVORCE PROCESS

Kressel and Deutsch (1977) and Irving (1981) have addressed one of the most crucial issues in the process of separating, i.e., the experience of the person who is left alone in this process. These clinicians and researchers encourage all involved to understand and accept the divorce process as a very painful experience. At the same time, they encourage acceptance as critically important in perceiving a balanced view of the marriage and to recognize that both have contributed to the dissolution process. Most important is the recognition that each partner must endure a process of learning about the reasons for one's choice of mate so that similar mistakes can be avoided in future relationships. The individual who feels abandoned in the process must assume greater autonomous functioning and more assertive qualities about their own rights and the utilization of both the health care delivery system and the legal process as instruments of society in the dissolution process.

EX-SPOUSE RELATIONSHIPS

The degree of stress and tension that is experienced in ex-spouse relationships has become the focus of several clinician-researchers. Weiss (1975) has demonstrated that even after the erosion of love and relationship, there is a continuation of attachment in some relationships. It is this attachment that works against the development of autonomy and independence necessary to function as a single adult or to seek new relationships beyond the relationship found in the initial marriage. Hynes (1979) has confirmed empirically that the higher the lingering attachment to the former spouse, the higher the stress associated with sudden divorce. Within the framework of family mediation, it becomes extremely important that the ex-spouses refrain from unnecessary contact with their former spouse but when contact is necessary, every attempt be made to work toward rational task oriented and goal directed interactions.

IMPACT ON THE SOCIAL SUPPORT SYSTEM

The patterns of friendship associated with the divorce or separation process have also gained the attention of several researchers (Berman and Turk, 1981; Miller, 1976; and Spanier and Casto, 1979). Individuals involved in the divorcing process, both adults and children, tend to experience a loss of support from some aspects of their friendship network and that these result in certain feelings of social isolation. Hetherington et al. (1976, 1978) indicate in their research that it is for about a period of two months following divorce that married friends remain supportive and spend considerable time with divorcing friends. To children of divorce, this becomes even more a critical problem because friendships are less well developed and networks of friendships have not been matured.

Likewise, relatives of divorced individuals are most likely to show some concern for the parties involved but eventually divorcing individuals will increase their contact with their own relatives but decrease contact with ex-spouse's relations (Booth, 1979).

More than half of all divorces involve minor children and virtually all of these divorces involve parents who are concerned about the key issues in family mediation, including child support, custody, and visitation. Hetherington et al. (1979); Wallerstein and Kelly (1977); Bane (1979); Wallerstein and Kelly (1980); and Berman and Turk (1981) suggest several key variables which must be considered in the adjustment of children to the divorce process. These include the following:

1. The psychological adjustment of the parents to the process of divorce and to the dissolution of the family.
2. The quality of the relationships that exist between the ex-spouses.
3. The level and intensity of the nurturing relationship toward the child from both the custodial and non-custodial parent.
4. The financial resources available and the integrity of the supporting spouse in the provision of financial support.
5. The involvement of all minor children in both the perceived and actual process of family dissolution wherein the child has input and understanding in the dissolution process and the new custodial relationship.

THE PERCEPTION OF FAILURE

Hetherington et al. (1978) addresses the impact of cultural norms about divorce and while they are perceived as quite liberal, many individuals involved in divorce still perceive themselves as failures because of it. There continue to be negative stereotypes and a variety of sanctions that society dictates toward individuals involved in divorce where divorce remains an ambiguous status for many and the traditional social norms argue against divorce being accepted within society. While the ambiguous state is a crucial issue toward adjustment, alternate sources of social support are extremely important. Kitson and Raschke (1981) suggest that high levels of social support are related to lower distress and better adjustment in the family mediation process. The quality of the social support, whether it be of a formal or informal nature, whether it be individual counseling or divorce adjustment groups, needs to address the emotional and post-trauma stress experienced by all concerned in the family mediation process.

SUMMARY

There is a clear evidence that the separation and subsequent divorce process is stressful for both parents and children. In addition, when parents and children are caught in the adversarial proceeding involving battling for custody, visitation and other crucial issues, the level of stress is considerably high and the potential for adjustment more difficult. A review of the literature herein has addressed the impact of separation and divorce on both adults and children and the potential for an innovative model of family mediation. Finally, several issues, primarily of a clinical nature that are experienced by both adults and children in the divorce process, have been enumerated to sensitize those involved in family mediation. Issues and concerns relative to the effective facilitation and resolution of the adversarial process.

REFERENCES

American Psychiatric Association (1980), *Diagnostic and Statistical Manual of Mental Disorders*, 3rd ed. Washington, DC: American Psychiatric Association.

Bachrach, L. L. (1975), Marital status and mental disorder: An analytic review. DHEW Publication No. (ADM) 75-217. Washington, DC: U.S. Government Printing Office.

Bahr, S. J. (1981), An evaluation of court mediation for divorce cases with children. *J. Fam. Iss.*, 14:29–34.

Bane, M. J. (1976), Marital disruption in the lives of children. *J. Soc. Iss.*, 32:103–117.

———— (1979), Marital disruption and the lives of children. In: *Divorce and Separation: Context, Causes and Consequences*, ed. G. Levinger & O. C. Moles. New York: Basic Books, pp. 187–206.

Baum, A., Singer, J. E., & Baum, C. S. (1981), Stress and the evironment. *J. Soc. Iss.*, 37:4–35.

Berman, W. H., & Turk, D. C. (1981), Adaptation to divorce: Problems and coping strategies. *J. Marr. & Fam.*, 43:1–139.

Bloom, B. L. (1975), *Changing Patterns of Psychiatric Care*. New York: Behavioral Publications.

———— Hodges, W. F. (1980), The predicament of the newly separated. Unpublished research report. University of Colorado, Denver.

Booth, G. V. (1979), Kinship and the crisis of divorce. Unpublished doctoral dissertation. Southern Illinois University of Carbondale.

Briscoe, C. W., Smith, J. B., Robins, E., Marten, S., & Gaskin, F. (1973), Divorce and psychiatric disease. *Arch. Gen. Psychiat.*, 29:119–125.

Chiriboga, D. A. (1979), Marital separation and stress: A life course perspective. *Alternat. Lifestyles*, 8:461–470.

———— Dean, H. (1978), Dimensions of stress: Perspectives from a longitudinal study. *J. Psychosom. Res.*, 22:47–55.

Deutsch, M. (1973), *The Resolution of Conflict*. New Haven, CT: Yale University Press.

Dohrenwend, B. S. (1975), Some issues in research on stressful life events. *J. Nerv. & Ment. Dis.*, 166:7–15.

Ebel, D. M. (1980), Bar programs: Other ways to resolve disputes. *Litigation*, 6:25–28.

Glenn, N. D. (1975), The contribution of marriage to the psychological well-being of males and females. *J. Marr. & Fam.*, 37:594–660.

Grant, I., Sweetwood, H., Yager, J., & Gerst, M. (in press), Quality of life events in relation to psychiatric symptoms. *Arch. Gen. Psychiat.*

Herman, M. S., McKenry, P. C., & Weber, R. E. (1979), Mediation and arbitration applied to family conflict resolution: The divorce settlement. *Arbitr. J.*, 34:17–21.

Hess, R. D., & Camara, K. A. (1979), Post-divorce family relationships as mediating factors and the consequences of divorce for children. *J. Soc. Iss.*, 35:79–96.

Hetherington, E. M., Cox, M., & Cox, R. (1976), Divorced fathers. *Fam. Coord.*, 25:417–428.

———— ———— ———— (1978), Family interaction and the social, emotional and cognitive development of children following divorce. Paper presented at a symposium on the family, "Setting Priorities," sponsored by the Institute for Pediatric Services of the Johnson & Johnson Baby Co., Washington, DC.

———— ———— ———— (1979), Play and social interaction in children following divorce. *J. Soc. Iss.*, 35:26–49.

Hynes, W. J. (1979), Single parent mothers and distress: Relationship between selected social and psychological factors and distress in low-income single parent mothers. Unpublished doctoral dissertation. The Catholic University of America, Washington, DC.

Irving, H. H. (1981), *Divorce Mediation: A Rational Alternative to the Adversary System*. New York: Universe Books.

Jacobsen, G. F., & Potuges, S. H. (1976), Relation of marital separation and divorce to suicide: A preliminary report. Paper presented at the annual meeting of the American Suicidology Association, Los Angeles, May 1.

Kalter, N. (1977), Children of divorce in an outpatient psychiatric population. *Amer. J. Orthopsychiat.*, 46:40–51.

Kitson, G., & Raschke, H. (1981), A review of Research on Divorce. *J. Divorce*, 23:11–18.

Kochen, T. A., & Jick, T. (1978), The public sector mediation process. *J. Conflict Resolut.*, 22:209–239.

Kressel, K., Jaffe, N., Tuchman, B., Watson, C., & Deutsch, M. (1980), A typology of divorcing couples: Implications for mediation and the divorce process. *Fam. Proc.*, 19:101–116.

——— Deutsch, M. (1977), Divorce therapy: An indepth survey of therapists' views. *Fam. Proc.*, 16:413–443.

Lazarus, R. S. (1980), The stress and coping paradigm. In: *Theoretical Bases in Psychopathology*, ed. C. Eisdorfer, D. Cohen, A. Kleinman, & P. Maxim. New York: Spectrum.

Miller, T. W. (1976), Effects of core facilitative conditions in mother on early adolescent self-esteem. *J. Soc. Psychol.*, 101:98–120.

——— (1977), The parental response inventory: An experimental research measure to assess family interaction patterns. In: *Tests and Measurements in Child Development*, Handbook 2, ed. O. G. Johnson. San Francisco: Jossey-Bass.

——— (1981), Measurement of locus of control in divorce mediation: An experimental instrument. Unpublished manuscript, State University of New York, Buffalo.

——— (1984), Paternal absence and its effect on adolescent self-esteem. *Internat. J. Soc. Psychiat.*, 30/4:293–297.

Mnoonkin, R. H., & Kornhauser, R. (1979), Bargaining in the shadow of the law: The case of divorce. *Yale Law J.*, 88:950–995.

Nada, I. (1971), Disease caused by alcoholism. In: *Alcoholism*, ed. I. Nada. Tokyo: Kinokumiya Shuten, pp. 68–83.

Pearson, J., & Thoennes, N. (1982), Mediating and litigating custody disputes: A longitudinal evaluation. Paper presented at the meeting of the International Society on Family Law, Cambridge, MA, June.

Rahe, R. H. (1979), Life change events and mental illness: An overview. *J. Hum. Stress*, 5:2–10.

Rutter, M. (1971), Parent-child separation: Psychological effects on children. *J. Child Psychol. & Psychiat.*, 12:233–260.

Spanier, G. B., & Casto, R. F. (1979), Adjustment to separation and divorce: A qualitative analysis. In: *Divorce and Separation: Context, Causes and Consequences*, ed. G. Levinger & O. C. Moles. New York: Basic Books, pp. 288–300.

Veltkamp, L., & Miller, T. W. (1984), The development and implementation of a therapeutic mediator module in contested court cases. Unpublished paper, University of Kentucky, Lexington.

Wallerstein, J. S., & Kelly, J. B. (1974), The effects of parental divorce: The adolescent experience. In: *The Child and His Family*, Vol. 3, ed. E. J. Anthony & C. Koupernic. New York: John Wiley, pp. 479–505.

——— ——— (1975), The effects of parental divorce: Experiences of the preschool child. *J. Amer. Acad. Child Psychiat.*, 14/4:600–616.

——— ——— (1976), The effects of parental divorce: Experiences of the child in later latency. *Amer. J. Opthopsychiat.*, 46/2:256–269.

——— ——— (1977), Divorce counseling: A community service for families in the midst of divorce. *Amer. J. Orthopsychiat.*, 47:4–22.

——— ——— (1980), *Surviving the Breakup: How Children and Parents Cope with Divorce*. New York: Basic Books.

Wechsler, H., Thum, D., Demone, H. W., & Dwinnell, J. (1972), Social characteristics and blood alcohol level. *Quart. J. Study Alcohol.*, 33:132–147.

Weiss, R. L. (1975), *Marital Separation*. New York: Basic Books.

Chapter 39
Factors Contributing to Teacher Stress

ROBERT G. HARRINGTON, PH.D., JUDITH A. BURRY, PH.D.,
AND DENNIS PELSMA, M.S.

There are many job-related pressures that teachers must try to endure. Popular reading as well as the research literature has amply demonstrated some of these pressures such as higher academic standing for students, better classroom discipline, more individualized instruction, and a host of other expectations. In addition, there is much data-based (Anderson, 1980; Ceckon and Koff, 1980; Coates and Thoreson, 1976; Fimian and Santoro, 1983; Greer and Wethered, 1984; Maslach and Jackson, 1981) and non-data-based documentation (Bloch, 1978; Fimian, 1980, 1982; Harrington, 1979; Styles and Cavanaugh, 1977) to attest to these stresses. As discussed by Fimian (1985), most current measures of teacher stress are unidimensional. That is, they either focus on those stimulus aspects of the environment that are demanding or disorganizing for the individual or they emphasize the responses of the individual to the events of the environment as being the primary defining features of stress. As a result, they may fail to take into account the full range of multivariate issues involved in teacher stress. Many environmental stimuli can contribute to a classroom

Acknowledgment. This chapter was presented at a meeting of the American Psychological Association, Los Angeles, August 26, 1985.

teacher's level of stress. Weiskopf (1980) noted the following stress sources: (1) work overload, (2) lack of recognition for success in one's role, (3) longer amounts of time in direct contact with students, (4) low staff/high child ratios, (5) undefined program structures and organizations, and (6) the constant responsibility to care for others. Fimian (1982) summarized 135 stress factors cited in the literature into 13 a priori categories: (1) personal competence, (2) self relationship, (3) conflicting values, (4) social approval, (5) isolation, (6) expectations, (7) self-fulfillment, (8) deficiencies in the physical environment, (9) unmet professional needs, (10) self-inflicted stress, (11) professional constraints, (12) student-teacher relationships, and (13) the miscellaneous demands of teaching. Cunningham (1983) reviewed some specific response oriented factors that may be related to teacher stress. These included the following:

1. Attitudes of teachers toward their perceived status versus desired status.
2. Attitudes of teachers toward the lack of respect shown them both from within and outside the profession.
3. Attitudes of teachers toward the lack of opportunity for job enrichment and redesign.
4. Lack of preservice preparation in areas of stress reduction; conflict management, etc.
5. Lack of appropriate supervision and support which often results in perceived isolation.
6. Perceived lack of opportunities for participation in school decision-making.

Although the connection between job satisfaction and job stress has been suggested it is unlikely that job stress is simply another term for job dissatisfaction (Maslach and Jackson, 1981). Thus, it appears the work climate, structure, and other facets inherent in the teacher's job may directly influence the quality of teacher work life through the amount of stress and the degree of satisfaction experienced by the individual. This approach to the measurement of teacher stress has come to be called the interactionist perspective because it emphasizes the characteristics of the organism as major mediation mechanisms between the stimulus characteristics of the environment and the responses they invoke. Interactional theorists have criticized the stimulus and the response theorists because they both overlook the person in the stress equation and their potential to mediate not only the impact of environmental stimulus events but also their own perceptual, cognitive, and physiological characteristics (Cox and Mackey, 1976; Lazarus, 1976, 1981). There have been very few new developments in stress measurement from the interactionist perspective, in part because the interactionist point of view is rather new in stress research. Previous efforts to measure teacher stress and job satisfaction have not been sound psychometrically. If progress is to be made in understanding the factors that lead to the improvement of the quality of teacher work life then more reliable and valid measures of teacher stress that assess the stimulus characteristics of the environment as well as the mediating response made to stress by the teacher must be developed.

This study focused on the development of a self-report inventory to assess those factors contributing to teacher stress from an interactionist perspective. The instrument is called the Quality of Teacher Work Life Scale (QTWL). The Quality of Teacher Work Life Scale combined the scores of two teacher ratings measuring: (1) the perceived satisfaction with specific aspects of the teachers' work environment, and (2) the degree of stress associated with each of these stimuli. Greer and Wethered (1984) have substantiated the idea that the belief system of the individual causes many events to be perceived as stressful. Thus, the belief systems held by some individuals may make them more or less susceptible to stress. The first purpose of this study was to investigate the psychometric characteristics of the QTWL including the construct validity of the "Stressed" and "Satisfied" scales, the relationship between the scales, and the reliability of the scales. The second purpose was to identify the major factors contributing to teacher dissatisfaction and stress using the newly developed QTWL Scale.

METHOD

INSTRUMENTATION

The Quality of Teacher Work Life Scale consisted of 50 items of which 36 were used to measure satisfaction and stress. The items were selected on the basis of previous studies in this area (Coates and Thoreson, 1976; Burry, Harrington, and Pelsma 1985) as well as judgments made by the authors of this chapter as to the hypothesized aspects of the quality of teacher work life. Following the lead of the Hasseles Scales (Lazarus and Cohen, 1977) and the Maslach Burnout Inventory (Maslach and Jackson, 1981) each statement was rated on two dimensions: satisfaction and stress experienced. The Satisfied scale was labeled at each point and ranged from 1 ("very dissatisfied") to 5 ("very satisfied"). The Stress scale ranged from 1 ("extreme stress") to 5 ("no stress"). The purpose for requesting such ratings was based on the assumption held by the authors and others (Maslach and Jackson, 1981) that the level of stress experienced was not simply a synonym for job dissatisfaction, but represented an interaction.

For example, each participant was asked: "Please write the appropriate number representing your *present* degree of *satisfaction* and the degree of *stress* you experience in each of the following job-related areas."

PARTICIPANTS

The QTWL Scale was sent to 511 certified teachers working in a relatively small suburban school district located in the Midwest. Surveys were sent in April 1984 and returned in May 1984. Usable responses were received from 251 teachers for a return rate of 49 percent. Demographic information for the subjects is presented in Table 39.1. For subjects completing the study, the mean age was approximately 40 years (ranging from

Table 39.1
Subjects Variables and Selected Survey Items ($n = 251$)

	M	SD	Range	Percent
1. Age	40.4	9.7	22–65	
2. Sex				
female				74
male				26
3. Education				
B.S.				38
M.S.				55
Ed.S.				1
Ed.D.				1
Ph.D.				2
Other				2
4. Level				
Preschool				2
Kindergarten				5
Elementary				43
Middle				12
Secondary				38
5. Total Years continuously employed in public schools (Item #7)	12.3	7.3	1–35	
6. No. of years employed in present school district (Item #8)	9.9	6.8	1–29	
7. No. of years in present position (Item #9)	8.0	6.2	1–26	
8. Do you plan to remain employed in education? (Item #10)			Yes No Undecided	87 2 11
9. Have reasons for choosing education been fulfilled? (Item #12)			Yes No	84 12

Table 39.1 (Continued)

10. How satisfied are you with your present position? (Item #13)	Very dissatisfied	7
	Mostly dissatisfied	8
	Neutral	6
	Mostly satisfied	43
	Very satisfied	36
11. If you had the choice to reconsider would you choose education? (Item # 14)	Definitely no	4
	Probably no	18
	Undecided	16
	Definitely yes	42

22–65). Almost 75 percent of the respondents were female. Over 55 percent of the subjects held at least a master's degree. The sample was divided equally between elementary teachers (50 percent) and junior high/high school teachers (50 percent). The mean years of employment in public schools was approximately 12 years with the number of years in the district almost 10. The next four global questions were intended to describe the attitudes of the sample toward the teaching experience in general. Of the sample 87 percent reported that they planned to remain employed in education and 84 percent said their reasons for choosing education had been fulfilled. Seventy-nine percent were either mostly satisfied or very satisfied with their present teaching positions, but only 42 percent said that if they had the choice to reconsider they would choose education. Correlations of the QTWL with certain demographic variables are presented in Table 39.2.

RESULTS AND DISCUSSION

The means, standard deviations, reliability coefficients, and standard errors of measurement for the Satisfied and Stressed scales of the QTWL are presented in Table 39.3. Out of a

Table 39.2
Means, Standard Deviations, Reliability Coefficients and Standard Errors of
Measurement for the Satisfied and Stressed Scales of the QTWL

Scale	Means	Standard Deviations	Reliability Coefficients	Standard Error of Measurement
Satisfied	116.91	16.25	0.87	5.86
Stressed	133.49	18.49	0.92	5.23

Table 39.3
Correlations of the Satisfied and Stressed Scales of the QTWL
with Demographic Variables

Scales	Age	Sex	Education	Level
Satisfaction	− .0019	− .0901	− .1242*	− .0739
Stressed	− .1083*	− .0001	− .0846	− .0056

*$p < .05$

possible raw score of 180 for either scale of the QTWL, the sample mean was 116.9 for the Satisfied scale and 133.49 for the Stressed scale. The reliability coefficients for the Satisfied ($r = .087$) and the Stressed ($r = 0.92$) scales were very acceptable as well as were the standard errors of measurement for the Satisfied ($±.586$) and the Stressed scales ($±.523$). The correlation coefficient between the Satisfied and Stressed scales was shown to be 0.70.

A factor analysis using varimax rotation, with unity (ones) on the diagonal was conducted on the two scales of the QTWL to test the construct validity of the scales. The factor loadings, percent of variances and cumulative percent for the 11 factors of the Satisfied scale and the 10 factors of the Stressed scale are presented in Tables 39.4 and 39.6. The factor loadings for individual items on the Satisfied and Stressed scales of the QTWL are presented in Tables 39.5 and 39.7. A listing of the factor names for both scales is presented in Table 39.8. The results of these factor analyses support the identification of the Satisfied and Stressed scales of the QTWL as two separate scales.

The eleven-component solution derived from the Satisfied scale accounted for 66.5 percent of the total scale variance. The ten-component solution derived from the stressed item scores accounted for 66.1 percent of the Stress scale variance associated with the item interrelationships. The factor loadings have similar patterns on both scales with two notable variations. Each factor for both the Satisfied and Stressed scales will be reported in the order of their importance to their respective scales based on their percent contributions to the total variance of the scales.

Factor I (22.3 percent of the total Satisfied scale variance; 26.8 percent of the total stressed scale variance) was called Administrative-Work Environment. The item content defining the scale suggested that teachers with low scores on this factor felt that there were problems in the work environment due to a lack of support from school administrators, incompetent administration, the administration's poor relationships with teachers, and lack of reinforcement other than pay, and to the kinds of formal evaluations of teaching performance used by the administration. Factor I is comprised of an almost identical item configuration for both the Satisfied and Stressed scales. This finding suggests that in fact the working environment created by the school administration contributes the most strongly to teachers' levels of dissatisfaction and stress and the overall quality of teacher work life.

Factor II on the Satisfied scale (8.4 percent of the total Satisfied scale variance) was called Relationships with Students and Parents. Teachers who scored low on this scale were dissatisfied with their present teaching assignments due to lack of student interest and motivation, student discipline problems, poor relationships and lack of support from parents. On the other hand, Factor II on the Stressed scale (7.4 percent of the total Stressed scale variance) was called Time Devoted to Specific Activities. Low scores meant that teachers felt that they did not have enough time for class preparation or time to recuperate between classes. There was too much time spent in clerical work and in adapting programs and in developing individualized programs for exceptional children. Too much

Table 39.4
Factor Loadings, Percent of Variance and Cumulative Percent for
Satisfied Scale of the QTWL

Factor	Factor Loadings	Percent of Variance	Cumulative Percent
I	8.03693	22.3	22.3
II	3.02669	8.4	30.7
III	2.37805	6.6	37.3
IV	1.81344	5.0	42.4
V	1.68662	4.7	47.1
VI	1.42151	3.9	51.0
VII	1.27431	3.5	54.5
VIII	1.20071	3.3	57.9
IX	1.05911	2.9	60.8
X	1.03797	2.9	63.7
XI	1.00900	2.8	66.5

time was spent in extracurricular activities, and large class sizes and resulting discipline problems were perceived as taking valuable class time.

Factor III (6.6 percent of the total Satisfied scale variance) was called Interruptions. Low scores meant that teachers were dissatisfied with students missing classes due to extracurricular activities and were dissatisfied with the number of breaks in the teaching process due to telephone calls, and school bells as well as support personnel interrupting the teaching process to get students for individualized instruction. Teachers wanted to have a greater say in decision-making affecting these and other areas related to teaching. Factor III (4.9 percent of the total Stressed scale variance) was called Student Evaluation-Outside School Support. All of the items on this factor related to a perceived lack of support from the community at large and from parents of students in particular. The public perception of education as well as the teachers' ability to evaluate student performance all added to the stress levels measured by this factor.

Factor IV (5.0 percent of the total Satisfied scale variance) was called Time. Class preparation time, no time to rest between class, extra time needed for large classes, and time spent in

Table 39.5

Factor Loadings for Items on the Satisfied Scale of the QTWL

No.	Item	I	II	III	IV	V	VI	VII	VIII	IX	X	XI	Final Communality Estimates
	Factor I: Administration												
38	Support from administrators	.83											.74
20	Competence of administration	.81											.74
44	Teacher relationships with administrators	.79											.70
48	Feedback or reinforcement other than pay	.50											.69
47	Formal evaluation of teaching performance	.49											.65
33	Work environment	.45											.56
	Factor II: Relationships with Students/Parents												
43	Amount of student interest		.83										.81
42	Amount of student motivation		.83										.78
39	Support from parents		.70										.69
45	Teacher relationship with parents		.57										.51
25	Student discipline		.56										.64
37	Present teaching assignment (e.g. subject area or grade level)		.38										.61

Factor III: Interruptions

28 Students missing class due to extracurricular activities	.75	.67
26 Number of breaks in the teacher process (i.e., telephone calls, announcements)	.74	.71
27 Number of breaks in the teacher process due to support personnel	.70	.70
50 Participation in decision-making affecting school policy	.40	.59

Factor IV: Time allowance

19 Daily time for preparation	.74	.64
18 Daily time for recuperation between work respossibilities	.70	.61
17 Class sizes	.69	.57
23 Time spent in extracurricular activities	.47	.52

Factor V: Work environment

34 School equipment	.79	.73
35 Educational curriculum materials	.76	.75
40 Support from the local community	.36	.58

Factor VI: Internal support

21 Competence of teachers	.86	.79
22 Competence of staff	.75	.71
36 Faculty relations	.53	.62

Table 39.5 (Continued)

Factor VII: Time devoted to specific activities						
32 Time spent in individualizing programs for special needs of children	.70					.68
46 Time required to adapt instruction to individual differences in utility, interest and needs	.63					.69
24 Time spent in clerical and administrative work	.43	.47				
Factor VIII: Job perceptions						
30 Availability of jobs within the educational professions		.78				.72
41 Opportunity for promotion or advancement		.65				.72
49 Public perceptions of education		.40				.52
Factor IX: Undefined						
31 Your ability to evaluate student performance			.73			.68
29 Job security			.70			.72
Factor X: Undefined						
16 Fringe benefits				.71		.68
Factor XI: Undefined						
15 Salaries					.81	.80

Table 39.6
Factor Loadings, Percent of Variance and Cumulative Percent for
Stressed Scale of the QTWL

Factor	Factor Loadings	Percent of Variance	Cumulative Percent
I	9.63870	26.8	26.8
II	2.66383	7.4	34.2
III	1.75038	4.9	39.0
IV	1.72697	4.8	43.8
V	1.64072	4.6	48.4
VI	1.54190	4.3	52.7
VII	1.42664	4.0	56.6
VIII	1.30939	3.6	60.3
IX	1.09772	3.0	63.3
X	1.00166	2.8	66.1

extracurricular activities were dissatisfying to teachers scoring low in this factor. On the Stressed scale, Factor IV (4.8 percent of the total Stressed scale variance) was called Work Environment. Low scores on this scale meant that those teachers were stressed about the available curriculum materials, the school equipment, and the formal evaluation of their teaching performance that may be impacted by this equipment.

Factor V (3.9 percent of the total Satisfied scale variance) was called Work Environment and was similar to Factor IV on the Stressed scale. The quality of school equipment and the availability of educational materials seemed to be related to the level of support received from the community. Factor V (4.6 percent of the total Stressed scale variance) was called Student Motivation and Interest. Teachers became stressed when student motivation and interest were low.

Factor VI (3.9 percent of the total Satisfied scale variance) was called Internal Support. This factor dealt with dissatisfaction due to conflicts in faculty relations, competence of fellow teachers, and the competence of other staff. Factor VI (4.3 percent of the total Stressed scale variance) was called Teaching Interruptions. This factor was similar to Factor III on the Satisfied scale and consisted of items describing various classroom interruptions.

Table 39.7

Factor Loadings for Items on the Stressed Scale of the QTWL

No.	Item	I	II	III	IV	V	VI	VII	VIII	IX	X	XI	Final Communality Estimates
	Factor I: Administration												
38	Support from administrators	.80											.68
20	Competence of administration	.77											.70
44	Teacher relationships with administrators	.75											.68
48	Feedback or reinforcement other than pay	.54											.64
50	Participation in decision-making affecting school policy	.50											.61
33	Work environment	.50											.53
37	Present teaching assignment (e.g., subject areas or grade)	.48											.62
	Factor II: Time												
19	Daily time for preparation		.76										.66
18	Daily time for recuperation between work responsibilities		.70										.60

	Loading				h^2
32 Time spent in individualizing programs for special needs of children	.56				.70
24 Time spent in clerical and administrative work	.55				.51
46 Time required to adapt instructions to individual differences in ability, interest and needs	.54				.69
23 Time spent in extracurricular activities	.46				.49
17 Class size	.43				.46
25 Student discipline	.34				.57
Factor III: Student evaluation—outside school support					
39 Support from parents		.75			.72
45 Teacher relationships with parents		.69			.71
40 Support from the local community		.68			.69
49 Public perception of education		.52			.58
31 Your ability to evaluate student performance		.39			.53
Factor IV: Work environment					
35 Educational curriculum materials			.78		.70
34 School equipment			.75		.71
47 Formal evaluation of teaching performance			.46		.58
Factor V: Student motivation and interest					
43 Amount of student interest				.89	.87
42 Amount of student motivation				.85	.85

Table 39.7 (Continued)

Factor VI: Teaching interruptions		
27 Number of breaks in the teaching process due to support personnel	.82	.75
26 Number of breaks in the teaching process (e.g., telephone calls, announcements, etc.)	.71	.68
28 Students missing class due to extracurricular activities	.49	.48
Factor VII: Internal support		
21 Competence of teachers	.86	.76
22 Competence of staff	.80	.77
36 Faculty relations	.57	.63
Factor VIII: Job market		
29 Job security	.79	.70
30 Availability of jobs within the educational profession	.78	.72
Factor IX: Job benefits		
16 Fringe benefits	.82	
15 Salaries	.76	.73
Factor X: Undefined		
41 Opportunity for promotion or advancement	.54	.69

Table 39.8
Factor Titles for the Satisfied and Stressed Scales of the QTWL

Factor	Satisfied	Stressed
I	Administrative-work environment	Administrative-work environment
II	Relationships with students and parents	Time
III	Interruptions	Local support
IV	Time allowances	Work environment
V	Work environment	Student motivation interest
VI	Internal support	Teaching interruptions
VII	Time devoted to specific teaching activities	Internal support
VIII	Job perceptions	Job market
IX	Undefined	Job benefits
X	Undefined	Undefined
XI	Undefined	

Factor VII (3.5 percent of the total Satisfied scale variance) was called Time Devoted to Specific Activities. Low scores on this factor were related to dissatisfaction with the amount of time necessary to complete certain activities such as individualizing for exceptional children and doing clerical work. Factor VII (4.0 percent of the total Stressed scale variance) was called Internal Support. This factor was identical to Factor VI on the Satisfied scale dealing with competence of teaching staff and faculty relations.

Factor VIII (3.3 percent of the total Satisfied scale variance) was called Job Perceptions. Satisfaction on this scale was related to availability of jobs within the educational profession, opportunity for promotion on advancement, and public perceptions of education. On the Stressed scale Factor VIII (3.6 percent of the total Stressed scale variance) and Factor IX (3.0 percent of the total Stressed scale variance) were related to the Job Market and Job Benefits respectively. Factor VIII related to job security and the availability of jobs within the educational profession while Factor IX dealt with stress related to job benefits and salaries.

Factors IX, X, and XI, on the Satisfied scale and Factor X on the Stressed scale were undefined because they contained only one item each.

When the factors on the Satisfied and Stressed scales are compared it is clear that the one factor that contributes most to teacher dissatisfaction and stress is the administrative component or Factor I on both scales. Likewise, interruptions to the teaching process, the level of internal support from peers in the teaching profession, the quality of the work environment including teaching materials and job perceptions as well as alternative job prospects were represented on both the Satisfied and Stressed scales. Where there were differences on the two scales was in relation to the impact of time on teacher stress and the effects of student/parent relationships with teachers and the levels of support they give teachers. On the Stressed scales there is only one general time factor operating while on the Satisfied scale there are two separate time factors. One factor on the Satisfied scale relates to a general lack of time allowances for class preparation and recuperation, while the other factor seemed to be related to time spent on adapting instructions for exceptional students. The Satisfied scale also included a dimension on Relationships with Students and Parents. This dimension became much less specific on the Stressed scale than on the Satisfied scale. This finding supported previous research (Maslach and Jackson, 1981; Fimian, 1982) that suggests that time pressures and personal relationships become distorted under stress. This research represents one of the first studies to identify and verify (Burry et al., 1985) the major factors that contribute most heavily to teacher stress.

CONCLUSION

The results of this study show the QTWL to be a reliable instrument with two valid scales that seem to be measuring separate but related constructs dealing with the quality of teacher work life. Several of the factors on the two scales did overlap somewhat and consequently were given similar factor titles. They were the following factors: Administrative-Work Environment, Teaching Interruptions, Work Environment and External Support. In addition, the Job Market and Job Benefits Factors on the Stressed scale contained item content similar to the Job Perceptions factor on the Satisfied scale. It is interesting to speculate about the differences in relationships and time that occur on the two scales and their implications for the beginning of a theory on the relationship between job satisfaction and stress and their impact on the quality of teacher life. It would appear that under stress teacher relationships with students and parents may be less positive. Stressed teachers may have greater difficulty in dealing with time management, activity management, and relating to people in general.

In summary, the QTWL appears to be a valid and reliable instrument for measuring the quality of teacher work life. Such an instrument has many potential uses in studying the effects of stressors within the public education system. The quality of teacher work life represents an area that certainly requires further study because it is these satisfying as well as stressful factors that affect the teachers' abilities to maintain quality levels of professional involvement and potentially their abilities to teach effectively.

REFERENCES

Anderson, M. B. (1980), A study of differences among perceived need deficiencies, perceived burnout, and select background variables for classroom teachers. Unpublished doctoral dissertation. University of Connecticut, Storrs.

Bloch, A. M. (1978), Combat neuroses in inner-city schools. *Amer. J. Psychiat.*, 135/10:118–192.

Burry, J. A., Harrington, R., & Pelsma, D. (1985), Diagnosing the effectiveness of teachers under stress: The development of a theory. Paper presented at the National American Psychological Association Convention, Los Angeles, CA, August.

Ceckon, D. J., & Koff, R. H. (1980), Stress and teaching. *NASSP Bull.*, 64/434:91–104.

Coates, T. J., & Thoreson, C. E. (1976), Teacher anxiety: A review with recommendations. *Rev. Ed. Res.*, 46/2:159–184.

Cox, T., & Mackey, C. J. (1976), A psychological model of occupational stress. Paper presented to the Medical Research Council Meeting on Mental Health in Industry, London.

Cunningham, W. (1983), Teacher burnout—Solutions for the 1980's: A review of the literature. *Urban Rev.*, 15:37–51.

Fimian, M. J. (1980), Stress reduction techniques for teachers. *The Pointer*, 1/2:64–70.

——— (1982), What is teacher stress? *The Clearing House*, 56/3:101–105.

——— (1985), The development of an instrument to measure occupational stress in teachers of exceptional students. *Techniques: J. Remed. Ed. & Counsel.*, 1:270–285.

——— Santoro, T. M. (1983), Sources and manifestations of occupational stress as reported by full-time special education teachers. *Except. Child.*, 49/6:540–543.

Greer, J. G., & Wethered, C. E. (1984), Learned helplessness: A piece of the burnout puzzle. *Except. Child.*, 50/6:524–530.

Harrington, R. G. (1979), Teacher burnout: How to cope when the world goes black. *Instructor*, 88/6:56–62.

Lazarus, R. S. (1976), *Patterns of Adjustment*. New York: McGraw-Hill.

——— (1981), The stress and coping paradigm. In: *Models for Clinical Psychopathology*, ed. C. Eisdorfer, D. Cohen, A. Kleinman, & P. Maxim. New York: Spectrum, pp. 218–236.

——— Cohen, J. (1977), Hasseles Scales: Development and validation study. Unpublished manuscript.

Maslach, C., & Jackson, S. E. (1981), The measure of experienced burnout. *J. Occupat. Behav.*, 2:99–113.

Styles, K., & Cavanaugh, G. (1977), Stress in teaching and how to handle it. *Eng. J.*, January, pp. 76–79.

Weiskopf, P. E. (1980), Burnout among teachers of exceptional children. *Except. Child.*, 47/1:18–23.

Chapter 40
Coping with Stress: Differences Among Working Families

ELAINE A. ANDERSON, PH.D., AND LEIGH A. LESLIE, PH.D.

INTRODUCTION

A major change in how American families live their lives is currently under way as increasingly larger numbers of families are being supported by two incomes. This change is largely due to the movement of greater numbers of women into the labor force. An average of more than one million women have joined the labor force in each year from 1971 to 1978, with most of this increase due to women with children. By 1979, 49 percent of all married women, with husband present, were in the labor force (U.S. Department of Labor, 1980). Accompanying this move to a "dual-income" lifestyle are, according to family theorists and researchers, new sources of stress for the family. These

Acknowledgments. Supported in part by the Graduate Research Board Grant and the Division of Human and Community Resources Grant, The University of Maryland, College Park.

This chapter was first presented at the Annual Convention of the American Psychological Association and adapted from a paper entitled "Satisfaction and stress in three types of working families." Published with permission.

sources of stress, though varying in form, originate largely from conflicts in the commitments of time and energy required to adequately fulfill worker, partner, and parent roles (Pleck, Staines, and Lang, 1980).

It has been suggested (Mortimer and London, 1984) that role overload is the major problem for the dual-income family, and is especially problematic for the employed woman. Although employed women enhance the family economic resources (Hayghe, 1979), their presence in the labor force strains the family resources; there is no full-time homemaker to provide child care, housework, and support of the husband's occupational role. Decisions such as who will care for the preschool children or provide afterschool supervision become paramount. Since there is no full-time homemaker, schedules may have to be juggled so that tasks such as meal preparation and housekeeping can be fulfilled. When both parents work and come home tired, handling the demands of children may strain resources beyond their ability to cope.

Whereas society is beginning to generally accept the two-provider family structure, the sharing of work within the family does not appear to be as accepted or expected. Pleck and Rustad (1980) found the difference in time spent in family work for husbands of employed women and homemakers was negligible. Women employed out of the home did 15 hours more work per week (including job and family work) and got a half hour less sleep per night than did homemakers. In addition, both males' and females' family roles vary according to their employment status; fully employed men do only about one-third of the family work that fully employed women do. VanVelsor and O'Rand (1984) also found that while working women spend fewer hours on housework per week than do homemakers, they still have more household responsibility than their employed husbands. One could conclude that although employment has a significant effect on family work, gender has a stronger effect and accounts for much more of the variance in an individual's family work.

A second type of role overload for the dual-income family

appears to be managing time schedules to meet both employment demands and family needs. Pleck et al. (1980) found men in two-income families to be concerned with the number of hours they could work per day while women in similar situations were more concerned with the scheduling of their work hours. This finding reflects the working mother's primary responsibility for their children. Women are more likely than men to get their children off to school, pick them up after school, and stay home with them when they're ill. In other words, women are more likely to be expected to disrupt their work to attend to their families. Given these expectations, it becomes most important that women hold jobs which offer them some flexibility in order to handle these day-to-day family tasks.

The aforementioned literature clearly suggests that dual-income families experience stressors unique from the traditional homemaker family. In addition, these studies also suggest that the responsibilities for working women are different than for working men; women appear to have taken on new functions in the labor force without relinquishing their traditional functions within the family.

As the dual-income family form increases in number, existing gaps in our knowledge must be addressed. First, the bulk of our empirical knowledge of working couples comes from studies of "dual-career" couples in which each partner is pursuing a profession requiring a high degree of commitment and which has a continuous development (Rapoport and Rapoport, 1971). It is likely, however, that the problems, as well as the resources, of these couples may differ from other working couples. As Dempster-McClain and Moen (1983) point out, dual-career couples make up only 12 percent of the families where both spouses are employed, while dual-earner (blue-collar) couples (defined as those engaged in gainful employment which does not have a developmental character) make up 60 percent of working couples and mixed-status couples (defined as one professional and one nonprofessional) make up the remaining 28 percent. This gap in the literature on dual-income blue-collar and mixed-status families is particularly noteworthy, given that dual-income families with below-average incomes have the highest rates of labor-force participation (Ryscavage, 1979). It is unclear to what extent the stressful life changes experienced by families and their resources for coping may vary among the work types.

A cursory glance at what we do know about families with different orientations to work should illustrate this point. Skinner (1980) classified the sources of stress in the dual-career couple into internal and external types of strain. The former deals with balancing career and family life, the latter includes the incongruity between the dual-career lifestyle and traditional norms and occupational pressures for mobility. In addition, as Rice (1979) described, if both spouses are struggling for advancement in their careers, and both simultaneously need emotional support and encouragement, there may be little reserve left for each other. The sharing of family tasks therefore becomes of crucial importance.

Issues for blue-collar dual-earner families may differ, however, from those of dual-career families. Decisions such as how one fulfills the traditional roles—for females the homemaker and for males the breadwinner—may produce stress (Rainwater, 1971; Kamarovsky, 1964; Rubin, 1976). If one chooses not to fill the traditional male/female role, what kinds of support are available to help meet these unique challenges. These are couples, by and large, who may not have the economic resources of the dual-career couple to hire support services. It has been suggested that one way blue-collar families cope with work and family is to use split shifts (Lein, 1979). This arrangement may address child care issues, but it probably restricts the type of jobs one can hold and would certainly limit the amount of time the spouses can spend together. It seems important, therefore, to consider the strategies couples in different work arrangements use to cope with the problems they face.

A second area which must be examined empirically is the factors which affect working couples' overall adjustment and satisfaction. There are few concepts in the family literature garnering more attention than marital adjustment/satisfaction.

In the last 45 years dozens of studies have attempted to define the concept as well as measure the amount of adjustment/satisfaction in all types of couples. We have chosen for this study to use the term "marital satisfaction." This term envelopes a range of marital experiences—namely satisfaction, happiness, adjustment, etc., which allows us to focus on and assess how the couples perceive the success of their marital dyad.

Thus, as Burgess and Cottrell (1939) assumed about well-adjusted and satisfied marriages:

1. Spouses have agreement on critical marital unity issues;
2. Spouses share common activities and interests;
3. Sharing of affection and confidences helps one to cope; and
4. Couples who are satisfied with their marriage have few complaints and doubts about the marriage's chance of success.

One of the major reasons the assessment of marital satisfaction in working families is important is because of the change in traditional male-female sex-roles. Employment of wives not only challenges our stereotyping of what are appropriate activities for males and females, but also an imbalance of division of labor may occur. What once was nicely delineated as the female's turf—the home—and the male's turf—the workplace—has become muddied. The result of these changes may be a duplication of efforts, possible competition for roles, absence of attention to the marital relationship because of this transitional time period, and increased marital dissatisfaction (Becker, 1973, 1974).

On the other hand, some studies have shown (Burke and Weir, 1976) that women employed out of the home are healthier and more communicative in their marriages than non-working wives. An argument could be made that these feelings of satisfaction about one's personal self also would bring feelings of satisfaction to one's marital relationship. However, most research has not looked at different types of working families and how satisfied they are with their marriage.

It is imperative that each employment group, including those following the "traditional" working arrangement of a breadwinner husband and a homemaker wife, be looked at for both the unique and common problems they face, their styles of coping, and the factors mediating the connection between stressful changes in family life and adjustment. This study considers both the stressful life changes faced by various types of working couples and whether or not these stressors influence how satisfied they are with their life. Three work-arrangement types are compared to determine if differences exist in the stressful life changes they experience or in their ability to cope with problems. We attempt to address such questions as do families experience different degrees of stressful life changes depending upon their type of work arrangement and are males and females in these different types of work groups experiencing these stressors to similar degrees.

Finally, marital and life satisfaction scores are determined for males and females. The extent to which an individual's work type, life-stressors, and coping style predict satisfaction with their marriage and their lives in general is considered. In summary, then, the present study examines stressful life changes experienced by American families in different work arrangements and their ability to cope. The association between this pattern and how satisfied the individuals are is also assessed.

STRESS AND SATISFACTION IN WORKING FAMILIES

SAMPLE

This research project compares two types of two-income families: dual-career and dual-earner. In addition, a sample of "traditional" work arrangement families was included in order to assess the extent to which stress experienced by two-worker families is unique and the extent to which it is common to all families regardless of their work arrangement. Dual-career is defined as a couple in which both partners are pursuing careers, while dual-earner refers to couples where both partners are employed but only one or neither partner has a career. Criteria for inclusion was that couples had to be married and living together and at least one spouse had to be employed a minimum of 30 hours a week. Due to the additional roles and demands placed on couples who are parents, a further criteria for inclusion was the presence of a child, 12 years of age or younger.

The sample was comprised of 38 couples; nine of which were homemaker families, 13 were dual-earner families, and 16 were dual-career families. The average age of the individuals was 34, with a range between 22 and 63. The average number of years these couples had been married was nine, with a range from 2 years to 21. Forty-seven percent of the individuals reported they had lived with their spouse at least three months prior to getting married.

The average amount of education for these individuals was a college degree. However, 38 percent were not four-year college graduates, while 38 percent reported having a graduate degree. Caucasian was the reported race for 84 percent of the sample, 5 percent were black, and 4 percent Hispanic. The average individual's income was between $20,000 and $25,000. Finally, 40 percent of the couples reported having one child, 39 percent had two, 19 percent had three, and 2 percent had more than three children.

Couples were identified through random mail-outs using lists provided by local day care centers and the University of Maryland staff and faculty directory. In addition, advertisements were placed in local newspapers, community newsletters, and a military base newspaper inviting couples to participate. An introductory letter explained the purpose of the study, informed the couples of a $10 payment for their participation, and invited them to volunteer by returning an enclosed postcard. Volunteers were surveyed through the use of a structured questionnaire, completed and mailed in at their convenience. The questionnaire included demographic information about the couple and family as well as standardized instruments to assess work and family related life changes in the previous 12 months (McCubbin, 1983), family coping style (McCubbin, Olson, and Larsen, 1982), adjustment in the marital dyad (Spanier, 1976), and overall life satisfaction (Campbell, Converse, and Rodgers, 1976). It should be noted that the family coping measures is composed of five subscales; each of which measures a different strategy that a family may use for coping with problems. These are: (1) acquiring social support, (2) reframing the problem to make it more manageable, (3) seeking spiritual support, (4) mobilizing the family to acquire professional and/or community help, and (5) passively accepting the problem (McCubbin et al., 1982).

RESULTS

The results presented in this paper are the preliminary data analyses to date on the sample as presently completed.

In order to assess the impact of their partner's work arrangement on the amount of stress they experience, a two-way analysis of variance was computed. Results suggest there were no significant effects for work type on family stress or life changes. A significant effect was found for gender ($F = 8.46$, $p < .01$) however, with females ($\bar{x} = 9.8$) reporting the presence of more family life stress in the previous year than did males ($\bar{x} = 7.8$).

Similarly, five two-way analyses of variance were computed to test the effects of type of work and gender or coping style. Results indicate no significant difference between males and females in their style of coping. However, couples in different work arrangements did appear to differ in the coping strategies they utilized most frequently. Though no differences were found for the coping strategies of reframing the problem or remaining passive, the three groups did differ in the extent to which they turned to family and friends ($F = 3.12$, $p = .05$)

relied on spiritual support ($F = 4.65$, $p = .01$), and mobilized the family to seek professional and community assistance ($F = 4.52$, $p < .05$). Means and standard deviations for the three groups on the five coping strategies can be seen in Table 40.1. Followup assessment using Tukey HSD indicated no significant difference between any two groups or utilization of social support, though an examination of the means shows that dual-earner couples had the highest mean on the social support subscale. Post hoc assessment indicated that the dual-career group was significantly less likely than each of the other two groups to utilize spiritual support. Finally, both the dual-earner and dual-career couples were significantly more likely to mobilize the family to seek community assistance.

Multiple regression was used to assess the contribution of work arrangement, life stress, and coping styles to general life satisfaction and marital satisfaction. Regression equations were computed separately for males and females because of a high correlation between husbands and wives on the dependent variables.

Looking first at general life satisfaction for men, three variables met the criteria and were entered into the regression equation (see Table 40.2). The amount of stress the man was experiencing, and his reliance on spiritual and social support together accounted for 14 percent of the variance in men's general life satisfaction, though the equation did not reach sta-

Table 40.1
Means and Standard Deviations on Coping Strategies by Work Type

	Traditional $n = 18$		Dual-Earner $n = 26$		Dual-Career $n = 32$	
	Mean	SD	Mean	SD	Mean	SD
Passive	8.50	2.01	9.06	2.43	8.96	1.9
Reframe	30.71	3.68	30.06	3.69	29.42	3.39
Social Support	27.86	5.09	31.78	5.39	28.25	5.22
Spiritual Support	12.79	5.12	13.89	3.21	9.96	4.36
Mobilize	10.36	3.64	13.39	2.36	12.25	2.58

Table 40.2
Multiple Regression for Life Satisfaction

Dependent Variable	Independent Variables	Multiple R	R²	Beta
Life Satisfaction (Males)	Family Life Stressors	.28	.08	−.346
	Spiritual Support	.34	.12	−.238
	Social Support	.38	.14	.176
Overall F = 1.69, n = 32				
Life Satisfaction (Females)	Social Support	.37	.14	.380
	Family Life Stressors	.48	.24	−.364
	Mobilize Family	.60	.35	−.350
Overall F = 5.36*, n = 34				

*$p < .01$

tistical significance. Men experiencing low stress, utilizing low levels of spiritual support and high levels of social support had high life satisfaction scores. When considering men's marital satisfaction, only the work arrangement was entered into the regression equation ($F = 3.88, p = .05$). The work arrangement a man was in accounted for 11 percent of the variance in his marital adjustment with those in the traditional work arrangement having the highest marital satisfaction.

In looking at women's life and marital satisfaction, somewhat similar patterns appear. Women's utilization of social support, amount of stress, and mobilization of family accounted for 35 percent of the variance in their general life satisfaction (see Table 40.2), with women high on social support, low in life stress, and low on mobility of family having higher life satisfaction scores. As with men, women's work arrangement accounted for the largest proportion of the variance (8 percent) in their marital satisfaction, with women in traditional work arrangements having the highest satisfaction scores (see Table 40.3). In addition, the level of stress experienced reached criteria for entrance into the equation, though the overall equation did not reach statistical significance.

Table 40.3
Multiple Regression for Marital Satisfaction

Dependent Variable	Independent Variables	Multiple R	R^2	Beta
Marital Satisfaction (Males)	Work Type	.34	.11	−.338
Overall F = 3.875*, n = 32				
Marital Satisfaction (Females)	Work Type	.29	.08	−.258
	Family Life Stressors	.37	.13	−.229
Overall F = 2.384, n = 34				

*p = .05

DISCUSSION AND CONCLUSIONS

The results indicate that females report more stressful family life changes than do males. This is a particularly interesting and perplexing finding given that husbands and wives were reporting on the same family events. This may speak to a perceptual difference in men and women, with women seen as acknowledging more family changes than men. Initially this finding may appear to be understood in light of Pleck and Rustad's (1980) suggestion that women who work out of the home spend more hours working per day than their husbands, and thus may perceive the stressors in life more acutely. However, given that no gender by work type interaction was found, this explanation seems questionable. As additional cases are added to this sample, this relationship can be more thoroughly investigated.

The result of the analysis of variance assessing the relationship between coping style and type of work is likewise worthy of further investigation. Perhaps most important to note is that dual-earner families score very high on the three coping strategies which require actively seeking assistance outside the family. These families not only have the highest utilization of social support, but they also are the most likely to seek spiritual support and are more likely than the traditional group to seek professional and community assistance. It may be, given the role overload of couples where both members are employed, that couples in this group need to turn to sources outside the nuclear family for help in coping with stress. It should be noted, in line with this argument that dual-career couples also turn to family, friends, and community resources for help and differ only in that they do not seek spiritual support.

Although the amount of variance in satisfaction scores accounted for in the multiple regressions was not large, one finding seems worthy of attention. It appears that both males and females in the traditional family arrangement, where the husband is employed and the wife is a homemaker, are more satisfied with their marriage than couples where both partners are employed. It seems likely the clear stratification of roles in these couples may lead to less complicated scheduling and decision-making issues, and hence, less stressful interactions. These findings do seem contradictory to previous research which suggests that employed women have higher marital satisfaction than homemakers. It is unclear why this contradiction exists, but it will need further investigation.

This chapter reports the results of the initial analysis as data collection stands to date. It is important to keep in mind that the numbers of couples in each work group are small. These numbers, particularly in the homemaker and dual-earner work groups reflect the difficulties of collecting data on a variety of families. When the larger study, of which this report is one part, is complete, there will be 20 families in each work type.

Given that the major structural change in the family, both in the past 15 years and in the coming decade, is that of both spouses working outside the home, it seems imperative that family scholars explore how this structure will affect family functioning, as well as its larger implications for both the public and private sectors. This study provides baseline information both on how varying organizations of work and family roles affect family functioning and on factors which may assist families in adjusting to the demands of a two worker life-style. These findings can therefore serve as a foundation for further research in the area, as data for family professionals who are working to assist families in coping with stress, and possibly as information to assist in policy decisions, within both the public and private sectors, concerning the work life of employees.

REFERENCES

Becker, G. (1973), A theory of marriage: Part I. *J. Polit. Econ.*, 81:813–846.
——— (1974), A theory of marriage: Part II. *J. Polit. Econ.*, 82:S11–S26.
Burgess, E., & Cottrell, L., Jr. (1939), *Predicting Success or Failure in Marriage*. New York: Prentice-Hall.
Burke, R., & Weir, T. (1976), Relationship of wives' employment status to husband, wife and pair satisfaction and performance. *J. Marr. & Fam.*, 38:279–287.
Campbell, A., Converse, P., & Rodgers, W. (1976), *The Quality of American Life: Perceptions, Evaluations, and Satisfactions*. New York: Russell Sage.
Dempster-McClain, D., & Moen, P. (1983), Work-time involvement and preferences of employed parents. Paper presented at the annual meeting of the National Council on Family Relations, Minneapolis, October.
Hayghe, H. (1979), Working wives' contributions to family income in 1977. *Monthly Lab. Rev.*, 102:62–64.
Kamarovsky, M. (1964), *Blue-collar Marriage*. New York: Random House.
Lein, L. (1979), Male participation in home life: Impact of social supports and breadwinner responsibility on the allocation of tasks. *Fam. Coord.*, 28:489–495.
McCubbin, H. (1983), Stress: The family inventory of life events and changes. In: *Marriage and Family Assessment*, ed. E. Filsinger. Beverly Hills, CA: Sage.
——— Olson, D., & Larsen, A. (1982), F-COPES: Family crisis oriented personal scales. In: *Inventories Used in a National Survey of Families Across the Family Life Cycle*, ed. D. Olson, H. McCubbin, H. Barnes, A. Larsen, M. Maxen, & M. Wilson. St. Paul: University of Minnesota.
Mortimer, J., & London, J. (1984), The varying linkages of work and family. In: *Work and Family*, ed. P. Voydanoff. Palo Alto, CA: Mayfield.
Pleck, J., Staines, G., & Lang, L. (1980), Conflicts between work and family life. *Monthly Labor Rev.*, March 103:29–32.

—— Rustad, M. (1980), Husbands' and wives' time in family work and paid work in 1975–76 study of time use. Unpublished paper. Wellesley College Center for Research on Women.

Rainwater, L. (1971), Making the good life: Working-class family and life-styles. In: *Blue Collar Workers: A Symposium on Middle America*, ed. S. A. Levitan. New York: McGraw-Hill, pp. 196–208.

Rapoport, R., & Rapoport, R. (1971), *Dual-Career Families*. Harmondsworth, UK: Penguin.

Rice, D. (1979), *Dual-Career Marriage: Conflict and Treatment*. New York: Free Press.

Rubin, L. B. (1976), *Worlds of Pain: Life in the Working Class Family*. New York: Basic Books.

Ryscavage, P. (1979), More wives in the labor force have husbands with above-average incomes. *Monthly Labor Rev.*, 102/6:40–42.

Skinner, D. (1980), Dual-career family stress and coping: A literature review. *Fam. Rel.*, 29:473–480.

Spanier, G. (1976), Measuring dyadic adjustment: New scales for assessing the quality of marriage and similar dyads. *J. Marr. & Fam.*, 38:15–28.

U.S. Department of Labor (1980), *Perspectives on Working Women: A Datebook*. Bulletin 2080, Bureau of Labor Statistics. Washington, DC: U.S. Government Printing Office.

VanVelsor, E., & O'Rand, A. (1984), Family life cycle, work career patterns, and women's wages at midlife. *J. Marr. & Fam.*, 46:365–373.

Chapter 41
The 50-Year-Old Woman and Midlife Stress

Shirley Campbell, M.S.S.W.

Although it is becoming apparent that virtually every age group has its own stresses, adjustments, and even "crises," there are some groups that have received relatively little attention. A group that has almost been ignored consists of women in their fifties, who have passed the mid-to-late forties and the end of childbearing, and who are not yet in the mid-sixties phase of incipient old age. Women in this age range are susceptible to numerous, more or less hidden, stresses, despite their freedom from the more obvious problems of the older and younger age groups.

The transitional nature of the fifties in itself entails a need for reevaluation and adjustment that may be quite disturbing. Peck and Berkowitz noted early that in their own studies, those women in their fifties rated "significantly lower on adjustment scales than either the 40-year-olds or the 60-year-olds," and concluded that possibly, a crisis occurs in the early fifties, when a new dissatisfaction with life and oneself seems to arise (Peck and Berkowitz, 1964). More recent findings tend to support this claim (Levinson, 1978).

Acknowledgment. This chapter was first published in the *International Journal of Aging and Human Development* (1983–1984), 18/4:295–307, and it is reprinted with permission.

Specific Problems: Widowhood, Divorce, Declining Income

There are some specific crises that women in this age group are likely to encounter. Widowhood has traditionally been regarded as the most disruptive crisis, and half of all widows are under 60 years of age (Troll, 1973), with the majority of these in their fifties. Moreover, in the last 20 years there has been a notable increase in the number of divorcées in this age group, increasing the number of 50-year-old women subject to severe emotional and financial strain. The married woman this age, noticing the prevalence of widowhood and divorce among her contemporaries, is almost bound to feel somewhat insecure, too, particularly as these contemporaries frequently have been abandoned for younger partners.

The widow or divorcée is almost certain to suffer from personal loss or rejection and loss of income, and to doubt that either of these losses can be recouped. The chances of a widowed or divorced woman over 50 finding lasting emotional or sexual relationship with a man are slim (Botwinnick, 1973); thus, she is confronted with 25–30 years of involuntary singleness, and probably celibacy. At all but the lowest socioeconomic levels she is likely to be in good health, and to have led a life which, although sometimes confining, has nonetheless been full and active. (This activity too may only recently have slowed down, depending on the age of her children.) She may thus quite suddenly find herself without children, husband, sex, and accustomed social supports.

As for loss of income, this is both a problem in itself and a contributing factor to psychosocial problems, as it fosters social isolation, loss of social status, and loss of self-esteem (Lopata, 1972). Most widows and divorcées, contrary to popular belief, are not adequately provided for (Qilliams, 1977), lack marketable skills, and are at an age when extensive training or education is not practical. Despite the increasing participation of older women in the work force, employment of those over 55 is not booming as much as for younger cohorts. The majority of women over 50 are still in low-paid, low-status, dead-end occupations (U.S. Department of Labor, 1977).

Edwards and Klemmack (1973) note that the primary determinant of life satisfaction in older adults is socioeconomic level, with family income the most important factor, and perceived health and informal social interaction second and third in importance. If she is still married, the woman at the upper socioeconomic levels may be lucky enough to have all three; if she is divorced or widowed, all three are likely to be absent, at least during a period of adjustment. For the woman at a lower socioeconomic level, the fifties may introduce a period of declining income even if she is married, as her husband retires, often early and involuntarily (Reno, 1971; Rones, 1978).

Very few women this age escape disruption and the need to make changes, for which their former lives have only poorly prepared them. The majority of women in this cohort have been socialized into more-or-less domestic roles and passive personality traits, both of which make it difficult for them to function in the labor force to their own best advantage. These roles and traits also hinder efforts to initiate new lifestyles, or to adopt new attitudes toward matters which may only now become crucial to women—employment, finances, and in many cases, the single life.

AGING AND DEVELOPMENTAL CHANGES

Even if none of the identifiable crises occur in the fifties, there are likely to be ongoing difficulties. There is the problem of aging itself, which often begins to take on new importance during this decade when the woman has to cope with the imminent transition from middle age to early old age. There are two related problems involved: the incongruence between the 50-year-old woman's self-image and the conceptions of others, and the realization of the passage of time and awareness of the finiteness of human life. More important yet, there are numerous developmental conflicts during this phase.

Several authors have noted the gap between self-image and society's definition of the "older" woman. Novak and Troll, for example, find that middle age is seen as the period between ages 40 and 55 by most people, and old age as between 65 and 80, with younger respondents specifying earlier onsets (Novak and Troll, 1974). Cameron also finds this discrepancy between younger and older respondents in the attribution of "middle-aged" and "old" statuses (Cameron, 1969). Interestingly, Drevenstedt finds that women are more likely to see the onset of middle and old age as occurring later than men do, although they agree with men that women become middle-aged or old earlier in life than do men (Drevenstedt, 1976). Not only is the 50-year-old woman between age statuses, she also tends to be perceived as older than the man in his fifties, and older than she sees herself. She is seen as passing from middle to old age by others, while she and her contemporaries see themselves as relatively young. Novak and Troll find that the divergence between chronological age and self-perception increases with the passing years.

Visscher claims that during this decade the experience of time accelerates and the years appear to everyone to be going faster, even though after this decade some see time as passing more slowly (Visscher, 1966). He points out that the need for security and fear of poverty increase markedly with the recognition that one is no longer young, a recognition which usually occurs in the fifties, as older associates (including relatives) begin to die off. Women are particularly likely to feel anxiety on this score; Bengtson, Cuellar, and Ragan (1977) note, "it is the forty-five to fifty-four-year-old group that expresses most fear of death" and women, they add, fear death considerably more than do men, at all ages.

The developmental changes encountered during this period are likely to be more profound and more disturbing than either aging or the passage of time. In an unpublished paper on women in their forties, Maya and Junge make several points that have relevance to 50-year-old women. They describe the upper middle class women they interviewed as caught between various pressures. Although most have chafed at the domestic role, now that they are free to pursue outside achievements they find themselves afraid of leaving the comfort and security of domestic life. They express guilt at not having taken advantage of options now seen as available to women (but not so apparent when they were young), but are aware of realistic obstacles to doing so now that they are older. At the same time, there is a resurgence of individuation, of the urge toward identity formation and attainment of psychological independence that, according to these authors, most women have postponed from early adulthood until after childbearing.

All of this can be expected to be true of women in their fifties, certainly at the same socioeconomic level, and according to Neugarten (1964), they are true of women at lower socioeconomic strata as well. Sangiuliano (1978) sees resurgent individuation as characteristic of women "in the late forties or early fifties," and claims that at this age women may suddenly become concerned with their personal and sexual identities.

These conclusions and a thesis introduced by Gutman (1964) in the 1960s are mutually supportive. Gutman (1976) claims that during their fifties, men and women tend to reverse emotional roles; women tend to become more assertive and managerial, while men become more attuned to the emotional and nurturing aspects of life.

Giambra (1979) in a study on day dreaming, found that in the forties, daydreams of nondomestic achievement are prominent for the first time in women, whereas for men during this decade achievement is for the first time not a prominent theme; i.e., there is a reversal of attitude toward achievement that can be seen as a precursor of the reversal of emotional roles or personality traits found in the fifties. That this reversal is a manifestation of major change, in women at least, is suggested by further findings that the most stereotyped views on sex roles are found in women aged 40 to 49 (who are the most conservative on this subject of all age and sex groups), and the least traditional views are held by women between 60 and 69 (Pepe and Wyly, 1976). Women in their fifties are doing a complete about-face in regard to their roles, and presumably in their self-images.

If, as the evidence suggests, women become more competitive in their fifties, they face objective difficulties in expressing their new desires for success, for example, lack of experience or education and lack of time for apprenticeship or training. They also face some internal difficulties.

A major psychological obstacle to later life achievement is the drop in motivation in women with age. It has been found that women in the 35 to 64 age group rate themselves lower on achievement/leadership measures than do women of any other age group (Monge, 1975). (The increase noted after 65, furthermore, is only slight and may be related to the change in family roles with the husband's retirement.) Bardwick (1971) cites Baruch (1966) as finding that in general there is a decline in achievement motivation with age, with a particularly large drop after age 55, for most women. There is an increase for college-educated women after the phase of mothering small children, but even for this group motivation peaks between 35 and 40, too early for the woman who finds herself with the need to achieve in her fifties.

The fifties are likely to be a time of inner conflict and complexity, which perhaps explains the dissatisfaction noted by Peck and Berkowitz (1964). The new-found desire to assert oneself and the psychosocial pressures to attain material success (the "status, rank and retirement benefits" listed by one of Maya and Junge's respondents) conflict with a realistic awareness of the difficulties in entering or reentering an occupation coupled with a decline in achievement motivation. Just at the time when a woman most needs and wants the fruits of success, she is least equipped to attain them.

Bloom (1961) found that self-acceptance rises between 20 and 50, peaks at 50, and declines after 60, contrary to Peck and Berkowitz (1964), but in accord with Novak and Troll's obser-

vation that in women concern with youthfulness gives way to
concern with attractiveness between 40 and 60, again suggesting
acceptance of the aging self. These findings suggest that during
the fifties either women come to accept themselves as individuals despite their dissatisfaction with their nondomestic achievement, or that the need for material success is primarily a
phenomenon of the forties, replaced in the fifties by the tendency to strive for the dominant role in interpersonal relations.
Such self-acceptance is itself no small achievement in a society
which, as Weinberg (1979) points out, emphasizes observable
activity and tangible success to an extent which makes acceptance of any other kind of life or personality difficult.

The fifties, then, are a time of transition for women; transition from middle age to incipient old age, from conservative
views of sex roles to relative flexibility, from dependence and
nurturance to assertiveness and desire for dominance, but also,
perhaps from dissatisfaction with oneself to more acceptance.
There is also transition from the wife-mother-daughter complex of roles to one which may be diminished by widowhood,
divorce, emancipation of children or death of parents, and may
possibly be augmented by addition of the role of worker or
family breadwinner.

How well this transitional decade is handled may be important not only in terms of a woman's current well-being, but also
because of its effect on the rest of her life. What she attains in
the fifties in psychological adjustment may determine how well
she copes with continued aging during the rest of her life. A
number of researchers (Neugarten, 1979; Reichard, Livson,
and Peterson, 1962) support Hendricks and Hendricks' (1979)
claim that aged personalities are most often merely the exten-
sions of middle-aged coping styles into later years. Newman
and Newman (1979) echo Visscher's claim that the fifties are
the decade when we begin the search for personal meaning that
lasts until death and is the major developmental task of age.

The fifties are the period when one takes the first steps
toward successful aging, i.e., toward a mode of coping with
normal later life, biological, sociocultural, and psychological

changes that will prove satisfying and will enable one to function as well as physical and social circumstances permit. Whether this means accepting a disappointing record with equanimity, focusing on a few available satisfactions while relinquishing broader social engagement, or remaining active and involved, has yet to be decided.

OBSTACLES TO SUCCESSFUL AGING

A number of prerequisites for successful adaptation to change, including the major change of aging, have been suggested. By the age of 50, a person's capacity to cope with aging, as with other changes, is bound to be influenced not only by the presence or absence of these factors at the time but also by their presence during the preceding decades. It can be argued that these factors are notably absent from the earlier lives of many of the current cohort of 50-year-old women.

The factors encouraging successful change tend to be those likely to foster competence and self-esteem at any age. Vaillant (1977) notes that in the case of the men he studied, those reporting most life satisfaction as well as the most materially successful lives were those who had been the most assertive, even to the point of aggressive competitiveness. He cites Claussen (1972) as giving four major variables affecting life-cycle developmental success: opportunities and obstacles, as influenced by "social class, ethnic membership, age, sex," individual investment of effort on one's own behalf; support and guidance orienting one toward one's (external) world; and individual personal resources, including intelligence and coping methods.

As numerous authors have pointed out (Horner, 1972; Barnett and Baruch, 1978), the experiences of today's 50-year-old woman have been such as to foster avoidance of assertive behavior. Opportunities for developing competences or strengths by interaction with the outside world have been minimized, and obstacles maximized, as has been amply documented. This has often been done in the name of guidance, if not support. Women of this age were usually discouraged from pursuing any but the domestic careers that Barnett and Baruch see as inimical to full adult growth: when they have pursued careers, they have rarely had available the input of mentors that is so helpful to the male. Investment of a woman's effort has rarely been on her own behalf; the current generation of 50-year-old women has been trained primarily to foster the well-being of others, to the detriment of their own personal or professional growth. The coping methods fostered have been those of unassertive compliance with the wishes of others. In short, whatever a woman's personal resources or advantages (intelligence, education, or material status, for example), these have usually been outweighted by the great mass of negative factors listed.

Assertiveness, success in either personal or professional spheres, and life satisfaction have all been found to be positively correlated with adequate self-esteem. There is little to foster self-esteem in either the life history of the 50-year-old woman or her current situation. Barnett and Baruch (1978) cite Brim (1976) as noting that two major requirements for self-esteem are "a feeling of being positively valued by others" and "a sense of mastery over one's environment," and note that these are conflicts for many traditionally raised women who have been taught that they will be valued for the very traits that preclude such mastery, compliance, nurturance, and self-effacement. This conclusion is supported by Rainwater's (1959) study of young working-class women, a cohort who are presently in their fifties. This study found that these women were totally absorbed by domestic roles, saw the outside world as dangerous, felt powerless to deal with others (even their own husbands), were rather passive, and were very insecure "about themselves and their own worth, about how acceptable they are to the world around them." Barnett and Baruch cite M. Brewster Smith as claiming that a sense of competence, which is essential to self-esteem, rests on a sense of power. The sense of power, he states, is unlikely to arise without both the respect of others and the opportunity to exercise some control [see Kivett, Watson, and

Busch (1977) on this, also], neither of which is likely to have played a large part in the life of the average 50-year-old woman.

Even the limited self-esteem to be gained from fulfilling the wife-mother role well is insecurely based. This source of self-worth lasts only through the early childrearing phase in an industrialized society, and may well be vanishing altogether. The older woman can take little pride in motherhood when her children are grown, or in the role of unemployed wife when even mothers of small children are employed in increasing numbers.

Other factors militating against successful aging for women in this age group have been noted in the early studies cited by Visscher. Kielholz's Basle study isolates several predisposing factors in involutional depression, i.e., the depression Kielholz sees as likely to strike women in their fifties. Several of these factors—feelings of not having worthwhile work and of being useless, and fear of income reduction—are likely to be present even in the married woman whose children are gone and whose husband nears retirement. The widow or divorcée is susceptible also to other factors that Kielholz identifies—lack of sources of emotional support, the need to move to a smaller home, and fear of the future in general. This leaves only two factors (religious crisis and the complex of alcoholism, sleep disturbance, and other somatic symptoms) which have only questionable relevance to the group under discussion in this article. Kielholz points out that the complete syndrome leads to pathological depression only given a predisposing personality type, but also claims that most middle-aged men and women have feelings that are similar, although less intense.

Even in the area least affected by participation in the non-domestic world, aging well through reflection, or Eriksonian integration of life experiences, it is doubtful that women have any particular advantage. As Visscher (1966) stresses, "psychic maturity requires conscious and deliberate reflection . . . it is not enough to simply amass experiences. . . . It is only consciously integrated experience which can stimulate, instruct and

encourage." He also mentions that "destiny and volition, constitutional and intentional factors all play their part and ma-
turation can only take place in people who lead conscious lives,
who do not simply allow themselves to be carried along by life.
Women, however, have been encouraged to allow themselves
to be carried along by life, rather than exercising their volitional
and intentional capacities.

Successful Aging and Role Inconstancy

Given this weight of negative evidence, one wonders what the
50-year-old woman does have in her favor. First, it is necessary
to consider the claim that role inconstancy, inherent in the
female life-cycle, confers major advantages in regard to aging.
Sinnott (1979) cites numerous authors as showing that late life
satisfaction, and even longevity itself, are correlated positively
with the high level of flexibility, including sex-role flexibility,
which allows the older adult to cope with role conflicts that arise
in later life. She claims further that these findings support the
thesis that it is sex-role inconstancy—the continual shifting from
one role to another (daughter, student, worker, wife, mother,
etc.) over a lifetime—that fosters such flexibility and allows for
successful adjustment to aging. Sinnott, in fact, goes so far as
to say that it is role inconstancy that allows a woman to approach
the androgynous personality type associated with successful
aging.

However, it should be noted that it is not only acceptance
and integration of male and female traits that marks the successfully aging, androgynous adult. It is also, as Sinnott notes,
autonomy, independence, persistence, acceptance of work as
well as family roles, and insight. With the possible exception of
the last, these are by and large traits which today's 50-year-old
woman has had little opportunity to develop. Although she may

indeed have had to shift from role to role, according to the dictates of chance or culture, this has usually been more a matter of successively accepting and relinquishing different sets of behaviors, a process requiring passivity rather than true flexibility or autonomy. Even sex-neutral roles, those of student or worker, for example, have been carried out within the framework of "feminine" attitudes and expectations, which, as Horner, Bardwick, and others have shown, dramatically influence the manner, duration, and outcome of such role participation (Horner, 1972). Even consideration of the feasibility of equivalent or convergent sex roles has become widespread only within the last 15 to 20 years, too late to seriously affect the youthful attitudes and behavior of women in this cohort. The fact that sex-role conservatism returns with the sixties, after the relative flexibility of the fifties, suggests that traditional sex-role behaviors are ingrained in past generations.

When androgynous traits do arise, as Gutman claims happens for most women in their fifties, their presence can be a mixed blessing. Even when the woman is able to adjust to the change and use her assertiveness constructively, she may have to cope with reactions on her husband's part which endanger marital stability. Gutman notes that many men in this age group are unable to accept the emergent "feminine" side of their nature, having held the life-long belief that aesthetic, emotional, and nurturing traits are unworthy of a male; they are particularly disturbed at no longer being able to project these characteristics onto their wives as in the past. The latter now explicitly reject such traits for themselves and, given their new assertiveness, are strikingly unsuitable objects of such projection. According to Gutman, at this point many men attempt to recapture the lost "real man" image through drink, liaisons with younger women (who do accept projection of "feminine" traits), or blatantly domineering behavior unacceptable to their wives. A woman in this situation is faced with an impossible choice: either she must stifle her own development and hamper her chance to age successfully, or risk marital conflict or breakdown.

FACTORS CONDUCIVE TO SUCCESSFUL AGING BY 50-YEAR-OLD WOMEN

Despite the lack of clear-cut preconditions for successful aging, and despite our lack of certainty as to what such preconditions should be, it is clear that many women weather the strains and crises of this decade and go on to successful old age. What makes them able to do so?

One positive factor is that if a woman now in her fifties has successfully resolved the late-forties conflicts, for example the delayed identity crisis, then she is indeed free, perhaps for the first time, to make and follow her own personal plans. A shift from family-centered life to a focus on an occupation or a study program (more accessible to the older woman now than ever before) can itself prove stimulating and refreshing, even when necessitated by widowhood or divorce. This kind of positive change is more likely to be available to women than to men in this age group. The traditional 50- to 60-year-old male characteristically shifts from work that has become tedious or draining to retirement, for which he is unprepared and which represents considerable loss of identity and status. The increase in self-esteem and psychic energy experienced by a woman who has started a "new life" may account for the fact that 82 percent of employed women this age say they would work even if not financially required to, and that 55 percent report more satisfaction from work than from leisure activities (Pfeiffer and Davis, 1971).

Furthermore, the psychological shift, noted by Gutman, to personality traits associated with the opposite sex, may well be less disturbing for a woman than for a man. The traits she is now adopting are those associated with a sense of competence and self-esteem, and those valued by society; unlike the male, she is not faced with having to accept a side of her nature that has hitherto been undervalued. Thus, her adoption of opposite sex traits is less likely to be fraught with self-doubt and fear of age-related inadequacy than is the case for the man, who may have long scorned the "feminine" qualities he now feels emerging. This is particularly true given the current social climate, in which women of all ages are being encouraged to assert themselves and to participate fully in all areas of society.

DeCarlo's (1974) study on leisure activity and successful aging shows that cognitive activities are most strongly associated with successful aging. If role inconstancy forces reevaluation and reflection (as an integral part of life rather than as leisure, admittedly) then women are in a good position to age well. If, however, it is cognitive activity purely for enjoyment that is important, participated in intensely, regularly and often (as DeCarlo claims is necessary), then it is doubtful that women have an advantage. Women in their fifties often have spent their lives fostering the intellectual development of their spouses, both professionally and recreationally, usually at the expense of their own opportunities for mental activity of a formalized kind.

Visscher (1966) stresses the point that a crisis may initiate the active reflection and conscious integration of experience that he sees as the key factor in successful aging. Either a major blow, such as widowhood, or the sort of ongoing inner turmoil Sangiuliano finds in the 45- to 55-year-old woman, may lead to developmental growth, in that each requires such reflection in order to surmount the present discomfort. The important feature of role inconstancy may be that although women accept and adjust (rather than initiate and act), they are nonetheless forced into continual reassessment throughout their lives. If men, on the other hand, are encouraged to act rather than to think, as may have been true for many older men, then women may be in a better position to age with satisfaction to themselves and to their associates.

Now more than ever before women in their fifties (and older) are employed, and the evidence is increasingly in favor of the benefits of a life that includes work outside the home, both at this age and in preceding decades. Middle-aged women who have not worked during the childrearing years profess to enjoy their present work, and plan to continue it. Professional women display higher self-esteem and see themselves as more attractive than homemakers at this age (Kasschau, 1976), and retired women report higher life satisfaction than housewives do, although they report slightly less life satisfaction than those still employed (Fox, 1979). Working women are reported to rank significantly lower on measures of psychological stress in all age and marital status groups (Kessler, 1975).

Even before the influx of older women into the labor force, there were suggestions that participation in roles other than, or in addition to, those of wife and mother makes for satisfaction in middle and late life. Lopata found this true of widows, just as Aldous (1975) found that it is a factor in marital satisfaction at the postparental ages. Neugarten (1964) found that active involvement with others increases life satisfaction even when such involvement is indicative of moderate personality disorder—i.e., when it is domineering or meddlesome (Sangiuliano, 1978). This suggests that the development trend toward greater dominance noted by Gutman must be expressed for a woman this age to be happy, and that when it has no constructive outlet, it will expend itself intrusively within the family or social circle.

Clearly, further study is needed before we can determine the prequisites of life satisfaction for the woman 50 or older. Meanwhile, it seems that expression of developmentally appropriate assertiveness in a suitable arena, usually outside the family circle, and serious reflection on and reevaluation of her life situation, are favorable to success for a woman in this and later stages of life.

REFERENCES

Aldous, J. (1975), *The Developmental Approach to Family Analysis*, Vol. 1. Athens, GA: University of Georgia.
Bardwick, J. M. (1971), *The Psychology of Women*. New York: Harper & Row.

Barnett, R. C., & Baruch, G. K. (1978), *The Competent Woman*. New York: John Wiley.

Baruch, R. (1966), The interruption and resumption of women's careers, Harvard Studies in Career Development, No. 50, Cambridge, MA.

Bengtson, V. L., Cuellar, J. B., & Ragan, P. K. (1977), Stratum contrasts and similarities in attitudes toward death, *J. Gerontol.*, 32:76–88.

Birnbaum, J. (1975), Life-patterns and self-esteem in gifted family-oriented and career-committed women. In: *Women and Achievement*, ed. T. Mednick. New York: Hemisphere-Halstead Press.

Bloom, K. L. (1961), Age and the self-concept. *Amer. J. Psychiat.*, 118:534–538.

Botwinnick, J. (1973), *Aging and Behavior*. New York: Springer.

Brim, O. J. (1976), Theories of the male mid-life crisis. *Counsel. Psychol.*, 6:2–9.

Cameron, P. (1969), Age parameters of young adulthood, middle age, and old age. *J. Gerontol.*, 24:201–202.

Claussen, J. (1972), The life course of individuals. In: *Aging and Society*, Vol. 3, ed. M. W. Riley, J. Johnson, & A. Foner. New York: Russell Sage Foundation.

DeCarlo, R. J. (1974), Recreation participation patterns and successful aging. *J. Gerontol.*, 29:416–422.

Drevenstedt, J. (1976), Perceptions of onsets of young adulthood, middle age, and old age. *J. Gerontol.*, 31:53–57.

Edwards, J. N., & Klemmack, D. L. (1973), Correlates of life satisfaction: A re-examination. *J. Gerontol.*, 28:497–502.

Fox, J. H. (1979), Effects of retirement and former work life on women's adaptation in old age. *J. Gerontol.*, 32:196–202.

Giambra, L. M. (1979), Adult sex differences in daydreaming. *Internat. J. Aging & Hum. Develop.*, 10:1–34.

Gutman, D. (1964), An exploration of ego configurations in middle and later life. In: *Personality in Middle and Later Life*, ed. B. L. Neugarten. New York: Atherton, pp. 114–148.

——— (1976), Individual adaptation in the middle years: Developmental issues in the masculine mid-life crisis. *J. Geriat. Psychiat.*, 9:41–59.

Hendricks, J., & Hendricks, C. D., eds. (1979), *Dimensions of Aging: Readings*. Cambridge, MA: Winthrop.

Horner, M. S. (1972), Toward an understanding of achievement-related conflicts in women. *J. Soc. Iss.*, 28:157–175.

Kasschau, P. L. (1976), Perceived age discrimination in a sample of aerospace employees. *Gerontologist*, 16:166–173.

Kessler, S. (1975), *The American Way of Divorce*. New York: Nelson-Hall.

Kivett, V. R., Watson, J. A., & Busch, J. C. (1977), The relative importance of physical, psychological, and social variables to locus of control orientation in middle age. *J. Gerontol.*, 32:203–210.

Levinson, D. J. (1978), *The Seasons of a Man's Life*. New York: Ballantine.

Lopata, H. Z. (1972), *Widowhood in an American City*. Boston: Schenkman.

Monge, R. H. (1975), Structure of the self-concept from adolescence through old age. *Exper. Aging Res.*, 1:281–291.

Neugarten, B. L. (1964), *Personality in Middle and Later Life*. New York: Atherton Press, pp. 114–118.

——— (1979), Time, age and the life cycle. *Amer. J. Psychiat.*, 137:887–984.

Newman, B. M., & Newman, P. R. (1979), Later adulthood: A developmental stage. In: *Dimensions of Aging*, ed. J. Hendricks & C. D. Hendricks, pp. 126–143.

Novak, C. A., & Troll, L. E. (1974), Age-concept in women: Concern with youthfulness and attractiveness relative to self-perceived age. Paper presented at the meetings of the Gerontological Society, Portland, OR.

Peck, R., & Berkowitz, H. (1964), Personality and adjustment in middle-age. In: *Personality in Middle and Later Life*, ed. B. L. Neugarten. New York: Atherton.

Pepe, E. A., & Wyly, M. B. (1976), Age and sex as determinants of sex-role identity. Paper presented at the meeting of the American Psychological Association, Washington, DC.

Pfeiffer, E., & Davis, G. C. (1971), The use of leisure time in middle life. *Gerontologist*, 11:187–195.

Qilliams, E. (1977), Alimony—The short goodbye. *Psychology Today*, 11:6, pp. 71–77.

Rainwater, L. (1959), *Workingman's Wife*. Social Research Press.

Reichard, S., Livson, F., & Peterson, P. (1962), *Aging and Personality*. New York: John Wiley.

Reno, V. (1971), Why men stop working at or before age 65: Findings from the survey of new beneficiaries. *Soc. Sec. Bull.*, 34/6:3–17.

Rones, P. (1978), Older men—The choice between work and retirement, *Monthly Labor Review*, 101/11:3–10.

Sinnott, J. D. (1979), Sex-role inconstancy, biology and successful aging. In: *Dimensions of Aging*, ed. J. Hendricks & C. D. Hendricks, pp. 144–149.

Sangiuliano, I. (1978), *In Her Time*. New York: Morrow.

Troll, L. E. (1973), *Early and Middle Adulthood*. Monterey, CA: Brooks/Cole.

U.S. Department of Labor, Bureau of Statistics, (1977), *U.S. Working Women: A Databook*, Bulletin No. 1977, Washington, DC: U.S. Government Printing Office.

Vaillant, G. G. (1977), *Adaptation to Life*. Boston: Little, Brown.

Visscher, A. L. (1966), *On Growing Old*. London: Allen & Unwin.

Weinberg, J. (1979), Psychopathology. In: *Dimensions of Aging: Readings*, ed. J. Hendricks & C. D. Hendricks. Cambridge, MA: Winthrop, pp. 160–172.

Chapter 42
Multifactoral Stressors in Life Change Events for the Elderly Patient

Thomas W. Miller, Ph.D., A.B.P.P., and
Louis L. Jay, R.Ph.

Considerable attention has been given in the literature to stress and life span development (Stein, Linn, Slater, Stein, 1984, see chapter 43, this volume). The latter portion of life is often seen as a period of particular stress with the departure of children from the home, issues related to menopause, retirement, diminished economic resources, and the death of lifelong friends and spouse. By the year 2000, it has been estimated that the older population of the United States will double to a number approaching 34 million people over the age of 65, and 6.8 million over the age of 85 (U.S. Bureau of Census, 1983). The group aged 85 and older has already grown at a rate in excess of 150 percent over the past two decades and while the older population as a whole is healthier than stereotypically assumed; by the age of 85 over half report being limited to or unable to carry out major life activities because of chronic illness.

Over the past 20 years, clinical research has addressed the

Acknowledgment. This chapter is adapted from a regional workshop presentation of the Southeastern Regional Medical Education Conference on Geriatrics (1985), Lexington, Kentucky.

issue of psychological stress and illness. Research (Linn, Hunter, and Harris, 1980) assessing life stress events has found correlations which approach .30, suggesting a relationship exists between psychological stress and illness, suggesting also that perhaps 10 percent of the variation in illness among individuals may best be explained by variations in stress. It is hypothesized that life stress and illness may well have concomitant factors which can over the periods of months and years substantially affect the health and well-being of an individual.

It is realized that stress can be either physical or psychological in nature, yet oftentimes an individual experiences a series of stages or phases in a stressful life situation which have been summarized by various individuals including Selye as a stage of alarm resistance and exhaustion. Stress is often a condition or situation that imposes demands for adjustment on the individual and that it is a non-specific response of the body to the demands that the environment or other individuals may place on the person. It is most frequently realized through a variety of symptomatology including motor tension, autonomic hyperactivity, apprehensive expectation, and vigilance of scanning. The symptoms one recognizes are the results of a process wherein internal cognitive capabilities and/or external demands exceed an individual's ability to cope, especially when the demand is perceived as important to the well-being of the individual.

LIFE CHANGE EVENTS: STRESS FOR THE ELDERLY

In recent years, a number of studies (Borup, 1983; Stein, Linn, Stein, and Linn, 1983; Wells and McDonald, 1981) recognized the process of relocation in the elderly as a stressful life event and while many of these studies have reported deleterious effects, usually in terms of higher mortality rates, others have failed to substantiate these findings. What has emerged is relocation in the elderly population, particularly institutionalization, has clear indications of being a life stress event. Lazarus (1975) has suggested that the individual's cognitive appraisal of the situation in coping with or defining stress associated with relocation is of critical importance. For the geriatric population who have already had a lifetime of mixed and changing circumstances, growing evidence suggests that it may be more appropriate to measure anticipated stress rather than the actual recent occurrence of life stress events. Stein, Linn, and Stein (1985) studied 223 patients newly admitted to 10 nursing homes and had these patients rate a 20-item scale listing potential stresses in the institution. Results were factor analyzed and factor scores were intercorrelated with the descriptive, attitudinal, psychological, and physical status of the patients. Five factors emerge that related in significant ways the psychological and physical variables recognized. The most significant stressors identified involve anticipatory stress with variables such as: (1) potential relationship to nursing staff, (2) level of treatment and respect the individual would receive, (3) physical care and well-being, (4) what other patients would be like, (5) whether there would be visitation from family and friends, (6) to a lesser degree adapting to institutional schedules, (7) retaining privacy, and (8) maintaining a sense of self within an institutional structure.

External events have also been recognized as critical issues facilitating stress in the geriatric population (Coffman, 1983). Most critical concerns include rising food costs and cut in Social Security benefits. Events that could threaten the immediate survival of the individual tended to be feared the most. Losing one's sight, having to live in a nursing home, and threat of physical harm to oneself were also critically important issues. While health and ability to function issues were of considerable concern, it was the fear of eventually relocating to a hospital or nursing home situation that was of utmost concern to the geriatric patient. Likewise, the loss of one's sight, an event that could considerably increase the level of dependency the individual might experience was also recognized as a significant stressor. Much more so, the question of impending death and concerns about health and disability could be considered among the most stressing factors facing our geriatric population today.

There are several critical factors which must be addressed within various components of relocation and change within the aging process. Just as with Abraham Maslow's hierarchy of needs (Table 42.1), geriatric patients are very much concerned at the first level with physical needs about issues related to physical pain (.79), course of their illness (.63), physical care they will receive (.75), personal privacy (.52), personal space (.47), the kind and quality of food (.51), and their possessions (.31). At the second level are safety issues and these include such concerns as the kind and appropriateness of medication (.65), seeing their doctor on a regular basis (.62), competency and care of nursing staff (.80), and security in institutional care (.53). In Maslow's third level of need hierarchy, social issues related to belonging become most prominent, and for the geriatric patient, this is also true in relocation issues. Potential stressors involve their acceptance by staff members in institutional care (.80), the likelihood of concern by families (.60), and regular contact and visits by family and friends (.66). Most prominent among esteem needs with the geriatric population include the desire to maintain a sense of oneself (.83) and being treated with respect by staff members (.80). In addition to that, however, the issue of becoming increasingly physically dependent on others for care and treatment probably has most serious impact on the esteem needs of the geriatric patient. Both physical and psychological information communicated to the patient by medical and nursing staff provide a crucial balance of the individual geriatric patient's ability to maintain a sense of self-respect and become realistic about physical dependence.

Beyond the internal stressors that are likely to occur with relocation, external stressors from society also raise key questions. Rising food costs and cuts in social security, events that could threaten immediate survival to the geriatric patient, were most feared. Beyond that, loss of one's sight and having to live under institutional care as well as the possibility of being robbed were also of great concern to the patients sampled. Close to 76

Table 42.1
**Maslow's Theoretical Need Hierarchy as It Relates to Stressful
Life Experiences in the Geriatric Patient**

Maslow's Theoretical Levels	Factoral Stressors in the Elderly
1. Physical Needs	Physical pain experienced Course of illness Physical care received Privacy Personal space Quality of food Personal possessions
2. Safety Needs	Appropriateness of medication Physician availability Competency of nursing care Security of personal self and possessions No harm from treatment
3. Social Needs	Acceptance by staff and peers Concern by family members Regular contact from friends and significant others
4. Esteem Needs	Maintaining a sense of oneself Treatment with respect by staff Self respect
5. Self Actualizing Needs	Fulfillment of personal and life goals

percent of the patients surveyed reported that they had been the object of burglary within the past six months when they were questioned about recent life event stressors. Though all of the health and ability to function items measured caused at least some concern, it was fear of having eventually to live in some form of institutional care that was of utmost concern to the geriatric population. While losing sight, an event which might well increase the issues related to dependency, external life stressors including assault, robbery, rising food costs, rent increase, and cuts in Social Security and disability benefits seemed to be most prominent.

Stein et al. (1984) report seven major categories of concern items for geriatric community residents. Included in the categories are: (1) financial concerns such as reductions in federal housing subsidies, food stamps, social security, and rising food costs, (2) health concerns which include fear of being disabled, loss of hearing or sight, experiencing a heart attack or developing a terminal illness such as cancer and the subsequent pain related to it, (3) concerns about how death will present itself and being the last survivor of a social group, and (4) functional status of the individual. Diagnostically relevant issues related to memory functioning, physical impairment, and greater dependence on others are of the most critical concern for the geriatric population. Certainly within the functional status is the potential for depressive episodes that are triggered most frequently by feelings of loneliness and uselessness. The experiences of depression might well be realized as a result of losing family members, friends, and neighbors through death; being forgotten by people; not being able to care for oneself or one's living situation and a general sense of loss of purpose to life. The overall results suggest that the geriatric population have moderately pervasive concerns which seem to be more reflective of a generalized level of anxiety about future than impending stressful life events. Within the framework of attempting to assist the geriatric patient in adjustment, it may be more beneficial to deal with the ideas of perceived stress in terms of anticipatory anxiety about potentially stressful life events. Recent research efforts on stress have sensitized health care professionals to question the geriatric patient on circumstances in their lives. Clearly the geriatric health care provider should be most concerned about the multiplicity of levels of needs of the geriatric patient. As Maslow emphasizes, concerns about physical health and well-being, safety and security, belongingness and a support network, and the self-respect and esteem that the geriatric patient must experience as a human being become critically important. In addition to endogenous and exogenous precipitators of stressful life events, personality of the individual becomes critically important. Personality is a guide to several lifestyle variables that influence health and emotional adjustment. Gaining a better understanding of personality make-up, psychological tests designed to assess personality components may be of considerable benefit.

ISSUES IN LIFE STRESS MEASUREMENT

There are potential limitations with respect to prospective studies in measuring life events. Most concern the time between initial assessment of life events and follow-up measurements. Length of time between events and intensity of events are also concerns. While some (Brown and Harris, 1978) have argued that some subjects may be more vulnerable to various psychiatric disorders for a considerable period of time after the stressful life event occurs, others emphasize the intensity of the event is different for each person. Most clinicians believe that a depressive response pattern is most common in the immediate aftermath of the stressful event. More recently, Murphy (1983) used Brown's (Brown, Harris, and Peto, 1973) more sensitive contextual measure of threat to life events in a sample of elderly depressed patients. Life events assessed at the initial admission did not predict relapse of 12-month follow-up. Grant, Yeager, Sweetwood, and Olshen (1982) followed a mixed sample of psychiatric patients and normal subjects over a three-year period. During that period of time, life events (SRE) and psychological symptoms were assessed every two months. Four different temporal patterns of relationships between events and symptoms were studied. The most crucial of these and the one in which a causal association between events and illness might be implicated was termed "coherent but one of phase." What this meant is that the events scores and symptom scores both fluctuated between high and low but did not alternate from one cycle to the next. It was extremely difficult to assess the causal relationship for when undesirable events were examined separately in similar analysis, only about 8 percent of the subjects exhibited a pattern consistent with causal association. The prospective studies in which life event stress is measured prior to the onset of psychological morbidity appear to add more controversy to the issue of accuracy of stressful life-event measurement. These studies are certainly to be distinguished from longitudinal studies in which events and illness are measured at the point in time to enhance the sensitivity of measures of stressful life events. Assessment of personality variables including premorbid personality and current personality functioning as well as estimates of the time difference and intensity of stress experienced would greatly enhance the accuracy and effectiveness of assessing stressful life events.

The efforts of Holmes and Rahe (1967) to assess stressful life events have been well recognized. The association between life change and illness susceptibility began with the research of Adolf Meyer and his creation of the "life chart" which organized medical data for demonstrating the relationship of biological and psycho-social phenomena to the processes of disease in man. The 43 items derived from this study and now used in the Schedule of Recent Events (SRE) are of two categories: those indicative of lifestyle and those indicative of occurrences involving the individual. From these findings, the Social Readjustment Rating Scale was used which ranked life events according to magnitude. The results of extensive testing exhibited that life change events are highly related to time of illness onset. Some of the life events measured in Holmes and Rahe's initial work would benefit from revisions of three types: (1) relevance of events listed for geriatric patients, (2) a rating of time-span from the event to the present, and (3) an estimate of the intensity. A suggested modification of the Social Readjustment Rating Scale is summarized in Figure 42.1.

COPING WITH STRESS AND LIFE CHANGE

Another key area of concern is one's ability to cope and while this is most often based on the personality composition of the individual, it also has to do with learned skills that the individual has developed throughout one's lifetime. As discussed earlier, anticipatory anxiety can be critically important in the way in which an individual perceives the world around him. As a result of that, one may well feel a state of learned helplessness because of the way in which he perceives the world around him and this may impair one's ability to cope effectively. The health care provider must be aware of the defense mechanisms or coping skills that the individual may use in dealing with stressful life experiences. Some researchers (Warheit, 1979) who have emphasized the study of coping mechanisms have noted that many defenses appear to be applied consciously and deliberately and that the coping has a dual purpose in that it attempts to provide an adequate solution to the stressful life situation and, furthermore, a reduction in physiological and psychological response. There is considerable debate, however, among those researchers who have explored in greater detail the variety of methods of handling stress through coping. Some theorists (Tennant, Bebbington, and Hurry, 1981) have suggested that coping mechanisms are problem focused while others are emotionally focused. Those that advocate the problem-focused mechanisms of coping tend to be more cognitive and stepwise oriented in their approach to situations whereas those who are more emotionally focused tend to concentrate on core facilitative conditions, expression of feelings, perceptions of concerns, and the likelihood of a lack of response contingent on positive reinforcement in the geriatric patient's life experience.

Those (Warheit, 1979) who have studied approaches to stress and coping have identified the role of autonomic or neuroendocrine division as a team mechanism in triggering organic pathology in the patient while there may well be a constitutional predisposition or a genetic base. Psychological adjustment becomes a critical issue in addressing the management of life stressors.

Considerable attention has addressed psychophysiologically based approaches to the management of autonomic hyperactivity (Miller, 1985). Biofeedback, progressive muscle relaxation, and cognitive meditation and cognitive imagery have been among the techniques that have been used to reduce the psychophysiological components of stress. There is a considerable

	Points (circle if applicable)	How Long?			How Intense?		
		Over a Year	Six Months	Week or Less	Mild	Moderate	Severe
		1	2	3	1	2	3
1. Death of spouse	100						
2. Divorce	73						
3. No contact from family members or loved ones	65						
4. Death of family member	63						
5. Hospitalization or nursing home placement	63						
6. Traumatic injury or illness	53						
7. Change in marital status	50						
8. Reprimand or firing from work	47						
9. Retirement from work	45						
10. Reconciliation with friend or spouse	45						
11. Change in health of family member	44						
12. Expressed concern by family members	40						
13. Gain of new family member	39						
14. Difficulties in sexual relations	39						
15. Readjustment in work or living setting	39						
16. Change in your financial status	37						
17. Death of a close friend or relative	36						
18. Change to routine or schedule	35						
19. Change in number of arguments with spouse	31						
20. Changes to privacy or personal space	30						

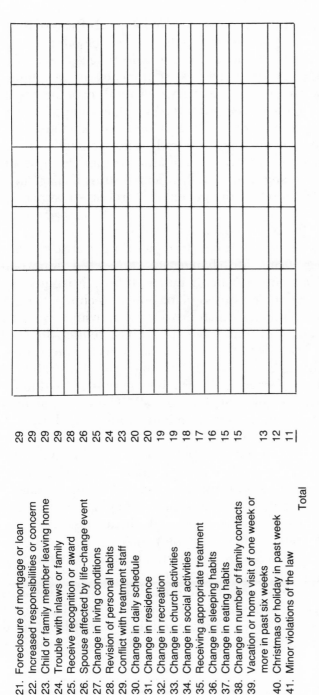

21. Foreclosure of mortgage or loan	29
22. Increased responsibilities or concern	29
23. Child or family member leaving home	29
24. Trouble with inlaws or family	29
25. Receive recognition or award	28
26. Spouse affected by life-change event	26
27. Change in living conditions	25
28. Revision of personal habits	24
29. Conflict with treatment staff	23
30. Change in daily schedule	20
31. Change in residence	20
32. Change in recreation	19
33. Change in church activities	19
34. Change in social activities	18
35. Receiving appropriate treatment	17
36. Change in sleeping habits	16
37. Change in eating habits	15
38. Change in number of family contacts	15
39. Vacation or home visit of one week or more in past six weeks	13
40. Christmas or holiday in past week	12
41. Minor violations of the law	11
Total	

Add up the points for each symptom you circle. Then in the section that asks "How Long?" add one point if you've experienced the event for weeks, two if it has gone on for months, and three if you've experienced the event over a year. In the second column, score the intensity of symptoms with one point for mild, two for moderate, and three for severe.

Figure 42.1. Stressful life-event scale. Adapted from Social Readjustment Scale by Homes and Rahe (1967).

body of literature that supports the physiological effects of these methods including prolonged reduction of blood pressure among borderline hypertensives in a wide range of age categories. Furthermore, biofeedback approaches as an adjunct therapy in the treatment of urinary and fecal incontinence in the elderly has shown some promise. As with most approaches, however, further research on the value of such methods in stress management must be explored. Where cognitive functioning permits the geriatric patient an acceptable level of autonomous functioning, behaviorally oriented stress management techniques related to how the patient can process stress may be most appropriate.

The role of cognitive-behavioral stress management procedures as adjunct intervention strategies for geriatric patients who are experiencing life change are considered important treatment options. Such patients may well benefit from stress management techniques. Stress management techniques refer to a variety of techniques which provide an individual with the skill of being able to voluntarily cope with or reduce the level of stress experienced by the patient. Some techniques utilize instrumentation to augment the training procedure referred to as biofeedback. Occasionally visual imagery is utilized to facilitate development of conscious control. The object of pain management training is to establish in the individual the ability to invoke a significant release of tension through the muscle systems in response to one's desire to do so. Training and practice are designed to habituate the relaxation response to identifiable environmental and internal cues. Stress management training has also been useful as a tool in helping geriatric patients learn control of affective arousal which causes or exaggerates symptomatic events including pain.

Cognitive and behaviorally oriented stress management training is integrally related to how the geriatric patient processes stress. The stress management training program involves four modules, each with specific therapeutic tasks and expected outcomes (Table 42.2). The initial module is one of behavioral assessment. The assessment phase involves the careful analysis

Table 42.2
Stress Management Training for Geriatric Patients

	Module	Therapeutic Tasks	Expected Outcome
I.	Behavioral Assessment	Assessment of the components of stress experienced by the person as it relates to life events.	Patient understands elements of stress and specific factors which trigger anxiety and result in stress.
II.	Cognitive Appraisal	Appraise the manner in which the patient perceives and communicates stress behavior in life stress events.	Patient understands how he/she processes the perception of stressful situations and uses this information to control stress producing experiences.
III.	Education and Training	Educate and train the patient to utilize a four model in dealing with stress and pain.	Patient understands and employs the four-step model in stress management skills training.
IV.	Stress Management Skills	Train the person in the use of cognitive imagery and muscle relaxation skills as the medium or reducing stress and pain.	Patient learns effective use of cognitive coping skills and employs them in the control of anxiety, stress, and tension.

of the variety of components of stress experienced by the patient. Significant life events initiate stress reaction in individuals mainly because it has some direct impact on our lives and this may be intensified. Because of this, it is essential that the patients take responsibility for the stress and discomfort that they are experiencing by carefully evaluating the circumstances that lead up to the stressful situation, how they are processing the information related to the stressful situation, and the extent to which they can cope with the stressful situation. Stress management training provides skills in assisting a person to evaluate and develop the coping mechanisms needed to relieve the physical and psychological features of anxiety and stress.

The second module of stress management involves a cognitive phase which aims to assess the specific process of cognitively interpreting stressful events. This cognitive phase recognizes that individuals perceive life events in a variety of different ways. The way in which life events are communicated, the way in which we have learned to perceive them tie into our own anticipatory anxiety, our aspirations and our threats to satisfactory adjustment in our everyday life. Cognitive appraisal becomes a key to satisfactory coping with life stress events and pain for the renal patient. The process of appraising a situation in life events has the potential of causing anxiety. The self statements that individuals make emphasize one's ability or inability to cope with that situation. While our cognitive appraisal is functioning, our body, including muscles, salivary glands and blood pressure, are producing comparable physiological responses. Some of these responses are in the form of muscle tension, perspiration, or a variety of other somatic concerns. They result in a self-fulfilling anxiety response and thus become the focus of control.

The third module of stress management training involves education and training. This module teaches four specific ingredients that are essential to the person's preparation for dealing with stress and painful experiences often a part of the renal patient's condition and/or treatment. The initial phase is to prepare for the anticipated stressful or painful situation. In preparing for this, an individual thinks through and carefully evaluates what triggers the pain or stress. Preparing for the triggering event allows the individual to carefully think through the options that one has in dealing with it. There is also an anxiety reducing effect in at least being able to visually imagine role playing the particular situation that one is anticipating a great deal of anxiety about. As part of preparing for this stress producing situation, an individual can call upon the use of muscle relaxation skills which can be used in conjunction with the visual imagery one considers using as a way of coping with the anticipated stressful situation.

The next phase is being able to confront the stressful situation or pain by cognitively rehearsing (rehearsing in your mind) the way in which the person has chosen to deal with this significant life event. Once this rehearsal phase has been completed, one is then ready to face the triggering event and to utilize both the cognitive imagery and relaxation skills that will allow the individual to see himself through this stress life event.

A third phase emphasizes coping with the stressful situation based on the preparation and cognitive-rehearsal phases. Reasoning things through and mentally preparing oneself for stressful life events means that the person can develop a mental preparedness for whatever situation is confronted. For renal patients who face both physical and psychological pain, this is especially true.

The final phase evaluates the level of satisfaction one has realized in coping with this particular stressful experience. This phase involves self-statements which support the individual's efforts to be in control and to manage the level of control he has realized in the utilization of stress management skills.

The fourth module of the stress management program is one of relaxation exercises. Relaxation exercises become the physical response experienced in conjunction with cognitive appraisal and coping skill. Relaxation exercises involve tensing and relaxing all 16 of the different muscle groups that are summarized in Table 42.3. As a part of the muscle relaxation training, geriatric patients are asked to listen to an audiotape

Table 42.3
Stress Management Training for Geriatric Patients
Utilizing Muscle Relaxation Skills[a]

Muscle Group	Self Directed Activity
Breathing exercises	Slowly inhale, hold and release. Repeat two or three times.
Right hand and forearm	Tense by making a tight fist. Hold and release.
Left hand and forearm	Tense by making a tight fist. Hold and release.
Biceps and triceps	Tense by bringing elbows in toward the body. Hold and release.
Forehead	Tense by raising eyebrows upward. Hold and release.
Facial muscles	Tense by squinting and wrinkling nose. Hold and release.
Mouth and jaw	Tense by clinching the teeth and lips. Hold and release.
Neck	Tense by pushing the head back, rolling in one continuous motion.
Shoulders and chest	Tense by pressing shoulder blades back and together.
Adbomen	Tense by tightening stomach muscles. Hold and release.
Lower back	Tense by arching back. Hold and release.
Thighs	Tense by raising leg (left then right) off ground. Hold and release.
Calves	Tense by pointing the toes toward head. Hold and release.
Feet and toes	Tense by curling the toes and pointing feet inward. Hold and release.

[a]Modified Jacobsen Muscle Relaxation Module

which leads the individual through the sequential phase of muscle relaxation training. Muscle relaxation recognizes that anxiety, stress, and tension are stored in the various muscle groups of the body. These same muscle groups that one deliberately tenses are the muscle groups that become tense and tight when anxiety, stress, and tension are experienced. The tensing and relaxing phase of muscle relaxation allows one to learn a physiological method of coping with pain and anxiety stored as muscle tension.

After the patient has had an opportunity to learn the progressive muscle relaxation sequence, a period of conditioning and reinforcement of both the cognitive and relaxation exercises is necessary for stress management to be effective. A cue controlled response can be obtained by the patient in a matter of seconds simply by utilizing the stress management skills learned, both cognitively and from the relaxation training, and allowing the individual's body systems which are often vulnerable to stress related concerns respond effectively by assuming a conditioned response cued by the experience already gained in doing the longer, more complete relaxation therapy.

The technique provides for several advantages by which the patient can voluntarily control the response to pain and produce a state of coping with chronic pain. The most obvious advantage is that the patient can employ pain management techniques even when reclining in a chair with eyes closed. Having a skill which can be employed to ease the pain state can greatly increase the patient's confidence. Another advantage is its inherent capacity to allow the patient to assume basic responsibilities for treatment, particularly as it may reduce the need for some pharmaceutical control. Once the patient has learned the skill, the patient retains it as one would any skill and its efficiency as directly related to practice.

Stress management procedures are best taught under the direction of a trained professional, usually a psychologist. Once the training procedures have been realized, an audiotape of the training procedures can be of benefit in systematically conditioning the patient to follow the proper procedures and to use the appropriate timing of the exercises. Without such a tape, it is possible that patients may tend to lose the numerous components and timing of the training exercises.

SUMMARY

The treatment of the geriatric patient is a complex one requiring the health care professional's understanding of the multifactoral stressors that the geriatric patient must face in a constantly changing life experience. The sequela of stress may well be manifested in a variety of forms including hyperirritability, disturbed interpersonal relations, withdrawal and detachment, eating and sleep disturbances. The increased withdrawal and detachment from daily life activities may often be representative of ego defense reaction against the possibilities of future disruption and a true indicator that the individual is experiencing a great deal of internal life stress. Holmes and Rahe (1967) have studied the relationship between the extent of life crises and the subsequent changes in health and shown that the frequency and severity of the illness increases in proportion to the extent of life change. It would, therefore, appear that the degree of forced change may well involve relocation or the reality of accepting oneself in a more frail and impaired sense and may result in the likelihood of a major affective disorder including depression. Sensitivity on the part of health care providers and proper planning and preparation can play a significant role in reducing the amount of anticipatory anxiety and experienced stress wherein voluntary relocation of the geriatric patient is required. Beyond that, follow-up programs after the relocation has occurred should be implemented to facilitate an integration of the person with the new environment, all of which should be enhanced by engaging family and significant others in the process of any major life change for the geriatric person.

REFERENCES

Borup, J. H. (1983), Relocation mortality research: Assessment, reply, and the need to refocus on the issues. *Gerontologist*, 23:235–242.

Brown, G. W., Harris, T. O., & Peto, J. (1973), Life events and psychiatric disorder. Part 2: Nature of the causal link. *Psychol. Med.*, 3:159–176.

———— ———— (1978). *The Social Origins of Depression*. London: Tavistock.

Coffman, T. L. (1983), Toward an understanding of geriatric relocation. *Gerontologist*, 23:453–459.

Grant, I., Yager, J., Sweetwood, H. L., & Olshen, R. (1982), Life events and symptoms. Fourier analysis of time series from a three-year perspective inquiry. *Arch. Gen. Psychiat.*, 39:598–605.

Holmes, T. H., & Rahe, R. H. (1967), The Social Readjustment Rating Scale. *J. Psychosom. Res.*, 11:213–218.

Lazarus, R. S. (1975), The self-regulation of emotions. In: *Emotions: Their Parameters and Measurement*, ed. L. Levi. New York: Raven Press.

Linn, M. W., Hunter, K., & Harris, R. (1980), Symptoms of depression and recent life events in the community elderly. *J. Clin. Psychol.*, 36:675–682.

Miller, T. W. (1985), Psychophysiological bases to hyperactivity. Colloquium Series, Department of Psychiatry, College of Medicine, University of Kentucky.

Murphy, E. (1983), The prognosis of depression in old age. *Brit. J. Psychiat.*, 142:111–119.

Stein, S., Linn, M. W., Stein, E. M., & Linn, B. S. (1983), The impact of environment on perception of stress and symptoms of the elderly. *Activities, Adaptation and Aging*, 3:39–48.

————— ————— Slater, E., & Stein, E. M. (1984), Future concerns and recent life events in the elderly. *J. Amer. Geriat. Soc.*, 32:431–434.

————— ————— Stein, E. M. (1985), Patients' anticipation of stress in nursing home care. *Gerontologist*, 25:88–95.

Tennant, C., Bebbington, P., & Hurry, J. (1981), The role of life events in depressive illness: Is there a substantial causal relation? *Psychol. Med.*, 11:379–389.

U.S. Bureau of the Census (1983), America in transition: An aging society. Current Population Reports, Series P-23, No. 128, Washington, DC: U.S. Government Printing Office.

Warheit, G. (1979), Life events, coping, stress and depressive symptomatology. *Amer. J. Psychiat.*, 136:502–507.

Wells, L., & Macdonald, G. (1981), Interpersonal networks and post-relocation adjustment of the institutionalized elderly. *Gerontologist*, 21:177–183.

Chapter 43
Future Concerns and Recent Life Events of Elderly Community Residents

SHAYNA STEIN, PH.D., MARGARET W. LINN, PH.D., ELISA SLATER, B.S.,
AND ELLIOT M. STEIN, M.D.

There is ample evidence in the literature to support a relationship between social factors, stressful life events, and illness (Rabkin and Struening, 1976). Though there has been controversy over the best methods for defining and measuring stressful events (Dohrenwend and Dohrenwend, 1978; Horowitz, Schaeffer, and Horito, 1977; Dohrenwend, 1973a) there is general agreement that past and current stressful life events can act as catalysts for changing a person's susceptibility to stress-related diseases (Renner and Birren, 1980).

Lazarus' (1976) work points out the importance of the individual's cognitive appraisal of a situation to their ability to cope with or define the associated stress. Reactions to stress have been said to be dependent on the person's initial appraisal

Acknowledgment. This chapter was first published in the *Journal of the American Geriatrics Society* (1984), 32/6:431–434, and it is reprinted with permission.

749

of the event, the subsequent affective reaction, and the cognitive elaboration that lends the event meaning (Dressler, Donovan, and Geller, 1976). In more general terms, a person's reactions to possible stressors can be anticipatory based on past experiences.

The question naturally arises as to what potential events are most worrisome to the aging, who already have had a lifetime of experience of changing circumstances. It may be that the fear of recurrence of a previously associated emotional reaction, rather than the event itself, would cause the most stress for this group in particular. For example, if losing a loved one in the past resulted in intense loneliness, worry about feeling lonely rather than losing a loved one may be the potential stressor.

The primary purpose of this study was to determine the level of concern that elderly persons who reside in the community attach to the occurrence of selected events or emotions. Whether personal characteristics or the actual recent occurrence of an event would bear more relationship to their worries also was examined.

METHOD

Fifty-eight aged community dwellers volunteered to participate in this study. Each person received a self-administered questionnaire in which background data, such as age and income, were first completed. Next, subjects were asked to rate their level of current concern, using a scale of 1 to 5—no concern to extremely concerned—about potential events and emotions on a 37-item "Concern Inventory." Items were selected partly through review of existing literature (Holmes and Rahe, 1967) and partly through consultation with professionals experienced in working with the elderly. The scale was pre-tested on 25 elderly persons, and item analyses showed that items correlated highly with a total score. Further, test-retest reliabilities on the items, based on a 3-day testing interval, were all above $r = 0.62$.

Though presented to subjects randomly, concerns were categorized as follows: financial, health, death, environmental, functional, victimization, and feelings of loneliness or uselessness. Each respondent was given a card listing the response categories for easy reference. Finally, a recent life-event checklist containing eight items to which subjects responded yes or no as having occurred in the past 6 months was completed. Items included robbery, assault, a rent increase, death of a family member, death of a close friend, change of residence, heart attack, and falls.

Mean and standard deviations were tabulated for all data, after which intercorrelations (Pearson correlations/r) were computed to determine if there were significant relationships between characteristics of subjects, recent events, and total score.

RESULTS

DESCRIPTION OF SUBJECTS

Of the 58 elderly persons in the sample, 30 were women and 28 were men. The average age was 72.8 years, and 44 percent were currently married. Thirty-two percent lived with their children. The group could be described as "high risk" in that they lived in predominantly poor neighborhoods, had an average annual income in the range of $4,000–$8,000, and had completed only about 9.5 years of school.

Many of the respondents were not only long-time residents of their neighborhoods but had lived at their present addresses for relatively long periods of time (13.4 and 11.3 years, respectively). There were exceptions to this, as evidenced by high standard deviations (10.9 and 11 years) for these items.

As a group, these elderly perceived their health to be in the good-to-fair range, with an average rating of 2.5 on a 5-point scale (1 = excellent). They reported visiting their doctors about three times over the past 6 months, had been sick in bed an

average of only 1.9 days during that same time, and had averaged 1.6 days in the hospital. Family histories of heart disease
were presented in 36 percent and family histories of cancer in
24 percent.

CONCERNS OF THE ELDERLY

Table 43.1 shows the means and standard deviations for the
concern items by category. Though mean ratings on the scale
items generally fell between "a little concerned" and "moderately concerned," there were five items with higher average
endorsements (mean = 3 or above). Rising food costs and cuts
in social security, events that could threaten immediate survival
for this group, were most feared. Losing sight, having to live
in a nursing home, and being robbed also were of great concern
for these elderly. The last item is not surprising, because 76
percent reported having been robbed in the last 6 months when
questioned about recent life events (see Table 43.2.). Though
all of the health and ability-to-function items caused at least
some concern, it was fear of having eventually to live in a nursing home that was of utmost concern for this group. Perhaps
losing sight, an event which would greatly increase dependency
if not corrected, threatens these elderly in a similar way. Interestingly, death itself was not so fearful. In fact, "life ending"
had the lowest mean concern score on the scale. Concerns about
health, and especially disability, caused more distress.

RECENT LIFE EVENTS

Table 43.2 shows the number who had an occurrence of each
of the life events during the last 6 months. As mentioned previously, the elderly group lived in poor neighborhoods. Nevertheless, it was alarming to find that so many had been recently
robbed. Considering the high percentage of robberies, it was
fortunate that only 11 had been assaulted.

Despite the fact that many of the group were long-time

Table 43.1
Means and Standard Deviations of Concern Items on a 37-Item Inventory
Administered to 58 Elderly Community Residents[a]

	Mean ± SD
Financial items	
Rising food costs	3.47 ± 1.59
Cuts in social security	3.36 ± 1.75
Cuts in medicaid for medical care	2.40 ± 1.84
Rent increase	2.29 ± 1.74
Cuts in federal housing subsidies	1.78 ± 1.58
Cuts in food stamps	1.72 ± 1.58
Health	
Losing your sight	3.16 ± 1.95
Becoming disabled	2.97 ± 1.77
Getting a lingering illness	2.97 ± 1.81
Someone close becoming disabled	2.90 ± 1.83
Getting appropriate medical attention	2.74 ± 1.79
Losing your hearing	2.56 ± 1.77
Being hospitalized	2.52 ± 1.75
Having a heart attack	2.40 ± 1.76
Getting cancer	2.40 ± 1.75
Pain	2.22 ± 1.60
Death	
Getting a fatal illness	2.59 ± 1.85
Being the last one in social group left alive	2.07 ± 1.54
Sudden death	1.88 ± 1.55
Life ending	1.62 ± 1.32
Environmental	
Having to move	2.36 ± 1.83
Bus strikes or transportation failures	2.24 ± 1.71
Functional status	
Having to live in a nursing home	3.19 ± 1.87
Falling down and hurting yourself	2.57 ± 1.75
Being able to remember things	2.52 ± 1.66
Becoming dependent	2.50 ± 1.80
Not being able to take care of living quarters	2.31 ± 1.77
Not being able to do what people expect of you	2.05 ± 1.57
Victimization	
Being robbed	3.16 ± 1.80
Being assaulted	2.53 ± 1.81

Table 43.1 (Continued)

Feelings of loneliness of uselessness	
Losing family members	2.76 ± 1.89
Feeling useless	2.50 ± 1.77
Being forgotten by people	2.33 ± 1.67
Losing friends	2.26 ± 1.54
Being lonely	2.17 ± 1.46
Feeling as though you have no purpose in life	2.07 ± 1.60
Not being able to see your children as often as you would like	2.07 ± 1.70

[a] Scale: 1 = no concern; 2 = a little concern; 3 = moderately concerned; 4 = very concerned; 5 = extremely concerned;

Table 43.2
Occurrence of Stressful Life Events (Within Last Six Months)
for 58 Community Elderly

	Number of Elderly
Robbery	44
Death of a close friend	18
Change of residence	17
Death of a family member	13
Assault	11
Falls	8
Rent increase	4
Heart attack	1

neighborhood residents, 17 had moved in the last 6 months, but only four had had a rent increase.

Recent death of a close friend or family member occurred for 18 and 13 of the group, respectively. Only one person had suffered a heart attack, but eight had fallen down.

FACTORS RELATING TO TOTAL CONCERN

All of the individual concern items correlated significantly ($p < .01$) with total score. In addition to being statistically significant, absolute values of the correlations were high. For this reason, a total score indicating degree of concern was used to correlate level of concern with personal characteristics of subjects and recent life events. Table 43.3 shows the factors for which this relationship was significant. As can be seen, the elderly with less education, shorter neighborhood tenure, poorer perceived health, and those living with their children expressed greater total concern.

In regard to actual events, only two—being assaulted and having a close friend die during the past 6 months—were associated significantly with degree of concern.

DISCUSSION

Results from this study suggest that, at least for the elderly poor, immediate economic survival is of utmost concern. Even the fear of being robbed could be considered an immediate survival issue, because income for these elderly was severely limited and most had been robbed during the previous 6 months. In addition to immediate economic survival, the most concern was shown about loss of functional capacities, as evi-

Table 43.3
Factors Significantly Related to Total Concern Score on a
37-Item Concern Inventory Administered to 58 Community Elderly

Subject characteristics	
Education	-0.33^*
Living with children	-0.26^*
Months living in neighborhood	-0.32^*
Health rating[a]	-0.38^*
Recent life events	
Assault	-0.28^*
Death of a close friend[b]	-0.29^*

* $p < 0.05$
[a] Scale: 1 = excellent health to 5 = very poor health
[b] Scale: 1 = yes; 2 = no

denced by greater fears of having to live in a nursing home and losing one's sight.

As one grows older and closer to the time of death, fear of the inevitable and yet unknown might be expected. It was interesting to find that "life ending" and "sudden death" were of relatively low concern for this group. It was surprising that although so many of the elderly had been robbed, it was the event of having been assaulted, not robbed, that correlated with total concern. Most probably the fear of bodily harm, which for this age group can have catastrophic consequences, caused this finding. In one study by Cook, Skogan, and Cook (1978), results showed that, although the elderly were attacked less frequently than other age groups, they were more likely to suffer injuries when attacked. Having to live in what has become a high-crime culture may make the event of robbery somewhat more commonplace.

The other event that correlated with total concern was having a close friend die. Having a family member die did not relate to total concern. There have been numerous studies that show that age-peer relationships fulfill many of the needs of the elderly (Arling, 1976). Losing a close friend can leave gaps that losing a family member might not do. In one study (Johnson, 1983) of 167 individuals aged 65 or older recently discharged from a hospital, over half of those in need of family supports while recuperating relied on an age-peer rather than a younger individual.

It was not surprising that the characteristics of poorer health and less education correlated with greater concerns. These factors have been shown to relate to stress in other research (Dohrenwend, 1973b). However, that the age, sex, income level, and marital status of the respondents did not relate to concerns was surprising and suggests that the elderly may be a unique group in terms of anticipated stressors. The high intercorrelations found for items on the concern scale point to the presence of a general anxiety state for the group as a whole.

Two characteristics that did relate to greater concerns and that may be distinct for the elderly were living with one's children and residing in the neighborhood for short periods of time. Perhaps not having as much access to networks of support in the neighborhood explains the latter finding. The importance of these networks for the elderly has been noted in previous research (Stein, Linn, and Stein, 1982). Living with one's children is a role reversal usually requiring compromises by both parties. It has been pointed out that although children are willing to care for their aging parent, they do so with ambivalence and conflict.

Whether the results of this study would be replicated with a more affluent, better-educated group of elderly is unknown. The results nonetheless do suggest goals for future research and treatment. One question needing further exploration is whether the extent or areas of concern relate to the current level of social functioning. For example, is someone with greater fear of being robbed more reclusive and thus potentially deteriorating in other areas of life? Also, could certain fears be modified by environmental manipulation? If it is known that newcomers to the neighborhood are more likely to feel stressed, would a "welcoming" program, perhaps initiated by the local senior center, alleviate some of the distress?

The results of this study show that the elderly poor in our sample had "moderate" pervasive fears, which were not necessarily concequences of life events that had occurred over the previous 6 months. Concerns seemed to be more reflective of a generalized level of anxiety about the future. Therefore, in attempting to measure stress in an elderly population, the recent-life-events approach may be of limited value. It may be more appropriate to measure perceived stress in terms of anticipated events or emotions.

REFERENCES

Arling, G. (1976), The elderly widow: Her family and friends. *J. Marr. & Fam.*, 38:737–746.

Cook, F. L., Skogan, W. G., & Cook, T. D. (1978), Criminal victimization of the elderly: The physical and economic consequences. *Gerontologist*, 18:338–346.

Dohrenwend, B. S. (1973a), Life events as stressors: A methodological inquiry. *J. Health & Soc. Behav.*, 14:167–220.

———— (1973b), Social status and stressful life events. *J. Persp. Soc. Psycho.*, 28:224–228.

———— Dohrenwend, B. P. (1978), Some issues in research on stressful life events. *J. Nerv. & Ment. Dis.*, 166:7–25.

Dressler, D. M., Donovan, J. M., & Geller, R. A. (1976), Life stress and emotional crisis: The idiosyncratic interpretation of life events. *Compr. Psychiat.*, 17:549–555.

Holmes, T. H., & Rahe, R. H. (1967), The Social Readjustment Rating Scale. *J. Psychosom. Res.*, 11:213–217.

Horowitz, M., Schaefer, C., & Hiroto, D. (1977), Life event questionnaires for measuring presumptive stress. *Psychosom. Med.*, 39:413–419.

Johnson, C. L. (1983), Dyadic family relations and social support. *Gerontologist*, 23:377–390.

Lazarus, R. S. (1976), The self-regulation of emotions. In: *Emotions—Their Parameters and Measurement*, ed. L. Levi. New York: Raven Press, pp. 47–56.

Rabkin, J. G., & Struening, E. L. (1976), Life events, stress, and illness. *Science*, 194:1013–1021.

Renner, V. J., & Birren, J. E. (1980), Stress: Physiological and psychological mechanisms. In: *Handbook of Mental Health and Aging*, ed. J. E. Birren & R. B. Stoane. Englewood Cliffs, NJ: Prentice-Hall, pp. 310–336.

Stein, S., Linn, M. W., & Stein, E. M. (1982), The relationship of self-help networks to physical and psychosocial functioning. *J. Amer. Geriat. Soc.*, 30:764–777.

Concluding Thoughts on Stressful Life Events

The health care delivery system has gained an increased awareness and significant interest in the psychology of health and how various components of health including stress have influenced our adaptational outcomes, our social functioning, and our quality of life. Considerable attention in the clinical research area has addressed stressful life events (Thoits, 1983) and the microstressors (Monroe, 1983), chronic role strains (Pearlin, 1983), and hassles of daily life (Lazarus, 1984). More recently, several researchers (Lazarus, Delonges, Folhman, and Gruen, 1985) have argued that stress lies not in the environmental input but in the person's appraisal of the relationship between the input and its demands and the person's agendas (e.g., beliefs, commitments, goals) and the capabilities of the individual to meet, mitigate, or alter these demands in the interest of well-being. Psychological stress must be recognized as a complex and multifactorial interactive variable. The clinician must explore the situational context that produces the perceptions and cognitions that result in "stressful" life events.

Theoretical formulations which address stressful life events raise for us a variety of questions and concerns. Some have argued (Dohrenwend, Dohrenwend, Dodson, and Shrout, 1984) that life stress events must be measured as pure environmental events uncontaminated by the perceptions, appraisals, or reactions that the individual experiences. Argued here is that known environmental stressors are experienced by vulnerable people whose personality make-up and ability to cope influence whether they will weather the experience of the life

759

stress event. Others (Lazarus, 1984) argue a relational approach to stress and encourage the consideration of widespread acceptance of the relational review of the disease itself as being an outcome of the organism's inability to deal with and cope with the measure and intensity of life stress events (Syme, 1984). Within this framework, stress is not defined as an environmental stimulus or an agent but rather is a relationship between stimulus and the vulnerability of the organism. A third approach addresses cognitive theories which involve the individual's perception, cognition and appraisal of the life stress experience. Lazarus et al. (1985) argue that the meaning and significance of stress is defined by a multiplicity of variables that are a component of the individual organism's appraisal of a relationship with the environment as relevant to one's physical and emotional well-being. These theoreticians further argue that the relationship and how it is appraised by the individual offer explanation of what we observe in the short-term and long-term effects of stressful life events on the organism. If we are to adopt this third model in describing the meaning and significance of stress and the environment, the term "environmentally induced stress" loses its significance because it is a person-environment relationship that is stressful or emotionally arousing. To verify such a theoretical position is to demand situational contexts that produce cognitive appraisals in the organism are unique and different for each personality and within the context of each environmental stressor. Efforts to examine individual differences within the context of personality characteristics and patterns of behavior within a multitude of life stress events appear to be the next significant step in mapping a clear picture of the relational effect between life stress events and emotional adjustment or maladjustment.

Several issues have emerged from the current state of life events study. With respect to the specificity of the measures and scales which have emerged, much work needs to be done to improve the sophistication of the measures. Few have applied the rigors of sound validity and reliability studies. Numerous measures which are published report only face validity and simplistic estimates of test-retest reliability. Efforts to apply more soundly developed statistical procedures including multivariate analysis or variance to parcel out significant differences especially with respect to mediating variables must be considered by future investigators. Multiple regression analysis to assess the predictive quality of the measures to be tested must be encouraged. Measures of the internal consistency of the instrument should be completed and reported along with factor analytic studies.

Other life events inventories have empirically relevant problems dealing specifically with the ambiguity, timing, and controllability of life events. Many of the unidimensional inventories generally have subjects rate events on a continuum defined a priori by the researcher and has come under criticism because the universe of life events is considerably more complex than a unidimensional total score might indicate. Researchers have addressed the problem of complexity and have designed an a priori class of events and clusters relating to economic factors, separation and/or death, interpersonal relations and life endangerment. Efforts such as this are an encouraging first step in considering the multiplicity and complexity of life stress events as precipitators of disease entities and the effort is valued as an improvement in the design and methodology of such inventories.

Neugarten (1979) has hypothesized underlying dimensions of life events and empirically investigated through factor analytic studies the structure of life-event scales. He has requested subjects to respond as to whether given events had happened to them within a certain time period. Studies such as these cluster events that tend to correlate with each other in actual occurrence. One must be cautious in the interpretation of such inventories, however, because covariance may well be unrelated to perceived stressfulness which is postulated as a crucial factor in disease onset and progression. One should not be discouraged however because multidimensional scaling techniques may well yield new and more empirically based multidimensional life stress event scales which could serve as a basis for hypothesizing specific events with specific outcomes.

With respect to scaling, several questions must be answered, including what life events are identifiable and ratable and are there mediating variables that have not been considered? All of this points to the necessity that life-event researchers first identify the onset of illness, the process of relapse, and map the pattern of disease. With this information, life events will assume significantly more impact when it is related to where in the course of illness the vents occur. The data must then be adjusted to an understanding of the psychological make-up and personality of the specific individual experiencing the illness and confronting the stressful life event.

There is a further consideration which deals with the definition of the universe to be scaled. Careful consideration must be given to the events listed in the life-event inventories for these must be events for which individuals in the study population would be at risk in the time span over which they are required to report. It is extremely difficult to conceptualize the universe of life events from a generalized perspective; furthermore, the inclusion of both desirable and undesirable events in the same measure has created some serious methodological concerns for researchers because undesirability rather than change factor appears to be more often associated with the gradients of change in health status.

There are other issues which address life events and their impact on measurement. Cultural bias can occur in the perception and response to life stress situations and some variables function as mediators for life events, including biological, psychological, social, and physical characteristics of the individual and the environment. There are large within- and between-person differences with respect to these variables. The better the individual's resources, the better the person is able to adapt to life events. Biological and intellectual variables set a lower limit on adaptation and they are necessary but not sufficient for adaptation. Finally there appears to be evidence that suggests virtually all stressful events over which subjects had any control were related to personality characteristics.

Finally, the timing of events and the clustering of events must be considered. Events may be particularly difficult when they cluster close together. Generally, adults adapt well to the occurrence of a single life event, as retirement, widowhood, departure of the last child from home, and illness but may demonstrate poorer adaptation when two or more events cluster. Several investigators have hypothesized that the individual's social support system may help moderate or buffer the effects of life events upon his or her psychological state. While the emergence of a buffering hypothesis suggests that individuals with a strong social support system should better cope with major life stresses, those with little or no social support may be more vulnerable to life changes, particularly undesirable ones and no efforts in the scaling process have begun to accommodate these particular issues. Certainly, these hypotheses concern an interaction effect, i.e., the occurrence of events in the presence of a social support system which should produce less stress than should the occurrence of events in the absence of social support systems. It becomes imperative that life-event studies involve an interactive measurement dimension if the life scaling process is to be understood and accurately researched.

Several methodological questions have come to the forefront of life-event research, the more notable of which include (1) the appropriate identification of events, (2) the degree of distress experienced, and (3) the measure of response of others to the impact of stressful life events on a subject population. Furthermore, the response to stressful life events must be examined from both a physiological perspective and from a social and cultural perspective. Some have contended that life stress analysis is supported more by faith than by specific evidence. The state of the science of life events remains in its infancy but the several efforts to date must be appreciated by the scientific community as efforts to identify and analyze a significant aspect of our growing understanding of the impact of life events on psychological and physical adjustment.

Another critical issue addresses the question of "how and why" well adjusted people deal with stressful life events and remain well adjusted in the process. Perhaps it should be viewed within the context that suggests the greater the life change, the more serious the occurrence of illness. Some studies completed contribute to the etiology and the onset of illness but systematic empirical study is necessary to assess idiographic components of the full range of psychologically adjusted persons as well as the multivariate treatment of stressful life events on each person in the range of stressful life events. A biopsychosocial approach to understanding stress, life events, and individual differences among human beings is clearly warranted from the research and several clinical studies which have emerged over the past two decades dealing with stressful life events.

It is realized that variables which may affect life events include socioeconomic status, income, and interpersonal support systems including family and friends. Supportive interpersonal relationships may serve as resources for the individual to the degree to which they provide physical, psychological, or financial support and the availability of these resources is likely to vary over the life span. Events such as marriage, divorce, birth of a child, and retirement can only yield unique responses affected by (1) the person's sociocultural world, including social structures (family social class and occupation and political affiliation), historic events such as war, and the economy; (2) the person's participation in this world, including both specific roles, such as husband, friend, worker, and parent, and the life events related to those roles, such as marriage, birth of a child, promotion, and retirement; and (3) aspects of the self including fantasies, moral values, talents, and skills.

Life events must also be explored further within the framework of interpersonal relations. Several researchers have focused on the issues in interpersonal qualities and various aspects of family or significant others interaction as a precipitator of stress. Miller (1981) has assessed the effects of communication style as a precipitator of relapse and developed a model of training family members and significant others in communicating so that expressed emotionality and verbal response style will be less influential in precipitating relapse or emotional breakdown. Stressful life events involving interactive patterns between family members or significant others must continue to be the focus for future research. While some prospective studies have questioned the significance of stressful life events as an antagonist for illness, there is growing evidence that certain individuals may have constitutional predispositions to illness which may be triggered by life stress. Should this be the case, the significant relationships reported in retrospective studies could be attributable to the accuracy of patient reporting or the sensitivity of the instruments used in collecting and classifying the data. It should not be a rationale for discounting stress as a precipitator of illness.

The work of Lazarus et al. (1985) has addressed a number of the confounding variables in understanding stressful life events. Argued is the fact that stress is an "unclean" variable because conceptually it depends on the interaction of two complex systems, the environment and the person, and it appears that the only way that this interlocking series of variables or systems can be separated for study is by addressing the temporal relationships cross-sectionally and mapping a pattern and style which will elucidate with some level of predictability but can be anticipated when given life stressors and personalities interact. There is a growing body of literature which assesses a relationship between major life events and psychological stress. Hyman and Woog (1982) have addressed carefully the assumption that stress, the organism's physiological and psychological response to life events, alters the organism's vulnerability and susceptibility and that this concept is a measurable dimension. Rabkin and Streuning (1976) have pointed to the fact that several of the life stress scales have emphasized events more often related to life happenings for people in young adulthood. This may well reflect the considerable level of life stress in early adulthood; however, the rationale from the existing studies is unclear. Issues such as this argue for the idiographic development of life events unique to different age range groups within the study population and encourages life-event scales be designed to address the entire life span development.

There is cause to be optimistic in understanding the role and function of life events in interpreting psychological adjustments; yet, those of us who continue to explore this area must be open to the possibility that stressful life events may be but extraneous variables. If we continue to focus *only* on generating lists of life events and apply them to various samples, we will have failed to recognize the important interchange which requires multivariate analysis of life events with locus of control, perceived self-esteem, state-trait anxiety, and numerous genetic, metabolic and biochemical measures. These adjacent areas *are* in the larger scope of successfully assessing and understanding stressful life events.

REFERENCES

Dohrenwend, B. S., Dohrenwend, B. P., Dodson, M., & Shrout, P. E. (1984), Symptoms, hassles, social supports and life events: The problem of confounded measures. *J. Abnorm. Psychol.*, 93:222–230.

Hyman, R. B., & Woog, P. (1982), Stressful life events and illness onset. *Res. in Nurs. & Health*, 5:155–163.

Lazarus, R. S. (1984), Puzzles in the study of daily hassles. *J. Behav. Med.*, 7:375–389.

———— DeLonges, A., Folhman, S., & Gruen, R. (1985), Stress and adaptational outcomes. *Amer. Psychol.*, 40/7:770–779.

Miller, T. W. (1981), Training schizophrenics and their families to communicate: A behavioral model. *Hosp. & Commun. Psychiat.*, 32/12:870–871.

Monroe, S. M. (1983), Major and minor life events as predictors of psychological distress: Further issues and findings. *J. Behav. Med.*, 6:189–205.

Neugarten, B. L. (1979), Time and the life cycle. *Amer. J. Psychiat.*, 136:887–893.

Pearlin, L. I. (1983), Role strains and personal stress. In: *Psychosocial Stress: Trends in Theory and Research*, ed. H. B. Kaplan. New York: Academic Press.

Rabkin, J. G., & Streuning, E. L. (1976), Life events, stress, and illness. *Science*, 194:1013–1020.

Syme, S. L. (1984), Sociocultural factors and disease etiology. In: *The Handbook of Behavioral Medicine*, ed. D. W. Gentry. New York: Guilford, pp. 13–37.

Thoits, P. A. (1983), Reconceptualizing mental illness: Deviations in feeling and expression. Paper presented at the meeting of the American Psychological Association, Anaheim, CA, August 1983.

Name Index

Abraham, K., 485, 496
Abram, H. S., 294, 298, 304
Abrams, R., 499, 504, 506
Acosta, F. X., 530, 549
Adams, J. E., 44, 46, 117, 118, 467
Adamson, J. D., 62, 85
Addell, J. M., 551
Adebimpe, V. R., 526, 550
Ader, R., 92, 99
Adler, D., 78, 85
Ainsworth, M., 646, 654, 656
Aitchison, R., 461, 467
Albee, G. W., 25, 27
Aldous, J., 21, 28, 725
Alexander, J., 481, 483
Alexander, M. S., 483
Alfert, E., 443, 466
Alkire, A., 433, 464
Allain, A. N., 543, 552
Allen, G. J., 182, 183, 194
Alpert, R., 183, 194
Altman, J., 646, 656
Ambonetti, A., 150, 161
Anderson, E. A., 606, 697
Anderson, M. B., 695
Anderson, M. P., 677
Andrews, G., 45, 46, 51, 85, 118, 119, 165,
    166, 168, 174, 177, 178, 212, 223,
    224, 225, 229, 234, 235, 258, 265,
    266, 270, 329, 346, 440, 462, 486,
    497, 610, 617
Angst, J., 497
Anson, O., 185, 194
Antelman, S. M., 238, 255
Anthony, E. J., 675
Antonovsky, A., 33, 43, 46, 57, 58, 72, 85,
    107, 119, 486, 497
Antonucci, T. C., 14, 15, 24, 28
Appley, M. H., 347
Archer, D., 556, 570
Archer, R. P., 543, 552
Archibald, H. C., 588, 599
Argyle, M., 447, 470
Arieti, S., 571

Arling, G., 756, 757
Arnold, M., 466
Arthur, A. Z., 422, 462
Arthur, R. J., 8, 10, 36, 48, 109, 121, 396,
    439, 441, 455, 459, 460, 469
Askenasy, A. R., 33, 47, 56, 86, 106, 119,
    129, 144, 145, 247, 254, 410, 463,
    504, 505
Asnes, R. S., 634, 641
Astrachan, B. M., 78, 85
Atchley, R. C., 13, 27
Atkins, H. G., 528, 551
Atkinson, B., 519, 522
Auerbach, S. M., 183, 195
Averill, J. R., 92, 99, 441, 466
Ayd, F. J., 594, 599
Ayer, W. A., 643, 656
Azima, H., 315

Babigian, H. M., 88, 348
Bachrach, L. L., 665, 672
Bahr, S. J., 662, 663, 666, 672
Baker, H., 298, 305
Baldessarini, R. J., 591, 594, 598, 599
Bale, R. M., 183, 194
Balter, M. D., 74, 88, 331, 348
Baltes, F., 27
Baltes, M., 28
Baltes, P. B., 16, 17, 27, 47, 49, 119
Bane, M. J., 660, 671, 673
Banton, M., 297, 304
Barbero, G. I., 640, 642
Barclay, R., 466
Bardwick, J. M., 716, 722, 726
Barehha, R., 62, 87
Bargmann, R. A., 240, 251
Barnes, H., 710
Barnett, R. C., 218, 719, 720, 726
Barrera, B., 271, 280
Barrett, J. E., 47, 221, 373, 463, 497
Bart, P., 19, 27
Baruch, G. K., 719, 720, 726
Baruch, R., 716, 726
Bateson, G., 424, 462

Battegay, R., 294, 305
Baughman, R., 308, 314, 315
Baum, A., 99, 664, 665, 673
Baum, C. S., 673
Bausell, R. B., 104, 197, 206
Beautrais, A. L., 609, 610, 611, 616, 618, 619, 621, 622, 630, 632, 634, 641
Bebbington, P., 82, 83, 85, 124, 126, 178, 739, 747
Bech, J., 128, 145
Beck, A. T., 562, 563, 570
Beck, J. C., 53, 76, 85, 339, 346, 366, 373, 417, 443, 462
Becker, G., 701, 709
Beech, H. R., 482
Beels, C., 451, 453, 462
Bell, W., 525
Bellack, A. S., 247, 255, 449, 462, 465
Belloc, N. B., 197, 206
Belza, M., 518, 573
Bemporad, J. R., 634, 641
Bendig, A. W., 185, 194
Bengtson, V. L., 18, 22, 27, 714, 726
Benjaminsen, S., 610, 618
Bennett, J. W., 110, 121
Bennett, L., 7, 10, 140, 146, 197, 206
Bergan, C., 110, 121
Berger, D., 452, 470
Berger, P. L., 25, 27, 284, 304
Bergson, H., 299, 304
Bergum, K., 272, 280
Berkowitz, H., 711, 712, 716, 717, 727
Berkowitz, R., 430, 431, 466, 470
Berman, M. A., 640, 641
Berman, W. H., 659, 670, 671, 673
Bernard, C., 6
Bernardes, J. F., 220, 222
Bernstein, J., 185, 194
Berto, F., 215
Beumont, P. J. V., 253
Bielski, R. J., 593, 599
Billings, A. G., 318, 323, 445, 468, 649, 656
Binik, Y. M., 288, 291, 293, 294, 295, 304
Birley, J. L. T., 33, 38, 45, 46, 57, 59, 60, 63, 66, 67, 68, 69, 70, 71, 72, 73, 74, 75, 76, 80, 81, 83, 85, 89, 107, 115, 119, 128, 131, 139, 145, 177, 178, 227, 233, 331, 341, 343, 344, 346, 355, 357, 358, 359, 362, 364, 365, 366, 367, 368, 369, 371, 373, 377, 378, 379, 380, 381, 383, 388, 391, 398, 399, 401, 403, 405, 406, 407,

408, 409, 414, 419, 462, 474, 481, 482
Birnbaum, J., 726
Birren, G., 27
Birren, J. E., 749, 758
Bixler, E. O., 257, 269
Black, A., 474, 482
Black, G. M., 232, 234
Black, J., 525
Black, O., 18, 27
Blanchard, E. B., 449, 464
Bleuler, D., 395, 462
Bleuler, M., 333, 346, 360, 366, 373, 394, 462
Bloch, A. M., 677, 695
Block, P. C., 233, 234
Bloom, B. L., 664, 665, 673
Bloom, F., 248, 254
Bloom, K. L., 717, 726
Blow, F. C., 2, 13
Blumenthal, D. L., 308, 314, 315
Blumenthal, J. A., 232, 234
Blumenthal, M. D., 169, 178
Blumer, D., 295, 304
Blundell, J. E., 249, 255
Bohannon, M. W., 111, 121
Bombardelli, S., 215
Booth, G. V., 670, 673
Borrow, M. G., 633, 641
Borup, J. H., 730, 746
Borus, J. F., 519, 523
Botkin, A., 185, 195
Botwinick, J., 712, 726
Boulanger, G., 527, 551
Boulton, D. M., 612, 618, 623, 632
Bowers, M. B., 422, 462
Bowlby, J., 14, 27
Box, G. E. P., 253
Boyce, W. T., 641
Boyd, J. L., 432, 464
Brady, J. V., 92, 99
Brantley, P. J., 543, 552
Breger, L., 257, 269
Brende, J. O., 556, 570
Brenner, J. I., 640, 641
Breslow, L., 197, 206
Bretches, P., 298, 306
Bretherton, I., 646, 654, 656
Breznitz, S., 468
Bridges, P., 473, 482
Bright, R. D., 308, 315
Brim, C. R., 28
Brim, O. G., 18, 27
Brim, O. G., Jr., 47, 49, 119

Brim, O. J., 719, 726
Briscoe, C. W., 664, 665, 673
Brockington, I. F., 488, 497
Brodie, H. K. H., 593, 594, 596, 599, 600, 601
Broen, W. W., 335, 346
Brown, D. E., 553
Brown, D. E., Jr., 571
Brown, G. W., 33, 38, 45, 46, 51, 52, 56, 57, 58, 59, 60, 61, 63, 66, 67, 68, 69, 70, 71, 72, 74, 75, 76, 77, 80, 81, 83, 85, 89, 107, 115, 119, 123, 124, 125, 126, 128, 131, 137, 139, 145, 149, 150, 160, 177, 178, 197, 206, 216, 221, 227, 233, 284, 304, 310, 315, 331, 332, 336, 341, 343, 344, 346, 352, 353, 355, 357, 358, 359, 362, 364, 365, 366, 367, 368, 369, 371, 373, 377, 378, 379, 380, 381, 383, 386, 387, 388, 389, 391, 398, 399, 401, 403, 405, 406, 408, 409, 414, 419, 420, 421, 425, 426, 427, 429, 430, 453, 457, 462, 469, 473, 481, 482, 508, 510, 513, 515, 610, 618, 735, 746
Brown, L. L., 249, 254
Brown, M. B., 614, 618
Bruder, G., 185, 194
Brunner, F., 294, 305
Brunson, B. I., 3, 91
Bryant, B., 447, 470
Bryant, T. E., 25, 28
Bubkoz, M. M. J., 19, 28
Buchbinder, J. T., 556, 564, 567, 568, 570, 571
Bucky, S. F., 183, 194
Burgess, E., 701, 709
Burke, R., 701, 709
Burroughs, J., 237, 255
Burry, J. A., 606, 677, 680, 694, 695
Burvill, J., 583, 585
Busch, J. C., 720, 727
Bush, J. P., 605, 643, 644, 645, 646, 649, 656, 657
Buszta, C., 293, 305
Butcher, J. N., 550
Byrne, D. G., 103, 165, 166, 169, 174, 176, 178, 210, 215, 221, 223, 224, 225, 226, 227, 230, 232, 234

Caddell, J. L., 562, 571
Cagahn, S. B., 633, 641
Calsyn, D. A., 300, 304

Camara, K. A., 660, 673
Cameron, P., 714, 726
Campbell, A., 704, 709
Campbell, D. T., 537, 550
Campbell, S., 606, 711
Cancro, R., 373, 465
Cannon, W. B., 6
Caplan, G., 374, 451, 463
Card, J. J., 527, 550
Cardenas, D. D., 292, 293, 294, 296, 300, 302, 304, 306
Carducci, B., 3, 91
Carlson, R., 21, 28
Carman, W. J., 197, 206
Carpenter, W. T., Jr., 363, 370, 374, 375, 444, 467
Carroll, E. M., 537, 550
Carstairs, G. M., 426, 462, 463
Casey, R. L., 140, 145
Casper, R. C., 237, 246, 253
Cassell, J. C., 14, 29, 641
Cassem, N. H., 444, 465
Casteneda, A., 185, 194
Casto, R. F., 670, 675
Cattell, R. B., 181, 194, 308, 314
Cauble, E., 607
Cavanaugh, G., 677, 696
Cavenar, J. O., 587, 589, 598, 600, 601
Ceckon, D. J., 677, 696
Cernovsky, Z. Z., 211, 257
Chamberlain, G., 271, 279
Chamberlin, K., 257, 269
Chan, R., 92, 99
Chandler, M., 337, 348
Charles, H. L., 528, 551
Chaudhry, L., 290, 305
Check, J. H., 277, 279
Cheng, L., 583, 585
Chesney, M., 232, 234
Chiriboga, D. A., 32, 37, 46, 664, 665, 673
Christenson, R. N., 588, 600
Chyatte, H., 298, 306
Cicchetti, D., 481, 483
Citler, L., 46
Clancy, J., 145, 417, 463
Clark, M., 15, 28
Clausen, J. A., 361, 373
Claussen, J., 718, 726
Clayton, P. J., 463, 505
Cleary, P. J., 51, 85
Clifton, R. K., 93, 99
Cloward, R. A., 528, 550
Coates, T. J., 677, 680, 696

Cobb, S., 183, 195, 197, 206, 451, 463
Cochrane, R., 150, 160
Cockrell, C. S., 605, 643
Coddington, R. D., 35, 36, 46, 109, 119, 211, 239, 243, 244, 253
Coelho, G., 468
Coelho, G. B., 46
Coelho, G. V., 118
Coffman, T. L., 731, 746
Cohen, B. D., 449, 463
Cohen, C., 452, 454, 467, 470
Cohen, D., 674, 680, 696
Cohen, H., 257, 269
Cohen, J., 696
Cohen, M. S., 481, 483
Cohen, R., 28
Cohen, R. M., 248, 255
Cohen, S., 93, 99
Cohler, 28
Cole, J. O., 220, 222
Collins, G., 570
Comstock, G. W., 132, 145, 165, 178
Connoly, J., 215, 221
Converse, P., 704, 709
Cook, F. L., 756, 758
Cook, T. D., 756, 758
Coons, H., 337, 344, 345, 348, 396, 409, 410, 418, 423, 470
Cooper, B., 353, 373
Cooper, J., 63, 89, 509, 515
Cooper, J. E., 129, 147, 357, 375, 379, 391, 427, 471
Copeland, J. R., 216, 221, 310, 315
Copley, J. B., 301, 305
Coppen, A., 272, 279
Corcoran, J. F. T., 560, 563, 570
Corfini, A., 215
Cornelison, A. R., 424, 467
Cornfield, R. B., 590, 591, 600
Costa, P. T., Jr., 46, 117, 119
Cottrell, L., Jr., 701, 709
Cowen, P. J., 475, 482
Cowie, V., 482, 483
Cox, B., 661
Cox, M., 659, 660, 661, 673, 674
Cox, R., 659, 660, 673, 674
Cox, T., 679, 696
Coyne, J., 282, 304
Crammond, W. A., 300, 301, 304
Crandall, J. E., 258, 269
Cromwell, R. L., 347, 463, 465, 469, 471
Cronbach, L. J., 622, 632
Cronkite, R. C., 318, 323
Crowder, J., 452, 468
Crowe, R., 145, 417, 463
Crumpton, E., 413, 470
Cuellar, J. B., 714, 726

Cunningham, W., 678, 696
Curran, J. P., 467, 471
Cutler, L., 37
Cutting, J. C., 475, 482
Czaczkes, J. W., 300, 305

D'Abrera, H. J. M., 133, 146
Dahlstrom, L. E., 532, 550
Dahlstrom, W. G., 528, 529, 532, 550
D'Amato, M. E., 91, 99
Damrosch, S. P., 104, 197
Daniels, G. E., 272, 280
Danish, S. J., 15, 25, 28
Datan, N., 47, 120
David, W. G., 119
Davies, L., 102, 123
Davin, T., 291, 305
Davis, G. C., 723, 727
Davis, J. M., 237, 253
Davis, W. G., 37, 47, 110
Dawson, M. E., 448, 455, 463, 468
Day, J., 424, 471
Day, R., 2, 51
Deale, R., 519, 522
Dean, A., 268, 269
Dean, H., 664, 673
De Andrade, J. R., 293, 304
DeCarlo, R. J., 724, 726
DeFazio, S., 554, 570
DeFrancisco, D., 452, 468
Dekirmenjian, H., 250, 254
De Kloet, E. R., 249, 255
De Konick, J. M., 257, 269
D'Elia, G., 488, 497
DeLong, W. B., 62, 86, 137, 145
DeLonges, A., 759, 766
Delvecchio Good, M. J., 284, 291, 305
Dembrowski, T. M., 234
Demone, H. W., 665, 675
Dempsey, G., 84, 88
Dempster-McClain, D., 699, 709
Depue, R. A., 252, 253, 255
Der, D., 296, 305
Descartes, R., 1, 5
Dessaursmith, J., 505
Deutsch, M., 662, 669, 673, 674
Devins, G. M., 288, 304
DeVito, A. J., 104, 181, 183, 186, 187, 194
Diamond, A., 554, 570
Diamond, S. R., 272, 279
Dienelt, M. N., 8, 10, 146, 149, 161, 338, 347, 481, 483
Diesenhaus, H., 182, 196
DiMascio, A., 255
Dimsdale, J. E., 233, 234
Dixon, R. A., 23, 28

Dixon, W. J., 614, 618
Doane, J., 431, 432, 434, 435, 436, 437, 463, 470
Docherty, J. P., 336, 346
Dodson, M., 759, 766
Dohrenwend, B. P., 29, 33, 38, 39, 43, 45, 47, 48, 51, 53, 56, 58, 80, 85, 86, 87, 106, 107, 119, 120, 128, 129, 137, 144, 145, 146, 147, 160, 178, 197, 206, 221, 222, 247, 254, 258, 269, 270, 326, 329, 344, 346, 348, 351, 353, 360, 364, 373, 374, 375, 391, 402, 406, 407, 410, 415, 418, 419, 463, 467, 497, 504, 505, 506, 546, 550, 749, 758, 759, 766
Dohrenwend, B. S., 29, 33, 43, 45, 47, 48, 51, 56, 58, 80, 86, 87, 106, 107, 112, 114, 119, 120, 128, 129, 144, 145, 146, 147, 160, 178, 197, 206, 221, 222, 247, 254, 258, 269, 270, 348, 353, 373, 374, 375, 391, 406, 410, 414, 463, 467, 497, 504, 505, 506, 546, 550, 673, 749, 756, 758, 759, 766
Dolan, M. P., 528, 551, 552
Donnellan, J., 551
Donovan, J. M., 227, 234, 339, 346, 750, 758
Doob, A. N., 92, 99
Dorsett, D., 525
Dressler, D. M., 227, 234, 750, 758
Dressler, L. M., 339, 346
Drevenstedt, J., 714, 726
Drew, F. L., 271, 279
Driscoll, J. M., 91, 92, 99
Dumas, 117
Dumas, M. A., 48, 120
Duncan-Jones, P., 131, 147, 166, 169, 170, 178, 179, 224, 234
Dunham, H. W., 365, 373
Dunleavy, D. L. F., 591, 600
Dunner, D. L., 272, 279, 504, 505
Durell, J., 54, 55, 88, 401, 470
Durkheim, E., 15, 28
Dwinnell, J., 665, 675
D'Zurilla, T. J., 447, 464

Eaton, W. W., 166, 177, 178
Ebel, D. M., 662, 663, 673
Eberly, R., 317
Ebling, F. J. G., 309, 316
Ebra, G., 296, 302, 305
Eckert, E. D., 237, 238, 253, 255
Edwards, A. E., 296, 305

Edwards, D. W., 42, 48, 146, 176, 179, 220, 222, 258, 270
Edwards, J. N., 713, 726
Egendorf, A., 526, 542, 548, 550
Egri, G., 326, 329, 344, 346, 351, 414, 419, 463
Eichhorn, R. L., 19, 28
Eisdorfer, C., 674, 696
Eisemann, M., 491, 498
Eisemberg, J. G., 220, 221
Eisenberg, L., 305
Eisler, R. M., 62, 86, 145, 417, 449, 464
Elder, G. H., Jr., 18, 28, 106, 119
Eliasson, M., 335, 347
Elkind, M. A., 104, 181
Emms, E. M., 217, 222
Endicott, J., 79, 84, 88, 474, 483
Engdahl, B., 317
Engel, G. L., 313, 315
Engelman, L., 614, 618
Epstein, S., 93, 99
Erdman, R., 43, 48, 117, 120
Erichsen, K., 302, 305
Erikson, E. H., 29
Eriksson, U., 491, 498
Escobar, J., 452, 453, 469
Evans, J. R., 433, 464
Evans, L. A., 530, 550
Eysenck, H. J., 230, 234
Eysenck, S. B. G., 230, 234

Faergeman, P. M., 83, 86
Faia, C., 443, 469
Fair, P., 298, 306
Fairbank, J. A., 537, 550
Fairbanks, D. T., 504, 505
Falloon, I. R. H., 407, 418, 428, 431, 432, 461, 464, 467, 471
Faravelli, D., 150, 161
Farber, E. M., 307, 308, 315
Farina, A., 368, 373
Farmer, R., 126, 161
Fava, G. A., 213, 217, 221, 309
Feibelman, N. D., 518, 553
Feighner, J. P., 84, 86, 340, 346, 487, 497, 500, 505
Ferguson, S., 272, 280, 623
Fergusson, D. M., 604, 609, 610, 618, 619, 620, 621, 630, 632, 634, 641
Ferman, L. A., 195
Field, S., 79, 86
Fields, L. G., 296, 305

Fiere, R. R., 272, 279
Fieve, R. R., 504, 505
Figley, C. R., 374, 519, 521, 523, 527, 536, 550, 551, 566, 567, 570, 571
Filsinger, E., 709
Fimian, M. J., 677, 678, 694, 696
Finch, A. J., 183, 195
Fine, S., 634, 642
Finkelman, J. M., 93, 99
Finney, J. W., 318, 323
Fisher, C., 591, 600
Fisher, D., 92, 99
Fisher, E., 454, 467
Fisher, M., 308, 315
Fisher, S., 272, 280
Fitts, W. H., 445, 464
Fitzgerald, R., 584, 585
Fleck, S., 424, 467
Fleiss, J. L., 125, 126
Fleming, R. H., 553, 571
Fletcher, J., 217, 222
Floderus, B., 166, 179
Floistad, R. L., 110, 121
Fogel, J., 28
Folhman, S., 759, 766
Folkman, S., 318, 323
Foner, A., 726
Fontana, A. F., 342, 346, 358, 373, 406, 407, 411, 412, 464
Foote, N., 21, 28
Fornasa, C. V., 307
Fox, J. H., 725, 726
Foy, D. W., 537, 544, 546, 550
Frank, C., 463
Frank, J. D., 368, 373
Fray, P. J., 238, 251, 252, 255
Frazier, H., 452, 468
Freedman, A. M., 120, 506
Freeman, A., 466
Freeman, C. W., 300, 304
Freeman, D., 425, 426, 464
Freeman, D. H., 614, 618
Freeman, W., 428, 471
Freud, S., 485, 497, 587, 600
Freyberger, H., 309, 316
Frey-Wouters, E., 527, 551
Friedel, R. D., 593, 599
Friedman, E. A., 290, 305
Friedman, M. M., 573, 585
Friedman, S. B., 9, 11, 92, 99, 640, 642
Froland, C., 451, 469
Fromm-Reichmann, F., 424, 464
Furedy, J. J., 92, 99

Gaind, R., 68, 86, 87, 128, 146, 358, 374, 377, 391, 399, 466
Gal, R., 446, 464
Galanter, E. H., 339, 348
Gale, E. N., 643, 656
Gallops, M. S., 527, 551
Gannon, L., 272, 279
Gansereit, K., 405, 468
Garber, J., 250, 251, 254
Garcia, A. M., 504, 505
Garcia, R., 497
Garfinkel, H., 60, 86
Garfinkel, P. E., 237, 246, 254
Garmezy, N., 343, 347, 360, 373
Garner, D. M., 237, 251, 254
Garner, R., 556, 570
Garrison, V., 452, 464
Garrity, I. F., 486, 497
Gaskin, F., 664, 673
Gastrof, J. W., 221, 222
Geiger, J., 452, 470
Gelenberg, A. J., 583, 585
Geller, R. A., 227, 234, 339, 346, 750, 758
Gentry, D. W., 766
George, G. C. W., 253
Georgopoulos, B. S., 306
Gerst, M. S., 145, 168, 178, 225, 234, 442, 465, 664, 673
Gersten, J. C., 220, 221
Giambra, L. M., 715, 726
Gift, T. E., 71, 86, 402, 409, 464, 465
Gigandet, J., 526, 550
Gilderman, A. M., 432, 464
Gillin, J. D., 264, 270
Ginsberg, L., 47, 120
Gittelman, R., 592, 600
Glaser, R., 550
Glasner, B., 505
Glass, D. C., 93, 99
Glassner, B., 328, 499, 501
Glenn, N. D., 664, 673
Goktepe, E. L., 473, 482
Goldberg, D. P., 165, 166, 169, 178
Goldberg, E. L., 132, 145
Goldberg, S. C., 237, 253, 368, 374, 400, 401, 413, 447, 464, 465
Goldberger, J., 468
Goldbourt, U., 453, 468
Goldfried, M. R., 447, 464
Goldsmith, L. A., 308, 314, 315
Goldstein, M., 433, 434, 435, 436, 437, 458, 463, 464, 467, 470
Goldthorpe, J. H., 216, 221, 310, 315

Gomez, J., 74, 88, 310, 316, 507, 515
Good, B., 284, 291, 305
Goode, D. J., 250, 254
Goodenough, D. R., 257, 269
Goodman, B. W., 639, 640, 642
Goodstein, L. D., 25, 28
Goodwin, N. J., 290, 305
Gordus, J. P., 195
Gorsuch, R. C., 182, 196
Gorusch, R. L., 649, 657
Gottesman, I. I., 352, 373, 393, 465, 470
Gould, E., 433, 464
Gould, M. S., 353, 373, 374, 467
Graffam, S. R., 114, 119
Graham, F. K., 93, 99
Graham, P., 63, 89
Grandison, L., 248, 254
Grant, I., 139, 145, 147, 168, 174, 178, 225, 234, 442, 465, 664, 673, 735, 747
Gray, H. L., 293, 298, 300, 301, 302, 303, 305, 306
Green, S. B., 541, 542, 548, 550
Greenbaum, P., 645, 656
Greenberg, M. T., 646, 654, 656
Greene, J. W., 605, 633
Greenhill, L., 438, 471
Greer, J. G., 677, 679, 696
Gregory, B., 272, 279
Grene, M., 306
Gretton, M. E., 619
Grinker, R., 402, 465
Grinker, R. P., 587, 589, 590, 600
Grinker, R. R., 257, 269
Grinspoon, L., 467
Griscom, H., 600
Groh, T., 368, 373
Gross, E., 633, 642
Gruen, R., 759, 766
Gruenberg, E. M., 351, 374
Guidotti, A., 248, 254
Guillemin, R., 248, 254
Gulledge, A. D., 293, 294, 301, 305
Gumenik, W. E., 91, 99
Gunderson, E. K. E., 36, 48, 109, 121, 140, 146, 222, 483
Gunderson, H., 235
Gurin, G., 79, 86
Gutman, D., 302,. 715, 722, 723, 725, 726
Gutman, R. A., 298, 301, 305
Guze, B. B., 487, 497, 500, 505
Guze, S., 84, 86, 340, 346
Gynther, M. D., 528, 529, 541, 542, 548, 550

Haber, R. N., 183, 194
Hackett, T. P., 233, 234, 444, 465
Haenel, T., 294, 305
Haertzen, C. A., 543, 550
Hagestad, G. O., 17, 18, 21, 22, 23, 26, 28
Haldipur, C. V., 328, 499, 501, 505
Haley, J., 424, 462
Halmi, K. A., 237, 253
Hamburg, D. H., 468
Hamilton, V., 269
Hammer, H. M., 220, 222
Hammer, M., 453, 465
Hammond, W. A., 587, 600
Hansen, D. N., 185, 195, 196
Hard, R. D., 498
Harder, D. W., 71, 86, 337, 348, 402, 403, 405, 406, 409, 419, 459, 464, 465
Hare, R. D., 92, 99
Harmon, D. K., 145
Harrington, R. G., 606, 677, 680, 695, 696
Harris, E., 526, 550
Harris, R., 730, 747
Harris, T. O., 51, 52, 56, 58, 59, 63, 77, 85, 123, 124, 126, 137, 145, 149, 177, 178, 216, 221, 227, 233, 310, 315, 332, 344, 346, 352, 373, 377, 389, 391, 598, 453, 462, 473, 481, 482, 508, 510, 513, 515, 610, 618, 735, 746
Harrow, M., 78, 85
Hassener, P. W., 523
Hatfield, W., 28
Haven, C., 14, 29
Havlicek, L. L., 262, 269
Hawk, A. B., 363, 374
Hawkins, D., 6
Hawkins, N. G., 37, 47, 110, 119
Hayghe, H., 698, 699
Hays, P., 499, 505
Healey, E. S., 257, 258, 267, 269
Hebb, D. O., 183, 194
Hedenberg, A. D., 302, 305
Hedl, J. J., Jr., 184, 194
Heilbronn, M., 295, 304
Heinrich, D. L., 185, 193, 195
Heinroth, 395
Hellerstein, H. K., 465
Henderson, A. S., 131, 166, 168, 169, 178, 224, 229, 230, 234
Henderson, J. M., 519, 522
Henderson, S., 147, 179
Hendricks, C. D., 717, 726, 727, 728
Hendricks, J., 717, 726, 727, 728
Hendrie, H. C., 610, 618

Herman, C. P., 232, 251, 254, 255
Herman, M. S., 662, 673
Herman, S., 234
Herr, M., 584, 585
Hersen, M., 247, 255, 449, 464, 465
Herz, M. I., 45, 47
Hess, J. L., 528, 552
Hess, R. D., 660, 673
Hetherington, E. M., 659, 660, 661, 670, 671, 673, 674
Hewson, D. M., 45, 46, 486, 497
Hickson, G., 605, 633
Hill, H. E., 543, 550
Hill, O. W., 316
Hill, R., 19, 21, 22, 28, 212, 297, 303, 305
Himmelhoch, J. M., 247, 255
Hinkel, L. E., 58, 86
Hiroto, D., 139, 145, 758
Hirsch, S. R., 68, 86, 87, 126, 128, 146, 161, 358, 374, 377, 391, 599, 424, 434, 465, 466
Hobfoll, S. E., 185, 194
Hoch, H., 99
Hocking, F., 53, 86
Hodges, W. F., 664, 673
Hofer, M. A., 9, 11
Hogarty, G. E., 368, 374, 400, 413, 420, 464, 465
Hogben, G. L., 590, 591, 600
Hohn, R. L., 182, 195
Hoiberg, A., 521, 523
Hollingshead, A. B., 239, 254
Holmes, T. H., 6, 7, 10, 32, 33, 34, 37, 44, 45, 47, 48, 51, 56, 57, 58, 60, 72, 86, 106, 107, 108, 110, 111, 119, 123, 124, 126, 140, 145, 146, 149, 161, 165, 166, 178, 179, 197, 207, 209, 212, 224, 225, 234, 258, 269, 272, 280, 308, 315, 338, 347, 390, 391, 395, 402, 407, 408, 409, 415, 441, 465, 501, 504, 505, 507, 508, 515, 611, 618, 619, 622, 632, 736, 746, 747, 750, 758
Homans, G. C., 15, 28
Hood, J., 251, 254
Hooke, J. F., 183, 195
Hope, K., 216, 221, 310, 315
Hor, L., 248, 254
Horito, 749
Horner, M. S., 719, 722, 726
Horowitz, M. J., 139, 145, 268, 269, 519, 523, 553, 555, 571, 779, 758
Horsley, J. S., 589, 600

Horwood, L. J., 604, 609, 619, 632
Hough, R. L., 33, 40, 47, 107, 113, 114, 119, 504, 505
House, J., 197, 206
Houston, B. K., 185, 195
Huberman, S. J., 331, 348
Hudgens, R. W., 32, 47, 58, 60, 62, 86, 87, 106, 119, 137, 145, 352, 353, 369, 374, 504, 505
Hudson, J. I., 246, 254
Hugi, R., 412, 467
Hultsch, D. R., 37, 47
Hummel, L., 583, 585
Humphries, H., 532, 551
Hunter, I., 257, 269
Hunter, K., 730, 747
Hurry, J., 124, 126, 739, 747
Hurst, M. W., 42, 45, 47, 74, 87, 140, 146, 169, 178
Hutchinson, T. A., 289, 305
Hutter, A. M., 233, 234
Huxley, P., 169, 178
Hyerstay, B. J., 300, 304
Hyman, R. B., 41, 47, 765, 766
Hynes, W. J., 670, 674

Ilfeld, F., 446, 465
Ingham, J. G., 150, 161, 165, 175, 179
Ingram, I. M., 473, 481, 482
Insel, P. M., 532, 551
Irving, H. H., 669, 674
Isaacs, A., 63, 89

Jablensky, A., 363, 375
Jackson, D. D., 424, 462
Jackson, S. E., 677, 678, 680, 694, 696
Jacobs, M. A., 197, 207
Jacobs, S. C., 51, 71, 72, 73, 74, 75, 77, 79, 80, 81, 83, 86, 87, 131, 145, 342, 343, 347, 355, 357, 365, 366, 369, 371, 374, 383, 388, 391, 405, 408, 409, 410, 411, 417, 465
Jacobsen, G. F., 665, 674
Jacobson, L., 486, 491
Jacobsson, J., 498
Jacobsson, L., 498
Jaffe, N., 662, 674
Jaffe, Y., 463
James, B., 215, 222
James, N. M., 499, 505
Janowsky, D. S., 248, 255
Jay, L. L., 607, 729

Jeger, A., 466
Jekyl, J. F., 614, 618
Jenkins, C. D., 47, 74, 87, 140, 142, 146, 169, 178, 215, 216, 220, 221, 233, 234
Jenkins, R., 475, 482
Jensen, E. W., 641
Jick, T., 662, 674
Johnsen, E. P., 182, 195
Johnson, C., 238, 252
Johnson, C. L., 254, 756, 758
Johnson, D. R., 258, 270
Johnson, J., 726
Johnson, J. H., 150, 161, 229, 234, 268, 269, 270, 272, 280, 636, 640, 642
Johnson, J. P., 301, 305
Johnson, O. G., 674
Jonas, J. M., 246, 254, 583, 585
Jones, B., 583, 585
Jones, F. D., 517, 519, 521, 523
Jones, J., 463
Jones, S., 428, 434, 471
Jones, T., 464
Judd, L., 433, 464
Jung, C., 395, 465
Junge, 715, 716

Kadushin, C., 527, 551
Kagay, M., 206, 207
Kahn, 421
Kahn, R. L., 14, 15, 24, 28
Kahn, S., 197, 206
Kaij, L., 343, 347
Kales, A., 257, 269
Kalin, N. H., 248, 255
Kalish, J. R., 28
Kallstrom, D. W., 182, 195
Kaloupek, D. G., 546, 551, 568, 569, 571
Kalter, N., 661, 674
Kalucy, R., 583, 585
Kalz, F., 315
Kamarovsky, M., 700, 709
Kaplan, B., 14, 29
Kaplan, H., 466
Kaplan, H. B., 222, 766
Kaplan, H. I., 120, 506
Kaplan-DeNour, A., 300, 302, 305
Kapur, R., 83, 87
Kardiner, A., 557, 571, 588, 600
Kasanin, J., 424, 466
Kasl, S. V., 183, 195, 197, 206
Kasschau, P. L., 725, 727
Kats, R., 46, 57, 58, 72, 85, 107, 119

Katschnig, H., 124, 126, 150, 159, 160, 161
Katz, S., 33, 43, 454, 467
Keane, T. M., 537, 544, 546, 550, 551, 562, 568, 569, 571
Kellam, S., 165, 178
Kelley, H. H., 15, 28
Kellner, R., 217, 221, 310, 311, 314, 315
Kelly, J. B., 660, 661, 664, 671, 675
Kelly, K., 272, 280
Kelsh, C., 306
Kelsh, K., 289
Kemball, C. P., 272, 280
Kendall, M. G., 477, 479, 482
Kendall, P. C., 183, 192, 195
Kendell, R. E., 486, 487, 488, 494, 497
Kenmy, K. A., 270
Kenmy, R. E., 267
Kerckhoff, A. C., 19, 28
Kerns, R. D., 657
Kesselman, M. S., 373
Kessler, S., 393, 466, 725, 727
Kety, S. S., 331, 347, 367, 374
Kielholz, 720
Kiesler, V., 28
Killam, K. F., 255
King, F. J., 185, 193, 195
Kinston, W., 53, 87
Kistner, R. W., 271, 274, 280
Kitson, G., 671, 674
Kivett, V. R., 720, 727
Kjellstrand, C. M., 291, 295, 305
Kleber, J. D., 546, 552
Klein, D. F., 592, 593, 600
Kleinman, A., 305, 674, 696
Klemmack, D. L., 713, 726
Klerman, G. L., 149, 161, 338, 347, 373, 463, 481, 483
Knight, E., 424, 466
Kobasa, S. C., 197, 206
Kochen, T. A., 662, 674
Koff, R. H., 677, 696
Kohn, M., 53, 87
Kokes, R. F., 71, 86, 402, 409, 464, 465
Kolb, J. C., 362, 374
Kolb, L. C., 402, 466
Komaroff, A. L., 146
Komarovsky, M., 19, 28
Kopple, J. D., 296, 305
Korman, M., 529, 548, 551
Kormos, H. R., 362, 374
Kornetsky, C., 335, 347
Kornhauser, R., 662, 674

Koulack, D., 257, 269
Koupernic, C., 675
Kraepelin, E., 393, 409, 466, 485, 497
Kraft, B., 308, 314, 315
Kramer, M., 270
Krantz, D. S., 444, 466
Krasnoff, L., 33, 47, 56, 86, 106, 119, 129, 145, 247, 254, 410, 463, 504, 505
Kreis, H., 302, 305
Kreisman, D. E., 45, 47, 120
Kressel, K., 662, 663, 666, 669, 674
Kretschmer, 421
Kringlen, E., 481, 482
Kubis, J. F., 186, 187, 194
Kuipers, L., 427, 430, 431, 466, 470
Kulchar, G. V., 308, 316
Kupfer, D. J., 601
Kurland, A., 405, 468
Kusanin, J., 466
Kutner, N. G., 293, 294, 296, 298, 300, 301, 302, 303, 304, 305, 306
Kutson, G., 674

Lachar, D., 550
Lader, M. H., 429, 470, 497
Lahniers, C. E., 128, 146, 366, 374, 466
Laing, R. D., 424, 466
Lamb, D. H., 182, 195
Lane, R. W., 257, 269
Lang, L., 698, 710
Langer, T. S., 220, 221
Langfeldt, G., 83, 87, 330, 347, 395, 466
Langlie, J. D., 198, 206
Lanzetta, J. T., 91, 92, 99
Larsen, A., 704, 709, 710
Larson, R., 238, 252, 254
Laufer, R. S., 527, 530, 547, 551
Lazarus, R. S., 166, 178, 183, 195, 209, 213, 224, 227, 234, 284, 306, 318, 323, 336, 347, 441, 443, 446, 464, 466, 664, 665, 674, 679, 680, 696, 731, 747, 749, 758, 759, 760, 765, 766
Lazowick, L. M., 185, 195
Leff, J., 51, 88, 120, 128, 146, 377, 383, 465, 466, 470, 471
Leff, J. F., 45
Leff, J. P., 49, 68, 70, 81, 82, 87, 121, 326, 342, 347, 358, 368, 374, 377, 378, 379, 385, 391, 399, 400, 405, 411, 416, 421, 424, 427, 428, 429, 430, 431, 434, 453, 456, 466, 470, 488, 497
Lehman, J., 105, 120
Lehman, R. E., 269

Lehmann, 443, 454
Lehmann, E. L., 133, 146
Lehmann, H., 466
Lehmann, S., 466
Lei, H., 36, 37, 48, 61, 87, 109, 110, 121
Leibowitz, S. F., 248, 249, 254
Lein, L., 700, 709
Lerner, R. M., 15, 17, 19, 29
Leslie, L. A., 606, 697
Lesse, S., 634, 642
Lester, E. P., 315
Lettieri, D., 551
Leventman, S. A., 527, 550
Levi, L., 747, 758
Levine, A. S., 238, 248, 255
Levine, P. M., 503, 506
Levine, S., 611, 618, 623, 632
Levinger, G., 673, 675
Levinson, D. J., 44, 47, 118, 120, 712, 727
Levis, D. J., 91, 100
Levitan, S. A., 710
Levy, N. B., 293, 294, 298, 306
Levy, S. M., 449, 467
Levy, S. T., 444, 467
Lewinsohn, P. M., 420, 467
Lewis, D. A., 412, 467
Lewis, J., 435, 467
Lewis, M., 656
Liberman, R. P., 450, 454, 455, 461, 463, 467
Liddell, H., 92, 99
Lidz, T., 424, 467
Lieberman, M. A., 47, 117, 120
Liem, J., 43, 47
Liem, R., 43, 47
Lilly, J. C., 422, 467
Lin, N., 268, 269
Lin, Y., 195
Lind, E., 166, 179, 215, 222
Lindemann, E., 44, 46, 117, 118
Lindenthal, J. J., 33, 48, 58, 87, 107, 120, 149, 161, 220, 222, 338, 347, 348, 355, 374, 481, 483, 490, 497
Lindzey, M. A., 28
Ling, N., 248, 254
Link, B., 353, 373, 374, 418, 467
Linn, B. S., 607, 747, 757
Linn, M. W., 729, 730, 731, 747, 749, 758
Lipinski, J. F., 331, 340, 348
Lipman, A., 19, 29
Lipman, R., 74, 88
Lipman, R. S., 220, 222, 331, 348
Lipowski, Z. J., 313, 315

Lipsit, L. P., 16, 27
Lipton, F., 454, 467
Lipton, M. A., 255
Livson, F., 717, 727
Lloyd, C., 52, 87, 504, 506
Lo, W. H., 473, 482
Locke, S. E., 197, 206
London, J., 698, 710
Lopata, H. T., 13, 29
Lopata, H. Z., 712, 727
Loranger, A. Q., 503, 506
Lord, M., 519, 523
Loviband, S. H., 91, 92, 99
Lowenthal, M. R., 29
Lubensky, A. W., 341, 348, 410, 471
Luckmann, T., 284, 304
Lukoff, D., 326, 393
Lukoff, I., 527, 529, 538, 542, 544, 545, 551
Lundberg, D., 227, 234
Lundberg, U., 7, 10, 146, 442, 467
Lundberg, V., 215, 222
Lundberg, Y., 166, 179
Lundin, A. P., 300, 306
Lundin, M. F., 300, 306
Lushene, R. E., 182, 196, 649, 657
Lynch, R. R., 291, 305
Lynn, E. J., 518, 573
Lytle, L. D., 248, 254

Maas, J. W., 250, 254
MacDonald, G., 747
MacDonald, R., 21, 28
MacGibbon, B., 289, 305
Mackey, C. J., 679, 696
Maddi, S. R., 197, 206
Magni, G., 210, 215
Mahan, W. J., 36, 48, 109, 121
Maher, B. A., 196, 346, 348
Maier, S. F., 250, 254
Malloy, P. F., 537, 550
Malmquist, A., 293, 306
Maltbie, A. A., 588, 600
Maltzman, I., 91, 100
Manley, M. J., 185, 195
Mann, A. H., 327, 473, 475, 476, 480, 482
Maratos, J., 473, 482
March, R. M., 28
Marcus, J. L., 346, 373, 464
Marcus, R. M., 342, 358, 406
Marder, S. R., 336, 346
Marshall, W., 569, 571

Marten, S., 664, 673
Martin, J., 527, 551
Martuza, V. R., 182, 195
Marvin, R. S., 646, 654, 656
Marx, M. B., 486, 497
Maslach, C., 677, 678, 680, 694, 696
Maslow, A., 732, 734
Masuda, M., 32, 45, 47, 51, 86, 106, 119, 140, 145, 146, 165, 179, 197, 207, 258, 269, 504, 505, 508, 515
Matthews, K. A., 3, 91, 94, 98, 100
Matthysse, S., 347, 463, 465, 469, 471
Mawson, A. R., 250, 254
Maxen, M., 710
Maxim, P., 674, 696
Maxwell, W. A., 184, 196
May, P. R. A., 433, 464
Maya, 715, 716
Mayer-Gross, W., 347, 395, 467
McArthur, R. A., 249, 255
McCabe, M., 83, 84, 87
McCabe, O., 405, 468
McCandless, B. R., 185, 194
McCary, R. W. A., 523
McCauley, C. R., 301, 305
McClelland, D. C., 341, 348, 410, 471
McColl, D., 481, 482
McCrae, R. R., 46, 117, 119
McCubbin, H. I., 603, 607, 704, 709, 710
McCutcheon, S., 636, 640, 642
McDonald, B. W., 140, 146
McGill, C. W., 432, 464
McGlashan, T. H., 444, 467
McGrath, M. M., 633, 641
McGuiness, B., 74, 88, 310, 316, 507, 515
McGuire, R. J., 302, 308, 314, 316
McKeachie, W. J., 195
McKenry, P. C., 662, 673
McKeon, J. P., 327, 473, 476, 481, 482
McMahon, B., 77, 87
McNeil, T. F., 343, 347
McPherson, S., 464
Meacham, J. A., 14, 29
Mechanic, D., 58, 87, 284, 306, 336, 347, 445, 450, 468
Medalie, J., 453, 468
Mednick, S. A., 335, 337, 347, 410, 468
Mednick, T., 726
Meehl, P. E., 344, 347
Melamed, B. G., 605, 643, 644, 645, 649, 650, 656, 657
Meltzer, H. Y., 250, 254
Mendels, J., 51, 75, 88, 140, 146, 508, 515

Mendelson, W. B., 264, 270
Merton, R. K., 15, 16, 29, 528, 551
Metzner, H. L., 197, 206
Metzner, R. J., 238, 256
Meyer, A., 6, 395, 468, 736
Meyer, M., 6, 10
Meyers, A. L., 527, 551
Meyers, J. K., 48
Micev, V., 569, 571
Michaux, W., 405, 468
Mikulka, P. J., 183, 195
Miles, R. C., 250, 256
Miller, E., 289, 306
Miller, J., 48
Miller, J. M., 296, 305
Miller, P. McC., 103, 149, 150, 161, 165, 175, 179, 449, 464
Miller, T. W., 2, 31, 48, 102, 105, 117, 120, 212, 281, 283, 295, 298, 306, 518, 553, 556, 562, 568, 571, 606, 607, 659, 668, 670, 674, 675, 729, 739, 747, 764, 766
Miller, W. R., 250, 254
Minick, S., 248, 254
Minter, R. E., 272, 280
Mintz, J., 527, 551
Miraglia, G., 215
Mirowsky, J., 146, 504, 506
Mirsch, S., 424, 471
Mitchel, A., 304
Mitchell, J. E., 238, 255
Mnoonkin, R. H., 662, 674
Moen, P., 699, 709
Mohler, I., 465
Moldofsky, H., 237, 254
Moles, O. C., 673, 675
Monck, E. M., 426, 463
Monge, R. H., 716, 727
Monroe, L. J., 257, 269
Monroe, S. M., 247, 255, 259, 270, 759, 766
Montague, D. K., 293, 305
Monti, P. M., 467, 471
Moore, G. L., 294, 304
Moore, T. E., 251, 254
Moos, R. H., 318, 323, 445, 468, 532, 551, 649, 656
Morgane, P. J., 254
Morganthau, T., 519, 523, 573, 585
Morley, J. E., 238, 248, 255
Morrell, W., 237, 255
Morrison, J. R., 62, 87, 417, 463
Mortimer, J., 698, 710

Moss, H. B., 432, 464
Moss, R., 407, 431, 464
Mueller, D. P., 42, 48, 146, 176, 179, 220, 222, 258, 270
Muhangi, J., 509, 515
Munari, F., 217, 221
Munoz, R., 340, 346, 487, 497
Murphy, D. L., 248, 255
Murphy, E., 197, 206, 735, 747
Murphy, H. B. M., 362, 374
Murray, P. J., 368, 373
Murthy, R. S., 51, 87
Musaph, H., 313, 316
Myers, J. K., 8, 10, 33, 48, 51, 56, 58, 71, 72, 73, 74, 75, 77, 78, 79, 80, 81, 83, 86, 87, 88, 120, 128, 131, 145, 146, 147, 149, 161, 220, 222, 259, 270, 338, 342, 343, 347, 348, 355, 357, 365, 366, 367, 369, 371, 374, 375, 403, 405, 408, 409, 410, 411, 414, 459, 465, 469, 474, 481, 483, 490, 497

Nace, E. P., 527, 551
Nada, I., 665, 674
Nader, R., 522
Nall, M. L., 308, 315
Nash, J. L., 587, 588, 589, 590, 600, 601
Naughton, J. P., 465
Ndetei, D. M., 328, 507, 508, 509, 513, 515
Nemiah, J. D., 309, 316
Neuchterlein, K. H., 326, 393, 448, 455, 463, 467, 468
Neufeld, R. W. J., 348, 470
Neugarten, B. L., 41, 48, 715, 717, 725, 726, 727, 761, 766
Neugarten, F., 29
Neugebauer, R., 102, 127, 131, 146, 353, 373, 374, 419, 467, 468
Neuhaus, R. J., 25, 27
Newman, B. M., 717, 727
Newman, P. R., 718, 727
Newmark, C. S., 182, 195
Ni Bhrolchain, M., 377, 391
Nies, A., 592, 600
Nisbet, W., 29
Nisula, B. C., 253, 255
Noel, B., 342, 346, 358, 373, 406, 464
Norton, J. P., 435, 436, 468, 470
Novak, C. A., 714, 717, 727
Nowak, C., 15, 28
Nuckolls, K. B., 14, 29
Nunnally, J. C., 139, 146

O'Brien, C. P., 527, 551
Odegard, O., 365, 375
Ohlin, L. E., 528, 550
Olshen, R., 735, 747
Olson, D., 704, 709, 710
Olson, M., 185, 195
O'Neil, H. F., Jr., 185, 195, 196
Oppenheim, H., 257, 270
Opton, E. M., Jr., 441, 466
O'Rand, A., 698, 710
Oreland, L., 498
Orzeck, C., 220, 221
Osler, 210
Osofsky, J. F., 272, 280
Oster, J., 633, 642
Ostrander, D. R., 58, 87, 107, 120, 490, 497
Oswald, I., 591, 600

Palermo, D. S., 185, 194
Palmore, E., 43, 48, 117, 120
Pandurangi, A., 83, 87
Pankratz, L. D., 583, 584, 585
Panksepp, J., 254
Pantell, R. H., 659, 640, 642
Park, L. E., 220, 222
Parkes, C. M., 71, 88
Parnas, J., 410, 468
Parry, G., 102, 123
Parsons, E. R., 526, 529, 530, 531, 538, 541, 542, 543, 544, 545, 548, 551, 556, 570
Paster, S., 361, 362, 375
Pasteur, L., 395
Patalano, 543
Patrick, V., 504, 505
Patterson, E. T., 528, 538, 543, 551, 552
Patterson, J. M., 603, 607
Pattison, E. M., 452, 468
Pavan, L., 217, 221
Pavlov, I., 5
Paykel, E. S., 8, 10, 33, 38, 42, 45, 48, 51, 57, 58, 59, 66, 71, 72, 74, 77, 78, 80, 87, 88, 107, 115, 120, 146, 149, 161, 166, 179, 217, 220, 222, 258, 259, 270, 310, 311, 313, 314, 316, 318, 323, 327, 338, 347, 359, 366, 374, 375, 383, 388, 390, 391, 403, 417, 442, 459, 465, 468, 470, 474, 475, 478, 481, 483, 486, 490, 497, 501, 506, 507, 515
Pearlin, L. I., 440, 445, 446, 450, 468, 759, 766

Pearson, J., 663, 666, 674
Peck, R., 711, 716, 717, 727
Pederson, J., 407, 431, 464
Pelsma, D., 606, 677, 680, 695
Penk, W. E., 517, 525, 528, 531, 537, 538, 541, 543, 546, 547, 551, 552, 553, 566, 571
Pepe, E. A., 716, 727
Pepitone-Arreola-Rockwell, F., 272, 280
Pepper, M., 48, 58, 87, 107, 120
Pepper, M. D., 33, 48
Pepper, M. P., 149, 161, 220, 222, 338, 348, 355, 374, 481, 483, 490, 497
Perini, G. I., 307
Perkins, C. C., Jr., 91, 100
Perlman, L. V., 272, 280
Perris, C., 486, 487, 488, 491, 497, 498
Perris, H., 327, 485, 486, 488, 491, 496, 498
Peterson, L., 644, 657
Peterson, N. L., 262, 269
Peterson, P., 717, 727
Peto, J., 51, 85, 332, 346, 352, 373, 398, 462, 735, 746
Pfeiffer, E., 723, 727
Phillips, B. N., 185, 193, 196
Phillips, L., 335, 348
Pierloot, R., 237, 246, 255
Pilisuk, M., 451, 469
Pillsbury, D. M., 308, 316
Pilowsky, I., 611, 612, 618, 623, 632
Platt, J. J., 447, 469, 470
Pleck, J., 698, 699, 707, 710
Plemmons, H., 551
Plemons, J. K., 37, 47
Poe, J., 272, 280
Polak, P., 62, 86, 145, 417, 464
Polivy, J., 251, 254, 255
Poll, I. B., 305
Pollitt, J., 473, 481, 483
Polner, M., 553, 571
Poon, L., 46
Pope, H. G., 246, 254, 331, 340, 348, 583, 585
Portuges, S. H., 665, 674
Post, R. M., 249, 255
Poznanski, E. O., 289, 306
Presley, A. S., 480, 481, 483
Prigogine, I., 212, 282, 286, 297, 299, 303, 306
Proudfoot, C. A., 117, 120
Pruchno, R. A., 2, 13
Prusoff, A., 58, 88

Prusoff, B., 71
Prusoff, B. A., 33, 48, 87, 107, 120, 146, 149, 161, 166, 179, 259, 270, 338, 347, 348, 366, 374, 383, 391, 417, 442, 465, 468, 474, 483, 507, 515
Pugh, T., 77, 87
Pugh, W. M., 140, 146
Pyle, R. L., 238, 255

Qilliams, E., 713, 727
Quitkin, E., 592
Quitkin, F., 600

Rabkin, J. G., 41, 48, 146, 272, 280, 329, 343, 348, 396, 419, 456, 469, 749, 758, 765, 766
Ragan, P. K., 714, 726
Rahe, R. H., 1, 5, 6, 7, 8, 10, 33, 34, 36, 37, 44, 47, 48, 56, 57, 58, 60, 72, 86, 106, 107, 108, 109, 110, 111, 119, 120, 121, 123, 124, 126, 140, 146, 149, 161, 166, 178, 197, 206, 209, 212, 215, 220, 222, 224, 225, 234, 235, 258, 270, 272, 274, 280, 308, 315, 338, 347, 348, 390, 391, 395, 396, 402, 407, 408, 409, 415, 439, 441, 455, 458, 459, 460, 465, 469, 483, 501, 505, 507, 515, 611, 618, 619, 622, 632, 664, 665, 675, 736, 746, 747, 750, 758
Rainwater, L., 700, 710, 719, 727
Rakusin, J. M., 342, 346, 358, 373, 406, 464
Ramer, J. D., 438, 471
Randolph, E., 452, 453, 469
Rapoport, R., 699, 710
Raschke, H., 672, 674
Rassaby, E. S., 217, 222
Ratskin, J., 51, 88
Rauscher, F., 84, 88
Ravaris, C. L., 592, 600
Razani, J., 432, 464
Ream, N., 527, 551
Rees, L., 308, 316
Reese, H. W., 16, 27
Reichard, S., 717, 727
Reichsman, F., 298, 306
Reinhold, M., 308, 316
Remington, M., 481, 483
Renner, V. J., 749, 758
Reno, V., 713, 727
Rhode, P., 68, 86, 87

Rice, D., 700, 710
Ridley-Johnson, R., 644, 657
Riegel, K. F., 14, 29, 106, 121
Rifkin, A., 592, 600
Riley, M. W., 16, 17, 18, 29, 726
Risch, S. S., 248, 255
Ritzler, B. A., 71, 86, 402, 409, 464, 465
Riviser, C., 248, 254
Rizzardo, R., 215
Roa, B., 327, 473, 476
Robbins, E., 84, 86, 88
Robbins, T. W., 238, 251, 252, 255
Roberts, W. R., 528, 551, 552
Robertson, A., 150, 160
Robinowitz, R., 517, 525, 528, 531, 538, 541, 543, 551, 552
Robins, E., 137, 145, 340, 346, 474, 483, 487, 497, 500, 505, 664, 673
Robins, L. N., 178, 463
Robinson, D. S., 592, 600
Robinson, R. R., 298, 305
Rochester, S. R., 449, 469
Rodgers, W., 704, 709
Rodnick, E. H., 433, 435, 463, 464, 467
Rodrigo, F., 291, 305
Roff, M., 88, 348
Rohde, P. D., 358, 374, 377, 391, 399, 466
Romo, M., 140, 146, 197, 206
Romo, T., 110, 121
Rones, P., 713, 727
Rook, A., 309, 316
Roper, M., 400, 464
Rosa, A. A., 291, 305
Rose, R. M., 47, 74, 87, 140, 146, 169, 178, 373, 463
Rosemier, R. A., 185, 195
Rosenbaum, M., 463
Rosenblum, L. A., 656
Rosenn, M., 92, 99
Rosenstock, I. M., 207
Rosenthal, D., 344, 347, 348, 367, 374, 394, 438, 469, 471
Rosenthal, S., 93, 99
Rosenzweig, N., 600
Ross, C. E., 146, 504, 506
Ross, D. R., 588, 600
Rosser, R., 53, 87
Rossi, A. S., 13, 16, 29
Rossier, J., 248, 254
Roth, M., 347, 395, 467
Rounsaville, B. J., 546, 549, 552
Rowland, N. W., 238, 255
Rubin, L. B., 700, 710

Rubin, R. T., 36, 48, 109, 121
Rubinstein, A. A., 272, 279
Ruch, L. P., 504, 506
Rudin, E., 473, 483
Rudnick, F. D., 238, 256
Rueger, D. B., 537, 550
Ruskin, A. P., 304
Russel, B., 307, 316
Rustad, M., 698, 707, 710
Rustin, S., 554, 570
Rutter, M. L., 379, 391, 426, 463, 469, 617, 618, 621, 622, 632, 660, 675
Ryckoff, L., 424, 471
Ryff, C. D., 15, 19, 29
Ryscavage, P., 700, 710

Sachs, D. A., 182, 196
Sadock, B. J., 466, 506
Sage, P., 424, 466
Sainsbury, P., 309, 316
Sale, I., 583, 585
Salguero, C., 289, 306
Salkin, B., 237, 255
Salt, P., 610, 618
Salter, D. P., 103, 149
Sameroff, A. J., 17, 29
Sandler, I., 25, 28
Sanger, M. D., 315, 316
Sangiuliano, I., 715, 725, 727
Santoli, A., 573, 584, 585
Santonastaso, P., 307
Santoro, T. M., 677, 696
Santulli, R., 634, 641
Sarason, I. G., 150, 161, 179, 183, 196, 229, 234, 258, 268, 269, 270, 272, 280, 642
Sarlin, B., 438, 471
Sartorius, N. M., 63, 89, 129, 147, 357, 363, 375, 379, 391, 427, 471, 509, 515
Sassenrath, E. N., 272, 280
Schaefer, C., 139, 145, 749, 758
Schaie, W., 27
Schalling, D., 490, 498
Scheier, I. H., 181, 194
Scheier, M. F., 3, 91
Schless, A. P., 51, 75, 88, 140, 146
Schmale, A., 62, 85
Schneider, K., 53, 88, 348, 362, 375, 395, 469
Schooler, C., 440, 445, 446, 450, 468
Schooler, N. R., 400, 464
Schulsinger, F., 331, 335, 337, 347, 367,
374, 410, 468
Schultz, R., 17, 29
Schulzinger, H., 410, 468
Schwartz, C., 74, 78, 79, 80, 81, 88
Schwartz, C. C., 128, 146, 147, 367, 375, 403, 410, 411, 414, 459, 469
Schwartz, C. D., 342, 348
Scott, D. H., 60, 88
Seaman, S. F., 250, 254
Seligman, M. E. P., 220, 222, 229, 234, 250, 254, 439, 469
Selye, H., 6, 209, 283, 306, 334, 348, 430, 439, 469, 730
Selzer, M. L., 258, 270
Serafetinides, E., 256
Serban, G., 421, 469
Seville, R. H., 308, 316
Seyman, R. G., 91, 100
Shabad, S., 519, 523, 573, 585
Shannon, F. T., 604, 609, 610, 618, 619, 632, 634, 641
Shapiro, D. A., 102, 123
Shapiro, L. E., 373
Shapiro, M. B., 124, 126
Shapiro, R., 363, 375
Shean, G., 442, 443, 469
Sheffield, B. F., 125, 310, 311, 314, 315
Sheras, P. L., 645, 656
Sherrard, D. J., 300, 304
Shidman, J. T., 291, 305
Shields, J., 352, 373, 393, 465, 470
Shigetomi, C., 644, 657
Shirin, K., 407, 431, 464
Shoemaker, R. J., 313, 316
Shrout, P. J., 61, 88, 147, 759, 766
Shure, M. B., 447, 470
Siegel, J. M., 150, 161, 229, 234, 258, 270, 272, 280, 447, 469
Sifneos, P. E., 309, 311, 316
Silsby, H. D., 517, 519
Siltanen, R., 110, 121
Silver, S., 573, 585
Simmons, O., 425, 426, 464
Singer, J. E., 99, 673
Singer, M., 434, 470
Singer, M. T., 424, 433, 471
Singh, K., 272, 280
Sinnott, J. D., 721, 727
Sipprelle, R. C., 537, 550
Siris, S. G., 336, 346
Skinner, B. A., 29
Skinner, D., 700, 710
Skinner, E. A., 17

Skinner, H. A., 36, 37, 48, 61, 87, 109, 110, 121
Sklair, F., 59, 85, 137, 145, 177, 178, 227, 233, 344, 346, 473, 482
Skogan, W. G., 756, 758
Slanger, J. L., 249, 255
Slater, E., 347, 395, 467, 481, 482, 483, 607, 729, 747, 749
Sloane, T., 27
Slotnick, R. W., 466
Smart, D. E., 253
Smelser, N. J., 29
Smith, A., 124, 126, 649, 656
Smith, J. B., 664, 673
Smith, M., 6, 10
Smith, M. B., 720
Smyer, M. A., 2, 13, 15, 21, 28
Snyder, F., 601
Snyder, K., 326, 393, 428, 471
Sobel, H. J., 445, 471
Sobel, R., 308, 314, 315
Sokolovsky, J., 452, 470
Soldatos, C. R., 257, 269
Solomon, G. F., 268, 269, 553, 555, 571
Somes, G. W., 486, 497
Sommer, B., 272, 280
Sorrell, G. T., 17, 29
Southerly, W. T., 567, 571
Spanier, G. B., 670, 675, 710
Sparr, B. W., 519, 522
Sparr, L., 584, 585
Spence, H., Jr., 91, 100
Spiegel, J. P., 257, 269, 402, 465, 587, 600
Spielberger, C. D., 161, 179, 181, 182, 183, 184, 185, 193, 194, 195, 196, 642, 649, 657
Spilkin, A. Z., 197, 207
Spinoza, 1, 5
Spittle, B., 215, 222
Spitzer, R. L., 79, 84, 88, 474, 483
Spivack, G., 447, 469, 470
Spring, B., 325, 329, 337, 344, 345, 348, 349, 394, 396, 397, 409, 410, 418, 420, 422, 423, 446, 454, 470, 471
Staines, G., 698, 710
Stanley, J. C., 537, 550
Starfield, B., 633, 642
Starr, R., 522, 523
Stead, W. W., 298, 305
Steele, G. P., 131, 132, 147, 169, 179
Stein, E. M., 607, 729, 730, 731, 747, 749, 757, 758
Stein, S., 607, 729, 730, 731, 733, 747,

749, 757, 758
Steinberg, H. R., 54, 55, 88, 401, 470
Steinberg, M. R., 433, 464
Stenbeck, K., 551
Stephenson, R. S., 185, 195
Stevens, B., 68, 86, 87
Stevens, B. C., 391
Stevens, B. S., 359, 374, 377, 399, 466
Stevens, S. S., 33, 49, 107, 121, 339, 348
Stewart, A. J., 610, 618
Stierman, K. L., 21, 28
Stoane, R. B., 758
Stodola, E., 212, 281, 295, 298, 306
Stokes, J. H., 308, 316
Stolk, J. M., 253, 255
Stolorow, R. D., 341, 348, 410, 471
Stone, R. T., 640, 642
Storms, L. H., 335, 346
Strandman, E., 496, 498
Strange, R. E., 553, 571
Straus, R., 282, 286, 306
Strauss, J. S., 71, 86, 88, 337, 348, 363, 370, 375, 402, 409, 464, 465
Stretch, R. H., 536, 550
Streuning, E. L., 41, 48, 765, 766
Strober, M., 211, 237, 246, 251, 253, 255
Strodbeck, F. L., 431, 470
Stromgren, E., 83, 88
Struening, E. L., 51, 88, 272, 280, 329, 348, 419, 469, 749, 758
Stuart, A., 477, 479, 482
Sturgeon, D., 430, 431, 466, 470
Styles, K., 677, 696
Sullivan, H. S., 424, 470
Suls, J., 221, 222
Surtees, P. G., 161
Susser, M., 83, 88, 177, 179
Susskind, W., 307, 308, 314, 316
Sutker, P. B., 543, 552
Suzman, N. M., 597, 600
Swank, R., 401, 470
Sweetwood, H. L., 139, 147, 168, 178, 225, 234, 664, 673, 735, 747
Swidler, A., 20, 29
Sydenham, A., 272, 280
Syme, S. L., 760, 766
Syzamanski, H., 45, 47
Szpiler, J., 93, 99

Talkington, J., 420, 467
Tarrier, N., 429, 430, 438, 470
Tausig, M., 460, 470
Taylor, H., 206, 207

Taylor, M., 499, 504, 506
Teasdale, T., 410, 468
Tennant, C., 31, 45, 46, 49, 51, 85, 124, 125, 126, 165, 168, 169, 178, 179, 212, 223, 224, 225, 229, 234, 235, 258, 265, 266, 270, 329, 346, 383, 440, 462, 486, 497, 739, 747
Terry, D., 424, 467
Theorell, T., 13, 29, 146, 166, 179, 215, 220, 222, 225, 227, 234, 235, 272, 280, 442, 467
Thibault, J. W., 15, 28
Thoennes, N., 663, 666, 674
Thoits, P. A., 49, 759, 767
Thomae, H., 32, 49
Thomas, D. C., 289, 305
Thompson, J., 605, 633
Thompson, K. C., 610, 618
Thoreson, C. E., 677, 680, 696
Thornton, D. R., 92, 99
Thum, D., 665, 675
Thurlow, H. J., 140, 147
Tizard, J. S., 617, 618, 621, 632
Tolsdorf, C. C., 452, 470
Topping, G. D., 426, 462
Toth, J. C., 296, 302, 305
Tracy, D. B., 182, 195
Trautman, E. C., 257, 270
Treas, L. L., 18, 27
Trent, J. T., 184, 196
Troll, L. E., 712, 714, 717, 727
Trower, P., 447, 470
Trumbull, R., 347
Tsuang, M. T., 84, 88
Tsushima, U., 182, 192, 196
Tuchman, B., 662, 674
Tuddenham, R. D., 588, 599
Tudiver, F., 212, 271
Turk, D. C., 657, 659, 670, 671, 673
Turner, S. M., 449, 465
Turpin, G., 430, 470
Tyler, P., 480, 481, 483

Uhlenhuth, E. H., 33, 48, 57, 58, 59, 60, 74, 88, 107, 120, 146, 161, 166, 179, 331, 338, 348, 403, 442, 468, 470, 507, 515
Ulrich, R. F., 420, 465

Vadher, A., 328, 507, 508, 509, 513, 515
Vaillant, G. E., 45, 46, 486, 497
Vaillant, G. G., 718, 728
Vale, W., 248, 254

Valins, S., 99
Valone, K., 435, 436, 438, 470
Vandereycken, W., 237, 246, 255
Van der Gugten, J., 249, 255
Van Kammen, D. P., 336, 346
Van Putten, T., 413, 422, 444, 470
Van Uitert, D., 213, 317, 323
Van Velsor, E., 698, 710
Vargo, T., 248, 254
Vaughn, C. E., 45, 49, 51, 81, 82, 87, 88, 120, 121, 326, 377, 378, 379, 391, 400, 416, 421, 427, 428, 429, 453, 456, 466, 470, 471
Veltkamp, L., 606, 659, 668, 675
Venables, P. H., 335, 348
Ventura, J., 326, 393
Veroff, J., 79, 86
Versteeg, D. H. G., 249, 255
Vickers, R., 232, 235
Viederman, G. E., 296, 306
Vinokur, A., 258, 270
Virchow, 395
Visscher, A. L., 714, 718, 720, 721, 724, 728
Volicer, B. J., 111, 121
Von Knorring, E., 497
Von Knorring, L., 486, 487, 488, 491, 498
Voydanoff, P., 710

Waal, H. J., 600
Wacks, J., 308, 315
Wagner, P. S., 361, 362, 375, 401, 402, 471
Wahl, C. W., 343, 348
Walker, I., 518
Walker, J. I., 519, 523, 573, 585, 587, 588, 589, 590, 593, 594, 596, 598, 599, 600, 601
Walker, L., 605
Walker, L. S., 633
Wallace, C. J., 448, 467
Wallace, C. W., 449, 461, 471
Wallerstein, J. S., 660, 661, 664, 671, 675
Walsh, B. T., 249, 256
Walton, H. J., 480, 481, 483
Warbuton, D. M., 269
Warheit, G., 739, 747
Waring, J., 16, 17, 18, 29
Watkins, V. B., 302, 306
Watson, C., 662, 674
Watson, J. A., 720, 727
Watt, N. F., 341, 348, 410, 471
Waxman, D., 569, 571

Weakland, J. H., 424, 462
Weber, R. E., 662, 673
Wechsler, H., 665, 675
Weidner, G., 91, 94, 98, 100
Weinberg, J., 717, 728
Weiner, B., 347
Weinstein, N., 508, 515
Weir, T., 701, 709
Weiskopf, P. E., 678, 696
Weiss, R. L., 670, 675
Weissman, M. M., 28, 318, 323, 546, 552
Welker, R. L., 250, 256
Wellman, B., 21, 29
Wells, L., 730, 747
Welsh, G. S., 532, 550
Wender, P. H., 331, 347, 367, 374, 438, 456, 458, 471
Wentz, A. C., 272, 280
West, K., 463, 464
Westervelt, F. B., 294, 304
Wethered, C. E., 677, 679
Wheatley, K. L., 250, 256
Wheeler, S., 18, 27
Whitacre, F., 271, 280
White, K., 128, 146, 366, 374, 466
Whitlock, F. A., 313, 316
Whitmore, K., 617, 618, 621, 632
Whyte, H. M., 169, 174, 176, 178, 215, 223, 224, 225, 226, 234
Whyte, M. M., 221
Wilbur, C. H., 546, 552
Wildman, R. C., 258, 270
Wilhelmsen, L., 215, 222
Wilkinson, D. S., 309, 316
Williams, T., 553, 571, 574, 586
Wilson, G. C., 48, 117, 120
Wilson, M., 710
Windle, C., 185, 196
Wing, J. K., 52, 53, 63, 67, 68, 86, 87, 89, 129, 147, 178, 357, 373, 375, 378, 379, 391, 401, 421, 422, 426, 427, 462, 463, 471, 509, 515
Winokur, G., 145, 340, 346, 417, 463, 487, 497

Winters, E., 468
Wiseman, L., 28
Witemberg, S. H., 221, 222
Witkin, H. A., 257, 269, 270
Wittkower, E. D., 307, 315, 316
Wolff, C. T., 11, 91, 100
Wolff, H. G., 6, 9
Wolpert, E. A., 503, 506
Wood, M., 633, 642
Wood, P., 452, 468
Woodruff, R. A., 340, 346, 487, 497
Woodward, W. A., 528, 551, 552
Woog, P., 47, 765, 766
Worden, J. W., 445, 471
Wortham, C., 298, 306
Worthen, J., 366, 373
Worthen, K., 53, 76, 85, 128, 145, 339, 346, 417, 443, 462
Wunsch-Hitzig, R., 353, 373, 374, 467
Wurtman, J. J., 254
Wurtman, R. J., 254
Wyatt, R. J., 264, 270, 601
Wyler, A. R., 197, 207
Wyly, M. B., 716, 727
Wynne, L. C., 347, 424, 433, 434, 437, 438, 463, 465, 469, 470, 471

Yager, J., 139, 140, 145, 147, 168, 178, 225, 234, 238, 256, 442, 465, 664, 673, 735
Yager, T., 551
Yale, C., 413, 470
Yamamoto, J., 530, 550
Yarvis, R. M., 42, 48, 146, 176, 179, 220, 222, 258, 270
Yurgelun-Todd, D., 246, 254

Zabin, M. A., 650, 657
Zimering, R. T., 551, 562, 571
Zinkin, J., 462
Zubin, J., 99, 344, 349, 394, 397, 410, 420, 422, 446, 454, 471

Subject Index

Absence of father, 243
Academic achievement, anxiety and, 192–193
trait, 184–185
Activities, life crises and, 57
Adjustment
of children to divorce process, 671
personal interpretations along dimensions of, 169
Administrative–Work Environment scale, teacher stress and, 684
Adolescent, somatic complaints in, 633–642
Adrenocortical steroids, 248, 249
ADTP; see Alcohol Dependence Treatment Program
Affective disorders, Umea Classification of, 488; see also Bipolar disorder
Affective style interaction measure, 431
Age, end-stage renal disease and, 289; see also Aging
Aggression
depression and, 486
life events and, 494
Aging
concerns of elderly of, 756
midlife stress and, 713–718
successful: factors conducive to, 723–725; obstacles to, 718–721; role inconstancy and, 721–722
Agitating parenting behavior, 651–652
Agreement on event dates, 137
Alcohol Dependence Treatment Program, 531
Alexithymia, 309, 312–313
Alienation
from peers, 243
Vietnam veterans and, 568
Amenorrhea, secondary, 271
American Psychiatric Association, 46, 84, 85, 105, 119, 239, 253, 370, 373, 401, 402, 462, 554, 570, 589, 599, 664, 672
Amitriptyline, 593
Amoxapine, 594
Amytal sodium, 589–590

Androgynous traits, midlife stress and, 722
Anger, personal interpretations along dimensions of, 169
Anorexia nervosa, 211
bulimia and stress in, 237–256: conclusion in, 252–253; discussion of, 245-252; method for, 239–241; methodological limitations in, 245–247; results in, 241–245; subgroups of, 238
as heterogeneous syndrome, 237
Anticholinergic medications, 596–597
Anticipated stress, measurement of, in elderly, 731
Anticipation of event, stress of, 183
Anticipatory socialization, 17
Antidepressants, tricyclic, 593–595
Antihistamines, 598
Antipsychotics
maintenance, stressors triggering schizophrenia and, 399–400
traumatic war stress and, 595–597
Anti-social acts, life-event ratings and, 150
Anxiety
Beck's definition of, 562
end-stage renal disease and, 298
maternal, 653
myocardial infarction and, 227-229
personal interpretations along dimensions of, 169
trait; see Trait anxiety
types of, 181
Vietnam veterans and, 568
Anxiety scale, trait anxiety inventory trait and, 181–196; see also Trait anxiety
Apathy, end-stage renal disease and, 298
Appraisal
cognitive, schizophrenia and, 441–443
stress and, 749–750, 759, 760
Arguments, schizophrenia and depressive neurosis and, 389
Artane; see Trihexyphenadyl
AS; see Affective style interaction measure

787

Assault concerns of elderly, 755, 756
Assertive behavior, midlife stress and, 719
Assessment and methodological issues, 101–208
    life-event interview in, 127–164; see also Life-event interview
    life-event ratings in, 123–126; see also Life-event measurements
    life-event scaling in, 105–121; see also Life-event scaling
    near future onset of psychological symptoms in, 165–179; see also Near future onset of symptoms
    overview of, 101–104
    stress as barrier to health in, 197–207
    trait anxiety scale in, 181–196; see also Trait anxiety
Atarax; see Hydroxyzine
Attachment, interdependent lives and, 14–15
Attachment behavior in child, reassuring parenting behavior and, 651
Attention directed toward stressor, 92–99
Autonomic nervous system activation, 335
    elderly and, 739
Aversive events, 91–99

Barbiturates, 598
Beck Depression Inventory, 318
Bedford Life Events and Difficulty Schedule, 149–150
Behavior
    child; see Child behavior
    life events and, 223
    measurement of change in, 106
Behavioral coping, schizophrenia and, 446–447, 456
Behaviorally oriented stress management training in elderly, 740
Behavioral medicine, life stress and, 209–324
    bulimia and anorexia nervosa in, 237–256
    dermatologic disorders and, 307–317
    dysfunctional uterine bleeding and, 271–280
    end-stage renal disease and, 281–306
    myocardial infarction and, 215–226
    sleep disorders in, 257–270
    strokes, coping of wives with husbands', 317–323
Behavior problems in child, 609; see also Child behavior

Benadryl; see Diphenhydramine
Benzodiazepines, 598
Benztropine, 596
Beta-endorphins, 248
Bias of recall, 220
    bulimia and, 246–247
    dysfunctional uterine bleeding and, 278
Bickering with parents, 243
Bilateral negotiation, 18
Biobehavioral model of stress, 286–288
Biochemical measure, multivariate analysis of life events and, 766
Biological fluctuation, schizophrenia and, 421–423
Biological level of behavior, 286
Biological response to stress, 335
Biological variables
    life stress situations and, 762
    schizophrenia and, 421–423
Biopsychosocial approach to stress, 764
Bipolar disorder, 328
    early and late onset of, 499–506: discussion of, 503–505; etiological differences in, 503; results in, 501–503
    multifactorial etiology of, 499
    polygenic etiology of, 499
    stress patterns in, age of onset and, 502
Birth complications, schizophrenia and, 343
Black combat veterans
    limited opportunity and deviant behavior in, 527–531
    racial prejudice and maladjustment among, 526–527
Black patients with end-stage renal disease, 300
Blue-collar, dual-earner families, 700
Bodily harm concerns of elderly, 756
Brief Psychiatric Rating Scale, 413
Brief reactive psychoses, 331
Brought-forward time, 77, 344, 359
Brown criteria for stress of life events, 115
Buffering hypothesis, 763
Bulimia, 211
    anorexia nervosa and, 237–256: bulimic subgroups of, 238; conclusion in, 252–253; discussion of, 245–252; method for, 239–241; methodological limitations in, 245–247; results in, 241–245
    definition of, 239
    severity of, 245
Burglary concerns among elderly, 733

Camberwell Family Interview, 379, 426, 427, 432
CAPD; *see* Continuous ambulatory peritoneal dialysis
Casual friendships, schizophrenia and, 454
Catastrophe theory model, posttraumatic stress disorder and, 564
Category program, 379
Causal factors pool, 82
CD; *See* Communication deviance
CDQ: *see* Child Development Questionnaire
Center for Study of Responsive Law, 522
CFI; *see* Camberwell Family Interview
Chaining of life events, 177
Change
    life crises and, 57
    state of life adjustment in, 107
Checklist format for life-event ratings, 38
    reliability of, 123–124
Chemical Use Questionnaire, 537
Chemotherapy
    of schizophrenia, 66
    traumatic war stress, 587–601: antipsychotics in, 595–597; benzodiazepines in, 598; lithium in, 599; monoamine oxidase inhibitors in, 590–593; posttraumatic stress disorder symptoms and, 587–589; propranolol in, 597–598; sedative-hypnotics in, 598; sodium amytal in, 589–590; soporifics in, 598–599; tricyclic antidepressants in, 593–595
Child behavior
    actual, maternal mood and, 631
    maternal and teacher descriptions of, 619–632: discussion of, 630–632; economic background and, 628–630; long-term life events in, 625–526, 631–632; materials and methods for, 621–624; maternal depression and, 624–626; results in, 624–630; short-term life events and, 620, 624–625, 631; social background and, 628–630
    score for: maternal, 621–622; teacher, 622
    see also Children
Child custody, contested, 659–675; *see also* Contested child custody
Child Development Questionnaire, 649, 652, 653, 654–655

Child Psychiatric Outpatient Clinic at University of Kentucky, 666
Child-rearing problems, 609–618
    discussion of, 616–617
    family background variables and, 612–613
    family life events score and, 611
    during fifth year, 611
    maternal depression score and, 611–612
    methods for, 611
    results in, 613–616
    social background variables and, 612–613
Children
    dependence concerns of elderly and, 757
    distress in, exploratory or prosocial behavior and, 650
    divorce process and, 671
    see also Child behavior
Chloral hydrate, 598–599
Choice of action, life-event ratings and, 150
Christchurch Child Development Study, 610, 621
Clinical interventions, schizophrenia and, 460–461
Clomipramine, 569
Clustering and timing of events, 117
    stress and, 763
CMPS, 496
Coddington Life Event Record, 640
Coddington modifications of Social Readjustment Rating Questionnaire, 109
Cogentin; *see* Benztropine
Cognitive responses to schizophrenia, 440–446
Cognitive deficit, 250–251
    end-stage renal disease and, 295–296
Cognitive framework, environmental experiences and, 166
Cognitive notions of stress, 227
Cognitive problem-solving skills, 446
    elderly and, 740, 743
    schizophrenia and, 447
Cognitive rehearsal, stress management in elderly and, 743
Collaborative Study Group, 413, 465
Colorado Bar Association, 663
Combat Experience Scale, 536
Combat stress
    psychotic symptoms and, 360–364

stages of adjustment to, 566
Combat veterans, black; *see* Black combat veterans
Commitment
 conflicts in, working families and, 698
 in family, conflict resolution and mediation and, 662
Common core in experiencing event, 60
Communication
 conflict resolution in family and, 662
 patterns of, schizophrenia and, 456
 style of, life events and, 764
Communication deviance, 433
Community-based patients and resilience in coping, 80
Competence, successful aging and, 718
Concept
 of change, 7
 of roles, 15
Conceptual model of stressful life events, 32–34
Concern Inventory, 750
Concerns in elderly, 754–755
Conciliation Counseling Service, 663
Confiding relationships, schizophrenia and, 453
Conflict
 in commitments, working families and, 698
 midlife stress and inner, 716
Contested child custody, 659–675
 mediation of: clinical issues in, 669–672; model for, 666–669; process of, 664–665; divorce and, 661–666
 separation and divorce in families and, 660–664
 summary of, 672
Contextual threat, 76, 150
Contingent events, 406
 schizophrenia and, 411
Continuous ambulatory peritoneal dialysis, 281–282
Contraceptives, dysfunctional uterine bleeding and, 275–276
Control
 cognitive strategies for, schizophrenia and, 443–446
 of future health, perceived, 200
 locus of, multivariate analysis of life events and, 766
 personal, 229–230
 sleep disorders and degree of, 265
 stroke of spouse and, 321

Convalescence, end-stage renal disease and, 298
Coping
 definition of, 440
 in elderly, 736–745
 resilience in, community-based patients and, 80
 schizophrenia and; *see* Coping responses in schizophrenia
 working families and strategies for, 704–705
Coping Questionnaire, 649
Coping responses in schizophrenia, 438–449
 alternatives and, 447–450
 behavioral coping and, 446–447
 breakdown of, 454, 455
 cognitive appraisal and, 441–443
 cognitive control strategies and, 443–446
 cognitive coping and, 440–441
 summary in, 450–451
Coronary heart disease, 216
Cortisol production, 249
Cost of living concerns of elderly, 752
Counseling, stroke of spouse and, 323
Crisis centers, 514
Criticalness of family, schizophrenia and, 455
Criticism
 depressive neurosis and, 386
 schizophrenia and, 386, 429
Cultural bias
 life-event response to, 116
 life stress situations and, 762
 measurement of life stress and, 42
Cultural level of behavior, 286
Culture specific psychological treatment, 529–530

Data reduction, need for, 24–25
Dating of illness onset, bulimia and, 246–247
DD214 discharge papers, factitious posttraumatic stress disorder and, 584
DDTP; *see* Drug Dependence Treatment Program
Death concerns in elderly, 734, 751, 752, 755, 756
Declining income, midlife stress and, 712–713
Degree of upset, life events and, 75–76
Delusions, depressive, 387
Demoralization, 368

Denial
    cognitive control and, 443
    of mental illness, grandiose patient and,
        445
Dependence, adaptive regression to, 296
Depression
    aggression and, 486
    black versus white Vietnam veterans
        and, 541, 542
    as both stressor and stress response, 282
    child-rearing problems and, 610
    end-stage renal disease and, 292–293
    events occurring before and after,
        507–515
    Feighner criteria for, 487
    involutional, midlife stress and, 720
    life events in, 359–360, 380–382
    maternal: child behavior and long-term
        life events and, 625–626, 631–632;
        child behavior and short-term life
        events and, 620, 624–625, 631;
        perceived child behavior and, 630
    personal interpretations along dimen-
        sions of, 169
    personality characteristics in, 485–498:
        assessment and, 490–492; diagnos-
        tic subdivision of, 488–489; discus-
        sion of, 492–496; life event
        assessment in, 489–490; methods
        for, 487–488; patients for, 487–488
    posttraumatic stress disorder and ma-
        jor, 595
    schizophrenia and, 377–391; conclu-
        sions on, 390–341; desirable events
        and, 382–385; discussion of,
        387–390; first admission in, 382;
        life-event rates in, 380–382; meth-
        ods for, 379–380; precipitated
        depression in, 386–387; results in,
        380–387; undesirable events in,
        382–385; unprecipitated depres-
        sion in, 386–387, 389
    severity of, 245
    stressful life events and, 5–11, 327–328
    Vietnam veterans and, 568
Depressive neurosis, schizophrenia and;
    see Schizophrenia, depressive neu-
    rosis and
Dermatologic disorders, 213, 307–317
Desipramine, 593
Desirable events, schizophrenia and de-
    pressive neurosis and, 382–385
Developmental changes, midlife stress and,
713–718
Developmental perspective on life-event
    webs, 19–27
Diabetes, end-stage renal disease and, 289
Dialysis, 288–296
    adjustment to, 296–301
    meaning of, 291–292
Diathesis-stress model, 344–345
Diet, 199
    end-stage renal disease and, 290, 300
Diphenhydramine, 596, 598
Disability
    concerns of elderly about, 752
    in spouse, 213
Disappointment in school activities, 243
Discharge papers, factitious posttraumatic
    stress disorder and, 584
Disease state, sufficient conditions for, 32
Dispute Resolution Act, 661
Disruption, personal interpretations along
    dimensions of, 169
Dissipative structures, 286–288
Distracting parenting behavior, 650
    positive reinforcement and, 652
    prosocial behavior in child and, 651,
        652
Distress in child, exploratory or prosocial
    behavior and, 650
Distress scores, 168
Divorce
    acceptance of, 669
    adjustment of children to, 671
    effects of, 26–27, 660–661
    failure fear and, 671–672
    mediation in separation and, 661–666
    midlife stress and, 712–713
    social support system and, 670–671
Double-bind hypothesis, schizophrenia
    and, 424
DPIS; see Dyadic Prestressor Interaction
    Scale
Drug abuse, 243
    treatment program for, 531
    Vietnam veterans and, 568
Drug Dependence Treatment Program,
    531
Drug-induced normality, psychosis and,
    413
Dual-career couples, 699
Dual-career families, 702
Dual-earner families, 700, 702
Dual-income lifestyle, 697
DUB; see Dysfunctional uterine bleeding

Dyadic Prestressor Interaction Scale, 645, 649, 650, 651, 652
Dysfunctional uterine bleeding, 271–280
Dysmenorrhea, 272, 273

Eating disorders, 211
  anorexia nervosa and; see Anorexia nervosa
  Vietnam veterans and, 568
Economic background, child behavior and, 628–630
Economic survival concerns of elderly, 733, 751, 755
Education, relationship of, to concerns of elderly, 756
EE; see Expressed emotion, index of
Elderly
  concerns of, 752
  future concerns of, 749–758: discussion of, 755–757; factors relating to, 754–755; methods for, 750–751; results in, 751–755
  life change events and, 729–747: coping patterns in, 736–745; life stress measurement and, 735–736; summary of, 745–746
  psychiatric disorders and stress in, 735
Emotional atmosphere, 81
Emotional attitudes of relatives, schizophrenia and, 389, 429
Emotional impact of life events, interpretive factors and, 224
Emotional reaction in elderly
  coping mechanisms and, 739
  fear of recurrence of previously associated, 750
Emotional upset, personal interpretations along dimensions of, 169
Emotion-focused parenting behavior, 644
Emotion psychoses, schizophrenia and, 330
Emotion recognition, schizophrenia and, 449
Employability, end-stage renal disease and, 301
End-stage renal disease, 212–213, 281–306
  adjustment to, 296–301: course of, 297–300; factors in successful, 300
  biobehavioral model of stress and, 286–288
  as both stressor and stress response, 283
  cognitive deficits in, 295–296
  depression and, 292–293

dialysis adjustment in, 296–301
dissipative structures in, 286–288
employability and, 301
fatigue and, 293–294
fluid and diet restrictions in, 290
machine dependence and, 289
marital functioning in, 291, 295
motor deficits in, 295–296
pain and, 295
patient mobility in, 290–291
quality of life issues in, 301–303
rehabilitation and, 301
sensory deficits in, 295–296
sexual problems and, 294
stress in, 288–296: biobehavioral definition of, 288; definition of, 282–285; interaction between stimulus and moderating factors and, 284–285; response to, 283–284; stimulus of, 285
suicide and, 294
time demands of treatment and, 290
uncertainty about survival and, 289
Environmental concerns in elderly, 751
Environmental experiences and personal cognitive framework, 166
Environmental level of behavior, 286
Environmental stressors, 759–760
Equilibrium, 286–287
ESRD; see End-stage renal disease
Euphoria, end-stage renal disease adjustment and, 298
Eutonyl; see Pargyline
Event agreement and item agreement, distinction between, 132–133
Events, desirable and undesirable, schizophrenia and depressive neurosis and, 382–385
Evolving reciprocity, 17
Examination stress conditions, 190–194
Exercise, dialysis adjustment and, 300
Experience
  common core in, 60
  integration of, midlife stress and, 724
Exploration behavior in child, 650, 651
Exposure to life events, schizophrenia and, 414–415
Expressed emotion
  in families, schizophrenia and, 400
  Family Project Interviews for, 435
  index of, 81–82, 379, 427, 428
  and relapse in schizophrenia, 423–432
Ex-spouse relationships, 670

External events
  personality characteristics and reactivity
    to, 496
  as stressor in elderly, 731, 732
External strain in dual-career couple, 700

Factitious posttraumatic stress disorder,
    573–585
  case reports of, 574–580
  conclusion in, 584–585
  discussion of, 580–584
  motives in, 581
Factor analysis, 41
  of Schedule of Recent Experience,
    109–110
Failure, divorce and perception of,
    671–672
Falling asleep, difficulty in, 259, 261, 262
Family, 22–23
  child behavior and, 631
  child-rearing problems and, 612–613
  end-stage renal disease and, 291
  and life span development, 603–758; see
    also Life span development
  mediation in; see Family mediation, sep-
    aration and divorce
  ripple effects and, 18–19
  schizophrenia and: expressed emotion
    and, 400; onset of, 433–439; pa-
    thology of, 366–367
  see also Relatives
Family background variables, child-rear-
    ing problems and, 612–613
Family constellations, 22–23
Family crisis framework of Hill, 297
Family Environment Scales, 532
Family life, end-stage renal disease and,
    291
Family life events
  child behavior and, 631
  in maternal depression and child-rear-
    ing problems, 609–618; see also
    Child-rearing problems
Family life events score, child-rearing
    problems and, 611
Family mediation, separation and divorce,
    661–664
  clinical issues in, 669–672
  effects of, 665–666
  model for, 666–669
  psychological factors in, 664–665
Family Project Interviews for expressed
    emotion, 435

Family studies predicting onset of schiz-
    ophrenia, 433–439
Fateful events, schizophrenia and, 409
Father, absence of, 243
Fatigue, end-stage renal disease and,
    293–294
Feelings of malaise, end-stage renal dis-
    ease and, 291
Feighner criteria for depression, 487
Females, anxiety and, 185, 193; see also
    Gender differences
Feminine side of male, midlife stress and,
    722
FES; see Family Environment Scales
Final straw role, life event, 77
Financial concerns in elderly, 733, 751,
    755
First admission to hospital, schizophrenia
    and depressive neurosis and, 382
Flight students, anxiety and, 183
Fluid restrictions, 290
Fluphenazine, 596
Flurazepam, 598
Food consumption
  aversive or stress-inducing events and,
    238
  regulation of, 248–249
  see also Anorexia nervosa
Formative effect of life events, 343–346,
    352—353
Formative stressors in schizophrenia, 398
Friedman test for aligned ranks, 133
Friendships, end-stage renal disease and,
    291
Frustration, Vietnam combat and, 565–566
Functional concerns in elderly, 734, 751,
    756
Fungal infections, 307–317
Future development of neurotic symp-
    toms, 165–179
  discussion of, 173–177
  methods for, 167–170
  procedure in, 167–168
  results in, 170–173
  study measures in, 168–170
  study sample in, 167
Future health, perceived control over, 200

Gender differences
  anxiety and, 185, 193
  concerns of elderly and, 756
  sleep disorders and, 265–266
  see also Male

Gender roles, 700–702
General Health Questionnaire, 169
Genetic measures, multivariate analysis events and, 766
GHQ; see General Health Questionnaire
Goal-directed pursuit of life events, 411–414
Goldberg Index, 447
Graffam Schedule of Nurse Response to Patients' Complaints of Distress, 114
Group involvement, 15
Group specific life-event scale, 40, 107–108, 113–114
Guilt, Vietnam veterans and, 568
Gurin Mental Status Index, 79

Haldol; see Haloperidol
Hallucinations, 79, 387
Hallucinatory-delusional factor, 79
Haloperidol, 596
Hassles of daily life, 759
Hazardousness scores, 76
Health
    concerns of elderly about, 734, 751, 752, 756
    dysfunctional uterine bleeding and, 276, 277, 279
    stress as barrier to, 197–207
Health Belief Model, 197–198
Health concerns of elderly, 734, 751, 752, 756
Health monitoring, 200
Health seeking behavior, stress and, 197, 199–200
Heart failure, end-stage renal disease and, 289
Helplessness, 229–230
    personal interpretations along dimensions of, 169
Hemodialysis, 281
Hierarchy of needs, Maslow's, 732–733
Hill family crisis framework, 297
Historical roots of stress, 5
Hollingshead two-factor index, 239
Holmes and Rahe life stress scale, 390, 504
Home-dialysis, 302
Hopeless situation, life-event ratings and, 150
Hormones, dysfunctional uterine bleeding and, 277
Hospitalization in schizophrenia, 411–414
    military service and, 54–55

Hospitalized patients and general population, differences in life-event rates between, 83
Hospital Stress Rating Scale, 111
Household tension, chronic, 68
HSRS; see Hospital Stress Rating Scale
Human development interventions, 25
Husbands' disabilities
    wives at risk after, 213
Hydrazine, 592
Hydroxyzine, 598
Hyperhidrosis, 309, 310
Hypochondriasis, black versus white Vietnam veterans and, 541, 543
Hypomania, black versus white Vietnam veterans and, 541, 544
Hypothalamic-pituitary-adrenal axis, 249
Hypothalamic-pituitary-ovarian axis, 277
Hysteria, black versus white Vietnam veterans and, 541, 542

ICD; see International Classification of Diseases
Identity
    personal, society definition of, 715
    psychological, racial prejudice and, 526
Ignoring parenting behavior, 655
    in medical situation, 650
    prosocial behavior in child and, 651
    punishment use and, 653
Illness
    in parent, 243
    requiring hospitalization, 243
Illness Onset Model, 8–11
Imaginal procedures in treating delayed combat stress reactions, 569
Income
    concerns of elderly and, 756
    declining, midlife stress and, 712–713
    end-stage renal disease and, 291
    life events and, 764
Independent life events, 406
    beyond respondent's personal control, 60–61
    schizophrenia and, 414
Inderal; see Propranolol
Index of Expressed Emotion, 81–82, 378, 427, 428
Individual interpretations of life-event distress, 227
Individual variables, life stress situations and, 762

Information overload, schizophrenia in, 448
Information-processing deficits, 449
Informing parenting behavior, 651
Inner conflict, midlife stress and, 716
Insomnia, 257–270
Instability of personality, 230
Institutionalization
 concerns of elderly poor and, 756
 as stressor in elderly, 731
Integration of experience, midlife stress and, 721, 724
Intellectualization, cognitive control and, 443
Intellectual variables, 762
Interactional approach, stress and, 284
Interactive measurement of life-event stress, 763
Interactive patterns between family members or significant others, 765
Interdependent lives, 13–29
 attachment and, 14–15
 life-event webs and, 15–19: developmental perspective in, 19–27
 role partners and, 14–15
Intergenerational studies, 22–23
Internal stressors
 in dual-career couple, 700
 in elderly, 732
Internal Support scale, teacher stress and, 689
International Classification of Diseases, 474, 475
Interpersonal relationships, 15
 life events and, 764
 supportive, 117–118
 variables affecting, 44–45
Interpersonal support, life events and, 764
Interrater agreement, 124–125
Interruptions scale, teacher stress and, 685
Interventions, human development, 25
Interview
 conditions of, 151–153
 life stress measurement and, 59
 probing and, 160
 rating of variables in, 153–154
 with relatives or significant others, 75
 reliability and, 123–126
 stress and bulimia in anorexia nervosa and, 240
 see also Life-event interview

Interviewer effect, 142–143
 on volume of elicited events, 137, 138–139, 142
Interview method of life-event rating, reliability of, 123–126
Intrafamilial milieu, 81
Intrapair agreement, 132–133
Intrauterine device, 276
Intrusiveness of family, schizophrenia and, 455
Inventory of life change events, 107
 unidimensional, 45
Involutional depression, 720
Irritability, Vietnam combat veterans and, 568
Isocarboxazid, 592
Issues and implications of life stress measurement, 40–46
Item agreement and event agreement, distinction between, 132–133
Item characteristics, life-event interviews and, 136–137
IUD; see Intrauterine device

J. Hillis Miller Health Center, 645
Job changes
 end-stage renal disease and, 291
 schizophrenia and, 365
Job Perceptions scale, teacher stress and, 693
Johnson and McCutcheon Life Events Checklist, 636, 640, 641

Kellner-Sheffield Symptom Rating Test, 310–311
Kendell hypothesis of depression and aggression, 486, 489, 494
KSP self-rating of personality characteristics, 490–491, 496

LCU; see Life change units
LCU score; see Life change unit score
Learned helplessness, 439
LEDS; see Life Events and Difficulty Schedule
Legacies of Vietnam, 527
Levine-Polowsky questionnaire, 611, 613
Life change events; see Life events
Life change score, 109
 negative, 637, 638
 positive, 637
 potential sources of error in, 59
 see also Life change units

Life change units, 35
  criticisms of, 57–59
  stress and bulimia in anorexia nervosa
    and, 240
  see also Life change score
Life charts, 395
Life ending concerns of elderly, 756
Life event; see Life events
Life-event chaining, 177
Life-event data, 168
  quantification of, 168–169
Life-event distress, individual interpreta-
    tions of, 227
Life-event interview, 149–164, 510
  discussion of study of, 159–160
  method of study of, 151–154
  reliability of, 127–147: comment on,
    139–143; methods for, 129–133;
    results in, 133–139
  results in, 133–139, 154–159
  see also Interview
Life-event inventories, 107
  ambiguity, timing, and controllability of
    life events and, 761
  sleep disorder frequency and, 258
  structure of, 761
  of Tennant and Andrews, 168, 224
  unidimensional, 45
Life-event measurements
  in hospitalized patients and general
    population, differences in, 83
  prominent scales in, 108–111
  reliability of, 123–126
  significant contributions to, 34–38
  schizophrenia and depressive neurosis
    and, 380–382
  see also Life-event scaling
Life Event Record, Coddington, 640
Life events
  and aggression, 494
  assessing impact of, 22
  assessment and methodological issues
    in, 101–208; see also Assessment
    and methodological issues
  behavior and increases or decreases in,
    223
  Brown criteria for stress of, 115
  change and, 56
  child-rearing problems and, 620
  classification of, 406: qualitative,
    217–218; quantitative, 217
  conceptual model of stressful, 32–34
  concluding thoughts on, 759–767

coping with stress in elderly and,
    736–745
  datable in terms of impact or first
    awareness, 56
  definition of, 56, 106
  depression and, 489–490
  and dermatologic disorders, 307–317
  emotional impact of, 225–226: in-
    terpretive factors in, 224
  of family, child behavior and, 631
  and hospitalization, goal-directed pur-
    suit of, 411–414
  individual interpretations of, 227
  internal and external cause for, 229
  inventory of, 107: unidimensional, 45
  long-term, child behavior and, 625–626,
    631–632
  and maternal depression, perceived child
    behavior in, 630
  mental illness and, 325–516; see also
    Mental illness
  myocardial infarction and, 215–222:
    personal determinants in, 223–236
  near future onset of psychological
    symptoms and, 165–179; see also
    Near future onset of symptoms
  and personality characteristics, 496
  proximal and distal effects of, 16–17
  schizophrenia and, 51–89, 403–415:
    background and research on,
    394–396; interaction with relatives'
    emotional attitudes in, 388; net-
    work of social support in, 73, 81;
    neuroleptic medications in, 68–70;
    studies of, 397–424; unrelatedness
    of, 415–423
  schizophrenia in absence of stressful,
    416–418
  short-term, child behavior and, 620,
    624–625, 631
  triggering effect of, 52, 343–346,
    352–353: schizophrenia and,
    397–404
  universal and group specific elements
    of stress in, 107–108
  variables affecting, 43, 44–45, 117
Life Events and Difficulty Schedule,
    149–150
Life-event scaling, 105–121
  definitions in, 106
  hospital stress rating scale and, 111
  major contributors to, 106–108
  other life-event measures and, 115–118

prominent scales in, 108–111
Psychiatric Epidemiological Research Interview—Life Events Scale and, 112–113
schedule of nurse response to patient distress and, 114
universal and group specific scales and, 113–114
see also Life-event measurements
Life Events Checklist, Johnson and McCutcheon, 636, 640, 641
Life events interview; *see* Life-event interview
Life events inventories; *see* Life-event inventories
Life-event stress; *see* Life events
Life-event webs, interdependent lives and, 15–19
research implications of, 21–25
Life experience integration, midlife stress and, 721
Life satisfaction
for men in working families, 705–706
for women in working families, 706–707
Life situation list, 161–164
Life span development, 603–758
child behavior and, 619–632; *see also* Child behavior
child-rearing problems in, 609–618; *see also* Child-rearing problems
contested child custody and, 659–675; *see also* Contested child custody
elderly adult and, 737–758; *see also* Elderly
family life events in, 609–618; *see also* Child-rearing problems
maternal depression in, 609–618; *see also* Child-rearing problems
midlife stress and, 711–728; *see also* Midlife stress
parenting children in medical situation, 643–657; *see also* Parenting children in medical situation
somatic complaints in adolescents and, 633–642
teacher stress in, 677–696; *see also* Teacher stress
working families and, 697–710; *see also* Working families
see also Family
Life-span orientation, 16
Life stress
behavioral medicine and, 209–324; *see*

also Behavioral medicine, life stress and
in elderly, measurement of, 735–736
and mental disorder, association between, 53–54
methodological questions in measurement of, 43–44
prospective studies and, 45–46
Life stress scales
of Holmes and Rahe, 390, 504
measurement of life stress and, 41–42
Life-style, 199
Life webs, interdependent lives and, 15–19
research implications of, 21–25
Limited opportunity hypothesis, 528, 529
Lithium
bipolar disorder and, 504
traumatic war stress and, 599
Living patterns, schizophrenia and stress prone, 404
Living with children, concerns of elderly and, 757
Locus of control, multivariate analysis of life events and, 766
London measure of threatening life events, reliability of, 123–126
London study of schizophrenia, 357–358
generalizability of results of, 369–371
main results from, 358–359
nature of life events described in, 364–368
Loneliness in elderly, 751
Long-term life events
child behavior and, 631–632
maternal depression, and child behavior, 625–626
as provoking agent in schizophrenia and depressive neurosis, 386

Machine dependence, end-stage renal disease and, 289
Magnitude-estimation, technique of, 107
Maintenance antipsychotic medication, schizophrenia and, 399–400
Major life events, psychological stress and, 765
Major role therapy, 400
Malaise, end-stage renal disease and, 291
Male
anxiety and, 185, 193
emergent feminine side of, midlife, 722
see also Gender differences
Manic-depressive disorder, 485

MAO inhibitors; *see* Monoamine oxidase inhibitors

Marital adjustment/satisfaction, 243, 701
  end-stage renal disease and, 291, 295
  schizophrenia and, 424

Marital status, concerns of elderly and, 756

Marplan; *see* Isocarboxazid

Masculinity-feminity
  black versus white Vietnam veterans and, 541
  midlife stress and, 722

Maslow's hierarchy of needs, 732–733

Material resources, psychiatric hospitalization and, 412

Maternal and teacher descriptions of child behavior, 619–632; *see also* Child behavior

Maternal anxiety, parenting behavior and, 653

Maternal depression
  child-rearing problems and, 609–618; *see also* Child-rearing problems
  and long-term life events, 625–626, 631–632
  and short-term life events, 620, 624–625, 631
  perceived child behavior and, 630: scoring of, 611–612

Maternal mood
  actual child behavior and, 631
  life stress and, 610
  perceived child behavior and, 630

Maternal rating of child behavior, 621–622
  scoring of, 611–612
  see also Child behavior

Maximum stress effect, nature and timing of, 342–346

Measurement of life stress, 31–49
  conceptual model of stressful life events and, 32–34
  contributions to, 34–38
  group specific life-events scales and, 40
  issues and implications of, 40–46
  methodological questions in, 43–44
  New Haven measure and, 38
  Psychiatric Epidemiological Research Interview—Life Events Scale and, 38–39
  schizophrenia in absence of stressful life events and, 418–420
  universal life-events scales and, 40

Mediating structures, 25

Mediation process
  family, 669–672
  model of, 662

Medical situations
  behavioral; *see* Behavioral medicine, life stress and parenting children in, 643–657; *see also* Parenting children in medical situation

Medication refusal, schizophrenia and, 413–424

Medications
  end-stage renal disease and, 291
  schizophrenic relapse and, 68–70, 413
  vulnerability reduction and, 368

Memory, problems of, 74–75; *see also* Recall

Menstrual irregularity, 272

Mental illness, 325–516
  bipolar disorder and, 499–506
  depression and, 485–498: Kenyan setting of, 507–515; *see also* Depression
  and life stress, association between, 53–54
  obsessive-compulsive neurosis and, 473–483; *see also* Obsessive-compulsive neurosis
  schizophrenia and, 377–391: psychogenesis of, 395; recent events in, 351–375; stress and, 329–350; *see also* Schizophrenia

Mental patient role, voluntary assumption of, 412

Meprobamate-like drugs, 598

Metabolic measures, multivariate analysis of life events and, 766

Methodological assessment of stressful life events, 101–208
  inadequacies in, schizophrenia and, 419
  see also Assessment and methodological issues

MI; *see* Myocardial infarction

Microstressors, 759

Midlife stress, 711–728
  aging and, 713–718: factors conducive to, 723–725; obstacles to successful, 718–721; role inconstancy and, 721–723; declining income and, 712–713; developmental changes and, 713–718; divorce and, 26–27, 712–713; role inconstancy and, 721–723; widowhood and, 712–715

Military service, schizophrenia during, 54–55, 401–402; *see also* Posttrau-

matic stress
Miller Health Center, 645
Minnesota Multiphasic Personality Inventory
  dermatologic disorder and, 308–309
  posttraumatic stress and, 518, 526, 532, 536, 537, 538, 542, 544, 547, 560, 561
  schizophrenia and, 447
Modeling parenting behavior, 652
Model of stressful life events, conceptual, 32–34
Moderating and stimulus factors, stress as interaction between, 336–337
Monoamine oxidase inhibitors, 590–593
Mood, maternal
  actual child behavior and, 631
  life stress and, 610
  perceived child behavior and, 630
Moos coping behavior inventory, 318
Mother, schizophrenia and pathology in, 366–367; see also Maternal depression
Motherhood, pride in, midlife stress and, 720
Motivation
  deficit of, 250–251
  midlife stress and, 716
Motor deficits, end-stage renal disease and, 295–296
Motor retardation factor, 79
MPI, dermatologic disorder and, 308–309
MRT; see Major role therapy
Munchausen's syndrome, 576, 583, 585
Myocardial infarction, 210–211
  anxiety surrounding, 227–229
  life-event stress and, 223–236: conclusions of, 233; method for, 224–225; results and discussion of, 225–233

Narcoanalysis, traumatic war stress and, 589
Nardil; see Phenelzine
Naturalistic stressors, schizophrenia and, 403
Navane; see Thiothixene
Near future onset of symptoms, 165–179
  cross-lagged correlations and, 175–176
  discussion of, 173–177
  measures for study of, 168
  method for, 167–168
  procedure for, 167–168
  results of, 170–173
  sample for, 167

Necessary cause, 32
Negative Life Change score, 637, 638
Network of social support, 81
  schizophrenia and, 73
  stability and change in, 20
Neurochemical deviations, bulimic eating and, 248
Neuroleptic medications, schizophrenia and, 68–70
Neurotic symptoms, 79, 309
  dermatologic disorders and, 314–315
  future development of, 165–179
  life-event measures and, 230
New Haven measure for life change, 38
New Haven Schizophrenia Index, 78, 79
New Haven study of schizophrenia, 355–357
  generalizability of results of, 369–371
  life events described in, 364–368
  main results from, 358–359
Nightmares, 259, 260
  frequency of recall of, 266–267
Noncontingent life events, 406
Nonindependent life events, 406
  schizophrenia and, 411
Non-precipitated depressions, 391
Noradrenergic mechanisms, 248–249
Norepinephrine, 248, 249
Normality
  end-stage renal disease and struggle for, 298
  psychosis and drug-induced, 413
Nortriptyline, 593
NSYMP; see Number of Symptoms Index
Number of Symptoms Index, 169, 171–173
Numbing-denial tendency, posttraumatic stress disorder and, 555
Nurse response to patient distress, 114
Nursing home concerns of elderly poor, 756

Objective items
  life-event interviews and, 136–137
  reliability and, 140
Observed parenting behavior, self-reported style and, 644
Obsessive-compulsive neurosis
  personality traits in, 473–483: method for, 474–477; results of, 477–480
  Research Diagnostic Criteria for, 474
Obsessive thought disorder, delayed stress syndrome and, 569
Older woman, society definition of, 714;

see also Elderly; Midlife stress
Onset
  of psychological symptoms, personal assessments and, 165–179; *see* Near future onset of symptoms
  versus recurrence of schizophrenia, 368–369
Operation Outreach, 573
Overinvolvement of family, schizophrenia and, 455

Pain
  end-stage renal disease and, 291, 295
  life crises and, 57
Paranoia, black versus white Vietnam veterans and, 541, 543, 544
Parent, illness in, 243
Parenting behavior
  agitating, 651
  distracting, 650: prosocial behavior in child and, 651, 652
  emotion-focused, coping efforts in child and, 644
  ignoring, 650: prosocial behavior in child and, 651; punishing parenting behavior and, 653
  informing, 651: exploration behavior in child and, 651
  modification of, in medical situation, 644; *see also* Parenting children in medical situation
  observed, self-reported style and, 644
  positive reinforcing, 652, 655
  problem-focused, 644
  punishing, 653
  reassuring, 650, 652: attachment behavior in child and, 651
  restraining, 650
  situational anxiety and, 644
Parenting children in medical situation, 643–657
  discussion of, 653–656
  method for, 645–650
  results in, 650–653
Pargyline, 592
Parnate; *see* Tranylcypromine
Patient mobility, end-stage renal disease and, 290–291
Patterns of living, stress-prone, 404
Pavlovian learning interpretation of stress-induced overeating, 251
Paykel checklist format for life event scaling, 115, 217, 475

Pentothal sodium, 589
Perceived control over future health, 200
Perceived life change events, 9
Perceived self-esteem, multivariate analysis of life events and, 766
Performance, anxiety and, 192–193
  trait, 184–185
PERI–LES; *see* Psychiatric Epidemiological Research Interview–Life Events Scale
Peritoneal dialysis, 281
Personal assessments of life-event stress and near future onset of symptoms, 165–179; *see also* Near future onset of symptoms
Personal cognitive framework and environmental experiences, 166
Personal control, 229–230
Personal identity, society definition of, 715
Personal interview; *see* Interview; Life-event interview
Personality, 117
  assessment of, 490–496
  depression and, 485–498
  instability of, life-event measures and, 230
  KSP self rating of, 490–491, 496
  life events and, 327, 496
  obsessive-compulsive neurosis and, 473–483
  and reactivity to external events, 496
  Srole's scales for, 425
  Standard Assessment of Personality in, 475, 479, 481
Personal loss, life-event ratings and, 150
Personal-social areas, dysfunctional uterine bleeding and, 276, 278, 279
Phenelzine, 590, 592
Phenothiazines, schizophrenia and
  reducing or stopping, 66, 68–70
  maintenance of, 385–386
Physical illness, stress and, 197
Physical symptoms, unpredictable events and, 91–99
Piton Foundation, 663
Polarizing filter model of cognitive appraisal, 441
Population controls, differences in life events and, 83
Positive Life Change score, 637
Positive reinforcing parenting behavior, 652, 655

Posttraumatic stress, 517–601
  adjustment related to significant life stressors and, 565–567
  chemotherapy and, 587–601; *see also* Chemotherapy, traumatic war stress
  clinical strategies with, 567–570
  criteria for diagnosing, 555
  depression and, 595
  diagnostic variables, 560–565
  DSM-III and, 554–558
  factitious, 573–586: case reports of, 574–580; conclusion in, 584–585; discussion of, 580–584; motives in, 581
  method for, 558
  psychometric assessment and race and, 524–552: discussion of, 545–549; limited opportunity and deviant behavior in, 527–531; method for, 531–538; Parsons' hypotheses in, 541–545; prejudice and maladjustment in, 526–527; results in, 538–541
  results in, 538–541, 558–560
  symptoms of, 587–588
  validity of, 554
  Vietnam, 519–523: Vietnam Experiences Questionnaire and, 526, 556, 567–568
Power, conflict resolution and mediation in family, 662
Precipitated depression, schizophrenia and depressive neurosis and, 386–387
Precision, 137
Predictability, 91–99
Pregnancy complications, schizophrenia and, 343
Premorbid personality, obsessive-compulsive neurosis and, 479–480
Preschizophrenic conditions, 341–342
Present State Examination, 379, 427, 509
Prigogine concept of dissipative structures, 286–288
Problem behavior in child; *see* Child behavior
Problem-focused coping mechanisms, 446
  in child, 644
  in elderly, 739
Prodromal features in psychosis, 332, 408–411
Prolixin; *see* Fluphenazine
Propanediols, 598
Propranolol, 597–598

Prosocial behavior in child
  distracting parenting behavior and, 651, 652
  distress in child and, 650
  ignoring parenting behavior and, 651
Prospective studies, life stress research and, 45–46
Protriptyline, 593
PSE; *see* Present State Examination
Pseudomutuality, schizophrenia and, 424
Psoriasis, 307–317
Psychasthenia, black versus white Vietnam veterans and, 541, 542, 543
Psychiatric Epidemiological Research Interview–Life Events Scale, 38–39, 112–113, 129
Psychiatric Evaluation Form, 79
Psychiatric symptomatology in extreme situations, 360–364
Psychogenesis of schizophrenia, 395
Psychological depression; *see* Depression
Psychological fluctuation, schizophrenia and, 421–423
Psychological identity, racial prejudice and integrity of, 526
Psychological level of behavior, 286
Psychological stress; *see* Stress
Psychometric assessment and race
  discussion of, 545–549
  limited opportunity and deviant behavior in, 527–531
  method for, 531–538
  Parsons' hypotheses in, 541–545
  racial prejudice and maladjustment and, 526–527
  results in, 538–541
Psychopathic deviate, Vietnam veterans and, 541, 542
Psychoses
  brief reactive, 331
  and drug-induced normality, 413
  prodromal features in, 332, 408–415
Psychosocial environment, schizophrenia and, 400–401
Psychosomatic symptoms, 395
  adolescent and, 633–642
  Vietnam combat veterans and, 568
Psychotic symptoms
  combat conditions and, 360–364
  stress and exacerbation of, 403
  Vietnam combat veterans and, 568
Punishing parenting behavior, 653, 654

QTWL; *see* Quality of Teacher Work Life Scale
Quality of life, end-stage renal disease and, 301
Quality of Teacher Work Life Scale, 679, 680
Quantification of life-event data, 168–169

Race, psychometric assessment and, 525–552; *see also* Psychometric assessment and race
Racial prejudice hypothesis, posttraumatic stress disorder and, 526–527
Reactive psychoses, brief, 331
Reactivity to external events, personality characteristics and, 496
Real man image, midlife stress and, 722
Reassuring parenting behavior, 650, 652
attachment behavior in child and, 651
Recall
biased, 220: bulimia and, 246–247; dysfunctional uterine bleeding and, 278
decrements in, 137, 138, 142
problems of, 74–75
Recent life change
and degree of stressfulness, 135–136
in elderly, 752–754
and Illness Onset Model, 8–11
and depression, 7–8
measurement of, 6–7
Recent Life Changes Questionnaire, 35, 274, 276
Recent Life Events Interview, revised, 217
Recruitment of social support in schizophrenia, 451–454
summary of, 454–455
Recurrence versus onset of schizophrenia, 368–369, 425–432
Reflection, midlife stress and, 724
Refusal of medication, schizophrenia and, 413
Regression, adaptive, 296
Rehabilitation, end-stage renal disease and, 301
Relapse, schizophrenia and, 368–369, 425–432
Relational approach to stress, 760
Relationships with Students and Parents scale, 684
Relative risk, measure of, 77–78
Relatives
interviewing of, 75

schizophrenia and: criticism and, 429; emotional attitudes and, 388; emotional overinvolvement and, 429
see also Family
Relaxation exercises, elderly and, 743–744
Reliability
of life-event interviews with outpatient schizophrenics, 127–147; *see also* Life-event interview
measurement of life stress and, 41
of SRE, 110
Relocation
schizophrenia and, 342, 365
as stress in elderly, 730, 757
Renal dialysis, 288–296
adjustment to, 296–301
meaning of, 291–292
Reproductive capacity, end-stage renal disease and, 291
Research Diagnostic Criteria for obsessive-compulsive disorder, 474
Residential changes
elderly and, 730, 757
schizophrenia and, 342, 365
Restraining, parenting behavior and, 650, 652
Restraint-interfering effects of stressors, 251
Restrictor subgroup of anorexia nervosa, 238, 239
Risk, measure of, 77–78
RLCQ; *see* Recent Life Changes Questionnaire
Robbery concerns of elderly, 752, 755, 756
Role inconstancy, successful aging and, 721–723
Role partners, interdependent lives and, 14–15
Roles
chronic strains in, 759
concept of, 14–15
for men and women, traditional, 700–702
successful aging and, 721–723
Rorschach Test, 433
Rutter Child Behaviour Questionnaire, 617, 621, 624

Safe driving behavior, 203, 206
Safety, 199
Salience, reliability and, 136
Sample bias, assessment in schizophrenia

and, 419; *see also* Bias of recall
Sample size, assessment in schizophrenia and, 419
SAP; *see* Standard Assessment of Personality
Schalling-Sifneos Personality Scale, 311
Schedule for life events, 115, 217, 475
Schedule of nurse response to patient distress, 114
Schedule of Recent Experience, 35–37, 108–111, 149–150
  elderly and, 736
  factor analysis of, 109–110
  reliability of, 110
  schizophrenia and, 395, 408, 409
  validity of, 109
Schizophrenia, 351–375, 393–471
  acute, 331: onset of, 333
  black versus white Vietnam veterans and, 541, 543, 544
  case-control studies of, 353–355
  clinical interventions and, 460–461
  conclusions in, 371–372, 455–456
  coping responses and, 438–449: alternatives in, 447–450; behavioral coping and, 446–447; cognitive appraisal in, 441–443; cognitive control strategies and, 443–446; cognitive coping in, 440–441
  defining characteristic in, 370
  definition of, 329–334
  definition of stress in, 334–339
  depressive neurosis and, 377–391: conclusions on, 390–391; desirable events and, 382–385; discussion of, 387–390; first admission in, 382; life-event rates in, 380–382; methods for, 379–380; precipitated depression in, 386–387; results in, 380–387; undesirable events in, 382–385; unprecipitated depression in, 386–387
  diagnosis of, clinical samples and, 83–84
  environment of, stressful life events and, 420–421
  expressed emotion and relapse in, 425–432
  familial stress in, 424–425
  family studies predicting onset of, 433–439: summary of, 437–438
  future research and, 456–460
  hospitalization and, 54–55, 411–414: consecutive first admission in, 71–72

  insidious onset of, 408–409
  life events and, 51–89, 359–360, 397–424: absence of stressful, 416–418; background and research on, 394–396; conceptual and methodological issues in, 52–61; conclusions in, 82–85; exposure to, 414–415; findings of controlled studies on, 62–82; goal-directed pursuit of, 411–414; neuroleptic medications and, 68–70; triggering role of, 397–404; unrelatedness of, 415–423
  London study of, 357–358: generalizability of results of, 369–371; life events described in, 364–368; main results from, 358–359
  maximum stress effect and, 342–346
  military service and hospitalization rates for, 54–55
  model for, 344–345
  New Haven study of, 355–357: generalizability of results of, 369–371; life events described in, 364–368; main results from, 358–359
  onset of, 331–334: unrelatedness of life events and, 415–423
  prodromal symptoms of, 332, 409–411
  psychiatric symptomatology in extreme situations and, 360–364
  recurrence of, 368–369: vulnerability/stress model in, 432
  reliability of life-event interviews with outpatient, 125–145; *see also* Life-event interview
  residual symptoms of, 409–411
  social support recruitment and, 451–454
  spectrum of disorders in, 410
  stress and, 325–327: conclusions on, 345–346; definition of, 334–339; environment and, 420–421; interaction between stimulus and moderating factors and, 336–337; measurement of, 339–342; response to, 334–336; stimulus of, 337–339
  stress-prone factors in, 408–415
  stress-prone patterns of living and, 404
  summary on, 432, 454–455
  support systems for, 452
  vulnerability/stress model of, 437
Schizophrenic factor, 79
Schizophreniform illness, 330

School activities, disappointment in, 243
SDS; *see* Self-Rating Depression Scale
Sealing over, cognitive control and, 444
Sedative-hypnotics, 598
Self-acceptance, midlife stress and, 717
Self-concept, effective coping and, 445
Self-disclosing statements, schizophrenia and, 449
Self-esteem
  midlife stress and, 719, 720
  perceived, multivariate analysis of life events and, 766
  successful aging and, 718
  Vietnam veterans and, 568
Self-image, midlife stress and, 714
Self-Rating Depression Scale, 169–170, 171–173
Self-reported parenting style and observed behavior, 644
Sending skills, schizophrenia and, 448, 450
Sensorily deprived environments, schizophrenia and, 422
Sensory deficits, end-stage renal disease and, 295–296
Sensory overload, schizophrenia and, 448
Separation and divorce
  family mediation in, 661–664
  impact of, 660–661
Sex differences
  anxiety and, 185, 193
  concerns of elderly and, 756
  sleep disorders and, 265–266
  see also Male
Sex roles, 700–702
Sexual identity, society definition of, 715
Sexual problems, end-stage renal disease and, 294
Sharing of work, workings families and, 698
Short-term life events, child behavior and, 620, 624–625, 631
Sick role, dialysis and, 300
Side-effects of medication, end-stage renal disease and, 291
Significant others, interviewing of, 75
Singer-Wynne measure of communication deviance, 433
Situational anxiety and parenting behavior, 644
SLCU score; *see* Subjective Life Change Unit score
Sleep, 203, 206

restless, 259, 261, 262
  unrefreshing, 259, 261, 262
Sleep disorders, 211–212
  reported frequency of, 257–270: discussion of, 267–269; method, 259–261; results, 261–267
  Vietnam combat veterans and, 568
Smoking, 203, 206
Social Adjustment Scale, 318
Social background
  child behavior and, 628–630
  child-rearing problems and, 612–613
Social introversion, black versus white Vietnam veterans and, 541, 542
Social isolation, schizophrenia and pursuit of, 411
Socialization, term of, 17–18
Social milieu, schizophrenia and, 81
Social networks; *see* Social support network
Social Readjustment Rating Scale, 33, 34, 106, 108–111
  child-rearing problems and, 611
  Coddington modifications of, 109
  criticisms of, 57–59
  dermatologic disorder and, 308–309
  maternal depression and, 619, 622
  modification of, 35–36
  schizophrenia and, 395, 396, 402, 407
  sleep disorder frequency and, 258
Social resources, hospitalization and, 412
Social Security cuts, concerns of elderly and, 752
Social skill deficit, schizophrenia and, 450
Social support network, 20
  dialysis and, 300
  and divorce, 670–671
  schizophrenia and, 73, 81, 451–454: summary of, 454–455
Socioeconomic status, 764
Sociological level of behavior, 286
Sodium amytal, 589–590
Sodium pentothal, 589
Somatic complaints in adolescents, 633–642; *see also* Psychosomatic symptoms
Soporifics, posttraumatic war stress and, 598–599
Specificity of patient-relative relationship, schizophrenia and, 457
Specific Stress Index, 405
SRE; *see* Schedule of Recent Experience
Srole's personality scales, 425

SRRS; *see* Social Readjustment Rating Scale
SRT; *see* Symptom Rating Test
Staff attitude toward dialysis, 300
Standard Assessment of Personality, 475, 479, 481
Startle reaction, Vietnam veterans and, 568
State anxiety, 181–182
State of helplessness, 229–230
State of life adjustment, change in, 107
State-trait anxiety, multivariate analysis of life events and, 766; *see also* Anxiety
State-Trait Anxiety Inventory, 649, 653
Statistical procedures, life stress measurement and, 41
Stelazine; *see* Trifluoperazine
Stimulus
  and moderating factors, stress as interaction between, 336–337
  stress as, 337–339
  and vulnerability, 760
Stress
  as barrier to health, 197–207
  biobehavioral definition of, 288
  biobehavioral model of, 286–288
  biological response to, 335
  and bulimia in anorexia nervosa, 237–256; *see also* Anorexia nervosa
  cognitive notions of, 227
  and coronary heart disease, 216
  definition of, 282–285, 334–339
  degree of, 136
  in elderly, coping and, 736–745
  end-stage renal disease and, 292
  historical roots of, 5
  as interaction between stimulus and moderating factors, 284–285, 336–337
  major life events and, 765
  maximum effect of, nature and timing of, 342–346
  as multifactorial interactive variable, 759
  as response, 283–284, 334–336
  schizophrenia and; *see* Schizophrenia
  as stimulus, 285, 337–339
  as variable, 765
Stress management training in elderly, 740, 743–744
Stressors
  attention directed toward, 92–99
  with end-stage renal disease and renal

dialysis, 288–296
Stress-prone factors in schizophrenia, 404, 408–415
Stress-transformation model, 297
Stroke victims, coping of wives of, 213
Student Motivation and Interest scale, 689
Subjective impressions of respondent, 60, 136–137
Subjective Life Change Unit score, 35, 109
Substance abuse, posttraumatic stress disorder and, 527, 530, 546, 547
  adjustment differences and, 566
  treatment of, 549
Success, desire for, midlife stress and, 716
Sudden death concerns of elderly, 756
Suicide, end-stage renal disease and, 294
Supportive interpersonal relationships, 117–118
Support network, 20
  dialysis and, 300
  and divorce, 670–671
  schizophrenia and, 73, 81, 451–454: summary of, 454–455
Surplus life events, schizophrenia and, 414
Survival, uncertainty about, 289
Symptom Rating Test, 310–311
Symptoms
  distinct dimensions of, 109
  near future onset of, 165–179; *see also* Near future onset of symptoms
  in schizophrenia, fluctuations in, 407
  unpredictable events and physical, 91–99
Syndrome, Munchausen's, 576, 583, 585
Systematic response prevention, delayed combat stress reactions and, 569

Tardive dyskinesia, 597
Target person, life-event web and, 21
TAT; *see* Thematic Apperception Test
Teacher descriptions of child behavior, 619–632
  scoring of, 622
  see also Child behavior
Teacher stress, 677–696
  conclusions on, 694–695
  method for, 680–681
  results and discussion of, 681–694
  unidimensional measures of teacher, 677
Temazepam, 598
Temporal level of behavior, 286
Tennant and Andrews life-event inven-

tory, 168, 224
Tennessee Self-Concept Scale, 445
Tension levels, schizophrenia and, 81
Thematic Apperception Test, 433
Theoretical consideration in stressful life events, 1–100
  interdependent lives and, 13–29; see also Interdependent lives
  measurement of life stress and, 31–49; see also Measurement of life stress
  psychological depression and, 5–11
  schizophrenia and, 51–89; see also Schizophrenia
  unpredicatable events and, 91–99
Thiothixene, 596
Thought disturbances, schizophrenia and, 448
Time demands of treatment, end-stage renal disease and, 290
Time Devoted to Specific Activities scale, 693
Time interval since event and degree of stressfulness, 135–136
Time scale, teacher stress and, 689
Timing of events
  clustering and, 117
  stress and, 763
Tinea, 309–310
Traditional roles for men and women, 700–702
Trait anxiety, 181–196
  definition of, 182
  discussion of, 190–194
  method for, 185–187
  results in, 187–190
  treatment implications for, 193–194
Trait anxiety inventory trait anxiety scale, 181–196; see also Trait anxiety
Transcultural therapy, 530
Transformation, crises and necessity for, 57
Transient symptomatology, 360–364
Transracially oriented therapy, 530
Tranylcypromine, 592
Treatment
  dialysis adjustment and, 300
  vulnerability reduction and, 368–369
  see also Chemotherapy
Tricyclic antidepressants
  overdose of, 594
  traumatic war stress and, 593–595
Trifluoperazine, 596
Triggering effect of life events, 52,

343–346, 352–353
  in schizophrenia, 397–404
Trihexyphenadyl, 596
Turbulence factor, 79
Type A behavior, 230–233
Tyramine avoidance, 593

UCLA Family Project, 40, 113–114, 435, 436, 437, 438
Umea Classification of affective disorders, 488
Uncertainty
  about survival, 289
  of outcome, life-event ratings and, 150
Uncontrolled life events, schizophrenia and, 414
Undesirable events, schizophrenia and depressive neurosis and, 382–385
Unemployment, 160
Universal elements of stressful life events, 107–108
Universal life-events scales, 40, 113–114
University of Kentucky, Department of Psychiatry, 660
Unphysiology, 291
Unprecipitated depression, schizophrenia and depressive neurosis and, 386–387
Unpredictable events and physical symptoms, 91–99
Upset, degree of, 75–76
Urticaria, chronic, 307–317
Uselessness, feelings of, in elderly, 751
Uterine bleeding, 212

Validity
  dysfunctional uterine bleeding study and, 278
  life stress measurement and, 41
  of Schedule of Recent Events, 109
Vanderbilt University Medical Center Adolescent Clinic, 634
Variables, life events mediated by, 117
VA/UCLA Life Change and Illness Research Project, 40, 113–114, 435, 436, 437, 438
VEQ; see Veterans Experiences Questionnaire
Veterans Experiences Questionnaire, 536, 556, 567–568
Victimization concerns in elderly, 751
Vietnam Experiences Questionnaire, 526, 556, 567–568

Vietnam posttraumatic stress syndrome, 519–523
Violence, Vietnam veterans and perceived capacity for, 568
Vision loss, concerns of elderly and, 752, 756
Visual analogue scales, 168–169
Vulnerability
    medication and reduction of, 368–369
    model for; *see* Vulnerability/stress model of schizophrenia
    and stimulus, stress and relationship between, 760
Vulnerability/stress model of schizophrenia, 344–345, 395, 403–404, 420, 437
    expressed emotion research and, 432
    support for, 397

Waking up at night, 259, 261, 262
Warrior status, factitious posttraumatic stress disorder and, 581

Web perspective, interdependent lives and, 15–19
    research implications of, 21–25
Weighted Life Events Inventories, 507, 508
Widowhood, midlife stress and, 712–713
Wilcoxon signed-rank test for paired comparisons, 133
Wives at risk after husbands' disabilities, 213
Work
    dialysis adjustment and, 300
    sharing of, working families and, 698
Work Environment scale, teacher stress and, 689
Working families, 697–710
    coping strategies for, 704–705
    discussion and conclusion of, 707–709
    life satisfaction in, 705–707
    stress and satisfaction in, 702–707